The Abolition of the Death Penalty in International Law

Third Edition

This is the third edition of William A. Schabas's highly praised study of the abolition of the death penalty in international law. Extensively revised to take account of developments in the field since publication of the second edition in 1997, the book details the progress of the international community away from the use of capital punishment, discussing in detail the abolition of the death penalty within the United Nations human rights system, international humanitarian law, European human rights law and Inter-American human rights law. New chapters in the third edition address capital punishment in African human rights law and in international criminal law. An extensive list of appendices contains many of the essential documents for the study of capital punishment in international law.

The Abolition of the Death Penalty in International Law is introduced with a foreword by Judge Gilbert Guillaume, President of the International Court of Justice.

The Abolition of the Death Penalty in International Law

Third edition

William A. Schabas

Irish Centre for Human Rights
National University of Ireland, Galway

PUBLISHED BY THE PRESS SYNDICATE OF THE UNIVERSITY OF CAMBRIDGE
The Pitt Building, Trumpington Street, Cambridge CB2 1RP, United Kingdom

CAMBRIDGE UNIVERSITY PRESS
The Edinburgh Building, Cambridge CB2 2RU, UK
40 West 20th Street, New York, NY 10011-4211, USA
477 Williamstown Road, Port Melbourne, VIC 3207, Australia
Ruiz de Alarcón 13, 28014 Madrid, Spain
Dock House, The Waterfront, Cape Town 8001, South Africa

http://www.cambridge.org

First edition 1993.
Second edition 1997.
Third edition 2002.
© Cambridge University Press 1993, 1997, 2002.

Printed in the United Kingdom at the University Press, Cambridge

Typeface Adobe Garamond 10.5/12.5pt   *System* LᴬTEX 2$_\varepsilon$ [TB]

A catalogue record for this book is available from the British Library

Library of Congress Cataloguing in Publication data

Schabas, William, 1950–
The abolition of the death penalty in international law /
William A. Schabas. – 3rd ed.
       p.   cm.
Includes bibliographical references and index.
ISBN 0 521 81491 X (hc.) ISBN 0 521 89344 5 (pb)
1. Capital punishment.   2. International law.   I. Title.
K5104.S33   1997
341.4′81 – dc20   96–29108 CIP

ISBN 0 521 81491 X hardback
ISBN 0 521 89344 5 paperback

Dedication

Socrates
Spartacus and Jesus Christ
Joan of Arc
Danton and Robespierre
John Brown
Louis Riel
Roger Casement
Sacco and Vanzetti
Julius and Ethel Rosenberg
Ken Saro-Wiwa

What is remarkable about such a list is how it permits history to be measured by executions: the apex of Greek philosophy, the decline of Rome and the birth of Christianity, the beginnings of the Renaissance, the French Revolution, the American Civil War, the cold war. It is a gruesome yardstick indeed of human 'progress' but, like every yardstick, it must have an end. The constant attention of international human rights law to the abolition of capital punishment has brought that end into sight.

Ni dans le coeur des individus ni dans les moeurs des sociétés, il n'y aura de paix durable tant que la mort ne sera pas mise hors la loi.

Albert Camus, 'Réflexions sur la guillotine'

Contents

Conclusion   363

Appendices   379

Foreword

William Schabas's work on the abolition of the death penalty could not be more timely, offering as it does a broad overview of the legal progress in the field over the last fifty years. In 1948, the *Universal Declaration of Human Rights* proclaimed the right to life. In 1966, the United Nations *Covenant on Civil and Political Rights* established that no one shall be arbitrarily deprived of life. It went on to add that in countries where the death penalty has not been abolished, a death sentence can only be pronounced for the most serious crimes in accordance with the law in force at the time of the commission of the crime. In 1989, an additional protocol to the *Covenant,* abolishing the death penalty in peacetime, was adopted. Thus we have moved from the proclamation of a principle to its regulation, and from regulation of that principle to abolition.

European law underwent an evolution parallel to that of the United Nations. The *European Convention on Human Rights* specified, in 1950, that

> Everyone's right to life shall be protected by law. No one shall be deprived of his life intentionally save in the execution of a sentence of a court following his conviction of a crime for which this penalty is provided by law.

The *Sixth Protocol* to the *Convention* abolished, in 1982, the death penalty, except in time of war or imminent danger of war.

In the Western hemisphere, a comparable progress took place. In 1948, the *American Declaration of the Rights and Duties of Man* proclaimed the right to life in terms similar to those of the *Universal Declaration.* In 1969, the *American Convention on Human Rights* regulated the death penalty in terms which were inspired largely by the UN *Covenant.* Even though no abolitionist protocol is yet in force within this system,[*] the *Convention* nevertheless specifies that the death penalty cannot be reestablished in States where it has been suppressed.

[*] Since these words were written, the *Additional Protocol to the American Convention on Human Rights to Abolish the Death Penalty*, OASTS 73, 29 *ILM* 1447, has entered into force.

ix

This final provision is particularly significant, illustrating as it does the close relationship between domestic and international law. The latter has developed because of the clear progress of the abolitionist movement, particularly in Europe. The parallel adoption and signature of international instruments on this subject has been inspired by the hope that they will lead to the abandonment of the death penalty by new States, and prevent retrogression in abolitionist States.

The debate is in fact far from resolved. Invoking Beccaria, Victor Hugo and Camus, partisans of abolition claim it to be cruel, no matter what the method of execution. They also doubt its utility, noting that criminality is no higher in abolitionist States than in retentionist States. They stress its irrevocable nature, especially in cases of judicial error, and add that the personality of the individual who is to be executed may be quite different from that of the offender at the time of the crime. Finally, they wonder how society can execute, in cold blood, a man whom it blames for having killed another.

But public opinion may remain somewhat unconvinced. Many people still accept the principle of 'an eye for an eye, a tooth for a tooth', particularly when atrocious crimes are involved. Some claim that the exemplary nature of the death penalty may play a preventive role, at least in certain cases. Others question the alternatives available in the case of dangerous repeat offenders. They fear that the victim's right to life may take second place to the right to life of the criminal.

This raises the question of whether, beyond the conventional instruments now in force, there also exist customary norms of international law concerning the death penalty.

William Schabas addresses all of these problems in this thought-provoking work. He successively analyses the *Universal Declaration of Human Rights*, the *International Covenant on Civil and Political Rights* and its *Second Protocol*, international humanitarian law, the *European Convention on Human Rights* and its *Sixth Protocol*, and the Inter-American instruments. In every case, he provides a detailed study of the texts and of their *travaux préparatoires*.

He then discusses the possible emergence of customary norms, noting that common article 3 to the four *Geneva Conventions of 1949* sets out rules that, in the view of the International Court of Justice, correspond to 'elementary considerations of humanity' (*Military and Paramilitary Activities in and Against Nicaragua (Nicaragua* v. *United States)*, [1986] ICJ Reports, paras. 218 and 255). He reasons that comparable rules must also apply in peacetime. From such a perspective, the death penalty cannot be pronounced in the absence of a judgment by an impartial tribunal after a trial which respects the rights of the accused. Such sentence can only be imposed for the most serious crimes, and cannot be carried out on pregnant women, on children under fifteen years of age, and on the insane.

These are particularly constructive conclusions. For though the death penalty has been abolished in many countries, it remains in force in several parts of the world, notably the United States, Africa and countries which follow Islamic law. It follows that the identification of minimum customary guarantees is consequently an extremely fruitful line of research.

I have taken both great personal pleasure and benefit in reading Mr Schabas's work. I hope that other readers share this same pleasure and derive like benefit.

Gilbert Guillaume, Judge
International Court of Justice
The Hague, January 1993

Preface to the third edition

Since the first edition appeared in 1993, the debate about capital punishment in international law has been utterly transformed. The astonishing speed of events has only confirmed the original thesis of the book, that there is an inexorable trend in international law towards the abolition of capital punishment. Indeed, in the first edition I noted that according to the lists prepared by Amnesty International, slightly less than half the countries in the world had abolished the death penalty, and that 'if the trend continues uninterrupted, sometime prior to the year 2000 a majority of the world's states will have abolished the death penalty'. That point was reached in the summer of 1995, shortly before I prepared the second edition. The trend has continued uninterrupted into the new millennium. Now a large majority of states have abolished capital punishment, and it is banned by the new international criminal courts. Those that still retain it now fight a rearguard action in the international arena, sensing that they are becoming the new pariahs of international human rights law.

My research assistants at the Université du Québec à Montréal (1991–2000) and, subsequently, at the National University of Ireland, Galway, have made important contributions to this study: Yanick Charbonneau, Dan Connelly, Julie Desrosiers, Geneviève Dufour, Laetitia Husson, David Koller, Carmel Morgan, Alexandre Morin, Audrey Murray, Angeline Northup and Nancie Prud'homme. My colleagues at the Irish Centre for Human Rights also gave me important encouragement, and I am delighted to have the opportunity to thank them publicly. The support of my wife, Penelope Soteriou, and my daughters, Marguerite and Louisa Schabas, is and always will be, as they well know, most dearly appreciated.

William A. Schabas
Oughterard, October 2001

Table of cases

International Court of Justice

Human Rights Committee

European Commission of Human Rights

Inter-American Commission of Human Rights

Table of international instruments

Abbreviations

AC	Appeal Cases
AI	Amnesty International
AIR	All India Reporter
AJIL	American Journal of International Law
All ER	All England Reports
Ann. Dig.	Annual Digest and Reports of Public International Law Cases
BFSP	British Foreign and State Papers
BYIL	British Yearbook of International Law
C. of E.	Council of Europe
CCC	Canadian Criminal Cases
CHR	Commission on Human Rights
CHRY	Canadian Human Rights Yearbook
CLR	Commonwealth Law Reports
Coll.	Collection of decisions of the European Commission of Human Rights
CTS	Consolidated Treaty Series
CYIL	Canadian Yearbook of International Law
DLR	Dominion Law Reports
DR	Decisions and Reports of the European Commission of Human Rights
Doc.	Document
EC	European Communities
EHRR	European Human Rights Reports
ESC	Economic and Social Council
ETS	European Treaty Series
F.	Federal Reporter
FC	Federal Court
FCR	Federal Court Reports
FCTD	Federal Court Trial Division

GA	General Assembly
HL	House of Lords
HRJ	Human Rights Journal
HRLJ	Human Rights Law Journal
HRQ	Human Rights Quarterly
ICC	International Criminal Court
ICJ	International Court of Justice
ICLQ	International and Comparative Law Quarterly
ICRC	International Committee of the Red Cross
ICTY	International Criminal Tribunal for the former Yugoslavia
ICTR	International Criminal Tribunal for Rwanda
ILC	International Law Commission
ILM	International Legal Materials
ILR	International Law Reports
JCPC	Judicial Committee of the Privy Council
L.Ed.	Lawyer's Edition
LNTS	League of Nations Treaty Series
LRC	Law Reports of the Commonwealth
LRTWC	Law Reports of the Trials of the War Criminals
Martens	Martens Treaty Series
NAC	National Archives of Canada
NILR	Netherlands International Law Review
NQHR	Netherlands Quarterly of Human Rights
OAS	Organization of American States
OASTS	Organization of American States Treaty Series
OAU	Organization of African Unity
RCADI	Recueil de cours de l'Académie du droit international de la Haye
RUDH	Revue universelle des droits de l'homme
Res.	Resolution
S-CHR	Sub-Commission on Prevention of Discrimination and Protection of Minorities
SA	South African Law Reports
SC	Supreme Court
SCR	Supreme Court Reports
S.Ct.	Supreme Court
TS	Treaty Series
TWC	Trials of the War Criminals
UKTS	United Kingdom Treaty Series
UN	United Nations
UNCIO	United Nations Conference on International Organization
UNTS	United Nations Treaty Series

US	United States
VR	Victoria Reports
WCR	War Crimes Reports
WIR	West Indies Reports
WLR	Weekly Law Reports
YECHR	Yearbook of the European Convention on Human Rights
ZSC	Zimbabwe Supreme Court

Introduction

This study could not have been written fifty-five years ago because its subject matter did not exist. International norms addressing the limitation and the abolition of the death penalty are essentially a post-Second World War phenomenon. As a goal for civilized nations, abolition was promoted during the drafting of the *Universal Declaration of Human Rights*[1] in 1948, although it found expression only implicitly in the recognition of what international human rights law designated 'the right to life'. At the time, all but a handful of States maintained the death penalty and, in the aftermath of a brutal struggle which had taken hundreds of millions of lives, few were even contemplating its abolition. When Uruguay objected to inclusion of the death penalty in the *Charter of the Nuremberg Tribunal*,[2] it was accused of having Nazi sympathies.[3] In 1946, a Norwegian court ruled that the death penalty was actually prescribed, by international law, and thus could be legitimately imposed despite the fact that it was inapplicable under the country's ordinary criminal law.[4] The United Nations Command, during the Korean War, formally provided for imposition of the death penalty on prisoners of war for post-capture offences.[5]

The idea of abolition gained momentum over the following decades. International lawmakers urged the limitation of the death penalty, by, for example, excluding juveniles, pregnant women and the elderly from its scope and by restricting it to an ever-shrinking list of serious crimes. Enhanced procedural

---

[1] GA Res. 217 A (III), UN Doc. A/810 (hereinafter, the *Universal Declaration* or *Declaration*).

[2] *Agreement for the Prosecution and Punishment of the Major War Criminals of the European Axis*, (1951) 82 UNTS 280, art. 27. On the debate about use of the death penalty for war crimes, see: Claude Pilloud, 'La protection pénale des conventions humanitaires internationales', [1953] *Revue internationale de la croix-rouge* 842, pp. 862–863.

[3] UN Doc. A/C.3/SR.811, para. 28.

[4] *Public Prosecutor* v. *Klinge*, (1946) 13 *Ann. Dig.* 262 (Supreme Court, Norway).

[5] 'Supplemental Rules of Criminal Procedure for Military Commissions of the United Nations Command', in Howard S. Levie, ed., *Documents on Prisoners of War*, Newport, R.I.: Naval War College Press, 1979, p. 592; 'Regulations Governing the Penal Confinement of Prisoners of War of the United Nations Command', *ibid.*, p. 614.

1

safeguards were required where the death penalty still obtained. Eventually, three international instruments were drafted that proclaimed the abolition of the death penalty, the first adopted in 1983 and the others only at the end of the 1980s.[6] Sixty-eight States are now bound by these international legal norms abolishing the death penalty,[7] and the number continues to grow rapidly.[8] Fifty-five years after the Nuremberg trials, the international community has now ruled out the possibility of capital punishment in prosecutions for war crimes and crimes against humanity.[9]

The importance of international standard setting was evidenced by parallel developments in domestic laws. From a handful of abolitionist States in 1945, the list grew steadily until, by 2001, considerably more than half the countries in the world had abolished the death penalty *de facto* or *de jure*. Those that still retain it find themselves increasingly subject to international pressure in favour of abolition, sometimes quite direct, for example, in the refusal to grant extradition where a fugitive will be exposed to a capital sentence. Abolition of the death penalty is generally considered to be an important element in democratic development for States breaking with a past characterized by terror, injustice and repression. In some cases, abolition is effected by explicit reference in constitutional instruments to the international treaties prohibiting the death penalty.[10] In others,

---

[6] *Protocol No. 6 to the Convention for the Protection of Human Rights and Fundamental Freedoms Concerning the Abolition of the Death Penalty*, ETS 114 (hereinafter *Protocol No. 6*) (see Appendix 15, p. 424); *Second Optional Protocol to the International Covenant on Civil and Political Rights Aiming at the Abolition of the Death Penalty*, GA Res. 44/128, (1990) 29 *ILM* 1464 (hereinafter the *Second Optional Protocol*) (see Appendix 4, p. 397); *Additional Protocol to the American Convention on Human Rights to Abolish the Death Penalty*, OASTS 73, 29 *ILM* 1447 (see Appendix 21, p. 438). A fourth treaty, the *American Convention on Human Rights*, (1979) 1144 UNTS 123, OASTS 36 (hereinafter the *American Convention*) (see Appendix 20, p. 436), is also an abolitionist instrument because it prevents countries which have already abolished the death penalty from reintroducing it. Thus, a State which has abolished the death penalty at the time of ratification of the *American Convention* is abolitionist from the standpoint of international law.

[7] Albania, Andorra, Argentina, Australia, Austria, Belgium, Bolivia, Bsonia and Herzegovina, Brazil, Bulgaria, Cape Verde, Chile, Colombia, Costa Rica, Croatia, Cyprus, Czech Republic, Denmark, Dominican Republic, Ecuador, El Salvador, Estonia, Finland, France, Georgia, Germany, Greece, Haiti, Honduras, Hungary, Iceland, Ireland, Italy, Latvia, Liechtenstein, Lithuania, Luxembourg, Macedonia, Malta, Mexico, Moldova, Monaco, Mozambique, Namibia, Nepal, Netherlands, New Zealand, Nicaragua, Norway, Panama, Paraguay, Peru, Poland, Portugal, Romania, San Marino, Seychelles, Slovakia, Slovenia, Spain, Sweden, Switzerland, Turkmenistan, Ukraine, United Kingdom, Uruguay, Venezuela and Yugoslavia. These States are abolitionist either *de jure* or *de facto*, and parties to one or more of the abolitionist treaties.

[8] Several European States have pledged to ratify *Protocol No. 6*, within twelve months as a condition for joining the Council of Europe.

[9] The Security Council has excluded use of the death penalty by the two international *ad hoc* tribunals created to deal with war crimes in the former Yugoslavia and Rwanda: *Statute of the International Tribunal for the Former Yugoslavia*, UN Doc. S/RES/827 (1993), annex, art. 24 §1; *Statute of the International Tribunal for Rwanda*, UN Doc. S/RES/955 (1994), annex, art. 23 §1. The death penalty is excluded from the *Rome Statute of the International Criminal Court*, UN Doc. A/CONF.183/9, art. 77.

[10] For example, the Arusha peace agreement of August 1993, which forms part of Rwandan fundamental law, provides for accession to all human rights treaties, and this is generally recognized as including the *Second Optional Protocol*: 'Protocole d'Accord entre le Gouvernement de la République Rwandaise et le

it has been the contribution of the judiciary, of judges applying constitutions that make no specific mention of the death penalty but that enshrine the right to life and that prohibit cruel, inhuman and degrading treatment or punishment.[11] Abolition of capital punishment features as one of the criminal law initiatives of the United Nations in its administration of Cambodia,[12] Kosovo[13] and East Timor.[14] The day when abolition of the death penalty becomes a universal norm, entrenched not only by convention but also by custom and qualified as a peremptory rule of *jus cogens*, is undeniably in the foreseeable future.

The death penalty has existed since antiquity. Anthropologists even claim that the drawings at Valladolid by prehistoric cave dwellers show an execution. The death penalty may well have had its origins in human sacrifices. In positive law, capital punishment can be traced back as early as 1750 bc, in the *lex talionis* of the Code of Hammurabi.[15] The Bible set death as the punishment for such crimes as magic, violation of the sabbath, blasphemy, adultery, homosexuality, relations with animals, incest and rape.[16] Yet the Jewish courts developed procedural safeguards for its employment. According to the Talmud, one rabbi called 'destructive' a Sanhedrin who imposed the death sentence once in seven years. Another said 'once in seventy years', and two others said they would never impose a death sentence.[17]

Front Patriotique Rwandais portant sur les questions diverses et dispositions finales signé à Arusha', 3 August 1993, *Journal officiel*, Year 32, no. 16, 15 August 1993, p. 1430, art. 15. The *Constitution of Bosnia and Herzegovina*, which forms Annex IV of the 'General Framework Agreement for Peace in Bosnia and Herzegovina', reached at Dayton, Ohio in November 1995, is even more explicit, providing that the new republic respect the protocols to the *Convention for the Protection of Human Rights and Fundamental Freedoms* (1955) 213 UNTS 221, ETS 5 (hereinafter the *European Convention*), including its *Protocol No. 6* at arts. II§2 and IV§3(c), and the *Second Optional Protocol* at Annex I, §7. See also Annex IV to the Dayton agreement, dealing with human rights, at arts. I and II§2(a) and Appendix §8. The Human Rights Chamber of Bosnia and Herzegovina has declared the death penalty to be unconstitutional: *Damjanovic v. Federation of Bosnia and Herzegovina* (Case No. CH/96/30), 5 September 1997, Decisions on Admissibility and Merits 1996–1997, p. 147.

[11] *S. v. Makuranyane*, 1995 (3) SA 391, (1995) 16 *HRLJ* 154 (Constitutional Court of South Africa); Ruling 23/1990 (X.31) AB, Constitutional Court of Hungary, Judgment of 24 October 1990, *Magyar Közlöny* (Official Gazette), 31 October 1991; Ukraine, Constitutional Court ruling, 30 December 1999; Albania, Constitutional Court ruling 10 December 1999.

[12] 'Provisions relating to the judiciary and criminal law and procedure applicable in Cambodia during the transitional period,' Supreme National Council decision of 10 September 1992.

[13] 'Regulation No. 1999/1, on the Authority of the Interim Administration in Kosovo', UN Doc. UNMIK/REG/1999/1.

[14] 'Regulation No. 1999/1, on the Authority of the Transitional Administration in East Timor', UN Doc. UNTAET/REG/1999/1, was promulgated by the United Nations Transitional Administrator on 27 November 1999. Death sentences were pronounced in East Timor in December 1997, apparently the first since the Indonesian occupation in 1975: 'Situation in East Timor, Report of the Secretary-General', UN Doc. E/CN.4/1998/58.

[15] Paul Savey-Casard, *La peine de mort: esquisse historique et juridique*, Geneva: Droz, 1968, at pp. 4–14.

[16] Exodus xxi, 14, xxii, 18; Leviticus xx, 13, 15, xxiv; Deuteronomy xxi, 21, xxii, 11, 25, xxix, 13; Numbers, xiii, 5, xvii, 7, xix, 19, xxii, 23, xxxiii 14, 37. See: Jean Imbert, *La peine de mort*, Paris: Presses universitaires de France, 1989, pp. 7–8.

[17] Charles L. Black Jr, *Capital Punishment: The Inevitability of Caprice and Mistake*, New York: Norton, 1974, at p. 94; F. Frez, 'Thou Shalt Not Execute. Hebrew Law Perspective on Capital Punishment', (1981) 19 *Criminology* 25.

The scourge of the death penalty cut short the life of one of ancient Greece's greatest thinkers, Socrates. Plato discussed the scope of the death penalty at length in his *Laws*.[18] Yet the death penalty had its opponents, even in early times. Thucydides reports a debate between Cleon and Diodotus concerning the implementation of the death penalty to suppress a rebellion of the island of Mitylene: 'We must not, therefore, commit ourselves to a false policy through a belief in the efficacy of the punishment of death, or exclude rebels from the hope of repentance and an early atonement of their error', said Diodotus, whose eloquent words rallied the majority of the Athenian assembly.[19]

During the Middle Ages, the death penalty was characterized by particular brutality.[20] Its legitimacy was defended by many of the great thinkers of the Renaissance and the Reformation. Grotius considered the issue at some length, finding it to be justified with reference to the Bible and other examples of Christian mores and in fact used the acceptance of capital punishment to justify the legality of warfare.[21] Both Thomas Hobbes and John Locke admitted that the death penalty was justifiable.[22]

Jean-Jacques Rousseau believed that in society man had a right not to be killed as long as he did not kill anyone else.[23] Diderot, too, was in favour of the death penalty: 'Il est naturel que les lois aient ordonné le meurtre des meurtriers.'[24] But the Enlightenment also saw the emergence of partial abolitionism. Montesquieu, for example, called for limitation of the death penalty to murder, attempted murder, certain types of manslaughter and some offences against property, although he did not commit himself to full abolition.[25]

---

[18] Plato, *The Laws*, Book VIII, Chapter 16, London: Harmondsworth, 1970, at pp. 353–366. Also on the death penalty in ancient Greece, see: P. Gelbert, 'L'exécution des condamnés à mort en Grèce antique', [1948] *Revue internationale de criminologie et de police technique* 38; Irving Barkan, *Capital Punishment in Ancient Athens*, Chicago, 1936; Jan Gorecki, *Capital Punishment, Criminal Law and Social Evolution*, New York: Columbia University Press, 1983, pp. 31–80.

[19] Thucydides, 'The Peloponnesian War', ch. 9, §§38–48, in *The Complete Writings of Thucydides*, New York: Modern Library, 1934, pp. 164–172.

[20] Jean Imbert, *La peine de mort*, at pp. 16–24; Richard J. Evans, *Rituals of Retribution, Capital Punishment in Germany 1600–1987*, Oxford: Clarendon Press, 1996.

[21] H. Grotius, *De jure belli ac pacis libri tres*, trans. Francis W. Kelsey, Oxford: Clarendon Press, 1925, at pp. 66–86. A similar connection between war and the death penalty was made by the Italian criminologist Garofolo: Raffaele Garofalo, *Criminology*, Montclair, N.J.: Patterson Smith, 1968, pp. 51–53.

[22] R. Zaller, 'The Debate on Capital Punishment During the English Revolution', (1987) 31 *American J. Legal History* 126.

[23] Jean-Jacques Rousseau, *Le contrat social*, Book II, ch. 5, Paris: Pléiade, Vol. III, pp. 376–377.

[24] Quoted in Jacques Goulet, *Robespierre, La peine de mort et la terreur*, Paris: Le Castor Astral, 1983, p. 13.

[25] Montesquieu, *De l'esprit des lois*, Paris: Société des belles lettres, 1950, pp. 159–161. See J. Graven, 'Les conceptions pénales et l'actualité de Montesquieu, [1949] *Revue de droit pénal et de criminologie* 161; Jean Imbert, 'La peine de mort et l'opinion au XVIIIᵉ siècle', [1964] *Revue de science criminelle et de droit pénal comparé* 521; Leon Radzinowicz, *A History of English Criminal Law and its Administration from 1750*, Vol. I, London: Stevens and Sons, 1948, pp. 268–284.

The modern abolitionist movement establishes its paternity with the great Italian criminologist, Cesare Beccaria. His work, *Dei delitti et delle pene*,[26] convinced such statesmen as Voltaire, Jefferson, Paine, Lafayette and Robespierre of the uselessness and inhumanity of capital punishment[27] and even led to ephemeral measures abolishing the death penalty in Austria and Tuscany.[28]

During debate on the adoption of the French *Code pénal* in 1791, Robespierre argued vigorously for the abolition of the death penalty.[29] He failed to convince the majority of the National Assembly, and the death penalty was retained, although in the relatively humane form proposed by his colleague, Dr Joseph-Ignace Guillotin. Robespierre later had a change of heart, calling for the execution of Louis XVI as a 'criminel envers l'humanité',[30] something that Thomas Paine, also an abolitionist, deemed a betrayal.[31] But the abolitionist ideal had not been completely obscured, and the Convention, in its final session, following the execution of Robespierre, decreed: 'À dater du jour de la publication générale de la paix, la peine de mort sera abolie dans la République française.'[32]

The abolitionist movement grew during the nineteenth century, rallying the support of such important English jurists as Bentham and Romilly.[33] In 1846, Michigan became the first jurisdiction to abolish capital punishment permanently.[34] Venezuela and Portugal abolished the death penalty in 1867,

[26] Cesare Beccaria, *On Crimes and Punishments*, trans. Henry Paolucci, Indianapolis: Bobbs-Merrill, 1963.

[27] Steven Lynn, "Locke and Beccaria: Faculty Psychology and Capital Punishment', in William B. Thesing, *Executions and the British Experience from the 17th to the 20th Century: A Collection of Essays*, Jefferson, N.C.: McFarland, pp. 29–44; Robert Badinter, 'Beccaria, l'abolition de la peine de mort et la Révolution française', [1989] *Revue de science criminelle et de droit pénal comparé* 245; Mireille Delmas-Marty, 'Le rayonnement international de la pensée de Cesare Beccaria', [1989] *Revue de science criminelle et de droit pénal comparé* 252; Jean Imbert, *La peine de mort*.

[28] Marcello Maestro, *Cesare Beccaria and the Origins of Penal Reform*, Philadelphia: Temple University Press, 1972; Radzinowicz, *A History*, pp. 290–293.

[29] Maximilien Robespierre, *Œuvres, VII*, Paris: Presses universitaires de France, 1952, pp. 432–437. See: Savey-Casard, *La peine de mort*, pp. 70–75; Goulet, *Robespierre*.

[30] Maximilien Robespierre, *Œuveres, IX*, Paris: Presses universitaires de France, 1952, p. 130.

[31] Thomas Paine, 'Preserving the Life of Louis Capet', in Michael Foot, Isaac Kramnick, *The Thomas Paine Reader*, London: Penguin, 1987, pp. 394–398.

[32] Decree of the fourth brumaire, year IV, quoted in Savey-Casard, *La peine de mort*, p. 80. It was not, however, until 1981 that France consigned its guillotine to the museum. On the history of capital punishment in France, see: Jean-Claude Chesnais, *Histoire de la violence en Occident de 1800 à nos jours*, Paris: Robert Laffont, 1981, pp. 138–154; Daniel Arasse, *La Guillotine et l'imaginaire de la terreur*, Paris: Flammarion, 1987.

[33] Radzinowicz, *A History*, pp. 497–525; Hugo Adam Bedau, 'Bentham's Utilitarian Critique of the Death Penalty', (1983) 74 *J. Criminal Law and Criminology* 1033; James E. Crimmins, ' "A Hatchet for Paley's Net": Bentham on Capital Punishment and Judicial Discretion', (1988) 1 *Canadian J. Law and Jurisprudence* 63. For the history of the English abolitionist movement during the nineteenth century, see Leon Radzinowicz, Roger Hood, *A History of English Criminal Law and its Administration from 1750*, Vol. V, London: Stevens and Sons, 1986, pp. 661–688.

[34] D. B. Davis, 'Movement to Abolish Capital Punishment in America, 1787–1861', (1957) 63 *American Historical Rev.* 23; Louis Filler, 'Movements to Abolish the Death Penalty in the United States', (1952) 284 *Annals of the American Academy of Political and Social Science* 124.

followed by the Netherlands (1870), Costa Rica (1882), Brazil (1889) and Ecuador (1897). Panama, created in 1903, never enacted the death penalty.[35] But abolition suffered a setback in the first decades of the twentieth century. Part of this was due to the influential criminological doctrines of Garofalo, Lombroso and Ferri, who argued that the death penalty was scientifically necessary as a social measure.[36] The rise of totalitarianism in Europe after the First World War was also responsible for a resurgence of the death penalty. Hitler, an enthusiast of the death penalty from his earliest days, wrote casually about the execution of 10,000 people in *Mein Kampf*.[37] Nazi use of the death penalty against prisoners and civilians was cited in the final judgment of the international war crimes tribunal at Nuremberg,[38] and Nazi judges and prosecutors were themselves punished by post-war tribunals for their cavalier resort to capital punishment.[39]

The international experts who assembled in the aftermath of the Second World War with the mission of enumerating fundamental rights and freedoms included in their lists a 'right to life'. As obvious as the right's importance appeared, its content was far from evident. Central to the preoccupations of these drafters was the issue of the death penalty. The post-war context had sensitized them to the terrible abuses of the death penalty prior to and during the armed conflict. Furthermore, they were conscious of giving effect to an abolitionist movement that had been gaining support, albeit with sporadic reversals, for the past two centuries. At the same time, the death penalty was almost universally applied, and even many of the most steadfast opponents of capital punishment were tempted to make exceptions in the cases of war criminals and collaborators. This was the dialectic that confronted those who first proclaimed, in international law, a 'right to life'.

The *Universal Declaration of Human Rights*, adopted by the United Nations General Assembly on 10 December 1948, declared the right to life in absolute fashion, any limitations being only implicit.[40] The same approach was taken in the *American Declaration on the Rights and Duties of Man*, adopted 4 May 1948.[41] In several subsequent international human rights instruments,

---

[35] See: Ricardo Ulate, 'The Death Penalty: Some Observations on Latin America', (1986) 12–13 *United Nations Crime Prevention and Criminal Justice Newsletter* 27.

[36] Raffaele Garofalo, *Criminology*, pp. 104–105, 376, 410; Cesare Lombroso, *Crime, Its Causes and Remedies*, Montclair, N.J.: Patterson Smith, 1968, pp. 426–428; Enrico Ferri, *Criminal Sociology*, New York: Agatha Press, 1967, p. 527.

[37] Adolf Hitler, *Mein Kampf*, Boston: Houghton Mifflin, 1943, p. 545.

[38] *France et al.* v. *Goering et al.*, (1946) 22 1MT 203.

[39] *United States of America* v. *Alstötter et al.* ('Justice trial'), (1948) 3 TWC 1, 6 LRTWC 1, 14 ILR 278 (United States Military Commission).

[40] Art. 3 (see Appendix 1, p. 379).

[41] OAS Doc. OEA/Ser.L./V/1.4, art. I (hereinafter, the *American Declaration*) (see Appendix 19, p. 435).

notably the *International Covenant on Civil and Political Rights*,[42] the *European Convention on Human Rights*[43] and the *American Convention on Human Rights*,[44] the death penalty is mentioned as a carefully worded exception to the right to life. In other words, from a normative standpoint, the right to life protects the individual against the death penalty unless otherwise provided as an implicit or express exception. The right to life in international law also ensures that the death penalty cannot be imposed without rigorous procedural safeguards, or against certain protected categories of persons, such as juveniles, pregnant women and the elderly.

There are some rather obvious exceptions to the right to life, indeed so obvious that there is really no need to make explicit mention of them in the international norms. An individual has the right to self-defence, including the right to take another's life where his or her own life is threatened by that person. In recognizing a defence of self-defence in its criminal legislation, the State breaches the right to life of the attacker. It is an exception that all but the most suicidal would quarrel with, and one that can also be justified in the name of the right to life, for it protects the right to life of the victim. The international law of armed conflict protects enemy combatants from criminal charges if captured, providing they bear arms, wear uniforms and meet the other requirements of the third *Geneva Convention*[45] and the *Protocol Additional I*.[46] Yet such protection, by tolerating the 'accidental' killing of civilians caught in the armed conflict, violates the right to life of these innocent victims. Here too, the exception to the right to life is an implicit one.

The *European Convention on Human Rights* is the only instrument to attempt an exhaustive list of exceptions to the right to life. The United Nations and the Inter-American systems chose to avoid such an approach, and instead declared simply that life could not be taken 'arbitrarily', leaving the scope of such exceptions to the interpreter. But all three instruments list separately what is the most striking exception to the right to life, the death penalty. Even the *European Convention* sets the death penalty apart from the other exceptions, dealing with it in a distinct paragraph. This is because, while the other exceptions are logical and self-evident, there is something contradictory and incompatible about recognizing a right to life and at the same time permitting

---

[42] (1976) 999 UNTS 171, art. 6 (hereinafter, the *Civil Rights Covenant* or *Covenant*) (see Appendix 2, p. 380).

[43] (1955) 213 UNTS 221, ETS 5, art. 2§1 (hereinafter the *European Convention*) (see Appendix 14, p. 423).

[44] See Appendix 20, p. 436.

[45] *Geneva Convention of August 12, 1949 Relative to the Treatment of Prisoners of War*, (1950) 75 UNTS 135.

[46] *Protocol Additional I to the 1949 Geneva Conventions and Relating to the Protection of Victims of International Armed Conflicts*, (1979) 1125 UNTS 3.

capital punishment. The drafters of the various instruments, intuitively, knew this.

The 'right to life' has been described at various times as 'the supreme right',[47] 'one of the most important rights',[48] 'the most fundamental of all rights',[49] 'the primordial right',[50] 'the foundation and cornerstone of all the other rights',[51] 'le droit suprême, . . . la condition nécessaire à l'exercice de tous les autres',[52] 'le noyau irréductible des droits de l'homme',[53] the 'prerequisite for all other rights',[54] and a right which is 'basic to all human rights'.[55] Basic as it appears, it is at the same time intangible in scope, and vexingly difficult to define with precision. The French scholar Frédéric Sudre describes it as an 'uncertain' right.[56] Perhaps more than any other, it is a right whose content is continuously evolving, in step with the hegemony of ever more progressive attitudes to capital punishment, nuclear arms, abortion and euthanasia, to mention only a few of the many issues that interpreters of the right to life have addressed.

There are two contending schools on the interpretation of the 'right to life'. The more restrictive school, one of narrow construction, would limit its scope to those issues considered by the drafters of the *Universal Declaration of Human Rights*, the *International Covenant on Civil and Political Rights* and the *European Convention on Human Rights*.[57] The narrow view confines the protection offered by the right to life to such matters as capital punishment, abortion, disappearances, non-judicial executions and other forms of intentional or reckless life-taking by the State.

---

[47] *General Comment 6(16)*, UN Doc. CCPR/C/21/Add.1, also published as UN Doc. A/37/40, Annex V, UN Doc. CCPR/3/Add. 1, pp. 382–383 (see Appendix 5, p. 402). See also, *de Guerrero* v. *Colombia* (No. 45/1979), UN Doc. C/CCPR/OP/1, p. 112, p. 117.

[48] *Stewart* v. *United Kingdom* (App. No. 10044/82), (1985) 7 EHRR 453.

[49] Theo C. Van Boven, 'The Need to Stop Deliberate Violations of the Right to Life', in Daniel Prémont, ed., *Essais sur le concept de 'droit de vivre' en mémoire de Yougindra Khushalani*, Brussels: Bruylant, 1988, pp. 285–292, p. 285.

[50] Bertrand G. Ramcharan, 'The Concept and Dimensions of the Right to Life', in Bertrand G. Ramcharan, ed., *The Right to Life in International Law*, Dordrecht/Boston/Lancaster: Martinus Nijhoff, 1985, pp. 1–32, p. 12; René Brunet, *La garantie internationale des droits de l'homme d'après la Charte de San-Francisco*, Geneva: Grasset, 1947, p. 211.

[51] Inter-American Commission of Human Rights, *Diez Años de Actividades, 1971–1981*, Washington, D.C.: Organization of American States, 1982, p. 339; *Annual Report of the Inter-American Commission on Human Rights, 1986–1987*, OAS Doc. OEA/Ser.L/V/II.71 doc. 9 rev. 1, p. 271.

[52] Frédéric Sudre, *La Convention européenne des droits de l'homme*, Paris: Presses universitaires de France, 1990, p. 87.

[53] A.-C. Kiss, J.-B. Marie, 'Le droit à la vie', (1974) 7 *HRJ* 338, p. 340.

[54] 'Initial Report of Uruguay', UN Doc. CCPR/C/1/Add.57.

[55] *General Comment 14(23)*, UN Doc. A/40/40, Annex XX, UN Doc. CCPR/C/SR.563, para. 1.

[56] Frédéric Sudre, *La Convention européenne*, pp. 87–88.

[57] Yoram Dinstein, 'The Right to Life, Physical Integrity, and Liberty', in Louis Henkin, ed., *The International Bill of Rights: The Covenant on Civil and Political Rights*, New York: Columbia University Press, 1981, pp. 114–137, p. 115; J. E. W. Fawcett, *The Application of the European Convention on Human Rights*, 2nd ed., Oxford: Clarendon Press, 1987, p. 37; F. Przetacnik, 'The Right to Life as a Basic Human Right', (1976) 9 *HRJ* 585.

The broader view of the right to life is considerably more recent and attempts to introduce an economic and social content, a 'right to live', as it is sometimes called.[58] According to this approach, the right to life includes a right to food, to medical care and to a healthy environment. This is the outlook that has been adopted by the Human Rights Committee in the interpretation of article 6 of the *International Covenant on Civil and Political Rights*[59] and is shared by some of the States parties.[60]

However, both schools agree that the issue of the death penalty is at the core of the right to life, and this is confirmed by an historical approach to the definition of the right. The early international instruments, notably the *Universal Declaration of Human Rights*, drew heavily on national declarations of fundamental rights that were inspired by the *Magna Carta*, the United States *Bill of Rights*, and the French *Déclaration des droits de l'homme et du citoyen*. There was nothing absolute about these early statements of the right to life; it was a right to protection of one's life from arbitrary deprivation by the State, in reality more of a licence to the State to execute, providing that procedural guarantees were observed. The earliest recognition of this protection is *Magna Carta*, whose chapter 26 provides:

> No freedman shall be taken or imprisoned, or be disseised of his freehold, or liberties, or free customs, or be outlawed, or exiled, or any other wise destroyed, nor will we pass upon him, nor condemn him, but by the lawful judgment of his peers, or by the law of the land.[61]

Declarations of the right to life appear in a number of pre-revolutionary American documents, authored by Puritans who had fled religious persecution in England. For example, the *Massachusetts Body of Liberties*, dated 10 December 1641, proclaims:

> No mans life shall be taken away . . . unlesse it be by bertue or equitie of some expresse law of the country narrating the same, established by a generall Cort and sufficiently published . . .[62]

---

[58] Bertrand G. Ramcharan, 'The Right to Life', (1983) 30 *NILR* 297; Ramcharan, 'The Concept', p. 6; Hector Gros Espiell, 'The Right to Life and the Right to Live', in Prémont, ed., *Essais*, pp. 45–53; Mikuin Leliel Balanda, 'Le droit de vivre', in Prémont, *ibid.*, pp. 31–41; Yougindra Khushalani, 'Right to Live', in Prémont, *ibid.*, p. 283; Thomas Desch, 'The Concept and Dimensions of the Right to Life – As Defined in International Standards and in International and Comparative Jurisprudence', (1985–86) 36 *Österreichische Zeitschrift für Öffentliches Recht und Völkerrecht 77.*
[59] *General Comment 6(16); General Comment 14(23).*
[60] E.g. 'Initial Report of Canada', UN Doc. CCPR/C/1/Add.43. See also: UN Doc. CCPR/C/SR.205, para. 26 (Opsahl).
[61] 6 Halsbury's Statutes (3rd edn) 401.
[62] Richard L. Perry, John C. Cooper, *Sources of Our Liberties*, Washington, D.C.: American Bar Association, 1952, p. 148.

The *Virginia Bill of Rights*, drafted by George Mason at the dawn of the American revolution, referred to 'inherent rights' to 'the enjoyment of life'.[63] The *Declaration of Independence*, which followed by a few weeks, stated:

> We hold these truths to be self-evident, that all men are created equal; that they are endowed by their Creator with certain unalienable rights; that among these are life, liberty, and the pursuit of happiness.

The fifth amendment to the United States *Constitution* specifically provides for procedural guarantees in cases of 'a capital or otherwise infamous crime', adding that no person shall:

> . . . be deprived of life, liberty, or property, without due process of law.

The fourteenth amendment, adopted on 28 July 1868, extended this protection to legislation of the States.

The drafters of the French *Déclaration des droits de l'homme et du citoyen* did not include the right to life, an omission that one scholar has explained with the observation that it is unnecessary to state a right without which all others have no *raison d'être*.[64] The *Déclaration* enumerates, at article 2, the 'inalienable rights of man' as being 'liberty, property, security, and resistance to oppression'. The Marquis de Lafayette, who had been inspired by American models and assisted by Thomas Jefferson, included the right to life in his drafts of the *Déclaration*,[65] as did Marat and others.[66]

Several national constitutions of the nineteenth and early twentieth century recognized the right to life, generally associated with a phrase acknowledging the exception of capital punishment. For example, Sweden's 1809 *Constitution* states: 'The King . . . shall not deprive anyone or permit anyone to be deprived of life without legal trial and sentence.'[67] In a study prepared by the Secretariat of the Commission on Human Rights in early 1947, twenty-six such provisions in various national constitutions were identified.[68]

The right to life is implicit in the early international humanitarian conventions. The random and arbitrary execution of prisoners of war was proscribed by article 23§c of the Hague *Regulations* of 1907,[69] an interdiction that codified

---

[63] *Ibid.*, p. 311. See also: *Constitution of Pennsylvania, ibid.*, p. 329; *Constitution of Massachusetts, ibid.*, p. 374; *Constitution of New Hampshire, ibid.*, p. 382.
[64] Brunet, *La garantie*, p. 211.
[65] Stéphane Rials, *La déclaration des droits de l'Homme et du citoyen*, Paris: Hachette, 1988, pp. 528, 567, 590; Julian P. Boyd, ed., *The Papers of Thomas Jefferson*, Vol. XIV, Princeton: Princeton University Press, 1958, pp. 438–440; *ibid.*, Vol. XV, pp. 230–233.
[66] Rials, *La déclaration*, p. 736 (Marat), p. 726 (Boislandry), pp. 717–718 (Pison de Galland), p. 707 (Georges-Cartou).
[67] Quoted in UN Doc. E/CN.4/AC.1/3/Add.1, p. 18.   [68] *Ibid.*, pp. 15–19.
[69] *Convention Regulating the Laws and Customs of Land Warfare (Hague Convention No. IV), Regulations Concerning the Laws and Customs of Land War*, 3 Martens (3rd) 461, 2 *AJIL Supp.* 2, [1910] TS 9.

customary international law and that, by the effect of the so-called 'Martens clause', extended to conflicts not covered by the *Regulations*. A 'right to life' *per se* probably first appeared in international law in an article by Antoine Rougier, published in 1910 in the *Revue générale de droit international public*. Rougier contemplated the question from the standpoint of humanitarian intervention, which he considered would be justified where a State violated the right to life of its subjects by wholesale massacres or even negligence in the provision of basic health care during an epidemic.[70]

The idea of an international declaration of human rights can be traced to 1929, with a document adopted by the International Law Institute at its meeting held at Briarcliff Manor, New York. Article 1 of that declaration recognized the right to life:

> It is the duty of every State to recognize the equal right of every individual to life, liberty and property, and to accord to all within its territory the full and entire protection of this right, without distinction as to nationality, sex, language, or religion.[71]

René Cassin credited the International Law Institute with playing an important role in the history of the *Universal Declaration of Human Rights*, noting in particular that the right to life was included as part of its 1929 declaration.[72] Hector Gros Espiell cited the International Law Institute declaration as 'the earliest recognition of the equal right to life of individuals'.[73] Already the implications that such an affirmation of the 'right to life' might have for the death penalty were evident. One participant at the 1929 session asked the *rapporteur*, André Mandelstam, for a declaration that the article be interpreted 'de façon raisonnable', suggesting it could not be used to suggest such 'extremes' as the

---

[70] Antoine Rougier, 'La theorie de l'intervention d'humanité', [1910] *Revue générale de droit international public* 468, at pp. 517–518.

[71] *Annuaire de l'Institut de droit international*, 1929, Vol. II, Brussels: Goemaere, 1929, pp. 118–120; the original is in French, but an English version was published many years later: Institut de droit international, 'Declaration of International Rights of Man', (1941) 35 *AJIL* 663.

[72] René Cassin, 'La déclaration universelle et la mise en oeuvre des droits de l'homme', (1951) 79 *RCADI* 237, p. 272. This Declaration was also examined by the drafters of the *American Declaration*: Inter-American Council of Jurists, *Recommendaciones e Informes, Documentos Oficiales, 1945–1947*, Washington, D.C.: Organization of American States, 1948, pp. 18–19. On the drafting of the declaration, see: John Herman Burgers, 'The Road to San Francisco: The Revival of the Human Rights Idea in the Twentieth Century', (1992) 14 *HRQ* 447.

[73] Espiell, 'The Right to Life', p. 50. In fact, the right to life was also recognized in several of the post-World War I minority treaties. Article 2 of the *Treaty of Peace Between the United States of America, the British Empire, France, Italy and Japan, and Poland*, [1919] TS 8, states: 'Poland undertakes to assure full and complete protection of life and liberty to all inhabitants of Poland without distinction of birth, nationality, language, race or religion.' Similar provisions appear in the *Treaty between the Principal Allied and Associated Powers and Roumania*, (1921) 5 LNTS 336, art. 1; *Treaty between the Principal Allied and Associated Powers and Czechoslovakia*, [1919] TS 20, art. 1; *Treaty between the Principal Allied and Associated Powers and the Serb–Croat–Slovene State*, [1919] TS 17, art. 1. The *Treaty of Saint-Germain-en-Laye*, [1919] TS 11, article 63, protects 'life and liberty, without distinction of birth, nationality, language, race or religion'.

abolition of the death penalty.[74] Mandelstam replied that the article's intention was certainly not to offer 'impunity' for breaches of law, yet addition of a phrase suggesting that the right to life be assured 'within the limits of the law' would only invite abuse.[75]

A resolution adopted the same year, on 8 November 1929, by the Académie diplomatique internationale also stated the right to life in absolute terms, with no suggestion of capital punishment as an exception:

> Tous les habitants d'un État ont le droit à la pleine et entière protection de leur vie et de leur liberté.[76]

The 1930 Hague Conference on the codification of international law adopted a resolution aimed at elaboration of a 'Declaration on the Leading Principles of International Law', and this led to the drafting of the 'Declaration on the Foundation and Leading Principles of Modern International Law', which was approved in 1936 by the International Law Association, the Académie diplomatique internationale and the Union juridique internationale. Its article 28 states:

> Tout État doit assurer à tout individu sur son territoire la pleine et entière protection du droit à la vie, à la liberté et à la propriété, sans distinction de nationalité, de sexe, de race, de langue ou de religion.[77]

Professor Hersch Lauterpacht, in his book *An International Bill of the Rights of Man* published in 1945, did not expressly include the right to life in the substantive provisions of his draft declaration. However, the preamble stated:

> Whereas the United Nations have decided that they were waging war for the defence of life, liberty, independence and religious freedom . . .[78]

Lauterpacht revised his draft for the 1948 Brussels conference of the International Law Association. Article 1 of the new draft stated: 'The life and liberty of the person shall be inviolate within the limits of the law', and it was submitted to the United Nations for consideration during the drafting of the *Universal Declaration of Human Rights*.[79] Recognition of the right to life in domestic constitutions followed much the same pattern; rarely recognized prior

---

[74] *Annuaire de l'Institut de droit international,* 1929, Vol. II, pp. 118–119.   [75] *Ibid.,* p. 119.

[76] André N. Mandelstam, 'La protection internationale des droits de l'homme', (1931) 38 *RCADI* 129, at p. 218.

[77] Alejandro Alvarez, *Exposé de motifs et déclaration des grands principes du droit international moderne,* Paris: Editions Internationales, 1936, pp. 10–11; an English translation of the text appears in [1956] II *Yearbook of the International Law Commission* 230.

[78] H. Lauterpacht, *An International Bill of the Rights of Man,* New York: Columbia University Press, 1945, p. 69.

[79] UN Doc. E/CN.4/89.

to the Second World War, it began to appear frequently in the years following 1945.[80]

Even if the right to life was present in these preliminary efforts to enumerate an international declaration of human rights, little thought had yet gone into the complex issues involved in defining the content of such a right. The brief discussion in 1929, at the time of adoption of the declaration of the International Law Institute, captures the problem in a nutshell. A right to life that allowed exceptions was of little value, yet the logical consequence of a right to life without exceptions, that is, abolition of the death penalty, was too radical for jurists of the time. This enigma confronted the members of the United Nations Commission on Human Rights, as well as their counterparts in the European and American human rights systems. To some extent, it has yet to be fully resolved, despite more than fifty years of development in international norms of human rights.

Our study of international norms dealing with abolition of the death penalty begins with the *Universal Declaration of Human Rights*,[81] a document that has served as a touchstone for all subsequent international instruments dealing with human rights and fundamental freedoms. Although silent on the subject of the death penalty, its consideration was nevertheless a focal point of debate during the drafting of article 3, which proclaims the right to life. The *Universal Declaration* was conceived as a 'common standard of achievement' and not as a binding legal norm. Indeed, even prior to its completion, the drafters of the *Universal Declaration* had commenced work on a second instrument that was to constitute a formal multilateral treaty, the *International Covenant on Civil and Political Rights*.[82] Article 6 of the *Covenant*, whose drafting was completed in 1957, recognizes the right to life in terms similar to those of the *Declaration*. However, it also provides for the death penalty as an exception to the right to life, and accompanies the provision with a substantial number of restrictions and safeguards on its use. In a final compromise with growing abolitionist sentiment, the drafters of the *Covenant* agreed to conclude article 6 with a call for the abolition of capital punishment.

Subsequent to 1957, and with the recognition that abolition of the death penalty was not on the immediate international agenda, the United Nations focused its energy on limiting its scope by, for example, reducing the number of capital offences, and by excluding certain groups from its ambit, and requiring strict procedural controls when it was still used. This study describes the elaboration of resolutions and other initiatives from various United Nations bodies, including the Commission on Human Rights, the Economic and Social Council, the General Assembly, the Committee on Crime Prevention and Control, and the

[80] Kiss, Marie, 'Le droit à la vie', p. 340.   [81] See n. 1 above.   [82] See n. 42 above.

Congresses on the Prevention of Crime and the Treatment of Offenders. These activities demonstrate a significant and constant evolution towards the goal envisaged in the final paragraph of article 6 of the *Covenant*. Indeed, they culminated, during the 1980s, in the elaboration of the *Second Optional Protocol to the International Covenant on Civil and Political Rights Aiming at the Abolition of the Death Penalty,*[83] a multilateral treaty which creates an international norm of abolition of the death penalty.

This volume proceeds to examine parallel developments within three regional human rights systems. The Council of Europe's *European Convention on Human Rights*[84] was the first international human rights treaty, completed in 1950. As such, it predates article 6 of the *Covenant* by seven years[85] and is not therefore as advanced in its approach to the death penalty. Article 2 of the *Convention* provides for the death penalty as an exception to the right to life but makes little provision for safeguards or limitations on its use and does not envisage abolition. In practice, by the late 1950s most European States were well on the way to abolition in their domestic law. *De facto* abolition of the death penalty soon became the rule within Western Europe[86] and, by 1980, the European institutions, notably the Council of Europe, were at work drafting a protocol to the *European Convention* abolishing the death penalty in peacetime.[87] *Protocol No. 6* came into force in 1985 and has been ratified by almost all of the forty-three members of the Council of Europe. The Council of Europe requires new members to undertake to ratify the *Protocol,* a condition that has resulted in abolition of the death penalty throughout Eastern Europe and deep into Asia.

Latin American States were pioneers in the abolition of the death penalty, and several of them promoted the ideal of abolition both within the United Nations and within their own regional system, under the aegis of the Organization of American States. The *American Convention on Human Rights,*[88] adopted in 1969 and in force since 1978, came the closest to actual abolition, before a last-minute change of heart that resulted in a text quite similar to that of article 6 of the *Covenant.* The *American Convention* does, however, go further in the provision of safeguards and limitations on the death penalty, excluding its use for political crimes and for the elderly. The notion that a State which has abolished the death penalty cannot reinstate it, something which some

[83] See Appendix 4, p. 397.   [84] See n. 42 above.
[85] The final version of article 6 of the *Covenant* was adopted in 1957 by the Third Committee of the General Assembly, although the complete instrument was not adopted by the Assembly until 1966.
[86] Of the original members of the Council of Europe, Turkey was the last to stop executions. It last imposed the death penalty on 25 October 1984.
[87] *Protocol No. 6 to the Convention for the Protection of Human Rights and Fundamental Freedoms Concerning the Abolition of the Death Penalty.*
[88] See Appendix 20, p. 436.

have argued is implicit in the *Covenant on Civil and Political Rights*, is stated expressly in the *American Convention*. As a result, the *American Convention* is an abolitionist instrument, at least for the many States parties that no longer have legislation providing for capital punishment.

The third of the major regional human rights systems still sends out ambiguous signals on capital punishment. Unlike the other general human rights treaties in the universal and regional systems, the *African Charter of Human and Peoples' Rights*, adopted in 1981 by the Organization of African Unity, makes no mention of the death penalty. It does, on the other hand, provide for an un-qualified right to life. There is a paucity of interpretative material on the *African Charter*, making construction of the scope of its right to life provision difficult. The African Commission on Human and Peoples' Rights has issued decisions in a few contentious cases dealing with the imposition of the death penalty, and in November 1999 it adopted a resolution calling for a moratorium on the use of capital punishment.[89]

In 1996, a meeting of thirty Asian governments held under United Nations auspices concluded that 'it was premature, at the current stage, to discuss specific arrangements relating to the setting up of a formal human rights mechanism in the Asian and Pacific region'.[90] As a region, Asia has made the least progress in terms of abolitionist practice. This does not mean that international legal norms on capital punishment do not reach into that continent. Not only are many Asian states active participants in the universal human rights system, there have also been important international initiatives aimed at restriction and abolition of the death penalty. For example, China is struggling with the limitations imposed on capital punishment as it prepares to ratify the *International Covenant on Civil and Political Rights*. European parliamentarians have threatened to withdraw Japan's observer status with the Council of Europe if it does not take steps to comply with international legal standards.[91]

A portion of Asia is covered by the Arab and Islamic systems, which are themselves very underdeveloped. In 1981 the Islamic Council adopted a *Universal Islamic Declaration of Rights*, which states:

> (a) Human life is sacred and inviolable and every effort shall be made to protect it. In particular no one shall be exposed to injury or death, except under the authority of the law.[92]

---

[89] 'Resolution Urging States to Envisage a Moratorium on the Death Penalty, Thirteenth Activity Report of the African Commission on Human and People's Rights', OAU Doc. AHG/Dec.153(XXXVI), Annex IV.

[90] 'Fourth Workshop on Regional Human Rights Arrangements in the Asian and Pacific Region', UN Doc. HR/PUB/96/3 (1996).

[91] Philippe Pons, 'Au Japan, il ne faut pas "troubler l'âme" des condamnés à mort', *Le Monde*, 9 March 2001, p. 4.

[92] *Universal Islamic Declaration of Rights*, (1982) 4 EHRR 433.

The final phrase appears to permit capital punishment and is in any case consistent with the practice of all Islamic states. The Organisation of the Islamic Conference has prepared a document on human rights and Islam, article 2 of which guarantees the right to life to 'every human being', and adds:

> il appartient aux individus, sociétés et Etats de protéger ce droit contre toute violation éventuelle, et il est interdit de mettre fin à une vie quelconque, sauf lorsque cela est en accord avec la chari'a.[93]

The Islamic system of human rights, still very rudimentary in comparison with the other regional systems, does not even contemplate abolition of the death penalty.

The more recent *Arab Charter of Human Rights*, adopted on 15 September 1994 but as yet ratified by only one of the members of the League of Arab States, proclaims the right to life in the same manner as the other international instruments. However, three distinct provisions, articles 10, 11 and 12, recognise the legitimacy of the death penalty in the case of 'the most serious crimes', prohibit the death penalty for political offences, and exclude capital punishment for crimes committed under the age of eighteen and for both pregnant women and nursing mothers, for a period of up to two years following childbirth.[94] In international fora such as the United Nations, Arab (and, more generally, Islamic) nations have been among the most aggressive advocates of the retention of the death penalty, often defending its use in the name of obedience to Islamic law and the strictures of the *chari'a*.[95]

A number of provisions exist in the related field of international humanitarian law, concerning imposition of the death penalty upon prisoners of war and civilians. Analysis of the provisions and of their *travaux préparatoires* shows that their goal is not only to limit and control the use of the death penalty but also to promote its abolition. Because the humanitarian treaties are much

---

[93] Organisation of the Islamic Conference, Secretary General, Doc. OIC/POL/MD/82–83/7, Djeddah, 25 April 1982.

[94] *Arab Charter on Human Rights*, (1997) 18 *HRLJ* 151.

[95] For example, during debate at the 1994 session of the General Assembly, the Sudanese delegate noted that 'capital punishment was a divine right according to some religions, in particular Islam . . . [C]apital punishment was enshrined in the Koran and millions of inhabitants of the Muslim world believed that it was a teaching of God' (UN Doc. A/BUR/49/SR.5, para. 13). Reynaldo Galindo Pohl, Special Rapporteur of the Commission on Human Rights on Iran, has observed that 'there are groups of Islamic legal scholars and practitioners who recommend the abolition of the death penalty for political crimes on the ground that it is contrary to Islamic law. They state that the number of crimes punishable by death is limited': UN Doc. E/CN.4/1989/26, para. 36. On capital punishment in Islamic law, see A. Wazir, 'Quelques aspects de la peine de mort en droit pénal islamique', (1987) 58 *Revue internationale de droit pénal* 421; Centre des Études de Sécurité (Arabie Saoudite), 'L'égalité et commodité de la peine de mort en droit musulman', (1987) 58 *Revue internationale de droit pénal* 431; N. Hosni. 'La peine de mort en droit égyptien et en droit islamique', (1987) 58 *Revue internationale de droit pénal* 407; M. Cherif Bassiouni, 'Death as a Penalty in the Shari'a', in International Commission of Jurists, *The Death Penalty: Condemned*, Geneva, 2000, pp. 65–84; William A. Schabas, 'Islam and the Death Penalty', (2000) 9 *William & Mary Bill of Rights Journal* 223.

more widely ratified than the human rights treaties, and because they apply in the extreme conditions of wartime, they provide guidance as to the core values of the international community with respect to the death penalty. The death penalty is also considered within the norms of international criminal law. Though once a punishment imposed by international tribunals for the most heinous crimes of international concern, it is now no longer so. The debate within the Security Council, the International Law Commission and the various bodies involved in establishing the International Criminal Court is also germane to the identification of customary legal rules whose implications go well beyond the specific tribunals that are involved.

Two challenges to the use of the death penalty within the United States have been brought before the International Court of Justice, one by Paraguay, the other by Germany, in cases concerning nationals of these states. The issue of capital punishment arises only indirectly, in that the matter in dispute involves notification of the right to seek consular assistance, as required by article 36(1)(b) of the *Vienna Convention on Consular Relations* of 24 April 1963.[96] Paraguay filed its application in April 1998, obtaining a provisional measures order from the International Court of Justice requiring the United States to stay the execution of Angel Breard until the merits of the matter had been examined.[97] The United States Supreme Court refused to intervene to enforce the order,[98] and the Governor of Virginia proceeded with the execution. Some months later, Paraguay discontinued its application. In March 1999, Germany filed a similar application with respect to the death sentence imposed upon two German nationals, Karl and Walter LaGrand, in the state of Arizona. Once again, the International Court of Justice requested a stay of the United States.[99] It noted cautiously that the case did not concern 'the entitlement of the federal states within the United States to resort to the death penalty for the most heinous crimes',[100] although it seemed obvious to all that the subtext of the litigation was growing international outrage, particularly in Europe, with United States

[96] (1963) 596 UNTS 261. See: Eva Rieter, 'Interim Measures by the World Court to Suspend the Execution of an Individual: The Breard Case', (1998) 16 *Netherlands Quarterly of Human Rights* 475; Constanze Schulte, 'Jurisprudence of the International Court of Justice: Order Issued in the Case Concerning the Vienna Convention on Consular Relations (Paraguay v. United States of America)', (1998) 9 *European Journal of International Law* 761; Alison Duxbury, 'Saving Lives in the International Court of Justice: The Use of Provisional Measures to Protect Human Rights', (2000) 31 *California Western International Law Journal* 141.

[97] *Vienna Convention on Consular Relations (Paraguay v. United States of America)*, Provisional Measures, Order of 9 April 1998, [1998] ICJ Reports 258.

[98] *Breard v. Greene, Paraguay v. Gilmore*, 66 *US Law Week* 3684 (SC, 1998).

[99] *LaGrand (Germany v. United States of America)*, Provisional Measures, Order of 3 March 1999, [1999] ICJ Reports 1, para. 29.

[100] *Ibid.*, para. 25. Betraying the human rights dimension of the litigation, Judge Oda, in the only individual declaration that accompanied the provisional measures order, said: 'if Mr Walter LaGrand's rights as they relate to humanitarian issues are to be respected then, in parallel, the matter of the rights of victims of violent crime (a point which has often been overlooked) should be taken into consideration' (para. 2).

death penalty practice. During the proceedings the issue was not raised directly by Germany, although Berlin had made its opposition to the death penalty quite clear in earlier diplomatic correspondence with the American authorities.[101] Karl LaGrand had already been executed when the application was submitted, so the Court only ordered that Walter LaGrand's execution be suspended, a request Arizona ignored. The Court later found that 'the various competent United States authorities failed to take all the steps they could have taken to give effect to the Court's Order'.[102] In its judgment on the merits, of 27 June 2001, the Court concluded that the United States had breached international law in proceeding with the execution of Walter LaGrand, although it was studiously neutral on the question of capital punishment.[103] The case is now authority for the binding nature of provisional measures orders.

But violations of the *Vienna Convention* provisions do indeed raise very significant human rights issues. Article 36(1)(b), in guaranteeing a foreign national a right to be informed of the right to consular assistance, provides a guarantee of procedural fairness that may be decisive in capital cases. The Inter-American Court of Human Rights, in its 1999 Advisory Opinion, focused precisely on these human rights aspects of the consular notification issue.[104] Some 120 foreign nationals, representing nearly forty nationalities, have been sentenced to death in the United States since capital punishment was reinstated in the 1970s, virtually all of them in breach of the *Vienna Convention*. The importance of this right was affirmed by the United Nations General Assembly in a resolution following the Inter-American Court's ruling.[105]

Until relatively recently, discussion of the death penalty in international human rights law focused on the norm protecting the right to life. The *travaux préparatoires* of the various instruments indicate that their drafters approached the question more or less strictly from the angle of the right to life. The provisions that deal explicitly with capital punishment are generally included within the articles on the right to life, as can be seen from article 6 of the *International Covenant on Civil and Political Rights*,[106] article 2 of the *European Convention on Human Rights*[107] and article 4 of the *American Convention on Human Rights*.[108] That the death penalty might also involve the norm prohibiting cruel, inhuman

---

[101] *LaGrand (Germany* v. *United States of America*), 27 June 2001, para. 26.   [102] *Ibid.*, para. 115.

[103] Judge Oda, again in dissent, suspected that a human rights agenda lay behind the German application: 'I would hazard a guess that the German Government was prompted to bring this case before the International Court of Justice by the outcry raised by some in Germany, by the emotional reaction on the part of some people there – where the death penalty has been abolished – to a case involving the existence and application of the death penalty in the United States.' *Ibid.*, Dissenting Opinion of Judge Oda, para. 9.

[104] *The Right to Information on Consular Assistance in the Context of the Guarantees of Due Process of Law*, Advisory Opinion OC-16/99 of 1 October 1999.

[105] 'Protection of Migrants', UN Doc. A/RES/54/166.   [106] See n. 42 above.

[107] See n. 43 above.   [108] See Appendix 20, p. 436.

and degrading treatment or punishment did not arise during the drafting of these instruments.[109] Precisely because the basic international human rights instruments appear to authorize the death penalty, some have turned to the prohibition of cruel punishment in order to attack capital punishment indirectly. Challenges have addressed such issues as the method of execution,[110] delay in informing offenders of reprieves,[111] and the 'death row phenomenon', that is, the prolonged wait that many condemned prisoners undergo between sentence and execution.[112] Cruel, inhuman and degrading treatment or punishment is also prohibited by certain specialized instruments, of which the most important is the United Nations *Convention Against Torture and Other Cruel, Inhuman and Degrading Treatment or Punishment.*[113] Adopted by the General Assembly in 1984, it completed work initiated with the *Declaration on the Protection of All Persons from Being Subjected to Torture and Other Cruel, Inhuman or Degrading Treatment or Punishment,*[114] adopted by the General Assembly in 1976. The treaty body created by the *Convention*, the Committee Against Torture, only occasionally addresses death penalty issues.

Taken as a whole, this review of international norms on the death penalty shows an inexorable progress towards abolition. In the early stages, abolition was only partial. Certain categories of individuals, such as juveniles, pregnant women and the elderly, were excluded from capital punishment, and its use was confined to an ever-shrinking list of serious crimes. By the 1980s, the abolitionist movement in international law had gained sufficient momentum that treaties proclaiming abolition of the death penalty could be drafted and opened for signature, ratification and accession. Nearly seventy States have now bound themselves to one or another of the conventional norms on abolition of the death penalty, and several others have signed the treaties or announced that they are contemplating ratification. Given the enormous and rapid progress in the development of international norms respecting the death penalty since the end of the Second World War, the general acceptance of abolition and its elevation to a customary norm of international law, perhaps even a norm of *jus cogens*, may be envisaged in the not too distant future.

---

[109] The actual wording of the provision varies from instrument to instrument, although its content is almost certainly identical: *Universal Declaration on Human Rights*, art. 5; *International Covenant on Civil and Political Rights*, art. 7; *European Convention on Human Rights*, art. 3; *American Declaration on the Rights and Duties of Man*, art. XXVI; *American Convention on Human Rights*, art. 5; *African Charter of Human and Peoples' Rights*, art. 5.

[110] *Ng* v. *Canada* (No. 469/1991), UN Doc. A/49/40, Vol. II, p. 189, (1994) 15 *HRLJ* 149: *Kindler* v. *Canada* (No. 470/1991), UN Doc. A/48/40, Vol. II, p. 138, (1993) 14 *HRLJ* 307, 6 *RUDH* 165; *Cox* v. *Canada* (No. 539/1993), UN Doc. CCPR/C/52/D/539/1993, (1995) 15 *HRLJ* 410.

[111] *Pratt and Morgan* v. *Jamaica* (Nos. 210/1986, 225/1987), UN Doc. A/44/40, p. 222.

[112] *Soering* v. *United Kingdom et al.*, 7 July 1989, Series A, Vol. 161, 11 EHRR 439; *Pratt* et al. v. *Attorney General for Jamaica* et al., [1993] 4 All E.R. 769, [1993] 2 LRC 349, [1994] 2 AC 1, [1993] 3 WLR 995, 43 WIR 340, 14 *HRLJ* 338, 33 ILM 364 (JCPC).

[113] GA Res. 39/46.   [114] GA Res. 3452 (XXX).

A parallel with the prohibition of torture and of slavery is helpful in this respect. Slavery was a common practice throughout history, and its prohibition, even in so-called civilized countries such as the United Kingdom and the United States, dates only to the 1800s. Torture was widely accepted and admitted, in certain circumstances, until the end of the Second World War. These two forms of barbarism are now proscribed in international human rights law, not only as conventional norms but also as customary norms. Although their prohibition naturally appears in the various international instruments, the mention is to some extent superfluous, because these are also peremptory norms, rules of *jus cogens*, enshrined by international custom.[115] The abolition of the death penalty may well be only a matter of decades behind the prohibition of slavery and torture.

Article 3 of the *Universal Declaration of Human Rights* is totally compatible with abolition of the death penalty, a testimony to the foresight of its authors, even though they stopped short of stating this expressly. As the international abolitionist trend gains hegemony, the *Universal Declaration* will not become outdated, its interpretation will merely be brought up to date. The *Universal Declaration* is often recognized as a statement of customary international law, and its very general wording permits it to grow and evolve in tandem with international custom. Dynamic or evolutive interpretation is fundamental to international human rights law.

This study seeks to demonstrate that since 1948, that is, since the first suggestion of the existence of an international norm limiting or abolishing the death penalty, there has been a clear and measurable progress towards that goal. The study does not endeavour to address the religious, moral, political and criminological arguments for the abolition or retention of the death penalty, these matters being the subject of an already enormous literature. The offences for which the death penalty may be imposed are increasingly limited. More and more categories of individuals who may never be subjected to the death penalty are being identified. International law is setting higher and higher standards for procedural requirements that are essential to any trial in which the death penalty may be imposed subject to law. These norms have been entrenched by convention, but in many cases it can be demonstrated that they are also customary in nature. These developments are, in effect, a form of partial abolition of the death penalty.

This progressive restriction has been crowned, in recent years, by the emergence of a norm that effectively abolishes the death penalty. Although still far from enjoying universal acceptance, its very existence testifies to its significance. Such instruments as the various protocols abolishing the death penalty

---

[115] Theodor Meron, *Human Rights and Humanitarian Norms as Customary International Law*, Oxford: Clarendon Press, 1989, pp. 220–222.

would have been unthinkable three or four decades ago. That they are now not only thinkable but also widely ratified shows how far the conception of the right to life, indeed how far human rights law in general, has developed and will continue to develop.

The first chapters of this study consider the universal norms. The drafting and interpretation of the relevant provisions in the three principal instruments, the *Universal Declaration*, the *International Covenant on Civil and Political Rights* and the *Second Optional Protocol* are considered successively. A generally chronological approach is followed in order to highlight the progressive evolution of abolitionist norms. Two treaties with their own particular missions, but which bear at least tangentially on death penalty issues, the *Convention Against Torture and Other Forms of Cruel, Inhuman and Degrading Treatment or Punishment* and the *Convention on the Rights of the Child* are discussed in the chapter on the *Covenant*. The 1984 'Safeguards Guaranteeing the Rights of Those Facing the Death Penalty'[116] are considered in the chapter dealing with the *Second Optional Protocol*, because these two instruments were drafted in parallel. Developments in international humanitarian law and international criminal law are treated in separate chapters, somewhat out of chronological order because the earliest norms dealing with the death penalty in international law appear in the 1929 *Geneva Convention*,[117] while the most recent were adopted in 1998. Three subsequent chapters deal with the main regional systems, those of the Council of Europe, the Organization of American States and the African Union. As has already been explained, because of their paucity the international legal developments in Asia have not received any detailed treatment. Developments on the death penalty within other European institutions, notably the European Union and the Organization on Security and Cooperation in Europe, are discussed within the chapter on European human rights law.

---

[116] ESC Res. 1984/50 (see Appendix 8, p. 413 below). Subsequently endorsed by GA Res. 39/118.
[117] *International Convention Concerning the Treatment of Prisoners of War*, (1932–33) 118 LNTS 343, art. 66.

1

The *Universal Declaration of Human Rights* and recognition of the right to life

The cornerstone of contemporary human rights law is the *Universal Declaration of Human Rights*,[1] adopted by the General Assembly of the United Nations on 10 December 1948. The *Universal Declaration* was complemented, some eighteen years later, by three international treaties, the *International Covenant on Civil and Political Rights*,[2] the *International Covenant on Economic, Social and Cultural Rights*,[3] and the *Optional Protocol to the International Covenant on Civil and Political Rights*.[4] A *Second Optional Protocol to the International Covenant on Civil and Political Rights Aiming at the Abolition of the Death Penalty*[5] was adopted by the United Nations General Assembly in December 1989, and came into force on 11 July 1991. Collectively, the five instruments comprise what is termed the 'International Bill of Rights'.

Although the *Universal Declaration* is not a binding treaty, it has played a seminal role not only in the United Nations system but also in the regional systems for the protection of human rights. The *Universal Declaration* is often cited, at least in part, as a statement or codification of customary international law, or as an authoritative interpretation of the human rights clauses in the *Charter of the United Nations*.[6] According to the International Court of Justice, 'General Assembly resolutions, even if they are not binding, may sometimes have normative value. They can, in certain circumstances, provide evidence important for establishing the existence of a rule or the emergence of an *opinio juris*.'[7] In June 1993 the World Conference on Human Rights at Vienna reaffirmed 'that the Universal Declaration of Human Rights, which constitutes a common standard

---

[1] GA Res. 217 A (III), UN Doc. A/810 (hereinafter, the *Universal Declaration* or *Declaration*).
[2] (1976) 999 UNTS 171 (hereinafter, the *Civil Rights Covenant* or *Covenant*).
[3] (1976) 993 UNTS 3.   [4] (1976) 999 UNTS 171.
[5] GA Res. 44/128, (1990) 29 *ILM* 1464 (hereinafter, *Second Optional Protocol*) (see Appendix 4, p. 397).
[6] John Humphrey, 'The International Bill of Rights: Scope and Implementation', (1976) 17 *William & Mary Law Review* 527; Thomas Buergenthal, 'International Human Rights Law and Institutions: Accomplishments and Prospects', (1988) 63 *William & Mary Law Review* 1.
[7] *Legality of the Threat or Use of Nuclear Weapons, Advisory Opinion*, [1996] ICJ Reports 226, para. 70.

of achievement for all peoples and all nations, is the source of inspiration and has been the basis for the United Nations in making advances in standard setting as contained in the existing international human rights instruments'.[8] Because of its role in the subsequent elaboration of international norms and its continuing significance as a benchmark for standards of human rights, it is essential to analyse the scope of the *Universal Declaration* with respect to the death penalty.

The *Universal Declaration* makes no mention of the death penalty. It does, however, enshrine the protection of the right to life in article 3. The debates in the Commission on Human Rights, in its Drafting Committee, and in the Third Committee of the General Assembly respecting adoption of the *Universal Declaration* indicate that the issue of abolition of the death penalty was crucial in the drafting of article 3. Three general approaches were considered by the drafters.

The first was to recognize in express form the death penalty as a limitation or an exception to the right to life. This approach was in fact followed in several subsequent international treaties, including the *Civil Rights Covenant*,[9] the *European Convention on Human Rights*[10] and the *American Convention on Human Rights*,[11] although it did not find favour with the drafters of the *Declaration*. Article 29 of the *Universal Declaration* recognizes that the human rights and fundamental freedoms stated in that document are subject to limits but gives no more precise indication of the scope of those limits or of whether there are in fact some rights which may not be limited. Critics of this first approach felt it suggested an endorsement of the death penalty by the United Nations and only harmed the eventual objective, which was abolition of the death penalty.

The second approach was to proclaim without equivocation the abolition of the death penalty. As the *Declaration* was a form of manifesto or statement of objectives, countries could recognize the goal of abolition even though their internal legislation still permitted capital punishment. This view found considerable support among delegates involved in the drafting process but failed to rally the majority, largely because of fears of isolating those States which still retained capital punishment. Nowhere in the *travaux* is there a defence of the death penalty as such, and the decision to exclude abolition was in no way intended as a statement that the United Nations in some way approved of or accepted the death penalty.

The third solution, one of compromise, stated the right to life in absolute terms, making no mention of either abolition or retention of the death penalty. This third approach, ambiguous and equivocating, eventually prevailed.

[8] 'Vienna Declaration and Programme of Action', UN Doc. A/CONF.157/24 (Part I), chap. III, 14 *HRLJ* 352.

[9] Art. 6.

[10] (1955) 213 UNTS 221, ETS 5, art. 2§1 (hereinafter the *European Convention*) (see Appendix 14, p. 423).

[11] (1979) 1144 UNTS 123, OASTS 36, art. 4 (hereinafter the *American Covention*) (see Appendix 20, p. 436).

Of course, the death penalty was not the only question debated by the drafters of the *Declaration* with respect to article 3. The other difficult issue was abortion. Many delegations to the United Nations would have preferred some mention that the right to life began 'from conception', thereby protecting the foetus. On this point, too, compromise dictated silence.

1.1 The origins of the Universal Declaration

The importance of an international declaration of human rights was recognized at the very earliest planning stages of the United Nations, at a time when the outcome of Second World War was still uncertain. As far back as 1942, United States State Department officials had given consideration to an international bill of rights as part of their scheme for the post-war united nations organization. A draft declaration, based on the American *Bill of Rights*, the French *Déclaration des droits de l'homme et du citoyen*, the English *Bill of Rights*, the post-World War I minority treaties and the 1929 declaration of the Institute of International Law, was prepared. It included guarantees of equality before the law with respect to 'life, liberty, property, enterprise and employment' and stated that nobody could be deprived of life without due process.[12]

The preliminary meetings for the organization of the United Nations were held in late 1944 at Dumbarton Oaks. The Dumbarton Oaks Proposals only set out the goals of the United Nations Organization and did not venture into the specific human rights that would be addressed. The phrase employed was: 'promote respect for human rights and fundamental freedoms'.[13] The following year at San Francisco the *United Nations Charter*[14] was adopted and the organization inaugurated. The *Charter* declared that the promotion and encouragement of respect for human rights was an obligation upon member States[15] and assigned the responsibility for human rights matters to the Economic and Social Council[16] and to Commissions that were to be set up by the Council.[17]

At San Francisco, there were unsuccessful efforts to adopt an 'international bill of rights' as part of the *Charter* or as an adjunct to it, and with this in mind drafts were submitted by Panama and Cuba. The Cuban draft proclaimed:

[12] Ruth B. Russell, *A History of the United Nations Charter*, Washington, D.C.: Brookings Institution, 1958, pp. 323–325; Louis B. Sohn, 'How American International Lawyers Prepared for the San Francisco Bill of Rights', (1995) 89 *AJIL* 540; Johannes Morsink, *The Universal Declaration of Human Rights, Origins, Drafting and Intent*, Philadelphia: University of Pennsylvania Press, 1998.
[13] *Dumbarton Oaks Proposals for a General International Organization*, Documents of the UN Conference on International Organization, San Francisco, 1945, Vol. III, p. 19.
[14] *Charter of the United Nations*, (1945) 39 *AJIL* Supp. 190, 145 BFSP 805.
[15] *Ibid.*, art. 55§c; see Jean-Bernard Marie, Nicole Questiaux, 'Article 55: alinéa c', in Jean-Pierre Cot, Alain Pellet, eds., *La Charte des Nations Unies*, Paris, Brussels: Economica, Bruylant, 1985, pp. 863–883; E. Schwelb, 'The International Court of Justice and the Human Rights Clauses of the Charter', (1972) 68 *AJIL* 337.
[16] *Charter of the United Nations*, arts. 60, 62§2.   [17] *Charter of the United Nations*, art. 68.

The right to life, to liberty, to personal security and to respect of his dignity as a human being.[18]

The Panamanian draft, derived from a version prepared by the American Law Institute, made no mention of the right to life.[19] The San Francisco conference did not proceed with the matter, leaving it as a priority for the future Commission on Human Rights.[20]

In order to give detailed direction to the Economic and Social Council for the establishment of the Commission, a 'nuclear commission on human rights' was convened in May 1946, with Anna Eleanor Roosevelt as its chair.[21] Although consideration of the Cuban[22] and Panamanian[23] drafts was on its agenda,[24] the Commission took the view that the actual drafting of the bill would be the task of he 'Permanent Commission on Human Rights', following the creation of that body.[25] The report of the nuclear commission to the Economic and Social Council contained recommendations to this effect.[26] Subsequently, the Commission on Human Rights was created by the Economic and Social Council and it was assigned responsibility for drafting the 'international bill of rights'.[27]

During the second part of the General Assembly's first session, in the autumn of 1946,[28] Panama asked that its draft declaration[29] be discussed, but the matter was referred to the new Commission.[30] Meanwhile, Chile submitted yet a third declaration, which was, in effect, the draft 'American Declaration' which had been prepared by the Inter-American Juridical Committee subsequent to the Chapultepec conference in the spring of 1945. Dated 31 December 1945, it was the work of Francisco Campos, F. Nièto del Rio, Charles G. Fenwick and A. Gómez Robledo, and contains the first specific mention of the issue of capital punishment in international human rights law.[31]

---

[18] UNCIO Doc. 2G/14(g), which mentioned the right to life.   [19] UNCIO Doc. 2G/7/(2).

[20] The First Committee did, on 1 June 1945, adopt a resolution that the General Assembly should examine the Panamanian text and give it an effective form (UNCIO Doc. 944, I–I, 34). See also Lilly E. Landerer, 'Capital Punishment as a Human Rights Issue Before the United Nations', (1971) 4 *HRJ* 511, at p. 513.

[21] UN Doc. A/125/Add.1, p. 7; UN Doc. E/HR/6, p. 3.

[22] UN Doc. E/HR/1; UN Doc. E/HR/13, p. 1; UN Doc. E/HR/15, pp. 4–5.

[23] UN Doc. E/HR/3; UN Doc. E/HR/13, p. 1; UN Doc. E/HR/15, pp. 4–5.

[24] UN Doc. E/HR/5.

[25] UN Doc. E/HR/13, p. 1; UN Doc. E/HR/15, pp. 4–5, UN Doc. E/HR/19, p. 5.

[26] UN Doc. E/38/Rev.1.   [27] UN Doc. A/125, para. 47.

[28] UN Doc. A/101, UN Doc. A/118.   [29] *Ibid.*   [30] UN Doc. A/234, p. 3.

[31] UN Doc. A/C.1/38; UN Doc. E/CN.4/2. See also Francisco Campos, F. Nièto del Rio, Charles G. Fenwick, A. Gómez Robledo, 'Report to Accompany the Draft Declaration of the International Rights and Duties of Man', (1946) 40 *AJIL Supp.* 100. The right to life provison, which was Article 1, read:

> Every person has the right to life. This right extends to the right to life from the moment of conception; to the right to life of incurables, imbeciles and the insane. It includes the right to

1.2 Drafting by the Commission on Human Rights

The first session of the Commission on Human Rights was held from 27 January to 10 February 1947.[32] In addition to the drafts from Cuba, Panama and Chile,[33] a fourth text had been submitted by the American Federation of Labor, which also made no mention of the right to life and focused its attention on economic and social rights.[34] The Commission's Secretariat, headed by John P. Humphrey, prepared a general memorandum on the proposed bill of rights,[35] a comparative analysis of the four drafts[36] and a study of the human rights provisions in trusteeship agreements endorsed by the General Assembly.[37] Another fourteen draft declarations from various individuals and groups completed the files of the Commission Secretariat,[38] and these too were analysed in a working paper prepared by the Secretariat. Proposals were also submitted by the United States[39] and India.[40]

The Secretariat suggested that the Bill might take one of three forms: a declaration in the General Assembly, a binding treaty or an amendment to the *Charter*.[41] The Secretariat classified the rights set out in the various drafts into

sustenance and support in the case of those unable to support themselves by their own efforts; and it implies a duty of the state to see to it that such support is made available.

The right to life may be denied by the state only on the ground of a conviction of the gravest of crimes, to which the death penalty has been attached.

See our discussion of the drafting of the *American Declaration of the Rights and Duties of Man* in Chapter 8 below.

[32] UN Doc. E/CN.4/SR.1*. For a history of the work of the Commission on Human Rights in the drafting of the *Universal Declaration* and the *Covenant*, see Jean-Bernard Marie, *La Commission des droits de l'homme de l'ONU*, Paris: Pedone, 1975.

[33] UN Doc. E/CN.4/2. It was also reproduced for the Drafting Committee in UN Doc. E/CN.4/AC.1/3/Add.1, at p. 14.

[34] UN Doc. E/CT.2/2, UN Doc. E/C.2/32.   [35] UN Doc. E/CN.4/W.4.

[36] UN Doc. E/CN.4/W.8.

[37] UN Doc. E/CN.4/W.13. There is nothing about the 'right to life' in this document.

[38] UN Doc. E/CN.4/W.16. See also Verdoodt, *Naissance*, p. 41. Almost all of the documents originated in the Western hemisphere. The earliest was the work of Alexandre Alvarez, and had been presented at the Havana meeting of the American Institute of International Law in January 1917. The second was adopted at the Briarcliff meeting of the International Law Institute in October 1929 (*Annuaire de l'Institut de droit international*, 1929, Vol. II, Brussels: Goemaere, 1929, pp. 118–120; Institut de droit international, 'Declaration of International Rights of Man', (1941) 35 *AJIL* 663). Several of the proposals were the work of individuals: H. G. Wells, Wilfred Parsons, Rollin McNitt, Irving Jacobs, Gustavoi Gutiérrez and H. Lauterpacht (from the book H. Lauterpacht, *An International Bill of the Rights of Man*, New York: Columbia University Press, 1945, p. 69; René Cassin said this work deserved 'une place exceptionnelle' in the history of the *Universal Declaration*: Cassin, 'La Déclaration universelle des droits de l'homme,' (1951) 79 *RCADI* 237, p. 272). Several were from non-governmental organizations: Free World, American Bar Association, World Government Association, American Association of the United Nations, American Jewish Conference, Commission to Study the Organization of Peace. The right to life was recognized in many of these drafts, according to an analysis by the Secretariat: UN Doc. E/CN.4/W.18. For a discussion of these drafts, see UN Doc. E/CN.4/Sub.2/7.

[39] UN Doc. E/CN.4/4, which did not mention the right to life.

[40] UN Doc. E/CN.4/11, which did not mention the right to life. It was entitled 'Draft of a Resolution for the General Assembly'.

[41] UN Doc. E/CN.4/W.4, p. 10.

three broad categories: 'the status of equality', 'the status of liberty' and 'the status of social security'. 'Life' was the first title enumerated in the 'status of liberty' category.[42] The Secretariat's analysis was discussed by the Commission at its thirteenth plenary meeting, where the 'right to life' was considered under the not altogether synonymous title of the 'right to existence'.[43] The summary records provide a *précis* of remarks by Colonel Hodgson of Australia, who considered the right to life to be so obvious that its mention was unnecessary:

> In his opinion certain rights enumerated in the list paragraph 2 were quite obvious, and already guaranteed. That applied, for example, to the right to existence which was, so to speak, a *sine qua non*. It was a right which was already assured by the laws of all countries . . . [44]

René Cassin replied immediately:

> As regards the right to existence, for example, the fundamental consideration was to assure the protection of human life. That certainly was not as elementary a right as one might believe for in 1933, when Germany violated those principles, there were many countries in the world who asked themselves whether they had a right to intervene. He considered that it was of fundamental importance to affirm the right of human beings to existence.[45]

During its first session, the Commission on Human Rights recognized that an *ad hoc* 'Drafting Committee' would be best suited to prepare the draft bill.[46] This approach was endorsed by the Economic and Social Council, which requested the Secretariat to prepare a documented outline.[47] The outline was to be studied by the Drafting Committee and mailed to Commission members by 25 June 1947. It would then be considered at the Commission's second session at the end of the year, returned to the Drafting Committee if necessary for a redraft, resubmitted to the Commission on Human Rights, and then sent on to the Economic and Social Council, with a view to adoption by the General Assembly at its 1948 session. The Drafting Committee was composed of representatives from Australia, Chile, China, France, Lebanon, the Soviet Union, the United Kingdom and the United States.

In preparation for this session, and according to its instructions, the Secretariat of the Commission on Human Rights drew up a draft outline bill

---

[42] UN Doc. E/CN.4.18; in its earlier working paper, the Secretariat had described this third category as the 'status of survival'. The initial working paper did not include the 'right to life' as part of the enumeration: UN Doc. E/CN.4/W.4., p. 12.

[43] However, when these comments were subsequently repeated in an analysis prepared by the Secretariat of the Commission on Human Rights (UN Doc. E/CN.4/AC.1/3), the expression 'right to existence' which had been used in the summary records was replaced by 'right to life'.

[44] UN Doc. E/CN.4/SR.13, p. 7.   [45] *Ibid.*

[46] UN Doc. E/CN.4/SR.9, p. 5; UN Doc. E/CN.4/SR.12, p. 5; UN Doc. E/259, §10(a).

[47] UN Doc. E/RES/46(IV), UN Doc. E/325.

consisting of a preamble and forty-eight articles.[48] The article on the right to life proposed by the Secretariat recognized the death penalty as the sole exception to the right to life:

> Everyone has the right to life. This right can be denied only to persons who have been convicted under general law of some crime to which the death penalty is attached.[49]

A lengthy annotated text was also prepared by the Secretariat,[50] containing the draft outline articles, accompanied by the observations made by members of the Commission on Human Rights at its first session,[51] equivalent articles in the draft international declarations or proposals submitted by Chile, Cuba, Panama, India and the United States of America, and relevant texts from national constitutions.[52]

The Commission had also received comments from individuals and non-governmental organizations, and these too were included in the document. The only submission relating to the death penalty came from the Comite Permanente de Relaciones Espiritualistas, in a letter dated 8 February 1947 to the Secretary-General, requesting that capital punishment be outlawed, 'as any form of violent death is unChristian'.[53]

In anticipation of the Drafting Committee session scheduled for June 1947, both the United Kingdom and the United States produced new proposals. The United Kingdom proposal, which specifically mentioned the death penalty as an exception to the right to life, would be discussed and then considered as an initial draft not of the declaration but of the covenant.[54] A few days later, the United States submitted a proposal that similarly expressed the death penalty as an exception to the right to life.[55]

---

[48] UN Doc. E/CN.4/AC.1/3.   [49] *Ibid.*; reprinted in UN Doc. E/CN.4/21, Annex A.

[50] UN Doc. E/CN.4/AC.1/3/Add.1.

[51] With respect to the 'right to life', Cassin's remarks, cited above, were reproduced.

[52] The provisions of twenty-six national constitutions dealing with the right to life were presented. There was nothing from countries with an unwritten constitution, such as the United Kingdom, Canada, and Australia, with the curious result that nowhere in the list was the *Magna Carta* mentioned. The United States *Constitution's* fifth amendment was reproduced, but not the fourteenth. Of the twenty-six constitutions, eighteen expressly addressed the issue of the death penalty and its exceptions.

[53] UN Doc. E/CN.4/AC.1/6, p. 2.

[54] UN Doc. E/CN.4/AC.1/4, p. 9; reprinted as Annex B of the Drafting Committee report, UN Doc. E/CN.4/21. The United Kingdom proposal and the Secretariat Draft Outline were reproduced in a comparative outline, UN Doc. E/CN.4/AC.1/3/Add.3. The right to life provision stated:
> Article 8. It shall be unlawful to deprive any person of his life save in the execution of the sentence of a court following on his conviction of a crime for which this penalty is provided by law.

[55] UN Doc. E/CN.4/AC.1/8; reprinted as Annex C of the Drafting Committee report, UN Doc. E/CN.4/21; the United Kingdom, United States and Secretariat proposals were reproduced in a comparative outline, UN Doc. E/CN.4/AC.1/11. It read:
> Article 8. The right to life is fundamental and may not be denied to any person except upon conviction for the gravest of crimes under general law providing for the penalty of death.

The Secretariat draft article 3, on the right to life, was considered at the second plenary meeting of the Drafting Committee, in June 1947, together with the United Kingdom draft. Eleanor Roosevelt read both articles to the Drafting Committee and then noted that there was a movement underway in some States to abolish the death penalty. She suggested that it might be better not to use the term 'death penalty'.[56] Her views found support from the Soviet delegate, Koretsky, who argued that the United Nations should not in any way signify approval of the death penalty.[57] René Cassin cautioned that even countries which had no death penalty must take into account the fact that some are in the process of abolishing it. He preferred the Secretariat draft article 3 to the United Kingdom draft article 8, adding that if the principle of universal abolition were to be adopted, it should not impose a strict obligation on States that wished to maintain the death penalty.[58]

At its third plenary meeting, the Drafting Committee compared the Secretariat's article 3 with the alternative text prepared by United the States. The expression 'gravest of crimes' in the United States alternative was criticized by Wilson of the United Kingdom for vagueness, because what might be considered grave in one country could be viewed differently in another.[59] By the close of its sixth plenary meeting, the Drafting Committee had agreed to set up a Working Group, composed of the representatives of France, Lebanon and the United Kingdom.[60] This Working Group in turn decided that it would be preferable for the draft declaration to be the work of a single individual and asked René Cassin to assume the responsibility. Cassin was to prepare a draft declaration based on those articles in the Secretariat outline that he felt belonged in the Bill, and he returned in a few days with a text consisting of a preamble and forty-four articles.[61]

Obviously influenced by the earlier discussion on the subject of capital punishment, Cassin had decided to delete any mention of the death penalty from the draft article on the right to life. His proposed provision on the 'right to life' read:

> No one shall be deprived of life or personal liberty, or be convicted or punished for crime in any manner, save by judgment of a competent and impartial tribunal, in conformity with law, after a fair public trial at which he has had the opportunity for a fair hearing, the right to be confronted with the witnesses against him, the right of compulsory process of obtaining witnesses in his favour, and right to consult with and be represented by counsel.

[56] UN Doc. E/CN.4/AC.1/SR.2, p. 10.
[57] UN Doc. E/CN.4/AC.1/SR.2, p. 11; his views were supported by Santa Cruz of Chile and Wilson of the United Kingdom. See Philippe de La Chapelle, *La Déclaration universelle des droits de l'homme et le catholicisme*, Paris; Librairie générale de droit et de jurisprudence, 1967, p. 94.
[58] UN Doc. E/CN.4/AC.1/SR.2, p. 10   [59] UN Doc. E/CN.4/AC.1/SR.3, p. 12.
[60] UN Doc. E/CN.4/AC.1/SR.6, p. 8; UN Doc. E/CN.4/21, §13.
[61] UN Doc. E/CN.4/AC.1/SR.7, p. 2; UN Doc. E/CN.4/21, §14; the draft is UN Doc. E/CN.4/AC.1/W.2/Rev.1.

Chapter 2. (Right to Life and Physical Inviolability)

> Article 7. Every human being has the right to life and to the respect of his physical inviolability. No person, even if found guilty, may be subjected to torture, cruelty or degrading treatment.[62]

The Working Group reviewed Cassin's text, studying only the preamble and the first six articles, and gave it back to him for another draft.[63] Cassin further revised his text[64] which was then examined by the Drafting Committee:[65]

> Article 7. Every human being has the right to life, to personal liberty and to personal security.[66]

Although in its early meetings in June 1947 there was no real distinction between the declaration and the convenant, by the close of its first session the Drafting Committee had determined to prepare two separate documents for the Commission, a draft declaration and a draft covenant.[67] The draft declaration was of course the text written by René Cassin, as modified, which made no mention of the death penalty. As for the covenant, the Drafting Committee agreed to submit the substantive proposals from the United Kingdom, also as modified,[68] together with an alternative proposal, from Lebanon, both of which referred explicitly to the death penalty as an exception to the right to life.[69]

The distinction in the approach to the two documents, with respect to the right to life, would persist. In fact, it remains to this day. The 'treaty', destined to impose binding legal obligations on states rather than mere goals or objectives, retained the death penalty as a permissible limit on the right to life through each of its successive drafts. On the other hand, nowhere in the draft declaration was the death penalty recognized as an exception to the right to life.

The notion that the 'International Bill of Rights' should consist of at lest two documents, the first a General Assembly resolution stating general principles

---

[62] UN Doc. E/CN.4/AC.1/W.2/Rev.1; it is also published as Annex D of UN Doc. E/CN.4/21.

[63] *Ibid.*   [64] UN Doc. E/CN.4/AC.W.2/Rev.2.   [65] UN Doc. E/CN.4/AC.1/SR.8, p. 4.

[66] UN Doc. E/CN.4/AC.1/W.2/Rev.2; UN Doc. E/CN.4/AC.1/SR.12; Annex F of UN Doc. E/CN.4/21.

[67] UN Doc. E/CN.4/21, para. 12.

[68] UN Doc. E/CN.4/AC.1/4, Annex I; is is also published as Annex G of UN Doc. E/CN.4/21. It does not seem entirely clear that the United Kingdom draft was intended to be a 'covenant' rather than a 'declaration'. The two notions were somewhat confused at this early stage, as can be seen by the fact that the Secretariat prepared a comparison of the Secretariat, United Kingdom and United States drafts (UN Doc. E/CN.4/AC.1/11). The Secretariat draft formed the basis of the future declaration, the United States draft was a commentary on it, and the United Kingdom draft was the antecedent of the future covenant.

[69] Annex G of UN Doc. E/CN.4/21:

> It shall be unlawful to deprive any person, from the moment of conception, of his life or bodily integrity, save in the execution of the sentence of a court following on his conviction of a crime for which this penalty is provided by law.

and the second a binding instrument or 'covenant', won rapid acceptance. Resolutions confirming this approach were drafted by the United Kingdom[70] and France.[71] In November 1947, the United States also presented two separate drafts along these lines.[72] Ecuador submitted a 'Draft Charter of International Human Rights and Duties', which borrowed heavily from an earlier Chilean proposal and had the distinction of being the first text to openly proclaim abolition of the death penalty. It began with the affirmation: 'There shall be no death penalty.'[73]

The Commission on Human Rights held its second session in December 1947. Eleanor Roosevelt presented the report of the Drafting Committee[74] and explained that the Commission had to decide whether there should be both a 'declaration' and a 'convention', and what measures of implementation should be adopted.[75] Three working groups were set up, one on the draft declaration, another on the draft convention and a third on the measures of implementation.[76] Roosevelt was named chair of the Working Group on the 'declaration', assisted by René Cassin, as *rapporteur*.[77] There was no discussion on the issue of capital punishment, debate centring on the economic and social dimensions of the right to life[78] and on the troublesome question of abortion.[79] The original Drafting Committee text was adopted by four votes, with two abstentions.[80] The Working Group on the draft covenant focused exclusively on the issue of abortion,[81] and this debate continued into the plenary session of the Commission.[82]

The death penalty did, however, become a significant issue when the report of the Working Party on the 'declaration' was submitted to the plenary Commission.[83] The delegate from Uruguay pointed out that many countries refused to apply the death penalty on philosophical, sociological and moral grounds. Uruguay said that the death penalty should in no case be imposed for political offences and proposed an amendment proclaiming that 'human life is

---

[70] UN Doc. E/CN.4/42 and UN Doc. E/CN.4/49.   [71] UN Doc. E/CN.4/48.
[72] UN Doc. E/CN.4/36 and Add. 1 and Add. 2; see also UN Doc. E/600, Annex A, p. 21.
[73] UN Doc. E/CN.4/32.

    Article I. (1) *Right to life*: There shall be no death penalty. Mutilation, flogging, and other tortures and degrading procedures are categorically forbidden, whether as penalties, corrective measures, or means of investigating offences.

        Everyone, including incurables, imbeciles, and the insane, has the right to life from the moment of conception.

        Persons unable to support themselves by their own efforts have the right to sustenance and support, and the State has the corresponding duty of seeing to it that such support is made available.

[74] UN Doc. E/CN.4/21.   [75] UN Doc. E/CN.4/SR.23, p. 4.
[76] UN Doc. E/CN.4/SR.29, p. 12.   [77] UN Doc. E/CN.4/57; UN Doc. E/600, para. 21.
[78] UN Doc. E/CN.4/AC.2/SR.3, p. 5.   [79] *Ibid.*, pp. 7–8.
[80] UN Doc. E/CN.4/AC.2/SR.3, p. 8.   [81] UN Doc. E/CN.4/56; UN Doc. E/600, para. 21.
[82] UN Doc. E/CN.4/SR.35, pp. 12–17.   [83] UN Doc. E/CN.4/57.

inviolable'.[84] At the request of Belgium, a separate vote was taken on each of the three paragraphs in the Uruguayan amendment, and the third paragraph, dealing with the death penalty, received three votes in favour, nine against and five abstentions.[85] As a result, the earlier Drafting Committee text that said 'Everyone has the right to life, to liberty and security of the person' was left unchanged by the Commission.[86] In fact, the text was to remain untouched throughout the subsequent debates, despite frequent attempts at amendment. The Commission adopted the text by sixteen votes in favour, with no recorded negative votes or abstentions.[87] The Commission's report on the second session included comments from the representative of Uruguay to the effect that the death penalty 'could not be justified by any philosophical or social arguments on any grounds of criminal or ethical policy'.[88]

Comments from Member States on the Commission's draft declaration and covenant were solicited by the Secretary-General.[89] Two States attempted to introduce reference to the death penalty as an express exception to the right to life in the declaration. Brazil said that the article on the right to life in the declaration should include the restriction contained in the draft covenant, namely 'save in the execution of the sentence of a court following his conviction for a crime for which this penalty is provided by law'.[90] New Zealand proposed an amendment to the draft declaration that would make the right to life 'subject to deprivation only in cases prescribed by law and after due process'.[91]

The Drafting Committee held its second and final session at Lake Success, New York, in May 1948, prior to the third session of the Commission on Human Rights. It studied both the draft declaration and the draft covenant. During consideration of the right to life article in the declaration, attention was almost entirely devoted to the abortion question, and the issue of capital punishment was virtually ignored.[92] The chair, Eleanor Roosevelt, brushed aside a suggestion from the representative of the American Federation of Labor that

---

[84] UN Doc. E/CN.4/SR.35, at p. 13.

> Human life is inviolable. The state shall grant protection to all persons born or those suffering from incurable diseases and those physically or mentally deficient are also entitled to it.
>
> The right to life includes the right of obtaining from the State minimum standards for a dignified and worthy life.
>
> The death penalty shall never be applied to political offenders. With regard to criminal offenders, it shall only be applied after sentence rendered under existing laws after a trial with the necessary guarantees for a just sentence.

[85] UN Doc. E/CN.4/SR.35, p. 14.   [86] UN Doc. E/600, Annex A, art. 4.

[87] UN Doc. E/CN.4/SR.35, p. 14.

[88] UN Doc. E/CN.4/77, UN Doc. E/600; the draft declaration is UN Doc. E/CN.4/77, Annex A, UN Doc. E/600, Annex A; the draft convention is UN Doc. E/CN.4/77, Annex B, UN Doc. E/600, Annex B; the report was considered by the Economic and Social Council: UN Doc. E/SR.128.

[89] UN Doc. SOA/17/1//01.   [90] UN Doc. E/CN.4/82/Add.2.

[91] UN Doc. E/CN.4/82/Add.12, p. 24.

[92] For discussion of the right to life, see UN Doc. E/CN.4/AC.1/SR.35, pp. 2–6.

the entire article in the draft declaration be replaced with the corresponding text in the *American Declaration on the Rights and Duties of Man*, which had been recently adopted at Bogotá.[93] The right to life provision in the declaration which had been adopted the previous year at Geneva by the Commission was again adopted by the Drafting Committee, this time by seven votes with one abstention.[94]

The Commission's discussion of the right to life provision of the declaration was rather perfunctory. Lebeau of Belgium questioned the need to say that every individual has the right to life, because in his opinion the declaration would only apply to those who were already alive. René Cassin answered that, at a time when millions of people had been deprived of their life, it was important for the Commission to emphasize that right.[95] Lebeau then said that, if this were the case, the wording should be changed to: 'Everyone has the right to protection of his life.' Otherwise, Belgium would have to abstain in voting on the draft article, he said.[96] The Soviet delegate suggested that the remarks of Lebeau were logical but that the article should nevertheless remain in its original form. He said that during discussion of the article in the Drafting Committee, he had criticized its lack of concreteness and its remoteness from reality, given that millions of people were dying of starvation, succumbing to epidemics and being exterminated in wars.[97] At Lebeau's request, the article was voted on in two stages. The first part, 'Every one has the right to life', was adopted by fourteen votes to none, with one abstention (presumably Lebeau); the second, 'Every one has the right to liberty and security of person', was adopted by fifteen votes to none.[98] Perhaps the most significant change made by the Commission at its third session to the draft declaration was the addition of article 29§2, providing for limitations on rights in a general form.[99]

The Commission's draft of the declaration was then submitted to the Economic and Social Council, where it received more or less summary approval.[100] At its August 1948 session, each of the Council members was invited to comment briefly on the drafts, although no amendments were ever proposed. Four delegates touched on the right to life. Santa Cruz, of Chile, described article 3 as containing 'the essence of the declaration'.[101] The Council agreed to submit the

[93] UN Doc. E/CN.4/AC.1/SR.35, p. 7. Article I of the *American Declaration*, OAS Doc. OEA/Ser.L./V/1.4, reads: 'Every human being has the right to life, liberty and the security of his person.'
[94] UN Doc. E/CN.4/AC.1/SR.35, p. 8.   [95] UN Doc. E/CN.4/SR.53, p. 2.
[96] *Ibid.*, p. 3.   [97] *Ibid.*   [98] *Ibid.*
[99] C. K. Boyle, 'The Concept of Arbitrary Deprivation of Life', in Bertrand G. Ramcharan, ed., *The Right to Life in International Law*, Boston: Martinus Nijhoff, 1985, pp. 221–244, p. 227.
[100] UN Doc. E/SR.180, UN Doc. E/SR.201, UN Doc. E/SR.202, UN Doc. E/SR.215, UN Doc. E/SR.218.
[101] UN Doc. E/SR.218, p. 3; see also UN Doc. E/SR.215, p. 28 (Venezuela); UN Doc. E/SR.215, p. 34 (Soviet Union).

Commission's draft 'International Declaration of Human Rights' to the General Assembly.[102]

1.3 Drafting by the Third Committee of the General Assembly

The General Assembly held the first part of its third session in Paris, in the autumn of 1948.[103] Before the text was submitted to the General Assembly for the final vote, article by article analysis of the draft declaration was conducted by the Third Committee. The debates in the Third Committee on article 3 were lengthy and heated, consuming five half-day sessions which sometimes degenerated into the tense polemics that characterized the dawn of the cold war.[104] The succinct text of article 3 that had been submitted by the Commission on Human Rights[105] eventually came through unscathed. It survived numerous attempts at amendment,[106] including one aimed at abolition of the death penalty,[107] and in a roll-call vote on the provision not one delegate opposed its adoption, although there were eight abstentions.

Most of the controversy surrounding the right to life provision of the declaration came from the delegations of the Soviet Union, the socialist States of Eastern Europe, and Latin America. The United States, the United Kingdom, France and a number of their allies consistently upheld the text of the Commission draft.[108] There was almost no discussion of the abortion issue, which had

[102] UN Doc. E/SR.218, p. 16.   [103] UN Doc. A/632, UN Doc. E/800.

[104] A first attempt at closure, after three days of discussion, was unsuccessful: UN Doc. A/C.3/SR.105, p. 2.

[105] UN Doc. E/800:
> Everyone has the right to life, liberty and security of person.

[106] Panama, UN Doc. A/C.3/220:
> Every human being has the right to exist and to maintain, develop, protect and defend his existence.

Cuba, UN Doc. A/C.3/224:
> Every human being has the right to life, liberty, security and integrity of the person.

Mexico, UN Doc. A/C.3/266:
> Add, as a second paragraph, the following: 'The right to maintenance, health, education and work, is considered essential in order to obtian an increase in the standard of living of the individual, as well as to secure the full existence of social justice and the full development of the human being.'

Uruguay: UN Doc. A/C.3/268:
> Everyone has the right to life, honour, liberty, and to legal, economic and social security.

Lebanon, Cuba and Uruguay: UN Doc. A/C.3/274/Rev.1 (as Belgium).

Belgium: UN Doc. A/C.3/274/Rev. 1:
> Everyone has the right to life, liberty, and respect of the physical and moral integrity of his person.

[107] Soviet Union, UN Doc. A/C.3/265:
> Everyone has the right to life. The State should ensure the protection of each individual against criminal attempts on his person. It should also ensure conditions that obviate the danger of death by hunger and exhaustion. The death penalty should be abolished in time of peace.

[108] See, for example, the comments of René Cassin: UN Doc. A/C.3/SR. 103, p. 6.

so troubled the members of the Drafting Committee and of the Commission on Human Rights.[109]

In a very general sense, the critics felt that the Commission draft was somewhat outmoded, patterned on an eighteenth-century concept of human rights that had emerged from the works of Rousseau, the United States *Declaration of Independence*, and the French *Déclaration des droits de l'homme et du citoyen*.[110] The Soviet Union attempted to address this point with a proposal to replace the Commission's right to life provision with a completely new text that imposed positive duties on States to protect individuals against hunger.[111] In addition to the expected support from Byelorussia and Ukraine, the first three sentences of the Soviet draft were also approved of by Yugoslavia,[112] Haiti,[113] the Dominican Republic,[114] Belgium[115] and Lebanon.[116] Even Cassin stated that the French delegation had no problem with the substance of the Soviet proposal, but that it considered it to be out of place.[117]

For the purposes of this study, the most significant feature of the Soviet proposal was its fourth sentence: 'The death penalty should be abolished in time of peace.' In the ensuing debate, hardly a voice was raised to defend capital punishment in peacetime, although a few were candid enough to admit that their governments had not yet abolished the death penalty.[118] The view was widespread among delegates that, although there was little quarrel with the principle contained in the death penalty article, it was controversial and therefore inopportune[119] or premature.[120] The United Kingdom representative said that its inclusion in the declaration might make it difficult for some States to accept.[121] Several delegates explained that they would abstain in the vote as a result.[122] The Netherlands, although agreeing with abolition of the death penalty, said it had no place in a declaration of human rights and should be reconsidered when a separate declaration of the rights and duties of States was being prepared.[123]

---

[109] See: UN Doc. A/C.3/SR.105, p. 9; UN Doc. A/C.3/SR.104/Corr.1.

[110] St Lot, the Haitian delegate and *rapporteur* of the Committee, said that the Commission draft had been overly influenced by the doctrine of individualism of Jean-Jacques Rousseau: UN Doc. A/C.3/SR.105, p. 3.

[111] UN Doc. A/C.3/265 (see n. 107 above).   [112] UN Doc. A/C.3/SR.103, p. 11.

[113] UN Doc. A/C.3/SR.105, p. 2.

[114] The Dominican delegate, Bernadino, also supported the joint amendment from Lebanon, Cuba and Uruguay: UN Doc. A/C.3/SR.105, p. 3.

[115] UN Doc. A/C.3/SR.103, p. 8.   [116] UN Doc. A/C.3/SR.102, pp. 4–5.

[117] UN Doc. A/C.3/SR.103, p. 6; the same criticism was made by Costa Rica: UN Doc. A/C.3/SR.105, p. 5.

[118] Belgium (UN Doc. A/C.3/SR.103, p. 9).

[119] UN Doc. A/C.3/SR.105, p. 5; Norway (UN Doc. A/C.3/SR.104, p. 12); Pakistan (UN Doc. A/C.3/SR.105, p. 8); Haiti (UN Doc. A/C.3/SR.105, p. 2); New Zealand (UN Doc. A/C.3/SR.105, p. 10); Australia (UN Doc. A/C.3/SR.103, p. 2); Turkey (UN Doc. A/C.3/SR.103, p. 11).

[120] UN Doc. A/C.3/SR.102, pp. 4–5.   [121] *Ibid.*, p. 9.

[122] Pakistan: UN Doc. A/C.3/SR.105, p. 8; Peru: UN Doc. A/C.3/SR.104, p. 10.

[123] UN Doc. A/C.3/SR.103, p. 10.

Brazil explained that, although it did not allow the death penalty, this was a matter for penal legislation and not an issue properly before the Third Committee.[124] Eleanor Roosevelt of the United States said that the Third Committee was not attempting to write criminal law, and that the declaration was not the place for the issue of capital punishement.[125]

The Soviet amendment was quite clearly restricted to abolition in peace-time only, and when the suggestion was made that this be extended to wartime as well, the Soviet delegate actually argued in favour of the death penalty.[126] No country which had suffered aggression and occupation could accept that point of view, said Pavlov. By accepting the principle of the abolition of the death penalty in time of war, the declaration would guarantee the defence of war criminals.[127]

It is difficult to appreciate this exception outside of the context of post-war Europe. The *Charter of the Nuremberg Tribunal*[128] had provided for the possibility of capital punishment, and the sentence was actually imposed on several of the Nazi leaders.[129] A report prepared by the Secretariat of the United Nations more than thirty years later noted that 'the post-war years were not conducive to allowing Member States to come to an unequivocal position on the issue. Some countries with a long abolitionist tradition argued for barring the death penalty during times of war, while other members proposed an exception for offenders guilty of crimes against mankind.'[130]

Several Latin American delegates were unhappy with the Soviet amendment because it did not go far enough; they simply could not accept the death penalty, even in wartime. Costa Rica's delegation said it would abstain from voting on the death penalty provision because of its restriction to times of peace.[131] The Venezuelan delegate said he could not support the Soviet proposal on the death penalty, because it implied that such punishment was legal in times of war,

---

[124] *Ibid.*, pp. 7–8. Virtually identical comments were made by the Syrian representative: UN Doc. A/C.3/SR.103, p. 8, and by the Egyptian delegate: UN Doc. A/C.3/SR.107, p. 6.

[125] UN Doc. A/C.3/SR.103, p. 12.

[126] On the use of the death penalty in the Soviet Union, see: W. Adams, 'Capital Punishment in Imperial and Soviet Criminal Law', (1970) 18 *American Journal of Comparative Law* 575; William Carty Quillin, 'The Death Penalty in the Soviet Union', (1977) 5 *American Journal of Criminal Law* 225; G. P. Van den Berg, 'The Soviet Union and the Death Penalty', (1983) 35 *Soviet Studies* 154; Andrew Scobell, 'The Death Penalty under Socialism, 1917–90: China, the Soviet Union, Cuba, and the German Democratic Republic', (1991) 12 *Criminal Justice History* 189.

[127] UN Doc. A/C.3/SR.104, p. 9. A review of the Soviet comments indicates that the argument was not so much about abolition of the death penalty in wartime as it was about the imposition of capital punishment on war criminals, something that might well take place in peacetime. The problem was accentuated when Denmark stated that it would vote against the Soviet amendment because, although it had been historically abolitionist, the death penalty had been reinstated *in peacetime* in order to deal with crimes arising during the war: UN Doc. A/C.3/SR.105, p.11. Belgium also refused to support the Soviet proposal because it made it impossible 'to shoot traitors in time of peace': UN Doc. A/C.3/SR.103, p. 9.

[128] (1951) 82 UNTS 279, art. 27.   [129] See Chapter 6.   [130] UN Doc. A/CONF.87/9, para. 4.

[131] UN Doc. A/C.3/SR.105, p. 6.

and this was contrary to his country's laws.[132] He said that he would have been able to vote in favour of the proposal if it had envisaged the complete abolition of the death penalty.[133] Uruguay's delegate proposed an amendment aimed at total abolition, but this was not voted upon.[134] The Ukrainian delegate argued that even if abolition were confined only to peacetime, something was gained, despite failure to reach agreement on total abolition.[135]

There were also suggestions that an abolitionist provision belonged in the declaration but not in the article on the right to life.[136] Uruguay felt it belonged with the provisions on legal rights, and Belgium proposed that it be placed with cruel, inhuman and degrading treatment or punishment.[137] Indeed, in the 1980s and 1990s, litigation dealing with capital punishment developed around construction of the norm prohibiting cruel punishment, specifically with respect to delay in imposition of the death sentence and method of execution.[138] However, during drafting of the basic norms, the death penalty debate revolved almost exclusively around the right to life.

The first of the amendments to be voted upon was that of the Soviet Union, which had been the focus of so much of the debate. It was agreed to vote on each sentence separately, and not to vote on the first sentence as this did not lead to any controversy.[139] After rejection of the second and third sentences,[140] the final sentence, dealing with the abolition of capital punishment, was defeated, on a roll-call vote, by twenty-one votes to nine, with eighteen abstentions.[141] Uruguay actually voted against the amendment, and other proponents of abolition abstained. The United Kingdom delegate expressed the view that the vote on the Soviet proposal aimed at abolition could in no way be interpreted as a vote for or against capital punishment.[142]

---

[132] UN Doc. A/C.3/SR.102.pp. 10–11.   [133] UN Doc. A/C.3/SR.104, p. 10.

[134] UN Doc. A/C.3/274/Rev.1.   [135] UN Doc. A/C.3/SR.105, p. 7.

[136] Ecuador reserved the right to make such a proposal: UN Doc. A/C.3/SR.104, p. 12.

[137] UN Doc. A/C.3/SR.103, p. 3.

[138] *Soering* v. *United Kingdom and Germany*, 7 July 1989 Series A, Vol. 161, 11 EHRR 439; *Ng* v. *Canada* (No. 469/1991), UN Doc. A/49/40, Vol.II, p. 189, (1994) 15 *HRLJ* 149; *Catholic Commission for Justice and Peace in Zimbabwe* v. *Attorney-General et al.*, (1993) 1 ZLR 242 (S), 4 SA 239 (ZSC), 14 *HRLJ* 323; *Pratt et al.* v. *Attorney General for Jamaica et al.*, [1993] 4 All E. R. 769, [1993] 2 LRC 349, [1994] 2 AC 1, [1993] 3 WLR 995, 43 WIR 340, 14 *HRLJ* 338, 33 ILM 364 (JCPC); *S.v. Makwanyane*, 1995 (3) SA 391, (1995) 16 *HRLJ* 154 (Constitutional Court of South Africa).

[139] UN Doc. A/C.3/SR.107, p. 4.   [140] *Ibid.*, p. 5.

[141] *Ibid.*, p. 6. *In favour.* Byelorussian Soviet Socialist Republic, Cuba Czechoslovakia, Dominican Republic, Mexico, Poland, Ukrainian Soviet Socialist Republic, Union of Soviet Socialist Republics, Yugoslavia.

Against: Afghanistan, Australia, Brazil, Canada, Chile, China, France, Greece, Guatemala, Haiti, Luxembourg, Panama, Philippines, Siam, Syria, Turkey, Union of South Africa, United Kingdom, United States of America, Uruguay, Yemen.

Abstained: Argentina, Belgium, Burma, Costa Rica, Denmark, Ecuador, Egypt, Ethiopia, Honduras, India, Lebanon, Netherlands, New Zealand, Norway, Peru, Saudi Arabia, Sweden, Venezuela.

[142] UN Doc. A/C.3/SR.103, p. 12.

The phrase 'right to life' was adopted by forty-nine votes to none, with two abstentions.[143] The phrase 'liberty and security of the person' was adopted by forty-seven votes to none, with four abstentions.[144] With the two phrases endorsed by the Committee, the chairman proceeded to put the entire article to a vote. Before doing so, however, the Soviet representative explained that his delegation objected to neither the first nor the second part of the provision but that it felt they did not form a complete article, as the guarantees of the right to life had been omitted.[145] According to the Soviet Union, the necessary guarantees were those in its amendment, including abolition of the death penalty in times of peace. As a result, the Soviet Union announced that it would abstain on the vote on the entire article.[146] Cuba,[147] Chile,[148] Mexico,[149] Panama[150] and Haiti[151] also presented justifications of their abstentions, based on various reasons unrelated to the death penalty issue. The right to life article, as originally drafted by the Commission on Human Rights, was voted on as a whole by the Third Committee, in a roll-call vote, and adopted by thirty-five votes in favour to none against, with twelve abstentions.[152]

The declaration was submitted to the General Assembly by the Third Committee on 7 December 1948.[153] A last-ditch attempt by the Soviet Union to postpone consideration of the declaration until the following year failed,[154] and what had now become the *Universal Declaration of Human Rights* was adopted by the General Assembly on 10 December 1948, without a dissenting vote but with several abstentions.[155]

1.4 Interpretation of the *Universal Declaration*

The *Universal Declaration* was not conceived of as an instrument creating binding norms at international law. Nevertheless, some jurists have since suggested that the *Declaration* represents a codification of customary norms.[156] The drafters

---

[143] UN Doc. A/C.3/SR.107, p. 14.   [144] *Ibid.*   [145] *Ibid.*, pp. 14–15.

[146] *Ibid.*, p. 15. Similar views were expressed by the delegates from Yugoslavia, the Byelorussian Soviet Socialist Republic and the Ukrainian Soviet Socialist Republic.

[147] *Ibid.*, at p. 15; similar view were expressed by the Ecuadorean delegate.

[148] *Ibid;* see also Philippines, UN Doc. A/C.3/SR.107, p. 17.

[149] *Ibid.*   [150] *Ibid.*   [151] *Ibid.*, p. 17.

[152] *Ibid.*, p. 16. *In favour*: Argentina, Australia, Belgium, Brazil, Canada, Chile, China, Denmark, Dominican Republic, Egypt, Ethiopia, France, Greece, Guatemala, Honduras, India, Iran, Luxembourg, Mexico, Netherlands, New Zealand, Norway, Peru, Philippines, Saudi Arabia, Siam, Sweden, Syria, Turkey, Union of South Africa, United Kingdom, United States of America, Uruguay, Venezuela, Yemen. *Abstained*: Byelorussian Soviet Socialist Republic, Cuba, Czechoslovakia, Ecuador, Haiti, Lebanon, Pakistan, Panama, Poland, Ukrainian Soviet Socialist Republic, Union of Soviet Socialist Republics, Yugoslavia.

[153] UN Doc. A/777.   [154] UN Doc. A/785/Rev.2.   [155] UN Doc. A/811.

[156] John P. Humphrey, 'The Universal Declaration of Human Rights: Its History, Impact and Judicial Character', in Bertrand G. Ramcharan, *Human Rights: Thirty Years After the Universal Declaration*, The

of the *Declaration* did not intend it as such, as they were working in parallel on a distinct instrument, the draft 'covenant', whose very purpose was to go beyond the *Declaration* and to create such binding obligations. Consequently, great care must be taken in drawing conclusions about the scope of article 3 of the *Universal Declaration* based on the *travaux préparatoires*, as if the exercise were truly one of treaty interpretation.[157]

Even in treaty interpretation, the *travaux préparatoires* are only a secondary source.[158] Just as in private municipal law the preliminary discussions between the parties to a contract can certainly assist in elucidating doubtful provisions, so in international law such materials are helpful where treaty provisions remain unclear. Resort to the *travaux préparatoires* is less appropriate in the context of international human rights law than with respect to other types of treaties, because the former merits an interpretation that goes beyond the intention of its drafters.[159] By its very nature, international human rights law must be dynamic, adapting and evolving with progress in social thought and attitudes. The only consequence of an exaggerated emphasis in the *travaux préparatoires* in the interpretation of human rights provisions is the imposition of a static view of their scope, the 'freezing' of their meaning at the time of their adoption. With respect to the specific case of the *Universal Declaration*, these comments are all the more relevant when we consider that the General Assembly and the subsidiary bodies never intended article 3 to constitute a binding norm.

It is useful in this respect to consider the experience of the Inter-American Commission on Human Rights in the interpretation of the *American Declaration of the Rights and Duties of Man*.[160] Like the *Universal Declaration*, it was not conceived of as a treaty imposing binding norms. Unlike the *Universal Declaration*, it was, some twenty years later, converted into a normative instrument by the Organization of American States.[161] Subsequently, litigants before the Inter-American Commission attempted to argue, in cases dealing

Hague: Martinus Nijhoff, 1984. See also the dissent of Judge Tanaka in *South West Africa Cases, Second Phase (Ethiopia v. South Africa, Liberia v. South Africa)*, [1966] ICJ Reports 6, pp. 288–293; and *United States Diplomatic and Consular Staff in Tehran (United States of America v. Iran)*, [1980] ICJ Reports 3, p. 42.

[157] Commissioner Marco Gerardo Monroy Cabra of the Inter-American Commission on Human Rights, in a dissenting opinion, said that it is an error to use the *Vienna Convention on the Law of Treaties* in order to interpret a human rights 'declaration' such as the *American Declaration on the Rights and Duties of Man* (and, by analogy, the *Universal Declaration of Human Rights*): *Roach and Pinkerton v. United States* (Case No. 9647), Resolution No. 3/87, reported in OAS Doc. OEA/Ser.L/V/II.71 doc. 9 rev. 1, p. 147, (1987) 8 *HRLJ* 345, p. 182.

[158] *Vienna Convention on the Law of Treaties*, (1979) 1155 UNTS 331, art. 32.

[159] *Loizidou v. Turkey (Preliminary objections)*, 23 March 1995, Series A, No. 310, paras. 71–72.

[160] See n. 93 above.

[161] *Charter of the Organization of American States*, (1952) 119 UNTS 4, *AJIL Supp.* 43, amended by *Protocol of Buenos Aires*, (1970) 721 UNTS 324, arts. 3j, 51e, 112, and 150. See: Thomas Buergenthal, 'The Revised OAS Charter and the Protection of Human Rights', (1975) 69 *AJIL* 828.

with the right to life, that the relevant provision of the *American Declaration* implicity includes the same content as the more prolix provisions of the *American Convention on Human Rights*, adopted in 1969 and in force only since 1978. The Inter-American Commission has had considerable difficulty with this argument and, on at least two occasions, has refused to use one instrument in order to construe the other.[162] More generally, it has found the challenge of finding a normative content in an instrument conceived of as a declaration or manifesto to be a dauting one. As far as the Inter-American Commission is concerned, the major assistance the *travaux préparatoires* provide in interpreting the *American Declaration* is in demonstrating how different that document is from the subsequent *Convention*.[163]

The *travaux préparatoires* of article 3 of the *Universal Declaration* are of great significance principally because the debates in the Commission on Human Rights and the Third Committee of the General Assembly represent the first major exchange on the subject of capital punishment within the context of international human rights law. The drafters of the *Universal Declaration* created an original norm, the right to life, inspired by incomplete formulations found in the instruments of the American revolution, but with a meaning going far beyond a mere right not to be deprived of life except with due process. The models on which the *Declaration* was based all recognized the death penalty as an explicit exception to the right to life. The *Universal Declaration* went one step further, removing any reference to the death penalty essentially because, in the words of Eleanor Roosevelt, there was a movement underway in some States to abolish capital punishment and, therefore, it might be better not to mention the death penalty.[164]

Participants in the debate attempted to breathe meaning into the provision with specific clauses, for example by emphasizing an economic and social content for the right to life or, in other words, the right to live, the right to a certain quality to life. There was even an attempt to make the declaration overtly abolitionist. But in the end prudence dictated a less precise statement, one which neither excluded the more radical approches to the right to life nor endorsed them. In this way, it accurately served the purpose of the *Declaration*, which was to be a manifesto whose scope could evolve over time, and not a detailed statement riddled with awkward exceptions.

The *travaux préparatoires* indicate that the drafters of the *Universal Declaration* considered that the question of capital punishment fell squarely

---

[162] *White and Potter* v. *United States* (Case no. 2141), Resolution No. 23/81, OAS Doc. A/Ser.L/V/II.52 doc.48, OAS Doc.A/Ser.L/V/II. 54 doc. 9 rev. 1, at pp. 25–54, Inter-American Commission on Human Rights, *Ten Years of Activities, 1971–1981*, Washington, D.C.: Organization of American States, 1982, pp. 186–209, (1981) 1 *HRLJ* 110; *Roach and Pinkerton* v. *United States* (Case No. 9647).
[163] See our discussion of the case law of the Inter-American Commission, pp. 315–325, 340–350 below.
[164] UN Doc. E/CN.4/AC.1/SR., p. 10.

within the context of the right to life. Furthermore, from the very beginning of the debates, its authors viewed the right to life as raising the matter not only of the death penalty, that is, of limitations on its implementation, but also of its abolition. Of course, they knew that most States in the world still imposed the death penalty and that the international community had also endorsed it, at least for war criminals. A proclamation of abolition of the death penalty might well have discredited and isolated the *Declaration*, making it a statement so out of step with the real world as to lose its potential significance.

Despite widespread support for abolition, there was no real consensus that the *Declaration* should take an abolitionist stance. Had, for example, the Soviets and the Latin American States truly desired that it reflect such a position, compromise would have been expected on the sole issue which divided them, namely, application of the death penalty in wartime or, rather, to war crimes and treason committed during wartime.

A final observation is in order. Nowhere, in any of the *travaux préparatoires* of the *Universal Declaration*, is a word spoken in support of the benefits of capital punishment, at least in time of peace. The death penalty was viewed virtually unanimously as a necessary evil, one whose existence could not be justified on philosophical or sceintific grounds. But its existence in the arsenal of domestic criminal law could not be questioned, and only a relatively small number of United Nations members had even contemplated abolition at the time. The fact that delegates to the Commission on Human Rights and the General Assembly made no attempt whatsoever to explain or account for the hiatus between their consideration of the right to life and the raw reality of their own legal systems is in itself quite striking. Their mission, to be sure, was one of elaborating a manifesto, a human rights beacon to guide domestic and international lawmakers over future decades. Of the twenty-one States that opposed the controversial Soviet amendment, more than half have now abolished the death penalty.

Publicists have provided little real guidance to interpretation of article 3 of the *Universal Declaration*. An article by Lilly Landerer describes the drafting of article 3, but makes no effort at interpretation.[165] Albert Verdoodt's exhaustive review of the drafting of the *Declaration* complains that the article is too vague, but admits that there is some implicit content with respect to the death penalty.[166] Verdoodt notes that there is no express condemnation of the death penalty 'for serious crimes', suggesting at the very least that some condition of proportionality in imposition of the death sentence is implicit in article 3.

The inescapable conclusion is that article 3 of the *Universal Declaration* is indeed abolitionist in outlook. By its silence on the matter of the death penalty,

---

[165] Landerer, 'Capital Punishment'.
[166] Albert Verdoodt, *Nuissance et signification de la Déclaration universelle des droits de l'homme*, Louvain, Paris: Nauwelaerts, 1963, pp. 99–100.

it envisages the abolition of capital punishment and, at the same time, admits its existence as a necessary evil, a relatively fine line which in hindsight appears to have been rather astutely drawn. A summary analysis of the death penalty debate in a report from the Secretariat of the United Nations has described the right to life provision in the *Universal Declaration* as being 'neutral' on the question of the death penalty.[167] Yet, several important resolutions of the General Assembly and the Economic and Social Council dealing with the limitation and ultimate abolition of capital punishment cite article 3 of the *Declaration* in their preambles,[168] implying that it is in fact favourable to abolition. The 'neutral' view is also in contradiction with the Secretary-General's report of 1973 on capital punishment, which claimed that article 3 of the *Declaration* implies limitation and abolition of the death penalty.[169] Clearly, the General Assembly has considered that article 3 of the *Declaration* and the abolition of the death penalty are indissociable.

In 1948, the death penalty was an almost universally recognized exception to the right to life, as can be seen by its constant inclusion in the early drafts of the *International Covenant on Civil and Political Rights* which was being prepared contemporaneously and by the same individuals. Eleanor Roosevelt's views against explicit reference to the death penalty in the *Universal Declaration*[170] were endorsed by Koretsky of the Soviet Union, Cassin of France, Santa Cruz of Chile and Wilson of the United Kingdom.[171] There was never any retreat from this position, despite the fact that the Soviet Union's abolitionist amendment failed to rally a majority of votes in the Third Committee. The true purpose of the *Universal Declaration* was to set goals for humanity, not to entrench the status quo, and this must be kept in mind in any construction of article 3.

Therefore, it is no exaggreation to state that article 3 of the *Universal Declaration* was aimed at eventual abolition of the death penalty, a role which it has admirably fulfilled, as our subsequent analysis of article 6 of the *Civil Rights Covenant,* the *Second Optional Protocol* and the various specialized and regional instruments should make clear. No better proof exists that the drafters of the *Declaration* contemplated the eventual abolition of the death penalty than the fact that article 3 has retained its pertinence during the evolution of more comprehensive abolitionist norms over subsequent decades.

---

[167] UN Doc. A/CONF.87/9, §4.
[168] GA Res. 2393 (XXIII); GA Res. 2857(XXVI); GA Res. 32/61; GA Res. 44/128; ESC Res. 1745 (LIV); ESC Res. 1930 (LVIII).
[169] UN Doc. E/5242, para. 11.   [170] UN Doc. E/CN.4/AC.1/SR.2, p. 10.
[171] *Ibid.,* p. 11.

2

The *International Covenant on Civil and Political Rights*: drafting, ratification and reservation

The drafting procedure of the *International Covenant on Civil and Political Rights*,[1] which began in the Drafting Committee of the Commission on Human Rights during the spring of 1947, was not completed until the final version of the instrument was adopted by the General Assembly in 1966.[2] Although a number of United Nations bodies were involved at various stages of the drafting, the Commission on Human Rights and the Third Committee of the General Assembly were its principal architects.

The Commission on Human Rights devoted its more or less continuous attention to the drafting of the *Covenant* from 1947 until 1954.[3] Successive drafts were reworked at its annual meetings and then transmitted to the Economic and Social Council and the General Assembly in the annual reports of the Commission. Occasionally, the General Assembly would redirect the Commission, as it did in 1951, when it divided the instrument into two separate 'covenants', one for civil and political rights and the other for economic, social and cultural rights.[4] The right to life provision remained in the civil rights covenant, despite the fact that it also has an economic and social dimension.[5]

---

[1] (1976) 999 UNTS 171.

[2] GA Res. 2200 A (XXI).

[3] The secondary sources on drafting of the *Covenant* include: Manfred Nowak, *CCPR Commentary*, Kehl: Engel, 1993; Dominic McGoldrick, *The Human Rights Committee*, Oxford: Clarendon Press, 1991; Vratislav Pechota, 'The Development of the Covenant on Civil and Political Rights', in Louis Henkin, ed., *The International Bill of Rights – the International Covenant on Civil and Political Rights*, New York: Columbia University Press, 1981, pp. 32–71; Marc J. Bossuyt, 'The Death Penalty in the "travaux préparatoires" of the International Covenant on Civil and Political Rights', in Daniel Prémont, ed., *Essais sur le concept de 'droit de vivre' en mémoire de Yougindra Khushalani*, Brussels: Bruylant, 1988, pp. 251–265; Lilly E. Landerer, 'Capital Punishment as a Human Rights Issue Before the United Nations', (1971) 4 *HRJ* 511.

[4] GA Res. 543 (VI). See John P. Humphrey, *Human Rights and the United Nations – A Great Adventure*, Dobbs Ferry, NY: Transnational, 1984, p. 129.

[5] Bertrand G. Ramcharan, 'The Concept and Dimensions of the Right to Life', in Bertrand G. Ramcharan, ed., *The Right to Life in International Law*, Dordrecht/Boston/Lancaster: Martinus Nijhoff, 1985, pp. 1–32; Hector Gros Espiell, 'The Right to Life and the Right to Live', in Daniel Prémont, ed.,

It was discussed at length by the Commission at its second, fifth, sixth and eighth sessions, in 1947, 1949, 1950 and 1952 respectively.

The final versions of the two draft covenants were adopted by the Commission on Human Rights at its tenth session, in 1954. They were then sent to the General Assembly, via the Economic and Social Council, for approval. At the time, few could have anticipated that the drafting procedure in the General Assembly would take another twelve years. The Third Committee of the General Assembly, meeting annually in the autumn of each year, examined the drafts in sometimes exhaustive detail. But consideration of the right to life provision of the *International Covenant on Civil and Political Rights*, the text which addressed the question of capital punishment, was the most time consuming. The article took up most of the twelfth session of the Third Committee, in 1957, undergoing extensive modifications, almost all of it related to the issue of capital punishment. For the purposes of this study, the most important development in the Third Committee was the addition of the notion of abolition of the death penalty to the *Covenant*. Article 6 of the *International Covenant on Civil and Political Rights*, as adopted by the Third Committee at the close of its 1957 session, was not subjected to any further debate or amendment in the General Assembly or its organs before formal adoption of the entire instrument in 1966. The final version of the right to life provision of the *Covenant*, article 6, is composed of six paragraphs, four of which (2, 4, 5 and 6) make direct reference to the death penalty:

> 1. Every human being has the inherent right to life. This right shall be protected by law. No one shall be arbitrarily deprived of his life.
>
> 2. In countries which have not abolished the death penalty, sentence of death may be imposed only for the most serious crimes in accordance with law in force at the time of the commission of the crime and not contrary to the provisions of the present Covenant and to the Convention on the Prevention and Punishment of the Crime of Genocide. This penalty can only be carried out pursuant to a final judgment rendered by a competent court.
>
> 3. When deprivation of life constitutes the crime of genocide, it is understood that nothing in this article shall authorize any State party to the present Covenant to derogate in any way from any obligation assumed under the provisions of the Convention on the Prevention and Punishment of the Crime of Genocide.
>
> 4. Anyone sentenced to death shall have the right to seek pardon or commutation of the sentence. Amnesty, pardon or commutation of the sentence of death may be granted in all cases.
>
> 5. Sentence of death shall not be imposed for crimes committed by persons below eighteen years of age and shall not be carried out on pregnant women.

Essais, pp. 45–53; Mikuin Leliel Balanda, 'Le droit de vivre', in Prémont, ed., *ibid.*, pp. 31–41; *General Comment 6(16)*, UN Doc. CCPR/C/21/Add.1, also published as UN Doc. A/37/40, Annex V, UN Doc. CCPR/3/Add.1, pp. 382–383 (see Appendix 5, p. 402).

6. Nothing in this article shall be invoked to delay or to prevent the abolition of capital punishment by any State party to the present Covenant.

The death penalty is the only exception to the right to life that is mentioned in article 6. The word 'arbitrarily' in paragraph 1 implies that there may be other exceptions but these are only left to implication. Yet even if the death penalty is recognized as an exception to the right to life, the word 'abolition' appears in two separate paragraphs, 2 and 6, indicating that the *Covenant* contemplates abolition, without however imposing an immediate obligation on States parties. This abolitionist perspective emerged only slowly during the protracted drafting process of the *Covenant*.

2.1 Drafting by the Commission on Human Rights

2.1.1 *The Drafting Committee phase*

The first suggestion that the International Bill of Rights would include a covenant was made in early 1947, in a general memorandum prepared by the Secretariat of the recently-formed United Nations Commission on Human Rights.[6] A proposal from the United Kingdom, which was deemed preparatory to the *Covenant*, provided for the right to life as follows:

> Article 8. It shall be unlawful to deprive any person of his life save in the execution of the sentence of a court following on his conviction of a crime for which this penalty is provided by law.[7]

Two other drafts, both of which spoke of the death penalty as an exception to the right to life, were submitted by Lebanon[8] and the United States.[9]

At the second session of the Commission on Human Rights, in December 1947, a Working Group, chaired by Lord Dukeston of the United Kingdom, with Charles Malik of Lebanon as *rapporteur*,[10] began study of the draft covenant.[11] Delegates were completely absorbed by the issue of abortion, and there was

---

[6] UN Doc. E/CN.4/W.4, p. 10.
[7] UN Doc. E/CN.4/AC.1/4, p. 9; reprinted as Annex B of the Drafting Committee report (UN Doc. E/CN.4/21); the United Kingdom proposal and the Secretariat Draft Outline were reproduced in a comparative outline (UN Doc. E/CN.4/AC.1/3/Add.3).
[8] Annex G of UN Doc. E/CN.4/21:
> It shall be unlawful to deprive any person, from the moment of conception, of his life or bodily integrity, save in the execution of the sentence of a court following on his conviction of a crime for which this penalty is provided by law.
[9] UN Doc. E/CN.4/37:
> It shall be unlawful for any state to deprive any person of his life save in the execution of the sentence of a court following on his conviction of a crime for which the penalty is provided by law.
[10] UN Doc. E/CN.4/56; UN Doc. E/600, para. 21.　　[11] UN Doc. E/CN.4/SR.29, p. 12.

virtually no discussion of the issue of capital punishment.[12] The Working Group adopted the United Kingdom's draft right to life article, with minor amendments.[13]

When comments from States were solicited by the Secretary-General,[14] Brazil felt that a phrase should be added to the draft covenant saying 'by law in force at the time when the offense was committed', making it clear that the death penalty could not be imposed *ex post facto*. Brazil also endorsed a suggestion from Uruguay for an additional article in the covenant that would ban the death penalty for political offences.[15] South Africa said the provision 'could hardly be acceptable to any country', because only one of many exceptions to the right to life had been set out explicitly. 'This leaves out of account the killings which may be necessary for the suppression of riots, or in self-defence, or in the defence of the life or limbs of another', it said. 'Why then has the most obvious exception, the execution of the death sentence, been specifically mentioned . . . ?'[16] France proposed an amendment that would enhance the procedural protections accompanying the death penalty.[17] New Zealand suggested a similar change.[18]

In the Drafting Committee session in the spring of 1948, the United States suggested that the right to life provision take a form virtually identical to the formulation of the right to life in the fifth amendment to the United States *Constitution*.[19] But, after discussion on the phrase 'due process of law', the United States delegate agreed to its replacement with 'save in execution of the sentence of a court'. Chile, in line with the Brazilian suggestion,[20] said that the article should provide that the death penalty could only be imposed under laws in force at the time the capital offence was committed.[21] The delegate from the United States answered that the issue of retroactive application of criminal law

---

[12] UN Doc. E/CN.4/AC.3/SR.1, pp. 4–6; UN Doc. E/CN.4/AC.3/SR.2, pp. 2–3.
[13] UN Doc. E/CN.4/AC.3/SR.2, p. 3, by three votes with one abstention. It read:

> It shall be unlawful to deprive any person, at any stage of his human development, of his life save in the execution of the sentence of a court following on his conviction of a crime for which this penalty is provided by law.

[14] UN Doc. SOA/17/1/01.   [15] UN Doc. E/CN.4/82/Add.2; UN Doc. E/CN.4/85, p. 60.
[16] UN Doc. E/CN.4/82/Add.4; UN Doc. E/CN.4/85, p. 60.
[17] UN Doc. E/CN.4/82/Add.8, p. 2:

> No one may be deprived of his life save in pursuance of a judicial sentence and in compliance with a provision of the criminal law prescribing such sentence.

[18] UN Doc. E/CN.4/82/Add. 12, p. 11:

> It shall be unlawful to deprive any person of his life save in the execution of the sentence of a court following his conviction of a crime for which this penalty is provided by law.

[19] UN Doc. E/CN.4/AC.1/19, p. 5:

> No one shall be deprived of his life, liberty or property, without due process of law.

[20] UN Doc. E/CN.4/85, p. 60; Eleanor Roosevelt reminded members of the Committee that the Economic and Social Council had suggested that comments received from governments be used as a basis for redrafting the articles.
[21] UN Doc. E/CN.4/AC.1/SR.22, p. 4.

was contemplated in a subsequent article of the draft covenant.[22] By a vote of three to zero with one abstention, that of the Soviet Union, the article was changed to read 'no one shall be deprived . . .'.[23] Anticipating a future debate, the Soviet delegate informed the Drafting Committee that his country had abolished the death penalty.[24]

The penchant of South Africa and the United States for exceptions such as self-defence led to the preparation of an enumeration of limitations to the right to life: suppression of rebellion or riot, self-defence, killing to effect arrest, killing by accident, killing to prevent escape, killing during surgical operation or in medical experiments, and killing during war.[25] The Drafting Committee voted to submit the list of limitations to the Commission together with the draft article:[26]

> No one shall be deprived of his life save in the execution of the sentence of a court following his conviction of a crime for which this penalty is provided by law.

But the Commission did not immediately consider the draft, deciding instead to set aside work on the covenant until its meeting in 1949 and to focus efforts on the draft declaration of rights.[27]

2.1.2 The Fifth Session of the Commission on Human Rights

The Drafting Committee's version of the right to life article returned to the Commission for further study at its fifth session in May 1949, accompanied by the list of exceptions based on submissions from the United States and the Union of South Africa. Inspired by this list, the United Kingdom then proposed a two-paragraph alternative that added the word 'intentionally' to the general statement of the right to life in the first paragraph and a precise and more succinct enumeration of exceptions in the second paragraph.[28] The United Kingdom's

---

[22] UN Doc. E/CN.4/AC.1/SR.22, p. 5.
[23] *Ibid.* At least, according to the summary records. The pencilled annotations of the late John P. Humphrey, who was secretary to the Commission, and whose archives are deposited in the Law Library of McGill University, Montreal, indicate that the phrase was changed to read 'no person shall be deprived of his life . . .'.
[24] UN Doc. E/CN.4/AC.1/SR.22, p. 5.
[25] UN Doc. E/CN.4/AC.1/38; reprinted in UN Doc. E/800, art. 5.
[26] UN Doc. E/CN.4/AC. 1/SR.29, p. 11; the list of exceptions is found at UN Doc. E/CN.4/95, p. 18.
[27] UN Doc. E/CN.4/95.
[28] UN Doc. E/CN.4/188:
    1.   No one shall be deprived of his life intentionally save in the execution of the sentence of a court following his conviction of a crime for which this penalty is provided by law.
    2.   This article shall not apply to killings resulting
    (a)   from the use of force which is no more than necessary
    (i)   in defence of person or property from unlawful violence;
    (ii)   in order to effect arrests for serious offences;

proposal was comparable to the draft article which was submitted the same year during preparation of the *European Convention on Human Rights* and which, with minor changes, was eventually incorporated in the final version of that instrument.[29]

However, the United States changed its mind about inclusion of any exceptions other than the death penalty, and came up with a new formulation.[30] Eleanor Roosevelt criticized the United Kingdom draft for accentuating the limitations to the right to life.[31] Such a list of exceptions only drew attention to the limitations, at the expense of the right itself. 'Had the Commission nothing better to do than to declare that it saw no objection in killings resulting from legitimate acts of war?' said Roosevelt.[32] The United States' proposal was defeated.[33] An adviser to the American delegation, James Simsarian, later explained that members of the Commission 'were not familiar with the substantive and procedural safeguards which have developed in American law around the concept of "due process of law" in the fifth and fourteenth amendments of the United States Constitution, and accordingly they were not willing to accept this proposal of the United States'.[34]

After rejection of the United States' amendment, Roosevelt asked the delegates from France, Lebanon and the United Kingdom to meet informally and to prepare a joint text for paragraph 1 of the right to life provision.[35] Their version closely resembled the United Kingdom's earlier proposal, with a first paragraph stating the right to life in conjunction with its principal exception, the death penalty, followed by an enumeration of other exceptions.[36]

(iii)   in order to prevent an escape from lawful custody;
(iv)   in order to prevent the commission of a crime of violence;
(v)   in action lawfully taken for the purpose of quelling a riot or insurrection; or
(b)   from the performance of lawful acts of war.

[29] *Collected Edition of the 'Travaux préparatoires' of the European Convention on Human Rights*, Vol. III, Dordrecht: Martinus Nijhoff, 1985, p. 28. The text was adopted as art. 2§1 of the *Convention*, (1955) 213 UNTS 221, ETS 5, art. 2§1 [hereinafter the *European Convention*) (see Appendix 14, p. 000).

[30] UN Doc. E/CN.4/170:

> In the punishment of crime, no State shall deprive any one of his life save in the execution of the sentence of a court following his conviction of a crime for which this penalty is provided by law.

[31] UN Doc. E/CN.4/SR.90, p. 9.

[32] UN Doc. E/CN.4/SR.91, p. 6; a point on which there was rare agreement from the Soviet Union: UN Doc. E/CN.4/SR.91, p. 9.

[33] *Ibid.*, p. 10 (seven votes to two, with three abstentions).

[34] James Simsarian, 'Draft International Covenant on Human Rights Revised at Fifth Session of United Nations Commission on Human Rights', (1949) 43 *AJIL* 779, pp. 780–781.

[35] UN Doc. E/CN.4/SR.91, p. 11.

[36] UN Doc. E/CN.4/204, jointly submitted by the United Kingdom and Lebanon, and approved by the French delegation:

> 1.   No one shall be deprived of his life intentionally save in the execution of the sentence of a court following his conviction of a crime for which this penalty is provided by existing law.
> 2.   There shall be no exception to this rule save in respect of killings resulting

The Commission then struck a sub-committee[37] which, unable to agree upon a single text, submitted drafts from the United Kingdom,[38] Chile,[39] the United States,[40] France[41] and the Soviet Union.[42] The Chilean amendment focused on the death penalty as the only exception to the right to life that would be mentioned explicitly and attempted to provide detailed norms aimed at limiting and regulating capital punishment: limitation of the death penalty to the 'most serious crimes' under 'ordinary law', prohibition of the death penalty for political crimes,[43] trial by a 'competent court' for a law in force prior to commission of the crime,[44] and amnesty and commutation of the death sentence

(a)   from the use of force which is no more than absolutely necessary in case of danger to human life;

(i)   in defence of person from unlawful violence;

(ii)   in order to effect arrests or to prevent an escape from lawful custody;

(iii)   in action lawfully taken for the purposes of quelling a riot or insurrection or for prohibiting entry to a clearly defined place to which access is forbidden on grounds of security.

(b)   from the performance of lawful acts of war.

[37] UN Doc. E/CN.4/SR. 93, p. 14; UN Doc. E/CN.4/SR.94, p. 4.

[38] UN Doc. E/CN.4/W.21.

[39] UN Doc. E/CN.4/W.22:

No one may deprive another person of his life arbitrarily.

In countries where capital punishment exists, sentence of death may be imposed only as a penalty for the most serious crimes under ordinary law and never for political offences.

No one may be executed save in virtue of the sentence of a competent court and in accordance with a law in force and prior to the commission of the crime so punished.

Amnesty, pardon or commutation of the sentence of death may be granted in all cases.

[40] UN Doc. E/CN.4/170/Add.5; the United States' proposal was simply to replace the entire text of the article with the first paragraph of the Chilean proposal.

[41] UN Doc. E/CN.4/W.23. A modification to add the phrase 'on pain of death' after the word 'forbidden' in subparagraph 2(b)(iii), suggested by the Iranian delegate, was accepted by Cassin, UN Doc. E/CN.4/SR.97, p. 9. The French amendment read:

1.   No one shall be deprived of his life intentionally.

2.   There shall be no exception to this rule save where the death results

(a)   in countries where capital punishment is lawful for the most serious crimes against the ordinary law, from the execution of a sentence pronounced by a competent court, if such penalty has not been commuted or pardoned; or

(b)   from the use of force which is no more than absolutely necessary in the case of danger to human life;

(i)   in the lawful defence of any person;

(ii)   in order to effect a lawful arrest or to prevent an escape from lawful custody; or

(iii)   in action lawfully taken for the purposes of quelling a riot or insurrection or for prohibiting entry to a clearly defined place to which access is forbidden on grounds of security.

[42] UN Doc. E/CN.4/241:

No one shall be deprived of his life except upon the grounds and in accordance with the procedure established by law.

The Soviet Union stated that its amendment was not being formally submitted, and that it was not seeking a vote on it: UN Doc. E/CN.4/SR.97, p. 3.

[43] After being briefly criticized on this point, the Chilean delegate withdrew reference to political crimes, indicating that in any case the point was implicit in the formulation that the death penalty could only be imposed for crimes under ordinary law: UN Doc. E/CN.4/SR.97, p. 4.

[44] Chile also withdrew the phrase 'and prior to the commission of the crime so punished' before the vote: UN Doc. E/CN.4/SR.98, p. 8.

(in paragraph 4).[45] It was the first attempt to provide a detailed limitation on the scope of capital punishment. Most of the debate, however, revolved around a choice between the words 'arbitrarily' and 'intentionally' in the first sentence, the United States, with the Soviet Union[46] and Chile, favouring the former, and the United Kingdom, France[47] and the Commonwealth countries preferring the latter.

The Chilean amendment was put to a vote. Its first paragraph, with the exception of the word 'arbitrarily',[48] was adopted. The second paragraph, with the exception of the phrase 'under ordinary law',[49] was also adopted.[50] The Uruguayan delegate, who was absent due to illness, later stated that he would have voted against the second paragraph of the Chilean amendment because his government was opposed in principle to the death penalty.[51] The third[52] and fourth[53] paragraphs were accepted without change, and then the entire Chilean amendment was adopted on a roll-call vote.[54]

A group led by the United Kingdom and France voted against the provision because it did not include the word 'intentionally'. Even after the vote, Australia vainly attempted to have the word 'intentionally' added, arguing that the Chilean amendment was 'illogical' without it.[55] Australia, France, Lebanon[56] and the United Kingdom then recorded their objections in an annex to the Commission's official report to the Economic and Social Council.[57] They explained that

[45] Paragraph 4 was put to a roll-call vote, and declared admissible by fourteen votes to none, with the United Kingdom abstaining: UN Doc. E/CN.4/SR.97, p. 5.

[46] UN Doc. E/CN.4/SR.98, p. 4.

[47] Comments by René Cassin: UN Doc. E/CN.4/SR.97, pp. 5–6, UN Doc. E/CN.4/SR.98, p. 8; supported by the United Kingdom: UN Doc. E/CN.4/SR.97, p. 6, Belgium: UN Doc/ E/CN.4/SR.97, p. 7.

[48] UN Doc. E/CN.4/SR.98, p. 12 (by fourteen votes to none, with one abstention). The word 'arbitrarily' was not adopted, because a vote on its insertion was tied, seven to seven with one abstention.

[49] *Ibid.*, five votes to four, with six abstentions.

[50] *Ibid.*, nine votes to four, with two abstentions.   [51] UN Doc. E/CN.4/SR. 101, p. 2.

[52] UN Doc. E/CN.4/SR.98, p. 12, eight votes to none, with six abstentions.

[53] *Ibid.*, nine votes to one, with five abstentions.

[54] UN Doc. E/CN.4/SR.98, p. 13. *In favour*: Chile, China, Egypt, Philippines, Ukrainian Soviet Socialist Republic, Union of Soviet Socialist Republics, United States, Yugoslavia.
Against: Australia, Belgium, Denmark, France, India, United Kingdom.
Abstaining: Iran.
The text adopted read:
    1.   No one shall be deprived of his life.
    2.   In countries where capital punishment exists, sentence of death may be imposed only as a penalty for the most serious crimes.
    3.   No one may be executed save in virtue of the sentence of a competent court and in accordance with a law in force and not contrary to the principles expressed in the Universal Declaration of Human Rights.
    4.   Amnesty, pardon or commutation of the sentence of death may be granted in all cases.

[55] E/CN.4/SR.98, p. 13.   [56] Lebanon had not been present during the voting.

[57] UN Doc. E/1371, UN Doc. E/CN.4/350:
    The Covenant is intended to be an international agreement imposing legal obligations and conferring legal rights, and the first requisite of a legal instrument is that it should state precisely

governments would not accede to the *Covenant* if such 'imprecise' terms as 'arbitrarily' were employed. Fresh drafts of article 5 were presented in these texts; they echoed the submissions of the United Kingdom to the fifth session of the Commission, and virtually mirrored the provisions that were eventually adopted by the Council of Europe in article 2 of the *European Convention*. According to explanatory comments accompanying the drafts, they allegedly showed:

> that it is possible ... to define all limitations of these rights which contracting States can reasonably require, in a form that is both brief and comprehensive and ... that a covenant drafted on such lines will be a much more effective instrument for the purpose for which it was intended, namely the guarantee of human rights.[58]

From the other camp, the United States gave notice that it would be insisting on inclusion of the word 'arbitrarily'.[59]

The fifth session of the Commission is important for its rejection of inclusion of a detailed enumeration of exceptions to the right to life, although proponents of this approach were to renew their efforts in subsequent years. The United Kingdom and its allies in the Commission had insisted upon the importance of a virtual codification of State-permitted killing. But the view that prevailed considered these exceptions to be implicit, their mention being unnecessary. Where the Commission opted for detailed provisions was in the description of the one exception which could not be left implicit, the death penalty. The Commission had therefore recognized that henceforth the right to life provision in the *Covenant* would principally address the issue of capital punishment. The fifth session produced detailed provisions that began to point the way towards limitation and abolition of the death penalty: the vague suggestion that some countries had already abolished the death penalty, its restriction to the 'most serious crimes', and the prospect of amnesty, pardon or commutation.[60] None of these points aroused any particular controversy at the time.

2.1.3 The Sixth Session of the Commission on Human Rights

At the sixth session of the Commission on Human Rights, in 1950, Sir Samuel Hoare of the United Kingdom charged that the draft right to life provision was 'practically meaningless from a legal point of view'.[61] The United Kingdom revived efforts to obtain an enumeration of exceptions to the right to life,[62] arguing

> the rights which it permits. Whereas the Covenant in general in the form in which it is now accepted by the majority of the Commission satisfies this requirement, two important articles, 5 [the right to life] and 9, appear not to do so.

[58] *Ibid.*   [59] UN Doc. E/CN.4/325.
[60] UN Doc. E/1371, UN Doc. E/CN.4/350; see also UN Doc. E/CN.4/SR.98, p. 121.
[61] UN Doc. E/CN.4/SR.139, paras. 15–16.
[62] UN Doc. E/CN.4/353/Add.2, UN Doc. E/CN.4/365, p. 23:

that the statement of general principles had been accomplished by the *Universal Declaration*[63] and that it was now time to draft a precise and clear treaty.[64]

The United States wanted to merge paragraphs 2 and 3 to create a single provision dealing with the specific issue of capital punishment.[65] Eleanor Roosevelt said that the United Kingdom proposal 'seemed intended rather to authorize killing than to safeguard the right to life'[66] and gave the provision a 'negative character'.[67] The United Kingdom was attempting to codify criminal law, she said, and offered a list of exceptions that had been omitted from the United Kingdom draft: ejection of an intruder from private property, prevention of trespassing on private property, prevention of wilful arson, prevention of attempted burglary, avenging of insult to honour in adultery cases, defence of the home and, in cases of extreme urgency, the killing of a few people to save the lives of many.[68]

France[69] and the Philippines[70] proposed new amendments, the latter adding the qualifier 'and only under extraordinary circumstances', so as to reflect

> 1.   No one shall be deprived of his life intentionally.
> 2.   There shall be no exception to this rule save where death results, in those States where capital punishment is lawful, from the execution of such a penalty in accordance with the sentence of a court.
> 3.   Deprivation of life shall not be regarded as intentional when it results from the use of force which is no more than absolutely necessary
> (i)   in defence of any person from unlawful violence;
> (ii)   in order to effect a lawful arrest or to prevent an escape from lawful custody; or
> (iii) in action lawfully taken for the purpose of quelling a riot or insurrection, or for prohibiting entry to a clearly defined place to which access is forbidden on grounds of national security.

[63] *Universal Declaration of Human Rights*, GA Res. 217 A (III), UN Doc. A/810 (hereinafter the *Universal Declaration or Declaration*).

[64] UN Doc. E/CN.4/SR. 139, para. 15.

[65] UN Doc. E/CN.4/353/Add.1 and Corr. 1; UN Doc. E/CN.4/365, p. 22. The substitute for paragraph 3 would read:
> In such countries, sentence of death may be executed only pursuant to the sentence of a competent court and in accordance with law.
The merging of paragraphs 2 and 3 would give the following result:
> In countries where capital punishment exists, sentence of death may be imposed only as a penalty for the most serious crimes pursuant to the sentence of a competent court and in accordance with law.

[66] UN Doc. E/CN.4/SR.139, para. 9.   [67] *Ibid.*, para. 12.

[68] *Ibid.*, para. 10; the United States later submitted observations that suggested seven exceptions that had been overlooked by the United Kingdom draft, relating to interference with property, arson, burglary, violation of honour and killing of a few to save the lives of many: UN Doc. E/CN.4/383. India later contributed its own example of an oversight in the United Kingdom enumeration, that of a doctor who, to save the life of the mother, intentionally killed the child during or before delivery: UN Doc. E/CN.4/SR.140, para. 42.

[69] France:
> Human life is sacred. To take life shall be a crime, save in the execution of a sentence or in self-defence, or in the case of enforcement measures authorized by the Charter.
UN Doc. E/CN.4/353/Add.8; UN Doc. E/CN.4/365, p. 24; UN Doc. E/CN.4/SR.139, p. 4. This was supported by Yugoslavia: UN Doc. E/CN.4/SR.140, §7. France later withdrew the first sentence of its amendment and replaced it with the text proposed by India: 'Everyone has the right to life', UN Doc. E/CN.4/SR.144, para. 4.

[70] UN Doc. E/CN.4/353/Add.3, UN Doc. E/CN.4/365, pp. 23–24.

the 'growing tendency all over the world either to abolish or restrict the death sentence'.[71] The amendment also included the word 'final' before 'sentence' and clarified the point that the penalty had to be in effect at the time of commission of the crime.[72] Uruguay's representative noted that it had submitted an abolitionist amendment. He said he now realized that most national legislations provided for capital punishment and that, as a 'practical consideration', the amendment could not succeed. He expressed the hope that, even if the Commission would not take an unequivocally abolitionist position, it would at least make every effort to limit the death penalty. These limits should include restrictions on its application to women, especially pregnant women, and children.[73]

It was agreed, in accordance with a solution originally proposed by the United States,[74] that paragraphs 2 and 3 be combined,[75] and Roosevelt urged that this provision be confined to capital punishment.[76] A new Lebanese text for paragraph 2 became the focus of the debate.[77] After refusing a number of amendments,[78] Malik of Lebanon accepted one from the United Kingdom, which added 'by the State' after the word 'effected'.[79] Several delegates rallied to an Egyptian suggestion that 'independent' be removed from the article,[80] and

[71] India also proposed an amendment that reproduced paragraph 1 of the Philippines' proposal: UN Doc. E/CN.4/385.

[72] UN Doc. E/CN.4/353/Add.3, UN Doc. E/CN.4/365, pp. 23–24.

    1.   In countries where capital punishment exists, sentence of death may be imposed only for the most serious crimes, and only under extraordinary circumstances.

    2.   No one may be executed save in virtue of the final sentence of a competent court and in accordance with a law in force at the time of the commission of the crime and not contrary to the principles expressed in the Universal Declaration of Human Rights.

    3.   Amnesty, pardon or commutation of the sentence of death may be granted in all cases.

Greece also proposed a compromise amendment that adopted the Philippines' suggestion of adding the word 'final': UN Doc. E/CN.4/SR.140, para. 16. India's amendment reproduced paragraph 2 of the Philippines' proposal, but substituted the words 'an independent tribunal' for 'a competent court': UN Doc. E/CN.4/385. India's amendment was withdrawn following the rejection of its first sentence, UN Doc. E/CN.4/SR.152, para. 10.

[73] UN Doc. E/CN.4/SR.139, para. 28.

[74] UN Doc. E/CN.4/393, UN Doc. E/CN.4/SR.149, para. 46.

[75] UN Doc. E/CN.4/SR.149, para. 66.   [76] UN Doc. E/CN.4/SR.152, para. 29.

[77] UN Doc. E/CN.4/413. The latest version of the Lebanese admendment read:

    Intentional deprivation of life may not be effected by the State save as capital punishment in countries where such punishment exists and then only:

    (a)   for the most serious crimes;

    (b)   in execution of a law not contrary to the principles expressed in the Universal Declaration of Human Rights and

    (c)   in virtue of the sentence of a competent court.

[78] Egypt sought the deletion of the words 'independent and competent', UN Doc. E/CN.4/SR.149, para. 29; the United Kingdom wanted to add the words 'by the State' after 'effected', UN Doc. E/CN.4/SR.149, para. 31; Uruguay wanted to add 'for the most serious crimes' after the words 'and then', UN Doc. E/CN.4SR.149, para. 33.

[79] UN Doc. E/CN.4/SR.149, para. 34.

[80] Australia: UN Doc. E/CN.4/SR.149, para. 42; United States: UN Doc. E/CN.4/SR.149, §43; Philippines: UN Doc. E/CN.4/SR.149, paras. 50, 57.

Malik finally agreed to withdraw it.[81] The Uruguayan proposal to add the phrase 'for the most serious crimes' was criticized by the United Kingdom because this would vary from one country to another.[82] Roosevelt supported it, because this would restrict application of the death penalty.[83] The delegates rallied to a proposal from the United States to revise paragraph 3 and reformulate it to include a 'due process' protection where the death penalty was being imposed.[84] In short order, the United States amendment was put to a vote in four parts and adopted in its entirety.[85] An Egyptian amendment that added 'in accordance with the procedure adopted by each country'[86] was rejected on a tied vote.[87]

A reference to the *Universal Declaration*, originally inserted during the fifth session, had been deleted from the amendments of the United States and Lebanon, although some delegates considered the cross-reference to be essential.[88] The United Kingdom insisted that only by mention of the *Declaration* would the phrase 'the most serious crimes' be adequately controlled and qualified.[89] The United Kingdom urged a vote on its new amendment,[90] which focused on an enumeration of exceptions. Five votes were cast in favour, five against, with four abstentions, and the amendment was rejected.[91] Ordonneau of France explained that he had abstained in the vote and, almost apologetically, said that the substance of the United Kingdom's amendments

---

[81]   *Ibid.*, paras. 45, 47.   [82]   *Ibid.*, para. 35.   [83]   *Ibid.*, para. 46.

[84]   UN Doc. E/CN.4/365, UN Doc. E/CN.4/393:

> In countries where capital punishment exists, sentence of death may be imposed only as a penalty for the most serious crimes pursuant to the sentence of a competent court and in accordance with law.

[85]   UN Doc. E/CN.4/SR.153, para. 12. The words 'In countries where capital punishment exists, sentence of death may be imposed only as a penalty for the most serious crimes' were adopted by thirteen votes to none, with one abstention. The words 'pursuant to the sentence of a competent court and . . .' were adopted by nine votes to none, with five abstentions. The words '. . . in accordance with law . . .' were adopted by twelve votes to none, with two abstentions. The words '. . . not contrary to the Universal Declaration of Human Rights . . .' were adopted by nine votes to two with three abstentions. The United States amendment as a whole was adopted by twelve votes to none, with three abstentions. The abstainers were Australia, UN Doc. E/CN.4/SR.153, para. 13, the United Kingdom, UN Doc. E/CN.4/SR.153, para. 14, and the Philippines, UN Doc. E/CN.4/SR.153, para. 15. The entire paragraph was then adopted: UN Doc. E/CN.4/SR.153, para. 17, by three votes in favour to three against, with eight abstentions.

[86]   UN Doc. E/CN.4/384.

[87]   UN Doc. E/CN.4/SR.153, para. 17; three votes in favour, three against, with eight abstentions.

[88]   Yugoslavia: UN Doc. E/CN.4/SR.149, paras. 58, 67; France: UN Doc. E/CN.4/SR.149, paras. 60, 64.

[89]   UN Doc. E/CN.4/SR.149, para. 61.

[90]   UN Doc. E/CN.4/417:

> Deprivation of life which results from the use, by an agent of public authority, acting in pursuance of his lawful powers, of force which is no more than absolutely necessary:
> (i)   in defence of any person from unlawful violence;
> (ii)   in effecting a lawful arrest or to prevent an escape from lawful custody; or
> (iii)   in action lawfully taken for the purpose of quelling a riot or insurrection, or for prohibiting entry to a clearly defined place to which access is forbidden on grounds of national security, shall be regarded as legitimate defence.

[91]   UN Doc. E/CN.4/SR.153, para. 16.

could be reconsidered on second reading of article 5. The vote should not be construed 'too rigidly'.[92]

A variety of reformulations were proposed for paragraph 4 (which became paragraph 3), dealing with 'amnesty, pardon and commutation'.[93] After a number of suggestions, none of which indicated any real substantive differences within the Commission, a Lebanese proposal[94] was adopted.[95] In effect, this added a final sentence to the draft article approved at the fifth session. An Egyptian proposal prohibiting execution of offenders under the age of seventeen was not voted upon.[96] Then the entire article on the right to life, as amended, was adopted by eleven votes to none, with three abstentions.[97]

Following the sixth session, the Secretary-General solicited views of Member States on the draft covenant.[98] Replies dealing with the right to life were

---

[92] *Ibid.*, para. 17.
[93] UN Doc. E/CN.4/365, p. 22 (United States of America):
Any one sentenced to death shall have the right to seek amnesty, or pardon, or commutation of the sentence.
(withdrawn, UN Doc. E/CN.4/SR.152, para. 58);
UN Doc. E/CN.4/365, p. 23:
Amnesty, pardon or commutation of the sentence of death shall be granted in all cases.
(note voted upon);
UN Doc. E/CN.4/371 (Yugoslavia):
Amnesty, pardon or commutation of the sentence of death may not be excluded in advance for any offence, person or category of persons.
(withdrawn, UN Doc. E/CN.4/SR.152, para. 59);
UN Doc. E/CN.4/386 (Lebanon):
A person sentenced to death shall have the right to apply for an amnesty, a pardon, or commutation of the sentence. It shall be possible in every case to grant an amnesty, a pardon or commutation of the sentence of death.
(not voted upon).
India would have preferred to remove the paragraph altogether, although this objection was 'not strong': UN Doc. E/CN.4/365, UN Doc. E/CN.4/SR.140, para. 15.
[94] UN Doc. E/CN.4/398.
[95] UN Doc. E/CN.4/SR. 153, para. 18, by thirteen votes to one, with no abstentions:
Anyone sentenced to death shall have the right to seek amnesty, or pardon or commutation of the sentence. Amnesty, pardon, or commutation of the sentence of death may be granted in all cases.
[96] UN Doc. E/CN.4/384:
Offenders under the age of 17 years shall not be sentenced to death or to imprisonment with hard labour for life.
[97] UN Doc. E/CN.4/SR. 153, para. 18. It now read:
1.   Everyone's right to life shall be protected by law.
2.   To take life shall be a crime, save in the execution of a sentence of a court or in self-defense, or in the case of enforcement measures authorized by the Charter.
3.   In countries where capital punishment exists, sentences of death may be imposed only as a penalty for the most serious crimes, pursuant to the sentence of a competent court and in accordance with law not contrary to the Universal Declaration of Human Rights.
4.   Anyone sentenced to death shall have the right to seek amnesty, or pardon, or commutation of the sentence. Amnesty, pardon or commutation of the sentence of death may be granted in all cases.
[98] UN Doc. SOA 317/1/01(1).

received from Chile,[99] Israel[100] and New Zealand.[101] The right to life provisions were considered summarily by the Economic and Social Council, at its eleventh session,[102] and by the Third Committee of the General Assembly, at its fifth session.[103] In the Third Committee, New Zealand observed that the circumstances in which the death penalty could be imposed were not sufficiently defined.[104]

2.1.4 The Eighth Session of the Commission on Human Rights

Given evident dissatisfaction with the existing draft from virtually all quarters, the Commission reconsidered the right to life provisions during its eighth session.[105] The Soviet Union,[106] the United States and Chile[107] all sought a return to the text which had been adopted at the fifth session, with some modifications. Chile and the United States proposed adding the word 'arbitrarily' to paragraph 1,[108] something Eleanor Roosevelt said 'filled a gap' in the Soviet amendment.[109] Uruguay restated its opposition to any article that would contain reference to the 'barbarous' death penalty.[110] Now it was joined by Sweden, which declared that the covenant should provide for the abolition of capital punishment.[111] Predictably, the United Kingdom renewed its insistence on an enumeration of exceptions.[112] The arguments were familiar ones,

[99] UN Doc. E/CN.4/515/Add.4.   [100] UN Doc. E/CN.4/515/Add.6.
[101] UN Doc. E/CN.4/515/Add.12.
[102] UN Doc. E/AC.7/SR.147, 148, 194; UN Doc. E/L.68; UN Doc. E/C.2/259.
[103] UN Doc. A/C.3/SR.288–291, UN Doc. A/C.3/354.   [104] UN Doc. A/C.3/SR.291, para. 39.
[105] The right to life provisions were considered summary by the Commission at its seventh session: UN Doc. E/1992, annex III, art. 3; UN Doc. E/CN.4/515/Add.4, Add.6, Add.12, paras. 87–94; and by the Economic and Social Council at its thirteenth session: UN Doc. E/C.2/SR.106.
[106] UN Doc. E/CN.4/L.122:
    1.   No one may be deprived of life. Everyone's right to life shall be protected by law.
    2.   In countries where capital punishment exists, sentence of death may be imposed only as a penalty for the most serious crimes.
    3.   No one may be sentenced to death except in pursuant of the sentence of a competent court and on the basis of the laws in force not contrary to the Universal Declaration of Human Rights.
    4.   Any one sentenced to death shall have the right to seek amnesty, or pardon, or commutation of the sentence. Amnesty, pardon or commutation of the sentence of death may be granted in all cases.
France proposed the deletion of the word 'amnesty' from paragraph 4: UN Doc. E/CN.4/L.160.
[107] UN Doc. E/CN.4/L.176, which was presented as a revision of the Soviet proposal (UN Doc. E/CN.4/L.122), so that it read as follows:
    1.   No one shall be arbitrarily deprived of life.
Roosevelt's explanation of the article appears at UN Doc. E/CN.4/SR.309, p. 4.
[108] *Ibid.*   [109] UN Doc. E/CN.4/SR.309, p. 4.
[110] UN Doc. E/CN.4/SR.310, p. 10.   [111] UN Doc. E/CN.4/SR.311, p. 3.
[112] UN Doc. E/CN.4/L.140, p. 1:
    1.   Everyone's right to life shall be protected by law. No one shall be deprived of his life intentionally, except in the execution of a sentence of a court following his conviction of a crime for which the death penalty is provided by law.

unchanged from those the United Kingdom had submitted at the fifth and sixth sessions.[113]

In an effort to promote compromise, the chairman of the Commission, René Cassin, explained that there were three approaches to the article on the right to life. The first was the Soviet view as amended by the United States and Chile, which had 'the greatest appeal because it was closest to the Sixth Commandment'. But despite its sentimental appeal, Cassin said that it could only be observed by States acting in good faith and did not provide for such important considerations as self-defence and national security.[114] The second was that of the United Kingdom, but Cassin said its great disadvantage was its resort to enumeration which could never be exhaustive: there would always be cases not covered by the covenant.[115] The third was the French approach, which was based on the fundamentally acceptable existing text of article 3 of the *Universal Declaration*, with some improvements. France agreed to insert the word 'intentionally' in paragraph 2, as proposed by the United Kingdom, the word 'justifiable', as proposed by the United States, and reference to the *Genocide Convention*, as proposed by Yugoslavia.[116]

The Yugoslav delegate had urged that the *Convention for the Prevention and Punishment of the Crime of Genocide*[117] be mentioned in the provision because of 'statements in the press' to the effect that its implementation would be made difficult by the covenants', right to life provision.[118] Cassin felt it should be made clear that the covenant was to be a general application of the *Universal Declaration*, whereas the *Genocide Convention* was a specific application.[119] Pakistan said the provision should in no way nullify the *Genocide Convention* or suggest that there were two conventions on the same subject.[120] According to Pakistan, it would be preferable to amend the draft covenant to make it clear

---

2.   Deprivation of life shall not be regarded an inflicted in contravention of this article when it results from the use of force which is no more than is necessary:
(i)   In defence of any person from unlawful violence;
(ii)   In order to effect a lawful arrest or to prevent the escape of a person lawfully detained;
(iii) In action lawfully taken for the purpose of quelling a riot or insurrection.
Subsequently, the United Kingdom accepted an Egyptian proposal to add the word 'competent' before 'court', UN Doc. E/CN.4/SR.310, p. 16.
[113] UN Doc. E/CN.4/SR.309, p. 3; a point that was not lost on Roosevelt, who noted that the article was almost identical to the one that had been proposed by the United Kingdom and rejected at the Sixth Session: UN Doc. E/CN.4/SR.309, p. 4.
[114] UN Doc. E/CN.4/SR.310, p. 4.   [115] *Ibid.*
[116] *Ibid.*, p. 5; Cassin's views were endorsed by the Greek delegate, Kyrou: UN Doc. E/CN.4/SR.310, p. 7.
[117] (1951) 78 UNTS 277.
[118] UN Doc. E/CN.4/L.178, UN Doc. E/CN.4/SR.309, p. 7. The same amendment was also proposed to the United States and Chile draft (UN Doc. E/CN.4/L.176), which had combined paragraphs 2 and 3 (UN Doc. E/CN.4/L.179), and to the Soviet Union's draft (UN Doc. E/CN.4/L.122): UN Doc. E/CN.4/L.180.
[119] UN Doc. E/CN.4/SR.310, p. 5; UN Doc. E/CN.4/SR.311, p. 5.   [120] *Ibid.*, p. 6.

that the two instruments were separate and that the covenant provision related to the right to life of the individual.[121]

It was agreed to consider the Soviet proposal first, together with the various amendments.[122] The reference to the *Genocide Convention* passed,[123] as did the amendment presented by the United States and Chile[124] which added the word 'arbitrarily' to paragraph 1.[125] Then the amended paragraph as a whole was adopted.[126] The Soviet Union said that it would accept paragraphs 2 and 3 of the United States–Chile amendment, obviating the need for a separate vote, and those provisions were in turn adopted.[127] The American approach to the right to life, which employed the term 'arbitrarily', had definitively triumphed over the United Kingdom's approach, which used the term 'intentionally'.[128] The United Kingdom and its allies on this point did not abandon the point, however, and renewed the proposals several years later in the Third Committee of the General Assembly, although with no more success than in the Commission.[129]

The French were unhappy with the use of the term 'amnesty' in paragraph 4, which was a broader concept than either pardon or commutation of sentence, but one which was also 'meaningless'. Individuals, groups and entire classes could seek amnesty.[130] Amnesty could be granted, it could not be sought, said the Yugoslav delegate.[131] Therefore it was inappropriate to describe amnesty as a right. The French proposal[132] was accepted,[133] and paragraph 4

---

[121] *Ibid.,* p. 7.   [122] UN Doc. E/CN.4/SR.311, p. 5.

[123] *Ibid.,* p. 5, by thirteen votes to two, with three abstentions.   [124] UN Doc. E/CN.4/L.176.

[125] UN Doc. E/CN.4/SR.311, p. 5, by ten votes to five, with three abstentions.

[126] *Ibid.,* p. 6, by twelve votes to four with two abstentions; see also UN Doc. E/2256, art. 5 [6]§1, UN Doc. E/2447, art. 6§1, and UN Doc. A/2929, p. 29.

[127] UN Doc. E/CN.4/SR.311, p. 6, by fourteen votes to one, with three abstentions; see also UN Doc. E/2556, art. 5 [6], UN Doc. E/2447, art. 6§2, and UN Doc. A/2929, p. 29.

[128] A memorandum by Sir Samuel Hoare, archived in the Public Record Office ('Draft United Nations Covenant on Civil and Political Rights', HO 274/2, 27 February 1953), indicates that the United Kingdom gave up the battle, because 'our amendments have been so decisively rejected by the Commission that it would be a waste of time to propose them again'. Referring to the right to life provision, Hoare wrote:

> This Article says that no one shall be arbitrarily deprived of his life. The United Kingdom method of setting out the categories of case in which intentional deprivation of life shall not be regarded as a crime (the method adopted in the European Convention) has been decisively rejected by the Commission, and the other alternatives to the present formulation of this Article are as objectionable to us as the present text – some are even worse than the present text. No one knows what "arbitrarily" means, and in the last resort it would have to be determined by the Human Rights Committee which is to be set up to deal with complaints between States parties to the Covenant of violation of its provisions. There is of course strong objection to drafting with such vagueness as is exemplified by the use of term "arbitrarily" (the objection is even stronger when we come to article 8). But it is extremely unlikely that any deprivation of life which occurred in this country would be challenged by another country party to the Covenant as a violation of this Article, or that if such a challenge were made a violation could ever be established against us.

[129] See pp. 70–73 below.   [130] UN Doc. E/CN.4/SR.309, p. 8.

[131] UN Doc. E/CN.4/SR.310, p. 13.   [132] UN Doc. E/CN.4/L.160.

[133] UN Doc. E/CN.4/SR.311, p. 6, by eleven votes to four, with three abstentions. Morozov of the Soviet Union later explained that he had voted against the French amendment because he mistakenly

of the Soviet draft, minus the word 'amnesty' in the first sentence, was adopted.[134]

The eighth session saw a further initiative aimed at limiting the use of the death penalty: a Yugoslav amendment, 'inspired by purely humanitarian considerations', proposed excluding pregnant women from execution.[135] Egypt proposed that the word 'inflicted' be replaced by 'put into effect'.[136] In response to questions as to whether the prohibition applied only during pregnancy and not afterwards,[137] Sir Samuel Hoare recommended that the provision read 'Sentence of death shall not be carried out on a pregnant woman', and the modification was accepted by Yugoslavia.[138] There is no doubt from the *travaux préparatoires* that the members of the eighth session only contemplated a prohibition on the death penalty while the woman was pregnant. The Yugoslav amendment was accepted.[139]

With all of the amendments in place, the delegates then adopted the right to life article as a whole.[140] René Cassin voted against, expressing the view that the article, while appearing to safeguard the right to life, in fact permitted its violation. He hoped the text would be changed subsequently.[141] With these comments, the Commission on Human Rights concluded its consideration of the right to life article in the covenant, which then read as follows:

1. No one shall be arbitrarily deprived of his life. Everyone's right to life shall be protected by law.

2. In countries where capital punishment exists, sentence of death may be imposed only as a penalty for the most serious crimes pursuant to the sentence of a competent court and in accordance with law not contrary to the principles of the Universal Declaration of Human Rights or the Convention on the Prevention and Punishment of the Crime of Genocide.

3. Any one sentenced to death shall have the right to seek pardon or commutation of the sentence. Amnesty, pardon or commutation of the sentence of death may be granted in all cases.

4. Sentence of death shall not be carried out on a pregnant woman.[142]

thought it referred to the mention of 'amnesty' in both the first and the second sentences of paragraph 4. In fact, it only applied to the first sentence: UN Doc. E/CN.4/SR.311, p. 6.

[134] *Ibid.*, by thirteen votes to one, with four abstentions.   [135] UN Doc. E/CN.4/SR.309, p. 3.
[136] UN Doc. E/CN.4/SR.311, p. 7.   [137] *Ibid.*   [138] *Ibid.*
[139] *Ibid.*, by twelve votes to one, with five abstentions.
[140] UN Doc. E/CN.4/SR.311, p. 7, by eleven votes to four, with three abstentions.
[141] *Ibid.*; others voting against were Greece, Uruguay (because of opposition to the death penalty in principle) and India. Sir Samuel Hoare said he had abstained in the vote, but that he felt some doubt whether he should not have voted against the article as a whole, because he fully shared Cassin's views (UN Doc. E/CN.4/SR.311, p. 8). Whitlam of Australia said he had abstained, but associated himself with Cassin's remarks (UN Doc. E/CN.4/SR.311, p. 8). Sweden had also abstained (UN Doc. E/CN.4/SR.311, p. 8). As a result of the comments, it is possible to identify those who voted in favour: Belgium, Chile, China, Egypt, Lebanon, Pakistan, Poland, Ukrainian Soviet Socialist Republic, Union of Soviet Socialist Republics, United States, Yugoslavia.
[142] UN Doc. E/2256, UN Doc. E/2447, UN Doc. A/2929.

Over its three sessions, the Commission had greatly expanded the reference to the death penalty, which now encompassed three of the four paragraphs in the draft provision. It had added procedural safeguards, contemplated amnesty, pardon and commutation, and excluded pregnant women from its scope. The progress was constant and pronounced, but there was as yet no explicit mention of abolition, merely a suggestion in the second paragraph that there were indeed some States which did not apply capital punishment. The draft article would, however, be completely reworked by the Third Committee of the General Assembly at its twelfth session, in 1957, and the abolitionist ideal considerably advanced.

2.2 Drafting by the Third Committee of the General Assembly

The draft covenant, as adopted by the Commission on Human Rights, was then submitted to the Economic and Social Council and, subsequently, to the General Assembly. The debate in the Third Committee of the General Assembly took twelve years to complete. At its twelfth session, in the autumn of 1957, the Committee devoted two full weeks to the right to life provision. The work of the Commission on Human Rights on the 'right to life' provision had first come before the General Assembly, at its ninth session, in 1954, where summary comments were made by members of the Third Committee about the draft text.[143] The United Kingdom repeated its complaints about the use of the term 'arbitrarily' in draft article 6, arguing that the provision would compel States whose systems of law and practice in the protection of life and liberty had been built up over the centuries to agree that their system be judged by an extra-legal and undefined standard.[144]

France said the draft article failed to take into account the inevitable exceptions, such as self-defence and attacks upon life that could result from enforcement actions authorized under the *Charter of the United Nations*, points that had been deliberately omitted from the draft. Although it acknowledged that a majority of the Commission had thought these limitations were implicit, the debates had shown that those who preferred the phraseology 'no one shall be arbitrarily deprived of his life' were themselves divided as to its interpretation.[145]

Uruguay's Rodriguez Fabregat considered it regrettable that the draft covenant contained a reference to the death penalty. He noted that his delegation

---

[143] Prior to the discussion in the Third Committee, the other references to the right to life are at the tenth session of the Commission: UN Doc. E/CN.4/Add.2, Add.6; Economic and Social Council thirteenth session, UN Doc. E/C.2/SR. 145.

[144] UN Doc. A/C.3/SR.562, para. 9. Also UN Doc. E/CN.4/694/Add.2.

[145] UN Doc. A/C.3/SR.566, para. 19.

had submitted a draft article calling for abolition of capital punishment, which had unfortunately been rejected, and he spoke for the benefits of abolition and the rehabilitation of criminals.[146]

As requested by the General Assembly,[147] the Secretary-General prepared a lengthy analysis of the Commission's text[148] to assist its article by article consideration of the covenant.[149] The 'Annotations' reviewed the two conflicting views on inclusion of a precise enumeration of the exceptions.[150] On paragraph 2, dealing with capital punishment, the Annotations stated:

> Some opposition was expressed to the inclusion in the article of provisions dealing with capital punishment since it might give the impression that the practice was sanctioned by the international community. The opinion was expressed that respect for human life required that a covenant on human rights should, as one of its main principles, provide for the abolition of capital punishment. On the other hand, it was pointed out that capital punishment existed in certain countries. It was recognized, however, that adequate safeguards should be provided in order that the death penalty would not be imposed unjustly or capriciously in disregard of human rights. It was agreed that the death sentence should be imposed only (a) as a penalty for the most serious crimes, (b) pursuant to the sentence of a competent court and (c) in accordance with the law not contrary to the principles of the Universal Declaration of Human Rights or in the Convention on the Prevention and Punishment of the Crime of Genocide.[151]

The Annotations probably gave more weight to abolitionist pronouncements in the Commission than the record justifies. The Annotations also explained that references to the *Universal Declaration* and to the *Genocide Convention* were included in the draft to provide a 'yardstick' for States to assess the justness of their own national laws concerning application of the death penalty.[152] The Annotations referred to debates on the scope of the 'most serious crimes',[153] the rejection of efforts to include political crimes as an exception,[154] the mention of amnesty, pardon and commutation,[155] and the prohibition on the execution of pregnant women.[156]

A number of comments and amendments were submitted prior to consideration of the right to life provision by the Third Committee. In a *note verbale* dated 12 July 1955, the United Kingdom stubbornly urged deletion of the first sentence of the right to life provision containing the term 'arbitrarily',[157] a debate it had fought and lost in the Commission. An Australian note complained that 'arbitrarily' was not defined, and that in the discussions no consensus on its meaning had emerged.[158] The Netherlands said 'arbitrarily' could only lead

---

[146] UN Doc. A/C.3/SR.573, para. 19.   [147] GA Res. 833 (IX), para. 2(a).
[148] UN Doc. E/2573, annex I.
[149] 'Annotations of the Text on the Draft International Covenants on Human Rights', UN Doc. A/2929.
[150] UN Doc. A/2929, Chap. VI, para. 1.   [151] *Ibid.*, para. 5.   [152] *Ibid.*, para. 8.
[153] *Ibid.*, para. 6.   [154] *Ibid.*, para. 6.   [155] *Ibid.*, para. 9.   [156] *Ibid.*, para. 10.
[157] UN Doc. A/2910/Add. 1.   [158] UN Doc. A/2910/Add.2; see also UN Doc. A/C.3/L.460.

to uncertainty; it preferred that the article be redrafted along 'the lines of the corresponding article 2 of the Convention for the Protection of Human Rights and Fundamental Freedoms'.[159] Thailand's *note verbale* suggested that article 6 provide that the death penalty never be inflicted for political offences which are not also non-political offences susceptible of capital punishment.[160]

Twelve meetings of the Third Committee, from 13 November to 26 November 1957, were consumed with debate on the right to life provision of the draft covenant.[161] Besides some further evolution on the subject of limitations and restrictions on the death penalty, the Committee directly addressed the issue of abolition of capital punishment, which was posed in the form of an amendment by Uruguay and Colombia. The issue of abolition had never been confronted by the Commission on Human Rights during its work. The amendment of Uruguay and Colombia was eventually defeated, but not before further compromises resulted in the entrenchment of new provisions that, while not prohibiting the death penalty, nevertheless indicated that abolition was to be its goal. Unlike the *Universal Declaration*, the *Covenant* was to have been a statement of binding norms subject to immediate implementation, but in the end it would in some aspects resemble a manifesto after all.

Debate in the Third Committee focused on four themes: abolition of the death penalty, use of the term 'arbitrarily', reference to the *Genocide Convention*, and prohibition of the execution of minors. Each of these themes is discussed in turn, not necessarily by order of position within article 6 of the *Covenant*, but by order of importance in the debate.

2.2.1 Abolition of the death penalty in the Covenant (paragraphs 2 and 6)

The abolitionist amendment presented by Uruguay and Colombia sought to replace the entire right to life article with the following:

> Every human being has the inherent right to life. The death penalty shall not be imposed on any person.[162]

The Uruguayan delegate explained that the death penalty was anachronistic, that it was sometimes carried out as a result of judicial error, and that

---

[159] UN Doc. A/1910/Add.3; see also UN Doc. A/C.3/L.460. Presented at UN Doc. A/C.3/SR.820 as A/C.3/L.651. The Netherlands amendment was virtually identical to the text submitted to the Commission at its eighth session by the United Kingdom, differing only in the omission of the word 'absolutely' before the word 'necessary'. Briefly presented by the Netherlands at UN Doc. A/C.3/SR.814, para. 24.
[160] UN Doc. A/2910/Add.2; see also UN Doc. A/C.3/L.460.
[161] For a popular account of the capital punishment debate during the 1957 meeting of the Third Committee, see James Avery Joyce, *Capital Punishment, A World View*, New York: Thomas Nelson, 1961, pp. 196–217.
[162] UN Doc. A/C.3/L.644.

it was immoral and pointless.[163] Nothing in the *Universal Declaration* could support the imposition of the death penalty, he added, and any paragraph in the covenant providing for its imposition, even in exceptional circumstances, would be *ipso facto* contrary to the *Universal Declaration*.[164] Co-sponsor Colombia argued eloquently for an abolitionist approach in article 6 and said that unless the draft were amended, it would be unable to support a text that sanctioned the taking of human life.[165] This bold call for abolition of the death penalty met with open support from Finland,[166] Panama,[167] Peru[168] and Ecuador.[169]

Many others were in favour of abolition and sympathetic to the objectives of the resolution but considered that such a measure was premature and might only prevent States that still applied the death penalty from ratifying the covenant. For example, Cuba agreed with the objectives of the resolution but urged Uruguay and Colombia to be more realistic.[170] Guatemala said the Colombian and Uruguayan proposal was of great interest, but it could only vote for an article if 'the abolition of the death penalty was merely described as desirable'.[171] Israel, which had abolished capital punishment in 1954,[172] said that States should commit themselves to progressive abolition.[173] The Dominican Republic said it could support an abolitionist article but respected the difficulties that this would cause for some States.[174] Bulgaria said that, despite its eventual intention to abolish the death penalty, it could not support the abolitionist provision, which would raise artificial obstacles to accession to the treaty.[175] Indonesia felt that abolition was desirable but premature.[176] Poland supported the aim of abolition but believed it could not be achieved in current circumstances.[177]

Thierry of France confessed that he had been deeply moved by the arguments of Uruguay and Colombia, yet added that the effect of adopting the Uruguayan–Colombian article on capital punishment would not be to abolish the death penalty, but only to prevent some States from ratifying the covenant.[178]

---

[163] UN Doc. A/C.3/SR.810, para. 22.
[164] *Ibid.*, para. 23. On the drafting and interpretation of the *Universal Declaration*, see Chapter 1 above.
[165] UN Doc. A/C.3/SR.811, paras. 10–15.   [166] *Ibid.*,§2; UN Doc. A/C.3/SR.819, para. 10.
[167] UN Doc. A/C.3/SR.819, para. 19.   [168] UN Doc. A/C.3/SR.812, para. 12.
[169] UN Doc. A/C.3/SR.813, paras. 23–24, UN Doc. A/C.3/SR.815, paras. 27–28.
[170] UN Doc. A/C.3/SR.811, para. 16. Romania (A/C.3/SR.814, paras. 25–26) and Afghanistan (UN Doc. A/C.3/SR.814, para. 30) called the amendment 'unrealistic'.
[171] UN Doc. A/C.3/SR.812, para. 5.
[172] Israel retained the death penalty for genocide and has since carried out only one execution, that of Adolph Eichmann: *A.G. Israel* v. *Eichmann*, (1968) 36 ILR 18 (DC); *A.G. Israel* v. *Eichmann*, (1968) 36 ILR 277 (SC). See also: Hannah Arendt, *Eichmann in Jerusalem, A Report on the Banality of Evil*, New York: Penguin Books, 1994.
[173] UN Doc. A/C.3/SR.814, para. 22.   [174] UN Doc. A/C.3/SR.812, para. 26.
[175] UN Doc. A/C.3/SR.813, para. 39. See also: Denmark (UN Doc. A/C.3/SR.819, §13); New Zealnd (UN Doc. A/C.3/SR.814, para. 46).
[176] UN Doc. A/C.3/SR.812, para. 30.   [177] UN Doc. A/C.3/SR.814, para. 2.
[178] UN Doc. A/C.3/SR.811, para. 26.

He said that a possible compromise solution would be to express the wish of the Committee to abolish the death penalty with a provision to the effect that States parties would undertake to develop their penal legislation in such a way as to move progressively towards abolition of capital punishment.[179] Brazil invited France to propose a resolution to that effect.[180]

The French suggestion quickly garnered wide support. Venezuela noted that as an abolitionist State, it sympathized with the Colombian–Uruguayan resolution, but that the moment for abolition had not yet arrived, and that it would support the French suggestion for gradual abolition of the death penalty.[181] Greece was of the opinion that the French suggestion was 'logical and satisfactory'. The death penalty should be abolished sooner or later, but this could not be done immediately because States first needed to reach a certain moral level, a level of civilization.[182] Even Colombia, which had proposed the abolitionist resolution with Uruguay, agreed that adoption of the French proposal would be a great improvement.[183]

Besides France, other delegations made attempts at compromise formulations. Panama preferred a phrase like: 'The States parties to this Covenant recognize the necessity of promoting the abolition of the death penalty.'[184] Peru agreed with abolition but said it had objections to the Colombian–Uruguayan proposal and proposed an alternative that began: 'In countries where capital punishment exists...'.[185] Similarly, Brazil suggested the provision be changed to read: 'In countries in which it has not been possible as yet to abolish capital punishment...'.[186] The Philippines proposed that its amendment[187] be changed to read: 'In countries where capital punishment still exists, sentence of death...'.[188] Costa Rica said it supported the amendment submitted by Colombia and Uruguay,[189] but it too suggested an amendment.[190] Ireland said it could not support the idea of progressive abolition but as a compromise proposed: 'Nothing in this article shall be invoked to prevent or to retard any

---

[179] *Ibid.*, para. 27.   [180] *Ibid.*, para. 35.   [181] UN Doc. A/C.3 SR.812, paras. 18–21.
[182] *Ibid.*, para. 34.   [183] UN Doc. A/C.3/SR.813, para. 12.
[184] *Ibid.*, paras. 26–29. El Salvador spoke in favour of the Panamanian proposal: UN Doc. A/C.3/SR.817, para. 29.
[185] UN Doc. A/C.3/SR.812, para. 12:
    In countries where capital punishment exists, such penalty shall be prescribed only for the most serious crimes and in accordance with the principles of article 14 of the present Covenant. Sentence of death shall not be imposed except in pursuance of the sentence of a competent court, pronounced in accordance with laws promulgated before the crime.
[186] UN Doc. A/C.3/SR.815, para. 6.
[187] UN Doc. A/C.3/L.646:
    Insert the words 'in force at the time of the commission of the crime and' after the word 'law' in paragraph 2. Insert the word 'final' before the word 'sentence'.
[188] UN Doc. A/C.3/SR.815, para. 17.   [189] UN Doc. A/C.3/SR.812, para. 10.
[190] UN Doc. A/C.3/L.648. Costa Rica's amendment, UN Doc. A/C.3/L.648, replaced article 6 by:
    Every human being shall have the inalienable right to his life and to the security of his person.

State party to the Covenant from abolishing capital punishment, either wholly or in part, by constitutional means.'[191] Panama submitted yet another solution, substituting the bluntly abolitionist phrase with 'The States parties to the Covenant recognize the propriety of promoting the abolition of the death penalty.'[192]

Many States expressed the view that they could not support such an amendment because their own legislation still provided for capital punishment. Japan said it 'valued the laudable intention of the Colombian–Uruguayan amendment', which it could not endorse because it had not yet abolished capital punishment.[193] Australia could not favour immediate abolition, because some of its states still retained the death penalty, but pledged its support for gradual abolition.[194] The Philippines said it shared abolitionist sentiments but retained the death penalty in its domestic law for the most serious crimes.[195]

A few delegates preferred that the covenant make no mention of abolition. Saudi Arabia noted that not all countries were as fortunate as Uruguay and Colombia, and that many States had not found it possible to abolish capital punishment, an issue which was far too complex for the Committee to deal with in any case.[196] Sir Samuel Hoare of the United Kingdom said he respected the intentions of Colombia and Uruguay about abolition, but could not accept the amendment because the United Kingdom had just come through a difficult debate on the subject and did not want to reopen the matter.[197] Mexico could not agree with the abolitionist paragraph proposed by Colombia and Uruguay, because it viewed the issue as a matter for the individual States. Mexico noted that article 2§7 of the United Nations *Charter* prevented the adoption of any mesure which might be regarded as intervention in matters within the domestic jurisdiction of States, and that administration of justice was such a measure.[198]

In telling observations, Uruguay's Tejera[199] and Colombia's Zea Hernandez[200] pointed out that none of the opponents of the amendment had attempted to defend the death penalty, comments that were basically valid for the entire *travaux préparatoires* of the right to life provision of the *Covenant*, in both the Commission on Human Rights and the Third Committee of the General Assembly.[201] There were only rare and equivocating hints of support for

[191] UN Doc. A/C.3/SR.813, para. 41.   [192] UN Doc. A/C.3/L.653.

[193] UN Doc. A/C.3/SR.814, para. 18.   [194] UN Doc. A/C.3/SR.812, para. 24.

[195] UN Doc. A/C.3/SR.815, para. 17. Others indicating that they had no immediate plans to abolish the death penalty included the Ukrainian Soviet Socialist Republic (UN Doc. A/C.3/SR.819, para. 4) and Canada (UN Doc. A/C.3/SR.814, para. 36).

[196] UN Doc. A/C.3/SR.811, para. 20.   [197] *Ibid.*, para. 40.

[198] A/C.3/SR.812, para. 8.   [199] UN Doc. A/C.3/SR.811, para. 32.

[200] UN Doc. A/C.3/SR.813, para. 10.

[201] On only one occasion during the *travaux préparatoires* was use of the death penalty defended, in 1948, in the Commission on Human Rights, by Soviet delegate A. P. Pavlov, who favoured it where traitors were concerned, UN Doc. E/CN.4/SR.98, p. 4.

capital punishment during the debates. India argued that there were several other well-recognized exceptions to the right to life, and said countries which had not abolished the death penalty should not be accused of being unethical and barbarous if adequate procedural guarantees were provided in its implementation.[202] New Zealand explained that it could not accept the notion that retention of the death penalty indicated a lack of social progress and would vote against if that were the implication.[203]

A Working Party was set up with a view to reaching a compromise. Already the initiative of Uruguay and Colombia had borne fruit, in that the Committee felt it necessary to give some recognition to the abolitionist position. Yet Uruguay was intransigent, refusing to participate in the Working Party because it said a compromise on capital punishment was impossible.[204]

The chairman of the Working Party presented its report to the Third Committee:

> the working party had co-ordinated the various amendments relating to paragraph 2 and the new paragraph to be added at the end of the article, and the texts agreed upon were given in the report. As to the other paragraphs of article 6, a number of suggestions were made on the voting procedure that might be followed. With reference to the text of paragraph 2 proposed by the working party, it was interesting to note that the expression: 'in countries which have not abolished the death penalty' was intended to show the direction in which the drafters of the Covenant hoped that the situation would develop.[205]

The Working Party proposed the following text:

> In countries which have not abolished the death penalty, sentence of death may be imposed only for the most serious crimes in accordance with the law which is in force at the time of the commission of the crime and that is not contrary to the provision of this Covenant and to the Convention on the Prevention and Punishment of the Crime of Genocide. This penalty can only be carried out pursuant to a final judgment rendered by a competent court.[206]

The Working Party also sought to reflect still further the abolitionist sentiment by the addition of a final phrase which set a goal of abolition of the death penalty:

> Nothing in this article shall be invoked to delay or to prevent the abolition of capital punishment by any State party to the present Covenant.

Delegations quickly rallied around the Working Party proposal. Indonesia said it could not support the Uruguayan–Colombian amendment, whose

---

[202] UN Doc. A/C.3/SR.813, paras. 34–35.   [203] UN Doc. A/C.3/SR.817, para. 10.
[204] UN Doc. A/C.3/SR.815, para. 51.   [205] UN Doc. A/C.3/SR.816, para. 19.
[206] UN Doc. A/3764, para. 102; UN Doc. A/C.3/L.655 and Corr. 1.

sentiment it appreciated, but that it would vote for the additional paragraph which did not bind States to abolition but simply held it out as a goal.[207] Ceylon said it sympathized with the abolitionist perspective but was grateful for a compromise, and it suggested that the new final paragraph should read 'nothing in this article shall be invoked to retard or to prevent progress towards the abolition of capital punishment by any State party to the Covenant'.[208] Chile could not support the Uruguayan–Colombian amendment because it retained the death penalty but, in view of the modern trend in favour of abolition, it accepted the Working Party draft.[209] El Salvador, an advocate of the abolitionist amendment, said it would now support the Working Party draft.[210]

Despite the consensus in favour of the Working Party compromise, Uruguay and Colombia did not withdraw their amendment, which was eventually defeated on a roll-call vote, by fifty votes to nine, with twelve abstentions.[211] It rallied only five other Latin American countries, plus Finland and Italy. Even vocal opponents of capital punishment who might have been expected to abstain, such as Israel, voted against the resolution. The socialist States, promoters of a similar abolitionist declaration in the *Universal Declaration*, opposed the Uruguayan and Colombian initiative.

The Working Party draft of paragraph 2 of the right to life article was adopted easily on a roll-call vote.[212] A separate vote on the phrase 'in force at the time of the commission of the crime and . . .' passed by a narrow margin.[213] Uruguay and Colombia voted against the phrase, but most of the others who had favoured the abolitionist amendment rallied in support of the Working Party's

[207] UN Doc. A/C.3/SR.819, para. 49. [208] UN Doc. A/C.3/SR.817, para. 6.
[209] UN Doc. A/C.3/SR.819, para. 39. [210] UN Doc. A/C.3/SR.817, para. 29.
[211] *In favour*: Colombia, Dominican Republic, Ecuador, Finland Italy, Panama, Uruguay, Venezuela, Brazil.
Against: Cambodia, Canada, Ceylon, China, Czechoslovakia, Denmark, Egypt, France, Ghana, Haiti, Hungary, India, Indonesia, Iran, Iraq, Ireland, Israel, Japan, Jordan, Liberia, Luxembourg, Malaya (Federation of), Mexico, Morocco, Nepal, Netherlands, New Zealand, Nicaragua, Norway, Pakistan, Philippines, Poland, Romania, Saudi Arabia, Sudan, Syria, Tunisia, Turkey, Ukrainian Soviet Socialist Republic, Union of Soviet Socialist Republics, United Kingdom, Yemen, Yugoslavia, Afghanistan, Albania, Australia, Belgium, Bulgaria, Burma, Byelorussian Soviet Socialist Republic.
Abstaining: Cuba, Ethiopia, Greece, Guatemala, Peru, Portugal, Spain, Sweden, Thailand, United States of America, Austria.
[212] UN Doc. A/C.3/SR.820, para. 13, by forty-five votes to seven, with nineteen abstentions. *In favour*: Italy, Japan, Liberia, Malaya (Federation of), Morocco, Norway, Pakistan, Panama, Peru, Philippines, Poland, Romania, Spain, Thailand, Tunisia, Turkey, Ukrainian Soviet Socialist Republic, Union of Soviet Socialist Republics, United Kingdom, Yugoslavia, Albania, Argentina, Australia, Austria, Brazil, Bulgaria, Burma, Byelorussian Soviet Socialist Republic, Canada, Ceylon, Chile, Cuba, Czechoslovakia, Dominican Republic, Ecuador, Ethiopia, Finland, France, Ghana, Greece, Guatemala, Haiti, Hungary, India, Iran.
Against: Iraq, Ireland, New Zealand, Uruguay, Venezuela, Colombia, Denmark.
Abstaining: Israel, Jordan, Luxembourg, Mexico, Nepal, Netherlands, Nicaragua, Portugal, Saudi Arabia, Sudan, Sweden, Syria, United States of America, Yemen, Afghanistan, Belgium, Cambodia, Egypt, Indonesia.
[213] UN Doc. A/C.3/SR.820, para. 12, by twenty-nine votes to twenty-five, with sixteen abstentions.

formulation. The final paragraph of the provision, proposed by the Working Party as amended, was also adopted by a generous majority.[214]

Because Uruguay and Colombia had insisted that the covenant contemplate abolition of the death penalty, two important references to abolition had been added to the right to life provision by the Third Committee. The first, in paragraph 2, indicated not only the existence of abolitionist countries but also the direction which the evolution of criminal law should take, and the second, in paragraph 6, set a goal for parties to the covenant. The *travaux préparatoires* indicate that these changes were the direct result of efforts to include a fully abolitionist stance in the covenant. They represented an intention, as France had said when it first introduced the compromise text, to express a desire to abolish the death penalty, and an undertaking by States to develop domestic criminal law progressively towards abolition of the death penalty.[215]

2.2.2 'Arbitrarily' (paragraph 1)

The other important focus of the debates in the Third Committee was the term 'arbitrarily' and the notion of an enumeration of exceptions to the right to life, matters that had vexed the Commission on Human Rights since the fifth session in the spring of 1949. The United Kingdom urged that paragraph 1 of the Commission draft be deleted.[216] The Netherlands government went even further, seeking deletion of the first sentence of paragraph 1, elimination of reference to the *Universal Declaration of Human Rights* and the *Convention for the Prevention and Punishment of the Crime of Genocide*, and provision of a list of enumerated exceptions along the lines of article 2 of the *European Convention on Human Rights*.[217] The Netherlands' amendment received support from a number of Western European States.[218] As had happened with previous efforts to introduce an enumeration of exceptions to the death penalty, this list was criticized as being incomplete.[219]

Sir Samuel Hoare, representing the United Kingdom, argued forcefully for the elimination of the term 'arbitrarily', which he said was ambiguous and confusing. Furthermore, he expressed fear that the consequence of the term

---

[214] UN Doc. A/C.3/SR.820, para. 26, by fifty-four votes to four with fourteen abstentions. No roll-call vote was requested.

[215] UN Doc. A/C.3/SR.811, paras. 26–27.

[216] The United Kingdom amendment, UN Doc. A/C.3/L.656, consisted in deleting the words 'which is' after the word 'law' and the words 'that is' before the word 'contrary' in the first sentence of paragraph 2. At the 819th meeting, these were incorporated into the text proposed by the Working Party.

[217] UN Doc. A/2291/Add.3, UN Doc. A/C.3/SR.809, paras. 24–26.

[218] UN Doc. A/C.3/SR.813, para. 25; also UN Doc. A/C.3/SR.819, para. 42 (Sweden); UN Doc. A/C.3/SR.815, para. 26 (Austria).

[219] UN Doc. A/C.3/SR.821, para. 13 (Canada); Un Doc. A/C.3/SR.819, para. 29 (Ghana); UN Doc. A/C.3/SR.815, para. 17 (Philippines); UN Doc. A/C.3/SR.817, para. 22 (El Salvador).

would be to give the future Human Rights Committee a mandate that had never been intended:

> the word 'arbitrarily' was not intended solely to require observance of the laws but also to require that the law should itself be in conformity with what was called 'natural justice'. He could understand and sympathize with the aim of preventing abuses under colour of law; but there was no accepted criterion in that field and the conception of the justice or injustice of laws was extremely subjective. He did not see how States could be asked to consent to having the justice of their laws decided upon, in the last analysis, by the Human Rights Committee to be set up under the Covenant. Such a task had never been envisaged by those, like his delegation, who supported the setting up of the Committee.[220]

Hoare reiterated his country's malaise with the absence of an enumeration of exceptions to the right to life.[221] He said that if 'arbitrarily' meant 'without due process of law', there was no need to include it, as the idea was already covered elsewhere in the covenant. Hoare said that 'arbitrarily' meant 'the essential justice of the law' and challenged those who said it meant only 'due process' to propose an amendment to that effect.[222]

Others had less difficulty with the term. The Philippines said it was obvious that the real meaning of 'arbitrarily' was 'without due process of law', the two terms being virtually synonymous.[223] Poland supported use of the word 'arbitrarily', saying that States knew what it meant, and that it was better than 'intentionally'.[224] Syria said that 'arbitrarily' meant the authorities could not act illegally and according to their own pleasure.[225] Even if it had not yet been accurately defined, it would acquire a specific meaning over time, as society progressed.[226]

Saudi Arabia noted that the word 'arbitrarily' leant itself to different interpretations. Its representative, Baroody, said he would give it the meaning 'summarily' or 'without due process of law' (i.e., illegally), but he realized that the United Kingdom did not share this view.[227] He suggested that the difficulty might be solved by replacing paragraph 1 with: 'No person shall be deprived of his life without due regard for the provisions of article 14 of this Covenant.'[228] But Hoare said inclusion of such a reference to article 14 would suggest that article 6 dealt only with the death penalty, which was not in fact the case.[229]

Chile said study of the debate on article 6 in the Commission on Human Rights would show that 'arbitrarily' had been accepted in a spirit of compromise to meet the position of countries which could not accept paragraph 1 without

---

[220] UN Doc. A/C.3/SR.809, para. 20.   [221] UN Doc. A/C.3/SR.809, para. 21.
[222] UN Doc. A/C.3/SR.815, para. 34; also UN Doc. A/C.3/SR.816, para. 4.
[223] *Ibid.*, para. 10.   [224] UN Doc. A/C.3/SR.814, paras. 1–2.
[225] UN Doc. A/C.3/SR.816, para. 1.   [226] *Ibid.*, para. 1.   [227] UN Doc. A/C.3/SR.811, para. 18.
[228] *Ibid.*, para. 23.   [229] *Ibid.*, para. 39.

qualification.[230] The Soviet Union stated that the United Kingdom proposal to delete the first sentence of the draft article amounted to a restatement of old arguments that had been rejected in the Commission on Human Rights. The Soviet Union was not particularly happy with inclusion of the word 'arbitrarily' but had accepted it in a spirit of compromise because no perfect definition could be found.[231]

Sir Samuel Hoare countered that the covenant was not concerned with statements of principle but rather with precise legal obligations. No State could fulfil the obligation to ensure that no one in its territory or jurisdiction should be deprived of life, as even the Soviet delegate had admitted, so it was necessary to qualify the absolute statement that 'no one shall be deprived of his life'.[232] The United Kingdom's proposal to enumerate exceptions had been rejected, a French amendment had been found unsatisfactory,[233] and use of the word 'arbitrarily' was no solution.[234] The only alternative was to delete the sentence, he argued.

However, a Costa Rican amendment aimed at removing the troublesome term 'arbitrarily'[235] was rejected,[236] and the Netherlands amendment, which added an enumeration of exceptions similar to that found in the *European Convention on Human Rights*,[237] was also defeated.[238] The Working Party draft of paragraph 1 of article 6 proceeded to clause by clause votes, each of which was adopted by a large majority.[239]

The Third Committee's report to the General Assembly reviewed the debate on the word 'arbitrarily' noting that, despite great controversy, the amendment

---

[230] UN Doc. A/C.3/SR.815, para. 22.   [231] UN Doc. A/C.3/SR.810, para. 17.

[232] *Ibid.*, para. 20.

[233] UN Doc. A/C.3/L.645:

> Amnesty, pardon or commutation of the sentence of death may be granted to a sentenced person in all cases.

[234] UN Doc. A/C.3.SR.810, para. 10.   [235] UN Doc. A/C.3/L.648.

[236] UN Doc. A/C.3/SR.820, para. 7, by fifty-eight votes to four, with ten abstentions.

[237] UN Doc. A/C.3/L.651.

[238] UN Doc. A/C.3/SR.820, para. 7, by fifty votes to nine, with eleven abstentions.

[239] The first clause ('Every human being has the inherent right to life') was adopted by sixty-five votes to three, with four abstentions, UN Doc. A/C.3/SR.820, para. 8. The second clause ('This right shall be protected by law') was adopted by sixty-nine votes to none, with one abstention, UN Doc. A/C.3/SR.820, para. 10. Previously, an amendment to include in paragraph 1 a clause protecting the right to life 'from the moment of conception' was rejected by thirty-one votes to twenty with seventeen abstentions. The third clause ('No one shall be arbitrarily deprived of his life') was adopted by forty-seven votes to twelve, with fourteen abstentions, on a roll-call vote, UN Doc. A/C.3/SR.820, para. 11: *In favour*: Bulgaria, Burma, Byelorussian Soviet Socialist Republic, Cambodia, Chile, Cuba, Czechoslovakia, Denmark, Dominican Republic, Ecuador, Egypt, Ethiopia, Ghana, Greece, Haiti, Hungary, Indonesia, Iraq, Ireland, Jordan, Liberia, Malaya (Federation of), Mexico, Morocco, Nicaragua, Norway, Panama, Peru, Philippines, Poland, Romania, Saudi Arabia, Spain, Sudan, Syria, Thailand, Tunisia, Turkey, Ukrainian Soviet Socialist Republic, Union of Soviet Socialist Republics, Yemen, Yugoslavia, Afghanistan, Albania, Austria, Belgium, Brazil. *Against*: Canada, Colombia, France, Israel, Morocco, Netherlands, New Zealand, Sweden, United Kingdom, Uruguay, Argentina, Australia. *Abstaining*: Ceylon, China, Finland, Guatemala, India, Iran, Italy, Japan, Luxembourg, Nepal, Pakistan, Portugal, United States of America, Venezuela.

from Costa Rica removing the term was convincingly defeated.[240] Implying that there was no consensus on the subject, it further noted that delegates had advanced a variety of definitions for the term: fixed or done capriciously or at pleasure; without adequate determining principle; depending on the will alone; tyrannical; despotic; without cause upon law; not governed by any fixed rule or standard.[241]

2.2.3 *Reference to the* Covenant *and the* Genocide Convention *(paragraphs 2 and 3)*

A third area of difficulty during the drafting of the right to life provision in the Third Committee was the cross-references to the *Universal Declaration* and the *Genocide Convention* that appeared in paragraph 2 of the proposal of the Commission on Human Rights. Some delegates suggested that these be omitted entirely. For example, the Iranian delegation argued for deletion because the covenants should form a comprehensive human rights code, containing all ideas and principles previously embodied in other conventions. Iran suggested that paragraph 6§2 be changed to read simply 'in accordance with law not contrary to the principles set forth in the Covenants'.[242] Sir Samuel Hoare of the United Kingdom felt that mention of the *Genocide Convention* was unnecessary, because nothing in paragraph 2 could suggest otherwise that genocide would be countenanced,[243] but he later said that he would not make an issue of the matter.[244]

Peru said that the draft covenant applied to individuals as well as to groups, so it was broader than the *Genocide Convention*, but that the *Genocide Convention* contained stronger provisions for implementation, and this was why Brazil and Peru had introduced their amendment.[245] Peru noted that the references were oriented towards mass death sentences imposed by Nazi tribunals after a travesty of the judicial process.[246] El Salvador said that the real purpose of the reference to the *Genocide Convention* was to prevent a State using an article of the covenant to prevent ratification of the *Convention*.[247] Ireland did not want mention of the *Genocide Convention*, to which it had not adhered.[248]

Australia proposed an amendment replacing the reference to the *Universal Declaration* with a reference to the *Covenant* itself.[249] This was justified by

---

[240] UN Doc. A/3764, para. 120.　　[241] *Ibid.*, para. 114.　　[242] UN Doc. A/C.3/SR.810, para. 6.
[243] UN Doc. A/C.3/SR.812, para. 38.　　[244] UN Doc. A/C.3/SR.815, paras. 39–40.
[245] UN Doc. A/C.3/SR.813, para. 1. The amendment is UN Doc. A/C.3/L.649.
[246] *Ibid.*, para. 2.　　[247] UN Doc. A/C.3/SR.817, para. 27.
[248] UN Doc. A/C.3/SR.813, para. 43.
[249] A/C.3/L.652:
　　Replace the phrase 'not contrary to the principles of the Universal Declaration of Human Rights' by the phrase 'that is not contrary to the provisions of this Covenant' in paragraph 2.
It was later incorporated into the Working Party text.

the argument that reference to the *Declaration* was inappropriate in a legally binding treaty, as it had never been intended that the *Declaration* be construed as such an instrument.[250] The rest of the paragraph was based on the Philippine amendment.[251] With regard to the addition of a new paragraph 3 to article 6, the Working Party had provided two very similar texts for the Committee to choose between. It should also be noted that France had withdrawn its amendment to the text of paragraph 3 as drafted by the Commission on Human Rights.[252]

2.2.4 Protection of juveniles and pregnant women

Another important modification to the right to life article by the Third Committee was the addition of the prohibition on the execution of young people. Two amendments, from Japan[253] and Guatemala,[254] attempted to address this matter. The idea of prohibiting execution of juveniles had been mentioned on a few occasions in the debates in the Commission[255] but had never crystallized in an amendment, something which is surprising given that the prohibition of execution of juveniles had already been recognized in international law in the fourth *Geneva Convention* of 1949.[256] Japan said that its amendment was aimed at protecting the lives of children and young persons, who already enjoyed special protection pursuant to the draft economic, social and cultural rights covenant.[257] The pitfall of Guatemala's amendment was, according to Japan, that it suggested that the death penalty could be imposed after attaining the age of majority.[258]

Canada objected to mention of the term 'minors', because it would be too difficult to agree upon the age.[259] New Zealand supported the proposal

---

[250] UN Doc. A/C.3/SR.814, para. 50.
[251] A/C.3/L.646:
> Insert the words 'in force at the time of the commission of the crime and' after the word 'law' in paragraph 2. Insert the word 'final' before the word 'sentence'.

It was incorporated into the Working Party text.
[252] A/C.3/L.645:
> (2) Replacement of paragraph 2 by the following: 'If the law provides for capital punishment, such penalty shall be prescribed only for the most serious crimes and in accordance with the principles of the Universal Declaration of Human Rights and the Convention on the Prevention and Punishment of the Crime of Genocide. The death penalty shall not be imposed except in pursuance of the sentence of a competent court'. Deletion of the first sentence of paragraph 3 [4] and addition of the words 'to a sentenced person' after the word 'granted' in the second sentence.

[253] UN Doc. A/C.3/L.655 and Corr. 1:
> Sentence of death shall not be imposed for crimes committed by minors, and shall not be carried out on children and young persons or on a pregnant woman.

[254] UN Doc. A/C.3/L.647:
> Sentence of death shall not be carried out on minors or on a pregnant woman.

This amendment was later withdrawn: UN Doc. A/C.3/SR.816, para. 19.
[255] For example, UN Doc. E/CN.4/SR.139, para. 28; UN Doc. E/CN.4/384.
[256] *Geneva Convention of August 12, 1949 Relative to the Protection of Civilians*, (1950) 75 UNTS 135, art. 68§4.
[257] UN Doc. A/C.3/SR.814, para. 19.   [258] *Ibid.*, para. 19.   [259] *Ibid.*, para. 42.

to protect persons under full age, but also did not like the term 'minors'.[260] Hoare observed that the term 'minors' had been debated at length with respect to article 10 of the draft economic, social and cultural rights covenant and that the term 'children and young persons' had been adopted because it was more flexible.[261] Others proposed the term 'juveniles'.[262]

Japan agreed to replace 'minors' with 'children and young persons' but opposed the United Kingdom's suggestion that 'for crimes committed by' be changed to 'on', because the purpose of the amendment was to prevent the death penalty for crimes committed while the individual was still a minor, even if arrest and conviction took place afterwards.[263] Hoare responded that, if it were to be construed that way, the United Kingdom could not support the provision, as it was inconsistent with his country's law. It might be difficult to determine the exact date of the crime, and in any case the Crown would 'ordinarily' commute such a sentence, he added.[264] Fujita of Japan replied that this was illogical; how could sentence be passed on a crime whose date had not been fixed? The purpose of paragraph 4 was to establish a date for criminal liability.[265] The United Kingdom's proposal to replace the phrase 'for crimes committed by' with the word 'on'[266] was rejected.[267]

Finland argued for reference to persons under eighteen, as this was the age used in the fourth *Geneva Convention*.[268] Norway preferred paragraph 4 to read: 'Sentence of death shall not be imposed for crimes committed by persons under eighteen years of age and by pregnant women.'[269] Australia liked the precision of the term 'persons below eighteen years of age'.[270]

Denmark preferred the original text of paragraph 4, which had been prepared by the Commission and which made no mention of minors. It reasoned that there were other classes that should also be excused from the scope of the death penalty, such as insane persons, and they had not been mentioned.[271] Japan answered that it would have no objection to the inclusion of such a provision dealing with the insane, but no formal amendment was ever submitted.[272]

Although the Working Party attempted to reach a compromise, there was no agreement on the proper formulation, and it submitted three alternatives to replace the controversial term 'children and young persons': 'minors', 'persons below eighteen years of age' and 'juveniles'. For no apparent reason, the chairman

---

[260] *Ibid.*, para. 49. [261] UN Doc. A/C.3/SR.730–738.
[262] UN Doc. A/C.3/SR.817, para. 40 (Saudi Arabia); UN Doc. A/C.3/SR.818, para. 23 (Philippines).
[263] UN Doc. A/C.3/SR.815, para. 53; UN Doc. A/C.3/SR.816, para. 18.
[264] UN Doc. A/C.3/SR.816, para. 3; also UN Doc. A/C.3/SR.817, para. 18.
[265] *Ibid.*, para. 18. [266] UN Doc. A/C.3/L.656.
[267] UN Doc. A/C.3/SR.820, para. 18, by forty-one votes to twelve, with nineteen abstentions.
[268] UN Doc. A/C.3/SR.819, para. 10. [269] UN Doc. A/C.3/SR.818, para. 1.
[270] UN Doc. A/C.3/SR.817, para. 33. [271] UN Doc. A/C.3/SR.819, para. 17.
[272] UN Doc. A/C.3/SR.820, para. 6.

suggested that the Committee vote first on the phrase 'persons below eighteen years of age',[273] which was adopted in a very close vote.[274] This meant that no vote was taken on the other options, and there is no way of knowing which of the three alternatives was the most popular. The paragraph as a whole was then adopted.[275] With respect to pregnant women, the only change to the provisions that was made at the Third Committee was replacement of the term 'a pregnant woman' by 'pregnant women', in response to the Japanese amendment.[276]

2.2.5 *Conclusion*

At the conclusion of the debates, upon a request by Colombia, a vote on the entire right to life article, as amended, was taken by roll call, and it was adopted by fifty-five votes to none, with seventeen abstentions.[277] By and large, the abstainers were European countries that had preferred a text similar to article 2 of the *European Convention on Human Rights*. The United Kingdom also rallied its Commonwealth allies to this position. The United States abstained on all votes, because it had earlier declared it had no intention of ratifying the instrument. Finally, Uruguay, Colombia and Venezuela also abstained, because they could not accept the provision's approbation of capital punishment, however mitigated it might be.

The death penalty is also addressed indirectly in article 4 of the *Covenant*, which deals with derogation. Article 4 specifies that no derogation is permitted in the case of article 6, thereby entrenching the death penalty provisions even in time of war or emergency.[278] The *travaux préparatoires* give no indication whatsoever of any discussion or controversy on this point. Other provisions of the *Covenant* also touch on the death penalty. Article 7, which prohibits cruel, inhuman and degrading treatment, is often linked to the issue of capital

---

[273] *Ibid.*, §19.

[274] *Ibid.*, para. 21, by twenty-one votes to nineteen, with twenty-eight abstentions.

[275] UN Doc. A/C.3/SR.820, para. 25, by fifty-three votes to five, with fourteen abstentions.

[276] UN Doc. A/C.3/L.650.

[277] UN Doc. A/C.3/SR.820, para. 27. *In favour*: Yemen, Yugoslavia, Afghanistan, Albania, Argentina, Austria, Brazil, Bulgaria, Burma, Byelorussian Soviet Socialist Republic, Cambodia, Ceylon, Chile, Cuba, Czechoslovakia, Dominican Republic, Ecuador, Egypt, Ethiopia, Finland, France, Ghana, Greece, Guatemala, Haiti, Hungary, India, Indonesia, Iran, Iraq, Ireland, Israel, Japan, Jordan, Liberia, Mexico, Morocco, Nepal, Nicaragua, Norway, Pakistan, Panama, Peru, Philippines, Poland, Romania, Saudi Arabia, Spain, Sudan, Syria, Thailand, Tunisia, Turkey, Ukrainian Soviet Socialist Republic, Union of Soviet Socialist Republics.
Abstaining: Australia, Belgium, Canada, China, Colombia, Denmark, Italy, Luxembourg, Malaya (Federation of), Netherlands, New Zealand, Portugal, Sweden, United Kingdom, United States of America, Uruguay, Venezuela.

[278] Thomas Buergenthal, 'To Respect and to Ensure: State Obligations and Permissible Derogations', in Louis Henkin, ed., *The International Bill of Rights: The Covenant on Civil and Political Rights*, New York: Columbia University Press, 1981, pp. 73–91.

punishment, and more specifically to such issues as method of execution and the death row phenomenon. The *travaux préparatoires* provide no evidence that the drafters of the *Covenant* made any such connection, however. Articles 14 and 15, dealing with procedural rights and protection against retroactive penal legislation, are also raised in cases dealing with the death penalty. Again, the link was not made during the drafting of the *Covenant.*

In the history of international treaties, it is surely unusual for the drafting of a single provision to be drawn out over eleven years, as it was for the right to life provision of the *International Covenant on Civil and Political Rights.* The detailed summary records and other documents of the Commission on Human Rights and the Third Committee of the General Assembly provide an exceptional opportunity to examine the evolving attitudes of international lawmakers to the issue of capital punishment.

The original drafts of the *Covenant* in 1947 gave few hints of either abolition or limitation of the death penalty. Early amendments recognized the fact that the death penalty could only be imposed for 'serious crimes' and pursuant to a regular trial. Over the years, further limitations were added, such as the prohibition of execution of pregnant women and, still later, of offenders for crimes committed while under the age of eighteen.

Only in 1957, at the conclusion of the drafting procedure, was there sufficient momentum for the ideal of abolition to incite its more militant advocates to an amendment aimed at banning capital punishment. Although the amendment failed to rally the majority of the Third Committee, it did provoke a compromise solution whose clear import is to set abolition as a goal. The progress had been inexorable since 1947, and it would continue in subsequent years, as further limitations were imposed on capital punishment. In the late 1980s, an additional protocol to the *International Covenant on Civil and Political Rights* was adopted which in effect completed the ambitious proposal of Uruguay and Colombia at the twelfth session of the General Assembly.

2.3 Ratification of the Covenant and Reservations to Article 6

The *International Covenant* was adopted by the United Nations General Assembly in 1966 and came into force on 23 March 1976, following the thirty-fifth ratification. By 1 May 2001, some 147 states had become parties to the *Covenant.* The *Covenant* makes no express provision for reservations, although subsequent State practice indicating them to be acceptable has been confirmed by the Human Rights Committee in a recent general comment.[279] Reservations

---

[279] *General Comment 24(52)*, UN Doc. CCPR/C/21/Rev.1/Add.6, (1994) 15 *HRLJ* 464.

to multilateral treaties,[280] including human rights treaties,[281] are permitted by international law providing that they remain compatible with the 'object and purpose' of the treaty, and this same general rule applies to the *Covenant*. But the practice is controversial, and its widespread use has undermined the effectiveness of human rights treaties. Moreover, many reservations made by States at the time of ratification are of doubtful legality. One of the ways in which States parties express their opposition to reservations is by making objections. There have been only three reservations to the right to life and to article 6 of the *Covenant*, by Norway, Ireland and the United States of America. The United States has also formulated a reservation to article 7 of the *Covenant*, which prohibits torture and cruel, inhuman and degrading treatment or punishment, to the extent that this provision may extend to capital punishment. Eleven States parties to the *Covenant* have objected to the reservations by the United States.

Norway ratified the *Covenant* on 13 September 1972, with a reservation to article 6§4.[282] Norway later explained that its legislation did not fully conform to article 6§4, because its military courts could rule that a death sentence be carried out irrespective of the existence of a right to appeal.[283] In practice, Norway had conducted no executions since the trials that followed the Second World War.[284] On 21 November 1979, Norway's reservation to article 6§4 was

---

[280] *Vienna Convention on the Law of Treaties*, (1979) 1155 UNTS 331, arts. 19, 20; *Reservations to the Convention on the Prevention of Genocide (Advisory Opinion)*, [1951] ICJ Reports 16.

[281] William A. Schabas, 'Reservations to International Human Rights Treaties', (1995) 32 *CYIL* 39.

[282] UN Doc. CCPR/C/2 and Add. 1 (see Appendix 2, p. 314).

[283] 'Initial Report of Norway', UN Doc. CCPR/C/1/Add.5:

Norwegian law does not fully conform to the requirement in *paragraph 4* prescribing that anyone sentenced to death shall have the right to seek pardon or commutation of the sentence. According to section 242 of the Military Criminal Procedures Act of 29 March 1900 No. 2, there are no legal remedies against judgements rendered by the Courts Martial and, according to section 243, a Court Martial's sentence of death shall be carried out immediately. Furthermore, according to section 208 of that Act (cf. section 211), the ordinary military courts may, in wartime and subject to specific conditions, decide that a sentence of death shall be carried out irrespective of the normal rules of procedure. According to section 18 of the Military Criminal Procedures Act and section 14 of the Act of 15 December 1950 No. 7 relating to Emergency Measures in Wartime, the King may in certain instances decide that the High Court (Criminal Division) shall act as the court of final instance so that the right of appeal ceases to apply.

The reason for these special provisions is that it may well happen that, in a wartime emergency, the Supreme Court will be cut off from contact with certain parts of the country or that for other reasons it may prove impossible to get appeals dealt with by the Supreme Court within a reasonable space of time.

Before Norway ratified the Covenant, due consideration was given to the question of amending Norwegian legislation on these points. However, it was instead decided to make a reservation in respect of paragraph 4, and the legal situation remains the same today.

Capital punishment may not be imposed under normal conditions, but military legislation does contain certain such provisions, but always as an *alternative* punishment to deprivation of liberty.

[284] CCPR/C/SR.79, §12; A/33/40*, §248. In one reported judgment, Norway's courts actually held that international law prescribed the death penalty in the case of war crimes: *Public Prosecutor* v. *Klinge*, (1946) 13 *Ann. Dig.* 262 (Supreme Court, Norway).

withdrawn,[285] following its abolition of the death penalty in wartime. Norway told the Human Rights Committee that the legislation had passed by a narrow margin after a deeply divided public debate.[286] There were no objections to Norway's reservation by other States parties within the twelve months that followed ratification.

Ireland ratified the *Covenant* with a reservation to article 6§5 that suggested its legislation was inconsistent with the *Covenant*. However, the reservation indicated that if the question of application of this legislation ever arose, the Irish government would take into account its obligations under the *Covenant*. As in the case of Norway, the reservation is of little more than theoretical interest, because Ireland has abolished the death penalty *de facto*. Again, no States parties have raised objections to the reservation. Ireland's reservation was withdrawn on 12 April 1994. In June 2001, Irish voters adopted a referendum effecting a constitutional prohibition of capital punishment.

The United States of America ratified the *Covenant*, effective 8 September 1992, with a reservation to the capital punishment provisions of article 6.[287] Moreover, it made the only reservation ever formulated to article 7 of the *Covenant*. These are far and away the most extensive reservations to the capital punishment provisions of any international human rights treaty.[288] The eleven objections are from States belonging to the European Union, whose members had previously thought it more expedient not to object to reservations. Sweden was the first, publicizing its objection to coincide with the World Conference

---

[285] CCPR/C/2/Add.4.

[286] CCPR/C/SR.301, §3. A brief account of the Norwegian debate on abolition is presented in H. Röstad, 'The International Penal and Penitentiary Foundation and the Death Penalty', (1987) 58 *Revue internationale de droit pénal* 345. Röstad notes that the Norwegian government announced it was abolishing the death penalty for wartime offences on the same day that it declared the award of the Nobel Peace Prize to Amnesty International.

[287] United States, 'Senate Committee on Foreign Relations Report on the International Covenant on Civil and Political Rights', (1992) 31 *ILM* 645, at p. 653 (for the text of the reservations, see Appendix 2, p. 314). See: John Quigley, 'Criminal Law and Human Rights: Implications of the United States Ratification of the International Covenant on Civil and Political Rights', (1993) 6 *Harvard Human Rights Journal* 59; Ved P. Nanda, 'The US Reservation to the Ban on the Death Penalty for Juvenile Offenders: An Appraisal under the International Covenant on Civil and Political Rights', (1993) 42 *Depaul Law Review*. 1311; David P. Stewart, 'US Ratification of the Covenant on Civil and Political Rights: The Significance of the Reservations, Understandings and Declarations', (1993) 14 *HRLJ* 77; E. F. Sherman Jr, 'The US Death Penalty Reservation to the International Covenant on Civil and Political Rights – Exposing the Limitations of the Flexible System Governing Treaty Formation', (1994) 29 *Texas International Law Journal* 69; William A. Schabas, 'Les réserves des États-Unis d'Amérique aux articles 6 et 7 du *Pacte international relatif aux droits civils et politiques*', (1994) 6 *RUDH* 137; Louis Henkin, 'US Ratification of Human Rights Conventions: The Ghost of Senator Bricker', (1995) 89 *AJIL* 341; William A. Schabas, 'Invalid Reservations to the International Covenant on Civil and Political Rights: Is the United States Still a Party?', (1995) 21 *Brooklyn Journal of International Law* 277.

[288] There have been no reservations to the capital punishment provisions of the *European Convention*, but several to article 4 of the *American Convention on Human Rights*, (1979) 1144 UNTS 123, OASTS 36 (hereinafter the *American Convention*) (see Appendix 20, pp. 436–437) and to article 68§2 of the *Geneva Convention of August 12, 1949 Relative to the Protection of Civilians* (see Appendix 10, pp. 416–419).

on Human Rights, in June 1993. The objections are worded in similar terms and suggest a considerable degree of cooperation.

In its reservation to article 6 of the *Covenant*, the United States reserves the right to impose capital punishment on any person, pursuant to any existing or future law, subject only to its own constitutional constraints. Oddly, what amounts to a blanket reservation includes one exception, pregnant women, whom the United States undertakes not to execute. For greater precision, probably because it has been the source of much criticism, the United States specifically mentions that it reserves the right to impose the death penalty for crimes committed under the age of eighteen. Some have suggested that the United States' reservation to article 6 only concerns juvenile executions,[289] but the specific and otherwise superfluous mention that the United States reserves the right to impose the death penalty 'including' the case of crimes committed under the age of eighteen makes it quite clear that much more is contemplated. The intention to give a broad scope to the reservation is also evidenced in the explanation submitted by the Bush administration to the Senate. It notes in particular 'the sharply differing view taken by many of our future treaty partners on the issue of the death penalty (including what constitutes 'serious crimes' under article 6(2))'.[290] There can be no doubt that the reservation extends far beyond the question of juvenile executions and seeks to exclude the United States from virtually all international norms concerning the death penalty.

The reservation to article 7 is intended to avoid the precedent established by the European Court of Human Rights in the case of *Soering* v. *United Kingdom*,[291] as the comments submitted by President Bush to Congress make abundantly clear.[292] The United States administration formulated a similar

[289] The reservation was presented in this fashion to the Human Rights Committee in the Initial Report of the United States, UN Doc. CCPR/C/81/Add.4, §§147–148. A similar view is expressed in Stewart, 'US Ratification', p. 290.

[290] United States, 'Senate Committee on Foreign Relations Report on the International Covenant on Civil and Political Rights', (1992) 31 *ILM* 645, p. 653. The report from the Committee on Foreign Relations is ambiguous, and seems to suggest that the Senators felt the only issue was imposition of the death penalty for juvenile offences (see *ibid.*, p. 650). Use of the *travaux préparatoires* in order to determine the real intent of the reserving State is not without its problems. The European Court of Human Rights, in *Belilos* v. *Switzerland*, 29 April 1988, Series A, Vol. 132, 10 EHRR 466, 88 ILR 635, para. 55, refused to rely on the *travaux préparatoires* in this context, insisting that preparatory materials cannot be used to obscure the objective reality of the text. See: Ronald St John MacDonald, 'Reservations Under the European Convention on Human Rights', (1988) 21 *RBDI* 428, at p. 444; Susan Marks, 'Reservations Unhinged: the Belilos Case before the European Court of Human Rights', (1990) 39 *ICLQ* 300, at pp. 308–309.

[291] *Soering* v. *United Kingdom and Germany*, 7 July 1989, Series A, Vol. 161, 11 EHRR 439. The Judicial Committee of the Privy Council has reached a similar conclusion: *Pratt* et al. v. *Attorney General for Jamaica* et al., [1993] 4 All ER 769, [1993] 2 LRC 349, [1994] 2 AC 1, [1993] 3 WLR 995, 43 WIR 340, 14 *HRLJ* 338, 33 ILM 364 (JCPC). See also a judgment of the Zimbabwe Supreme Court: *Catholic Commission for Justice and Peace in Zimbabwe* v. *Attorney-General et al.*, (1993) 1 ZLR 242 (S), 4 SA 239 (Z.SC), 14 *HRLJ* 323.

[292] United States, 'Senate Committee on Foreign Relations Report on the International Covenant on Civil and Political Rights', (1992) 31 *ILM* 645, at p. 654.

condition, known as 'the Soering understanding',[293] to accompany its ratification of the *Convention Against Torture and Other Cruel, Inhuman and Degrading Treatment or Punishment.*[294]

By making such a broad reservation to article 6, the United States leaves open the possibility of execution of very young children,[295] or of the insane and the severely mentally handicapped.[296] By reserving the norm requiring that the death penalty be imposed for only the 'most serious crimes', even in the future, the United States allows for the imposition of capital punishment for crimes without violence, crimes against morality or political crimes. In making a reservation to the 'arbitrary' use of the death penalty, the United States permits imposition of death sentences in the absence of stringent procedural safeguards, going as far as the suspension of the presumption of innocence.[297] The method of execution is also excluded from the scope of the *Covenant* by the reservation to article 7. Consequently, the reservation would allow the United States to impose unquestionably inhuman punishments, such as stoning or public beheading, without running afoul of its obligations under the *Covenant.*

Although an argument can be made to the effect that all of the substantive provisions of the *Covenant* are essential to its 'object and purpose', and that as a consequence, reservation to any such provision is illegal,[298] State practice generally indicates that reservations to substantive provisions of human rights treaties in general and the *Covenant* in particular are not in and of themselves incompatible with the object and purpose of the treaty. A large number of such reservations have been made to various international human rights instruments, without any opposition based on the notion that these are *prima facie* unacceptable. The Inter-American Court of Human Rights has recognized that reservations to substantive provisions of human rights treaties cannot be excluded.[299] The Human Rights Committee reached the same result

[293] Richard B. Lillich, 'The *Soering* case', (1991) 85 *AJIL* 128.

[294] GA Res. 39/46, Annex (1985). On 27 October 1990 the Senate gave its advice and consent to ratification of the *Torture Convention.* The United States ratified the *Convention* in 1994, with the following reservation: 'That the United States considers itself bound by the obligation under article 16 to prevent "cruel, inhuman or degrading treatment or punishment", only insofar as the term "cruel, inhuman or degrading treatment or punishment" means the cruel, unusual and inhumane treatment or punishment prohibited by the Fifth, Eighth and/or Fourteenth Amendments to the Constitution of the United States.'

[295] Several of the States in the United States have no restriction on execution of children. Others set minimum ages as low as twelve. The age limit for executions according to the *Constitution* is still unclear: *Thompson* v. *Oklahoma,* 487 US 815, 108 S.Ct. 2687, 101 L.Ed.2d 702 (1988).

[296] See: William A. Schabas, 'International Norms on Execution of the Insane and the Mentally Retarded', (1993) 4 *Criminal Law Forum* 95.

[297] At the very least, in time of national emergency, where the fair trial provisions could be suspended, pursuant to article 4 of the Covenant. Although procedural safeguards in the United States are at present fairly comprehensive, there is still much room for improvement.

[298] *Belilos* v. *Switzerland* (concurring opinion of Judge De Meyer).

[299] *Restrictions to the Death Penalty (Arts. 4§2 and 4§4 American Convention on Human Rights),* Advisory Opinion OC–3/83 of 8 September 1983, Series A No. 3, 4 *HRLJ* 352, 70 ILR 449, para. 61.

in its 1994 *General Comment* on reservations.[300] Within the substantive provisions of the *Covenant*, a relatively small number of provisions are classified as non-derogable provisions, rights so fundamental and so essential that they brook no exception, even in emergency situations.[301] Articles 6 and 7 of the *Covenant* belong to this category.[302] Reservations to the non-derogable provisions of the *Covenant* are very rare. When the Congo made a reservation to article 11 (imprisonment for debt), citing its domestic law which provided for the possibility of detention when an individual was in default on financial obligations, Belgium and the Netherlands objected because they did not want to set a precedent by which reservations to non-derogable articles might be tolerated. Indeed, the Netherlands, in its objection to the reservation by the United States to article 7, declares that 'this reservation has the same effect as a general derogation from this Article, while according to Article 4 of the Covenant, no derogations, not even in times of public emergency, are permitted'.[303]

The Inter-American Court of Human Rights has taken the position that reservations to non-derogable provisions are not *a priori* unacceptable, although it affirms that blanket reservations to the right to life are incompatible with the object and purpose of the *Convention*.[304] According to the Court, reservations seeking only to restrict certain aspects of a non-derogable right cannot be presumed to be invalid providing they do not deprive the right as a whole of its basic purpose.[305] The problem with the United States reservations to article 6 of the *Covenant* is that they do much more than restrict certain aspects of the right to life.

The Human Rights Committee takes a similar view in its *General Comment* on reservations. It notes that not all rights of fundamental importance are deemed non-derogable, citing in this respect article 9 (protection of persons detained or arrested) and article 27 (minority rights). Some rights have been made non-derogable, suggests the Committee, merely because their suspension is irrelevant to the legitimate control of the state of national emergency. An example is imprisonment for debt, prohibited by article 11 of the *Covenant*. In other cases, derogation is forbidden because it is impossible to control in any case (article 18,

---

[300] *General Comment 24(52)*, para. 3. See also the remarks of Human Rights Committee chairman Francisco Jose Aguilar Urbina, UN Doc. HR/CT/405 (1995).

[301] Art. 4. See: Buergenthal, 'To Respect and to Ensure', pp. 73–91.

[302] Support for the idea that article 6 constitutes a norm of *jus cogens* may be found in W. Paul Gormley, 'The Right to Life and the Rule of Non-derogability: Peremptory Norms of *jus cogens*', in Ramcharan, ed., *The Right to Life*, pp. 120–159, at p. 125; 'Human Rights in Chile', UN Doc. E/CN.4/1983/9 (1983).

[303] Similar statements were made by Denmark, Norway and Finland.

[304] *Vienna Convention on the Law of Treaties*, art. 20§1.

[305] *Restrictions to the Death Penalty (Arts. 4§2 and 4§4 American Convention on Human Rights)*, para. 61.

freedom of conscience).[306] The Committee concludes: 'While there is no automatic correlation between reservations to non-derogable provisions, and reservations which offend against the object and purpose of the Covenant, a State has a heavy onus to justify such a reservation.'[307] But at least two members of the Committee, Fausto Pocar and Prafullachandra Natwarlal Bhagwati, still appear favourable to the thesis that reservations directed against non-derogable rights under the *Covenant* are questionable.[308]

The Human Rights Committee also suggests another test to assist in establishing whether a reservation is compatible with the *Covenant*'s 'object and purpose'. In its *General Comment*, the Human Rights Committee declares that provisions in the *Covenant* that are also norms of customary international law may not be the subject of reservations. It provides a list of such customary norms:

> Accordingly, a State may not reserve the right to engage in slavery, to torture, *to subject persons to cruel, inhuman or degrading treatment or punishment*, to arbitrarily deprive persons of their lives, to arbitrarily arrest and detain persons, to deny freedom of thought, conscience and religion, to presume a person guilty unless he proves his innocence, *to execute pregnant women or children*, to permit the advocacy of national, racial or religious hatred, to deny to persons of marriageable age the right to marry, or to deny to minorities the right to enjoy their own culture, profess their own religion or use their own language. And while reservations to particular clauses of Article 14 may be acceptable, a general reservation to a fair trial would not be.[309] [my emphasis]

The *General Comment* implies that the reservation by the United States to article 6§5 of the *Covenant*, with respect to the execution of individuals for crimes committed while under the age of eighteen, is illegal because it violates a customary norm. The *General Comment* could have been more explicit, for it refers only to a prohibition 'to execute pregnant women or children', whereas article 6§5 of the *Covenant* speaks of 'crimes committed by persons below eighteen years of age'. The Inter-American Commission on Human Rights has already held that there is a customary norm prohibiting execution of children, but that

---

[306] A curious comment: if the State cannot limit freedom of conscience, why bother including it in the *Covenant* at all.

[307] *General Comment No. 24(52)*, para. 12. Scholars have also taken this position: Quoc Dinh Nguyen, Patrick Daillier, Alain Pellet, *Droit international public*, 4th ed., Paris: Librairie générale de droit et de jurisprudence, 1993, p. 175.

[308] UN Doc. HR/CT/405 (1995).

[309] *General Comment No. 24(52)*, para. 8. Note, however, that in the past the Human Rights Committee has given effect to reservations or interpretative declarations concerning provisions that are almost certainly declaratory of customary norms: *C.L.D.* v. *France* (No. 228/1987), UN Doc. A/43/40, p. 257.

the norm only extends to some unspecified age which is lower than eighteen.[310] The United States has also taken this position in comments addressed to the United Nations Special *Rapporteur* on Extrajudicial, Summary and Arbitrary Executions: 'the [United States] Government's view was that general international law did not prohibit the execution of those committing capital crimes under age 18, provided that adequate due process guarantees were provided and that, although a number of nations prohibited the execution of such offenders, the practice of these States lacked the uniformity and *opinio juris* necessary to create a norm of customary international law'.[311] The Special *Rapporteur*, on the other hand, has taken the view that article 6 as a whole has become a rule of customary international law.[312] The *Convention on the Rights of the Child* defines a 'child' (the term used in the Human Rights Committee's *General Comment*) as a person under eighteen.[313]

The provision in article 6 of the *Covenant* that is indisputably incompatible with United States practice is the prohibition on execution of juveniles. On this point, United States constitutional law, as interpreted by the United States Supreme Court, falls two years short of the eighteen-year threshold set by article 6§5 of the *Covenant*.[314] As for the 'most serious crimes' standard, executions in the United States are only permitted in the case of killing, and there can be little doubt about its status as a 'most serious crime'. The Human Rights Committee would probably consider that the United States also respects, in a general sense, the procedural safeguards in article 6 and article 14,[315] although this assessment would be disputed by the many critics of the death penalty within the United States.[316] The reservation is therefore far broader than needed, but by its excessive scope, it must surely cross the line set by the Inter-American Court concerning reservations that 'restrict certain aspects of a non-derogable right'.

---

[310] *Roach and Pinkerton v. United States* (Case No. 9647), Resolution No. 3/87, reported in: OAS Doc. OEA/Ser.L/V/II.71 doc. 9 rev. 1, p. 147, *Inter-American Yearbook on Human Rights, 1987*, Dordrecht/Boston/London: Martinus Nijhoff, 1990, p. 328, 8 *HRLJ* 345, §60. See: Dinah Shelton, 'Note', (1987) 8 *HRLJ* 355; Dinah Shelton, 'The Prohibition of Juvenile Executions in International Law', (1987) 58 *Revue internationale de droit pénal* 773; David Weissbrodt, 'Execution of Juvenile Offenders by the United States Violates International Human Rights Law', (1988) 3 *American U. J. Int'l Law & Policy* 339. See also the reply to Professor Weissbrodt's criticism of the Inter-American Commission's report by a lawyer for the Commission: Christina M. Cerna, 'US Death Penalty Tested Before the Inter-American Commission on Human Rights', (1992) 10 *NQHR* 155.
[311] UN Doc. E/CN.4/1990/22, para. 431.   [312] UN Doc. E/CN.4/1993/46, para. 678.
[313] *Convention on the Rights of the Child*, GA Res. 44/25, Annex (1989), art. 1.
[314] *Stanford v. Kentucky; Wilkins v. Missouri*, 492 US 361, 109 S.Ct. 2969, 106 L.Ed.2d 306 (1989).
[315] It has examined the question, at least indirectly, in three Canadian communications challenging extradition to the United States for capital crimes: *Kindler v. Canada* (No. 470/1991), UN Doc. A/48/40, Vol. II, p. 138, 14 *HRLJ* 307, 6 *RUDH* 165; *Ng v. Canada* (No. 469/1991), UN Doc. A/49/40, Vol. II, p. 189, 15 *HRLJ* 149; *Cox v. Canada* (No. 539/1993), UN Doc. CCPR/C/52/D/539, (1994) 15 *HRLJ* 410.
[316] General works on the subject include: Hugo Adam Bedau, ed., *The Death Penalty in America*, Oxford: Oxford University Press, 4th ed., 1997.

When the initial report by the United States to the Human Rights Committee was examined on 30–31 March 1995, the Committee affirmed that at least some elements of the reservations dealing with the death penalty are 'incompatible with the object and purpose of the Covenant'.[317] The Committee considers that the reservations to article 6§5 (but not to article 6 as a whole) and to article 7 should be held to be invalid. The Committee does not address the legality of the reservation to article 6 as a whole, leaving some uncertainty as to its position. Although the Committee says it is concerned by the excessive number of offenses punishable by the death penalty in a number of States', it does not pronounce itself on this aspect of the reservation.[318] The Committee is silent as to the consequences of its ruling, although other authorities, notably a recent judgment of the European Court of Human Rights,[319] as well as the objections of other States parties, suggest that despite its reservations the United States is bound at law by the *Covenant* as a whole, including articles 6§5 and 7.

In accordance with Committee practice, the comments were adopted by consensus, and there is no further explanation or justification for such a conclusion. Some guidance as to the views of the Committee may, however, be found in the individual comments of members of the Committee made during examination of the initial report. Several members noted that international law prohibited the execution for crimes committed while under eighteen. Cecilia Medina Quiroga described this as a 'consensus in international law against capital punishment of juveniles'.[320] Fausto Pocar described the prohibition as a part of international customary law,[321] and as a 'peremptory rule of customary law'.[322] Members of the Committee referred to article 24§1 of the *Covenant*, concerning the protection of children, as well as article 37(a) of the *Convention on the Rights of the Child*, in support of this view.[323] Other members challenged whether it was fair to claim, as the American delegation had suggested, that public opinion was strongly favourable to the retention of capital punishment.[324] Concerns

---

[317] 'Consideration of reports submitted by states parties under article 40 of the Covenant, Comments of the Human Rights Committee, United States – Initial Report', UN Doc. CCPR/C/79/Add.50 (1995), para. 14.

[318] *Ibid.*, para. 16.

[319] *Loizidou* v. *Turkey* (*Preliminary Objections*), 23 March 1995, Series A, Vol. 310.

[320] UN Doc. CCPR/C/SR.1401, para. 52. Also: UN Doc. CCPR/C.SR.1402, para. 38 (Lallah); UN Doc. CCPR/C/SR.1401, para. 44 (Prado Vallejo); UN Doc. CCPR/C/SR.1402, para. 51 (Aguilar Urbina).

[321] UN Doc. CCPR/C/SR.1402, para. 34.   [322] UN Doc. CCPR/C/SR.1406, para. 11.

[323] UN Doc. CCPR/C/SR.1406, para. 11 (Pocar); UN Doc. CCPR/C.SR.1406, para. 11 (Bruni Celli); UN Doc. CCPR/C/SR.1406, para. 28 (El Shafei); UN Doc. CCPR/C/SR.1406, para. 44 (Ando).

[324] UN Doc. CCPR/C/SR.1402, paras. 12, 51 (Francis). Also: UN Doc. CCPR/C/SR.1406, para. 21 (Bruni Celli). But see the comments of the legal advisor to the State Department, Conrad Harper: UN Doc. CCPR/C/SR.1405, para. 12.

were also expressed about the use of capital punishment on mentally retarded persons[325] and about methods of execution.[326]

The conservative United States Senate reacted to the Human Rights Committee's finding that the reservations were at least partially illegal by proposing an amendment to new legislation providing for appropriations to the State Department, presented in June 1995. The amendment noted that the Committee's position was 'to seek to nullify as a matter of international law the reservations, understandings, declarations, and proviso contained in the Senate resolution of ratification, thereby purporting to impose legal obligations on the United States never accepted by the United States'.[327] It went on to restrict any expenditure of funds relating to the reporting procedure before the Committee until it changes its position on the subject of reservations, and 'expressly recognize[s] the validity as a matter of international law of the reservations, understandings, and declarations contained in the United States instrument of ratification of the International Covenant on Civil and Political Rights'.[328] This legislation was subsequently vetoed by President Clinton.

The United States' reservation to article 6 was also criticised by the Special Rapporteur on Extrajudicial, Summary and Arbitrary Executions, who took the view that the reservation goes considerably beyond the narrow issue of juvenile executions. He pointed out, for example, that it allows for execution of the mentally disabled. Moreover, use of the word 'future', when it refers to 'future laws' allowing capital punishment, is incompatible with the restrictive spirit of article 6.[329]

The legality of the reservation to article 6 has also been challenged before the national courts of the United States. In *Domingues* v. *Nevada*, the United States Supreme Court considered the imposition of capital punishment upon an individual aged sixteen at the time the crime was committed. The Court requested the Solicitor General of the United States to present it with the government's view of its international obligations on this point. The Solicitor General submitted an *amicus curiae* brief maintaining that the reservation to article 6 was valid and that the United States was therefore not bound by any customary legal obligation with respect to juvenile executions. Shortly afterwards, the Supreme Court ruled that it would not consider the appeal.[330]

---

[325] UN Doc. CCPR/C/SR.1402, para. 21 (Bhagwati).
[326] UN Doc. CCPR/C/SR.1406, para. 33 (Klein).
[327] S. Rep. No. 95, 104th Cong., 1st Sess., §314(a)(5) (1995) (Draft of Bill S. 908).
[328] *Ibid.*, §314(b)(2)(B).
[329] UN Doc. E/CN.4/1998/68/Add.3, para. 30; also paras. 140–141.
[330] *Domingues* v. *Nevada*, 114 Nev. 783, 961 P.2d 1279 (1998), *cert. denied* 526 US 1156, 120 S.Ct. 396, 145 L.Ed.2d 309 (1999). See also *Austin* v. *Hopper*, 15 F.Supp.2d 1210, 1260 (1998); *Faulder* v. *Johnson*, 99 F.Supp.2d 774, 777 (1999); *Ex parte Pressley*, 770 So.2d 143, 148 (2000); *Beazley* v. *Johnson*, 242 F.3d 248, 264–265 (5th Circ. 2001).

In its February 2000 declaration, prompted by the execution of Sean Sellers for crimes committed at the age of sixteen, the European Union condemned the United States reservation to article 6, saying it should be withdrawn as 'a matter of urgency'. Citing the Human Rights Committee's position on the matter, it said the reservation should be withdrawn because it was incompatible with the object and purpose of the *Covenant*.[331]

Thailand formulated an interpretative declaration to article 6§5, noting the theoretical possibility that a juvenile aged seventeen could be sentenced to death. Thailand's declaration attempts to reassure its treaty partners that 'the Court always exercises its discretion under Section 75 to reduce the said scale of punishment, and in practice the death penalty has not been imposed upon any persons below eighteen years of age. Consequently, Thailand considers that in real terms it has already complied with the principles enshrined herein.' Nevertheless, the Netherlands objected, stating that it considered the declaration to be a reservation: 'The Government of the Kingdom of the Netherlands objects to the aforesaid declaration, since it follows from the text and history of the Covenant that the declaration is incompatible with the text, the object and purpose of article 6 of the Covenant, which according to article 4 lays down the minimum standard for the protection of the right to life. This objection shall not preclude the entry into force of the Covenant between the Kingdom of the Netherlands and the Kingdom of Thailand.'

An indirect reservation to the death penalty provisions of the *Covenant* was formulated by Trinidad and Tobago on 26 May 1998, not to the *Covenant* itself but to the *Optional Protocol to the International Covenant on Civil and Political Rights*,[332] which allows individual petitions or 'communications' to be filed with the Human Rights Committee. Irritated by a series of individual communications to the Human Rights Committee from death row inmates, pursuant to the *Optional Protocol to the International Covenant on Civil and Political Rights*, Trinidad and Tobago denounced the *Protocol* and then re-acceded to it.[333] The reservation purported to deny the Committee jurisdiction over individual communications dealing with sentence of death as of the coming into force of the *Protocol* on 26 August 1998. It stated:

> Trinidad and Tobago re-accedes to the Optional Protocol to the International Covenant on Civil and Political Rights with a Reservation to article 1 thereof to the effect that the Human Rights Committee shall not be competent to receive and consider communications relating to any prisoner who is under sentence of death in respect

---

[331] 'EU Demarche on the Death Penalty', 25 February 2000.
[332] *Optional Protocol to the International Covenant on Civil and Political Rights*, (1976) 999 UNTS 171.
[333] On the legality of withdrawing from a contentious regime and then rejoining it, see *Fisheries Jurisdiction (Spain v. Canada)*, 4 December 1998, para. 39.

of any matter relating to his prosecution, his detention, his trial, his conviction, his sentence or the carrying out of the death sentence on him and any matter connected therewith.

Trinidad and Tobago attempted to justify this measure with reference to the 1993 decision of the Judicial Committee of the Privy Council, holding that prolonged detention on death row constituted a form of inhuman or degrading punishment or other treatment, which would be contrary to the country's constitution.[334] Trinidad and Tobago said it was therefore required by law to ensure that the appellate process was expedited.

> In the circumstances, and wishing to uphold its domestic law to subject no one to inhuman and degrading punishment or treatment and thereby observe its obligations under article 7 of the International Covenant on Civil and Political Rights, the Government of Trinidad and Tobago felt compelled to denounce the Optional Protocol. Before doing so, however, it held consultations on 31 March 1998, with the Chairperson and the Bureau of the Human Rights Committee with a view to seeking assurances that the death penalty cases would be dealt with expeditiously and completed within 8 months of registration. For reasons which the Government of Trinidad and Tobago respects, no assurance could be given that these cases would be completed within the timeframe sought.[335]

With respect to a communication filed the day before the reservation was to come into effect, two members of the Committee, Martin Scheinin and Fausto Pocar, anticipated that Trinidad's reservation would be judged ineffective.[336] In December 1998, Rawle Kennedy, who had been on death row for more than ten years, filed a communication alleging a number of violations of the *Covenant* respecting his death sentence. The Committee issued an interim measures request pursuant to article 86 of its *Rules.* Trinidad and Tobago challenged the Committee's jurisdiction to consider the matter, invoking the reservation it formulated when it re-ratified the *Protocol.* The Committee cited its General Comment 24, affirming it had the jurisdiction to rule on whether such a reservation could validly be made. It said the issue was whether such a reservation could be considered compatible with the object and purpose of the *Optional Protocol,* in accordance with article 19 of the *Vienna Convention on the Law of Treaties.* The Committee recalled that in General Comment 24 it had warned that reservations to the *Protocol* would not be considered permissible because they would constitute an indirect way of formulating reservations to the *Covenant* itself.[337]

---

[334] *Pratt et al.* v. *Attorney General for Jamaica et al.*
[335] *Kennedy* v. *Trinidad and Tobago* (No. 845/1999), UN Doc. CCPR/C/67/D/845/1999, para. 6.3.
[336] *Bethel* v. *Trinidad and Tobago* (No. 830/1998), UN Doc. CCPR/C/65/D/830/1998, Individual Opinions by Committee Members Fausto Pocar and Martin Scheinin (concurring).
[337] See General Comment 24, para. 13.

But in its admissibility ruling in *Kennedy*, it advanced another rationale. According to the Committee:

> The present reservation, which was entered after the publication of General Comment No. 24, does not purport to exclude the competence of the Committee under the Optional Protocol with regard to any specific provision of the Covenant, but rather to the entire Covenant for one particular group of complainants, namely prisoners under sentence of death. This does not, however, make it compatible with the object and purpose of the Optional Protocol. On the contrary, the Committee cannot accept a reservation which singles out a certain group of individuals for lesser procedural protection than that which is enjoyed by the rest of the population. In the view of the Committee, this constitutes a discrimination which runs counter to some of the basic principles embodied in the Covenant and its Protocols, and for this reason the reservation cannot be deemed compatible with the object and purpose of the Optional Protocol. The consequence is that the Committee is not precluded from considering the present communication under the Optional Protocol.[338]

Four members dissented from the Committee's conclusions, declaring: 'If a State party is free either to accept or not accept an international monitoring mechanism, it is difficult to see why it should not be free to accept this mechanism only with regard to some rights or situations, provided the treaty itself does not exclude this possibility. All or nothing is not a reasonable maxim in human rights law.'[339] The dissenters found the reasoning of the Committee, based on discrimination against those condemned to death, to be unconvincing, because not all distinction or differentiation runs counter to the *Covenant*. They said they found nothing to indicate that the reservation was incompatible with the object and purpose of the *Optional Protocol* and felt that as a result the communication should be deemed inadmissible.

The Committee did not properly consider the important issue of severability, something that the four dissenters pointed out in their individual opinions. Assuming the reservation to be invalid, the question necessarily arises as to whether the ratification or accession itself is valid. A State's consent to an international instrument may well be conditional upon the acceptance of any accompanying reservations. In *Loizidou* v. *Turkey*, the European Court of Human Rights devoted considerable attention to this matter.[340] The Human Rights Committee passed over the matter without meaningful comment although the dissenters said that the issue was hardly 'self-evident'. They said they presumed the Committee had adopted the approach set out in General Comment 24, by which '[t]he normal consequence of an unacceptable reservation is not that the

---

[338] *Kennedy* v. *Trinidad and Tobago*, para. 6.7.
[339] *Ibid.*, Individual Dissenting Opinion of Committee Members Nisuke Ando, Prafulachandra N. Bhagwati, Eckart Klein and David Kretzmer, para. 6.
[340] *Loizidou* v. *Turkey* (Preliminary Objections).

Covenant will not be in effect at all for a reserving party. Rather, such a reservation will generally be severable, in the sense that the Covenant will be operative for the reserving party without benefit of the reservation.'

The position taken by the European Court, and in some rather old jurisprudence of the International Court of Justice,[341] holds that reservations are not severable when it is clear that the reserving State's agreement depends upon the acceptability of the reservations. For the dissenters in *Kennedy*, the circumstances surrounding Trinidad and Tobago's reservation were such that it could not be severed from the re-accession.[342] In conclusion, they note that developments in the case law of the Judicial Committee of the Privy Council may have made the reservation unnecessary.

Guyana took an initiative similar to Trinidad and Tobago's on 5 January 1999, withdrawing from the *Optional Protocol* and then acceding to the instrument with the following reservation:

> the Government of Guyana feels compelled to denounce the Optional Protocol. Before doing so, however, it held public discussions and obtained Parliamentary approval for the denunciation of the aforesaid Protocol.
>
> Notwithstanding that, it is the desire of the Government of Guyana to recognize the competence of the Human Rights Committee to receive and consider communications from individuals, in terms of that Instrument, to the extent that no constraints upon its constitutional authority set out above would arise. To this end, Guyana re-accedes to the Optional Protocol to the International Covenant on Civil and Political Rights with a Reservation to Article 6 thereof with the result that the Human Rights Committee shall not be competent to receive and consider communications from any person who is under sentence of death for the offences of murder and treason in respect of any matter relating to his prosecution, detention, trial, conviction, sentence, or the execution of the death sentence and any matter connected herewith.

Nine States filed objections to the reservation made by Trinidad and Tobago, and another seven to that of Guyana.[343] Essentially, they complained that the reservation 'raises doubts as to the commitment of Trinidad and Tobago to the object and purpose of the Optional Protocol'. Some of the States argued that the reservations were contrary to the rules of the law of treaties that prohibit formulating reservations after ratification. Others described them more modestly as a 'bad precedent'. Several noted, nevertheless, that the reservations did not preclude entry into force of the Optional Protocol for Trinidad and Tobago and for Guyana with respect to the objecting State. Only a few explicitly endorsed the

---

[341] *Interhandel Case (Switzerland v. United States)*, [1959] ICJ Reports 6, p. 117; see also Judge Lauterpacht's Dissenting Opinion in the *Norwegian Loans Case (France v. Norway)*, [1957] ICJ Reports 9, pp. 43–66.

[342] *Kennedy v. Trinidad and Tobago*, Individual Dissenting Opinion of Committee Members Nisuke Ando, Prafulachandra N. Bhagwati, Eckart Klein and David Kretzmer, para. 17.

[343] For the texts, see Appendix 3, pp. 390–396.

view of the Human Rights Committee by which States cannot use the Optional Protocol as a vehicle to enter reservations to the International Covenant on Civil and Political Rights.

On 27 March 2000, Trinidad and Tobago notified the United Nations Secretary-General that it had decided to denounce the *Optional Protocol* for the second time with effect from 27 June 2000. This time, it shows no intention of attempting to accede with a new reservation. This may be taken as an unfortunate consequence of the aggressive stance taken by the Human Rights Committee. Indeed, the 'excessive pretentions'[344] of the Committee's approach to reservations have been criticized by the Special Rapporteur of the International Law Commission, Alain Pellet, as being 'contrary to general international law'.[345] But Professor Pellet's critique is not shared by all members of the International Law Commission,[346] and it has been contested by the Human Rights Committee.[347] As Gérard Cohen-Jonathan has observed, although many had threatened that the boldness of the Human Rights Committee's approach would provoke other denunciations and discourage ratification, these fears have not really been borne out.[348]

[344] 'Report of the International Law Commission on the Work of Its Forty-Ninth Session, 12 May–18 July 1997', UN Doc. A/52/10, para. 87.
[345] *Ibid.*, para. 85.   [346] *Ibid.*, paras. 129–130 and 133–147.
[347] 'Third Report on Reservations to Treaties by Mr Alain Pellet, Special Rapporteur', UN Doc. A/CN.4/491, para. 16.
[348] Gérard Cohen-Jonathan, 'La décision du Comité des droits de l'homme des Nations Unies du 2 novembre 1999 dans l'affaire *Kennedy contre Trinité-et-Tobago*, Des réserves au premier protocole facultatif', (2000) 12 *Revue universelle des droits de l'homme* 209.

3

Interpretation of the *International Covenant on Civil and Political Rights*

The *International Covenant on Civil and Political Rights*, as a multilateral convention, is subject to the general rules of treaty interpretation. A treaty is to be interpreted in good faith, in accordance with the ordinary meaning to be given to the terms of the treaty in their context and in the light of its object and purpose.[1] Subsequent practice in the application of the treaty is among the elements to be considered in treaty interpretation.[2] The *travaux préparatoires*, which are of great historical interest and which provide strong evidence of a growing trend in favour of abolition of the death penalty, are in fact only supplementary means for the purposes of interpretation.[3] This rule is all the more relevant in human rights treaties, which are 'designed rather to protect the fundamental rights of individual human beings from infringements . . . than to create subjective and reciprocal rights' among States.[4] An undue emphasis on the *travaux préparatoires* may in fact frustrate the dynamic and evolutive approach that human rights treaties require.

Under the *Covenant* and its *Optional Protocol,* a considerable body of 'jurisprudence' has developed, principally the work of the Human Rights Committee, the eighteen-member expert body created by the *Covenant* that considers the obligations of States parties in the context of three implementation mechanisms, one mandatory and the other two optional. The mandatory procedure involves the submission of periodic reports in accordance with article 40 of the *Covenant.* The initial report is due one year after ratification. Thereafter, every five years States parties are required to present detailed reports on the measures they have adopted to give effect to the rights recognized in the *Covenant* and on the progress made in the enjoyment of those rights. These reports are published as unrestricted documents, and then presented in public sessions of the Human

---

[1] *Vienna Convention on the Law of Treaties*, (1979) 1155 UNTS 331, art. 31.
[2] *Ibid.*, art. 31§3(b).   [3] *Ibid.*, art. 32.
[4] *Austria v. Italy* (App. No. 788/60), (1961) 4 *YECHR* 116, p. 140.

Rights Committee. The Committee members discuss the reports, expressing their personal opinions. Since 1992, the Committee has also issued 'concluding observations', which represent its formal position on problems of compliance with human rights norms within the state concerned. The periodic reports are of great assistance in interpreting article 6 of the *Covenant*. Aside from providing useful factual information on the death penalty, they also furnish an indication of each State party's views on the scope of the article.

In the context of its examination of periodic reports, the Human Rights Committee has adopted a number of 'general comments', issued in accordance with article 40§4 of the *Covenant*. The Committee has explained that the purpose of its general comments is to assist States parties in fulfilling their reporting obligations, by sharing the experience gleaned from the many periodic reports already studied, drawing attention to insufficiencies, and suggesting improvements.[5] These general comments come very close to being a form of official or authentic commentary on the *Covenant*. Two general comments address the right to life provisions of the *Covenant*, although only the first deals with capital punishment.[6]

The first optional procedure, established by article 41 of the *Covenant*, envisages inter-State petitions. Since the coming into force of the *Covenant* in 1976, the mechanism has never been invoked.

The second optional procedure is established by the *Optional Protocol*. It creates a mechanism by which individuals may petition the Human Rights Committee alleging breaches of their rights under the *Covenant*. The Committee may release what the hesitant language of the *Protocol* designates as 'views', in reality a judgment on the allegation that a State party has violated one or several provisions of the *Covenant*. A large number of death penalty cases have come

---

[5] UN Doc. CCPR/C/21; also published in UN Doc. A/36/40, Annex VII, UN Doc. CCPR/3/Add.1, pp. 298–299.

[6] *General Comment 6(16)*, UN Doc. CCPR/C/21/Add.1, UN Doc. A/37/40, Annex V, UN Doc. CCPR/3/Add.1, pp. 382–383 (see Appendix 5, p. 402 below). The second comment on the right to life, *General Comment 14(23)*, UN Doc. A/40/40, UN Doc. CCPR/C/SR.563, para. 1, deals with issues of war and nuclear weapons. *General Comment 6(16)* was originally proposed as Conference Room Paper 1982/1 (the initial draft was reprinted in the summary records: UN Doc. CCPR/C/SR.369, para. 10). Some members of the Human Rights Committee felt it important to stress the need to eliminate the social and economic conditions that lead to crime as preliminary to the abolition of capital punishment, but no amendment in this sense was ever made (UN Doc. CCPR/C/SR.369, para. 22; UN Doc. CCPR/C/SR.369, para. 24; UN Doc. CCPR/C/SR.369, para. 29; UN Doc. CCPR/C/SR.370, para. 19; UN Doc. CCPR/C/SR.370, para. 29). Only minor drafting changes were made to the paragraphs dealing with capital punishment in the final version adopted by the Committee. In the Third Committee, at the thirty-seventh session of the General Assembly, there was widespread satisfaction with *General Comment 6(16)*. One of the few critical voices was the German Democratic Republic, which felt that describing the abolition of the death penalty as being 'desirable' was inappropriate, because states had a duty laid down in article 6 that went well beyond the merely 'desirable' (UN Doc. A/C.3/37/SR.52, para. 4).

before the Committee, most of them from Jamaica[7] and other Commonwealth Caribbean States that still retain the death penalty, and from Canada, which does not, although it has extradited fugitives to the United States for capital crimes. Considerable improvements have been effected in the imposition of the death penalty within Jamaica, some of this no doubt attributable to the intense scrutiny provided by the Committee's petition procedure.[8] But ostensibly frustrated with delays in the treatment of cases by the Human Rights Committee, Jamaica withdrew from the *Optional Protocol* with effect from 22 January 1998, followed by Trinidad and Tobago in 2000.

Article 6 has also been considered by several domestic tribunals addressing issues relating to the death penalty.[9] Because the Inter-American Court of Human Rights is entitled to interpret 'other treaties', it will occasionally construe provisions of the *Covenant*, and has in fact considered the scope of the guarantee of a free trial enshrined in article 14 as it relates to capital cases.[10]

3.1 The right to life (article 6) and capital punishment

Article 6 of the *International Covenant on Civil and Political Rights* enshrines the right to life. It is derived from article 3 of the *Universal Declaration of Human Rights*,[11] which it completes and, depending upon the interpretation that is given to article 3, limits. For, in effect, while article 6 begins by proclaiming the right to life, it proceeds to recognize capital punishment as a permissible exception to the right to life, and then spells out limitations on the use of capital punishment. At the same time, in two places article 6 also contemplates abolition of the death penalty. Interpreters of article 6 have been torn in two directions, between viewing article 6 as being essentially permissive, and therefore 'recognizing' that the death penalty is beyond the scope of the right to life, and being restrictive, admitting the existence of the death penalty as a regrettable and temporary compromise, but viewing it as ultimately incompatible with the right to life in its most pure expression.

[7] According to the High Commissioner for Human Rights, as of July 2000 the Human Rights Committee had adopted Views in 113 Jamaican death penalty cases, finding a violation of the *Covenant* in ninety-four of them.

[8] 'Report of the Human Rights Committee, 1998', UN Doc. 53/40, para. 75.

[9] *Stanford* v. *Kentucky*, *Wilkins* v. *Missouri*, 492 US 361, 109 S.Ct. 2969 (1989); *Thompson* v. *Oklahoma*, 487 US 815, 108 S.Ct. 2687 (1988); *Kindler* v. *Canada*, [1991] 2 SCR 779; *Bachan Singh* v. *State of Punjab*, (1980) 67 AIR (Supreme Court) 898; *S.* v. *Makwanyane*, 1995 (3) SA 391 (Constitutional Court of South Africa); *Pratt* et al. v. *Attorney General for Jamaica* et al., [1993] 4 All ER 769, [1993] 2 LRC 349, [1994] 2 AC 1, 33 ILM 364 (JCPC); *Catholic Commission for Justice and Peace in Zimbabwe* v. *Attorney-General et al.*, (1993) 1 ZLR 242 (S), (4) SA 239 (ZSC), 14 *HRLJ* 323.

[10] *The Right to Information on Consular Assistance in the Context of the Guarantees of Due Process of Law*, Advisory Opinion OC-16/99 of 1 October 1999. This decision is discussed at greater length in Chapter 8.

[11] GA Res. 217 A (III), UN Doc. A/810 (hereinafter the *Universal Declaration* or *Declaration*). On the *Universal Declaration*, see Chapter 1.

3.1.1 The 'inherent' right to life, and the prohibition of its 'arbitrary' deprivation

Article 6 of the *Covenant* begins with the sentence: 'Every human being has the inherent right to life.' This phrase was added during the debates in the Third Committee of the General Assembly, the notion that the right to life was 'inherent' not having been raised during the lengthy meetings of the Commission on Human Rights. The term itself came from the provocative amendment submitted by Uruguay and Colombia that called for abolition of the death penalty:

> Every human being has the inherent right to life. The death penalty shall not be imposed on any person.[12]

The abolitionist second sentence did not survive the drafting process, although it did result in an important compromise and reference to abolition of the death penalty in two other places in the provision on the right to life.[13] The first sentence, on the other hand, quickly won widespread support[14] and was even borrowed by other amendments.[15] During drafting of the *Covenant*, the view that the right to life is 'inherent' suggested that the right is not conferred on an individual by society,[16] but rather that society is obliged to protect the right to life of an individual.[17] Despite criticism that the phrase was declaratory and inappropriate in a full-fledged legal instrument,[18] the sentence was adopted by an enormous majority.[19]

During the drafting of the *Covenant*, a large number of possible exceptions to the right to life were discussed. These included, aside from the death penalty, suppression of rebellion or riot, self-defence, killing to effect arrest, killing by accident, killing to prevent escape, killing during surgical operation or in medical experiments, and killing during war. A number of States insisted that article 6 include an enumeration of such exceptions, similar to what appears in article 2 of the *European Convention on Human Rights*.[20] Yet the death penalty was the only exception actually mentioned in the *Covenant*. Some or all of these exceptions may be subsumed within paragraph 1 of article 6.

---

[12] UN Doc. A/C.3/L.644.

[13] For detailed discussion on the drafting of the *Covenant*, see Chapter 2.

[14] UN Doc. A/C.3/SR.811, para. 3 (Spain); UN Doc. A/C.3/SR.815, para. 36 (United Kingdom); UN Doc. A/C.3/SR.818, para. 13 (Pakistan); UN Doc. A/C.3/SR.814, para. 36 (Canada); UN Doc. A/C.3/SR.811, para. 4 (El Salvador).

[15] UN Doc. A/C.3/L.654 (Belgium, Brazil, El Salvador, Mexico and Morocco).

[16] UN Doc. A/C.3/SR.810, para. 10 (France); UN Doc. A/C.3/SR.814, para. 21 (Italy).

[17] UN Doc. A/C.3/SR.810, para. 10 (France); UN Doc. A/C.3/SR.813, para. 35 (India).

[18] UN Doc. A/C.3/SR.814, para. 3, UN Doc. A/C.3/SR.817, para. 12 (Poland); UN Doc. A/C.3/SR.819, para. 14 (Denmark).

[19] UN Doc. A/C.3/SR.820, para. 8, by sixty-five votes to three, with four abstentions.

[20] *Convention for the Protection of Human Rights and Fundamental Freedoms*, (1955) 213 UNTS 221, ETS 5.

According to Professor Yoram Dinstein, use of the word 'inherent' in paragraph 1 may indicate that the right to life is entrenched as part of customary international law and that it applies even to States that have not ratified or acceded to the *Covenant*.[21] This conclusion does not find any support in the *travaux préparatoires*. In any case, even if there is little doubt that the 'right to life' forms part of customary international law, the real problem is in defining the scope of that right.

In his individual dissenting opinion in *Kindler* v. *Canada*, Human Rights Committee member Bertil Wennergren stated that by guaranteeing to every human being 'the inherent right to life', article 6 makes clear that its object as a whole is the protection of human life. According to Wennergren, the other provisions of article 6 concern 'a secondary and subordinate object, namely to allow States parties that have not abolished capital punishment to resort to it until such time they feel ready to abolish it'. Wennergren wrote: 'The principal different between my and the Committee's views on this case lies in the importance I attach to the fundamental rule in paragraph 1 of article 6, and my belief that what is said in paragraph 2 about the death penalty has a limited objective that cannot by any reckoning override the cardinal principle in paragraph 1.'[22]

But are there exceptions to this 'inherent' right to life? Wennergren, in his individual dissenting opinion, recognized only two: the death penalty, which is codified in paragraphs 2, 4, 5 and 6 as a 'necessary evil', and the rule of necessity, which is implicit. He said that only if absolute necessity so requires will it be justifiable to deprive an individual of life, in order to prevent the individual from killing others or in order to avert man-made disasters. 'For the same reason, it is justifiable to send citizens into war and thereby expose them to a real risk of their being killed', he concluded. 'In one form or another, the rule of necessity is inherent in all legal systems; the legal system of the Covenant is no exception.'[23]

The second sentence of paragraph 1 ('This right shall be protected by law') expresses the principle of legality. In all cases where life may be taken by the state, this must be provided for by legislative provisions.[24] Furthermore, the State must protect the individual by legislating to repress those who would breach the right

---

[21] Yoram Dinstein, 'The Right to Life, Physical Integrity, and Liberty', in Louis Henkin, ed., *The International Bill of Rights – The International Covenant on Civil and Political Rights*, New York: Columbia University Press, 1981, pp. 114–138, at p. 115; see also Richard Lillich, 'Civil Rights', in Theodor Meron, ed., *Human Rights in International Law: Legal and Policy Issues*, Oxford: Clarendon Press, 1984, pp. 115–170, at p. 121.

[22] *Kindler* v. *Canada* (No. 470/1991), UN Doc. A/48/40, Vol. II, p. 138, 14 *HRLJ* 307, 6 *Revue universelle des droits de l'homme* 165, p. 157. See also the individual dissenting opinion of Francisco Jose Aguilar Urbina, *ibid.*, at p. 175.

[23] *Ibid.*   [24] Dinstein, 'The Right to Life', p. 115.

to life of others, by, for example, penalizing the crime of homicide.[25] It is a provision that may even be invoked on occasion by supporters of the death penalty, who argue that repression of the crime of murder necessitates a penalty that is an effective deterrent. They may say that the only way to protect life is with the threat that murderers will themselves be executed.[26] Certainly, the State is under an obligation to criminalize the killing of human beings, and does this by legislating against murder, homicide and manslaughter.[27]

The final sentence of paragraph 1 declares: 'No one shall be arbitrarily deprived of his life.' The Human Rights Committee has stated that 'arbitrariness' should not be equated with 'against the law', but that it should be interpreted more broadly, to include notions of inappropriateness, injustice and lack of predictability.[28] In *Kindler*, the Human Rights Committee answered the charge that the right to life had been violated 'arbitrarily' because the petitioner had been extradited to the United States without assurances he would not be executed. It said the decision to extradite had been taken after hearing argument from both sides, and that it was based on reasons, namely the absence of exceptional circumstances, the availability of due process in the United States, and prevention of Canada becoming a safe haven for murderers.[29] In an individual dissenting opinion in that case, Rajsoomer Lallah discussed the scope of the term 'arbitrarily'. Lallah observed that individuals in Canada were entitled to full protection of the right to life, because it had abolished the death penalty, at least for non-military offences. Yet 'Canada might be free to abrogate that level of respect and protection by the deliberate and coercive act of sending the individual away from its territory to another State where the fatal act runs the real risk of being perpetrated'. According to Lallah this amounted to 'arbitrary' deprivation of the right to life, and was therefore contrary to the provisions of article 6§1 of the *Covenant*: 'Canada, through its judicial arm, could not sentence an individual to death under Canadian law whereas Canada, through its executive arm, found it possible under its extradition law to extradite him to face the real risk of such a sentence.'[30]

---

[25] *De Guerrero* v. *Columbia* (No. 45/1979), UN Doc. CCPR/C/OP/1, p. 112, at p. 117. See also: C. K. Boyle, 'The Concept of Arbitrary Deprivation of Life', in Bertrand G. Ramcharan, ed., *The Right to Life in International Law*, Boston: Martinus Nijhoff, 1985, pp. 221–244, at p. 234.

[26] A study prepared by criminologist Norval Morris for the United Nations, and cited by Justice Thurgood Marshall of the United States Supreme Court in both *Furman* v. *Georgia* and *Gregg* v. *Georgia*, states: 'It is generally agreed between the retentionists and abolitionists, whatever their opinions about the validity of comparative studies of deterrence, that the data which now exist show no correlation between the existence of capital punishment and lower rates of capital crime': *Capital Punishment*, UN Doc. ST/SOA/SD/9, UN Doc. ST/SOA/SD/10 (1968), Vol. II, p. 123.

[27] *Kindler* v. *Canada* (No. 470/1991), p. 158 (*per* Wennergren, dissenting); *ibid.*, p. 160 (*per* Lallah, dissenting).

[28] *Van Alphen* v. *the Netherlands* (No. 305/1988), UN Doc. A/45/40, Vol. II, p. 108, para. 5.8.

[29] *Kindler* v. *Canada* (No. 470/1991), para. 14.6.

[30] *Ibid.*, p. 161. On the Kindler case, see: Sharon A. Williams, 'Extradition and the Death Penalty Exception in Canada: Resolving the Ng and Kindler Cases', (1991) 13 *Loyola Los Angeles International*

When the *Covenant* was being drafted, the debate around the term 'arbitrarily' was inextricably linked to proposals that an enumeration of exceptions to the right to life be included, along the lines of that of the *European Convention*,[31] an approach that was ultimately not taken. Yet the *European Convention* also makes a distinction between the death penalty and the other exceptions. Use of the word 'arbitrarily' was one of the great controversies in the drafting of article 6, and scholars continue to wrestle with the meaning that the term is to be given. Kevin Boyle has commented: 'No reading of the *travaux* of Article 6 of the *Covenant* could possibly conclude there was any consensus as to the meaning of arbitrary or as to its appropriateness in that Article.'[32]

According to a United Nations expert committee charged with analyzing the term 'arbitrary', as it appears in article 9 of the *Universal Declaration of Human Rights* and article 9 of the *Covenant*, 'illegal' is not synonymous with 'arbitrary'; something can be 'legal' and yet also 'arbitrary'.[33] Daniel Nsereko has said that deprivation of life is 'arbitrary' if it is made without due regard to the rules of natural justice or the due process of law, if it is made in a manner contrary to the law, or if it is made in pursuance of a law which is despotic, tyrannical and in conflict with international human rights standards or international humanitarian law.[34]

While it is evident that the term 'arbitrarily' was intended to cover other exceptions to the right to life, there is nothing to suggest that it was not also

and Comparative Law Journal 799; Sharon A. Williams, 'Extradition to a State that Imposes the Death Penalty', [1990] *Canadian Yearbook of International Law* 117; Sharon A. Williams, 'Nationality, Double Jeopardy, Prescription and the Death Sentence as Bases for Refusing Extradition', (1991) 62 *International Review of Penal Law* 259; Sharon A. Williams, 'Human Rights Safeguards and International Cooperation in Extradition: Striking the Balance', (1992) 3 *Criminal Law Forum* 191; Donald K. Piragoff and Marcia V. J. Kran, 'The Impact of Human Rights Principles on Extradition from Canada and the United States: The Role of National Courts', (1992) 3 *Criminal Law Forum* 191; William A. Schabas, 'Extradition et la peine de mort: le Canada renvoie deux fugitifs au couloir de la mort', (1992) 4 *Revue universelle des droits de l'homme* 65; William A. Schabas, 'Kindler and Ng: Our Supreme Magistrates Take a Frightening Step into the Court of Public Opinion', (1991) 51 *Revue du Barreau* 673.

[31] Yoram Dinstein has written that the *travaux préparatoires* of the *Covenant* indicate that the exceptions found in article 2 of the *European Convention* indicate deprivations of life that are not 'arbitrary' and are therefore permissible: Dinstein, 'The Right to Life', p. 119. See also Parvez Hassan, 'The Word "Arbitrary" As Used in the Universal Declaration of Human Rights, Illegal or Unjust?', (1969) 10 *Harvard International Law Journal* 225; L. Marcoux Jr., 'Protection from Arbitrary Arrest and Detention Under International Law', (1982) 5 *Boston College International and Comparative Law Review* 345; 'United Nations Study of the Right of Everyone to be Free From Arrest, Detention and Exile', UN Doc. E/CN.4/826/Rev.1

[32] Boyle, 'The Concept of Arbitrary Deprivation of Life', p. 225.

[33] 'Study of the right of everyone to be free from arbitrary arrest, detention and exile', UN Doc. E/CN.4/826/Rev.1, para. 27. See also, on the term 'arbitrary': *Anglo-Iranian Oil, Competence (United Kingdom v. Iran)*, [1952] ICJ Reports 89, p. 168; *X. v. United Kingdom*, 5 November 1981, Series A, Vol. 46, (1982) 4 EHRR 188, 67 ILR 466; *Winterwerp v. Netherlands*, 24 October 1979, Series A, Vol. 33, (1980) 2 EHRR 387, 59 ILR 653.

[34] Daniel D. Nsereko, 'Arbitrary Deprivation of Life: Controls on Permissible Deprivations', in Bertrand G. Ramcharan, ed., *The Right to Life*, pp. 245–283, at p. 248.

intended to cover the death penalty. Even if the other provisions of article 6 offer more specific limitations, these were not meant to be exhaustive, and there will be cases where execution is consistent with paragraphs 2, 4, 5 and 6, and yet where it is also 'arbitrary'. For example, paragraph 5 excludes juveniles and pregnant women from the death penalty but neglects to include other categories of individuals, such as the insane. The insane were not intentionally excluded from paragraph 5. The drafters merely seemed unwilling to make the text more cumbersome with a comprehensive list of exclusions.[35] Execution of the insane is contrary to the domestic law of practically every State and is probably a customary norm of international human rights law.[36] Any attempt to execute the insane, while not contrary to paragraph 5, would nevertheless be 'arbitrary' and therefore in breach of the *Covenant*. Similarly, the general prohibition of arbitrary executions may also extend to the mentally disabled.[37] Although the *Covenant* only excludes women who are pregnant from the death penalty, would it not be 'arbitrary' to execute a nursing mother within days of giving birth? Virtually all States provide for a stay of execution during a period of confinement subsequent to birth.

The term 'arbitrarily' may limit the categories of crimes for which capital punishment may be imposed, although this issue is also addressed in article 6§2 with its prohibition of the death penalty except for 'the most serious crimes'. Mandatory imposition of the death penalty, where capital murder was defined as an intentional act of violence resulting in the death of a person, irrespective of whether there was an intent to cause the death, was deemed to be an 'arbitrary' violation of the right to life, contrary to article 6§1, in *Thompson* v. *St Vincent and the Grenadines*, in which the Committee said:

> [M]andatory imposition of the death penalty under the laws of the State party is based solely upon the category of crime for which the offender is found guilty, without regard to the defendant's personal circumstances or the circumstances of the particular offence . . . The Committee considers that such a system of mandatory capital punishment would deprive the author of the most fundamental of rights, the right to life, without considering whether this exceptional form of punishment is appropriate in the circumstances of his or her case.[38]

But in another *Optional Protocol* case, filed against Jamaica, the Human Rights Committee dismissed an argument by which the mandatory death sentence for capital murder was 'an arbitrary and disproportionate punishment', noting that

---

[35] UN Doc. A/C.3/SR.819, para. 17; UN Doc. A/C.3/SR.820, para. 6.

[36] See the discussion of this issue at p. 170 below.

[37] UN Doc. E/CN.4/1998/68/Add.3, para. 145.

[38] *Thompson* v. *St. Vincent and the Grenadines* (No. 806/1998), UN Doc. CCPR/C/70/D/806/1998, para. 8.2. These views were endorsed by the East Caribbean Court of Appeal in *Spence v. The Queen*, *Hughes v. The Queen*, Criminal Appeal Nos. 20 of 1998 and 14 of 1997, Judgment of 2 April 2001.

Jamaican law distinguished between capital and non-capital murder, and that capital murder was murder committed under aggravated circumstances.[39]

According to some, procedural issues related to application of the death penalty should also be examined within the context of paragraph 1 of article 6. On this point, Bertil Wennergren disagreed with the majority view of the Human Rights Committee which relied on paragraph 2 of article 6 in holding that any breach of the procedural safeguards of article 14 of the *Covenant* violates the right to life. Wennergren contrasted cases where capital punishment resulted from a more or less proper trial, albeit defective in certain respects, and cases of what were in effect summary executions. The latter should be contemplated by the term 'arbitrarily', he said. When a trial does not display all the characteristics of a fair trial, article 6§2 would no longer be relevant.[40]

In the case of truly 'summary' executions, death sentences are usually rendered by a special court, a 'people's court', a 'revolutionary court' or a 'military tribunal', in the absence of ordinary rules of procedure.[41] Often the proceedings are held *in camera*, the accused is denied proper counsel, and the 'judges' are recent recruits, usually from the military. There is no recognition of a right of appeal or to seek pardon or clemency, and execution follows sentence in short order. The former United Nations Special *Rapporteur* on extrajudicial, summary or arbitrary executions, Amos Wako, has said that trials held without fulfilling the guarantees of article 14 of the *Covenant* are to be considered 'summary executions' and therefore a breach of article 6, where a capital sentence is imposed. Wako has supported his position with reference to both paragraphs 1 and 2 of article 6.[42]

Public executions are increasingly rare, although still very much a feature of death-penalty practice in many States. In its Concluding Observations on Nigeria's periodic report, the Human Rights Committee said: 'Public executions are also incompatible with human dignity.'[43] No specific provision of the *Covenant* was cited. The term 'dignity' appears in the preamble ('[human rights]

---

[39] *Brown* v. *Jamaica* (No. 775/1997), UN Doc. CCPR/C/65/D/775/1997, para. 6.14. Jamaica's *Offences Against the Person (Amendment) Act 1992* classifies murder as capital when it is committed, *inter alia*, in the furtherance of robbery, burglary or housebreaking. Despite what the Human Rights Committee suggests, this would seem to be a mandatory death sentence in such cases.

[40] *Pinto* v. *Trinidad and Tobago* (No. 232/1987), UN Doc. A/45/40, Vol. II, pp. 75–76; *Reid* v. *Jamaica* (No. 250/1987), UN Doc. A/45/40, Vol. II, p. 85, 11 *HRLJ* 319, pp. 94–95.

[41] Nsereko, 'Arbitrary Deprivation of Life', p. 250. For an example, see: 'Iran: Islamic Revolutionary Tribunals' Rules of Procedure', (1980) 25 *ICJ Review* 20.

[42] 'Report – Summary or Arbitrary Executions', UN Doc. E/CN.4/1983/16, p. 15. See the discussion of this point by Theodor Meron, *Human Rights in Internal Strife, Their International Protection*, Cambridge: Grotius Publications, 1987, pp. 61–62; Theodor Meron, *Human Rights Law-Making in the United Nations, A Critique of Instruments and Process*, Oxford: Clarendon Press, 1986, pp. 93–99. Also: Stephanos Stavros, 'The Right to a Fair Trial in Emergency Situations', (1992) 41 *International and Comparative Law Quarterly* 343.

[43] 'Concluding Observations, Nigeria', UN Doc. CCPR/C/79/Add.16, para. 16.

derive from the inherent dignity of the human person'), and the concept ought to inform the term 'arbitrarily' in article 6§1.

3.1.2 'In countries which have not abolished the death penalty . . .'

The draft initial phrase of paragraph 2 of article 6, as adopted by the Commission on Human Rights, did not use the term 'abolished', and said: 'In countries where capital punishment exists . . .'[44] It was changed by the Working Party of the General Assembly's Third Committee so as to satisfy the many delegates who had supported abolition of the death penalty. The report of the Working Group explained that the phrase was 'intended to show the direction in which the drafters of the Covenant hoped that the situation would develop'.[45] In *General Comment 6(16)*, the Human Rights Committee states that paragraph 2 suggests that 'abolition is desirable'.[46] By referring to the importance of 'all measures of abolition' in its *General Comment*, the Committee also implies that even partial abolition or limitation of the death penalty should be considered within the rubric of 'abolition'.[47]

The phrase 'in countries which have not abolished the death penalty' indicates that paragraph 2 is inapplicable to those States that have abolished the death penalty. It has been suggested that this phrase also implies that there can be no retraction of abolition of the death penalty; once a State has abolished the death penalty, it cannot reinstate it.[48] An express provision to this effect appears in article 4§3 of the *American Convention on Human Rights*.[49] A Committee of Experts of the Council of Europe felt that it is 'not clear' whether the *Covenant* prohibits reintroduction of the death penalty in a country where it has already been abolished, and noted that this did not appear to be the intention of its drafters.[50]

The majority of the Human Rights Committee has yet to take the view that article 6§2 of the *Covenant* prevents a State from reintroducing the death penalty if it has already been abolished. In 2000, in *Piandong* v. *Philippines*, the

---

[44] UN Doc. E/2256, UN Doc. E/2447, UN Doc. A/2929.   [45] UN Doc. A/C.3/SR.816, para. 19.
[46] During consideration of the 'Initial Report of Barbados', Sir Vincent Evans said that article 6 'looks towards abolition' (UN Doc. CCPR/C/SR.264, para. 22). Evans made similar comments during presentation of the 'Initial Report of Mali' (UN Doc. CCPR/C/SR.284, para. 20).
[47] UN Doc. CCPR/C/21/Add.1, UN Doc. A/37/40, Annex V, UN Doc. CCPR/3/Add.1, pp. 382–383, para. 6.
[48] R. Sapienza, 'International Legal Standards on Capital Punishment', in Bertrand G. Ramcharan, *The Right to Life*, pp. 284–296, at p. 289.
[49] (1979) 1144 UNTS 123, OASTS 36: 'The death penalty shall not be reestablished in states that have abolished it.'
[50] 'Problems arising from the co-existence of the United Nations Covenants on Human Rights and the European Convention on Human Rights', C. of E. Doc. H(70)7, para. 91.

Committee did not speak to the issue because 'neither counsel nor the State party has made submissions in this respect'.[51] But by raising it despite the silence of the parties, the Committee may have been suggesting that it was open to the argument that reinstatement of the death penalty might be prohibited by article 6.[52]

Varied individual opinions on the subject have been expressed by Committee members over the years. Kurt Herndl and Waleed Sadi opposed interpreting article 6§2 as an implied prohibition on reintroduction of capital punishment. Making reference to article 31 of the *Vienna Convention on the Law of Treaties*, they stressed that treaties must be interpreted '*in good faith* in accordance with the ordinary meaning to be given to the terms in their context' (emphasis in the original). They said that the context of article 6 of the *Covenant* was determined by paragraph 2, 'which does not prohibit the imposition of the death penalty for the most serious crimes; part of the context to be considered is also the fact that a large majority of States – at the time of the drafting of the Covenant and still today – retain the death penalty. One may not like this objective context, but it must not be disregarded.'[53] Herndl and Sadi noted that, by comparison, article 4§3 of the *American Convention on Human Rights* specifically prohibits reintroduction of capital punishment, and that it could also be 'read into' the *Second Optional Protocol.*

Several members of the Committee have taken the contrary view. When Guatemala reintroduced the death penalty in 1982, Prado Vallejo described the measure as 'scandalous'. But he was unsuccessful in attempts to address the issue in *General Comment 6(16).*[54] For Christine Chanet, the wording of article 6§2 is 'negative and refers not to countries in which the death penalty exists but to those in which it has not been abolished'. As a result, it '*rules out the application of the text to countries which have abolished the death penalty*'.[55] She said the majority of the Committee viewed paragraph 2 as 'an authorisation to re-establish the death penalty', whereas it was merely 'an implicit recognition of its existence'.[56] A similar opinion was expressed by Bertil Wennergren in *Cox* v. *Canada*: 'What article 6, paragraph 2, does not, in my view, do is to permit States parties that have abolished the death penalty to reintroduce it at a later stage.'

---

[51] *Piandong et al.* v. *Philippines* (No. 869/1999), UN Doc. CCPR/C/70/D/869/1999, para. 7.4.

[52] One of the members of the Committee who participated in the decision has described this portion of the Committee's views as an *obiter dictum.* See: Martin Scheinin, 'Capital Punishment and the International Covenant on Civil and Political Rights: Some Issues of Interpretation in the Practice of the Human Rights Committee', p. 13.

[53] *Cox* v. *Canada* (No. 539/1993), UN Doc. CCPR/C/52/D/539/1993, (1994) 15 *HRLJ* 410.

[54] UN Doc. CCPR/C/SR.369, para. 35.

[55] *Kindler* v. *Canada* (No. 470/1991), p. 164 (emphasis in the original). Chanet repeated these comments in *Cox v. Canada* (No. 539/1993).

[56] *Cox v. Canada* (No. 539/1993), p. 421.

The most compelling argument in favour of such a view relies on the relationship between paragraphs 2 and 6 of article 6. Abolition is more than just a fact that conditions the application of paragraph 2, it is also a goal of the *Covenant*. The drafting history of the *Covenant* justifies such a connection, as the two references to abolition were both introduced at the same time, and for the same reason. In his dissenting opinion in *Kindler* v. *Canada*, Fausto Pocar wrote:

> [T]he wording of paragraphs 2 and 6 clearly indicates that article 6 tolerates – within certain limits and in view of future abolition – the existence of capital punishment in States parties that have not yet abolished it, but may by no means be interpreted as implying for any State party an authorization to delay its abolition or to introduce or reintroduce it. Consequently, a State party that has abolished the death penalty is in my view under the legal obligation, according to article 6 of the Covenant, not to reintroduce it. This obligation must refer both to a direct reintroduction within the State party's jurisdiction, and to an indirect one, as is the case when the State acts – through extradition, expulsion or compulsory return – in such a way that an individual within its territory and subject to its jurisdiction may be exposed to capital punishment in another State.[57]

May a country extend the scope of the death penalty without violating article 6? The Human Rights Committee has stated that '[e]xtension of the scope of application of the death penalty raises questions as to the compatibility with article 6 of the Covenant'.[58] The Committee has criticised Lebanon for extending the death penalty to new crimes, noting that this was 'not compatible' with article 6.[59] But its members did not object on this ground when Mauritius, in presentation of its second periodic report,[60] stated it was reintroducing the death penalty for drug traffickers after a twenty-three-year moratorium.[61] The Special *Rapporteur* on extrajudicial, summary or arbitrary executions has also expressed the view that the expansion of the scope of the death penalty violates the spirit of article 6 of the *Covenant*, which promotes the progressive reduction in the number of crimes subject to capital punishment.[62]

3.1.3 'the most serious crimes . . .'

Paragraph 2 of article 6 also declares that the death penalty may only be applied for the 'most serious crimes'. The provision was frequently criticised during the

---

[57] The same opinion was expressed in virtually identical terms by Pocar, this time joined by his colleague Francisco Jose Aguilar Urbina, in *Cox v. Canada* (No. 539/1993).

[58] 'Preliminary Observations on the Third Periodic Report of Peru', UN Doc. CCPR/C/79/Add.67, para. 15.

[59] 'Concluding Observations, Lebanon', UN Doc. CCPR/C/79/Add.78, para. 20; 'Annual Report of the Human Rights Committee, 1997', UN Doc. 52/40, para. 350.

[60] 'Second Periodic Report of Mauritius', UN Doc. CCPR/C/28/Add.12.

[61] UN Doc. CCPR/SR.904–906, UN Doc. A/44/40, para. 508.

[62] UN Doc. E/CN.4/1998/68/Add.3, paras. 145 and 156(d). Also: UN Doc. E/CN.4/1994/7, para. 677; UN Doc. E/CN.4/1994/7/Add.2, para. 74.

drafting, and some delegates had argued for a specific enumeration of serious crimes.[63] It has since been attacked for allowing too much divergence in State practice and for being ineffectual as a check on some States' proneness to resort to capital punishment.[64] The 'Safeguards Guaranteeing Protection of Those Facing the Death Penalty', adopted by the Economic and Social Council in 1984 and subsequently endorsed by the General Assembly, declare that the ambit of the term 'most serious crimes' 'should not go beyond intentional crimes, with lethal or other extremely grave consequences'.[65] According to the Secretary-General, this means 'the offences should be life-threatening, in the sense that this is a very likely consequence of the action'.[66] The Commission on Human Rights, in its 1999 resolution, echoing the views of the Special *Rapporteur* on extrajudicial, summary or arbitrary executions,[67] urged States not to impose the death penalty for non-violent financial crimes or for non-violent religious practice or expression of conscience.[68]

Other treaties with similar provisions are of interest but do not provide much assistance in interpreting article 6§2 of the *Covenant*. The fourth *Geneva Convention* enumerates the only capital crimes that may be applied to civilians in occupied territories: espionage, serious crimes of sabotage of military installations, and intentional murder.[69] Article 33 of the *Convention on the Status of Refugees* uses the term 'particularly serious crime' to limit the principle of *non-refoulement*.[70] Atle Grahl-Madsen has written that a 'particularly serious crime' is 'any offence for which the maximum penalty in the majority of countries of Western Europe and North America is imprisonment for more than five years or death', rejecting a narrower interpretation which would confine the scope of the term to offences against life or limb.[71]

The Secretary-General has distinguished between three categories of 'most serious offences': ordinary offences, offences against the State, and military and wartime offences.[72] The 1990 report, prepared by criminologist Roger Hood and based on replies to a questionnaire from forty-one Member States, noted that not all of the offences appeared to comply with the standards of the *Covenant*. 'For example', says the report, 'offences aimed at the domination of a social class or at overthrowing the basic economic and social orders (as reported by Turkey), and theft in aggravated circumstances, sexual intercourse with a female

---

[63] UN Doc. A/C.3/SR.814, para. 12. [64] Nsereko, 'Arbitrary Deprivation of Life', pp. 254–255.
[65] ESC Res. 1984/50; GA Res. 39/118. [66] UN Doc. E/2000/3, para. 79.
[67] UN Doc. E/CN.4/1999/39, para. 63. [68] UN Doc. E/CN.4/1999/RES.61.
[69] *Geneva Convention of August 12, 1949 Relative to the Protection of Civilians*, (1950) 75 UNTS 135, art. 68§2.
[70] (1951) 189 UNTS 137.
[71] A. Grahl-Madsen, *The Status of Refugees in International Law*, Vol. I, Leyden: Sijthoff, 1966, p. 284. See also: Guy S. Goodwin-Gill, *The Refugee in International Law*, Oxford: Clarendon Press, 1983, pp. 69–100.
[72] UN Doc. E/1995/78, paras. 53–60.

relative under 15 or arousing of religious and sectarian feelings and propagation of Zionist ideas (as reported by Cuba), may not stand the test of a "most serious crime" in the sense of article 6 of the Covenant.'[73]

Reports to the Human Rights Committee, the Committee Against Torture, the Committee on the Rights of the Child, the Secretary-General, the Special *Rapporteur* on extrajudicial, summary or arbitrary executions, and the other special *rapporteurs* and special representatives, indicate that, in addition to such undisputedly serious crimes as premeditated murder and treason, the death penalty is also applied in some States for economic crimes,[74] embezzlement,[75] industrial espionage,[76] misuse of public funds,[77] destruction of food warehouses,[78] counterfeiting,[79] trafficking in currency,[80] in toxic waste,[81] and in women and children,[82] kidnapping,[83] banditry,[84] political crimes,[85] terrorism,[86] anarchy,[87] theft,[88] vehicle theft,[89] piracy,[90] activities in an illegal organization,[91] the use,

[73] UN Doc. E/1990/38, para. 41.

[74] 'Initial Report of Bulgaria', UN Doc. CCPR/C/SR.131, para. 30, UN Doc. CCPR/C/SR.132, para. 37; 'Initial Report of Mali', UN Doc. CCPR/C/1/Add.49, UN Doc. CCPR/C/SR.283, para. 11; 'Report on the Situation of Human Rights in Iraq', UN Doc. E/CN.4/1998/67, para. 18; 'Concluding Observations, Algeria', UN Doc. CCPR/C/79/Add.1, para. 7; 'Concluding Observations, Iraq', UN Doc. CCPR/C/79/Add.84, para. 10; 'Report by the Special Rapporteur, Mr. Bacre Waly Ndiaye, Submitted Pursuant to Commission on Human Rights Resolution 1993/71', UN Doc. E/CN.4/1994/7, paras. 209 (China); 'Report by the Special Rapporteur, Mr. Bacre Waly Ndiaye, Submitted Pursuant to Commission on Human Rights Resolution 1993/71', UN Doc. E/CN.4/1994/7, para. 377 (Iraq).

[75] UN Doc. E/CN.4/1992/30, para. 42 (Algeria); UN Doc. E/CN.4/1993/46, para. 176 (China).

[76] UN Doc. E/CN.4/1988/22, para. 117.

[77] 'Initial Report of Romania', UN Doc. CCPR/C/1/Add.33, UN Doc. CCPR/C/SR.135, para. 37.

[78] UN Doc. CAT/C/SR.202, para. 13.

[79] 'Report on the Situation of Human Rights in the Democratic Republic of the Congo', UN Doc. E/CN.4/1999/31, para. 72.

[80] 'Initial Report of Sudan', UN Doc. CCPR/C/45/Add.3, UN Doc. CCPR/C/SR.1065–1067, UN Doc. A/46/40, para. 509.

[81] 'Second Periodic Report of Cameroons', UN Doc. CCPR/C/63/Add.2, para. 49.

[82] UN Doc. E/2000/3, para. 83.

[83] *Ibid.*, para. 82; UN Doc. E/CN.4/1996/4 and Corr.1, para. 210; UN Doc. E/2000/3, para. 83.

[84] 'Initial Report of Bulgaria', para. 14.

[85] 'Initial Report of Jordan', UN Doc. CCPR/C/1/Add. 56, 'Initial Report of Iraq', UN Doc. CCPR/C/1/Add.45; UN Doc. CCPR/C/SR.200, para. 19, para. 42; 'Initial Report of Japan', UN Doc. CCPR/C/10/Add.1; 'Initial Report of Libyan Arab Jamahiriya', UN Doc. CCPR/C/1/Add.3*, UN Doc. CCPR/C/1/Add.20; 'Report on the Situation of Human Rights in Iraq', UN Doc. E/CN.4/1998/67, para. 34; 'Report Submitted by the Special Rapporteur [on Iraq], Mr Max van der Stoel, in Accordance with Commission Resolution 1998/65', UN Doc. E/CN.4/1999/37, para. 8.

[86] 'Report by the Special Rapporteur, Mr. Bacre Waly Ndiaye, Submitted Pursuant to Commission on Human Rights Resolution 1993/71', UN Doc. E/CN.4/1994/7, para. 136.

[87] *Ibid.*.

[88] 'Report on the Situation of Human Rights in Democratic Republic of Congo (former Zaire)', UN Doc. E/CN.4/1998/65, para. 102

[89] 'Report by the Special Rapporteur, Mr. Bacre Waly Ndiaye, Submitted Pursuant to Commission on Human Rights Resolution 1993/71', UN Doc. E/CN.4/1994/7, paras. 373 and 375 (Iraq).

[90] UN Doc. E/CN.4/1993/46, para. 225 (Cuba).

[91] 'Report of the Special Rapporteur [on Sudan], Mr Gaspar Biro', UN Doc. E/CN.4/1998/66, para. 10.

possession[92] and trafficking in narcotic drugs,[93] homosexuality,[94] offences against sexual morality,[95] adultery,[96] rape,[97] blasphemy,[98] apostasy,[99] armed robbery,[100] robbery with violence,[101] arson,[102] espionage,[103] terrorism,[104] avoiding military service,[105] cowardice,[106] threatening judges in open court,[107] an attempt on the life of a militiaman[108] and involuntary crimes.[109]

General Comment 6(16) states that the expression 'most serious crimes' must be 'read restrictively', because death is a 'quite exceptional measure'.[110] Moreover, the Human Rights Committee considers that, while article 6 of the *Covenant* does not require States to abolish the death penalty altogether, the combined effect of paragraphs 2 and 6 is that they must abolish it for other than the 'most serious crimes'. The *General Comment* states: 'Accordingly, they ought to consider reviewing their criminal laws in this light and, in any event, are obliged to restrict the application of the death penalty to the "most serious

---

[92] 'Initial Report of Iran', UN Doc. CCPR/C/1/Add.58; UN Doc. E/CN.4/1994/7, para. 352.

[93] 'Initial Report of Sudan'; UN Doc. E/2000/3, para. 81.

[94] 'Initial Report of Iran'; UN Doc. E/2000/3, para. 82; UN Doc. E/CN.4/1998/82, annex.

[95] 'Initial Report of Togo', UN Doc. CCPR/C/36/Add.5, UN Doc. CCPR/C/SR.870, 871, 874, 875, 876, UN Doc. A/44/40, para. 259; 'Second Periodic Report of Yemen', UN Doc. CRC/C/70/Add.1, para. 95.

[96] 'Initial Report of Iran'; UN Doc. CCPR/C/SR.365, paras. 7 and 8; UN Doc. E/CN.4/1999/39/Add.1, para. 103; UN Doc. E/2000/3, para. 82; 'Report of the Special Rapporteur [on Sudan], Mr Leonardo Franco', UN Doc. E/CN.4/1999/38/Add.1, para. 91.

[97] 'Third Periodic Report of the Union of Soviet Socialist Republics', UN Doc. CCPR/C/52/Add.2 and 6, UN Doc. CCPR/C/SR.928–932, UN Doc. A/45/40, para. 93; UN Doc. CCPR/C/SR.119, para. 14 (Bulgaria); 'Fourth Periodic Report of Tunisia', UN Doc. CCPR/C/84/Add.1, para. 82d); UN Doc. E/CN.4/1990/22, para. 266 (Iraq); UN Doc. E/2000/3, para. 82.

[98] 'Report by the Special Rapporteur, Mr. Bacre Waly Ndiaye, Submitted Pursuant to Commission on Human Rights Resolution 1993/71', UN Doc. E/CN.4/1994/7, para. 475; UN Doc. E/CN.4/1995/61, para. 247; 'Report Submitted by Mr Abdelfattah Amor, Special Rapporteur [on religious intolerance]', UN Doc. E/CN.4/1999/58, para. 85 (Mauritania).

[99] 'Report Submitted by Mr Abdelfattah Amor, Special Rapporteur [on religious intolerance]', UN Doc. E/CN.4/1999/58, para. 78 (Mauritania); 'Report Submitted by Mr Abdelfattah Amor, Special Rapporteur [on religious intolerance]', UN Doc. E/CN.4/1998/6, para. 62.

[100] 'Initial Report of Kenya', UN Doc. CCPR/C/1/Add.47, UN Doc. CCPR/C/SR.271, para. 29; 'Second Periodic Report of Cameroons', para. 49; UN Doc. E/CN.4/1989/25, paras. 195–198.

[101] UN Doc. E/CN.4/1992/30, para. 96 (China).

[102] UN Doc. E/CN.4/1990/22, para. 113 (China).

[103] 'Second Periodic Report of Iraq', UN Doc. CCPR/C/46/Add.4, UN Doc. CCPR/C/SR.1077–1079, UN Doc. A/46/40, para. 632.

[104] 'Concluding Observations, Egypt', UN Doc. CCPR/C/79/Add.23 (1993), para. 8.

[105] 'Report on the Situation of Human Rights in Iraq', UN Doc. E/CN.4/1998/67, para. 37; 'Concluding Observations, Iraq', para. 11. See also the 1999 resolution of the Sub-Commission on the Protection and Promotion of Human Rights: 'The Death Penalty, Particularly in Relation to Juvenile Offenders', UN Doc. E/CN.4/Sub.2/RES/1999/4.

[106] 'Report on the Situation of Human Rights in Democratic Republic of Congo (former Zaire)', UN Doc. E/CN.4/1998/65, para. 102.

[107] 'Fourth Periodic Report of Tunisia', para. 82d). [108] UN Doc. A/52/44, para. 135 (Ukraine).

[109] UN Doc. CCPR/C/SR.136, paras. 39–40. [110] *General Comment 6(16)*, para. 7.

crimes".'[111] During consideration of the periodic reports of States parties under article 40 of the *Covenant*, members of the Human Rights Committee have indicated the restrictive interpretation to be given to the term 'serious crimes'. Often, they have focused solely on the length of the list of capital offences. For example, during presentation of a report from Jordan, a Committee member said that eleven capital crimes was 'a high number'.[112] In response to criticism from members of the Committee that the number of capital crimes was too large, the representative of Tunisia, during presentation of its third periodic report, agreed that the list was long and that 'it should be shortened as a first step'.[113] In its comments on the third periodic report of Belarus, the Committee said it was troubled by the large number of crimes for which the death penalty was still provided, despite the fact that in practice it is of limited application.[114] Often, reports have indicated that the list of capital crimes is in the process of being shortened. Algeria, in its initial report, said that the reduction of capital crimes is under consideration by a commission responsible for revising the Penal Code and that opinion favours abolition of the death penalty for economic offences.[115] But in its comments on the Algerian report, the Committee recalled that economic crimes could not be sanctioned by the death penalty.[116] When Japan failed to make good on a pledge to shorten the list, the Committee said it was gravely concerned and implied a violation of article 6§2.[117] The Supreme Court of India has concluded that Indian legislation is in accordance with article 6§2 of the *Covenant*, because the death penalty only applies in the case of seven offences.[118]

The Human Rights Committee has singled out a number of individual offences, suggesting that they do not meet the standard of article 6§2 of the *Covenant*: apostasy,[119] abetting suicide,[120] homosexual acts,[121] illicit sex,[122]

[111] *Ibid.*, para. 7.
[112] UN Doc. CCPR/C/SR.362, para. 43. See also: 'Initial Report of Madagascar', UN Doc. CCPR/C/1/Add.14, UN Doc. CCPR/C/SR.87, para. 19; UN Doc. A/33/40*, para. 282; 'Initial Report of Democratic Yemen', UN Doc. CCPR/C/50/Add.2, UN Doc. CCPR/C/SR.927, SR.932, UN Doc. A/45/40, para. 45; 'Initial Report of Viet Nam', UN Doc. CCPR/C/26/Add.3, UN Doc. CCPR/C/SR.982, SR.983, SR.986, SR.987, UN Doc. A/45/40, para. 465.
[113] 'Third Periodic Report of Tunisia', UN Doc. CCPR/C/52/Add.5, UN Doc. CCPR/C/SR.990–992, UN Doc. A/45/40, paras. 513–514.
[114] 'Comments on the Third Periodic Report of Belarus', UN Doc. CCPR/C/79/Add.5, para. 6.
[115] 'Initial Report of Algeria', UN Doc. CCPR/C/62/Add.1, para. 84.
[116] 'Comments on the Initial Report of Algeria', UN Doc. CCPR/C/79/Add.1, para. 5.
[117] 'Concluding Observations, Japan', UN Doc. CCPR/C/79/Add.102, para. 20.
[118] *Bachan Singh* v. *State of Punjab*, p. 931.
[119] 'Concluding Observations, Sudan', UN Doc. CCPR/C/79/Add.85, para. 8.
[120] 'Concluding Observations, Sri Lanka', UN Doc. CCPR/C/79/Add.56, para. 14.
[121] 'Concluding Observations, Sudan', UN Doc. CCPR/C/79/Add.85, para. 8.
[122] 'Second Periodic Report of Sudan'; 'Annual Report of the Human Rights Committee, 1998', UN Doc. 53/40, para. 119;

espionage,[123] evasion of military responsibility,[124] economic crimes,[125] currency offences,[126] offences against property,[127] embezzlement by state officials,[128] theft by force,[129] misappropriation of state or public property,[130] misuse of public funds[131] and crimes against the economy.[132] It has been particularly insistent with respect to political crimes.[133] Attempts during drafting of the *Covenant* to prohibit the death penalty in the case of political crimes were unsuccessful.[134] During drafting of the *General Comment* on article 6, one Committee member sought a last-minute amendment stating that capital punishment should not be imposed for political offences but was told that it was too late in the drafting process to make any changes to the text.[135] An explicit provision prohibiting capital punishment for political crimes appears in the *American Convention on Human Rights*.[136] If political crimes are not 'the most serious crimes' within the meaning of the *Covenant*, then the death penalty is forbidden in such cases even in the absence of a specific provision. On this basis, the Human Rights Committee has challenged States parties that impose the death penalty for political offences in general,[137] as well as for refusal to divulge previous political activities,[138] conspiracy between civil servants and soldiers,[139] secession[140] and treason.[141]

---

[123] 'Concluding Observations, Cameroons', UN Doc. CCPR/C/79/Add.116, para. 14.

[124] 'Fourth Periodic Report of Iraq'; 'Concluding Observations, Iraq', para. 11.

[125] 'Concluding Observations, Libyan Arab Jamahiriya', UN Doc. CCPR/C/79/Add.45 (1994), para. 8; 'Concluding Observations, Libyan Arab Jamahiriya', UN Doc. CCPR/C/79/Add.101, para. 8.

[126] UN Doc. CCPR/SR.1628, para. 37 (Sudan).

[127] 'Concluding Observations, Sri Lanka', para. 14.

[128] 'Second Periodic Report of Sudan'; 'Concluding Observations, Sudan', UN Doc. CCPR/C/79/Add.85, para. 8.

[129] 'Concluding Observations, Sudan', UN Doc. CCPR/C/79/Add.85, para. 8

[130] 'Initial Report of Mongolia', UN Doc. CCPR/C/1/Add.38; UN Doc. CCPR/C/SR.197, para. 6 (Janca); UN Doc. CCPR/C/SR.198, para. 21 (Koulishev); UN Doc. CCPR/C/SR.198, para. 32 (Sadi).

[131] UN Doc. A/33/40, para. 153.

[132] UN Doc. CCPR/C/1/Add.3 para. 7; Also: 'Initial Report of Democratic Yemen'; 'Initial Report of Viet Nam'; 'Initial Report of Algeria'.

[133] Z. P. Separavic, 'Political Crimes and the Death Penalty', (1987) 58 *Revue internationale de droit pénal* 755; Marc Ancel, 'Le crime politique et le droit pénal au XXe siècle', [1938] *Revue d'histoire politique et constitutionnelle* 87.

[134] UN Doc. E/CN.4/82/Add.2; UN Doc. E/CN.4/85, p. 60; UN Doc. E/CN.4/SR.97, at p. 4; UN Doc. A/C.3/L.460.

[135] UN Doc. CCPR/C/SR.378, para. 54.

[136] Art. 4§4. Resolutions of the General Assembly have criticized politically motivated executions: GA Res. 35/172; GA Res. 36/22. The Sub-Commission on Prevention of Discrimination and Protection of Minorities has called for the abolition of the death penalty for political offences: S-CHR Res. I(IV), UN Doc. E/CN.4/1512, UN Doc. E/CN.4/Sub.2/495. Execution of opponents to *apartheid* was criticised in a number of Security Council resolutions: SC Res. 191 (1964); SC Res. 253 (1968); SC Res. 503 (1982).

[137] UN Doc. CCPR/C/SR.200, para. 19 (1980); 'Initial Report of Viet Nam'.

[138] UN Doc. CCPR/C/SR.200, para. 42 (Prado Vallejo).

[139] 'Initial Report of Mali'; UN Doc. CCPR/C/SR.284, para. 6 (Tarnopolsky).

[140] 'Concluding Observations, Cameroons', para. 14

[141] UN Doc. CCPR/C/SR.258, para. 10 (Tomuschat).

Examining Democratic Yemen's initial report, members of the Human Rights Committee objected to 'vaguely defined crimes' subject to the death penalty, including offences against 'peace, humanity or human rights' or war crimes 'motivated by hostility towards the Republic'.[142]

Recent case law of the Committee suggests that its interpretation of 'most serious crimes' is confined to murder,[143] although the possibility that it might cover other crimes of violence with grave consequences, such as aggravated forms of rape, cannot be excluded. There have been isolated suggestions that it might even consider capital punishment for drug trafficking to be consistent with article 6§2 of the *Covenant*.[144] But commenting on Iran's second periodic report, the Committee said imposition of the death penalty for crimes that do not result in loss of human life is contrary to the *Covenant*.[145] In its Concluding Observations on Sri Lanka, it said 'drug-related offences' were not 'serious crimes' within the meaning of article 6.[146] In *Lubuto* v. *Zambia*, the Committee concluded that there had been a violation of article 6§2 because the petitioner had been sentenced to death under a law imposing a mandatory sentence of death for aggravated robbery in which firearms are used. The Committee observed that 'use of firearms did not produce the death or wounding of any person and that the court could not under the law take these elements into account in imposing sentence'.[147]

Where the term 'murder' is confined to intentional homicide, there can be little doubt that it meets the 'most serious crimes' test. But in focusing the debate upon the result alone, namely the loss of human life, relatively less serious offences such as manslaughter (negligent homicide) or felony murder (that is, when there is unintended loss of life during the commission of another criminal act) might be deemed consistent with the *Covenant*. In *Piandong* v. *The Philippines*, although neither counsel nor the State party had addressed the fact that one or more of the applicants had been convicted of felony murder, the Committee referred to the issue, hinting that it might find this to be contrary to article 6§2.[148] According to Professor Martin Scheinin, himself a member of the Human Rights Committee, 'one should be careful not to put too much importance on the fact

---

[142] 'Initial Report of Democratic Yemen'; also: 'Concluding Observations, Kuwait', UN Doc. CCPR/CO/69/KWT, para. 464.

[143] In *Cox v. Canada* (No. 539/1993), para. 16.2, the Committee noted that the applicant was to be tried for complicity in two murders, and that these were 'undoubtedly very serious crimes'.

[144] 'Second Periodic Report of Mauritius', p. 113; see also 'Initial Report of Bolivia', UN Doc. A/44/40, p. 95; UN Doc. A/44/40, para. 508. For a spirited argument that execution of drug offenders is compatible with the Covenant, see Singapore's letter to the Special Rapporteur on extrajudicial, summary or arbitrary executions of 27 June 1997, UN Doc. E/CN.4/1998/13.

[145] UN Doc. CCPR/C/79/Add.25, para. 8.

[146] 'Concluding Observations, Sri Lanka', para. 14. Also: 'Concluding Observations, Kuwait', para. 464; 'Concluding Observations, Cameroon', para. 14..

[147] *Lubuto* v. *Zambia* (No. 390/1990), UN Doc. CCPR/C/55/D/390/1990/Rev.1, para. 7.2.

[148] *Piandong et al.* v. *Philippines*, para. 7.4.

that the Human Rights Committee, in paragraph 7 of its General Comment No. 6 and also in the Lubuto case emphasised the gravity of the consequences of a crime in defining whether it belongs to the most serious ones ... Classifying the gravity of a crime merely or primarily with reference to the consequences of the act is not in line with current thinking in the field of criminal law.'[149]

Because of the requirement in article 6§4 that all death sentences be subject to commutation or reprieve, it appears that the spirit of the *Covenant* opposes mandatory death sentences. Although the Human Rights Committee has addressed the issue of mandatory capital punishment under paragraph 6§1, as being 'arbitrary', it seems that it is also inconsistent with the 'most serious crimes' norm. The Secretary-General has noted that 'a mandatory death penalty can make it difficult if not impossible for the court to take into account a variety of mitigating or extenuating circumstances that might remove a particular offence from the category of most serious crimes'.[150] In *Lubuto* v. *Zambia*, adopted in October 1995, the offender had received a mandatory sentence of death for armed robbery. The Human Rights Committee wrote: 'Considering that in this case use of firearms did not produce the death or wounding of any person and that the court could not under the law take these elements into account in imposing sentence, the Committee is of the view that the mandatory imposition of the death sentence under these circumstances violates article 6, paragraph 2, of the *Covenant*.'[151]

3.1.4 'the law in force at the time of the commission of the crime...'

The phrase 'in accordance with the law in force at the time of the commission of the crime' was added to article 6 by the Working Party of the Third Committee, in 1957,[152] after a suggestion from the Philippines,[153] after unsuccessful attempts in the Commission on Human Rights to introduce a similar formulation.[154] It appears redundant, being merely a specific expression of the principle *nullum crimen, nulla poena sine lege* stated in article 15 of the *Covenant*. Actually, article 15 goes further, providing for the benefit of the lesser penalty if the legislation is changed between the date of the infraction and the date of the sentence. Perhaps the main interest in the reference to 'the law in force' is its demonstration of the imperfections in the drafting process of the *Covenant* and, consequently, the inherent defect in efforts to discern the 'intent' of its drafters.

---

[149] Martin Scheinin, 'Capital Punishment and the International Covenant on Civil and Political Rights: Some Issues of Interpretation in the Practice of the Human Rights Committee', p. 13.
[150] UN Doc. E/2000/3, para. 87.   [151] *Lubuto* v. *Zambia*, para. 7.2.
[152] UN Doc. A/C/3/L.655.   [153] UN Doc. A/C.3/L.646.
[154] UN Doc. E/CN.4/365; UN Doc. E/CN.4/384; UN Doc. E/CN.4/385.

No cases have come before the Committee where the death penalty has been pronounced when it was not in fact in force at the time of the commission of the crime. The retroactivity issue was raised in a Trinidadian death penalty case, but with respect to essentially procedural and evidentiary rather than strictly substantive issues. The impugned legislation adopted had been designed specifically for a particular prosecution. It allowed for an unlimited number of potential jurors and permitted use of a deposition of a deceased witness as evidence. Although the Committee summarily dismissed the complaint, in an individual opinion, Martin Scheinin said that 'article 15, paras. 1 and 2, must be understood to limit the enactment of retroactive legislation even in the procedural field when such legislation is designed for a concrete case'.[155] Probably the classic example is the imposition of capital punishment at Nuremberg and Tokyo for 'crimes against peace'. Authorised by the majority, this prompted considerable outrage from some dissenting judges at the Tokyo trial. Judge Röling, although clearly not opposed to the death penalty in principle, challenged its use in cases where the accused were found guilty of crimes against peace, which he believed should not be considered a capital crime.[156] More recently, the retroactivity argument has tended to go in the other direction. Judges at the international *ad hoc* tribunals for the former Yugoslavia and Rwanda impose lengthy custodial sentences explaining to the condemned that these are extraordinarily clement given that the death penalty was provided for similar crimes under the domestic system in force where the crime was committed.[157]

3.1.5 Procedural guarantees

Imposition of the death penalty following an unfair trial is a breach not only of procedural norms but also of the right to life itself. Pursuant to article 6§2, the death penalty can only be imposed in accordance with law 'not contrary to the provisions of the present Covenant' and 'pursuant to a final judgment rendered by a competent court'. According to *General Comment 6(16)*, this reference to the *Covenant* in paragraph 2 in effect adds, by reference, the provisions of article 14 to article 6: 'The procedural guarantees therein prescribed must be observed, including the right to a fair hearing by an independent tribunal, the presumption of innocence, the minimum guarantees for the defence, and the right to review

---

[155] *Chadee* et al. v. *Trinidad and Tobago* (No. 813/1998), UN Doc. CCPR/C/63/D/813/1998, Individual opinion by Mr. Scheinin (dissenting), para. 9.

[156] B. V. A. Röling and Antonio Cassese, *The Tokyo Trial and Beyond*, Cambridge: Polity Press, 1993. According to Röling, three of the Tokyo Tribunal judges voted systematically against death sentences. In Hirota's case, the vote was six to five in favour of execution. 'I consider that a scandalous way of arriving at the penalty of hanging', wrote Judge Röling (p. 64).

[157] *Prosecutor* v. *Serushago* (Case No. ICTR-98-39-S), Sentence, 2 February 1999, para. 17; *Prosecutor* v. *Kayishema and Ruzindana* (Case No. ICTR-95-1-T), Judgment, 21 May 1999, paras. 6–7; *Prosecutor* v. *Kordic and Cerkez* (Case No. IT-95-14/2-T), Judgment, 26 February 2001, para. 849.

by a higher tribunal.'[158] In other words, if article 14 of the *Covenant* is violated during a capital trial, then article 6 of the *Covenant* is also breached. In *Reid* v. *Jamaica*, the Human Rights Committee referred to its *General Comment 6(16)*:

> The Committee is of the opinion that the imposition of a sentence of death upon the conclusion of a trial in which the provisions of the Covenant have not been respected constitutes, if no further appeal against the sentence is available, a violation of article 6 of the Covenant. As the Committee noted in its general comment 6(16), the provision that a sentence of death may be imposed only in accordance with the law and not contrary to the provisions of the Covenant implies that 'the procedural guarantees therein prescribed must be observed, including the right to a fair hearing by an independent tribunal, the presumption of innocence, the minimum guarantees for the defence, and the right to review by a higher tribunal'. In the present case, since the final sentence of death was passed without having met the requirements for a fair trial set forth in article 14, it must be concluded that the right protected by article 6 of the Covenant has been violated.[159]

The Committee added that 'in capital punishment cases, the duty of States parties to observe rigorously all the guarantees for a fair trial set out in article 14 of the Covenant is even more imperative'.[160] Some recent pronouncements of the Committee seem to go even further, holding that a capital trial in which there is any breach of the *Covenant* also constitutes a breach of article 6.[161] But in practice, the Committee does not generally rule that there is a violation of article 6 when sentence of death is imposed following a trial 'in which the provisions of the Covenant have not been respected'. It makes this finding in cases where there is a denial of the right to counsel, for example, but not in cases where trial has been unduly delayed. In *Steadman* v. *Jamaica*, for example, violations of article 9 and several subparagraphs of article 14 were established, but the Committee concluded: 'In the present case, since the final sentence of death was passed without effective representation for the author on appeal, there has consequently also been a violation of article 6 of the Covenant.'[162]

An important corollary of the linkage between articles 14 and 6 is to make article 14 non-derogable, at least in death penalty cases. Article 4 of the *Covenant* allows States parties to suspend or derogate from certain provisions, including article 14 but not article 6, '[i]n time of public emergency which threatens the life of the nation'.

---

[158] The phrase is routinely repeated in views issued by the Committee where a violation of article 14 occurs in a death penalty case.

[159] *Reid* v. *Jamaica* (No. 250/1987), para. 11.5. See *The Right to Information on Consular Assistance in the Context of the Guarantees of Due Process of Law*, para. 132, where these views are endorsed.

[160] *Ibid.*, para. 12.2.

[161] *Domukovsky, Tsiklauri, Gelbakhiani and Dokvadze* v. *Georgia* (Nos. 623–624 and 626–627/1995), UN Doc. CCPR/C/62/D/623, 624, 626 and 627/1995, para. 18.10.

[162] *Steadman* v. *Jamaica* (No. 528/1993), UN Doc. CCPR/C/59/D/528/1993, para. 10(4).

The reference to the *Covenant* in article 6§2 can be traced back to the fifth session of the Commission on Human Rights, in 1949, and was 'intended to ensure that no person should be deprived of his life pursuant to unjust laws'.[163] At the time, the draft referred to the *Universal Declaration of Human Rights*, but this was changed to the *Covenant* by the Third Committee in response to the observation that the *Declaration* was not a legally binding document.[164] The term 'provisions' was also adopted to replace 'principles' in the earlier draft.

The Human Rights Committee has found violations of article 14, and consequently of article 6, in many death penalty cases. Petitions are examined in light of the detailed provisions of article 14. Most of these concern issues of undue delay in proceedings, of right to counsel and of the other very specific norms enumerated in paragraph 3 of article 14. Rather more occasionally, the Committee addresses issues raised by paragraph 1, which ensures the right to equality before the courts, and to 'a fair and public hearing by a competent, independent and impartial tribunal established by law'. In *Alrick Thomas* v. *Jamaica*, the complainant alleged that he had been informed of the date of his appeal hearing only after it had taken place. The Human Rights Committee concluded that there was a violation of the requirements of a fair trial, contrary to article 14§1 of the *Covenant*.[165] In another Jamaican case, the accused was charged with manslaughter and pleaded guilty to the offence at the arraignment. The proceedings were adjourned to enable the defendant to produce evidence in mitigation of punishment. But before the next stage in the proceedings, the Department of Public Prosecution decided that manslaughter was not the appropriate charge, and that the accused should be indicted for murder, a capital offence. The prosecutor entered a *nolle prosequi* on the manslaughter indictment, and then proceeded to obtain a conviction for murder in a trial by jury. Publicity had been given to the fact that he had already entered a plea of guilty to the manslaughter charge. The Committee considered that there had been a breach of the right to a fair trial, as guaranteed by article 14§1. The obvious breach, it would seem, was of the presumption of innocence, set out in article 14§2, but no finding was made in this respect.[166]

Some legal proceedings relating to imposition of capital punishment are not, strictly speaking, part of the trial or appeal procedure. An example is the reclassification procedure introduced in Jamaica during the 1990s, by which cases of those sentenced to death were reassessed and then redefined as either capital or non-capital. Several cases dealing with the reclassification procedure have been

---

[163] UN Doc. A/2929, Chapter VI, para. 8; also UN Doc. E/CN.4/SR.98, p. 9; UN Doc. E/CN.4/SR.140, para. 4; UN Doc. E/CN.4/SR.149, paras. 58–61 and 64.
[164] UN Doc. A/C.3/SR.809, para. 25; UN Doc. A/C.3/SR.810, para. 6; UN Doc. A/C.3/SR.812, para. 24.
[165] *Alrick Thomas* v. *Jamaica* (No. 272/1988), UN Doc. A/47/40, p. 261, paras. 11.4 and 13.
[166] *Richards* v. *Jamaica* (No. 535/1993), UN Doc. CCPR/C/59/D/535/1993/Rev.1, para. 7.2.

submitted to the Committee. The Committee considered that the procedure was not a 'determination of a criminal charge', with the consequence that the detailed safeguards of article 14§3 were inapplicable, but that the more general and limited safeguards set out in article 14§1 – which apply to all judicial proceedings, including administrative matters – did apply. An initial screening exercise by a single judge, in the absence of the accused, prior to a proper hearing before a three-judge panel, did not constitute a violation of article 14§1, it said.[167]

The communication under the *Optional Protocol* is itself a special procedure in capital cases whose integrity must be respected. In communications involving imposition of capital punishment by the State party itself, as well as those where expulsion or extradition by a State party to another State that threatens use of the death penalty, the Human Rights Committee will usually issue a 'request for interim measures' pursuant to Rule 86 of its Rules of Procedure.[168] Generally, this is the responsibility of its Special *Rapporteur* for new communications. No explicit power to issue interim measures requests is set out in the *Optional Protocol*, however, and several States parties seem to contest the Committee's authority. Canada appears to have been the first State party to challenge the Human Rights Committee in this area. It extradited Joseph Kindler and Charles Ng to the United States following a final judgment by the Supreme Court of Canada, despite an interim measures request from the Committee. In the third Canadian death penalty case, however, the Canadian Government honoured the interim measures requested by the Committee and did not extradite Keith Cox until the Committee's Views had been released. Since then, other States have been similarly defiant of the Committee.[169] The European Court of Human Rights, in a debate on the same point, concluded that such a power was not implicit and did not exist if not set out expressly in the applicable treaty.[170]

The Committee meekly 'expresse[d] its regret that the State party did not accede to the Special Rapporteur's request' not to extradite Kindler.[171] As for *Ng*, in which the Committee concluded there was a breach of article 7 of the

---

[167] *Levy* v. *Jamaica* (No. 719/1996), UN Doc. CCPR/C/64/D/719/1996, para. 7.1. Also *Morgan and Williams* v. *Jamaica* (No. 720/1996), UN Doc. CCPR/C/64/D/720/1996, para. 7.1; *Marshall* v. *Jamaica* (No. 730/1996), UN Doc. CCPR/C/64/D/730/1996, para. 5.4. But see: *Bailey* v. *Jamaica* (No. 709/1996), UN Doc. CCPR/C/66/D/709/1996, para. 7.5; *Gallimore* v. *Jamaica* (No. 680/1996), UN Doc. CCPR/C/66/D/680/1996, para. 7.2.

[168] UN Doc. CCPR/C/SR.17, paras. 25 and 26, UN Doc. CCPR/C/3/Rev.1; UN Doc. CCPR/C/OP/1, Annex II, p. 155.

[169] *Ashby* v. *Trinidad and Tobago* (No. 580/1994), UN Doc. CCPR/C/54/D/580/1994; *Rogers* v. *Trinidad and Tobago* (No. 494/1992), UN Doc. CCPR/C/53/D/494/1992; *Simms* v. *Jamaica* (No. 540/1993), UN Doc. CCPR/C/53/D/541/1993; *Bradshaw* v. *Barbados* (No. 489/1992), UN Doc. A/49/40, Vol. II, p. 305, para. 5.3; *Roberts* v. *Barbados* (No. 504/1992), UN Doc. A/49/40, Vol. II, p. 322, para. 6.3; *Kandu-Bo* et al. v. *Sierra Leone* (Nos. 839, 840 and 841/1998), UN Doc. CCPR/C/64/D/839, 840 and 841/1998; *Piandong et al. v. Philippines*, paras. 5.1–5.4.

[170] *Cruz Varas* et al. v. *Sweden*, 20 March 1991, Series A, No. 201, 14 EHRR 1.

[171] *Kindler* v. *Canada* (No. 470/1991), para. 17.

Covenant, the Views did not even criticize Canada for its contemptuous attitude, stating only that Canada should 'make such representations as might still be possible to avoid the imposition of the death penalty'.[172] Only Francisco José Aguilar Urbina, in his individual dissenting opinion, took Canada to task, saying that Canada 'failed to display the good faith which ought to prevail among the parties to the Protocol and the Covenant'. In its concluding observations on Canada's fourth periodic report, the Committee 'expresse[d] its concern' that Canada considered it was not required to comply with requests for interim measures, and urged Canada to revise its policy.[173] Recently, the Committee has become more aggressive on the subject. In November 2000, the Committee said States parties to the *Optional Protocol* had made an implicit undertaking to cooperate with the Committee in good faith. 'It is incompatible with these obligations for a State party to take any action that would prevent or frustrate the Committee in its consideration and examination of the communication, and in the expression of its Views', the Committee said.[174] The Committee added that a State that proceeded with an execution after being notified of a communication, even in the absence of an interim measures request, and before the Committee had concluded its consideration and examination of the case, was in 'grave breach' of its obligations under the *Optional Protocol.*[175] In July 2001, in its Views in a series of Sierra Leonean applications, where petitioners were executed by firing squad despite an interim measures request from the Committee, it wrote: '[T]he State party would be committing a serious breach of its obligations under the Optional Protocol if it engages in any acts which have the effect of preventing or frustrating consideration by the Committee of a communication alleging any violation of the Covenant, or to render examination by the Committee moot and the expression of its Views nugatory and futile.'[176]

Generally, the Human Rights Committee stops short of reconsidering issues of fact and evidence that arise in the course of capital trials,[177] unless it is clear that evaluation of the evidence was arbitrary or amounted to a denial of justice.[178] According to the Committee's established jurisprudence, 'it is generally for the appellate courts of States parties to the Covenant to evaluate the facts and evidence in a particular case'.[179] The relationship between article 6

---

[172] *Ng* v. *Canada* (No. 469/1991), UN Doc. A/49/40, Vol. II, p. 189, 15 *HRLJ* 149, para. 18.

[173] UN Doc. CCPR/C/79/Add.105, para. 14.   [174] *Piandong et al. v. Philippines,* para. 5.1.

[175] *Ibid.,* para. 5.2. Also *Mansaraj* et al. v. *Sierra Leone* (Nos. 839/1998, 840/1998 and 841/1998), UN Doc. CCPR/C/72/D/840/1998, para. 6.2.

[176] *Mansaraj* et al. v. *Sierra Leone* (Nos. 839/1998, 840/1998 and 841/1998), UN Doc. CCPR/C/72/D/840/1998, para. 5.2.

[177] *Smith* v. *Jamaica* (No. 282/1988), UN Doc. A/48/40, Vol. II, p. 28, para. 8.

[178] *Wright* v. *Jamaica* (No. 349/1989), UN Doc. A/47/40, p. 300, 13 *HRLJ* 348.

[179] *G.H.* v. *Jamaica* (No. 370/1989), UN Doc. A/48/40, Vol. II, p. 181, para. 4.2. Also: *V.B.* v. *Trinidad and Tobago* (No. 485/1991), UN Doc. A/48/40, Vol. II, p. 222, para. 5.2; *Allen* v. *Jamaica* (No. 332/1988), UN Doc. A/49/40, Vol. II, p. 31, para. 8.4; *R.M.* v. *Trinidad and Tobago* (No. 384/1989),

and other violations of the Covenant has not always been consistent, however. In a Georgian case, where two of four applicants had been sentenced to death, the Committee found violations of several provisions of article 14 as well as a breach of article 9 (illegal arrest), but did not consider that there was also an article 6 issue.[180]

It is only appropriate that the Committee, in examining individual communications under the *Optional Protocol,* propose measures that constitute a remedy. Furthermore the *Covenant* imposes a specific obligation, in article 2§3, upon States parties to ensure that those whose rights are violated 'shall have an effective remedy'. A specific right to compensation for arrest or detention that is unlawful either under the *Covenant* or domestic law is set out in article 9§5. With respect to the appropriate remedy when the right to a fair trial has been violated in a death penalty case, the Committee's jurisprudence has not always been consistent, and the reasoning behind its choice among several options difficult to understand in its tersely worded decisions. In its earliest death penalty cases, it stated that capital punishment 'should not be imposed in circumstances where there have been violations by the State party of any of its obligations under the Covenant'.[181] But over the years it appears to have retreated from such an unequivocal position.

Sometimes, the Committee declares that the petitioner is entitled to an effective remedy entailing release.[182] Rather more occasionally, it has proposed

UN Doc. A/49/40, Vol. II, p. 246, para. 5.2; *Barry* v. *Trinidad and Tobago* (No. 471/1991), UN Doc. A/49/40, Vol. II, p. 283, para. 7.4; *R.M.* v. *Trinidad and Tobago* (No. 476/1991), UN Doc. A/49/40, Vol. II, p. 291, para. 5.3; *Lambert* v. *Jamaica* (No. 517/1992), UN Doc. A/49/40, Vol. II, p. 333, para. 6.2; *Chadee et al* v. *Trinidad and Tobago*, paras. 8.3–8.4; *Gonzales* v. *Trinidad and Tobago* (No. 673/1995), UN Doc. CCPR/C/65/D/673/1995, para. 5.2; *Uton Lewis* v. *Jamaica* (No. 527/1993), UN Doc. CCPR/C/57/D/527/1993, para. 6.4; *Henry and Douglas* v. *Jamaica* (No. 571/1994), UN Doc. CCPR/C/57/D/571/1994, para. 6.4; *Adams* v. *Jamaica* (No. 607/1994), UN Doc. CCPR/C/58/D/607/1994, para. 6.3; *Steadman* v. *Jamaica*, para. 6.4; *Walker and Richards* v. *Jamaica* (No. 639/1995), UN Doc. CCPR/C/60/D/639/1995, para. 6.3; *McIntosh* v. *Jamaica* (No. 640/1995), UN Doc. CCPR/C/61/D/640/1995, para. 6.3; *Jones* v. *Jamaica* (No. 585/1994), UN Doc. CCPR/C/62/D/585/1994, para. 6.3; *Everton Morrison* v. *Jamaica* (No. 635/1995), UN Doc. CCPR/C/63/D/635/1995, paras. 11.3 and 12.3; *Smart* v. *Trinidad and Tobago* (No. 672/1995), UN Doc. CCPR/C/63/D/672/1995, para. 6.6; *Whyte* v. *Jamaica* (No. 732/1997), UN Doc. CCPR/ C/63/ D/732/1997, para. 7.6; *Pennant* v. *Jamaica* (No. 647/1995), UN Doc. CCPR/ C/64/D/647/1995, para. 6.4; *Ajaz and Jamil* v. *Korea* (No. 644/1995), UN Doc. CCPR/ C/66/D/644/1995, para. 14.2; *Piandong et al. v. Philippines*, paras. 7.2–7.3.

[180] *Domukovsky, Tsiklauri, Gelbakhiani and Dokvadze* v. *Georgia*, para. 18.10.

[181] *Pratt and Morgan* v. *Jamaica* (Nos. 210/1986, 225/1987), UN Doc. A/44/40, p. 222, 11 *HRLJ* 150, para. 15.

[182] For example, *Pinto* v. *Trinidad and Tobago* (No. 512/1992), UN Doc. CCPR/C/57/D/512/1992, para. 13.2; *Kelly* v. *Jamaica* (No. 253/1987), UN Doc. A/46/40, p. 241, paras. 6–7 (but see also the dissenting views of W. Sadi; *Raphael Henry* v. *Jamaica* (No. 230/1987), UN Doc. A/47/40, p. 218, para. 10; *Little* v. *Jamaica* (No. 283/1988), UN Doc. A/47/40, p. 276, paras. 8.5 and 10; *Campbell* v. *Jamaica* (No. 307/1988), UN Doc. A/48/40, Vol. II, p. 41, para. 8; *Yasseen and Thomas* v. *Guyana* (No. 676/1996), UN Doc. CCPR/C/62/D/676/1996, para. 9; *McCordie Morrison* v. *Jamaica* (No. 663/1995), UN Doc. CCPR/C/64/D/663/1995, para. 10; *Jones* v. *Jamaica*, para. 11. It does

retrial[183] or a new appeal,[184] failing which the complainant should be entitled to release. In some circumstances, it has also urged 'early release', which is presumably not the same thing as 'release' but involves some shortening of the period in detention.[185] Reduction of parole ineligibility periods has also been proposed.[186] In most death penalty cases, the Committee confines its proposed remedies to compensation and, where appropriate, commutation of sentence and access to medical care.[187] In many cases, commutation may already have been awarded before the Committee's views are issued; sometimes, it goes no further,[188] while in other cases it may urge a 'further measure of clemency'.[189] In a series of individual opinions, Martin Scheinin has written that 'when a person has been sentenced to death in violation of the Covenant or treated contrary to the provisions of the Covenant while awaiting execution, the remedy should include an irreversible decision not to implement the death penalty'.[190] Nevertheless, commutation is not systematically proposed in death penalty cases. In a case involving beatings and inhumane conditions on death row, and where the sentence was already commuted, the Committee proposed compensation, but also that Jamaica 'carry out an official investigation into the beating by wardens with a view to identify the perpetrators and punish them accordingly'.[191] Where a death row inmate was killed in a disturbance, following a flawed trial, the Committee

---

not appear that the Committee's calls for release have been very productive. In one case, a successful litigant before the Committee filed a new communication complaining that Trinidad and Tobago had failed to release him. He even noted that he had been told by the authorities that his applications for the prerogative of mercy had been dismissed precisely because of his successful international petitions, a claim that the Committee said was a violation of article 10§1 of the *Covenant*: *Pinto* v. *Trinidad and Tobago* (No. 512/1992), para. 8.3. But the Committee could only reiterate its appeal to the State party for release given that the original trial had been flawed: *ibid.*, para. 12.

[183] *Simmonds* v. *Jamaica* (No. 338/1988), UN Doc. A/48/40, Vol. II, p. 78 (Appendix, *per* Julio Prado Vallejo, Waleed Sadi and Bertil Wennergren), at p. 84; *Brown v. Jamaica*, para. 8.

[184] *McLeod* v. *Jamaica* (No. 734/1997), UN Doc. CCPR/C/62/D/734/1997, para. 8.

[185] *Daley* v. *Jamaica* (No. 750/1997), UN Doc. CCPR/C/63/D/750/1997, para. 9; *Nicholas Henry* v. *Jamaica* (No. 610/1995), UN Doc. CCPR/C/64/D/610/1995, para. 10.

[186] *Gallimore* v. *Jamaica*, para. 9.

[187] *Pratt and Morgan* v. *Jamaica*, para. 13.7; *Bailey* v. *Jamaica* (No. 334/1988), UN Doc. A/48/40, Vol. II, p. 72, para. 11.1; *Levy* v. *Jamaica*, para. 9; *Marshall* v. *Jamaica*, para. 8; *McLawrence* v. *Jamaica* (No. 702/1996), UN Doc. CCPR/C/60/D/702/1996, para. 7; *Patrick Taylor* v. *Jamaica* (No. 707/1996), UN Doc. CCPR/C/60/D/707/1996, para. 10; *Barrington Campbell* v. *Jamaica* (No. 618/1995), UN Doc. CCPR/C/64/D/618/1995, para. 9; *Smart* v. *Trinidad and Tobago*, para. 12; *Shaw* v. *Jamaica* (No. 704/1996), UN Doc. CCPR/C/62/D/704/1996, para. 9; *Desmond Taylor* v. *Jamaica* (No. 705/1996), UN Doc. CCPR/C/62/D/705/1996, para. 9; *Everton Morrison* v. *Jamaica*, para. 25.

[188] *Richards* v. *Jamaica*.

[189] *LaVende* v. *Trinidad and Tobago* (No. 554/1993), UN Doc. CCPR/C/61/D/554/1993, para. 7.

[190] *McLeod* v. *Jamaica*, Individual opinion by Mr. Martin Scheinin; *McTaggart* v. *Jamaica* (No 749/1997), UN Doc. CCPR/C/62/D/749/1997, Individual opinion (partly dissenting) by Mr. Scheinin. Also, *Neville Lewis* v. *Jamaica* (No. 708/1996), UN Doc. CCPR/C/60/D/708/1996, Individual opinion by Committee member Martin Scheinin (partly dissenting), where he insists upon commutation in cases where there has been a 'multiple violation' of the *Covenant*.

[191] *Colin Johnson* v. *Jamaica* (No. 653/1995), UN Doc. CCPR/C/64/D/653/1995, para. 10. Also: *Hylton* v. *Jamaica* (No. 407/1990), UN Doc. A/49/40, Vol. II, p. 79, para. 11.1.

said that compensation to the family was in order.[192] Generally, it also orders that there not be a repeat of the violation.

It may seem logical that, where a trial has been unfair, the conviction cannot stand. Release, then, can be the only option. But this is not in fact how appellate courts generally treat the matter, nor is it the appropriate approach for the Human Rights Committee. Some procedural flaws are more serious than others, some clearly imperil the conviction whereas others, while unacceptable violations of fundamental norms, do not genuinely put in doubt the validity of the verdict itself. It is hard to develop general principles, and decisions must be taken on a case-by-case basis. Nevertheless, a few themes emerge. Where a person has been detained under sentence of death for a lengthy period following an unfair trial, the Committee will tend to propose release, 'as so many years have elapsed since his conviction'.[193] Where an individual had been convicted of a crime committed while under eighteen years of age, and thirteen years had already been served on death row before commutation, the Committee said he was entitled to immediate release.[194] In a matter concerning conditions on death row, the Committee recommended early release, 'especially in view of the fact that the author was already eligible for parole in December of 1996'.[195] In a case involving not only undue delay but also a clearly unfair trial because of denial of legal aid, which affected access to alibi witnesses, the Committee concluded that 'in view of the fact that the author has spent over fifteen years in prison, the State party consider the author's release'.[196]

3.1.5.1 Competent, independent and impartial tribunal

According to article 6§2, the court that pronounces a final judgment of the death sentence must be 'competent'. The term was introduced at the sixth session of the Commission in the Chilean amendment.[197] The word 'competent' must surely mean that the court must have jurisdiction under applicable law, and not that it must be 'competent' in respect of its abilities. The term is superfluous, because a court which is not competent cannot render any sentence, let alone a death sentence. Article 14§1 goes beyond this, requiring trial by 'a competent, independent and impartial tribunal established by law'. A death sentence not rendered by such a court would be a summary execution and would doubtless fall within the scope of the word 'arbitrarily' in article 6§1. Of course, any sentence depriving an individual of liberty that is not rendered by a court falls afoul of

---

[192] *Burrell* v. *Jamaica* (No. 546/1993), UN Doc. CCPR/C/57/D/546/1993, para. 11. Also: *Henry and Douglas* v. *Jamaica*, para. 11.
[193] *Wright* v. *Jamaica*, para. 10.
[194] *Clive Johnson* v. *Jamaica* (No. 592/1994), UN Doc. CCPR/C/64/D/592/1994, para. 12.
[195] *Pennant* v. *Jamaica*, para. 10.
[196] *Samuel Thomas* v. *Jamaica* (No. 532/1993), UN Doc. CCPR/C/61/D/532/1993, para. 8.
[197] UN Doc. E/CN.4/W.22.

article 14. The words 'court', used in article 6, and 'tribunal', in article 14, would appear to be synonyms.

A considerable body of case law exists with respect to the competent tribunal provision in article 14, all of it relevant to capital punishment cases of course even if it is derived from non-capital cases. Although it has often been argued before the Human Rights Committee that capital trials were not held before competent, independent and impartial tribunals, few challenges have been successful. Most of them have involved jury trials in Jamaica, with a focus on the judge's charge or instructions. The Committee has dismissed most of these at the admissibility stage, using a stock paragraph asserting that it will not intervene 'unless it can be ascertained that the instructions to the jury were clearly arbitrary or amounted to a denial of justice, or that the judge manifestly violated his obligation of impartiaplity'.[198] In one case, the Committee dismissed a complaint in which the applicant filed affidavits from jury members claiming the foreman had acted irregularly in exhorting them to reach a verdict.[199] A communication whose only serious ground was that a capital trial was conducted 'in a biased way' was declared inadmissible.[200] Similarly, the trial judge's decision not to grant a request for change of venue will not engage the Human Rights Committee 'barring any evidence of arbitrariness or manifest inequity'.[201]

In *Collins* v. *Jamaica*, the complainant argued that the judge who presided over his trial for murder did not meet such a standard. 'Justice G.', sitting as

---

[198] *Sawyers and McLean* v. *Jamaica* (Nos 226/1987 and 256/1987), UN Doc. A/46/40, p. 226, para. 13.5. See also: *Reynolds* v. *Jamaica* (No. 229/1987), UN Doc. A/46/40, p. 235, paras. 6.2 and 6.3; *Kelly* v. *Jamaica* (No. 253/1987), para. 5.13; *D.S.* v. *Jamaica* (No. 234/1987), UN Doc. A/46/40, p. 267, para. 5.2; *A.H.* v. *Trinidad and Tobago* (No. 302/1987), UN Doc. A/46/40, p. 274, para. 6.2; *D.S.* v. *Jamaica* (No. 304/1988), UN Doc. A/46/40, p. 281, para. 5.2; *Pinto v. Trinidad and Tobago*, paras. 12.3–12.4; *G.J.*v. *Trinidad and Tobago* (No. 331/1988), UN Doc. A/47/40, p. 345, para. 5.2; *Collins* v. *Jamaica* (No. 356/1989), UN Doc. A/48/40, Vol. II, p. 85, para. 8.3; *Reid* v. *Jamaica* (No. 250/1987), para. 11.2; *N.P.* v. *Jamaica* (No. 404/1990), UN Doc. A/48/40, Vol. II, p. 187, para. 5.3; *Tomlin* v. *Jamaica* (No. 589/1994), UN Doc. CCPR/C/57/D/589/1994, para. 6.3; *Neville Lewis* v. *Jamaica*, para. 6.5; *McLeod* v. *Jamaica*, para. 6.2; *McTaggart* v. *Jamaica*, para. 6.3; *Leslie* v. *Jamaica* (No. 564/1993), UN Doc. CCPR/C/63/D/564/1993, para. 6.5; *Finn* v. *Jamaica* (No. 617/1995), UN Doc. CCPR/C/63/D/617/1995, para. 6.9; *Perkins* v. *Jamaica* (No. 733/1997), UN Doc. CCPR/C/63/D/733/1997, para. 7.3; *Clive Johnson* v. *Jamaica*, para. 6.4; *Nicholas Henry* v. *Jamaica*, para. 6.3; *Pennant* v. *Jamaica*, para. 6.4; *Colin Johnson* v. *Jamaica*, para. 6.4; *McCordie Morrison v. Jamaica*, para. 6.4; *Marshall* v. *Jamaica*, para. 5.3; *Bennett* v. *Jamaica* (No. 590/1994), UN Doc. CCPR/C/65/D/590/1994, para. 6.5; *Samuel Thomas* v. *Jamaica* (No. 614/1995), UN Doc. CCPR/C/65/D/614/1995, para. 9.4; *Amore* v. *Jamaica* (No. 634/1995), UN Doc. CCPR/C/65/D/634/1995, para. 6.2; *Fraser and Fisher* v. *Jamaica* (No. 722/1996), UN Doc. CCPR/C/65/D/722/1996, para. 6.4; *Brown v. Jamaica*, para. 6.10; *Brown and Parish* v. *Jamaica* (No. 665/1995), UN Doc. CCPR/C/66/D/665/1995, para. 6.2; *Gallimore* v. *Jamaica*, para. 6.3.

[199] *Samuel Thomas* v. *Jamaica* (No. 614/1995), Individual opinion of Committee member Hipólito Solari Yrigoyen (dissenting).

[200] *A.W.* v. *Jamaica* (No. 290/1988), UN Doc. A/45/40, Vol. II, p. 172, para. 8.2. Also *G.S.* v. *Jamaica* (No. 329/1988), UN Doc. A/45/40, Vol. II, p. 189, para. 3.2. Christine Chanet prepared an individual opinion arguing that, even if the allegations were 'insufficiently substantiated', this was not a matter to be settled at the admissibility stage.

[201] *Chung v. Jamaica* (No. 591/1994), UN Doc. CCPR/C/62/D/591/1994, para. 8.3.

a judge in the Portland Magistrates' Court, heard Collins' bail application and motion for change of venue. Collins was well known in the Portland area, notably to the associates of 'Justice G.', with whom he had 'bad business relations'. At the hearing of the application, 'Justice G.' allegedly said, 'apparently only as an aside, that if he were to try the author he would ensure that a capital sentence be pronounced'.[202] At trial, Collins complained to his lawyer that 'Justice G.' was biased against him. His attorney, a senior counsel, told him that nothing could be done about this. The Committee refused to consider that there had been a denial of justice. It appeared to doubt the veracity of Collins' version of the alleged statement by the judge, and observed that the matter was not raised on appeal. According to the Committee, 'counsel opined that it was preferable to let the trial proceed', and 'in the absence of professional negligence on the part of counsel, it is not for the Committee to question the latter's professional judgment'.[203]

Four members of the Committee, Chanet, Herndl, Aguilar Urbina and Wennergren, were in disagreement with the majority in *Collins*. They said that, irrespective of the content and the impact of the comments attributed to 'Justice G.', the fact that he had taken part in bail and other proceedings gave him a knowledge of the case prior to trial. According to the minority, 'a magistrate who has been involved in one phase of the proceedings concerning the pertinent albeit preliminary evaluation of charges against a person, may not take part in any capacity whatsoever in the trial of that person on matters of substance'.[204]

3.5.1.2 Equality of arms

The expression 'equality of arms' is used in both United Nations and European jurisprudence to refer to several of the fair trial rights, including adequate time and facilities for preparation of the defence, communication with counsel, the right to be represented by counsel including funded counsel, and the right to summon and question witnesses. These are developed in the sub-paragraphs of article 14§3. One due process right not explicitly included in article 14 is that of a foreign national to be informed of his or her right to consular assistance, in accordance with article 36§1(b) of the *Vienna Convention on Consular Relations*. According to the Inter-American Court of Human Rights, this right to information about consular assistance is necessary to ensure the right to due process of law set out in article 14 of the *Covenant*. It is especially important in capital cases.[205]

---

[202] *Collins* v. *Jamaica* (No. 240/1987), UN Doc. A/47/40, p. 227, para. 2.3. See also: *Alrick Thomas* v. *Jamaica*, para. 11.3.
[203] *Ibid.*, para. 8.3; *Leslie* v. *Jamaica*, paras. 9.4–9.5; *Hixford Morrisson* v. *Jamaica* (No. 611/1995), UN Doc. CCPR/C/63/D/611/1995, para. 6.4; *Perkins* v. *Jamaica*, para. 7.4.
[204] *Collins* v. *Jamaica* (No. 240/1987), p. 13.
[205] *The Right to Information on Consular Assistance in the Context of the Guarantees of Due Process of Law*, para. 124.

The Human Rights Committee considers that what constitutes 'adequate time' for preparation of a defence is to be assessed in the circumstances of each individual case.[206] In *Reid* v. *Jamaica*, the complainant was only able to communicate with his legal aid attorney for the first time on the day of the trial. His lawyer asked for a postponement in order to prepare the case, but the judge refused.[207] The Committee said this violated article 14§3(b) of the *Covenant*.[208] In *Alrick Thomas* v. *Jamaica*, the accused met his court-appointed lawyer for the first time on the day of the trial. The trial continued the same day and, according to Thomas, his attorney did not present all of the facts to the judge and jury. But, in the absence of evidence of a request for postponement or adjournment, this and similar complaints have been dismissed.[209]

In *Little* v. *Jamaica*, the complainant's argument that he had been denied adequate time and facilities for the preparation of the defence was accepted by the Committee. Little had been assigned two attorneys by the court, who met with him briefly before the preliminary hearing and for about thirty minutes one month prior to the trial. At the appeal, a court-appointed attorney did not consult with Little, despite several letters requesting an interview. 'Bearing in mind particularly that this is a capital punishment case and that the author was unable to review the statements of the prosecution's witnesses with counsel, the Committee considers that the time for consultation was insufficient to ensure adequate preparation of the defence, in respect of both trial and appeal', it noted.[210]

The right to counsel is protected by article 14§3(b), which guarantees the right of an accused person 'to communicate with counsel of his own choosing', and article 14§3(d), which declares the right 'to defend himself in person or through legal assistance of own choosing; to be informed, if he does not have legal assistance, of this right; and to have legal assistance assigned to him, in any case where the interests of justice so require, and without payment by him in any such case if he does not have sufficient means to pay for it'.

The right is violated when an individual is held in custody for five days after arrest without being able to communicate with counsel.[211] This requirement is not satisfied merely by efforts which the trial judge may otherwise make to

---

[206] Socrates objected to the haste of his capital trial, and told the jury, according to Plato's *Apology*: 'if there were a law at Athens, as there is in other cities, that a capital cause should not be decided in one day, then I believe that I should have convinced you'.

[207] *Reid* v. *Jamaica* (No. 250/1987), para. 4.

[208] *Ibid.*, para. 11.3. See also: *Smith* v. *Jamaica*, para. 10.4; 'Annual Report of the Human Rights Committee, 1998', UN Doc. 53/40, para. 82.

[209] *Alrick Thomas* v. *Jamaica*, para. 11.4. See also: *Kelly* v. *Jamaica* (No. 253/1987), para. 5.9; *Sawyers and McLean* v. *Jamaica*, para. 13.6; *Nicholas Henry* v. *Jamaica*, paras. 7.5, 8.2; *Campbell* v. *Jamaica* (No. 248/1987), UN Doc. A/47/40, p. 240, para. 6.5; *Robinson* v. *Jamaica* (No. 223/1987), UN Doc. A/44/40, p. 241, para. 10.4; *Perkins* v. *Jamaica*, para. 11.5; *McCordie Morrison* v. *Jamaica*, para. 6.3; *Marshall* v. *Jamaica*, para. 6.4; *Brown & Parish* v. *Jamaica*, para. 9.2.

[210] *Little* v. *Jamaica*, para. 8.4.

[211] *Kelly* v. *Jamaica* (No. 537/1993), UN Doc. CCPR/C/57/D/537/1993, para. 9.3.

assist the accused in the handling of his defence, in the absence of counsel.[212] Some Jamaican applicants were unsure whether they had been represented at the appeal stage, given that appellants often do not attend such proceedings personally. If the State party was unable to resolve doubts about the matter, the Committee has found a violation of the right to counsel.[213] Counsel cannot be imposed upon an accused against his or her will; an accused is entitled to defend himself or herself, or to be defended by counsel of his or her own choosing.[214] The right to representation applies at all stages of the proceedings, including any preliminary hearings,[215] an appeal and even a constitutional challenge.[216] According to Christine Chanet, 'in cases involving criminal offences punishable by the death sentence, the presence of a lawyer should be required at all stages of the proceedings, regardless of whether the accused requests it or not or whether the measures carried out in the course of an investigation are admitted as evidence by the trial Court'.[217]

Article 14§3(d) of the *Covenant* provides that, where an accused is indigent, counsel must be provided 'where the interests of justice so require'.[218] Obviously, this is a requirement in all capital cases. In *Reid* v. *Jamaica*, the Human Rights Committee said that 'it is axiomatic that legal assistance must be made available to a convicted prisoner under sentence of death'.[219] According to the Committee, 'in cases involving capital punishment, in particular, legal aid should enable counsel to prepare his client's defence in circumstances that can ensure justice. This does include provision for adequate remuneration for legal aid.'[220] The provision has been interpreted, in capital cases, to mean a right to state-funded counsel at all stages of the proceedings, including constitutional litigation.[221]

When incompetent representation by counsel is alleged, a distinction is generally made between assigned counsel and privately retained counsel. The conduct of assigned counsel can be imputed to the State party, whereas that of

---

[212] *Yasseen and Thomas* v. *Guyana*, para. 7.8.

[213] *Lumley* v. *Jamaica* (No. 662/1995), UN Doc. CCPR/C/65/D/662/1995, para. 7.4.

[214] *Domukovsky, Tsiklauri, Gelbakhiani & Dokvadze* v. *Georgia*, para. 18.9.

[215] *Wright and Harvey* v. *Jamaica* (No. 459/1991), UN Doc. CCPR/C/55/D/459/1991, para.10.2; *Levy* v. *Jamaica*, para. 7.2; *Clive Johnson* v. *Jamaica*, para. 10.2; *Marshall* v. *Jamaica*, para. 6.2; *Brown* v. *Jamaica*, para. 6.6; *Piandong et al.* v. *Philippines*, Individual opinion by Mr. Martin Scheinin (partly dissenting).

[216] *Currie* v. *Jamaica* (No. 377/1989), UN Doc. A/49/40, Vol. II, p. 73, paras. 13.2–13.4; *LaVende* v. *Trinidad and Tobago*, para. 5.8; *Henry* v. *Trinidad and Tobago* (No. 752/1997), CCPR/C/64/D/752/1997, para. 7.6; *Kelly* v. *Jamaica* (No. 537/1993), para. 9.7; *Patrick Taylor* v. *Jamaica*, para. 8.2; *Shaw* v. *Jamaica*, para. 7.6; *Desmond Taylor* v. *Jamaica*, para. 7.3.

[217] *Piandong et al. v. Philippines*, Individual opinion by Ms. Christine Chanet (partly dissenting).

[218] *Samuel Thomas* v. *Jamaica* (No. 532/1993), paras. 6.2 and 6.4.

[219] *Reid* v. *Jamaica* (No. 250/1987), para. 11.4. Also: *Grant* v. *Jamaica* (No. 353/1988), UN Doc. A/49/40, Vol. II, p. 50, para. 8.6.

[220] *Reid* v. *Jamaica* (No. 250/1987), para. 13. See also: *Reid* v. *Jamaica* (No. 355/1989), UN Doc. A/49/40, Vol. II, para. 14.2; *Campbell* v. *Jamaica*, para. 6.6; *Pratt and Morgan* v. *Jamaica*, para. 13.2; *Little* v. *Jamaica*, para. 8.4; *Kelly* v. *Jamaica* (No. 253/1987), para. 5.10.

[221] *LaVende* v. *Trinidad and Tobago*, para. 5.8.

privately retained counsel cannot, 'unless it was manifest to the judge that the lawyer's behaviour was incompatible with the interests of justice'.[222] But, even where counsel is retained privately, the court – and therefore the State party – has a duty to ensure respect for the right to counsel. In *Yasseen v. Guyana*, privately retained counsel withdrew from the case shortly before trial. The accused engaged a new attorney, whose request for an adjournment because of a scheduling conflict was refused. The trial proceeded, and for four days the accused was not represented. Guyana argued that he was assisted by the trial judge, but the Committee was not impressed. The Committee said that, in capital cases, the right to counsel was axiomatic, 'even if the unavailability of private counsel is to some degree attributable to the author'.[223]

The Committee also found a violation where counsel failed to obtain crucial evidence and was absent during most of the judge's summing up.[224] But the Committee has also said that 'the mere absence of defence counsel at some limited time during the proceedings does not in itself constitute a violation of the Covenant'.[225] It concluded that there was a violation when John Campbell only learned the name of his attorney after his appeal had been dismissed, and he was consequently unable to consult with him or give instructions.[226] Several *Optional Protocol* cases have involved counsel who abandoned appeals, or at least failed to advance certain grounds of appeal, without any prior consultation or agreement with the client. According to the Committee, the right to counsel includes 'consulting with, and informing, the accused if he intends to withdraw an appeal or to argue, before the appellate instance, that the appeal has no merit'.[227]

Where counsel is assigned, the Committee has said there is no right to counsel of one's choice.[228]

---

[222] *Raphael Henry* v. *Jamaica*, para. 8.3; *Collins* v. *Jamaica* (No. 240/1987), para. 8.5; *Berry* v. *Jamaica* (No. 330/1988), UN Doc. A/49/40, Vol. II, p. 20, para. 11.3; *Uton Lewis* v. *Jamaica*, paras. 6.6, 10.3; *Henry and Douglas* v. *Jamaica*, para. 6.5; *Edwards* v. *Jamaica* (No. 529/1993), UN Doc. CCPR/C/60/D/529/1993, para. 5.2; *Patrick Taylor* v. *Jamaica*, para. 6.3; *Desmond Taylor* v. *Jamaica*, para. 6.2; *McLeod* v. *Jamaica*, para. 6.1; *McTaggart* v. *Jamaica*, para. 6.2; *Daley* v. *Jamaica*, para. 7.3; *Finn* v. *Jamaica*, para. 6.7; *Smart* v. *Trinidad and Tobago*, para. 10.3; *Whyte* v. *Jamaica*, para. 9.2; *Everton Morrison* v. *Jamaica*, para. 11.4; *Hixford Morrisson* v. *Jamaica*, para. 6.4; *Leslie* v. *Jamaica*, paras. 9.4–9.5; *Marshall* v. *Jamaica*, para. 6.5; *Nicholas Henry* v. *Jamaica*, para. 7.4; *Barrington Campbell* v. *Jamaica*, para. 7.3; *Forbes* v. *Jamaica* (No. 649/1995), UN Doc. CCPR/C/64/D/649/1995, para. 7.1; *Fraser and Fisher* v. *Jamaica*, para. 6.5; *Smith and Stewart* v. *Jamaica* (No. 668/1995), UN Doc. CCPR/C/65/D/668/1995, para. 7.4.

[223] *Yasseen and Thomas* v. *Guyana*, para. 7.8.   [224] *Brown v. Jamaica*, para. 6.8.

[225] *Marshall* v. *Jamaica*, para. 6.3.

[226] *Campbell* v. *Jamaica*, para. 6.2. Also: *Simmonds* v. *Jamaica*, para. 8.4.

[227] *Collins* v. *Jamaica* (No. 356/1989), para. 8.2; *Campbell* v. *Jamaica*, para. 6.2; *Kelly* v. *Jamaica* (No. 537/1993), para. 9.5; *Burrell* v. *Jamaica*, para. 9.3; *Price* v. *Jamaica* (No. 572/1994), UN Doc. CCPR/C/58/D/572/1994, para. 9.2; *Adams* v. *Jamaica*, para. 8.4; *Steadman v. Jamaica*, para. 10.3; *Jones* v. *Jamaica*, paras. 9.5, 10; *McLeod* v. *Jamaica*, para. 6.4; *Daley* v. *Jamaica*, para. 7.5; *McCordie Morrison v. Jamaica*, para. 8.6; *Marshall* v. *Jamaica*, para. 6.5; *Smith and Stewart* v. *Jamaica*, para. 7.3; *Gallimore* v. *Jamaica*, para. 7.3.

[228] *Bennett* v. *Jamaica*, para. 6.6.

In its Views in *Reid* v. *Jamaica,* the Committee also took the occasion to comment on the legal aid system in Jamaica:

> On the basis of the information before it, the Committee considers that this system, in its current form, does not appear to operate in ways that would enable legal representatives working on legal aid assignments to discharge themselves of their duties and responsibilities as effectively as the interests of justice would warrant. The Committee considers that in cases involving capital punishment, in particular, legal aid should enable counsel to prepare his client's defence in circumstances that can ensure justice. This does include provision for adequate remuneration for legal aid. While the Committee concedes that the State party's authorities are in principle competent to spell out the details of the Poor Prisoner's Defence Act, and while it welcomes recent improvements in the terms under which legal aid is made available, it urges the State party to review its legal aid system.[229]

Provision of legal aid, and for that matter many of the other accoutrements of a fair trial, involves economic resources which are scarce or unavailable in underdeveloped countries. Yet, when Zambia argued that this should be taken into account in assessing whether article 14 of the *Covenant* was being respected in capital cases, the Committee replied: 'The Committee acknowledges the difficult economic situation of the State party, but wishes to emphasize that the rights set forth in the Covenant constitute minimum standards which all States parties have agreed to observe.'[230]

Equality of arms also involves the right of a person charged with a capital offence '[t]o examine, or have examined, the witnesses against him and to obtain the attendance and examination of witnesses on his behalf under the same conditions as witnesses against him' (art. 14§3(e)). In a Jamaican case, the petitioner had attempted to obtain his girlfriend's testimony, which would have corroborated an alibi defence. The trial transcript showed that his attorney had contacted the witness and asked the judge to have her summoned to court. The judge instructed the police to contact the witness, but she said she could not attend because she had no money to travel. The police replied that they had no vehicle to furnish such transport. The Committee considered that there had been a breach of article 14§3(e), and expressed its opinion that 'bearing in mind that this is a case involving the death penalty, the judge should have adjourned the trial and issued a subpoena to secure the attendance of [the witness] in court. Furthermore, the Committee considers that the police should have made transportation available to her.'[231]

In a Guyanese case, evidence that might have been exculpatory disappeared after being considered at an initial hearing that resulted in a mistrial. During the subsequent proceedings, when the accused were sentenced to death, this material

---

[229] *Reid* v. *Jamaica* (No. 250/1987), para. 13. [230] *Lubuto* v. *Zambia,* para. 7.3.
[231] *Grant* v. *Jamaica,* para. 8.5.

evidence was unavailable. Absent any valid explanation by the State party, the Committee considered there had been a breach of paragraphs 14§3(b) and (e).[232]

But in *Compass* v. *Jamaica,* where testimony from a preliminary hearing was filed in the trial record, the applicant's complaint that he was denied the right to cross-examine was rejected, because he had been given the opportunity to cross-examine the witness during the preliminary hearing. Thus, the witness was examined under the same conditions for both prosecution and defence, and the principle of equality of arms was respected.[233]

3.5.1.3 Trial without undue delay

All stages of judicial proceedings should take place without undue delay, the Human Rights Committee has said in its General Comment on article 14 of the *Covenant.*[234] As with other procedural guarantees, respect of the norm is all the more acute and scrutiny the more severe in cases involving capital punishment. According to the Committee, 'in particular in capital cases, the accused is entitled to trial and appeal proceedings without undue delay, whatever the outcome of these judicial proceedings may turn out to be'.[235] In *Lubuto* v. *Zambia,* the Committee considered that a period of eight years between arrest and final decision of the Supreme Court, dismissing the offender's appeal, was incompatible with the requirements of article 14§3(c),[236] although this is one of the most extreme cases of abuse. The general rule, set out in article 14§3(c), is that any person charged with a criminal offence has the right '[t]o be tried without undue delay'. But other provisions are also relevant, among them article 9§3, guaranteeing that persons 'arrested or detained on a criminal charge shall be brought promptly before a judge or other officer authorized by law to exercise judicial power and shall be entitled to trial within a reasonable time or to release'. Article 9§2 may also be involved, guaranteeing anyone who is arrested the right to be informed, at the time of arrest, of the reasons for arrest and to be informed promptly of any charges against the person.

Violations of paragraphs 2 and 3 of article 9, dealing with arrest and pre-trial delay, have often been alleged in death penalty litigation before the Committee, although only rarely will it associate such a breach with a violation of article 6§2 as well,[237] something that it does rather more frequently when a violation of article 14 is involved. In some cases of pre-trial delay, the Committee has

---

[232] *Yasseen and Thomas* v. *Guyana,* para. 7.10.

[233] *Compass* v. *Jamaica* (No. 375/1989), UN Doc. A/49/40, Vol. II, p. 68, para. 10.3.

[234] *General Comment No. 13 (21),* para. 10.

[235] *Kelly* v. *Jamaica* (No. 253/1987), para. 5.12. See also: *E.B.* v. *Jamaica* (No. 303/1988), UN Doc. A/46/40, p. 278, para. 5.3; *R.M.* v. *Jamaica* (No. 315/1987), UN Doc. A/46/40, p. 290, para. 6.3.

[236] *Lubuto* v. *Zambia,* para. 7.3.

[237] *Steadman v. Jamaica,* paras. 10.1 and 10.4. In *McLawrence* v. *Jamaica,* para. 5.6, and *Patrick Taylor* v. *Jamaica,* para. 8.3, the Committee found violations of article 9§3 and article 14, but associated the violation of the right to life with article 14 only.

concluded that there is a breach of article 9§3, saying it does not therefore need to consider 14,[238] while in others it adds a violation of article 14§3(c) to that of article 9§3.[239] There do not seem to be any principles at work in the Committee's determinations. In order to give the Committee's case law more consistency, because article 14§3(c) speaks of the right 'to be tried', application of this provision probably should be confined to the length of the trial itself, an approach taken by the European Court of Human Rights in its case law.[240] Accordingly, article 9§3 would then be reserved for pre-trial delay, as its wording indicates.

As for the initial delay in appearance before a judge, protected by article 9§2, in capital cases the Human Rights Committee has held that it should not exceed a few days,[241] and periods of three weeks[242] and six weeks[243] but not one week[244] have been ruled incompatible with article 9§2.[245] With respect to pre-trial delays *per se*, the Committee examines the period from arrest until the beginning of trial, generally within the context of article 9§3 although it sometimes invokes article 14§3(c) as well. Delays of twelve months,[246] fourteen months[247] and eighteen months have not been deemed undue or unreasonable,[248] although they were not 'desirable'[249] and were 'a matter of concern'.[250] One member considered that in the absence of an explanation, even eighteen months was too long.[251] But a delay of twenty-one months between a court of appeal judgment and the beginning of a retrial, that could not 'be solely attributed to the State party', did not disclose a violation.[252] At about twenty-one months, the Committee's threshold of tolerance starts to break down, and it has generally condemned violations that exceed this amount as being excessive.[253]

---

[238] *Neville Lewis* v. *Jamaica*, para. 9; *Perkins* v. *Jamaica*, para. 11.3.

[239] *Whyte* v. *Jamaica*, para. 9.1; *Finn* v. *Jamaica*, para. 9.4; *Patrick Taylor* v. *Jamaica*, para. 8.4; *Shaw* v. *Jamaica*, para. 7.4; *Smart* v. *Trinidad & Tobago*, para. 10.2; *Steadman* v. *Jamaica*, para. 10.1.

[240] *Wemhoff* v. *Federal Republic of Germany*, 27 June 1968, Series A, No. 7, 1 EHRR 55, 41 ILR 281.

[241] *McLawrence* v. *Jamaica*, para. 5.6; *Shaw* v. *Jamaica*, para. 7.3. Also, *General Comment 8(16)*, para. 2.

[242] *Whyte* v. *Jamaica*, para. 9.1.   [243] *Daley* v. *Jamaica*, para. 7.1.

[244] *Neville Lewis* v. *Jamaica*, Individual opinion by Committee member Martin Scheinin (partly dissenting).

[245] *Daley* v. *Jamaica*, para. 7.1

[246] *Everton Morrison* v. *Jamaica*, Dissenting opinion by Mr. Justice P. N. Bhagwati, co-signed by Mr. Nisuke Ando, Mr. Th. Buergenthal and Mr. Maxwell Yalden.

[247] *Samuel Thomas* v. *Jamaica* (No. 532/1993), para. 9.5; *Leehong* v. *Jamaica* (No. 613/1995), UN Doc. CCPR/C/66/D/613/1995, para. 6.6.

[248] *Everton Morrison* v. *Jamaica*, para. 21.3.   [249] *McTaggart* v. *Jamaica*, para. 8.2.

[250] *Everton Morrison* v. *Jamaica*, para. 21.3.

[251] *Ibid.*, Individual opinion by Ms. Cecilia Medina Quiroga (dissenting).

[252] *Brown* v. *Jamaica* (No. 775/1997), para. 6.11.

[253] Twenty-one months: *Perkins* v. *Jamaica*, para. 11.3; twenty-two months: *Smart* v. *Trinidad and Tobago*, para. 10.2; twenty-three months: *Neville Lewis* v. *Jamaica*, para. 8.1; 'nearly two years': *Walker and Richards* v. *Jamaica*, para. 8.2; twenty-four months: *Yasseen and Thomas* v. *Guyana*, para. 7.11; twenty-six months: *Everton Morrison* v. *Jamaica*, para. 22.3; twenty-seven months: *Shaw* v. *Jamaica*, para. 7.4; *Smart* v. *Trinidad and Tobago*, para. 10.2; *Desmond Taylor* v. *Jamaica*, para. 7.1; *Steadman* v. *Jamaica*, para. 10.1; twenty-eight months: *Patrick Taylor* v. *Jamaica*, para. 8.4; twenty-nine-months: *Leslie* v. *Jamaica*, para. 9.3;

Almost all of the litigation before the Committee has concerned Jamaican cases, and the Committee takes care to note that the State party rarely provides any explanation for the delay. This implies, of course, that the length of time before arrest and trial, or between trial and appeal, must normally be weighed against other factors, including the complexity of the case, when these other factors exist.[254] The Committee will also take into account the role of the accused in delaying proceedings,[255] and it has frequently dismissed complaints because the delay 'cannot be solely attributed to the State party'.[256] But the Committee has not usually been impressed when the State party argues that trial was delayed because a preliminary hearing was held.[257] In the case of pre-trial delay, it also notes that the length of the delay must be considered in light of the fact that the accused has been detained without bail. Although article 9§3 creates a presumption in favour of interim release, most national legal systems would consider as an exception cases of the 'most serious crimes' likely to attract capital punishment.[258] The Committee seems to accept that it is normal that those charged with murder be detained prior to trial.[259]

Although article 14§3(c) speaks more directly to the issue of delay within the trial itself than to pre-trial delay, there have been no cases complaining that hearings were unnecessarily or unfairly prolonged. Once trial actually begins, the Jamaican cases that have come before the Committee have been models of expedited justice, with trials rarely lasting more than a few days. This of course raises other problems concerning respect for norms of due process.

Like the trial, the appeal must also take place within a reasonable time, and this involves breaches of article 14§5 in addition to article 14§3. With respect to appeal delays, the operative period is that between conviction at trial and the disposition of the appeal. The Committee has judged delays exceeding twenty-three months to be contrary to the provisions of the *Covenant*.[260] But

Finn v. *Jamaica*, para. 9.4; thirty months: *Henry and Douglas* v. *Jamaica*, para. 9.3; *Everton Morrison* v. *Jamaica*, para. 21.3; thirty-one months: *Samuel Thomas* v. *Jamaica*, para. 6.2; *McLawrence* v. *Jamaica*, para. 5.11; *Brown and Parish* v. *Jamaica*, para. 9.5; thirty-three months: *Hamilton* v. *Jamaica* (No. 616/1995), UN Doc. CCPR/C/66/D/616/1995, para. 8.3; thirty-six months: *Whyte* v. Jamaica, para. 9.1.

[254] *Shaw* v. *Jamaica*, para. 7.4; *Henry & Douglas* v. *Jamaica*, para. 9.3.

[255] See, in this respect, *Neville Lewis* v. *Jamaica*, Individual opinion by Committee member Lord Colville (dissenting); *Neville Lewis* v. *Jamaica*, Individual opinion by Committee member Nisuke Ando (dissenting); *Neville Lewis* v. *Jamaica*, Individual opinion by Committee member Rajsoomer Lallah (dissenting).

[256] *Brown* v. *Jamaica*, para. 6.11.

[257] *Desmond Taylor* v. *Jamaica*, para. 7.1. But see: *Everton Morrison* v. *Jamaica*, para. 21.3.

[258] This is even the case for international criminal justice: *Rome Statute of the International Criminal Court*, UN Doc. A/CONF.183/9, art. 59(4); *Rules of Procedure and Evidence*, UN Doc. IT-14, Rule 65; *Prosecutor* v. *Simic* et al. (Case No. IT-95-9-AR65), Decisions on Simo Zaric's and Miroslav Tadic's Applications for Provisional Release, 4 April 2000.

[259] *Everton Morrison* v. *Jamaica*, para. 21.3.

[260] Twenty-three months: *Samuel Thomas* v. *Jamaica*, para. 9.5; twenty-five months: *Smith and Stewart* v. *Jamaica*, para. 7.4; twenty-seven months: *Bennett* v. *Jamaica*, para. 10.5; twenty-eight months: *Brown and Parish* v. *Jamaica*, para. 9.5; thirty months: *Walker and Richards* v. *Jamaica*, para. 8.2; thirty-one months: *Daley* v. *Jamaica*, para. 7.4; three years: *Kelly* v. *Jamaica* (No. 253/1987), para. 5.12; *E.B.* v. *Jamaica*,

delay of five months from lodging of petition for special leave to appeal to the Judicial Committee of the Privy Council and its dismissal was not considered a breach.[261] On appeal, there are also frequent delays between the actual hearing and the delivery of written judgments,[262] or of the trial transcripts,[263] which are necessary before further challenges to death sentences may be lodged.

3.5.1.4 *Presence at trial*

Article 14§3(d) ensures the right of a person charged with a criminal offence '[t]o be tried in his presence'. Nazi war criminal Martin Bohrman was tried *in absentia* at Nuremberg and sentenced to death, although decades later DNA testing on human remains found in Berlin determined that he was actually dead before the trial even began. The Human Rights Committee has taken the view that *in absentia* trials are not necessarily contrary to article 14 of the *Covenant*, because an accused may renounce the right to be tried in his or her presence. Even common law courts, which are generally unfriendly to the idea of *in absentia* trials, will in certain circumstances allow justice to proceed in the absence of an accused when, for example, he or she is disrupting the hearing or absconds while on interim release. The Human Rights Committee has held that where an accused disrupts a capital trial, the court must take 'all reasonable measures' to ensure that the proceedings continue in his or her presence, failing which there is a violation of the right to be present.[264]

In *Mbenge* v. *Zaire*, the former governor of Shaba province had fled his country and set up residence in Belgium. He was twice sentenced to death, *in absentia*, learning of this in the press. He had not been 'duly summoned at his residence in Belgium to appear before the tribunals'. The judgments condemning Mbenge to death explicitly stated that summonses had been issued by the clerk of the court, but the summons was issued only three days before the beginning of the hearing. This deprived Mbenge of the time necessary for preparation of a proper defence. The Committee concluded that there was a breach of articles 14§3(a), (b), (d) and (e), and this necessarily resulted in a breach of article 6§2 as well.[265]

3.5.1.5 *Revision or appeal*

Article 14§5 guarantees a right to have a criminal conviction and sentence 'reviewed by a higher tribunal according to law'.[266] Many judicial systems provide

para. 5.3; *R.M.* v. *Jamaica* (No. 315/1987), para. 6.3; *McCordie Morrison* v. *Jamaica*, para. 8.5; *Samuel Thomas* v. *Jamaica*, para. 6.2; three years and four and a half months: *Henry and Douglas* v. *Jamaica*, para. 9.4; seven years: *Neptune* v. *Trinidad and Tobago* (No. 523/1992), UN Doc. CCPR/C/57/D/523/1992, para. 9.3.

[261] *Bennett* v. *Jamaica*, para. 10.6.
[262] *McCordie Morrison* v. *Jamaica*, para. 8.5; *Nicholas Henry* v. *Jamaica*; *Little* v. *Jamaica*.
[263] *Walker and Richards* v. *Jamaica*, para. 8.3.
[264] *Domukovsky, Tsiklauri, Gelbakhiani & Dokvadze* v. *Georgia*, para. 18.9.
[265] *Mbenge* v. *Zaire* (No. 16/1977), UN Doc. CCPR/C/OP/2, p. 76, at p. 78.
[266] 'Concluding Observations, Iraq', para. 15.

for an appeal of right or *de plano* in the case of death sentences. But, in a Jamaican death penalty case, the Human Rights Committee said 'a system not allowing for automatic right to appeal may still be in conformity with article 14, paragraph 5, as long as the examination of an application for leave to appeal entails a full review, that is, both on the basis of the evidence and of the law, of the conviction and sentence and as long as the procedure allows for due consideration of the nature of the case'.[267] However, judicial review, at which there is no hearing, which is confined to matters of law only, and which does not permit a full reassessment of the trial procedure and of the evidence, does not satisfy the requirements of article 14§5.[268]

The Committee has stated that article 14§5 of the *Covenant* does not require States parties to provide for several instances of appeal in death penalty cases.[269] However, if the law provides for several levels of appeal, a convicted person must have effective access to each level, and this includes availability of written judgments permitting an accused to advance in the appeal process.[270] Where the Jamaican Court of Appeal failed to issue a written judgment in a death penalty case, in effect obstructing further appeal to the Judicial Committee of the Privy Council,[271] the Committee held there had been a breach of article 14§5 of the *Covenant*.[272]

---

[267] *Lumley* v. *Jamaica*, para. 7.3; *Mansaraj* et al. v. *Sierra Leone* (Nos. 839/1998, 840/1998 & 841/1998), UN Doc. CCPR/C/72/D/840/1998, para. 5.6.

[268] *Domukovsky, Tsiklauri, Gelbakhiani & Dokvadze* v. *Georgia*, para. 18.11.

[269] *Nicholas Henry* v. *Jamaica*, para. 8.4.

[270] *Reid* v. *Jamaica* (No. 250/1987), para. 11.6; *Barrett and Sutcliffe*, v. *Jamaica* (Nos 270/1988 and 271/1988), UN Doc. A/47/40, p. 254, para. 8.4; *Nicholas Henry* v. *Jamaica*; *Little* v. *Jamaica*; *Francis* v. *Jamaica* (No. 320/1988), UN Doc. CCPR/C/47/D/320/1988, para. 12.2; *Griffiths* v. *Jamaica* (No. 274/1988), UN Doc. A/48/40, Vol. II, p. 22, para. 7.4; *Martin* v. *Jamaica* (No. 317/1988), UN Doc. A/48/40, Vol. II, p. 57, para. 12.1; *Kindler* v. *Canada* (No. 470/1991), para. 15.2; *Cox* v. *Canada* (No. 539/1993), para. 17.2; *Hamilton* v. *Jamaica* (No. 333/1988), UN Doc. A/49/40, Vol. II, p. 37, para. 9.1; *Currie* v. *Jamaica*, para. 13.5; *Lumley* v. *Jamaica*, para. 7.5.

[271] In practice, the Judicial Committee of the Privy Council has systematically dismissed any petition unsupported by the relevant court documents: *M.F.* v. *Jamaica* (No. 233/1987), UN Doc. A/47/40, p. 338, para. 5.2; *Smith* v. *Jamaica*, para. 10.5; *Currie* v. *Jamaica*, para. 13.5. Prior to the Privy Council's ruling in *Pratt* et al. v. *Attorney General for Jamaica* et al. [1993] 4 All ER 769, [1993] 2 LRC 349, [1994] 2 AC 1, 14 *HRLJ* 338, 33 ILM 364 (JCPC), in November 1993, observers were very critical about the efficacy of such appeals: R. M. B. Antoine, 'The Judicial Committee of the Privy Council – An Inadequate Remedy for Death Row Prisoners', (1992) 41 *International and Comparative Law Quarterly* 179; R. M. B. Antoine, 'International Law and the Right to Legal Representation in Capital Offence Cases – A Comparative Approach', (1992) 12 *Oxford Journal of Legal Studies* 284; David Pannick, *Judicial Review of the Death Penalty*, London: Duckworth, 1982. But despite a high failure rate of Privy Council appeals, the Human Rights Committee has considered them to be available domestic remedies: *N.A.J.* v. *Jamaica* (No. 246/1987), UN Doc. A/45/40, Vol. II, p. 137, para. 10.3, p. 139; *A.A.* v. *Jamaica* (No. 251/1987), UN Doc. A/45/40, Vol. II, p. 141; *L.R. and T.W.* v. *Jamaica* (No. 258/1987), UN Doc. A/45/40, Vol. II, p. 145; *D.B.* v. *Jamaica* (No. 259/1987), UN Doc. A/45/40, Vol. II, p. 149; *C.B.* v. *Jamaica* (No. 260/1987), UN Doc. A/45/40, Vol. II, p. 153; *N.C.* v. *Jamaica* (No. 278/1988), UN Doc. A/45/40, Vol. II, p. 166; *C.G.* v. *Jamaica* (No. 281/1988), UN Doc. A/45/40, Vol. II, p. 169; *A.S.* v. *Jamaica* (No. 231/1987), UN Doc. A/44/40, p. 274, para. 9.3. The Privy Council decision in *Pratt and Morgan* showed the correctness of this view.

[272] *Raphael Henry* v. *Jamaica*; *Little* v. *Jamaica*; *Francis* v. *Jamaica* (No. 320/1988); *Hamilton* v. *Jamaica* (No. 333/1988); *Collins* v. *Jamaica* (No. 356/1989); *Smith* v. *Jamaica*, para. 10.5; *Champagnie,*

Under common law systems most death sentences are issued following jury trials and, in some cases, the jury itself makes the determination about whether or not to impose capital punishment. As a rule, juries do not give reasons for their decisions and they are often under an obligation to remain silent about their deliberations. This makes any right to revision or appeal somewhat problematic. In *Young* v. *Jamaica*, two jury members filed affidavits swearing that they had been cajoled and exhorted by the trial judge and the jury foreman to reach a guilty verdict in a case involving mandatory imposition of the death penalty. But the Committee stuck with its established jurisprudence whereby it defers to national courts on such issues, noting furthermore that neither juror had manifested any objection to the procedure during the trial itself.[273]

The question of a right of appeal is closely related to the issue of exhaustion of local remedies. Where the right of appeal is not effective, not only is the *Covenant* breached, the individual litigant is also relieved of the obligation to undertake such an appeal prior to filing a communication with the Human Rights Committee. The Judicial Committee of the Privy Council took the Human Rights Committee to task on this point in its judgment in *Pratt and Morgan*. According to the Lords, '[i]n practice it is necessary to have the reasons of the Court of Appeal available at the hearing of the application for special leave to appeal, as without them it is not usually possible to identify the point of law or serious miscarriage of justice of which the appellant complains'. But '[t]he availability of the reasons is not, however, a condition precedent to lodging an application for special leave to appeal'.[274] The Human Rights Committee subsequently took note of the Privy Council's position whereby review on appeal was possible even in the absence of a written judgment, but said this did not resolve the problem, because a remedy must not only be available in a formal sense, it must also be effective. The Human Rights Committee has since concluded that despite the Privy Council's admonition, if written reasons have not been provided by the lower courts, it will not consider the absence of an application for leave to appeal to be a failure to exhaust domestic remedies.[275] In at least one Jamaican death row case, the adoption by the Committee of a decision declaring a communication admissible where the Court of Appeal had failed to provide written reasons was sufficient to provoke the Court to issue such reasons.[276]

Palmer and Chisholm v. *Jamaica* (No. 445/1991), UN Doc. A/49/40, Vol. II, p. 136, paras. 7.2–7.3.
[273] *Young* v. *Jamaica* (No. 615/1995), UN Doc. CCPR/C/61/D/615/1995/Rev.1, para. 5.4. See especially, in the *Young* case, Individual opinion by Mr. Prafullachandra N. Bhagwati.
[274] *Pratt* et al. v. *Attorney General for Jamaica* et al., para. 24.
[275] *Hamilton* v. *Jamaica* (No. 333/1988), para. 8.3.
[276] *M. F.* v. *Jamaica*, paras. 6.1–6.2. Subsequently, the Committee revised its decision and declared the communication inadmissible, given the possibility of petition to the Judicial Committee of the Privy Council.

3.1.6 Reference to the Genocide Convention

The reference to the *Convention for the Prevention and Punishment of the Crime of Genocide* [277] in paragraph 2 of article 6 was introduced at the eighth session of the Commission of Human Rights, where it was intended 'to provide a further yardstick to which national laws authorizing the imposition of the death sentence should conform'.[278] The norms of the *Genocide Convention* are regarded as declaratory of customary law.[279] Advocates of the reference also insisted that an individual's right to life could not be safeguarded if the existence of the group he or she belonged to were menaced with extinction.[280]

In the final version of the *Covenant*, there is in fact a second reference to the *Genocide Convention*, in paragraph 3, which states that nothing in this article shall authorize any derogation by a State party. This provision is most certainly redundant, as article 5 of the *Covenant* prohibits any restriction upon or derogation from rights recognized or existing pursuant to any law, conventions, regulations or custom on the pretext that the *Covenant* did not recognize such rights or recognized them to a lesser extent.

3.1.7 Amnesty, pardon or commutation

Pardon implies complete release, whereas commutation is the substitution of a death sentence with a usually lengthy term of imprisonment. The availability of pardon or commutation frequently proves to be highly important, because it is often through executive intervention that the first steps towards abolition take place.[281] In many countries, *de facto* abolition is the result of generous application of the prerogative of pardon or commutation, followed years later by *de jure* abolition. Its use is vulnerable to political vicissitudes, although were it to be exercised in a discriminatory fashion, capital punishment would be conducted 'arbitrarily' and, therefore, in breach of paragraph 1. Several periodic reports to the Human Rights Committee have provided information on the availability of pardon or commutation.[282] In many States, a death

---

[277] (1951) 78 UNTS 277. See: William A. Schabas, *Genocide in International Law*, Cambridge: Cambridge University Press, 2000.
[278] UN Doc. A/2929, para. 8.
[279] *Reservations to the Convention on the Prevention of Genocide (Advisory Opinion)*, [1951] ICJ Reports 16; *A.G. Israel* v. *Eichmann*, (1968) 36 ILR 18 (DC); *United States of America* v. *Ohlendorf* et al. ('Einsatzgruppen trial'), (1948) 15 *Ann. Dig.* 656, 3 LRTWC 470 (United States Military Tribunal).
[280] UN Doc. A/C.3/SR.813, para. 1-2; UN Doc. A/C.3/SR.814, para. 5; UN Doc. A/C.3/SR.815, para. 3; UN Doc. A/C.3/SR.816, para. 1.
[281] Amnesty International, *When the State Kills . . .*, *The Death Penalty: A Human Rights Issue*, New York: Amnesty International, 1989, at pp. 33–34.
[282] 'Initial Report of the Byelorussian Soviet Socialist Republic', UN Doc. CCPR/C/1/Add.27; 'Initial Report of Mongolia'; 'Initial Report of Bulgaria'; 'Initial Report of Chile', UN Doc. CCPR/C/1/Add.25; 'Fourth Periodic Report of Tunisia', para. 83(e); 'Second Periodic Report of El Salvador', UN Doc. CCPR/C/51/Add.8, paras. 103–122; 'Second Periodic Report of Cameroons', paras. 51 and 54.

sentence cannot be carried out until the dismissal of an application for pardon or commutation.[283]

The term 'amnesty' only appears in the second sentence of the paragraph, because it is granted by the State and not applied for.[284] Consequently, it is inappropriate to describe it as a 'right'.

3.1.8 Juveniles and pregnant women

Paragraph 5 of article 6 provides that in no case shall the death penalty be carried out on a person who was under eighteen at the time of commission of the crime or on a pregnant woman. Other instruments of international law recognize additional excluded categories, for example, the elderly,[285] mothers having dependent infants,[286] mothers of young children,[287] the insane[288] and the mentally disabled.[289] Examination of the *travaux préparatoires* indicates that these other categories were not intentionally excluded, and that the drafters merely proceeded in a piecemeal fashion. This suggests an interpretative approach that considers the enumeration in article 6§5 to be non-exhaustive. In other words, other categories of individuals, such as young mothers, the elderly and the insane may be sheltered from capital punishment, if not by article 6§5, then by the term 'arbitrarily' in article 6§1 of the *Covenant*. For example, the

---

[283] 'Initial Report of Czechoslovakia', UN Doc. CCPR/C/1/Add.12; 'Initial Report of Madagascar'; 'Initial Report of Hungary', UN Doc. CCPR/C/1/Add.11.

[284] UN Doc. E/CN.4/SR.310, at p. 13.

[285] *American Convention on Human Rights*, (1979) 1144 UNTS 123, OASTS 36, art. 4§5; 'Safeguards Guaranteeing Protection of the Rights of Those Facing the Death Penalty', ESC Res. 1984/50, art. 3.

[286] *Protocol Additional I to the 1949 Geneva Conventions and Relating to the Protection of Victims of International Armed Conflicts*, (1979) 1125 UNTS 3, art. 76§3; 'Safeguards Guaranteeing Protection of the Rights of Those Facing the Death Penalty', art. 3.

[287] *Protocol Additional II to the 1949 Geneva Conventions and Relating to the Protection of Victims of Non-International Armed Conflicts*, (1979) 1125 UNTS 609, art. 6§4.

[288] 'Safeguards Guaranteeing Protection of the Rights of Those Facing the Death Penalty', art. 3. See the appeal from the Special Rapporteur on extrajudicial, summary and arbitrary executions in the case of *John Selvage* v. *United States*: UN Doc. E/CN.4/1989/25, paras. 279–283. Also: William A. Schabas, 'International Norms on Execution of the Insane and the Mentally Retarded', (1993) 4 *Criminal Law Forum* 95. That it is contrary to the *Covenant* to execute an insane person was raised in a Jamaican communication under the *Optional Protocol*. But after the sentence was commuted the Human Rights Committee said the matter was moot and did not pronounce itself on this most interesting question: *Williams* v. *Jamaica* (No. 609/1995), UN Doc. CCPR/C/61/D/609/1995, para. 6.2.

[289] 'Implementation of the Safeguards Guaranteeing Protection of the Rights of Those Facing the Death Penalty', ESC Res. 1989/64, para. (d). In an appeal for urgent action, the Special *Rapporteur* on extrajudicial, summary and arbitrary executions has challenged the United States Government in a case involving execution of a mentally retarded individual: UN Doc. E/CN.4/1992/30, paras. 577–578. See also: UN Doc. E/CN.4/1993/46, paras. 629–630, 632 and 679; UN Doc. E/CN.4/1994/7, paras. 620 and 686. The United States offered its justification for the execution of those with mental disability in a report to the Secretary-General, noting that many people with mental disabilities, however, are not legally insane. Some persons with mental disabilities have been found legally capable of resisting impulses and acting responsibly. 'Question of the Death Penalty, Report of the Secretary-General Submitted Pursuant to Commission Resolution 1997/12', UN Doc. E/CN.4/1998/82, Annex.

International Court of Justice has held that, for the purposes of its application during armed conflict, the term 'arbitrarily' in article 6§1 'falls to be determined by the applicable lex specialis, namely, the law applicable in armed conflict which is designed to regulate the conduct of hostilities'.[290] Instruments of this *lex specialis* refer to nursing mothers[291] and young mothers.[292] It does seem an absurd result that these international law norms prohibit execution of young mothers during non-international armed conflict yet might allow the same during peacetime.

When the *Covenant* was being drafted, the prohibition of the execution of juveniles had already been included in the *Geneva Convention of August 12, 1949 Relative to the Protection of Civilians*.[293] However, the norm applied only to non-combatants in occupied territories. An Egyptian proposal to prohibit the death penalty for offenders under the age of seventeen years,[294] an amendment whose purpose was to ensure the rehabilitation of juvenile offenders,[295] was debated during the fifth session of the Commission in 1949. China opposed the Egyptian amendment, arguing it would 'overload the articles of the draft covenant with details';[296] these views were endorsed by the chair, Eleanor Roosevelt.[297] The existing provision is the result of an amendment adopted during the debates in the Third Committee in 1957.[298]

The first suggestion that pregnant women be protected was made by Uruguay during the fifth session of the Commission. Uruguay preferred to extend this to women in general.[299] The amendment in the eighth session of the Commission that led to the eventual provision for pregnant women was proposed by Yugoslavia, 'inspired by purely humanitarian considerations'.[300] The Secretary-General's Annotations suggest that the provision was added out of 'consideration for the interests of the unborn child'.[301] The inclusion of other groups, specifically the insane and the elderly, arose during the debates, but no formal amendments to this effect were ever made.[302]

Paragraph 6§5 does not apply the same rules to juveniles that it does to pregnant women. For the former, sentence of death shall not be imposed for

---

[290] *Legality of the Threat or Use of Nuclear Weapons, Advisory Opinion,* [1996] ICJ Reports 226, para. 25.
[291] *Protocol Additional I,* art. 76§3.   [292] *Protocol Additional II,* art. 6§4.
[293] *Geneva Convention of August 12, 1949 Relative to the Protection of Civilians,* art. 68§4.
[294] UN Doc. E/CN.4/SR.149, para. 68. See also the comments of the Uruguayan delegate, UN Doc. E/CN.4/SR.139, para. 28.
[295] UN Doc. E/CN.4/SR.149, para. 77.   [296] *Ibid.,* para. 83.   [297] *Ibid.,* para. 86.
[298] UN Doc. A/C.3/L.647; UN Doc. A/C.3/L.650; UN Doc. A/C/3/L.655.
[299] UN Doc. E/CN.4/SR.139, para. 28.   [300] UN Doc. E/CN.4/SR.309, p. 3.
[301] UN Doc. A/2929, Chapter VI, para. 10. An unsuccessful amendment, submitted by Belgium, Brazil, El Salvador, Mexico and Morocco, UN Doc. A/C.3/L.654, protected the right to life 'from the moment of conception'. Speaking in support of the proposal, the Belgian delegate said that the principles underlying paragraph 6§5, which was designed to protect the unborn child whose mother had been sentenced to death, should be extended to all unborn children: UN Doc. A/C.3/SR.810, para. 2.
[302] UN Doc. A/C.3/SR.819, para. 17 (Denmark); UN Doc. A/C.3/SR.820, para. 6 (Japan).

crimes committed by persons below eighteen years of age, whatever the current age of the individual. It is a consequence of generally recognized criminal policy that limits the liability of juveniles, on the premise that they are too young to be fully responsible for their acts. For the pregnant woman, it is the unborn child's protection that is envisaged, and the sentence may well be 'imposed' although it may not be 'carried out'. In other words, a pregnant woman may be sentenced to death but the sentence must not be carried out while she is pregnant. Is the prohibition a permanent one, or does the prohibition fall into abeyance once pregnancy is at an end? According to Yoram Dinstein, once a pregnant woman has delivered or otherwise ended her pregnancy, she becomes open to execution.[303] During drafting of the provision, discussion took place both in the Commission and the Third Committee as to whether the prohibition applied after the child's birth as well, but the matter was never resolved.[304] The text is consistent with a more generous interpretation by which, once a women accused of a capital crime or sentenced to death becomes pregnant, the sentence can never be carried out. This interpretation is reinforced by the abolitionist orientation of article 6, notably by the first phrase of paragraph 2 and by paragraph 6.

The periodic reports indicate that in some States parties the prohibition on execution comes to an end upon the termination of pregnancy[305] or upon the completion of some subsequent delay which may cover the period of lactation or extend up to two years.[306] Other periodic reports suggest that the sentence of death is permanently stayed if the condemned woman becomes pregnant.[307] Still others indicate rules that do not strictly conform to the *Covenant*, such as a prohibition on pronouncement of a sentence of death on a pregnant woman (implying no particular protection if the woman becomes pregnant subsequent to sentencing)[308] or a total absence of any relevant norm in national law.[309]

[303] Dinstein, 'The Right to Life', p. 117.   [304] UN Doc. A/3764, para. 118.

[305] 'Third Periodic Report of Senegal', UN Doc. CCPR/C/64/Add.5, para. 34; 'Supplementary Report of Denmark', UN Doc. CCPR/C/1/Add.19; 'Initial Report of Bulgaria'; 'Fourth Periodic Report of Tunisia', para. 77e).

[306] 'Initial Report of Madagascar'. The Supplementary Report provides more detail on the case of mothers: there is a stay of three months following birth, and, in the case of breast-feeding mothers, of two years, where it is evident that damage would be inflicted on the child if the sentence were to be carried out: UN Doc. CCPR/C/1/Add.26; 'Initial Report of Algeria', para. 81; 'Initial Report of Libyan Arab Jamahiriya'; 'Initial Report of Iraq'; 'Second Periodic Report of Yemen', UN Doc. CCPR/C/82/Add.1, para. 16.

[307] 'Initial Report of the Byelorussian Soviet Socialist Republic'; 'Initial Report of Czechoslovakia'; 'Initial Report of Chile'; 'Initial Report of Japan'; 'Additional Supplementary Report of Jordan', UN Doc. CCPR/C/1/Add. 56; UN Doc. CCPR/C/SR.68, para. 11 (German Democratic Republic); 'Second Periodic Report of Bulgaria', UN Doc. CCPR/C/32/Add.17, para. 56; 'Third Periodic Report of Jordan', UN Doc. CCPR/C/76/Add.1, para. 13.

[308] 'Initial Report of Jamaica', UN Doc. CCPR/C/1/Add.53; 'Supplementary Report of Cyprus', UN Doc. CCPR/C/1/Add.28.

[309] 'Initial Report of Canada', UN Doc. CCPR/C/1/Add.43, UN Doc. CCPR/C/SR.202, para. 6.

When Morocco, in its initial report, informed the Committee that pregnant women were not executed until forty days after delivery,[310] Bouziri and others said that it was 'cruel' to execute a woman after delivering a child.[311] During consideration of the initial report of Mali, Bouziri found a similar provision to be unduly harsh, asking who would look after the infant. 'After all, the ultimate aim of article 6 of the Covenant was to prevail upon countries to abandon the death penalty', he said.[312] In reply, the representative of Mali told the Committee that the death penalty had never in fact been carried out on a mother.[313]

One way to avoid any ambiguity or confusion is to abolish the death penalty for women altogether. Ukraine, in its third periodic report, indicated that new criminal legislation currently being prepared would outlaw the death penalty in the case of women in general.[314] But when Mongolia reported that its Penal Code also prevents the death sentence for women,[315] this was criticized as being inconsistent with the principle of non-discrimination on the basis of sex.[316] The Mongolian representative ably explained that women were exempted, first, because they were mothers and required humane treatment and, second, because it was a step towards total abolition.[317]

In practice, the execution of pregnant women must be extremely rare,[318] which probably explains why there has been no litigation and little scholarly comment on the subject. The same cannot be said of the execution of juveniles, notably because of a decision of the United States Supreme Court allowing the execution of individuals who have committed crimes while under the age of eighteen.[319] The *Covenant* provision is clear and has posed no significant

---

[310] 'Initial Report of Morocco', UN Doc. CCPR/C/10/Add.10.

[311] UN Doc. CCPR/C/SR.327, para. 8; see also: UN Doc. CCPR/C/SR.327, para. 29 (Aguilar); UN Doc. CCPR/C/SR.328, para. 22 (Evans). In its Third Periodic Report, Morocco informed the Committee that no woman had been executed since independence: 'Third Periodic Report of Morocco', UN Doc. CCPR/C/76/Add.3, para. 31.

[312] UN Doc. CCPR/C/SR.284, para. 15. See also Bouziri on the 'Initial Report of Italy', UN Doc. CCPR/C/6/Add.4, para. 26: UN Doc. CCPR/C/SR.258, para. 58.

[313] UN Doc. CCPR/C/SR.289, para. 27.

[314] 'Third Periodic Report of the Ukrainian Soviet Socialist Republic', UN Doc. CCPR/C/58/Add.8, para. 30.

[315] UN Doc. CCPR/C/SR.197, para. 8.

[316] *Ibid.*, para. 6; see also Koulishev, UN Doc. CCPR/C/SR.198, para. 21.

[317] UN Doc. CCPR/C/SR.202, para. 6.

[318] Committee member Walter Tarnopolsky questioned Iran about reports that pregnant women had been executed: UN Doc. CCPR/C/SR.365, para. 9.

[319] *Stanford* v. *Kentucky*, *Wilkins* v. *Missouri*, in which the minority of the United States Supreme Court, at pp. 2985–2986 (S.Ct.), relied on article 6§5 of the *International Covenant*, art. 4§5 of the *American Convention on Human Rights*, art. 68 of the *Geneva Convention Relative to the Protection of Civilian Persons in Time of War*, and the 'Safeguards Guaranteeing Protection of the Rights of Those Facing the Death Penalty'. The previous year, in *Thompson* v. *Oklahoma*, the Court had decided that execution for a crime committed while under sixteen was 'cruel and unusual punishment'; in that decision, the majority cited the three international treaties prohibiting execution for crimes committed while under eighteen (pp. 2696–2697, S.Ct.).

problem of interpretation.[320] In a few Jamaican cases, alleged victims have argued that they were under eighteen when the crime was committed. In *Perkins*, the Human Rights Committee concluded, after examining birth certificates and assessing the competing arguments, that the applicant was not in fact under eighteen when the crime was committed.[321] In another case, Jamaica did not really quarrel with the claim, but said the sentence had been commuted so the question was moot. Nevertheless, the Committee said there had been a violation of article 6§5 of the *Covenant*.[322]

The periodic reports indicate general compliance with the norm,[323] although there are occasional examples of violation, where the age of majority is below eighteen years[324] or where there is no provision at all.[325] The Cyprus Criminal Code set a limit of sixteen years, but its representative told the Committee that the provision would be declared inoperative in view of its conflict with article 6§5 of the *Covenant*.[326] Several States will not sentence a minor to death, but this leaves open the possibility of an individual over eighteen years of age being sentenced for a crime committed while still a minor.[327] In many cases, lengthy prison sentences are imposed as an alternative, a measure that while lacking the horror of the death sentence does little to further the principle of mitigated criminal responsibility for minors.[328] During presentation of its supplementary report, Hungary's representative said its legislation previously provided that the death penalty could not be imposed on persons under twenty except those enlisted in military service, and this meant that some people under twenty were subject to the death penalty. When the new Criminal Code was

---

[320] In *Baker* v. *The Queen* [1975] 3 WLR 113, [1976] Crim LR 49 (JCPC), Jamaican law provided that no sentence of death could be pronounced or imposed on a person under eighteen. Baker had committed a capital crime while under eighteen but was sentenced when over eighteen. On appeal to the Judicial Committee of the Privy Council, his argument that this violated the Constitution, which guaranteed him the right to the less severe penalty, was rejected.

[321] *Perkins* v. *Jamaica*, para. 11.6.　　　[322] *Clive Johnson* v. *Jamaica*, para. 10.3.

[323] 'Initial Report of Mongolia'; 'Initial Report of Japan'; 'Initial Report of Czechoslovakia'; 'Initial Report of the Byelorussian Soviet Socialist Republic'; 'Initial Report of Bulgaria'.

[324] 'Initial Report of Morocco', sixteen years; Morocco was criticized in this respect by Bouziri, UN Doc. CCPR/C/SR.327, para. 8, Aguilar, UN Doc. CCPR/C/SR.327, para. 29, and Evans, UN Doc. CCPR/C/SR.328, para. 22. Also 'Initial Report of Jordan', where the age is unspecified; 'Additional Supplementary Report of Jordan', fifteen years; 'Second Periodic Report of Iraq', sixteen years.

[325] 'Initial Report of Canada'; 'Initial Report of Saint Vincent and the Grenadines', UN Doc. CCPR/C/26/Add.4, UN Doc. CCPR/C/SR.953–954, UN Doc. A/45/40, paras. 249 and 266.

[326] UN Doc. CCPR/C/SR.166, para. 8; also UN Doc. CCPR/C/SR.166, para. 46; 'Second Periodic Report of Cyprus', UN Doc. CCPR/C/32/Add.18, para. 30.

[327] 'Initial Report of Madagascar'; 'Initial Report of Chile'; 'Initial Report of Jamaica'; 'Initial Report of Iraq'; 'Third Periodic Report of the Union of Soviet Socialist Republics'.

[328] 'Third Periodic Report of Senegal', para. 34, a sentence of ten to twenty years; UN Doc. CCPR/C/SR.289, para. 27 (Mali), twenty years; 'Initial Report of Algeria', para. 80, a sentence of ten to twenty years; 'Initial Report of Togo', ten years; 'Initial Report of Libyan Arab Jamahiriya', a sentence of not less than five years; 'Supplementary Report of Denmark', life imprisonment (for military offences); 'Initial Report of Democratic Yemen', three to ten years.

elaborated, an *ad hoc* committee reviewed Hungary's international obligations and proposed to eliminate that anomaly.[329]

The principal, and perhaps now the sole,[330] offender of the prohibition on juvenile executions found in paragraph 5 is the United States. The United States continues to sentence offenders to death for crimes committed while under the age of eighteen, and has in fact carried out several such sentences since ratifying the *Covenant* in 1992. The United States formulated a reservation whose purpose was to exclude the prohibition on juvenile executions from the obligations it assumed at the time of ratifying the *Covenant*. Eleven States parties objected to this reservation as being incompatible with the object and purpose of the *Covenant*. In March 1995, during presentation of the United States' initial report under article 40 of the *Covenant*, the Human Rights Committee expressed the opinion that the reservation was invalid.[331] In its General Comment on reservations, the Human Rights Committee said that it was contrary to customary law 'to execute pregnant women or children'. Consequently, any reservation to this effect would be inconsistent with the object and purpose of the *Covenant*.[332]

3.1.9 Delay or prevention of abolition

The sixth paragraph of article 6 points the *Covenant* in the direction of abolition of the death penalty. Like the reference to abolition at the beginning of paragraph 2, it was added by the Third Committee in the hopes of giving expression to a sentiment favourable to abolition, even if the drafters were reluctant to impose this as a binding obligation. Paragraph 6 is in a sense 'preambular' in nature, in that it is intended only to colour interpretation of the other normative provisions. Marc Bossuyt has described paragraph 6 as creating 'a strong presumption in favour of the abolition of the death penalty'.[333] By placing it within article 6 itself, the drafters not only set a goal for States parties in the future but also set a standard to be taken into account in the construction of the single explicit exception to the protection of the right to life.

Paragraph 6 gives the Human Rights Committee a licence to promote abolition of the death penalty, despite the fact that other provisions of article 6 seem

---

[329] UN Doc. CCPR/C/SR.225, para. 10. In 1990, by judgment of its Constitutional Court, Hungary eliminated the death penalty altogether: Ruling 23/1990 (X.31) AB, Constitutional Court of Hungary, Judgment of 24 October 1990, *Magyar Közlöny* (Official Gazette), 31 October 1991. See: Tibor Horvath, 'L'abolition de la peine de mort en Hongrie', [1992] 2 *Revue internationale de criminologie et de police technique* 167.

[330] Also: Algeria, 'Annual Report of the Human Rights Committee', UN Doc. 53/40, para. 359.

[331] For our discussion on the United States reservations, see Chapter 2, above.

[332] *General Comment 24(51)*, para. 8.

[333] Marc J. Bossuyt, 'The Death Penalty in the "Travaux Préparatoires" of the International Covenant on Civil and Political Rights', in Daniel Prémont, ed., *Essais sur le concept de 'droit de vivre' en mémoire de Yougindra Khushalani*, Brussels: Bruylant, 1988, pp. 251–265, at pp. 264–265.

to authorize or at least tolerate its continued use. In accordance with paragraph 6, during consideration of the periodic reports of States parties it will insist upon information concerning measures to limit or abolish the death penalty. This may be particularly effective in the many States where the death penalty is abolished *de facto* but not *de jure*, the public embarrassment of submission of periodic reports being an incentive to complete the process of abolition. For example, the Republic of Korea, in its initial report, indicated that it was not prepared to abolish the death penalty but that it was in the course of revising its criminal legislation in order to limit the crimes subject to the death penalty, 'in consideration of . . . the international trend toward the abolition of the death penalty'.[334] Libya announced, in its second periodic report, that its objective is to abolish the death penalty.[335]

3.1.10 *Extradition, expulsion, deportation and the death penalty*

The *Covenant* says nothing explicitly about whether States parties may extradite, expel or deport individuals who may be facing the threat of capital punishment. By contrast, the *Convention Against Torture* provides that 'no State Party shall expel, return ("*refouler*") or extradite a person to another State where there are substantial grounds for believing that he would be in danger of being subjected to torture'.[336] Several cases have come before the Human Rights Committee involving extradition, expulsion and deportation in death penalty situations. In three Canadian applications, the Human Rights Committee took the view that, because capital punishment was not contrary to the *Covenant*, it was therefore not a breach to extradite fugitives to the United States where they would be subject to the death penalty.[337] Although it agrees that 'States parties must be mindful of their obligations to protect the right to life of individuals subject to their jurisdiction when exercising discretion as to whether or not to deport said individuals', it does not consider that the terms of article 6 require a State party to refrain from extraditing or deporting a person to a State that retains capital punishment.[338] Several dissenting opinions have developed the argument that a country that has already abolished capital punishment cannot apply it indirectly.[339]

---

[334] 'Initial Report of the Republic of Korea', UN Doc. CCPR/C/68/Add.1, paras. 101–109. See also: 'Second Periodic Report of New Zealand, including reports of Niue and Tokelau', UN Doc. CCPR/C/37/Add.8, UN Doc. CCPR/C/37/Add.11 and 12, UN Doc. CCPR/C/SR. 888–891.
[335] 'Second Periodic Report of Libyan Arab Jamahiriya', UN Doc. CCPR/C/28/Add.16, para. 19.
[336] *Convention Against Torture and Other Cruel, Inhuman or Degrading Treatment or Punishment*, (1987) 1465 UNTS 85, art. 3.
[337] *Kindler* v. *Canada* (No. 470/1991); *Ng* v. *Canada*; *Cox* v. *Canada* (No. 539/1993).
[338] *A. R. J.* v. *Australia* (No. 692/1996), UN Doc. CCPR/C/60/D/692/1996, para. 6.13.
[339] *Kindler* v. *Canada* (No. 470/1991); *Cox v. Canada* (No. 539/1993).

According to the Committee's jurisprudence, a person may not be extradited, expelled or deported to a country where there is a 'necessary and foreseeable' threat that the *Covenant* will be violated.[340] The Committee seems to consider that extradition or deportation to a State where an aspect of article 6 would be breached, for example where the death penalty is mandatory for a given crime, would in itself constitute a breach of article 6. For these purposes, it is relevant that a State may have ratified the *Second Optional Protocol* to the *Covenant*.[341] Two dissenting members of the Committee, Eckart Klein and David Kretzmer, have expressed the view that expulsion from Australia to Malaysia, where a person could be subject to mandatory imposition of the death penalty for possession of a relatively small quantity of heroin, constituted a breach of article 6 of the *Covenant*.[342] But the potential violation of article 6 by Malaysia is unclear in their reasons, which seem to imply that the violation of article 6 is the death penalty itself, a claim that appears to run against the text of paragraph 6§2. A third member, Martin Scheinin, while stating that he agreed with the other two, said it was article 7 that would be violated.[343] Here, Scheinin seemed to be indicating that article 7 may neutralize the tolerance of the death penalty found in article 6.[344]

During presentation of periodic reports, the Committee has expressed appreciation that States refuse to extradite without assurances the death penalty will not be carried out.[345]

3.2 Cruel, inhuman and degrading treatment or punishment (article 7) and conditions on 'death row' (article 10)

Article 7 of the *Covenant* addresses torture and inhuman treatment or punishment. Most interpreters would consider that, while article 7, standing alone, might prohibit capital punishment, the recognition of capital punishment as an exception to the right to life also applies implicitly to the prohibition of inhuman treatment. Nevertheless, article 7 is of considerable relevance to the practice of the death penalty. For example, it applies to the 'death row phenomenon',

---

[340] *T.* v. *Australia* (No. 706/1996), UN Doc. CCPR/C/61/D/706/1996, para. 5.3; *A. R. J.* v. *Australia* para. 6.8.

[341] *T.* v. *Australia*, para. 8.4.

[342] *Ibid.*, Individual opinion by Committee members Eckart Klein and David Kretzmer (dissenting).

[343] *Ibid.*, Individual opinion by Committee member Martin Scheinin (dissenting).

[344] Similar to the argument of Judge De Meyer of the European Court of Human Rights in *Soering* v. *United Kingdom and Germany*, 7 July 1989, Series A, No. 161, 11 EHRR 439, p. 51, and of Hélio Bicudo of the Inter-American Commission of Human Rights in *Lamey et al.* v. *Jamaica* (Case Nos. 11.826, 11.843, 11.846, 11.847), Report No. 49/01, 4 April 2001 and *Knights* v. *Grenada* (Case No. 12.028), Report No. 47/01, 4 April 2001.

[345] 'Annual Report of the Human Rights Committee, 1997', UN Doc. 52/40, para. 313 (Portugal).

that is, the inhuman treatment resulting from the special conditions on death row [346] and the often prolonged wait for executions or where the execution itself is carried out in a way that inflicts gratuitous suffering. Also, where confessions are extracted as a result of treatment constituting a violation of article 7, in death penalty cases, the Committee has considered this to breach the right to a fair trial (article 14 together with article 6), and to justify a remedy entailing release.[347] Finally, the method of implementation of capital punishment must not cause unnecessary or superfluous suffering.

3.2.1 The 'death row phenomenon'

Prolonged delay following sentence of death prior to execution may be deemed a form of cruel, inhuman and degrading treatment or punishment. In 'death row phenomenon' cases, the European Court of Human Rights as well as several prominent constitutional courts have taken the view that there is a violation of fundamental human rights.[348] The Human Rights Committee's General Comment 20(44) on article 7 of the *Covenant* states that 'when the death penalty is applied by the State party . . . it must be carried out in such a way as to cause the least possible physical pain and mental suffering'.[349] However, the Committee has refused to construe article 7 of the *Covenant* as a prohibition of lengthy detention prior to execution, taking the view that, because article 6 points towards abolition as a goal, it is preferable for death row inmates to be kept alive as long as possible. It says that it cannot adopt an approach to the *Covenant* whereby a State fulfils its obligations by executing somebody. A minority of the Committee, consisting of perhaps one-third of its members (although this varies somewhat as the membership changes), takes the view that the 'death row phenomenon' is a breach of article 7.

The first major case before the Committee to raise the 'death row phenomenon' was that of Earl Pratt and Ivan Morgan. Pratt and Morgan were arrested in 1977 for murder and have been held in custody ever since. Their conviction and sentence to death on 15 January 1979 was followed by a long saga of appeals and other remedies, to domestic courts, the Judicial Committee of the Privy Council and international human rights bodies.[350] Although the Human Rights Committee concluded there had been a violation of articles 7 and 14 of the *Covenant*, it dismissed the argument based on the death row phenomenon. The Views were released in April 1989, only a few months before the

[346] For example, *Francis* v. *Jamaica* (No. 320/1988), para. 12.4. [347] *Berry* v. *Jamaica*.
[348] *Soering* v. *United Kingdom and Germany*, *Catholic Commission for Justice and Peace in Zimbabwe* v. *Attorney-General et al.*; *Pratt* et al. v. *Attorney General for Jamaica* et al.; *Andrews* v. *United States* (Case No. 11.139), Report No. 57/96, 6 December 1996; *United States* v. *Burns*, [2001] 1 SCR 283.
[349] *General Comment 20(44)*, UN Doc. CCPR/C/21/Rev.1/Add.3, para. 6.
[350] The procedural history of *Pratt and Morgan* is discussed in some detail in Chapter 8.

European Court of Human Rights rendered its judgment in *Soering* v. *United Kingdom*. In contrast to the European body, the Human Rights Committee declared that '[i]n principle prolonged judicial proceedings do not *per se* constitute cruel, inhuman or degrading treatment, even if they can be a source of mental strain for the convicted prisoners. However, the situation could be otherwise in cases involving capital punishment and an assessment of the circumstances of each case would be necessary.'[351]

The duration of detention on death row was again challenged, in 1992, in *Barrett and Sutcliffe* v. *Jamaica*. The Committee confirmed its conclusions in *Pratt and Morgan*, refining somewhat the statements in the earlier decision, and declared:

> that prolonged judicial proceedings do not *per se* constitute cruel, inhuman and degrading treatment, even if they may be a source of mental strain and tension for detained persons. This also applies to appeal and review proceedings in cases involving capital punishment, although an assessment of the particular circumstances of each case would be called for. In States whose judicial system provides for a review of criminal convictions and sentences, an element of delay between the lawful imposition of a sentence of death and the exhaustion of available remedies is inherent in the review of the sentence; thus, even prolonged periods of detention under a severe custodial regime on death row cannot generally be considered to constitute cruel, inhuman or degrading treatment if the convicted person is merely availing himself of appellate remedies. A delay of ten years between the judgment of the Court of Appeal and that of the Judicial Committee of the Privy Council is disturbingly long. However, the evidence before the Committee indicates that the Court of Appeal rapidly produced its written judgment and that the ensuing delay in petitioning the Judicial Committee is largely attributable to the authors.[352]

But, unlike *Pratt and Morgan*, the Committee was no longer unanimous. Christine Chanet refused to accept the blame being placed on Barrett and Sutcliffe for the length of their detention on death row. 'The conduct of the person concerned with regard to the exercise of remedies ought to be measured against the stakes involved', she wrote. 'Without being at all cynical, I consider that the author cannot be expected to hurry up in making appeals so that he can be executed more rapidly.' Citing *Soering*, Chanet concluded: 'A very long period on death row, even if partially due to the failure of the condemned prisoner to exercise a remedy, cannot exonerate the State party from its obligations under article 7 of the *Covenant*.'[353]

---

[351] *Pratt and Morgan* v. *Jamaica*, para. 13.6.

[352] *Ibid.*, para. 8.4; also *Reid* v. *Jamaica* (No. 250/1987), para. 11.6 (in which the Committee said such allegations were 'insufficiently substantiated'); *Martin* v. *Jamaica* , para. 12.2; *Griffiths* v. *Jamaica*, para. 7.4.

[353] *Barrett and Sutcliffe* v. *Jamaica*, p. 254 (*per* Chanet). Christine Chanet's dissenting views were later described, by Chief Justice Gubbay of the Zimbabwe Supreme Court, as being 'more plausible and persuasive': *Catholic Commission for Justice and Peace in Zimbabwe* v. *Attorney-General, Zimbabwe, et al.*

The Committee revisited the issue in *Kindler*, recalling its earlier jurisprudence.[354] It noted that it had paid 'careful regard' to the *Soering* judgment of the European Court of Human Rights, but stressed the many distinctions between the two cases, particularly the age and mental state of the offenders and the prison conditions in Pennsylvania: 'important facts leading to the judgment of the European Court are distinguishable on material points from the facts in the present case.'[355] Kurt Herndl[356] and Waleed Sadi penned an individual opinion, saying they agreed with the Committee's established jurisprudence, whereby 'the so-called 'death row phenomenon' does not *per se* constitute cruel, inhuman and degrading treatment, even if prolonged judicial proceedings can be a source of mental strain for the convicted prisoners.[357] In early 1994, the Committee debated the implications of the Privy Council decision in *Pratt and Morgan*.[358] It also held a meeting with the Solicitor General of Jamaica to discuss the growing number of pending death row cases.

In *Simms* v. *Jamaica*, the Committee declared a 'death row phenomenon' petition to be inadmissible, in light of its 'established jurisprudence', but added that 'prolonged detention on death row does not in itself constitute cruel and inhuman treatment *in the absence of some further compelling circumstances*'. The Committee expressly cited the Privy Council's judgment in *Pratt and Morgan*, noting that it conflicted with its own established case law.[359] That there might be an evolution in the Committee's thinking became more apparent in 1995. In *Shalto* v. *Trinidad*, the Committee ruled that a four-year delay between reversal by the Court of Appeal and a new trial constituted a breach of articles 9§3 and 14§3(c) of the *Covenant*, although there was no violation of articles 6 or 7. But, in light of the fact that Shalto had spent sixteen years in prison, the Committee recommended his early release from prison as an appropriate remedy under the circumstances.[360] In *Francis* v. *Jamaica*, in which Views were issued at the Committee's July 1995 session, the Committee concluded that a thirteen-year delay by the Court of Appeal in issuing a written judgment was, of course, attributable to the State party. 'Whereas the psychological tension created by prolonged detention on death row may affect persons in different degrees, the evidence before the Committee in this case, including the author's confused

---

[354] *Kindler* v. *Canada* (No. 470/1991), para. 15.2.   [355] *Ibid.*, para. 15.3.

[356] At the time Herndl issued his individual opinion in *Kindler*, he was also Austrian ambassador to Canada. There is nothing in the public record to indicate that he declared this potential conflict of interest to counsel for the alleged victim, or that his recusal was considered by the Committee.

[357] *Kindler* v. *Canada* (No. 470/1991), p. 315. See also the concurring views of Herndl and Sadi in *Cox* v. *Canada* (No. 539/1993).

[358] *Pratt* et al. v. *Attorney General for Jamaica* et al. See: Markus G. Schmidt, 'The Complementarity of the Covenant and the European Convention on Human Rights – Recent Developments', in D. H. Harris, ed., *The ICCPR – Its Impact on United Kingdom Law*, Oxford: Oxford University Press, 1995, pp. 635–665, at p. 652.

[359] *Simms* v. *Jamaica*, para. 6.5 (emphasis added). Also: *Berry* v. *Jamaica* , para. 11.8.

[360] *Shalto* v. *Trinidad* (No. 447/1991), UN Doc. CCPR/C/53/D/447/1991.

and incoherent correspondence with the Committee, indicates that his mental health seriously deteriorated during incarceration on death row.'[361]

Despite these hints that its views were evolving, the Committee did not change its mind on the 'death row phenomenon'. In April 1996, in *Errol Johnson* v. *Jamaica*, both the majority[362] and the minority[363] of the Committee staked out their positions. Johnson had been held on death row, in the appalling conditions of Jamaica's St. Catherine's Prison, for more than eleven years. Nevertheless, while the length of pre-execution detention was a matter of 'serious concern',[364] there were no 'compelling circumstances' advanced in the communication 'that would turn Mr. Johnson's detention into a violation of articles 7 and 10'.[365] The Committee said it was aware its jurisprudence on the subject of prolonged detention on death row had given rise to controversy, and it wished to set out its position in detail. The majority said that three relevant factors had to be considered:

> (a) The Covenant does not prohibit the death penalty, though it subjects its use to severe restrictions. As detention on death row is a necessary consequence of imposing the death penalty, no matter how cruel, degrading and inhuman it may appear to be, it cannot, of itself, be regarded as a violation of articles 7 and 10 of the Covenant.
>
> (b) While the Covenant does not prohibit the death penalty, the Committee has taken the view, which has been reflected in the Second Optional Protocol to the Covenant, that article 6 'refers generally to abolition in terms which strongly suggest that abolition is desirable'. (See General Comment 6[16] of 27 July 1982; also see Preamble to the Second Optional Protocol to the Covenant Aiming at the Abolition of the Death Penalty.) Reducing recourse to the death penalty may therefore be seen as one of the objects and purposes of the Covenant.
>
> (c) The provisions of the Covenant must be interpreted in the light of the Covenant's objects and purposes (article 31 of the Vienna Convention on the Law of Treaties). As one of these objects and purposes is to promote reduction in the use of the death penalty, an interpretation of a provision in the Covenant that may encourage a State party that retains the death penalty to make use of that penalty should, where possible, be avoided.[366]

The majority of the Committee reasoned that, because of these factors, if a State party executes a condemned prisoner after time has elapsed on death row, it does not breach the Covenant, 'whereas if it refrains from doing so, it will violate the

---

[361] *Francis* v. *Jamaica* (No. 320/1988), para. 9.2. See also: *Stephens* v. *Jamaica* (No. 373/1989), UN Doc. CCPR/C/55/D/373/1989.

[362] Shortly after the views in *Johnson* were issued, the Committee adopted a practice of naming those members present who participate in a case. But it is not possible to specify exactly how many of the twelve non-dissenting members of the Committee signed the majority opinion, or who they were.

[363] Christine Chanet, Prafullachandra N. Bhagwati, Marco T. Bruni Celli, Fausto Pocar, Julio Prado Vallejo and Francisco José Aguilar Urbina.

[364] *Errol Johnson* v. *Jamaica* (No. 588/1994), UN Doc. CCPR/C/56/D/588/1994, paras. 8.1; also: *Forbes* v. *Jamaica*, para. 7.4.

[365] *Ibid.*, para. 8.6.   [366] *Ibid.*, para. 8.2.

Covenant'. Setting a cut-off date – the approach of the Judicial Committee of the Privy Council – only exacerbates the problem, giving the State party a clear deadline for executing a person if it is to avoid violating its obligations under the Covenant, says the majority of the Committee. The fear is that, by focusing on the time factor *per se*, 'States parties which seek to avoid overstepping the deadline will be tempted to look to the decisions of the Committee in previous cases so as to determine what length of detention on death row the Committee has found permissible in the past'.[367]

The second implication of making the time factor determinative, said the majority of the Committee, is that it encourages States to carry out executions as expeditiously as possible.

> This is not a message the Committee would wish to convey to States parties. Life on death row, harsh as it may be, is preferable to death. Furthermore, experience shows that delays in carrying out the death penalty can be the necessary consequence of several factors, many of which may be attributable to the State party. Sometimes a moratorium is placed on executions while the whole question of the death penalty is under review. At other times the executive branch of government delays executions even though it is not feasible politically to abolish the death penalty. The Committee would wish to avoid adopting a line of jurisprudence which weakens the influence of factors that may very well lessen the number of prisoners actually executed. It should be stressed that by adopting the approach that prolonged detention on death row cannot, per se, be regarded as cruel and inhuman treatment or punishment under the Covenant, the Committee does not wish to convey the impression that keeping condemned prisoners on death row for many years is an acceptable way of treating them. It is not. However, the cruelty of the death row phenomenon is first and foremost a function of the permissibility of capital punishment under the Covenant.[368]

In conclusion, the majority noted that, in dismissing arguments based on the length of detention on death row, it does not mean to imply that other circumstances connected with detention on death row may not amount to cruel, inhuman and degrading treatment or punishment. 'The jurisprudence of the Committee has been that where compelling circumstances of the detention are substantiated, that detention may constitute a violation of the Covenant', it says.[369]

Six of the Committee's eighteen members signed one of three dissenting opinions. The most moderate of the three dissents was set out by four members, Prafullachandra N. Bhagwati, Marco T. Bruni Celli, Fausto Pocar and Julio Prado Vallejo, who said that they agreed with the proposition that prolonged detention on death row was not *per se* contrary to article 7. They felt, however, that the position taken in *Johnson* was simply too rigid, in that it would not allow a case-by-case assessment of whether prolonged detention on death row constitutes

---

[367] *Ibid.*, para. 8.3.   [368] *Ibid.*, para. 8.4.   [369] *Ibid.*, para. 8.5.

cruel, inhuman or degrading treatment within the meaning of article 7. The four members associated themselves with the two other individual opinions, particularly that of Christine Chanet, who reiterated the position that she had initially set out in 1992, in *Barrett and Sutcliffe*, when she was the only member to recognise the 'death row phenomenon'.[370]

In *Johnson*, Chanet said it was wrong to postulate that awaiting death is preferable to death itself, because it was not exceptional to find persons suffering from incurable illness who opt for immediate death 'rather than the psychological torture of a death foretold'. Moreover, the Committee was overly subjective to anticipate that recognition of the 'death row phenomenon' would encourage States to proceed with a hasty execution. The analysis, said Chanet, should be based on 'consideration of humanity' at the 'strictly legal level of the Covenant itself'. The issue, then, is not what is preferable for the condemned person. Chanet said she believed that being on death row cannot in itself be considered cruel, inhuman or degrading treatment. However, it must be assumed that the psychological torture inherent in waiting for execution must be reduced to the minimum length of time necessary for the exercise of remedies. Because the *Covenant* does not prohibit capital punishment, 'its imposition cannot be prohibited, but it is incumbent on the Human Rights Committee to ensure that the provisions of the Covenant as a whole are not violated on the occasion of the execution of the sentence'. Chanet added that such factors as the physical and psychological treatment of the prisoner, age and state of heath were all relevant factors in the assessment of whether there had been a violation of articles 7 and 10.[371]

Francisco José Aguilar Urbina began his individual opinion with the assertion that 'capital punishment in itself constitutes inhuman, cruel and degrading punishment', although he also said he agreed that the *Covenant* does not prohibit the death penalty. He echoed the approach of Christine Chanet, saying he disagreed with the majority when it said it was 'preferable for a condemned person to endure being on death row, regardless in any case of the length of time spent there'. Like Chanet, he said it was wrong to speculate about how Jamaica would react to the Committee's jurisprudence, especially in light of the fact that for fifteen years it had failed to respect its obligation under the *Covenant* to submit periodic reports. He noted that States parties were under an obligation to 'minimize the psychological torture involved in awaiting execution'.[372]

---

[370] *Errol Johnson* v. *Jamaica*, Individual opinion by Committee members Prafullachandra N. Bhagwati, Marco T. Bruni Celli, Fausto Pocar and Julio Prado Vallejo.

[371] *Ibid.*, Individual opinion by Committee member Christine Chanet.

[372] *Ibid.*, Individual opinion by Committee member Francisco José Aguilar Urbina. See also: *Uton Lewis* v. *Jamaica*, Individual opinion of Committee member Francisco José Aguilar Urbina; *Spence* v. *Jamaica* (No. 559/1994), UN Doc. CCPR/C/57/D/599/1994, Individual opinion of Committee member Francisco José Aguilar Urbina; *Hylton* v. *Jamaica* (No. 600/1994), UN Doc. CCPR/C/57/D/600/1994, Individual opinion of Committee member Francisco José Aguilar Urbina.

The Committee returned to the point in 1997, in two cases involving sixteen and eighteen years on death row in Port of Spain, Trinidad, periods that it described as 'unprecedented and a matter of serious concern'.[373] Two new members of the Committee had joined the dissenters, Pilar Gaitan de Pombo and Maxwell Yalden, but because of its changing composition they still only numbered six as against ten for the majority.[374] The arguments were essentially the same as those in *Johnson* and since then the Committee has stuck unwaveringly to the majority position by which delayed detention on death row does not *per se*, in the absence of 'compelling circumstances', constitute cruel, inhuman and degrading treatment.[375]

But what are 'compelling circumstances'? In one case, the petitioner submitted that 'as a result of judicial delays, the lack of proper legal representation and his confinement on death row, his uncertainty and distress intensified; on that basis, he claimed that he was subjected to cruel, inhuman and degrading treatment'. Two dissenting members considered this enough to substantiate the claim, at least for purposes of admissibility,[376] but the majority disagreed.[377] In death row cases where detention under harsh conditions is extremely protracted,[378] where it is accompanied by serious medical consequences[379] or lack of psychiatric treatment[380] or where there is evidence of beatings and

---

[373] *LaVende* v. *Trinidad and Tobago*, para. 5.2; *Bickaroo* v. *Trinidad and Tobago* (No. 555/1993), UN Doc. CCPR/C/61/D/555/1993, para. 5.2.

[374] *Bickaroo* v. *Trinidad and Tobago*, Individual opinion by Committee member Fausto Pocar, approved by Mr. Prafullachandra N. Bhagwati, Ms. Christine Chanet, Ms. Pilar Gaitan de Pombo, Mr. Julio Prado Vallejo and Mr. Maxwell Yalden regarding the cases of *LaVende* and *Bickaroo*. However, by the time of *Bickaroo* the Committee was publishing the names of all members who participated in its findings. The following members of the Committee (as of November 1997) subscribed to the Committee's position on the inadmissibility of the 'death row phenomenon': Nisuke Ando, Thomas Buergenthal, Lord Colville, Omran El Shafei, Elizabeth Evatt, Eckart Klein, David Kretzmer, Cecilia Medina Quiroga, Martin Scheinin and Abdallah Zakhia.

[375] *Hylton* v. *Jamaica* (No. 600/1994), para. 8; *Spence* v. *Jamaica*, para. 7.1; *Sterling* v. *Jamaica* (No. 598/1994), UN Doc. CCPR/C/57/D/598/1994, para. 8.1; *Uton Lewis* v. *Jamaica*, para. 6.9; *Adams* v. *Jamaica*, para. 8.1; *Reynolds* v. *Jamaica* (No. 587/1994), UN Doc. CCPR/C/59/D/587/1994, para. 6.3; *McLawrence* v. *Jamaica*, para. 5.3; *Patrick Taylor* v. *Jamaica*, para. 6.3; *Edwards* v. *Jamaica*, paras. 5.3 and 8.2; *Williams* v. *Jamaica*, para. 6.4; *McIntosh* v. *Jamaica*, para. 6.2; *Samuel Thomas* v. *Jamaica*, para. 5.3; *Jones* v. *Jamaica*, para. 6.8; *Deidrick* v. *Jamaica* (No. 619/1995), UN Doc. CCPR/C/62/D/619/1995, para. 6.2; *Desmond Taylor* v. *Jamaica*, para. 7.4; *Levy* v. *Jamaica*, para. 6.5; *Marshall* v. *Jamaica*, para. 5.7; *McCordie Morrison* v. *Jamaica*, para. 6.6; *Chung* v. *Jamaica*, para. 6.1; *Daley* v. *Jamaica*, para. 7.6; *Hixford Morrisson* v. *Jamaica*, para. 6.5; *Smart* v. *Trinidad and Tobago*, para. 6.2; *Finn* v. *Jamaica*, para. 6.5; *Forbes* v. *Jamaica*, para. 7.4; *Colin Johnson* v. *Jamaica*, para. 8.1; *Barrington Campbell* v. *Jamaica*, para. 7.1; *Morgan and Williams* v. *Jamaica*, para. 6.3; *Pennant* v. *Jamaica*, para. 8.5; *Nicholas Henry* v. *Jamaica*, para. 7.2; *Amore* v. *Jamaica*, para. 6.3; *Bennett* v. *Jamaica*, para. 6.7; *Brown* v. *Jamaica*, para. 6.12; *Gonzales* v. *Trinidad and Tobago*, para. 5.3; *Samuel Thomas* v. *Jamaica* (No. 614/1995), para. 6.4; *Leehong* v. *Jamaica*, para. 6.5; *Gallimore* v. *Jamaica*, para. 7.3.

[376] *Samuel Thomas* v. *Jamaica* (No. 532/1993), Individual opinion by Messrs. Fausto Pocar and Rajsoomer Lallah.

[377] *Ibid.*, para. 5.3.   [378] *Edwards* v. *Jamaica*, para. 8.3

[379] *Henry and Douglas* v. *Jamaica*, para. 9.5; *Brown* v. *Jamaica*, para. 6.13; *Whyte* v. *Jamaica*, para. 9.4. See also: 'Annual Report of the Human Rights Committee, 1998', UN Doc. 53/40, para. 458.

[380] *Williams* v. *Jamaica*, para. 6.5.

destruction of belongings by jailers,[381] the Committee tends to conclude there has been a violation of article 7, although there are exceptions where it only finds a breach of article 10§1.[382] As for harsh conditions on death row *per se*, these are dealt with under article 10§1.

The Committee has held that 'compelling circumstances' are not the same as 'deplorable conditions of detention' on death row.[383] The exact legal significance of this point is difficult to grasp, as the Committee regularly concludes that 'deplorable conditions of detention' on death row are a violation of articles 7 and 10§1 of the *Covenant*.[384] In its comments on Japan's third periodic report, the Committee also expressed concern with conditions of detention on death row, citing undue restrictions on visitors and correspondence, as well as the fact that families of offenders were not informed of execution dates.[385] In numerous decisions, the Committee has condemned the deplorable conditions of detention in Jamaica's St. Catherine's District Prison, including confinement to unfurnished cells for most of the day, lack of mattresses, sharing of mattresses, generally unsanitary conditions, use of slop pails as toilets, infestations of ants, cockroaches, other insects and rats, unpalatable food, lack of natural light, enforced darkness, inadequate ventilation, proximity to sewage pipes, no potable water, mentally ill cellmates, isolation from other prisoners, denial of visitors, no access to recreational facilities, books, work or education, and lack of medical or dental treatment and facilities for the disabled.[386] The Committee

---

[381] *Collins* v. *Jamaica* (No. 240/1987), paras. 8.6–8.7; *Francis* v. *Jamaica* (No. 320/1988), para. 12.4; *Bailey* v. *Jamaica* (No. 334/1988), para. 9.3; *Hylton* v. *Jamaica* (No. 407/1990), para. 9.3; *Raphael Thomas* v. *Jamaica* (No. 321/1988), UN Doc. A/49/40, Vol. II, p. 1, para. 9.2; *Sterling* v. *Jamaica*, paras. 2.2–2.3, 3.2 and 8.2; *Spence* v. *Jamaica*, paras. 3.2 and 7.2; *Reynolds* v. *Jamaica* (No. 587/1994), paras. 10.2–10.4; *Walker and Richards* v. *Jamaica*, para. 8.1; *Young* v. *Jamaica*, para. 5.2; *McTaggart* v. *Jamaica*, para. 8.7; *Chung* v. *Jamaica*, para. 8.2; *Jones* v. *Jamaica*, para. 9.4; *Deidrick* v. *Jamaica*, para. 9.3; *Everton Morrison* v. *Jamaica*, para. 23.3; *Leslie* v. *Jamaica*, para. 9.2; *Whyte* v. *Jamaica*, para. 9.4; *Nicholas Henry* v. *Jamaica*, para. 7.3; *Colin Johnson* v. *Jamaica*, para. 8.1.

[382] *Marshall* v. *Jamaica*, para. 6.7.

[383] *Levy* v. *Jamaica*, para. 6.5; *Morgan and Williams* v. *Jamaica*, para. 6.3; *Marshall* v. *Jamaica*, para. 5.7.

[384] *Francis* v. *Jamaica* (No. 320/1988), para. 12.4. See also: *Raphael Thomas* v. *Jamaica*, para. 9.2; *Bailey* v. *Jamaica* (No. 334/1988), para. 9.3; *Hylton* v. *Jamaica*, para. 9.3; *Berry* v. *Jamaica*, para. 11.2 (violation of article 10 but not article 7).

[385] 'Comments on the Third Periodic Report of Japan', UN Doc. CCPR/C/79/Add.28, para. 12.

[386] *Francis* v. *Jamaica* (No. 320/1988), para. 12.4; *Bailey* v. *Jamaica* (No. 334/1988), para. 9.3; *Raphael Thomas* v. *Jamaica*, para. 9.2; *Hylton* v. *Jamaica* (No. 407/1990), para. 9.3; *Berry* v. *Jamaica*, para. 11.2; *Kelly* v. *Jamaica* (No. 253/1987), para. 3.8; *Collins* v. *Jamaica* (No. 240/1987), paras. 8.6–8.7; *Uton Lewis* v. *Jamaica*, para. 10.4; *Spence* v. *Jamaica*, paras. 3.2 and 7.2.; *Henry and Douglas* v. *Jamaica*, para. 9.5; *Edwards* v. *Jamaica*, para. 8.3; *Patrick Taylor* v. *Jamaica*, para. 8.1; *McTaggart* v. *Jamaica*, paras. 8.6–87; *McLeod* v. *Jamaica*, para. 6.4; *Deidrick* v. *Jamaica*, para. 9.3; *Shaw* v. *Jamaica*, para. 7.2; *Desmond Taylor* v. *Jamaica*, para. 7.4; *Yasseen and Thomas* v. *Guyana*, para. 7.6; *Daley* v. *Jamaica*, para. 7.6; *Finn* v. *Jamaica*, para. 9.3; *Everton Morrison* v. *Jamaica*, para. 23.3; *Perkins* v. *Jamaica*, para. 11.7; *Whyte* v. *Jamaica*, para. 9.4; *Leslie* v. *Jamaica*, para. 9.2; *Morgan and Williams* v. *Jamaica*, para. 7.2; *Pennant* v. *Jamaica*, para. 8.4; *Forbes* v. *Jamaica*, para. 7.5; *Nicholas Henry* v. *Jamaica*, para. 7.3; *McCordie Morrison* v. *Jamaica*, para. 8.2; *Barrington Campbell* v. *Jamaica*, para. 7.2; *Marshall* v. *Jamaica*, para. 6.7; *Colin Johnson* v. *Jamaica*, para. 8.2; *Levy* v. *Jamaica*, para. 7.4; *Bennett* v. *Jamaica*,

generally notes that these allegations have gone generally uncontested by Jamaica. Trinidad and Tobago has fared somewhat better before the Committee because it has provided detailed refutation of allegations,[387] although when uncontested by the State party the Committee has found article 10§1 to be violated by degrading prison conditions (crowded cells, poor lighting, inedible food).[388] The Committee considers it important that petitioners demonstrate they are specifically and personally affected by the conditions.[389]

The Standard Minimum Rules for the Treatment of Prisoners[390] are the international human rights reference for conditions of detention, and the Committee has cited them as a benchmark for the application of article 10. For the Human Rights Committee, 'these are minimum requirements which the Committee considered should always be observed, even if economic or budgetary conditions may make compliance with these obligations difficult'.[391] But the Committee has not cited the Rules in death penalty cases and one member, Nisuke Ando, has written that while they are 'desirable' then cannot be considered 'binding norms of international law'.[392]

Where a death row inmate was killed by guards in the aftermath of a prison disturbance, the Committee concluded that it had failed to take adequate measures to protect his life, constituting a violation of article 6§1.[393] Conditions on death row may also raise issues relating to article 17. In *Whyte v. Jamaica*, the Committee dismissed as inadmissible complaints that a death row inmate's personal belongings and legal papers, including trial transcript and correspondence with counsel, had been burned by prison guards, and that prison authorities had failed to deliver a new set of documents sent by counsel.[394]

The Committee seemed to contradict its traditional position in a case involving an individual who was sentenced to death for crimes committed while under the age of eighteen, and who had spent eight years on death row: 'In the circumstances, since the author of this communication was sentenced to

para. 10.8; *Brown v. Jamaica*, para. 6.13; *Hamilton v. Jamaica* (No. 616/1995), para. 8.2; *Leehong v. Jamaica*, para. 9.2; *Bailey v. Jamaica* (No. 709/1996), Individual opinion of Ms Elizabeth Evatt, co-signed by Ms Pilar Gaitin de Pombo, Ms Cecilia Medina Quiroga and Mr. Maxwell Yalden; *Gallimore v. Jamaica*, para. 7.1.

[387] *Chadee et al v. Trinidad and Tobago*. But see the dissenting views of Martin Scheinin on this point. Also: *Pinto v. Trinidad and Tobago*, para. 7.

[388] *Neptune v. Trinidad and Tobago*, para. 9.1; *Henry v. Trinidad and Tobago*, para. 7.3.

[389] *Daley v. Jamaica*, para. 7.6; *Patrick Taylor v. Jamaica*, para. 8.1; *Desmond Taylor v. Jamaica*, para. 7.4.

[390] ESC Res. 663 C (XXIV), 2076 (LXII).

[391] *Mukong v. Cameroon* (No. 458/1991), UN Doc. CCPR/C/51/D/458/1991, para. 9.3; *Potter v. New Zealand* (No. 632/1995), UN Doc. CCPR/C/60/D/632/1995, para. 6.3.

[392] *Yasseen and Thomas v. Guyana*, Dissenting opinion of Nisuke Ando.

[393] *Burrell v. Jamaica*, para. 9.

[394] *Whyte v. Jamaica*, paras. 6.6–6.7. But see: *Whyte v. Jamaica*, Individual opinion by Mr. Martin Scheinin (dissenting); *Whyte v. Jamaica*, Individual opinion by Ms. Cecilia Medina Quiroga (dissenting), para. 2.

death in violation of article 6(5) of the Covenant, and the imposition of the death sentence upon him was thus void ab initio, his detention on death row constituted a violation of article 7 of the Covenant.'[395] Thus, detention on death row *per se*, in the absence of any particular information about conditions of detention or other 'compelling circumstances', was deemed a form of cruel, inhuman or degrading treatment. Although there is no explanation, presumably the Committee considered that its reasoning in *Johnson* did not apply because one of its premises, namely that imposition of the death penalty was not contrary to the *Covenant*, did not apply in the case of a child. David Kretzmar drafted concurring reasons by way of explanation. Although supporting the consistent jurisprudence of the majority of the Committee, Kretzmar conceded that a person on death row 'suffers from the anxiety over his pending execution' and that this 'may certainly amount to cruel and inhuman punishment, especially when that detention lasts longer than necessary for the domestic legal proceedings required to correct the error involved in imposing the death sentence'.[396]

Although surely inadvertently, Kretzmar's explanation seems to get at the heart of the weakness in the Committee's position on the death row phenomenon. In effect, it takes the view that if the initial conviction and death sentence is flawed, as was the case with seventeen-year-old Clive Johnson, then it will recognise that his prolonged wait on death row constituted, absent any other circumstances, a form of cruel, inhuman and degrading treatment in breach of article 7. The Committee does not take the same position, however, in the case of adult offenders. But surely when an eighteen-year-old is sentenced to death following an unfair trial, in breach of article 14 and therefore of article 6§2 of the *Covenant*, his or her suffering on death row while awaiting execution is just as outrageous as that experienced by Clive Johnson who was, it should be added, of the age of majority while on death row. But the contradiction in the Committee's position on this point only leads to another aspect of incoherence. Why should the suffering on death row of a guilty person be any less unacceptable than that of an innocent one, or of a person who has been wrongfully convicted or wrongfully sentenced to death?

Within death rows there are often 'death cells' where those sentenced to execution are taken to spend their final days or hours. In *Francis v. Jamaica*, the Human Rights Committee described how the petitioner was placed in the death cell adjacent to the gallows for five days and subjected to round the clock surveillance. During this period, he was weighed in order to calculate the length of the rope that would be required for an efficient and successful 'drop'. Moreover, he was taunted by the executioner about the impending execution date, and could

---

[395] *Clive Johnson* v. *Jamaica* (No. 653/1995), para. 10.4.
[396] *Ibid.*, Individual opinion by member David Kretzmer (concurring).

hear the gallows being tested. For the Committee, these were among the factors in his case justifying the conclusion that he had been subject to torture or cruel, inhuman and degrading treatment or punishment.[397]

In another Jamaican case, Carlton Linton was transferred to the death cells in St. Catherine's Prison together with four of his colleagues. The warders began teasing Linton and the inmate in a neighbouring cell, describing in detail all of the stages in the execution. The Committee's Views even speak of a 'mock execution', although no details are provided. It concluded that this constituted cruel and inhuman treatment, within the meaning of article 7.[398]

As for the delay itself in the death cell, *Pennant* v. *Jamaica* concerned a two-week stay in a 'death cell' after reading of the warrant of execution. In the absence of a detailed explanation by the State party as to the reasons for this stay, the Committee said it was incompatible with the provisions of the *Covenant* 'to be treated with humanity' and accordingly contrary to article 7.[399] But in another case, a seventeen-day stay in the death cell awaiting execution, where all relevant procedures were respected, was not judged a breach of article 7.[400] In the case of *Pratt and Morgan*, a temporary stay of execution was granted by Jamaican authorities on 23 February 1988, but the accused were not notified for twenty hours, leaving them in the agony of imminent execution until forty-five minutes before the scheduled hanging. According to the Committee, from the time the stay of execution was granted until the time they were removed from their death cell Pratt and Morgan were subjected to cruel and inhuman treatment within the meaning of article 7.[401]

3.2.2 Method of execution

The norm prohibiting torture and inhuman treatment also applies to the method of execution. In *General Comment 20(44)*, issued on 7 April 1992, the Committee noted: 'when the death penalty is applied by a State party for the most serious crimes, it must not only be limited in accordance with article 6 but it must be carried out in such a way as to cause the least possible physical and mental suffering',[402] a reference to the method of capital punishment. Charles Ng successfully argued that use of the gas chamber might expose him to torture or cruel, inhuman and degrading treatment or punishment, in breach of article 7 of the

---

[397] *Francis* v. *Jamaica* (No. 606/1994), UN Doc. CCPR/C/54/D/606/1994, para. 9.2.

[398] *Linton* v. *Jamaica* (No. 255/1987), UN Doc. A/47/40, p. 12.

[399] *Pennant* v. *Jamaica*, para. 8.6.   [400] *Martin* v. *Jamaica*, para. 12.3.

[401] *Pratt and Morgan* v. *Jamaica*, para. 13.7.

[402] *General Comment 20(44)*, UN Doc. CCPR/C/21/Rev.1/Add.3, para. 6. The Committee also took the occasion to reiterate that 'article 6 of the Covenant refers generally to abolition of the death penalty in terms that strongly suggest that abolition is desirable'.

International Covenant on Civil and Political Rights. Ng's petition was directed against Canada, which had extradited him to California. The Committee agreed with him, concluding rather laconically:

> In the present case, the author has provided detailed information that execution by gas asphyxiation may cause prolonged suffering and agony and does not result in death as swiftly as possible, as asphyxiation by cyanide gas may take over ten minutes. The State party had the opportunity to refute these allegations on the facts; it has failed to do so. Rather, the State party has confined itself to arguing that in the absence of a norm of international law which expressly prohibits asphyxiation by cyanide gas, 'it would be interfering to an unwarranted degree with the internal laws and practices of the United States to refuse to extradite a fugitive to face the possible imposition of the death penalty by cyanide gas asphyxiation.'
>
> In the instant case and on the basis of the information before it, the Committee concludes that execution by gas asphyxiation, should the death penalty be imposed on the author, would not meet the test of 'least possible physical and mental suffering', and constitutes cruel and inhuman treatment, in violation of article 7 of the Covenant . . .
>
> The Committee need not pronounce itself on the compatibility, with article 7, of methods of execution other than that which is at issue in this case.[403]

The Committee noted that asphyxiation by cyanide gas may take more than ten minutes, and this suggests that it adopts the criterion of instantaneity. In fact, Canada apparently did contest the issue of the gas chamber on the facts, stating that 'none of the methods currently in use in the United States is of such a nature as to constitute a violation of the Covenant or any other norm of international law'.[404] Two members of the Committee, Andreas Mavrommatis and Waleed Sadi, dissented with the majority, stating that the evidence before the Committee did not justify a conclusion that execution by gas asphyxiation constituted cruel and inhuman treatment within the meaning of article 7:

> Every known method of judicial execution in use today, including execution by lethal injection, has come under criticism for causing prolonged pain or the necessity to have the process repeated. We do not believe that the Committee should look into such details in respect of execution such as whether acute pain of limited duration or less pain of longer duration is preferable and could be a criterion for a finding of violation of the Covenant.[405]

Mavromattis and Sadi added that '[a] method of execution such as death by stoning, which is intended to and actually inflicts prolonged pain and suffering, is contrary to article 7'.[406]

A similar opinion was expressed by Kurt Herndl, who said: 'To attempt to establish categories of methods of judicial executions, as long as such methods are not manifestly arbitrary and grossly contrary to the moral values of a democratic society, and as long as such methods are based on a uniformly applicable

---

[403] *Ng* v. *Canada*, paras. 16.3–16.5.　　[404] *Ibid.*, p. 213.　　[405] *Ibid.*, p. 209.　　[406] *Ibid.*

legislation adopted by democratic processes, is futile, as it is futile to attempt to quantify the pain and suffering of any human being subjected to capital punishment.'[407]

Fausto Pocar said he agreed that there was a violation of article 7 of the *Covenant*, because 'by definition, every execution of a sentence of death may be considered to constitute cruel and inhuman treatment within the meaning of article 7 of the Covenant'.[408] Francisco José Aguilar Urbina said that he too considered the death penalty as such to constitute cruel, inhuman and degrading treatment, in violation of article 7 of the *Covenant*.[409] Christine Chanet declared:

> As regards article 7, I share the Committee's conclusion that the provision has been violated in the present case. However, I consider that the Committee engages in questionable discussion when, in paragraph 16.3, it assesses the suffering caused by cyanide gas and takes into consideration the duration of the agony, which it deems unacceptable when it lasts for over ten minutes. Should it be concluded, conversely, that the Committee would find no violation of article 7 if the agony lasted nine minutes?[410]

And she concluded: 'By engaging in this debate, the Committee finds itself obliged to take positions that are scarcely compatible with its role as a body monitoring an international human rights instrument.'[411]

Turning to execution by lethal injection, in *Kindler* the Committee dismissed an argument that this violated article 7, but noted that the applicant had not adduced evidence.[412] Subsequently, in *Cox v. Canada*,[413] it rejected the argument by citing *Kindler*. Yet in *Cox* there was substantial evidence presented to the Committee of suffering during execution by injection. An affidavit, supplied by Professor Michael Radelet of the University of Florida, an authority on the subject, described several 'botched' executions using lethal injection. Canada had argued that death by lethal injection could not be inhuman, because it was the same method proposed by advocates of euthanasia.

---

[407] *Ibid.*, p. 214.   [408] *Ibid.*, p. 208.   [409] *Ibid.*, p. 218.   [410] *Ibid.*, p. 220.   [411] *Ibid.*

[412] *Kindler v. Canada* (No. 470/1991). The subject was discussed in some detail by Bertil Wennergren in his individual opinion in *Ng v. Canada*, p. 210: '[T]he State of California, in August 1992, enacted a statute law that enables an individual under sentence of death to choose lethal injection as the method of execution, in lieu of the gas chamber. The statute law went into effect on 1 January 1993. Two executions by lethal gas had taken place during 1992, approximately one year after the extradition of Mr. Ng. By amending its legislation in the way described above, the State of California joined twenty-two other States in the United States. The purpose of the legislative amendment was not, however, to eliminate an allegedly cruel and unusual punishment, but to forestall last-minute appeals by condemned prisoners who might argue that execution by lethal gas constitutes such punishment. Not that I consider execution by lethal injection acceptable either from a point of view of humanity, but – at least – it does not stand out as an unnecessarily cruel and inhuman method of execution, as does gas asphyxiation.'

[413] *Cox v. Canada* (No. 539/1993).

4

Towards abolition: the *Second Optional Protocol* and other developments

Abolitionist States were encouraged by the debate in 1957 surrounding adoption of the right to life provision of the *International Covenant on Civil and Political Rights*[1] in the Third Committee of the General Assembly. They quickly took the initiative in the General Assembly, even before the *Covenant* was formally adopted in 1966. Recognizing that there might be no short-term gain in terms of norms on the death penalty, it was essential to keep the issue on the agenda of the political bodies of the United Nations. The campaign began slowly, with an innocuous call for a study of the death penalty and of its effectiveness as a deterrent. The results of this research were submitted to an expert committee, which confirmed that modern science found little to redeem the death penalty. Fortified by this support, the resolutions in the General Assembly and the Economic and Social Council became more demanding, citing article 3 of the *Universal Declaration of Human Rights*[2] and implying that only when capital punishment was abolished would the right to life be truly assured.[3] In the early 1980s, the momentum of this patient activity coupled with a significant evolution in the domestic law of many States culminated in important legal developments.

In 1984, the United Nations Committee on Crime Prevention and Control (now the 'Commission')[4] drafted the 'Safeguards Guaranteeing Protection of the Rights of Those Facing the Death Penalty',[5] a document which was inspired in large part by articles 6, 14 and 15 of the *Civil Rights Covenant* but which went further, detailing the scope of the phrase 'most serious crimes' and adding new mothers and the insane to the categories of individuals upon whom the death

---

[1] (1976) 999 UNTS 171 (see Appendix 2, p. 380). The *travaux préparatoires* of article 6 of the *Covenant* are reviewed in Chapter 2 above.
[2] GA Res. 217 A (III), UN Doc. A/810.
[3] GA Res. 2393 (XXIII); GA Res. 2857 (XXVI).
[4] Roger S. Clark, *The United Nations Crime Prevention and Criminal Justice Program, Formulation of Standards and Efforts at Their Implementation*, Philadelphia: University of Pennsylvania Press, 1994, pp. 58–62.
[5] ESC Res. 1984/50 (see Appendix 8, p. 413). Subsequently endorsed by GA Res. 39/118.

penalty could never be carried out. The Congress on the Prevention of Crime and the Treatment of Offenders, held every five years, examined the death penalty and endorsed the 'Safeguards', as did the Economic and Social Council and the General Assembly. In 1988, the 'Safeguards' were themselves strengthened by a new resolution of the Committee on Crime Prevention and Control, which addressed additional matters, such as the prohibition of execution of the mentally handicapped.[6]

The heightened activity in the Committee on Crime Prevention and Control and in the Congress on the Prevention of Crime and the Treatment of Offenders did not create new treaty norms, in the strict sense, but it did elaborate various standards that may help to define customary norms. At the same time, however, other United Nations bodies, notably the Sub-Commission on Prevention of Discrimination and Protection of Minorities, drafted the *Second Optional Protocol to the International Covenant on Civil and Political Rights Aiming at the Abolition of the Death Penalty*.[7] This instrument was finally adopted by the General Assembly in 1989 and entered into force in July 1991, the fruit of the process that began in 1959 with the first resolutions on the death penalty adopted within the United Nations.

4.1 From 1959 to 1980: United Nations resolutions and reports

In 1959, Austria, Ceylon, Ecuador, Sweden, Venezuela, and Uruguay proposed a resolution in the General Assembly inviting the Economic and Social Council to begin a study on the question of capital punishment.[8] These countries, several of which had been prominent on the abolitionist side in the debate two years earlier at the time of the adoption of article 6 of the *Covenant*, managed to rally support from a spectrum of United Nations member States, including Ghana, India, Israel, Japan, Pakistan, the Philippines and the United Kingdom.

The proposed study was to be based on the relevant articles of the *Universal Declaration of Human Rights* and on article 6 of the draft covenant.[9] The Soviet Union and Poland challenged the resolution, arguing that capital punishment was a matter of domestic jurisdiction and that it should not be the subject of United Nations studies. Austria, Italy and others replied that, as the United Nations had addressed such issues as prostitution, traffic in narcotic drugs and punishment of genocide, it was also competent to study the question of capital punishment.

---

[6] ESC Res. 1989/64.　　[7] GA Res. 44/128 (see Appendix 4, pp. 397–401).
[8] UN Doc. A/C.3/L.767. The idea of such a study had originally been suggested by Sweden, during the 1957 debate on article 6 of the draft *Covenant*: UN Doc. A/C.3/SR.813.
[9] UN Doc. A/4250, para. 55.

There was also debate about whether the Social Commission (now known as the Commission for Social Development) or the Commission on Human Rights should take responsibility. Those favouring the Social Commission argued that capital punishment had nothing whatsoever to do with human rights.[10] In fact, the Social Commission had been marginally involved in the death penalty issue since the beginnings of the United Nations. In 1950, the functions of the International Penal and Penitentiary Commission, a body which had sporadically considered the death penalty since its origins in the nineteenth century,[11] were formally transferred to the Social Defence Section of the Social Commission.[12] However, the following year, the Social Commission decided to defer the question of 'capital and corporal punishment' for consideration at a later date,[13] apparently as the result of pressure from the United States, the United Kingdom and the Soviet Union.[14] Nor was the issue of capital punishment considered at the First United Nations Congress on the Prevention of Crime and the Treatment of Offenders, held in Geneva in 1955.[15]

A compromise was reached: the Commission on Human Rights would carry out the study in consultation with the Social Commission, leaving it to the Economic and Social Council to decide which Commission should address the issue first.[16] The amendment was accepted by the sponsors of the resolution, with some further modifications,[17] and subsequently adopted by the Third Committee[18] and the General Assembly.[19] The following spring, the Economic

---

[10] UN Doc. A/C.3/SR.939.

[11] Thorsten Sellin, 'Lionel Fox and the International Penal and Penitentiary Commission', in Manuel Lopez-Ray, Charles Germain, eds., *Studies in Penology Dedicated to the Memory of Sir Lionel Fox, C.B., M.C.,* The Hague: Martinus Nijhoff, 1964, p. 194: H. Röstad, 'The International Penal and Penitentiary Foundation and the Death Penalty', (1987) 58 *Revue internationale de droit pénal* 345; Roger S. Clark, 'Human Rights and the UN Committee on Crime Prevention and Control', (1989) 506 *Annals of the American Association of Political and Social Science* 68; William Clifford, 'The Committee on Crime Prevention and Control', (1978) 34 *International Review of Criminal Policy* 11.

[12] GA Res. 415 (V).

[13] 'United Nations Programme of Research and Study in the Field of the Prevention of Crime and the Treatment of Offenders', (1952) 1 *International Review of Criminal Policy* 21, §20.

[14] James Avery Joyce, *Capital Punishment, A World View,* New York: Thomas Nelson, 1961, p. 195.

[15] UN Doc. A/CONF/6/1.

[16] UN Doc. A/C.3/L.775, sponsored by Italy; UN Doc. A/4250, §58. The Italian amendment added a preambular paragraph: 'Recalling Economic and Social Council resolution 731F (XXVIII) on the future of the United Nations social defence programme' and, at the end of the operative paragraph, the phrase: 'and, as appropriate, be carried out in consultation with the Social Commission'.

[17] UN Doc. A/4250, para. 60; UN Doc. A/C.3/L.767/Rev. 1. The change was the addition in the preamble of a reference to ESC Res. 624B (XXII) on reports and studies in the field of human rights. At Sweden's suggestion, a further preambular paragraph was also added: '*Invites* the Economic and Social Council to request the Commission on Human Rights to undertake a study of the question of capital punishment, of the laws and practices relating thereto, and of the effects of capital punishment, and the abolition thereof, on the rate of criminality. The study should begin as soon as the work programme of the Commission permits and, as appropriate, be carried out in consultation with the Social Commission.'

[18] A/C.3/SR.940, by forty-three votes to one, with thirty abstentions.

[19] GA Res. 1396 (XIV), by fifty-seven votes to zero, with twenty-two abstentions, UN Doc. A/SR.841.

and Social Council requested the Secretary-General to prepare an analysis of the question.[20]

Marc Ancel, an eminent French jurist and Director of the Criminal Science Section of the Institute of Comparative Law in Paris, was engaged to prepare the study. Ancel was also *rapporteur* of a special sub-committee of the European Committee on Crime Problems, a body under the aegis of the Council of Europe and for which he was then conducting a similar review of the death penalty in Europe.[21] In 1962, Ancel presented the Economic and Social Council with his study.[22] Discussing the consequences of abolition and the issue of deterrence, Ancel observed that 'all the information available appears to confirm that such a removal [of the death penalty] has, in fact, never been followed by a notable rise in the incidence of the crime no longer punishable with death'.[23] According to Ancel, the 'modern tendency' was towards a discretionary and not a mandatory death penalty, the latter being used only in exceptional cases, such as capital murder or crimes against the external security of the State.[24] Ancel also concluded that most legal systems protected juveniles and pregnant women from the death penalty and that, in practice, a stay of execution for pregnant women nearly always led to commutation of the sentence.[25]

In accordance with the Economic and Social Council resolution, comments on the report were submitted by the *ad hoc* Advisory Committee of Experts on the Prevention of Crime and the Treatment of Offenders.[26] The Committee said that Ancel's conclusion was confirmed by its own knowledge and experience, namely 'that if one looked at the whole problem of capital punishment in a historical perspective it became clear that there was a worldwide tendency towards a considerable reduction of the number and categories of offences for which capital punishment might be imposed'.[27] The Committee also noted that the major trend among experts and other practitioners was towards abolition and that 'even those who do not support abolitionist policy tend to take an increasingly restrictive view of the use of capital punishment'.[28]

---

[20] Proposed by Chile: UN Doc. E/SR. 1095, para. 28; UN Doc. E/L.857/Rev. 1. Adopted unanimously on 6 April 1960: UN Doc. E/SR. 1096, §37, as ESC Res. 747 (XXIX).

[21] Marc Ancel, *The Death Penalty in European Countries*, Strasbourg: Council of Europe, 1962. See our discussion of Ancel's European report, at pp. 279–280 below.

[22] Marc Ancel, *Capital Punishment*, UN Doc. ST/SOA/SD/9, Sales No. 62.IV.2.

[23] *Ibid.*, p. 54. There is a great deal of literature on the subject of deterrence. See the references cited in Chapter 3, above.

[24] *Ibid.*, p. 12.   [25] *Ibid.*, pp. 13, 25.

[26] UN Doc. E/CN.5/371; UN Doc. E/3724. In 1965, the *ad hoc* Committee became a ten-person Advisory Committee of Experts on the Prevention of Crime and the Treatment of Offenders (UN Doc. ESC Res. 1086 (IX)B), which was expanded to fifteen members in 1971 and renamed the Committee on Crime Prevention and Control (UN Doc. 1584(L)). For a brief history of the Committee, see Clark, *The United Nations Crime Prevention and Criminal Justice Program*.

[27] UN Doc. E/CN.5/371, para. 18.   [28] *Ibid.*, para. 32.

In the Eeconomic and Social Council, Italy and Austria proposed a resolution expressing appreciation for the Ancel report and requesting further work in the area of capital punishment. The resolution also called on governments to review capital offences, removing the death penalty from the criminal law for any crime to which it was not applied or intended, and to examine facilities for medical and social investigation in the case of every offender so as to ensure the most careful legal procedures and the greatest possible safeguards for the accused.[29] The United Kingdom said that its government was not in favour of abolishing capital punishment at the present time.[30] This was a matter for individual governments, there was no need for a resolution, and the United Kingdom would abstain during the vote.[31] France, too, said that, as a matter of principle, the question came within the exclusive competence of individual Member States.[32] Ancel's report had been criticized by the *ad hoc* Committee for overlooking the issue of military courts. Colombia and Uruguay reiterated these complaints[33] and proposed an amendment to cover this omission.[34] The change was agreed to by the sponsors,[35] and the resolution adopted.[36]

Later that year, a resolution was proposed in the General Assembly aimed at maintaining the issue of capital punishment on the United Nations' agenda.[37] It referred the Ancel report to the Commission on Human Rights for further study and asked the Secretary-General, after examining the report of the Commission on Human Rights and with the cooperation of the *ad hoc* Advisory Committee, to report back to the General Assembly.[38]

The proponents of abolition decided to seek more substantive developments. In the 1967 session of the Commission on Human Rights,[39] Austria and Sweden submitted a resolution inviting governments to amend their laws to provide for a six-month moratorium before implementation of the death penalty,

---

[29] UN Doc. E/L/986, orally amended by India and Uruguay; UN Doc. E/SR.1249, para. 6.

[30] UN Doc. E/SR.1249, para. 7. Interestingly, the same year (1964) the United Kingdom carried out its last execution, and by 1973 it had abolished the death penalty for ordinary crimes.

[31] UN Doc. E/SR.1249, para. 10; UN Doc. E/SR.1251, para. 11.

[32] UN Doc. E/SR. 1249, para. 36.   [33] *Ibid.*, para. 26 (Colombia); *ibid.*, para. 40 (Uruguay).

[34] UN Doc. E/SR. 1250, para. 21; together with a minor change suggested by India, UN Doc. E/SR.1249, para. 28, UN Doc. E/SR.1250, para. 17.

[35] UN Doc. E/SR. 1251, para. 6.

[36] *Ibid.*, para. 13, by sixteen votes to none with two abstentions, probably France and the United Kingdom.

[37] UN Doc. A/C.3/L. 1143/Rev. 1, proposed by Ceylon, Ecuador, Sweden, Uruguay and Venezuelz.

[38] GA Res. 1918 (XVIII), UN Doc. A/PV. 1274, para. 74. Adoption in the Third Committee: UN Doc. A/C.3/SR.1255, para. 5.

[39] The Commission had been unable to consider the matter for three years (UN Doc. E/4184, UN Doc. E/CN.4/916). During the 1966 session, it resolved to treat the matter in 1967 'as a matter of priority' (CHR Res. 15 (XXII)). The resolution was proposed by Austria and Sweden, UN Doc. E/CN. 4/L.837. The Soviet Union proposed an amendment deleting the words 'as a matter of priority', which was rejected by four votes to ten, with six abstentions, UN Doc. E/4184, UN Doc. E/CN.4/916, para. 497.

to provide for a right of appeal or to petition for pardon or reprieve, and to inform the Secretary-General of death sentences pronounced and carried out and the crimes for which they were imposed.[40] Because of lack of time, the resolution was not discussed that year,[41] but the General Assembly resolved to discuss the matter at its 1968 session.[42]

The draft resolution proposed in the 1968 session of the Commission on Human Rights strengthened the wording of the earlier efforts.[43] Its preamble noted that 'the major trend among experts and practitioners in the field is to-wards the abolition of capital punishment' and repeated the new safeguards that had been proposed in the previous drafts, respecting appeal, pardon and reprieve, and delay of execution until in the exhaustion of such procedures.[44] It also urged the fixing of a time limit before the expiry of which no death sentence could be carried out, 'as has already been recognized in certain international conventions dealing with specific situations'.[45] It took note of the new study entitled *Capital Punishment: Developments, 1961–1965*, which had been requested by the General Assembly in 1963 and prepared by criminologist Norval Morris, a member of the Advisory Committee of Experts on the Prevention of Crime and the Treatment of Offenders.[46] The draft resolution also sought a periodic report on the death penalty to be prepared by the Secretary-General every three years, based on information which Member States would be obliged to provide on application of the death penalty.[47] The reporting obligations were controversial, and the Swedish representative suggested they be placed in parentheses

[40] UN Doc. E/CN.4/L.930.

[41] UN Doc. E/4322, UN Doc. E/CN.4/940, p. 198. Sweden and Venezuela submitted a similar draft resolution to the Economic and Social Council (UN Doc. E/AC.7/L.514 and Rev. 1) which was also not discussed, but instead forwarded to the General Assembly (UN Doc. E/L.1164; ESC Res. 1243 (XLII)), by nineteen votes to zero, with five abstentions, UN Doc. E/SR.1479; the debates in the Social Committee are reported at UN Doc. E/C.2/SR.562–575, 577–579.

[42] GA Res. 2334 (XXII), adopted unanimously, UN Doc. A/PV.1636, after being adopted unanimously in the Third Committee, UN Doc. A/C.3/SR.1553, para. 35. The draft resolution, UN Doc. A/C.3/L.1514, was sponsored by Austria, Costa Rica, Denmark, Dominican Republic, Ecuador, Finland, Iceland, Ireland, Italy, Libya, Mauritania, Mexico, New Zealand, Sierra Leone, Sweden, Uruguay and Venezuela. An amendment by the USSR was accepted by the sponsors, UN Doc. A/C.3/L.1515, UN Doc. A/C.3/SR.1553, para. 34.

[43] UN Doc. E/CN.4/L.1013 and Add. 1, sponsored by Austria, Italy, Sweden and Venezuela.

[44] UN Doc. E/4475, UN Doc. E/CN.4/972, pp. 134–136, 162–164.

[45] Presumably a reference to the *International Convention Concerning the Treatment of Prisoners of War*, (1932–33) 118 LNTS 343, art. 66; *Geneva Convention of August 12, 1949 Relative to the Treatment of Prisoners of War*, (1950) 75 UNTS 135, art. 101.

[46] *Capital Punishment: Developments, 1961–1965*, Sales No. E.67.IV.15. The two reports, by Ancel and Morris, were published in a single volume in 1968: UN Doc. ST/SOA/SD/9, UN Doc. ST/SOA/SD/10.

[47] Some periodic reports on compliance with the *Universal Declaration of Human Rights* by member States had been submitted to the Commission on Human Rights since 1958, pursuant to ESC Res. 624B (XXII), UN Doc. E/2844, para. 23. Under the 'right to life', the Commission had divided comments into three areas, one of which was 'provisions concerning the death penalty'. See UN Doc. E/CN.4/757, paras. 175–207.

with the rest of the resolution.[48] The resolution related abolition of the death penalty not only to article 3 of the *Universal Declaration of Human Rights* but also, apparently for the first time, to article 5, which prohibits inhuman and degrading treatment or punishment.

During the brief discussion in the Commission on Human Rights,[49] some voices opposed the mention of a general trend towards abolition, agreeing however with the idea that there was a trend to reducing the number and categories of offences.[50] There were also objections to what one delegate termed the 'pejorative nuance' that States that had not abolished the death penalty were in breach of article 3 of the *Universal Declaration of Human Rights*.[51] The United States supported the resolution, noting a trend in its country towards reducing the number of executions and the federal government's contemplation of abolition of the death penalty.[52] After Sweden toned down the draft resolution slightly, the text was adopted by the Commission.[53] As requested the previous year, the views of the Consultative Group on the Prevention of Crime and the Treatment of Offenders were also transmitted to the General Assembly,[54] and they indicated unanimous support within that body for abolition of the death penalty.

In the General Assembly, even many retentionist States supported the draft resolution, noting that it confined itself to the 'humanitarian' aspect of the question,[55] while more militant abolitionist States criticized its timidity, saying it would not 'induce Governments to abolish the death penalty'.[56] France sought the elimination of preambular paragraph 6, which took note of the views of the Advisory Committee that 'the trend among experts and practitioners in the field is towards the abolition of capital punishment'.[57] Sweden replied with an amendment referring to 'the view of the [Consultative] Group that there is a strong trend towards the abolition of capital punishment or at least towards fewer executions'.[58] The Philippines submitted an amendment that referred to the need for provision of legal assistance to indigent defendants charged with capital offences.[59] The resolution' took note of the conclusion in the Advisory Committee that, 'if one looked at the whole problem of capital punishment in a historical perspective, it became clear that there was a world-wide tendency

[48] UN Doc. E/CN.4/SR.990, p. 265.   [49] *Ibid.*, pp. 265–269.
[50] France, India, Poland, Union of Soviet Socialist Republics.
[51] UN Doc. E/CN.4/SR.990, p. 267.   [52] *Ibid.*, p. 266.
[53] *Ibid.*, by nineteen votes to none, with three abstentions. The Economic and Social Council eliminated the obligation of Member States to report on application of the death penalty, a point that had sharply divided the Commission (ESC Res. 1337 (XLIV), adopted unanimously, E/SR. 1530, E/C.2/SR.605, E/4535 and Add. 1). However, the provision was reinstated by the General Assembly.
[54] UN Doc. ST/SOA/SD/CG.2.
[55] UN Doc. A/C.3/SR. 1557, para. 17 (China); UN Doc. A/C.3/SR.1558, para. 10 (France).
[56] UN Doc. A/C.3/SR.1558, para. 2 (Austria).   [57] *Ibid.*, para. 11.
[58] UN Doc. A/C.3/L.1554/Rev.1.
[59] UN Doc. A/C.3/L.1556/Rev.1; amended orally, UN Doc. A/C.3/SR.1559, §32.

towards a considerable reduction in the number and categories of offences for which capital punishment might be imposed'. The resolution, together with the amendments that had been proposed, was adopted with virtual unanimity.[60] In an explanation of its vote, the United States said that the reference to articles 3 and 5 of the *Universal Declaration of Human Rights* in the preamble did not necessarily mean that respect for the *Universal Declaration* implied approval of abolition of the death penalty.[61] At the same session, the Assembly also adopted a resolution condemning imposition of the death penalty on opponents of *apartheid* in South Africa.[62]

Pursuant to Resolution 2393 (XXIII), in 1971 the Secretary-General prepared a note on information received from Member States on the subject of the death penalty which in effect updated the previous reports by Ancel and Morris.[63] The report was submitted to the Economic and Social, Council, together with a draft resolution reminding States of the principle of progressive restriction, of the number of offences for which capital punishment should be imposed, and of the desirability of full abolition.[64] Operative paragraph 3 of the draft stated that the 'main objective to be pursued is that of progressively restricting the number of offences for which capital punishment might be imposed with a view to total abolition of this punishment in all countries, so that the right to life, provided for in article 3 of the *Universal Declaration*, may be fully guaranteed'. During debate in the Social Committee of the Economic and Social Council, the sponsors agreed to change the term 'total abolition' to 'desirability of abolishing'.[65] After addition of an operative paragraph requesting the Secretary-General to prepare a separate report on practices and statutory rules which may govern the right to petition for pardon, commutation or reprieve, the resolution[66] was adopted by the General Assembly, with a lone negative vote, Saudi Arabia, and a large number of abstentions.[67]

[60] GA Res. 2393 (XXIII). UN Doc. A/PV.1727, by ninety-four votes to zero, with three abstentions. Adoption in the Third Committee: UN Doc. A/C.3/SR.1559, para. 34.
[61] UN Doc. A/C.3/SR.1560, para. 1.   [62] GA Res. 2394 (XXIII).
[63] UN Doc. E/4947 and Corr. 1 and Add. 1.
[64] UN Doc. E/AC.7/L.578, proposed by Italy, Norway, United Kingdom and Uruguay. Amendments were proposed by the Soviet Union: UN Doc. E/AC.7/L.579.
[65] UN Doc. E/4993, para. 6. The resolution was adopted as ESC Res. 1574 (L); UN Doc. E/SR. 1769, by fourteen votes to zero with six abstentions.
[66] UN Doc. A/C.3/L.1908, sponsored by Austria, Costa Rica, Italy, Netherlands, New Zealand, Norway, Sweden, United Kingdom, Uruguay and Venezuela.
[67] GA Res. 2857 (XXVI), UN Doc. A/PV.2027, adopted by fifty-nine votes to one, with fifty-four abstentions. In the Third Committee, a separate vote was taken on the term 'total abolition' in the first preambular paragraph, UN Doc. A/C.3/SR.1905, para. 69, and it was retained by twenty-four votes to eight, with sixty-one abstentions. A separate vote was taken on the term 'total abolition' in operative paragraph four, UN Doc. A/C.3/SR. 1905, para. 69, and it was retained by twenty-three votes to nine, with sixty-two abstentions. The request for a new report from the Secretary-General was also accepted on a separate vote, UN Doc. A/C.3/SR.1905, para. 69, adopted by thirty-three votes to none, with sixty-two

The following year, the Secretary-General submitted a note summarizing information received since the previous report to the Council.[68] The report suggested that further action be deferred until 1973 or 1974, when the separate report requested in the 1971 resolution on the right to petition for pardon, commutation or reprieve would be prepared.[69] Later that year, the General Assembly considered a resolution requesting the Secretary-General to prepare a report that would update the earlier studies by Ancel and Morris, and that would include its examination of the issue of petitioning for pardon, commutation or reprieve.[70] After perfunctory discussion in the Third Committee,[71] the resolution was adopted by the Assembly.[72]

The Secretary-General's report on capital punishment was presented to the Economic and Social Council in February 1973.[73] Citing article 3 of the *Universal Declaration of Human Rights* and suggesting it implied limitation and abolition of the death penalty,[74] the report observed that 'the United Nations has gradually shifted from the position of a neutral observer concerned about, but not committed on, the issue of capital punishment to a position favouring the eventual abolition of the death penalty'.[75] The report noted that the suggestion that there be a time delay between final judgment and execution had been rejected by an overwhelming majority of States, in their replies to the Secretary-General.[76] Pessimistically, the report said that governments were inclined to favour the death penalty, and that the impression of a steadily abolitionist evolution was a misconception created by trends in a few large countries.[77]

The Economic and Social Council called on the Secretary-General to prepare similar reports every five years.[78] It also asked the Committee on Crime

---

abstentions. In the Third Committee, the resolution was adopted, UN Doc. A/C.3/SR.1905, para. 69, by thirty-three votes to none, with sixty-two abstentions.

[68] UN Doc. E/5108.

[69] The Economic and Social Council resolved that States that had not yet provided the information requested by the General Assembly in its earlier resolutions should do so: ESC Res. 1656 (LII), adopted without objection, UN Doc. E/SR.1816. The resolution, UN Doc.E/AC.7/L.609, was proposed by Austria, Finland, Italy, Netherlands, New Zealand, Sweden and the United Kingdom, and approved by consensus in the Social Committee, UN Doc. E/5163.

[70] The draft resolution, UN Doc. A/C.3/L.1964, was sponsored by Austria, Costa Rica, Ecuador, Finland, Italy, Netherlands, New Zealand, Norway, Sweden, United Kingdom, Uruguay and Venezuela.

[71] UN Doc. A/C.3/SR.1943, paras. 26, 30.

[72] GA Res. 3011 (XXVII), by eighty-six votes to zero, with thirty-two abstentions. The draft resolution, UN Doc. A/C.3/L.1964, was sponsored by the following states: Austria, Costa Rica, Ecuador, Finland, Italy, Netherlands, New Zealand, Norway, Sweden, United Kingdom, Uruguay and Venezuela.

[73] UN Doc. E/5242 and Add. 1. See also UN Doc. E/AC.57/12 and Corr. 1, paras. 1–6; UN Doc. E/AC.57/18.

[74] UN Doc. E/5242, para. 11.   [75] *Ibid.*, para. 16.

[76] *Ibid.*, paras. 59–60. This had been proposed in GA Res. 2392 (XXIII).

[77] UN Doc. E/5242, §§73, 76.

[78] UN Doc. E/5298. Six quinquennial reports have now been produced: UN Doc. E/5616 and Add. 1 and Corr. 1 and 2 (covering the period 1969 to 1973); UN Doc. E/1980/9 and Corr. 1 and 2. Add. 1.

Prevention and Control and the United Nations Social Defence Research Institute to study the Secretary-General's report and propose appropriate areas for further scientific examination.[79] The resolution, 'with a view to the desirability of abolishing this punishment in all countries', reaffirmed that progressive restriction of capital offences was the main objective to be pursued. Indonesia suggested deletion of the phrase 'in all countries' from this paragraph,[80] and this was accepted on a separate vote.[81]

The Secretary-General submitted the first of the five-year reports in 1975, and it, too, painted a rather discouraging picture:

> It remains extremely doubtful whether there is any progression towards the restriction of the use of the death penalty. Periods of abolition or non-use may be succeeded by widespread executions in a highly unstable political situation or by a sudden return to the death penalty as a sanction where a State feels insecure. Moreover, in a few States where serious forms of terror and violence have been experienced, the death penalty has been used increasingly as counter-terror, or deterrence.[82]

Later the same year, the Economic and Social Council reaffirmed the commitment to progressive restriction and the desirability of abolition.[83] It requested the Committee on Crime Prevention and Control, with the cooperation of the United Nations Social Defence Research Institute, to study appropriate ways of analysing existing trends towards the restriction of the number of capital offences. The resolution also asked the Secretary-General to proceed with a report on practices and statutory rules which might govern the right to petition for pardon, commutation or reprieve, and to include this information in its next report, due in 1980.[84]

---

and Corr. 1, and Add. 2 and 3 (1974 to 1979) UN Doc. E/1985/43 and Corr. 1 (1979–1983); UN Doc. E/1990/38/Rev.1 and Corr. 1 and Add. 1 (1984–1988); UN Doc. E/1995/78 (1989–1993); UN Doc. E/2000/3.

[79] UN Doc. E/AC.7/L.624, sponsored by Austria, Finland, Italy, Netherlands, New Zealand, Sweden and Venezuela. Following suggestions from Chile (UN Doc. E/AC.7/L.624), Trinidad and Tobago (UN Doc. E/AC.7/L.625) and Ghana (UN Doc. E/AC.7/L.626), the resolution was revised by its sponsors (UN Doc. E/AC.7/L.624/Rev.1), who were joined by the United Kingdom. For the Secretary-General's communication with the Committee on Crime Prevention and Control, see UN Doc. E/AC.3/18. On the work of the Social Defence Research Institute, see: U. Leone, 'UNSDRI's Activities Related to the Death Penalty Issue', (1987) 58 *Revue internationals de droit pénal* 325.

[80] UN Doc. E/AC.7/L.624/Rev.2.

[81] UN Doc. E/5298, para. 16, by twenty-five votes to ten, with seven abstentions. The draft resolution was adopted in the Social Committee, UN Doc. E/5298, para. 16, by twenty-three votes to one with twenty abstentions, and in the Council: ESC Res. 1745 (LIV), UN Doc. E/SR.1833, by thirteen votes to zero with twelve abstentions. See also UN Doc. A/9003, paras. 965–972.

[82] UN Doc. 5616, para. 48.

[83] UN Doc. E/AC.7/L.678/Rev. 1, sponsored by Austria, Ecuador, Italy, Netherlands, Norway and Venezuela.

[84] ESC Res. 1930 (LVIII), UN Doc. E/SR.1948, by twenty-seven votes to zero with nine abstentions. See also: UN Doc. A/10003, paras. 296–302.

Attempts to raise the issue of capital punishment at the Fifth United Nations Congress on the Prevention of Crime and the Treatment of Offenders, held in Geneva in September 1975,[85] failed because the issue was not on the agenda.[86] The Congress had been presented with a proposal from twenty-six non-governmental organizations asking the General Assembly to adopt a declaration urging worldwide abolition of the death penalty.[87] After the vain attempt to raise the matter in 1975, efforts focused on plans for the 1980 Congress. A European Regional Preparatory Meeting, held in Bonn in October 1977, supported inclusion of the question of capital punishment on the Congress agenda, although not unanimously.[88] The Latin American Regional Preparatory Meeting reflected the traditional support for abolition in that continent,[89] and the African Regional Preparatory Meeting anticipated difficulties on the matter.[90]

At the General Assembly session of 1977, a draft resolution on capital punishment adopted the formulation of several earlier Economic and Social Council resolutions, affirming that the main objective in the field of capital punishment was progressive restriction of the number of offences for which it might be imposed, with the desirability of overall abolition.[91] It urged member States to cooperate with the Secretary-General in providing information for his five-year study and called upon the 1980 Congress to consider the matter. The Committee on Crime Prevention and Control was to make the necessary preparations for that discussion. The General Assembly undertook to consider, 'with high priority', the question of capital punishment at its 1980 session, which would follow the Congress by a few weeks. After brief discussion[92] and some minor revisions,[93] the resolution was adopted.[94]

The Committee on Crime Prevention and Control addressed the matter of capital punishment at its 1978 session.[95] The members of the Committee

---

[85] UN Doc. A/CONF.56/10.

[86] UN Doc. A/CONF.56/1/Rev.1. Capital punishment had been discussed in the African Regional Preparatory Meeting, where it was noted that there was still 'widespread reliance on capital punishment': 'Report on the African Regional Preparatory meeting of Experts on the Prevention of Crime and the Treatment of Offenders', UN Doc. A/CONF.56/BP/4, para. 33.

[87] Amnesty International, *The Death Penalty*, London: Amnesty International, 1979, at p. 33.

[88] UN Doc. A/CONF.87/BP/1, para. 70; also considered summarily by the Asia and Pacific Regional Preparatory Meeting: UN Doc. A/CONF.87/BP/2, para. 59.

[89] UN Doc. A/CONF.87/BP/3, para. 58.   [90] UN Doc. A/CONF.87/BP/4, para. 53.

[91] UN Doc. A/C.3/32/L.21, sponsored by Austria, Costa Rica, Denmark, Ecuador, Finland, Honduras, Italy, Netherlands, New Zealand, Norway, Portugal, Senegal, Sweden, Venezuela. See also UN Doc. A/C.3/32/SR.40, paras. 46–47.

[92] UN Doc. A/C.3/32/SR.39–41, 49.

[93] UN Doc. A/C.3/32/L.21/Rev.1. Canada joined the sponsors after the revision (UN Doc. A/C.3/32/SR.49, para. 33).

[94] GA Res. 32/61. UN Doc. A/PV.98, adopted without a vote. In the Third Committee: UN Doc. A/C.3/SR.49, para. 35.

[95] UN Doc. E/CN.5/558, paras. 1, 58–67, UN Doc. E/AC.57/33. The Committee had earlier considered the matter at its 1972 session (UN Doc. E/AC.57/5, paras. 27–33). At its 1978 meeting, at the request

agreed with the reduction in use of capital punishment and the desirability of its eventual abolition, although the short-term difficulty of such a goal was noted.[96] The Committee recommended that the issue of capital punishment be dealt with at the 1980 Congress under the agenda heading 'United Nations norms and guidelines in criminal justice'.[97] It adopted a resolution[98] urging as complete a report as possible by the Secretary-General in preparation for the Congress.[99] The same resolution, with minor changes, was adopted by the Economic and Social Council.[100]

In 1980, the Secretary-General submitted the second of the five-year reports to the Economic and Social Council, based on information received from seventy-four member States of the United Nations over the period 1974–1978.[101] It was not quite as discouraging as the 1975 report. The Secretary-General noted that although there was a slight increase in the number of abolitionist States, several retentionist States had expanded the use of the death penalty. Most retentionist States provided a variety of means for delaying, commuting or avoiding the death penalty, as well as mechanisms for review, pardon, commutation, and reprieve, and for exclusion of the death penalty on grounds of age, pregnancy or mental or physical illness.

Besides the quinquennial report, a working paper was prepared by the Secretariat for the 1980 Congress, dealing with commutation, pardon and reprieve in capital cases.[102] Reviewing the history of the death penalty debate within the United Nations, the paper explained that 'the post-war years were not conducive to allowing member states to come to an unequivocal position on the issue. Some countries with a long abolitionist tradition argued for barring the death penalty during times of war, while other members proposed an exception for offenders guilty of crimes against mankind.'[103] The paper characterized the General Assembly debates during adoption of the *Universal Declaration* as 'neutral'.[104] The Secretariat working paper recommended the creation of fact-finding commissions to study the evidence for and against the deterrent effect of the death penalty, experience in countries where the death penalty had been abolished, and factors determining public opinion.[105]

---

of Sweden, the 'Declaration on the Abolition of the Death Penalty', made at Stockholm on 11 December 1977 by Amnesty International, was circulated (UN Doc. E.AC.57/30).

[96] UN Doc. E/CN.5/558, §61.   [97] *Ibid.*, para. 64.

[98] *Ibid.*, para. 67, without a vote.   [99] UN Doc. E/AC.57/L.12.

[100] ESC Res. 1979/22, adopted without a vote. The resolution was proposed by the Second (Social) Commission, UN Doc. E/1979/55, para. 19, upon the recommendation of the Commission for Social Development, UN Doc. E/1979/24, UN Doc. E/CN.5/582, §132.

[101] UN Doc. E/1980/9 and Corr. 1 and 2 and Add. 1–3.   [102] UN Doc. A/CONF.87/9.

[103] *Ibid.*, para. 4.   [104] *Ibid.*   [105] *Ibid.*, para. 86.

The Sixth United Nations Congress on the Prevention of Crime and the Treatment of Offenders was held from 25 August to 5 September 1980 in Caracas. At the Congress, more time was devoted to the issue of capital punishment than to any other question.[106] The report of Committee II noted that many delegations representing countries which still retained capital punishment 'expressed their interest in the attainment of its abolition as a possible final goal'.[107] But there were also strong voices raised in support of the death penalty, something which had not previously been a feature of United Nations debates on the subject.[108] A draft resolution called for restriction and eventual abolition of the death penalty and added that abolition would be 'a significant contribution to the strengthening of human rights, in particular the right to life'.[109] States retaining the death penalty were invited to respect the terms of articles 6 and 14 of the *International Covenant on Civil and Political Rights*, which codified 'generally accepted international human rights standards'. A controversial provision urged States which had not abolished capital punishment to 'consider establishing a moratorium in its application, or creating other conditions under which capital punishment is not imposed or is not executed, so as to permit those States to study the effects of abolition on a provisional basis'.

Egypt challenged the draft resolution with an 'amendment', which added preambular paragraphs stressing the importance of general deterrence in providing for penalties, including capital punishment, and referred to 'the importance of providing for capital punishment in order to instill the necessary fear in the hearts of people.'[110] Faced with stiff opposition and inadequate time to complete the discussions, the sponsors withdrew the revised draft resolution.[111] For abolitionists, the results of the desultory discussion[112] were disappointing, although, had the resolution proceeded to a vote and been defeated, the movement might have been seriously set back. [113]

---

[106] See comments of the Chief, Crime Prevention and Criminal Justice Branch, UN Doc. A/C.3/35/SR.74, para. 40.

[107] UN Doc. A/CONF.87/14/Rev. 1, para. 98.   [108] *Ibid.*, paras. 99–100.

[109] UN Doc. A/CONF.87/C.1/L.1. Sponsored by Austria, Ecuador, the Federal Republic of Germany and Sweden. It was revised following informal discussions (UN Doc. A/CONF.87/14/Rev. 1, para. 111; UN Doc. A/CONF.87/C.1/L.1/Rev.1). The resolution is reproduced as an Annex to the Congress Report (UN Doc. A/CONF.87/14/Rev. 1, pp. 58–60).

[110] UN Doc. A/CONF.87/C.1/L.9. The amendment is reproduced as an Annex to UN Doc. A/CONF.87/14/Rev. 1, p. 60.

[111] UN Doc. A/CONF.87/14/Rev. 1, para. 111.

[112] Clark, 'Human Rights', p. 75. Also Ann Marie Clark, *Diplomacy of Conscience*, Princeton and Oxford: Princeton University Press, 2001, pp. 108–109.

[113] Later that year a draft resolution in the General Assembly was aimed at the same moratorium on the death penalty that had failed in Caracas (UN Doc. A/C.3/35/L.67, sponsored by Austria, Costa Rica, Denmark, Ecuador, Federal Republic of Germany, Italy, Norway, Panama, Papua New Guinea, Portugal, Spain, Sweden and Venezuela). It was criticized for reviving the Caracas debate, and effectively shelved

4.2 The 'Safeguards'

Although 'summary and arbitrary executions' are in fact forms of capital punishment, they have generally been treated distinctly from the issue of capital punishment within the United Nations. In summary executions, the procedural safeguards found in articles 14 and 15 of the *International Covenant on Civil and Political Rights* are not observed. In arbitrary executions, there is no legal process whatsoever.[114] The issue has been addressed in a large number of General Assembly resolutions,[115] and a Special *Rapporteur* has been presenting reports on the subject to the Commission on Human Rights since 1983.[116]

To assist in delineating where 'legitimate' capital punishment, under article 6 of the *Covenant*, leaves off and where summary executions begin, in 1981 the General Assembly assigned the Committee on Crime Prevention and Control to examine the subject.[117] The Committee was also respecting instructions from the Sixth United Nations Congress on the Prevention of Crime and Treatment of Offenders, held in Caracas in 1980. The Congress had failed to adopt a resolution on the issue of capital punishment that expressed the goal of 'further restriction in the application of capital punishment',[118] but in its report it 'took note' of the draft resolution and agreed that it should be considered further by United Nations legislative bodies. [119]

The Secretary-General prepared a report on summary and arbitrary executions,[120] based on a questionnaire sent to Member States, and in 1982 the Committee on Crime Prevention and Control prepared a series of draft 'guidelines' or 'safeguards' that were to be respected where the death penalty was being imposed.[121] Eight 'guidelines' were enumerated, in essence repeating the terms of articles 6, 14 and 15 of the *Covenant*. According to the draft, capital punishment could only be imposed for the most serious crimes, in accordance with the law in force at the time of commission of the crime, and not for crimes committed while under eighteen or on pregnant women, and always pursuant to a final judgment by a competent court, for which legal assistance would be available at all stages of the proceedings. The death penalty must be suspended pending any appeal or proceedings relating to pardon or commutation, there

by procedural motions from two retentionist States, Morocco and India: UN Doc. A/C.3/35/SR.76, UN Doc. A/C.3/35/SR.84.
[114] UN Doc. E/AC.57/1984/16, para. 33.
[115] GA Res. 36/22, GA Res. 37/182, GA Res. 38/96, GA Res. 39/110, GA Res. 40/143, GA Res. 41/144, GA Res. 42/141, GA Res. 43/151, GA Res. 44/159, GA Res. 45/162.
[116] The work of the Special *Rapporteur* is discussed later in this Chapter.
[117] GA Res. 36/22.
[118] UN Doc. A/CONF.87/C.1/L.1. See our discussion of the Congress, pp. 166–167 above.
[119] UN Doc. A/CONF.87/14/Rev.1; *Yearbook of the United Nations, 1980*, New York: United Nations, 1983, at pp. 781, 783.
[120] UN Doc. E/AC.57/1982/4 and Add. 1.
[121] UN Doc. E/CN.5/1983/2, chap. I, sect. A, para. 1, draft resolution I; also chap. V, §174.

must be a right to appeal and a right to apply for pardon or commutation, and there must be the possibility of seeking amnesty, pardon, or commutation at all stages. The Committee did not have time to complete its consideration of the subject at its 1982 meeting and referred the draft 'guidelines' to its next session, two years hence.[122]

The Secretariat proposed a number of changes to the text in preparation for the 1984 meeting of the Committee. It suggested expanding the guideline referring to 'the most serious crimes', mentioning that the scope of this term is limited to intentional lethal offences and that it excludes political offences.[123] On the guideline prohibiting the death penalty for juveniles and pregnant women, the report urged the addition of new mothers and persons over seventy years of age,[124] groups that had not been included in article 6§5 of the *Covenant* but that appeared in other instruments drafted subsequently.[125] Returning to an old proposal,[126] the Secretary-General recommended a temporary stay of the death penalty following sentencing, that could vary from two to six months.[127] The Secretary-General also urged that the guidelines specify that an appeal procedure be automatic in capital cases.[128]

The Committee adopted the 'Safeguards Guaranteeing Protection of the Rights of Those Facing the Death Penalty' at its March 1984 session, proposing that they be entrenched in a resolution of the Economic and Social Council.[129] Many of the changes suggested by the Secretary-General were accepted, but the Committee made some innovations of its own. For example, in article 1, providing that the death penalty could only be imposed for 'the most serious

---

[122] The Economic and Social Council confirmed that the Committee was to study the guidelines at its 1984 session: ESC Res. 1983/24.

[123] UN Doc. E/AC.57/1984/16, para. 43:
> ... it being understood that its scope should be limited to intentional lethal offences. Accordingly, it should be excluded for offences which are considered to be of a merely political nature, or for cases in which the political nature of the offence exceeds its criminal aspects.

[124] UN Doc. E/AC.57/1984/16, para. 49.

[125] The elderly, in article 4§5 of the *American Convention on Human Rights*, (1979) 1144 UNTS 123, OASTS 36 (see Appendix 20, p. 436), drafted in 1969; 'mothers having dependent children' in article 76§3 *of the Protocol Additional I to the 1949 Geneva Conventions and Relating to The Protection of Victims of International Armed Conflicts*, (1979) 1125 UNTS 3 (see Appendix 11, p. 420), drafted in 1977; 'mothers of young children' in article 6§4 of the *Protocol Additional II to the 1949 Geneva Conventions and Relating to The Protection of Victims of Non-International Armed Conflicts*, (1979) 1125 UNTS 609 (see Appendix 12, p. 421), drafted in 1977.

[126] GA Res. 2393 (XXIII), art. 1§b.

[127] UN Doc. E/AC.57/1984/16, para. 55:
> ... and in any case, not until a specific minimum period of time has elapsed, ranging on average between two and six months, and established in accordance with the legal practice and social circumstances of each non-abolitionist country, after all the legal remedies in capital proceedings have been exhausted and taking into account the physical and mental health condition of the condemned person.

[128] UN Doc. E/AC.57/1984/16, para. 87.

[129] 'Draft resolution VII', UN Doc. E/1984/16, UN Doc. E/AC.57/1984/18.

crimes', the Committee accepted the suggestion that it refer to crimes with lethal consequences but added a rather large loophole with the addition of the phrase 'or other extremely grave consequences'.[130] Article 2 essentially provided for the rule against retroactive imposition of the death penalty and for the benefit of the lesser penalty where the law has been changed.

For article 3, the Committee took up one of the Secretary-General's suggestions, adding the term 'new mothers', but it rejected the other suggestion and did not add the elderly. A new category, the insane, had not been mentioned in earlier drafts of the 'Safeguards'. The final version of article 3 said of the death penalty:

> persons below 18 years of age at the time of the commission of the crime shall not be sentenced to death, nor shall the death sentence be carried out on pregnant women, or on new mothers or on persons who have become insane.[131]

The category of the insane had been considered briefly by the Third Committee in 1957 for addition to article 6§5 of the *Covenant*, but no action was taken.[132] In his 1962 study, Marc Ancel discussed the widespread practice of staying the execution of a person who has become insane after being sentenced to death.[133] The rule exists in English common law,[134] under the eighth amendment to the United States *Bill of Rights*,[135] and in the positive law of most contemporary legal systems.[136]

Article 4, dealing with the burden of proof in capital cases, was an innovation. It declared that capital punishment could not be imposed unless there was 'clear and convincing evidence leaving no room for an alternative explanation of the facts'. This went considerably further than anything in the *Covenant*, although article 14§2 of the latter instrument does enshrine the presumption of innocence and therefore the requirement could be considered implicit.

Article 5 was in some respects a rewrite of article 6§2 of the *Covenant*. It stated that capital punishment may only be carried out pursuant to a final

---

[130] According to Sir Nigel Rodley, who attended the meeting as an observer for Amnesty International, the term 'or other extremely grave' was added upon the representations of a member of the Committee, who said that some acts, such as provision of secret information to an enemy in wartime, could result in large-scale loss of life, although the lethal results of the offence might not easily be proven. See: Nigel Rodley, *The Treatment of Prisoners Under International Law*, Paris: Unesco, Oxford: Clarendon Press, 1987, p. 174.

[131] UN Doc. E/1984/16, UN Doc. E/AC.57/1984/18. No summary records are kept of the sessions of the Committee.

[132] UN Doc. A/C.3/SR.819, para. 17; UN Doc. A/C.3/SR.820, para. 6. William A. Schabas, 'International Norms on Execution of the Insane and the Mentally Retarded', (1993) 4 *Criminal Law Forum* 95.

[133] UN Doc. ST/SOA/SD/9, §71.

[134] 4 W. Blackstone, Commentaries 24, 25; Coke, Third Institutes 6 (1644); Hawkins, Pleas of the Crown 2 (1716); *Re Tait*, [1963] VR 532; *Solesbee* v. *Balkcom*, 339 US 9 (1950); J. D. Feltham, 'The Common Law and the Execution of Insane Criminals', (1964) 4 *Melbourne University L. J.* 434.

[135] *Ford* v.*Wainwright*, 477 US 399, 106 S.Ct. 2595, 91 L.Ed.2d 335 (1986).

[136] For example: 'Initial Report of Italy', UN Doc. CCPR/C/6/Add.4, para. 26; 'Initial Report of Algeria', UN Doc. CCPR/C/62/Add.1, para. 81.

judgment rendered by a competent court but adds something that the *Covenant's* drafters had left implicit, namely that the guarantees of a fair trial must be 'at least equal to those contained in Article 14 of the International Covenant'. Article 5 of the 'Safeguards' also stated that adequate legal assistance must be available at all stages of the proceedings.

Article 6 of the 'Safeguards' took up the suggestion of the Secretary-General that appeals should be mandatory. Article 7 recognized the right to seek pardon or commutation, and article 8 stated that the death penalty could not be imposed while proceedings in appeal or other recourse are still underway. Article 9 added that capital punishment should be carried out so as to inflict the minimum possible suffering, a point which had previously received little attention in the international law debate on the death penalty. The question of the mode of execution is a matter falling within the scope of article 7 of the *Covenant*, which protects offenders against inhuman or degrading treatment or punishment.[137]

After adoption by the Committee, the 'Safeguards' were submitted to the Economic and Social Council. There were concerns that the 'Safeguards' might appear to legitimize capital punishment, and an amendment from staunchly abolitionist States replaced, in article 3, the more neutral phrase 'not to be interpreted as affecting the consideration of the question of the abolition or retention of capital punishment' with the abolition-leaning 'not to be invoked to delay or to prevent the abolition of capital punishment'.[138] In the Council, the United States made an oral amendment calling for reinstatement of the original article 3, but this was rejected.[139] The phrase 'In countries which have not abolished the death penalty', borrowed from article 6§2 of the *Covenant*, was added at the beginning of paragraph 1 of the 'Safeguards'. Its value is twofold, recalling that abolition is the goal and suggesting that States which have already abolished the death penalty may not revive it. Another amendment, providing for a minimum period of three months from judgment until execution,[140] was withdrawn. There is no record or even suggestion of any debate on the subject of the prohibition of execution of the insane or opposition to inclusion of the point in the 'Safeguards'.[141]

---

[137] See: *General Comment No. 20(44)*, UN Doc. CCPR/C/21/Rev.1/Add.3, para. 6. See also our discussion of method of execution in Chapter 3, at pp. 151–153.

[138] UN Doc. E/1984/C.2/L.8, sponsored by Austria, Costa Rica, Italy, Netherlands, Sweden and Uruguay. The amendment was adopted by twenty-nine votes to one, with seventeen abstentions.

[139] UN Doc. E/1984/SR.21, para. 22, by twenty-three votes to six, with sixteen abstentions.

[140] Similar to provisions in: *International Convention Concerning the Treatment of Prisoners of War*, art. 66; *Geneva Convention of August 12, 1949 Relative to the Treatment of Prisoners of War*, art. 101; and in two draft resolutions submitted to the Commission on Human Rights in the late 1960s: UN Doc. E/CN.4/L.930; UN Doc. E/CN.4/L.1013 and Add. 1.

[141] UN Doc. E/1984/SR.21, para. 24.

After adoption by the Economic and Social Council,[142] the 'Safeguards' were endorsed by the General Assembly[143] and by the Seventh United Nations Congress on the Prevention of Crime and the Treatment of Offenders, held in Milan in 1985,[144] which called in a resolution for their widespread dissemination and implementation.[145] The Economic and Social Council, in 1986, requested the Secretary-General to prepare a new study on the question of the death penalty together with a report on implementation of the 'Safeguards'.[146]

Containing a review of the replies from seventy-four governments to a questionnaire dealing with respect of the 'Safeguards',[147] the report was submitted to the Committee on Crime Prevention and Control at its 1988 session.[148] At the same time, a study of the death penalty by criminologist Roger Hood was presented.[149] The Committee adopted a resolution dealing with implementation of the 'Safeguards' that in fact added some new standards to be applied in examining the implementation of the death penalty. The resolution declared that not only must there be adequate assistance of counsel, as found in article 5 of the 'Safeguards', but also this must go 'above and beyond the protection afforded in non-capital cases'.[150] The resolution also stated that a maximum age should be established above which the death penalty cannot be imposed or carried out.[151] However, the 1988 resolution did not set a specific age, as had been proposed, unsuccessfully, in 1984. The 1984 'Safeguards' had excluded the insane from the death penalty; the 1988 resolution added 'persons suffering from mental retardation or extremely limited mental competence'.[152] The change in emphasis was due to developments in Washington. In 1988, the docket of the United States Supreme Court included a case dealing with execution of the mentally retarded. At first glance, a prohibition

---

[142] ESC Res. 1984/50, adopted without a vote.
[143] GA Res. 39/118, UN Doc. A/PV.101, para. 79, without a vote.
[144] UN Doc. A/CONF.121/22/Rev. 1, pp. 83–84, 131–132.
[145] UN Doc. A/CONF.121/C.1/L.9, sponsored by Austria, Denmark, France, Greece, India, Italy, Norway, Uruguay and Yugoslavia. Adopted by consensus at the fifteenth meeting of Committee I, UN Doc. A/CONF.121/22/Rev. 1, para. 195; adopted by the Congress at its fourteenth plenary meeting, UN Doc. A/CONF.121/22/Rev. 1, para. 214. The resolution adopted at the Congress had been drafted at the Varenna preparatory meeting for the Congress, held in 1984: UN Doc. A/CONF.121/IPM/3, §§61–68. A Secretariat note on capital punishment had been submitted to the Varenna meeting: UN Doc. A/CONF.121/CRP.2.
[146] ESC Res. 1986/10.   [147] UN Doc. E/1988/20, UN Doc. E/AC.57/1988/17, p. 56.
[148] UN Doc. E/AC.57/1988/9 and Corr. 1 and 2.
[149] UN Doc. E/AC.57/1988/CRP.7. See: UN Doc. E/1988/20, para. 72. The report was subsequently published commercially: Roger Hood, *The Death Penalty: A Worldwide Perspective*, Oxford: Clarendon Press, 1989.
[150] UN Doc. E/1988/20, UN Doc. E/AC.57/1988/17, pp. 28–29. Draft resolution E/AC.57/1988/L.19, art. 1§a.
[151] *Ibid.*, art. 1§c.   [152] *Ibid.*, art. 1§d.

on executing the 'insane' and one on executing the 'mentally disabled' might appear to have fundamentally the same *raison d'être*. But, in the 1989 case of *Penry* v. *Lynaugh*,[153] the United States Supreme Court distinguished between the two, concluding that it was not 'cruel and unusual' to execute the mentally disabled.

The new resolution, entitled 'Implementation of the Safeguards Guaranteeing Protection of the Rights of Those Facing the Death Penalty', was adopted by the Economic and Social Council, following approval by the Second (Social) Committee.[154] The principal addition to this second resolution was the recommendation favouring '[e]limination of the death penalty for persons suffering from mental retardation or extremely limited mental competence, whether at the stage of sentence or execution'. The resolution also recognized the obligation imposed upon death penalty states to allow adequate time for the preparation of appeals to a court of higher jurisdiction and for the completion of appeal proceedings, as well as petitions for clemency.[155] The resolution was reconfirmed in 1996 when the United Nations Commission on Crime Prevention and Control declared that 'there appears to have been lack of protection from the death penalty of those mentally retarded'.[156]

Neither the 'Safeguards' nor the 1988 resolution on their implementation are treaties. Drafted by an expert committee, they were, however, endorsed by consensus by the Economic and Social Council, thus showing their unanimous acceptance within the international community. Their implementation has been monitored in the reports of the Secretary-General.[157] The only source of discord in the adoption of the 'Safeguards' by the Economic and Social Council was over whether they would be abolitionist in orientation or simply neutral on the subject, a point unrelated to the substance of the individual safeguards themselves. The effect of the 'Safeguards' is probably to elevate the norms of articles 6 and 14 of the *International Covenant on Civil and Political Rights*, in death penalty cases, to the status of customary international law. The only possible exception to this generalization might be the issue of execution of juveniles, the United States and some others refusing to accept the age of eighteen as a cut-off. This problem aside, the 'Safeguards' represent an invaluable benchmark and an important development in the limitation – that is, the partial abolition – of the death penalty. While the 'Safeguards' and their implementation were being considered, an even more important development was underway, the preparation of the *Second Optional Protocol.*

---

[153] 109 S.Ct. 2934 (1989).   [154] UN Doc. E/1989/91, para. 36.
[155] ESC Res. 1989/64, adopted without a vote.   [156] ESC Res. 1996/19.
[157] UN Doc. E/1985 and Corr.1; UN Doc. E/1990/38/Rev.1 and Corr.1; UN Doc. E/1995/78; UN Doc. E/2000/3.

4.3 The *Second Optional Protocol*

4.3.1 Drafting of the Protocol

The first universal treaty abolishing the death penalty was submitted in draft form to the United Nations General Assembly at its 1980 session.[158] Annexed to a resolution was the 'Second Optional Protocol to the International Covenant on Civil and Political Rights'.[159] There was no preamble, although space had been left to add some paragraphs later. Of the nine operative paragraphs in the protocol, article 1 quickly established the substance:

> 1. Each State party shall abolish the death penalty in its territory and shall no longer foresee the use of it against any individual subject to its jurisdiction nor impose nor execute it.
>
> 2. The death penalty shall not be re-established in States that have abolished it.

Article 2 provided that article 1 would be regarded as an additional article to the *International Covenant on Civil and Political Rights* 'as between the States parties'. Furthermore it stated that no derogation whatsoever could be permitted from article 1. The remainder of the draft dealt with such matters as communications to the Human Rights Committee and the formalities of signature, ratification or accession, federal States, and coming into force.

The sponsors of the draft protocol advanced with considerable caution, admitting that their proposal was 'breaking new ground' and that it might be years before any action was taken. Their real goal, they said, was for the Secretary-General to take note of the proposal and seek information from Member States, with a view to a more thorough discussion the following year.[160] Reformulated as a 'draft decision' aimed at further work on the possibility of such a protocol,[161] the original resolution was adopted by consensus in the Third Committee[162] and in the General Assembly.[163] Several delegates expressed opposition to the proposal, implying that had it been put to a vote they would have been opposed[164] or would have abstained.[165]

[158] The General Assembly had been committed to a debate on capital punishment at that session since 1977: GA Res. 32/61.

[159] UN Doc. A/C.3/35/L.75. Submitted by Austria, Costa Rica, Dominican Republic, Federal Republic of Germany, Italy, Portugal and Sweden. Another draft resolution, UN Doc. A/C.3/35/L.80, dealt with summary executions.

[160] UN Doc. A/C.3/35/SR.74, para. 56.   [161] UN Doc. A/C.3/35/L.97.

[162] UN Doc. A/C.3/35/SR.84, paras. 9–10.   [163] GA Decision 35/437, UN Doc. A/35/PV.96.

[164] UN Doc. A/C.3/35/SR.84, para. 12 (Philippines), para. 13 (Yemen), para. 14 (Japan), para. 15 (Morocco), para. 17 (United Kingdom).

[165] UN Doc. A/C.3/35/SR.84, para. 18 (Uganda, Oman, Bangladesh, Benin, Pakistan, Jordan, United Arab Emirates).

The Secretary-General received comments on the proposal from twenty-five governments, and these were published prior to the 1981 session of the General Assembly.[166] Austria, Finland, Italy,[167] the Federal Republic of Germany, the Netherlands, Norway, Spain, Sweden and Switzerland supported the proposed protocol. Many States, including the United States of America and the United Kingdom, insisted that they could not ratify such an instrument but refrained from opposing its drafting, and the United States actually said 'it would have no reason to object if other countries wished to adopt and accede to the draft Protocol'.[168] Only Japan expressed formal disagreement with the draft instrument.

The General Assembly decided to seek further submissions from Member States, with a view to a full debate on the subject in the 1982 session.[169] The Federal Republic of Germany noted that not only abolitionist States, but those contemplating abolition, should be in a position to support the protocol.[170] It also stressed the optional nature of the protocol. Several States, including Iran,[171] the German Democratic Republic,[172] Hungary[173] and the Ukrainian Soviet Socialist Republic,[174] were opposed. Nevertheless, the resolution was adopted by consensus in the Third Committee[175] and in the General Assembly.[176]

Sixteen governments sent replies to the Secretary-General, although these included additional comments from Austria, the Federal Republic of Germany, Italy and the Dominican Republic, all staunch partisans of abolition.[177] The replies over the two years were almost equally divided between abolitionist and retentionist States.[178] Several retentionist States indicated that their laws could not permit ratification of such a treaty, Pakistan adding ominously that abolition of the death penalty was inconsistent with Islamic law.

A new draft resolution was framed that assigned the Commission on Human Rights with the mission to 'consider the idea of elaborating a draft second optional protocol' and to submit a report on the subject in two years.[179] Several governments argued on the merits of abolition of capital punishment,

---

[166] UN Doc. A/36/441 and Add. 1 and 2. [167] UN Doc. A/36/441/Add. 1.
[168] UN Doc. A/36/441, at p. 20.
[169] UN Doc. A/C.3/36/L.33/Rev.1, sponsored by Austria, Costa Rica, Dominican Republic, Ecuador, Federal Republic of Germany, Italy, Netherlands, Nicaragua, Norway, Panama, Peru, Portugal, Sweden, Uruguay.
[170] UN Doc. A/C.3/36/SR.27, para. 15. Other speakers in favour included The Netherlands (UN Doc. A/C3/36/SR.27, paras. 26–31) and Canada (UN Doc. A/C.3/36/SR.31, para. 9).
[171] UN Doc. A/C.3/36/SR.29, para. 15. [172] UN Doc. A/C.3/36/SR.30, para. 5.
[173] UN Doc. A/C.3/36/SR.34, para. 39. [174] *Ibid.*, para. 28.
[175] UN Doc. A/C.3/36/SR.38, para. 83. [176] GA Res. 36/59, UN Doc. A/36/PV.73.
[177] UN Doc. A/37/407 and Add. 1. [178] See: UN Doc. E/CN.4/Sub.2/1987/20, para. 83.
[179] UN Doc. A/C.3/37/L.60/Rev.1, sponsored by Austria, Cape Verde, Costa Rica, Denmark, Dominican Republic, France, Federal Republic of Germany, Greece, Honduras, Iceland, Ireland, Italy, Luxembourg, Netherlands, Nicaragua, Norway, Panama, Portugal, Solomon Islands, Spain, Sweden, Uruguay.

pointing to its humanitarian dimension, the fact that capital punishment was not a useful deterrent, and the fact that abolitionist States had not encountered a breakdown in public order.[180] Several emphasized the optional nature of the draft protocol and reminded other States that adoption of the resolution left them free to choose whether or not to accede to the draft protocol.[181] Some States said they could support the resolution because it was only procedural, it did not go to the substance of the issue, and it would permit a continuing dialogue on the matter.[182]

Japan opposed the draft protocol, saying the matter should be left to individual governments, although it voted in favour of the resolution.[183] As a general rule, countries with a strong Moslem population voted against the resolution, and in many cases they cited the fact that Islamic law permitted the death penalty as the justification for their vote.[184] Some Islamic countries abstained for the same reason.[185] Mauritania explained its favourable vote as being a mistake, because 'it was well known that the Islamic Republic of Mauritania was in favour of capital punishment'.[186] Kuwait said there could be no question of abolishing the death penalty, which was part of the Kuwaiti religion.[187] The draft resolution was adopted in the Third Committee on a recorded vote[188] and in the General Assembly by consensus.[189]

The Commission on Human Rights did not address the matter until its 1984 session, when it decided to transmit the draft second protocol to its Sub-Commission on Prevention of Discrimination and Protection of Minorities,[190]

---

[180] Austria (UN Doc. A/C.3/36/SR.29, paras. 1–4, UN Doc. A/C.3/37/SR.55, paras. 63–65); Federal Republic of Germany (UN Doc. A/C.3/37/SR.64, paras. 8–9); Finland, speaking on behalf of Denmark, Iceland, Norway and Sweden (UN Doc. A/C.3/37/SR.50, para. 1); Italy (UN Doc. A/C.3/37/SR.51, para. 33); Netherlands (UN Doc. A/C.3/37/SR.55, paras. 26–31, UN Doc. A/C.3/36/SR.50, paras. 32–33); Nicaragua (UN Doc. A/C.3/36/SR.29, para. 69); Venezuela (UN Doc. A/C.3/37/SR.53, para. 11).

[181] Canada (UN Doc. A/C.3/36/SR.31, para. 9); Costa Rica (UN Doc. A/C.3/37/SR.67, para. 58); Norway (UN Doc. A/C.3/36/SR.35, para. 55); Portugal (UN Doc. A/C.3/36/SR.35, paras. 36–37, UN Doc. A/C.3/37/SR.56, para. 6); Uruguay (UN Doc. A/C.3/37/SR.56, paras. 56–59).

[182] Chile (UN Doc. A/C.3/37/SR.67, para. 58); United Kingdom (UN Doc. A/C.3/37/SR.67, para. 91); United States of America (UN Doc. A/C.3/36/SR.29, para. 81). Others announced that they would abstain from the vote for essentially the same reason: Morocco (UN Doc. A/C.3/36/SR/31, para. 14); Niger (UN Doc. A/C.3/37/SR.67, para. 57); Uganda (UN Doc. A/C.3/37/SR.36, para. 23).

[183] Japan (UN Doc. A/C.3/37/SR.32, para. 44, UN Doc. A/C.3/37/SR.53, para. 4, UN Doc. A/C.3/37/SR.67, para. 84).

[184] Afghanistan (UN Doc. A/C.3/37/SR.37, para. 59); Iran (UN Doc. A/C.3/37/SR.67, para. 49); Iraq (UN Doc. A/C.3/37/SR.67, para. 53); Jordan (UN Doc. A/C.3/37/SR.67, para. 48); Kuwait (UN Doc. A/C.3/37/SR.67, para. 47); Libyan Arab Jamahiriya, (UN Doc. A/C.3/37/SR.67, para. 52); Oman (UN Doc. A/C.3/37/SR.67, para. 45); Somalia (UN Doc. A/C.3/37/SR.67, para. 50); Sudan (UN Doc. A/C.3/37/SR.67, para. 46).

[185] Pakistan (UN Doc. A/C.3/37/SR.67, para. 67); Tunisia (UN Doc. A/C.3/37/SR.67, para. 67).

[186] UN Doc. A/C.3/37/SR.67, para. 84.   [187] *Ibid.*

[188] *Ibid.*, by fifty-two votes to twenty-three, with fifty-three abstentions.

[189] GA Res. 37/192, UN Doc. A/37/PV.111.   [190] CHR Res. 1984/19, UN Doc. E/1984/14.

a body of experts who are not, strictly speaking, representatives of their govern-ments.[191] Views in the Commission on Human Rights were generally favourable to adoption of the draft protocol.[192] Only the German Democratic Republic stated its opposition, claiming that article 6 of the *Covenant* 'regulated the question of abolishing or maintaining capital punishment in a balanced and flexible manner that took account of the possible practice of all States'.[193]

The Sub-Commission considered the issue in August 1984.[194] Several speakers voiced support for abolition of the death penalty.[195] Others emphasized the complex and controversial nature of the problem and the fact that the various positions of Member States were based on different legal, philosophical, religious and social backgrounds.[196] It was pointed out that the Sub-Commission's man-date was not to determine the advantages and disadvantages of abolition, but rather to examine the possibility of drawing up a second optional protocol.[197] This did not inhibit the members of the Sub-Commission, however, from ven-turing into debate on the merits. The weight of opinion was clearly in favour of abolition, but some views supporting retention were expressed.[198] The Jordanian Awn Shawkat Al Kwasawneh argued strongly against the protocol, given the great divergence of world opinion on the matter. He urged, as an alternative, a protocol on prevention or minimization of abuse of capital punishment.

The Sub-Commission proposed that one of its members, Marc Bossuyt, be designated special *rapporteur*, charged with the task of preparing an analysis of the question.[199] Bossuyt had earlier spoken in favour of elaboration of the second optional protocol, saying such an instrument could become a 'pole of attraction' for States considering abolition of the death penalty. Bossuyt had

---

[191] Louis Joinet, 'La Sous-Commission des droits de l'homme', in Hubert Thierry, Emmanuel Decaux, eds., *Droit international et droits de l'homme*, Paris: Montchrestien, 1990, pp. 153–162.

[192] Argentina (UN Doc. E/CN.4/1984/SR.18, para. 79); Bangladesh (UN Doc. E/CN.4/1984/SR.18, para. 49); Canada (UN Doc. E/CN.4/1984/SR.17, para. 58); France (UN Doc. E/CN.4/1984/SR.18, para. 74); Federal Republic of Germany (UN Doc. E/CN.4/1984/SR.15, paras. 54–55); Spain (UN Doc. E/CN.4/1984/SR.15, para. 46); Sweden (UN Doc. E/CN.4/1984/SR.17, para. 23).

[193] UN Doc. E/CN.4/1984/SR.17, para. 7.   [194] UN Doc. E/CN.4/Sub.2/1984/SR. 14–16.

[195] Louis Joinet, France (UN Doc. E/CN.4/Sub.2/1984/SR.14, para. 31); Jules Deschênes, Canada (UN Doc. E/CN.4/Sub.2/1984/SR. 14, para. 42); Ahmed M. Khalifa, Egypt (UN Doc. E/CN.4/Sub.2/ 1984/SR. 16, para. 19); Erica-Irene A. Daes, Greece (UN Doc. E/CN.4/Sub.2/1984/SR.16, §7); the observer for Argentina (UN Doc. E/CN.4/Sub.2/1984/SR.15, para. 46).

[196] Awn Shawkat Al Kwasawneh, Jordan (UN Doc. E/CN.4/Sub.2/1984/SR.15, paras. 10–15); Viktor M. Tchikvadze, Union of Soviet Socialist Republics (UN Doc. E/CN.4/Sub.2/1984/SR.15, paras. 18–19); John P. Roche, United States of America (UN Doc. E/CN.4/Sub.2/1984/SR.15, para. 35); Miquel Alfonso Martinez, Cuba (UN Doc. E/CN.4/Sub.2/1984/SR.16, para. 11); Dumitru Mazilu, Romania (UN Doc. E/CN.4/Sub.2/1984/SR.16, para. 15); the observer of the Federal Republic of Germany (UN Doc. E/CN.4/Sub.2/1984/SR.15, paras. 42–45).

[197] Ahmed M. Khalifa, Egypt (UN Doc. E/CN.4/Sub.2/1984/SR.16, para. 19).

[198] Viktor M. Tchikvadze, Union of Soviet Socialist Republics (UN Doc. E/CN.4/Sub.2/1984/SR.15, paras. 18–19); Dumitru Mazilu, Romania (UN Doc. E/CN.4/Sub.2/1984/SR.16, para. 15).

[199] S-CHR Res. 1984/7, UN Doc. E/CN.4/Sub.2/1984/L.8, UN Doc. E/CN.4/1985/3.

said that the time had come to take the further step of supplementing the *Covenant* by a second optional protocol that would make abolition an obligation under international law for States that had already decided upon abolition in their domestic law, adding that the Sub-Commission should avail itself of the opportunity to make a contribution to the development of human rights law.[200] The Sub-Commission resolution stressed that Bossuyt was to take into account views both for and against a protocol and to submit his recommendations to the Sub-Commission in 1986.[201]

Technically, the Sub-Commission resolution had to return to the Commission on Human Rights, which would not meet until early 1985. But, in the autumn of 1984, a General Assembly resolution endorsed the initiatives of the Commission and the Sub-Commission and allowed three years for those bodies to complete their analysis of the question.[202] Again, there was some vocal opposition to the proposal in the Third Committee. The Japanese representative said it was not desirable to abolish the death penalty, which served not only as a punishment for especially grave crimes but also as a deterrent.[203] A number of Islamic States, namely Saudi Arabia, the United Arab Emirates, Yemen, Kuwait and Morocco, also expressed support for capital punishment.[204] Several States, including Burundi, Canada, Mali, Rwanda, the United Kingdom and the United States, said they could easily support a text which was procedural in nature, but insisted that their votes were not to be interpreted as affecting their positions on the merits of the question.[205] The resolution was adopted in the Third Committee[206] and the General Assembly[207] on recorded votes that showed strong opposition, almost exclusively from Islamic States, and an extraordinary number of abstentions. The Sub-Commission's proposal to appoint Marc Bossuyt as special *rapporteur* was endorsed the following year by the Commission on Human Rights in a resolution[208] adopted by consensus.[209] Even Saudi Arabia joined the consensus, although it declared that it would maintain

---

[200] UN Doc. E/CN.4/Sub.2/1984/SR.14, paras. 29–30.

[201] The result of insistence by the retentionist member, Al Kwasawneh, who threatened to break the consensus unless Bossuyt's mandate was sufficiently objective: UN Doc. E/CN.4/Sub.2/1984/SR.33, para. 172.

[202] UN Doc. A/C.3/39/L.48/Rev.1. *Sponsors*: Argentina, Austria, Belgium, Cape Verde, Colombia, Costa Rica, Cyprus, Denmark, Dominican Republic, Ecuador, Finland, Federal Republic of Germany, Greece, Honduras, Iceland, Italy, Luxemburg, Netherlands, Nicaragua, Norway, Panama, Portugal, Solomon Islands, Spain, Sweden and Uruguay. There were minor oral amendments (UN Doc. A/C.3/39/L.48/Rev.1).

[203] UN Doc. A/C.3/39/SR.49, para. 3.   [204] UN Doc. A/C.3/SR.44–52, 56, 57, 60.   [205] *Ibid.*

[206] UN Doc. A/39/707, UN Doc. A/C.3/SR.60, by fifty-seven votes to eighteen with fifty abstentions.

[207] GA Res. 39/137, UN Doc. A/39/PV.101, by sixty-four votes to eighteen with fifty abstentions.

[208] UN Doc. E/CN.4/1985/L.75, sponsored by Austria, Colombia, Costa Rica, Cyprus, Denmark, Finland, Netherlands, Nicaragua, Norway, Peru, Senegal, Sweden and the United Kingdom.

[209] CHR Res. 1985/46, UN Doc. E/1985/22, para. 439, UN Doc. E/CN.4/1985/L.76/Rev.1. The Commission recommendation was subsequently incorporated in a resolution of the Economic and Social Council, adopted by consensus: ESC Res. 1985/41.

the right not to abolish the death penalty, as this would run counter to Islamic law.[210]

Bossuyt's report was submitted to the Sub-Commission, on schedule, in 1987.[211] The analysis included a review of the international law provisions dealing with the death penalty, the decisions of the Human Rights Committee under the *Optional Protocol*, the periodic reports submitted to the Committee pursuant to article 40 of the *Covenant*, the comments of the Committee on those reports, and the case law of the Inter-American Commission and Court of Human Rights. Bossuyt also reviewed the third of the five-year reports by the Secretary-General, concerning the situation, trends and safeguards in capital punishment.[212]

Bossuyt proposed a number of modifications to the original draft that had been submitted to the General Assembly in 1980. The protocol would be self-executing, and reservations would be possible with respect to the death penalty in time of war. Bossuyt said the purpose of his analysis was not to press States to abolish capital punishment but only to 'take note of the growing trend in the world today towards abolition of the death penalty'.[213] He warned that there was often confusion between the issue of abolition as such and the issue of the desirability of adopting a second optional protocol. Although one abolitionist government had expressed opposition to the instrument[214] and two retentionist States saw no objection to it,[215] by and large the attitudes of governments to the draft protocol were consistent with their attitudes towards capital punishment. 'There is nevertheless a considerable difference between not being able at the present moment to accept such a commitment and preventing others from accepting that commitment', he wrote.[216]

Bossuyt's analysis and revised draft protocol were accepted by the Sub-Commission and transmitted to the Commission on Human Rights on 1 September 1988.[217] The draft was approved by the Commission on Human Rights[218] and the Economic and Social Council[219] the following spring and then submitted to the General Assembly at its forty-fourth session in the autumn of 1989. The draft protocol and its accompanying resolution were presented to the Third Committee of the General Assembly by the Federal Republic of Germany,[220] which reminded delegates that 'its sole aim [was] to provide

---

[210] UN Doc. E/1985/95 and Corr. 1 (in the Second Committee).
[211] UN Doc. E/CN.4/Sub.2/1987/20.   [212] UN Doc. E/1985/43.
[213] UN Doc. E/CN.4/Sub.2/1987/20, para. 182.
[214] United Kingdom (UN Doc. A/36/441, pp. 18–19).
[215] United States of America (UN Doc. A/36/441, p. 20); UN Doc. A/C.3/36/SR.36, para. 23, UN Doc. A/C.3/37/SR.67, para. 89.
[216] UN Doc. E/CN.4/Sub.2/1987/20, para. 185.
[217] S-CHR Decision 1988/22, UN Doc. E/CN.4/Sub.2/1987/28.
[218] CHR Res. 1985/25, UN Doc. E/1989/20, pp. 83–84.   [219] ESC Res. 1989/139.
[220] As draft resolution UN Doc. A/C.3/44/L.42.

States which chose to become parties to the protocol with an international legal instrument'.[221] The German representative, perhaps naively, hoped that the resolution could be adopted in the Third Committee by consensus, but one of the most vocal retentionist States, Saudi Arabia, insisted upon a recorded vote.[222]

Apart from a few speeches in favour of the draft,[223] there were several comments by its opponents, almost all countries with a significant Moslem population.[224] Several speakers made explicit reference to Islamic law and the Koran. Saudi Arabia argued that the death penalty was the only fitting sanction for those who took life, as provided for in Islamic law.[225] Jordan maintained that the death penalty had a positive, deterrent effect.[226] Iraq and Morocco implied that there was a hidden agenda behind the protocol, and that it was aimed at embarrassing or exerting pressure on States which had not abolished the death penalty, States, they hastened to point out, constituting the majority of the members of the United Nations.[227] Japan argued that the instrument was 'premature'.[228] A few Islamic countries preferred to abstain.[229]

The *Second Optional Protocol to the International Covenant on Civil and Political Rights, Aiming at the Abolition of the Death Penalty* was adopted by the General Assembly on 29 December 1989, with fifty-nine votes in favour, twenty-six votes against and forty-eight abstentions.[230] It was unchanged from the draft that Marc Bossuyt had proposed in the Sub-Commission. The General

[221] UN Doc. A/C.3/44/SR.50, para. 72.   [222] UN Doc. A/C.3/44/SR.52, para. 23.

[223] In the Third Committee, a few representatives made essentially perfunctory comments in favour: Australia (UN Doc. A/C.3/44/SR.40, para. 8), Italy (UN Doc. A/C.3/44/SR.40, para. 43), Portugal (UN Doc. A/C.3/44/SR.42, para. 6).

[224] Egypt (UN Doc. A/C.3/44/SR.52, para. 7), Afghanistan (UN Doc. A/C.3/44/SR.52, para. 19), Somalia (UN Doc. A/C.3/44/SR.52, para. 20), Pakistan (UN Doc. A/C.3/44/SR.52, para. 21), Oman (UN Doc. A/C.3/44/SR.52, para. 18), Iran (UN Doc. A/C.3/44/SR.52, para. 13), Indonesia (UN Doc. A/C.3/44/SR.52, para. 14).

[225] UN Doc. A/C.3/44/SR.52, para. 12.   [226] *Ibid.*, para. 16.

[227] *Ibid.*, para. 11 (Iraq), para. 17 (Morocco).   [228] UN Doc. A/C.3/44/SR.42, para. 35.

[229] Algeria, in the Third Committee: UN Doc. A/C.3/44/SR.52, para. 10; Democratic Yemen, in the General Assembly: UN Doc. A/44/PV.82.

[230] GA Res. 44/128, UN Doc. A/44/824, UN Doc. A/44/PV.82, p. 11.

In favour: Argentina, Australia, Austria, Belgium, Bolivia, Brazil, Bulgaria, Byelorussian Soviet Socialist Republic, Canada, Cape Verde, Colombia, Costa Rica, Cyprus, Czechoslovakia, Democratic Kampuchea, Denmark, Dominican Republic, Ecuador, El Salvador, Finland, France, German Democratic Republic, Federal Republic of Germany, Greece, Grenada, Guatemala, Haiti, Honduras, Hungary, Iceland, Ireland, Italy, Luxemburg, Malta, Mexico, Mongolia, Nepal, Netherlands, New Zealand, Norway, Panama, Paraguay, Peru, Philippines, Poland, Portugal, Saint Kitts and Nevis, Saint Lucia, Saint Vincent and the Grenadines, Samoa, Spain, Sweden, Togo, Ukrainian Soviet Socialist Republic, Union of Soviet Socialist Republics, United Kingdom of Great Britain and Northern Ireland, Uruguay, Venezuela, and Yugoslavia. Nicaragua later advised the Secretariat that it had intended to vote in favour.

Against: Afghanistan, Bahrain, Bangladesh, Cameroon, China, Djibouti, Egypt, Indonesia, Islamic Republic of Iran, Iraq, Japan, Jordan, Kuwait, Maldives, Morocco, Nigeria, Oman, Pakistan, Qatar, Saudi Arabia, Sierra Leone, Somalia, Syrian Arab Republic, United Republic of Tanzania, United States of America, and Yemen. Malaysia and Sudan later advised the Secretariat that they had intended to vote against.

Abstaining: Algeria, Antigua and Barbuda, Bahamas, Barbados, Bhutan, Botswana, Brunei Darussalem, Burkina Faso, Burundi, Chile, Congo, Côte d'Ivoire, Cuba, Democratic Yemen, Dominica, Ethiopia, Fiji,

Assembly resolution referred twice to his report, which in effect amounts to the principal *travaux préparatoires* of the instrument. The *Protocol* entered into force on 11 July 1991, following its tenth ratification. Ten years later, it had obtained forty-one ratifications. If this number seems modest, it might be well to bear in mind that it took ten years for the *International Covenant on Civil and Political Rights* to obtain thirty-five ratifications, the amount necessary for its entry into force.

In the consideration of periodic reports under article 40 of the *Civil Rights Covenant*, the Human Rights Committee asks States parties whether they intend to ratify the *Second Optional Protocol*. During the presentation of Canada's second and third periodic reports,[231] the Canadian delegation replied that, although the matter was receiving careful consideration with a view to possible accession, no decision had yet been taken.[232] Finland, during consideration of its third periodic report,[233] indicated its intention to ratify the *Protocol* within a matter of months.[234] During consideration of its third periodic report,[235] Spain stated that the instrument of ratification had already been submitted to the *Cortes*, but that Spain would enter a reservation allowing the death penalty to be applied in extremely serious cases in wartime, as permitted by the text of the *Protocol*.[236] Costa Rica answered that the death penalty had been abolished in 1882, that there was no opposition to such ratification, but that it would take 'some time' before it could be ratified.[237] Uruguay, in its third periodic report, reminded the Committee that it had supported all initiatives aimed at abolition, including the *Second Optional Protocol*, and that it had acceded to the *Protocol* on the day it was opened for signature.[238] The second periodic report of Cyprus informed the Committee that legislative amendments were planned in order to enable ratification of the *Protocol*.[239] Denmark announced its ratification, and was congratulated, during presentation of its third periodic report.[240] During

---

Gambia, Ghana, Guinea, Guyana, India, Israel, Jamaica, Kenya, Lebanon, Lesotho, Liberia, Libyan Arab Jamahiriya, Madagascar, Malawi, Mali, Mauritius, Mozambique, Myanmar, Romania, Rwanda, Senegal, Singapore, Solomon Islands, Sri Lanka, Suriname, Trinidad and Tobago, Turkey, Uganda, Vanuatu, Zambia, Zimbabwe. Saint Vincent and the Grenadines later advised the Secretariat that it had intended to abstain.

[231] UN Doc. CCPR/C/51/Add.1, UN Doc. CCPR/C/64/Add.1, UN Doc. CCPR/C/SR.1010–1013, UN Doc. A/46/40, pp. 10–25.

[232] UN Doc. A/46/40, paras. 64–65.

[233] UN Doc. CCPR/C/58/Add.5, UN Doc. CCPR/C/SR.1014–1016, UN Doc. A/46/40, pp. 26–34.

[234] UN Doc. A/46/40, paras. 118–119.

[235] UN Doc. CCPR/C/58/Add.1 and 3, UN Doc. CCPR/C/SR.1018–1021, UN Doc. A/46/40, pp. 35–45.

[236] UN Doc. A/46/40, paras. 156–157. For the text of Spain's reservation, see Appendix 4, p. 399.

[237] 'Second Periodic Report of Costa Rica', UN Doc. CCPR/C/37/Add.10, UN Doc. CCPR/C/SR.958–960, UN Doc. A/45/40, paras. 294–295.

[238] 'Third Periodic Report of Uruguay', UN Doc. CCPR/C/64/Add.4, paras. 32–36. In fact, Uruguay had only signed the *Protocol*.

[239] 'Second Periodic Report of Cyprus', UN Doc. CCPR/C/32/Add.18, para. 34.

[240] 'Annual Report of the Human Rights Committee, 1997', UN Doc. 52/40, para. 58.

presentation of its initial report, Lithuania informed the Committee it had suspended executions, was adopting a new criminal code with no death penalty, and was planning to ratify the *Second Optional Protocol.*[241] Slovakia was urged to ratify the *Second Optional Protocol,* given that it had abolished capital punishment.[242] Even Libya said that its goal was to abolish capital punishment, prompting the Committee to urge that it ratify the *Second Optional Protocol.*[243]

4.3.2 Interpretation of the Protocol

The original 1980 draft of the *Protocol* had left space for preambular paragraphs, but made no specific proposals. The five preambular paragraphs added by Bossuyt cite article 3 of the *Universal Declaration of Human Rights* and article 6 of the *International Covenant on Civil and Political Rights,* noting that the *Covenant* 'refers to abolition of the death penalty in terms that strongly suggest that abolition is desirable'. The preamble also states that all measures of abolition should be considered as progress in enjoyment of the right to life.

Article 1 consists of two paragraphs. The first provides that no one within the jurisdiction of a State party shall be executed. Bossuyt introduced this provision in response to a suggestion from the Netherlands, which felt the treaty should be self-executing in States whose constitution would permit this.[244] Such a self-executing provision means that ratification of the *Protocol* effects abolition of the death penalty within the ratifying State, without need of any implementing legislation in domestic law. Bossuyt considered that the first paragraph had been worded 'in a manner sufficiently clear and complete' to effect direct application within domestic law, where appropriate.[245] However, Bossuyt departed from the Netherlands' proposal by adding a second sentence to article 1, imposing an obligation on States parties to abolish the death penalty.[246] Article 1 of the *Protocol* declares:

> 1. No one within the jurisdiction of a State party to the present Optional Protocol shall be executed.
> 2. Each State party shall take all necessary measures to abolish the death penalty within its jurisdiction.

The original 1980 draft had included, in article 1, a provision stating that the death penalty would not be re-established in States which had abolished it. Such a provision echoed article 4 of the *American Convention on Human Rights,* but Bossuyt felt that it was superfluous. 'It is obvious that a State party to the

[241] 'Annual Report of the Human Rights Committee, 1998', UN Doc. 53/40, para. 162.
[242] 'Annual Report of the Human Rights Committee, 1997', para. 369.
[243] UN Doc. CCPR/C/79/Add.45 (1994), para. 16.   [244] UN Doc. A/36/441, p. 12.
[245] UN Doc. E/CN.4/Sub.2/1987/20, §159.   [246] *Ibid.*, §160.

second optional protocol could not re-establish the death penalty without manifestly violating that protocol', he wrote. 'Indeed, a re-establishment of capital punishment would be contrary to the very object and purpose of the second optional protocol.'[247] The view that the a prohibition of reinstatement of the death penalty may be 'read into' the *Protocol* has also been expressed by two members of the Human Rights Committee, Waleed Sadi and Kurt Herndl.[248]

Article 2 of the *Second Optional Protocol* permits reservation of the application of the death penalty in time of war, pursuant to a conviction for 'a most serious crime of a military nature committed during wartime'. The 1980 draft had provided that there would be neither reservation nor derogation to the second optional protocol, but Bossuyt favoured a more nuanced position. He noted that about a dozen abolitionist States retained the death penalty for crimes committed under military law or in exceptional circumstances, such as wartime. Furthermore, five of the seven States that had proposed the original draft second optional protocol had also, in December 1982, adopted *Protocol No. 6 to the European Convention on Human Rights,*[249] whose article 2 provided for derogation in respect of acts committed in time of war or of imminent threat of war.[250] A similar approach in the second optional protocol, said Bossuyt, might make it possible for more States to become parties. He suggested it might be 'unrealistic' to expect States to assume obligations in a United Nations instrument that they were unwilling to assume in a regional system.[251]

Reservations to the *Protocol* are only permitted at the time of ratification or accession and must be accompanied by a notice to the Secretary-General of the United Nations of the relevant provisions in the national legislation applicable during wartime. It is therefore impossible for a State to modify indirectly its reservation by changing its national legislation. Bossuyt had insisted on this point, saying that any possibility of subsequent reservation 'would very likely be incompatible with the object and purpose of the second optional protocol'.[252]

Such reservations must provide for the death penalty only 'in time of war'. A broad construction of this term could encompass internal armed conflict or civil war. Commentators on the European *Protocol No. 6,* whose wording is similar, have suggested that this is not the case and that the term 'civil war' would have been used specifically if this were the intention. International law generally uses the term 'war' only in connection with international armed conflict.[253]

---

[247] UN Doc. E/CN.4/Sub.2/1987/20, §162.

[248] *Cox* v. *Canada* (No. 539/1993), UN Doc. CCPR/C/52/D/539/1993, (1994) 15 *HRLJ* 410, at p. 418.

[249] *Protocol No. 6 to the Convention for the Protection of Human Rights and Fundamental Freedoms Concerning the Abolition of the Death Penalty,* ETS 114 (see Appendix 15, pp. 424–429). For our discussion of the drafting and interpretation of the European protocol, see Chapter 7.

[250] UN Doc. E/CN.4/Sub.2/1987/20, paras. 163–164.

[251] *Ibid.,* para. 165.   [252] *Ibid.,* para. 166.

[253] Rodley, *The Treatment of Prisoners,* p. 173. Also: Jacques Velu, Rusen Ergec, *La Convention européenne des droits de l'homme,* Brussels: Bruylant, 1990, p. 185.

The Appeals Chamber of the International Criminal Tribunal for the former Yugoslavia has defined the related term of 'armed conflict' as existing 'whenever there is a resort to armed force between States or protracted armed violence between governmental authorities and organized armed groups or between groups within a State'.[254]

On its face, the term 'state of war' is considerably narrower than the comparable provision of *Protocol No. 6* to the *European Convention*, which adds the phrase 'or of imminent threat of war'. However, Bossuyt's report explained that use of the expression 'state of war' would encompass the terms 'time of war' and 'time of imminent threat of war'.[255] If this is indeed the correct interpretation, problems associated with identifying the beginning of a state of war are avoided. Furthermore, States are required, under article 2§3, to notify the Secretary-General of the United Nations of any beginning or ending of a state of war applicable to their territory. Bossuyt observed: 'Particularly in case of an "imminent threat of war", it is not the factual situation itself, but the legal declaration of such a situation which provides to the individual the necessary legal security with regard to the applicable law.'[256] Naturally, the factual situation of a war or an imminent threat of war must also be objectively present.

Normally, a 'state of war' at international law is a precise legal status that must be declared by at least one party and that creates specific rights and obligations.[257] The *Geneva Conventions* refer, in common article 2, to 'all cases of declared war or of other armed conflict ..., even if a state of war is not recognized by one of them'.[258] Because the purpose of the *Geneva Conventions* is protection of the victims of armed conflict, common article 2 provides for an especially broad definition of wartime. Article 2 of the *Second Optional Protocol* is different in nature, an exceptional provision creating rights for States in a treaty whose purpose is protection of the individual. The argument that 'war' should be construed narrowly, applying only to war declared by at least one of the belligerents, is therefore a persuasive one.

Reservations are admissible only for 'the most serious crimes of a military nature' committed during wartime. The term 'most serious crimes' is borrowed from article 6§2 of the *Covenant*, but it is further qualified by the term 'of a military nature'. Said Bossuyt: 'The crimes thus envisaged are those provided for in the military code. As, however, some States do not have a military code

---

[254] *Prosecutor* v. *Tadic* (Case no. IT-94-1-AR72), Decision on the Defence Motion for Interlocutory Appeal on Jurisdiction, 2 October 1995, (1997) 105 ILR 453, 35 ILM 32, para. 70.

[255] UN Doc. E/CN.4/Sub.2/1987/20, para. 168.   [256] *Ibid.*

[257] Rodley, *The Treatment of Prisoners*, p. 172.

[258] *Geneva Convention of August 12, 1949 For the Amelioration of the Condition of the Wounded and Sick in Armed Forces in the Field*, (1950) 75 UNTS 31, art. 2; *Geneva Convention of August 12, 1949 For the Amelioration of the Condition of Wounded, Sick and Shipwrecked Members of Armed Forces at Sea*, (1950) 75 UNTS 85, art 2; *Geneva Convention of August 12, 1949 Relative to the Treatment of Prisoners of War*, (1950) 75 UNTS 135, art. 2; *Geneva Convention of August 12, 1949 Relative to the Protection of Civilians*, (1950) 75 UNTS 287, art. 2.

separate from the Penal Code, the larger notion of "crimes of a military nature" is proposed.' Bossuyt also noted that the scope of reservation would continue to be limited by the State's obligations under international humanitarian law, notably the 1949 *Geneva Conventions* and *Additional Protocols I* and *II*.[259] Article 68§2 of the fourth *Geneva Convention* limits the scope of the death penalty during wartime, at least as far as civilians in an occupied territory are concerned, to espionage, serious acts of sabotage against the military installations of the occupying power or intentional offences which have caused the death of one or more persons. This widely ratified provision is a good guide to the scope of the term 'most serious crimes of a military nature'. As a further qualification, such offences must be committed 'during wartime', precluding capital punishment in peacetime for crimes committed during the conflict as well as eliminating its imposition during the conflict for crimes committed prior to the outbreak of hostilities. In fact, there have been two reservations to the *Protocol*, by Spain and Malta. Both take the terms of the instrument a bit further. Spain limits its reservations to 'exceptional and extremely serious cases', whereas Malta speaks of 'exceptional and serious cases'. According to the Human Rights Chamber of Bosnia and Herzegovina, the term 'application' which is used in article 2 of the *Second Optional Protocol* covers both the imposition and the carrying out of the death penalty. In other words, the *Protocol* prohibits absolutely both the imposition and the carrying out of capital punishment in peacetime.[260]

There have been five reservations to the *Second Optional Protocol*, by Spain, Malta, Azerbaijan, Greece and Cyprus.[261] Spain limits its reservations to 'exceptional and extremely serious cases', Malta speaks of 'exceptional and serious cases'. Greece and Cyprus more prudently stick to the text of article 2 in their reservations. Azerbaijan's reservation refers to the fact that its legislation allows for application of the death penalty for 'grave crimes, committed during the war or in condition of the threat of war'. Both Spain and Malta have since withdrawn their reservations.

Four European States have objected to Azerbaijan's reservation, noting that the reference to 'condition of the threat of war' was inconsistent with article 2, which only allows the death penalty 'during wartime'. Finland and Sweden said that this did not preclude the *Protocol* coming into force between the two States, but added that it should 'become operative between the two states without

---

[259] UN Doc. E/CN.4/Sub.2/1987/20, para. 167. The provisions are: *Geneva Convention of August 12, 1949 Relative to the Treatment of Prisoners of War*, arts. 100, 101 (see Appendix 9, pp. 414–415); *Geneva Convention of August 12, 1949 Relative to the Protection of Civilians*, arts. 68, 75 (see Appendix 10 pp. 416–419); *Protocol Additional I to the 1949 Geneva Conventions and Relating to the Protection of Victims of International Armed Conflicts*, articles 76§3, 77§5 (see Appendix 11, p. 420); *Protocol Additional II to the 1949 Geneva Conventions and Relating to The Protection of Victims of Non-International Armed Conflicts*, art. 6§4 (see Appendix 12, p. 421).

[260] *Damjanovic* v. *Federation of Bosnia and Herzegovina* (Case no. CH/96/30), 5 September 1997, Decisions on Admissibility and Merits 1996–1997, p. 147, para. 36.

[261] For the text of the reservations and objections to the *Second Optional Protocol*, see Appendix 4.

Azerbaijan benefiting from the reservation'. Germany and the Netherlands confined themselves to saying that the objection did not preclude the entry into force of the *Protocol* between Azerbaijan and Germany. Subsequently, Azerbaijan communicated to the Secretary-General a modification to its reservation. According to the Secretary-General:

> In keeping with the depositary practice followed in similar cases, the Secretary-General proposes to receive the modification in question for deposit in the absence of any objection on the part of any of the Contracting States, either to the deposit itself or to the procedure envisaged, within a period of twelve months from the date of the present depositary notification. In the absence of any such objection, the above modification will be accepted for deposit upon the expiration of the above-stipulated twelve-month period, that is on 5 October 2001.

Articles 3, 4 and 5 provide for the same implementation mechanism as that of the *Covenant* and the first *Optional Protocol*, to the extent that States parties to the *Second Optional Protocol* have made the appropriate declarations respecting inter-State and individual communications. If a State party does not wish these mechanisms to apply automatically, it must make a reservation at the time of accession or ratification. The 1980 draft had specified that States parties to the *Optional Protocol* would be obliged to make a new declaration recognizing the competence of the Human Rights Committee to receive communications under that instrument.[262]

Article 3 of the *Second Optional Protocol* requires States parties to include information about progress in abolition of the death penalty in their periodic reports to the Human Rights Committee,[263] and no exception by reservation is permitted to this obligation. According to articles 4 and 5, if a State party has already accepted the inter-State and individual communications procedures for the *Covenant*, these are also applicable to the *Second Optional Protocol*. However, a State may declare otherwise at the time of ratification or accession. Bossuyt felt that it was clear enough in his draft that a communication to the Human Rights Committee alleging a violation of article 1 of the *Second Optional Protocol* would be admissible from the moment of a potential threat of execution. Obviously, actual execution of the death sentence would prevent an individual from making a communication. 'The fact that a person would have to live under a threat of execution would in itself violate the obligation of a State party to the second optional protocol in view of its article 1, paragraph 2, which requires it to take all necessary measures to abolish the death penalty', he wrote.[264]

Article 6 describes the provisions of the *Second Optional Protocol* as additional provisions to the *International Covenant on Civil and Political Rights*.

---

[262] UN Doc. E/CN.4/Sub.2/1987/20, paras. 171–174.
[263] See also the 1990 Annual Report of the Human Rights Committee (UN Doc. A/45/40, para. 21).
[264] UN Doc. E/CN.4/Sub.2/1987/20, para. 175.

According to Bossuyt, this emphasizes that the requirements of due process, provided by article 14 of the *Covenant*, apply to cases of the military death penalty as well as the relevant provisions of humanitarian law, by the effect of article 5§2 of the *Covenant*. Bossuyt noted that articles 3, 100 and 101 of the third *Geneva Convention*, dealing with execution of prisoners of war, are particularly relevant in this respect. In assessing whether a State has violated article 6 of the *Covenant* by extraditing an individual to a country where he or she might be executed, the Human Rights Committee considers it relevant that a State may have ratified the *Second Optional Protocol* to the *Covenant*.[265]

4.4 The *Convention on the Rights of the Child*

Paragraph 5 of article 6 of the *International Covenant on Civil and Political Rights* prohibits execution of persons for crimes committed while under the age of eighteen.[266] The norm also appears in the 'Safeguards Guaranteeing the Rights of Those Facing the Death Penalty'.[267] The prohibition on execution of individuals for crimes committed while under the age of eighteen was reiterated in the *Convention on the Rights of the Child*, which was adopted by the General Assembly in 1989.[268]

A 1980 Working Party draft of the *Convention on the Rights of the Child* included a rather summary provision dealing with criminal procedure, which specified that a child not be liable to capital punishment, and that '[a]ny other punishment shall be adequate to the particular phase of his development'.[269] In 1985, Canada proposed the addition of a detailed provision guaranteeing the rights of a child upon being accused or convicted of a criminal offence.[270] Canada's text included a statement that no child could be sentenced to death. At the time, a 'child' was defined in the draft convention as being a person under eighteen, 'unless, under the law of his State, he has attained his age of majority earlier'.[271] The next year, Canada revised its proposal, rephrasing the provision and making a cross-reference to article 6§5 of the *Covenant*.[272] A competing Polish text stated that 'no child shall be . . . sentenced to death'.[273]

An informal Working Party formulated a text that prohibited capital punishment 'for crimes committed by persons below eighteen years of age', removing any possible ambiguity relating to the definition of the term 'child' and making the provision consistent with the *Covenant*.[274] The United States' representative

---

[265] *T. v. Australia* (No. 706/1996), UN Doc. CCPR/C/61/D/706/1996, para. 8.4.
[266] See pp. 136–138 above for our discussion of this provision.   [267] See Appendix 8, p. 413.
[268] *Convention on the Rights of the Child*, GA Res. 44/25, 28 ILM 1448 (see Appendix 7, p. 406).
[269] UN Doc. E/CN.4/1349*, article 20§2.   [270] UN Doc. E/CN.4/1985/64, Annex II, p. 4.
[271] UN Doc. E/CN.4/1985/64, Annex I, p. 2.
[272] UN Doc. E/CN.4/1986/39, para. 90.   [273] UN Doc. A/C.3/40/3, para. 2.
[274] *Ibid.*, para. 93. The text read:
     The following sentences shall not be imposed for crimes committed by persons below eighteen years of age: (a) capital punishment; (b) life imprisonment.

objected to the draft paragraph, stating that reference to 'persons below eighteen years of age' was too arbitrary, and proposed its deletion. The United States said that it did not consider the eighteen-year age limit to be 'an appropriate general rule', but added that it would not insist upon an amendment which would block consensus, providing it be understood that the United States maintained its right to make a reservation on this point.[275] Amnesty International and the International Commission of Jurists opposed the United States.[276]

In the 1986 Working Group, the Japanese representative questioned the phrase 'or life imprisonment' and proposed its deletion.[277] According to the Working Group report, Canada sought to accommodate' the Japanese position and suggested adding the words 'without possibility of release' after the words 'life imprisonment'.[278] The Report indicates that the United Kingdom placed on record its reservation to the provision, but does not suggest why; presumably, the United Kingdom was troubled by the life imprisonment provision, which was probably inconsistent with its legislation.[279] Eventually, the Working Group adopted the following text: 'Capital punishment or life imprisonment without possibility of release is not imposed for crimes committed by persons below eighteen years of age.'[280]

The article was reviewed in a special Working Party session in late 1988. Besides the Working Group text, the Working Party had another version proposed by the Crime, Prevention and Criminal Justice Branch of the Centre for Social Development and Humanitarian Affairs, United Nations Office at Vienna, which revived the blanket prohibition on both capital punishment and life imprisonment: 'The death penalty or a term of life imprisonment is not imposed for offences committed by children below 18 years of age.'[281] A drafting group attempted to devise a compromise, but eventually submitted a text in which the reference to 'without possibility of release' was square-bracketed.[282] During debate on the point, Austria, the Federal Republic of Germany, Senegal and Venezuela urged that the phrase 'without possibility of release' be deleted, while China, India, Japan, Norway, the Soviet Union and the United States took the contrary position.[283] A suggestion that compromise be sought by simply removing any reference to life imprisonment, leaving the prohibition on the death penalty to stand alone, was opposed by Senegal, which said its omission would leave judges 'at liberty to use life imprisonment as a substitute for capital punishment'.[284] Eventually, those States that had fought to delete

---

[275] *Ibid.*, paras. 105, 107. The United States made such a statement concerning the draft provision on more than one occasion. See, for example: UN Doc. E/CN.4/1989/48, para. 544.
[276] *Ibid.*, para. 105.   [277] *Ibid.*, para. 104   [278] *Ibid.*   [279] *Ibid.*, para. 107.
[280] *Ibid.*, para. 106. See also: UN Doc. E/CN.4/1988/WG.1/WP.1/Rev.2.
[281] UN Doc. E/CN.4/1989/WG.1/WP.2.   [282] UN Doc. E/CN.4/1989/WG.1/WP.67/Rev.1.
[283] UN Doc. E/CN.4/1989/48, para. 541.   [284] *Ibid.*, para. 542.

the square-bracketed reference to possibility of release withdrew their insistence, '[i]n a spirit of compromise'.[285] The Working Party draft[286] was adopted by the Commission on Human Rights by consensus,[287] by the Third Committee in an unrecorded vote,[288] and ultimately by the General Assembly.[289]

Article 51 explicitly permits reservations, but only to the extent that they are compatible with the object and purpose of the *Convention*. There have been three reservations to article 37§a of the *Convention*, although none has explicitly referred to the death penalty.[290] Myanmar's reservation said it 'accepts in principle the provisions of article 37 as they are in consonance with its laws, rules, regulations, procedures and practice as well as with its traditional, cultural and religious values'. Myanmar withdrew its reservation on 19 October 1993.[291] Singapore formulated what it called a 'declaration' saying that article 37 does not prohibit 'the application of any prevailing measures prescribed by law for maintaining law and order in the Republic of Singapore' and 'measures and restrictions which are prescribed by law and which are necessary in the interests of national security, public safety, public order, the protection of public health or the protection of the rights and freedoms of others'. According to Malaysia's reservation, article 37§a is applicable only to the extent it is 'in conformity with the Constitution, national laws and national policies of the Government of Malaysia'.

All three reservations have provoked objections. Germany, Portugal and Ireland reacted to Myanmar's reservation, adding that the objection was not an obstacle to the coming into force of the *Convention* between themselves and Myanmar. Germany, Portugal and Ireland objected to Malaysia's reservation in similar terms, although Ireland did not specify whether the *Convention* entered into force. Finland objected, saying Malaysia's reservation was 'devoid of legal effect'. Belgium and Denmark did not formulate their objections within the one-year period provided for in the *Vienna Convention on the Law of Treaties* of 1969.[292] In explanation, they said that no time limit applied to objections against reservations that are inadmissible under international law. Germany, Belgium, Italy, the Netherlands, Finland, Norway, Portugal and Sweden objected to Singapore's declaration.

During the presentation of periodic reports, the issue of juvenile executions has arisen on several occasions before the Committee on the Rights of the Child.

---

[285] *Ibid.*, para. 543.   [286] UN Doc. E/CN.4/1989/48/Rev.1, p. 15.
[287] UN Doc. E/CN.4/1989/L.88. The debates are found at UN Doc. E/CN.4/1989/SR.54, UN Doc. E/CN.4/1989/SR.55, UN Doc. E/CN.4/1989/SR.55/Add.1.
[288] UN Doc. A/C.3/SR.44, para. 63, UN Doc. A/C.3/44/L.44.
[289] UN Doc. A/44/PV.61, as GA Res. 44/25.
[290] For the text of the reservations and the objections, see Appendix 7, p. 406.
[291] 'Initial Report of Myanmar', UN Doc. CRC/C/8/Add.9, para. 31.
[292] *Vienna Convention on the Law of Treaties*, (1979) 1155 UNTS 331, art. 20§5.

Many States simply remind the Committee that they have abolished the death penalty.[293] Others explain that their domestic legislation complies with the *Convention.*[294] Some have stated that their legislation does not permit executions of 'juveniles', but without providing details.[295] Occasionally, the Committee seems to blur the scope of article 37§a, suggesting that it prohibits execution of persons under the age of eighteen, whereas in fact it also prohibits execution of adults for crimes committed below that age.[296] With respect to the Egyptian initial report, which is silent on the subject of juvenile executions,[297] the Committee said '[c]oncern is expressed, in general, as to the compatibility with articles 37 and 40 of the Convention of the juvenile justice institutions and the administration of justice system in so far as it relates to juvenile justice', although there is nothing specific to indicate that capital punishment was a concern.[298] Sudan's initial report declared that 'with the exception of offences punishable by penalties and sanctions, the death penalty may not be imposed on a person under the age of eighteen or over the age of seventy. A juvenile delinquent may be sentenced to death only for an offence punishable by penalties and sanctions, in accordance with provisions of Islamic law.'[299] During discussion of the report, the issue of juvenile executions was not even raised by the Committee,[300] although it did express 'its concern as to the issues of criminal responsibility'.[301] Barbados testified to the positive effects of article 37 of the *Convention* when it noted, in its initial report to the Committee, that since ratification it has been concerned with the issue of imposition of capital punishment for crimes committed while under eighteen years of age. Barbados informed the Committee that it had adopted the Juvenile Offenders Act, which prohibits imposition of the death penalty when it appears that the accused was under eighteen when the offence was committed.[302]

---

[293] 'Initial Report of Namibia', UN Doc. CRC/C/3/Add.12, para. 454; 'Initial Report of Sweden', UN Doc. CRC/C/3/Add.1, para. 83; 'Initial Report of El Salvador', UN Doc. CRC/C/3/Add.9, para. 194; 'Initial Report of Bolivia', UN Doc. CRC/C/3/Add.2, para. 92.

[294] 'Initial Report of the Russian Federation', UN Doc. CRC/C/3/Add.5, para. 162; 'Initial Report of Iraq', UN Doc. CRC/C/41/Add.3, paras. 124, 132, 133; 'Initial Report of Bangladesh', UN Doc. CRC/C/3/Add.38, para. 145; 'Initial Report of Barbados', UN Doc. CRC/C/3/Add.45, para. 48; 'Initial Report of Iraq', UN Doc. CRC/C/41/Add.3, para. 133; 'Initial Report of Myanmar', UN Doc. CRC/C/8/Add.9, para. 71(c)(i); UN Doc. CRC/C/SR.61, paras. 25–26 (Viet Nam).

[295] 'Initial Report of Indonesia', UN Doc. CRC/C/3/Add.10, para. 107; 'Initial Report of Viet Nam', UN Doc. CRC/C/3/Add.4, para. 228.

[296] 'Concluding Observations of the Committee on the Rights of the Child, Nigeria', UN Doc. CRC/C/15/Add.61, para. 39.

[297] 'Initial Report of Egypt', UN Doc. CRC/C/3/Add.6.

[298] 'Preliminary Observations of the Committee on the Rights of the Child: Egypt', UN Doc. CRC/C/15/Add.5, para. 8; also UN Doc. CRC/C/16, para. 100.

[299] 'Initial Report of Sudan', UN Doc. CRC/C/3/Add.4, para. 228.

[300] UN Doc. CRC/C/SR.70, paras. 42–48.

[301] 'Preliminary Observations of the Committee on the Rights of the Child: Sudan', UN Doc. CRC/C/15/Add.6, para. 11; also UN Doc. CRC/C/16, para. 120.

[302] 'Initial Report of Barbados', UN Doc. CRC/C/3/Add.45, paras. 7–8, 48; UN Doc. CRC/C/SR.535, para. 22.

When Barbados was challenged by a member of the Committee, who said there were reports it intended to lower the age for capital punishment to sixteen,[303] these were strenuously denied by the government representative.[304] Bangladesh did not provide satisfactory answers when challenged about the possibility of juvenile executions. Its initial report indicated that the death penalty could not be imposed upon 'children', but elsewhere the report indicated the lack of an unambiguous definition of what constitutes a 'child'.[305]

Seven countries are known to have executed offenders who were under eighteen at the time the crime was committed since 1990: Congo (Democratic Republic), Iran, Nigeria, Pakistan, Saudi Arabia, United States and Yemen.[306] All but the United States are parties to the *Convention on the Rights of the Child*,[307] and none has made a reservation to article 37§a. When Pakistan's report indicated its legislation was compatible with the *Covenant*, the Committee urged it to review this keeping in mind its concerns with such matters as the possible imposition of capital punishment for crimes committed under the age of eighteen.[308] Pakistan's representatives failed to answer a challenge that its laws were inconsistent with article 37§a.[309] In 2000, Pakistan set the minimum age for the death penalty at the age of eighteen at the time of the offence, in accordance with article 37§a. Examining Nigeria's report, the Committee noted that it was possible for children to be sentenced to death, in violation of article 37§a.[310] Nigeria indicated that its present legislation only limits the death penalty to seventeen, but that a draft decree will increase this to eighteen.[311] The periodic reports of Yemen have seemed to suggest that persons over fifteen can be executed,[312] and its answers on this point have appeared evasive.[313] Yemen raised the minimum age for execution to eighteen at the time of the offence in 1994. In its conclusions with respect to the periodic report of the Democratic Republic

---

[303] UN Doc. CRC/C/SR.535, para. 14.   [304] *Ibid.*, para. 22.

[305] UN Doc. CRC/C/SR.382, para. 18. But see: 'Initial Report of Bangladesh', UN Doc. CRC/C/3/Add.38, para. 145, which claims that '[t]he Children's Act of 1974 categorically prohibits the death sentence'. Also paras. 42–46.

[306] Amnesty International, 'Facts and Figures on the Death Penalty', AI Index: ACT 50/002/2001, p. 2. The United States has executed fourteen juvenile offenders since 1990, the greatest number of known executions of this sort.

[307] The United States signed the *Convention* in 1995 without reservation. It is obliged to refrain from acts which would defeat the object and purpose of the *Convention* pending ratification, unless it makes clear its intention not to ratify, something it has not done: *Vienna Convention on the Law of Treaties*, art. 18§a.

[308] 'Final Observations of the Committee on the Rights of the Child, Pakistan', UN Doc. CRC/C/15/Add.18, para. 23.

[309] UN Doc. CRC/C/SR.133, para. 11.

[310] 'Concluding Observations of the Committee on the Rights of the Child: Nigeria', UN Doc. CRC/C/15/Add.61, paras. 20, 39; also: UN Doc. CRC/C/SR.323, paras. 56, 73, 84.

[311] UN Doc. CRC/C/SR.323, para. 73.

[312] 'Second Periodic Report of Yemen', UN Doc. CRC/C/70/Add.1, para. 82(g).

[313] UN Doc. CRC/C/SR.262; CRC/C/SR.523, para. 28.

of Congo, the Committee noted its concern that children aged sixteen or more can be sentenced to death, although it recognised that a presidential pardon had recently been accorded in such cases.[314] In its initial report to the Committee on the Rights of the Child, Saudi Arabia said capital punishment could not be imposed upon children 'who have attained the age of majority in accordance with Islamic law'.[315] In its concluding observations on Saudi Arabia, the Committee 'strongly recommend[ed] that the State party take immediate steps to halt and abolish by law the imposition of the death penalty for crimes committed by persons under 18'.[316] With respect to Iran, the Committee said it was 'seriously disturbed' at the application of the death penalty for crimes committed under the age of eighteen.[317]

4.5 The *Convention Against Torture and Other Cruel, Inhuman and Degrading Treatment or Punishment*

The *Convention Against Torture and Other Forms of Cruel, Inhuman and Degrading Treatment or Punishment* was adopted by the General Assembly in 1984 and entered into force on 26 June 1987.[318] As of 1 May 2001, the *Convention* had been ratified by 126 states. Like several of the other human rights treaties of the United Nations system, the *Convention* creates a committee of experts charged with overseeing its implementation. Composed of ten members, the Committee Against Torture's principal activity has been the consideration of periodic reports, filed by States parties pursuant to article 19 of the *Convention*. The *Convention* also provides for an individual petition mechanism, similar to that set out in the *Optional Protocol to the International Covenant on Civil and Political Rights*. It requires a supplementary declaration by States parties.[319] In the first years of its operations, only a handful of petitions came before the Committee, although this has picked up somewhat. *Refoulement* (return) to a country where the death penalty might be imposed has been raised in a few individual petitions to the Committee Against Torture, but it has avoided pronouncing itself on the question directly.[320]

---

[314] 'Concluding Observations, Democratic Republic of the Congo', UN Doc. CRC/C/15/Add.153, para. 74. Also: UN Doc. CRC/C/SR.705, para. 58.

[315] UN Doc. CRC/C/61/Add.2, para. 253.

[316] 'Concluding Observations, Saudi Arabia', UN Doc. CRC/C/15/Add.148, para. 27. Also: UN Doc. CRC/C/SR.688, para. 42.

[317] 'Concluding Observations, Iran (Islamic Republic of)', UN Doc. CRC/C/15/Add.123, para. 29. Also: UN Doc. CRC/C/SR.617, paras. 46–47.

[318] GA Res. 39/46.

[319] The *Convention* also creates an optional procedure for inter-State petitions, but, like the comparable mechanism under the *International Covenant on Civil and Political Rights*, it has never been used.

[320] *P.Q.L. v. Canada* (No. 57/1996), UN Doc. CAT/C/19/D/57/1996. See also: *I.A.O. v. Sweden* (No. 65/1997), UN Doc. CAT/C/20/D/65/1997; *M.R.P. v. Switzerland* (No. 122/1998), UN Doc. CAT/C/25/D/122/1998, para. 3.2.

A literal reading of the *Convention* might suggest that the death penalty does not fall within its scope, because article 1, which defines torture, excludes 'pain or suffering arising only from, inherent in or incidental to lawful sanctions'. Nevertheless, pursuant to article 16 of the *Convention*, '[e]ach State Party shall undertake to prevent in any territory under its jurisdiction other acts of cruel, inhuman or degrading treatment or punishment which do not amount to torture as defined in article 1, when such acts are committed by or at the instigation of or with the consent or acquiescence of a public official or other person acting in an official capacity'. On at least one occasion, early in the work of the Committee, a member of the Committee said that 'the death penalty theoretically did not come within the Committee's mandate'.[321] More recently, in its concluding observations, the Committee has expressed its concern at 'the continuing use of the death penalty'.[322] In its conclusions and recommendations on periodic reports, the Committee has often expressed satisfaction with measures towards total abolition of the death penalty.[323] When Armenia's initial report was being considered, Andreas Mavrommatis said that, while he welcomed the statement that the death penalty was confined to particularly heinous crimes, pending its abolition, 'he would have expected a moratorium on capital punishment under the circumstances'.[324] During presentation of the Republic of Korea's periodic report, the Committee's country *rapporteur* said 'all were agreed that the death penalty was a cruel, inhuman and degrading punishment' and he requested Korea to abolish it.[325]

Many of the periodic reports of States parties to the Committee Against Torture make reference to norms concerning the application of the death penalty,[326]

[321] UN Doc. CAT/C/SR.120, para. 6 (Sorensen)

[322] 'Concluding Observations: Belarus', UN Doc. CAT/C/XXV/Concl.2/Rev.1, para. 6(i).

[323] Annual Report of the Committee Against Torture, UN Doc. A/53/44, para. 125 (Spain); Report of the Committee Against Torture, UN Doc. A/52/44, para. 79 (Algeria); UN Doc. CAT/C/SR.283, para. 36 (Burns); 'Concluding observations: Armenia', UN Doc. CAT/CXXV/Concl/1, para. 3(a); UN Doc. CAT/C/SR.383, para. 3(a) (Luxemburg); UN Doc. CAT/C/SR.379, para. 4(c) (Bulgaria); UN Doc. C/CAT/SR.375, para. 3 (Mauritius); UN Doc. CAT/C/SR.419 (Poland).

[324] UN Doc. CAT/C/SR.440, para. 17.

[325] UN Doc. CAT/C/SR. 246, para. 44. Also: UN Doc. CAT/C/SR.405, para. 29 (Uzbekistan).

[326] 'Initial Report of Bulgaria', UN Doc. CAT/C/5/Add.28, paras. 50–54; 'Initial Report of Ukraine', UN Doc. CAT/C/17/Add.4, paras. 13–14; 'Initial Report of Libya', UN Doc. CAT/C/9/Add.7, paras. 28, 40; 'Initial Report of Libya', UN Doc. CAT/C/9/Add.12, pp. 19–20; 'Initial Report of Libya', UN Doc. CAT/C/9/Add.12/Rev.1, paras. 89–92; 'First Supplementary Report of China', UN Doc. CAT/C/7/Add.14, paras. 38–42, 123–129; 'Initial Report of Cyprus', UN Doc. CAT/C/16/Add.2, para. 23; 'Initial Report of Senegal', UN Doc. CAT/C/5/Add.19, paras. 4–6; 'First Supplementary Report of Belarus', UN Doc. CAT/C/17/Add.6, para. 3; 'Initial Report of Netherlands (Aruba)', UN Doc. CAT/C/25/Add.5, para. 51; 'Initial Report of Mauritius', UN Doc. CAT/C/24/Add.3, para. 36; UN Doc. CAT/C/SR.28, paras. 41, 74 (Soviet Union); UN Doc. CAT/C/SR.52, para. 11 (Ukrainian SSR); UN Doc. CAT/C/SR.77, para. 7, 12 (Chile); 'Initial Report of Algeria', UN Doc. CAT/C/25/Add.8, para. 43; UN Doc. CAT/C/SR.335/Add.1, para. 5 (Kuwait); UN Doc. CAT/C/SR.169, para. 25 (Cyprus); UN Doc. CAT/C/SR.125, para. 4 (Ukraine); UN Doc. CAT/C/SR.381, para. 28 (Libya); 'Initial Report of Malta', UN Doc. CAT/C/12/Add.7, para. 29;

extradition to other States for capital crimes,[327] efforts towards abolition,[328] or the fact that it has been or is being abolished.[329] This may be due to the fact that, prior to the presentation of periodic reports, the Committee indicates subjects on which it desires to receive information. At the very top of the list is '[a]bolition of the death penalty'.[330] Luxemburg's second periodic report provides information on abolition of the death penalty, noting that it is '[i]n reply to the views expressed by several members of the Committee during the presentation of the initial report regarding the advisability of eliminating all reference to the death penalty in legal provisions'.[331] Sometimes quite direct questions are asked of States about whether or not capital punishment is practicsed, the method of execution and whether it is carried out in public.[332] The United Kingdom representative referred to how 'the Committee had exhorted the British Government to have the Crown dependencies bring their practice regarding

UN Doc. CAT/C/SR.419 (Poland); 'Initial Report of Armenia', UN Doc. CAT/C/Add.4/Rev.1, para. 14; 'Initial Report of Uzbekistan', UN Doc. CAT/C/32/Add.3, paras. 58–59.

[327] 'Initial Report of Panama', UN Doc. CAT/C/17/Add.7, para. 23(k); 'Initial Report of Italy', UN Doc. CAT/C/9/Add.9, para. 24; 'Initial Report of Argentina', UN Doc. CAT/C/17/Add.2, para. 23;. 'Initial Report of Portugal', UN Doc. CAT/C/15, para. 61;. 'Initial Report of Canada', UN Doc. CAT/C/17/Add.5, paras. 17–19; UN Doc. CAT/C/SR.64, para. 42 (Netherlands); 'Initial Report of Mexico', UN Doc. CAT/C/5/Add.7, paras. 19–20; 'Initial Report of Czech Republic', UN Doc. CAT/C/21/Add.2, para. 41; UN Doc. CAT/C/SR.63, para. 91, UN Doc. CAT/C/SR.64, para. 41 (Netherlands (Netherlands Antilles)); UN Doc. CAT/C/SR.96, para. 40 (Australia); UN Doc. CAT/C/SR.335/Add.1, paras. 5, 9 (Kuwait); UN Doc. CAT/C/SR.276, para. 8 (Poland); 'Initial Report of Namibia', UN Doc. CAT/C/28/Add.2, para. 11 (Namibia); UN Doc. CAT/C/SR.373, para. 8 (Macedonia); UN Doc. CAT/C/SR.306, para. 14 (Portugal); UN Doc. CAT/C/SR.123, para. 11 (Norway). When Canada was questioned by the Committee Against Torture about the extradition of Kindler and Ng, government spokesperson Martin Low informed the Committee that the matter was pending before the Human Rights Committee, and hoped the Committee would appreciate the 'impropriety' of further discussion. He added that 'some delay was inevitable when, following conviction, a person had invoked legal procedures that were intended to ensure that the execution could not take place before the most exhaustive review and legal scrutiny': UN Doc. CAT/C/SR.140, para. 36.

[328] UN Doc. CAT/C/SR.278, para. 12 (Georgia); UN Doc. CAT/C/SR.161, para. 8 (Poland); UN Doc. CAT/C/SR.283, para. 6 (Ukraine); 'Third Periodic Report of Poland', UN Doc. CAT/C/44/Add.5, paras. 27–29.

[329] 'Initial Report of Romania', UN Doc. CAT/C/16/Add.1, para. 7; UN Doc. CAT/C/SR.167, para. 20 (Portugal); 'Initial Report of Hungary', UN Doc. CAT/C/17/Add.8, paras. 6–8; 'Initial Report of Uruguay', UN Doc. CAT/C/12/Add.3, para. 4; 'Initial Report of Poland', UN Doc. CAT/C/9/Add.13, para. 6; 'Second periodic Report of Poland', UN Doc. CAT/C/25\Add.9, para. 11; 'Initial Report of Switzerland', UN Doc. CAT/C/17/Add.12, paras. 27–28; 'Initial Report of Senegal', UN Doc. CAT/C/5/Add.19, para. 6; 'Initial Report of Philippines', UN Doc. CAT/C/5/Add.18, para. 29; 'Second Periodic Report of Mauritius', UN Doc. CAT/C/43/Add.1, para. 1; UN Doc. CAT/C/SR.276, para. 8 (Poland); UN Doc. CAT/C/SR.372, para. 5 (Bulgaria); UN Doc. CAT/C/SR.301, para. 24 (Cyprus); UN Doc. CAT/C/SR.401, para. 8 (Azerbaijan); 'Initial Report of Azerbaijan', UN Doc. CAT/C/37/Add.3, para. 259; UN Doc. CAT/C/SR.307, para. 2 (Switzerland); 'Second Periodic Report of Bulgaria', UN Doc. CAT/C/17/Add.19, para. 5; UN Doc. CAT/C/SR.311, para. 7 (Spain); UN Doc. CAT/C/SR.142/Add.2, para. 9 (Hungary); 'Third Periodic Report of the Netherlands (Antilles and Aruba)', UN Doc. CAT/C/44/Add.4, para. 95; 'Second Periodic Report of Switzerland', UN Doc. CAT/C/17/Add.12, para. 27; 'Initial Report of Macedonia', UN Doc. CAT/C/28/Add.4, paras. 46–47.

[330] See, for example, 'Second Periodic Report of Luxemburg', UN Doc. CAT/C/17/Add.20.

[331] 'Second Periodic Report of Luxemburg', UN Doc. CAT/C/17/Add.20, para. 33.

[332] For example, UN Doc. CAT/C/SR.442, para. 46.

corporal punishment and the death penalty into line with that of the United Kingdom'.[333]

In many cases, comments on the subject are provoked by questions from the Committee.[334] One of the most aggressive examples is the question raised by Committee member Peter Burns during examination of China's second periodic report:

> With regard to the manner in which capital punishment was applied in China, first of all, he wished to know the number of convictions and executions in 1994 and 1995. According to Amnesty International, 2,780 death sentences had been handed down in 1994 and 2,050 executions had taken place. In the first half of 1995, 1,800 persons had apparently been convicted and 1,147 executions had taken place. Although the application of the death penalty did not in itself constitute a violation of the Convention, it was clearly evident that, in the spirit of article 1 thereof, capital punishment could be imposed only for the most serious offences. However, according to some information, it was applied in China for a very large range of offences. He wished to know whether that information was correct, in which case the Committee would have cause for concern. Moreover, the Committee might be seriously disturbed at the way in which executions were carried out. They apparently took place in public and the condemned persons were paraded in chains. It also seemed that, contrary to the assertion that there should be a two-year time-lag between the sentence and the execution in order to give the condemned person an opportunity to demonstrate his penitence and have his penalty commuted, guilty persons were sometimes executed very soon after being sentenced at a public hearing. Similarly, if it was confirmed, the practice mentioned by Amnesty International of chaining persons condemned to death until they were executed could, like the other circumstances surrounding the execution, constitute cruel and degrading treatment under article 16 of the Convention. The removal of organs from the bodies of condemned persons for commercial purposes and without their prior consent, which had been reported by Amnesty International, if confirmed, also seemed to be a reprehensible practice.[335]

---

[333] UN Doc. CAT/C/SR.355, para. 34.

[334] 'Initial Report of Uruguay', UN Doc. CAT/C/5/Add.30, p. 25; UN Doc. CAT/C/SR.62, para. 5 (Turkey); UN Doc. CAT/C/SR.98, para. 54 (Bulgaria); UN Doc. CAT/C/SR.161, para. 8 (Poland); UN Doc. CAT/C/SR.146/Add.2, para. 19 (China); UN Doc. CAT/C/SR.169, para. 25 (Cyprus); UN Doc. CAT/C/SR.160, para. 17 (Poland); UN Doc. CAT/C/SR.130, para. 15, UN Doc. CAT/C/SR.135, para. 26 (Libya); UN Doc. CAT/C/SR.133, para. 18 (Belarus); UN Doc. CAT/C/SR.107, paras. 31, 45 (Luxemburg); UN Doc. CAT/C/SR.140, para. 36 (Canada); UN Doc. CAT/C/SR.80, para. 25 (Algeria); UN Doc. CAT/C/SR.76, para. 22 (Panama); UN Doc. CAT/C/SR.14, para. 65, UN Doc. CAT/C/SR.14, para. 44 (Philippines); UN Doc. CAT/C/SR.28, para. 27 (Switzerland); UN Doc. CAT/C/SR.32, para. 29, UN Doc. CAT/C/SR.33, para. 14 (Byelorussian SSR); UN Doc. CAT/C/SR.34, para. 35 (Cameroon); UN Doc. CAT/C/SR.34, para. 60, 67, UN Doc. CAT/C/SR.35, para. 59 (Hungary); UN Doc. CAT/C/SR.46, para. 43, 57, UN Doc. CAT/C/SR.47, para. 29 (Tunisia); UN Doc. CAT/C/SR.50, para. 15, UN Doc. CAT/C/SR.51, paras. 18–19, 37, 41, 46 (China); UN Doc. CAT/C/SR.52, para. 30, 43, UN Doc. CAT/C/SR.53, para. 8 (Ukrainian SSR); UN Doc. CAT/C/SR.79, paras. 24, 27 UN Doc. CAT/C/SR.80, para. 25 (Algeria); UN Doc. CAT/C/SR.79, para. 34 (Chile); UN Doc. CAT/C/SR.93, para. 88 (Libya); Report of the Committee Against Torture, UN Doc. A/52/44, paras. 135, 150 (Ukraine); UN Doc. CAT/C/ST.213, para 20 (Mauritius); UN Doc. CAT/C/SR.252/Add.1, para. 22 (China).

[335] UN Doc. CAT/C/SR.251, para. 20.

By contrast, the Committee was remarkably gentle during its consideration of the initial report of the United States, focusing on the treatment of asylum seekers and steering clear of capital punishment altogether.[336]

The Committee seems prepared to address death penalty issues more directly when it can relate them to other international obligations of the State party. During consideration of Ukraine's third periodic report, in 1997, at a time when abolitionist pressure from the Council of Europe upon that country was at its height, the Committee Against Torture said it was 'seriously concerned about the scale on which the death penalty is applied as being contrary to the European Convention on Human Rights and the European Convention on the Prevention of Torture and Inhuman or Degrading Treatment or Punishment'. The Committee also expressed its concern about the large number of crimes subject to capital punishment, such as an attempt on the life of a militiaman. 'This situation is contrary to the obligation assumed by Ukraine to introduce a moratorium on the imposition of the death penalty', the Committee concluded. It recommended that the moratorium on application of the death penalty in Ukraine be given permanent effect.[337] During presentation of Guatemala's third periodic report, the country rapporteur noted that extension of the death penalty was prohibited by the *American Convention on Human Rights*, yet the country's Supreme Court seemed to have allowed the contrary.[338] With respect to Peru, the Committee's country rapporteur observed that extension of the death penalty to terrorism, and a provision in the constitution saying that international obligations could not affect the death penalty, was a violation of the *International Covenant on Civil and Political Rights*.[339]

The possibility that the Committee Against Torture or that other States parties might interpret the *Convention* as encompassing death penalty issues led the United States, when it ratified the instrument in 1994, to formulate what is known as the '*Soering* understanding'.[340] The understanding is aimed at the 'death row phenomenon', which the European Court of Human Rights has held to violate the norm prohibiting inhuman and degrading treatment: 'The United States understands that international law does not prohibit the death penalty, and does not consider this Convention to restrict or prohibit the United States from applying the death penalty consistent with the Fifth, Eighth and/or Fourteenth Amendments to the Constitution of the United States, including any constitutional period of confinement prior to the imposition of the death penalty.' The United States also formulated a general reservation to

---

[336] UN Doc. CAT/C/SR.424.
[337] UN Doc. CAT/C/SR.287, para. 28; Report of the Committee Against Torture, UN Doc. A/52/44, paras. 122, 135, 150.
[338] UN Doc. CAT/C/SR.450, para. 16.   [339] UN Doc. CAT/C/SR.193, para. 35.
[340] Richard B. Lillich, 'The Soering Case', (1991) 85 *AJIL* 128.

the *Convention*, which makes no explicit reference to death penalty issues but which implicitly addresses them: 'That the United States considers itself bound by the obligation under article 16 to prevent "cruel, inhuman or degrading treatment or punishment", only insofar as the term "cruel, inhuman or degrading treatment or punishment" means the cruel, unusual and inhumane treatment or punishment prohibited by the Fifth, Eighth and/or Fourteenth Amendments to the Constitution of the United States.' The United States Supreme Court does not consider capital punishment to breach the *Constitution*,[341] although it has yet to determine whether prolonged detention prior to execution might constitute cruel and unusual punishment.[342]

Finland, the Netherlands and Sweden have objected to the general reservation made by the United States. Finland's objection notes that such general reservations violate the general principle of treaty interpretation according to which a State may not invoke the provisions of its internal law as justification for failure to perform a treaty obligation. It makes specific reference to its objection to the United States reservation to article 7 of the *International Covenant on Civil and Political Rights*, which was aimed at the *Soering* precedent. Sweden also referred to its objections to the United States reservation to article 7 of the *Covenant*. The Netherlands said that the 'understanding' concerning death row appeared to restrict the scope of the definition of torture, and that it considered the statement to have no impact on the obligations of the United States under the *Convention*. The Netherlands added that its objection did not preclude the entry into force of the *Convention* with the United States.

4.6 *International Convention on the Elimination of All Forms of Racial Discrimination*

Death penalty issues have occasionally been taken up by members of the Committee for the Elimination of Racial Discrimination.[343] The issue arises in the context of article 5§a of the *International Convention for the Elimination of all Forms of Racial Discrimination*, by which States parties 'undertake to prohibit and to eliminate racial discrimination in all its forms and to guarantee the right of everyone, without distinction as to race, colour, or national or ethnic origin, to equality before the law, notably in the enjoyment of the following rights . . . The right to equal treatment before the tribunals and all other organs administering justice.'[344] For example, country rapporteur Sadiq Ali said Swaziland's decision

---

[341] *Gregg* v. *Georgia*, 428 US 153, 96 S.Ct. 2909, 49 L.Ed.2d 859 (1976).
[342] *Lackey* v. *Texas*, 115 S.Ct. 1421, 63 L.W. 3705, 131 L.Ed.2d 304 (1995).
[343] UN Doc. CERD/C/SR.1190, para. 21, UN Doc. CERD/C/SR.1191, para. 19 (Guatemala); UN Doc. CERD/C/SR.1198, para. 13 (Pakistan).
[344] *International Convention on the Elimination of All Forms of Racial Discrimination*, (1969) 660 UNTS 195, art. 5§a.

to maintain the death penalty ran counter to this provision. She requested information about seven people whose death sentences were then under appeal.[345] During presentation of the twelfth periodic report of the Holy See, Theo van Boven questioned its position on the death penalty, noting that 'the Committee had been concerned to note that persons of a particular origin, race or colour were far more frequently subject to the death penalty than others, which was clear evidence of racial discrimination'.[346] But Michael Banton said 'he was not sure that the issue of the death penalty was relevant'. Moreover, he said that, if the Committee wished to pursue the issue, it should do so in the context of a report from the State party responsible.[347]

4.5 Recent developments

At the 1990 Congress on the Prevention of Crime and the Treatment of Offenders, held in Havana, a resolution on capital punishment was proposed which returned to the idea of a moratorium on the death penalty, 'at least on a three year basis'.[348] Promoted by the Italian delegation, the resolution was adopted in Committee by forty votes to twenty-one, with sixteen abstentions,[349] but was rejected in plenary session because it failed to obtain a two-thirds majority.[350] The issue of capital punishment was absent from the agenda of the 1995 Congress, held in Cairo.

Also in 1990, the Economic and Social Council mandated a change in the five-year reports, requesting that the next report, due in 1995, draw on all available data, including current criminological research, and that it also cover the implementation of the safeguards guaranteeing protection of the rights of those facing the death penalty.[351] English criminologist Roger Hood was commissioned to prepare the report, which was finally published in June 1995.[352] Professor Hood reviewed replies that had been submitted by fifty-seven States, most of them abolitionist, and he warned against the dangers of conclusions based on such a relatively limited sample. Nevertheless, he proceeded to careful analysis of information from those States that had replied, making distinctions between States that were totally or only partially abolitionist, and those that were *de jure* or *de facto* abolitionist, in order to determine trends as accurately as possible. His conclusion, based on the fifty-seven replies, was that 'there has been a

---

[345] UN Doc. CERD/C/SR.1209, para. 12.   [346] UN Doc. CERD/C/SR.991, para. 23.
[347] *Ibid.*, para. 31.   [348] UN Doc. A/CONF.144/C.2/L.7, as amended orally.
[349] A/CONF.144/28/Rev.1, para. 350.
[350] A/CONF.144/28/Rev.1, §358. See: Roger S. Clark, 'The Eighth United Nations Congress on the Prevention of Crime and the Treatment of Offenders, Havana, Cuba, August 27–September 7, 1990', (1990) 1 *Criminal Law Forum* 513, at pp. 518–519.
[351] ESC Res. 1990/51. See also: ESC Res. 1989/64.
[352] Pursuant to ESC Res. 1994/206. For the report itself, see: UN Doc. E/1995/78.

considerable shift towards the abolition of the death penalty both de jure and in practice' in the years 1989 to 1993.[353] After consulting other sources, Professor Hood observed that 'it appears that since 1989 twenty-four countries have abolished capital punishment, twenty-two of them for all crimes in peacetime or in wartime'.[354] Over the same period, the death penalty was reintroduced in four States.[355] Despite the caveats of a scrupulous researcher, Professor Hood concludes that 'the picture that emerges is that an unprecedented number of countries have abolished or suspended the use of the death penalty'.[356]

In 1994, at the forty-ninth session, a draft General Assembly resolution called for a moratorium on the death penalty.[357] A series of preambular paragraphs referred to earlier General Assembly resolutions on the death penalty, the 1984 'Safeguards', relevant provisions in the *Universal Declaration of Human Rights*, the *International Covenant on Civil and Political Rights* and the *Convention on the Rights of the Child*, the statutes of the *ad hoc* criminal tribunals for the former Yugoslavia and Rwanda and the draft statute of the proposed International Criminal Court. The first of three dispositive paragraphs invited States that still maintain the death penalty to comply with their obligations under the *International Covenant* and the *Convention on the Rights of the Child*, and in particular to exclude pregnant women and juveniles from execution. The second paragraph invited States which had not abolished the death penalty to consider the progressive restriction of the number of offences for which the death penalty may be imposed, and to exclude the insane from capital punishment. The final paragraph 'encourge[d] states which have not yet abolished the death penalty to consider the opportunity of instituting a moratorium on pending execution with a view to ensuring that the principle that no state should dispose of the life of any human being be affirmed in every part of the world by the year 2000'.

Italy initiated the resolution with a request addressed to the Office of the Presidency of the General Assembly that the item 'capital punishment' be added to the agenda. Pakistan, speaking on behalf of the Organization of the Islamic Conference, opposed modification of the agenda to include the item, adding that if the resolution were to be considered, this should be in the Sixth Committee, dealing with legal issues, and not the Third Committee, dealing with human rights issues.[358] Pakistan argued that capital punishment was 'a highly sensitive and complicated issue, and warranted further and thorough consideration'. The representative of Sudan described capital punishment as 'a divine right according to some religions, in particular Islam'.[359] Iran, Malaysia

---

[353] UN Doc. E/1995/78, para. 32.   [354] *Ibid.*, para. 33.

[355] *Ibid.*, para. 38.   [356] *Ibid.*, para. 87.

[357] UN Doc. A/49/234 and Add. 1 and Add. 2 (1994), later revised by UN Doc. A/C.3/49/L.32/Rev.1 (1994).

[358] UN Doc. A/BUR/49/SR.6, para. 2.   [359] UN Doc. A/BUR/49/SR.5, para. 13.

and Egypt also opposed discussing the draft resolution, while Uruguay, Malta, Cambodia, Austria, Burundi, Guinea-Bissau, Nicaragua, France, Ukraine and Andorra urged it be included on the agenda of the Third Committee.[360] The item 'capital punishment' was added to the agenda of the Third Committee not by consensus, as many had hoped, but on a vote of the General Assembly, with seventy States in favour, twenty-four opposed and forty-two abstentions.[361]

Italy eventually obtained forty-nine co-sponsors for the resolution.[362] During debate in the Third Committee, Singapore took the initiative in attacking the draft resolution. According to the Singapore representative, 'it strongly opposed efforts by certain States to use the United Nations to impose their own values and system of justice on other countries'. He added that it was evident, from the wording of the *International Covenant on Civil and Political Rights*, that no universal consensus held capital punishment to be contrary to international law. The abolition of the death penalty did not necessarily contribute to the advancement of human dignity, he said. Rather, its retention had served to preserve and safeguard the interests of society. He cited, in particular, use of capital punishment to repress drug trafficking.[363] Other States opposing the resolution during the debate included Malaysia, Jamaica, Bangladesh, China, Sudan, Saudi Arabia, Libya, Egypt, Iran, Japan and Jordan.[364]

Germany spoke on behalf of the European Union, of which it held the Presidency at the time, supporting the resolution and noting that capital punishment was not applied by any of its members. The German representative cited its lack of significant deterrent effect, and a preference of European States for rehabilitation rather than retribution as a goal of punishment. He reminded delegates that the main purpose of the draft resolution was 'to promote further reflection on the highly complex and delicate question of capital punishment'. The text did not create new standards, but did urge that while 'looking ahead' towards abolition, the *status quo* of persons currently on death row should be preserved.[365] Slovenia, Sweden, Italy, Ireland, Nicaragua, New Zealand, Andorra, Malta, Portugal, Cambodia and Namibia took the floor to support the draft resolution.[366]

---

[360] UN Doc. A/BUR/49/SR.5-6.   [361] UN Doc. A/49/610, para. 2.

[362] Andorra, Argentina, Australia, Austria, Belgium, Bolivia, Cambodia, Cape Verde, Chile, Colombia, Costa Rica, Cyprus, Czech Republic, Denmark, Dominican Republic, Ecuador, El Salvador, Finland, France, Germany, Greece, Haiti, Honduras, Hungary, Iceland, Ireland, Liechtenstein, Luxemburg, Malta, Marshall Islands, Micronesia, Monaco, New Zealand, Nicaragua, Norway, Panama, Paraguay, Portugal, Romania, San Marino, Sao Tomé and Principe, Slovak Republic, Solomon Islands, Spain, Sweden, Uruguay, Vanuatu and Venezuela.

[363] UN Doc. A/C.3/49/SR.33, paras. 23–27. For Singapore's spirited defence of its policy on capital punishment, see UN Doc. E/CN.4/1998/113.

[364] UN Doc. A/C.3/49/SR.33-UN Doc. A/C.3/49/SR.43.

[365] UN Doc. A/C.3/49/SR.36, paras. 7–15.

[366] UN Doc. A/C.3/49/SR.33-UN Doc. A/C.3/49/SR.43.

At the conclusion of the debate in the Third Committee, the Chair attempted to summarize the debates:

> the Committee had clearly been divided into two camps: those favouring the abolition of capital punishment and those wishing to retain it. Arguments in favour of abolishing the death penalty had been the following: States could not impose the death penalty as a means of reducing crime because there was no evidence that it had a deterrent effect; the right to life was the most basic human right and, consequently, States did not have the right to take the life of any individual; the death penalty sometimes veiled a desire for vengeance or provided an easy way of eliminating political opponents; the death penalty, once applied, could not be reversed in the event of judicial error; and capital punishment was excluded from the penalties used by international tribunals, including those established to deal with the situations in the former Yugoslavia and Rwanda, and should consequently become less prevalent in national legislation.
>
> Arguments in support of maintaining the death penalty had been the following: certain legislative systems were based on religious laws; it was not possible to impose the ethical standards of a single culture on all countries; there was a need to discourage extremely serious crimes; and, in some countries, capital punishment was a constitutional or even a religious obligation.
>
> At the same time, all members had agreed on certain fundamental points: the death penalty should be applied only in exceptional circumstances and subject to strict preconditions; and its scope of application should be extremely limited.[367]

Singapore initially attempted to block the resolution by proposing a 'no action' motion, a familiar procedural gambit that effectively sabotages a genuine vote. This ploy was rejected, sixty-five States voting in favour to seventy-four against, with twenty abstentions. Singapore then proposed an 'amendment' that in effect distorted the original purpose of the resolution, by adding the following preambular paragraph: 'Affirming the sovereign right of states to determine the legal measures and penalties which are appropriate in their societies to combat serious crimes effectively . . .'.[368] In order to save the resolution, Italy then modified its original text by incorporating the Singapore amendment, while at the same time adding a reference to the *Charter of the United Nations* and to international law, aimed at making Singapore's reactionary appeal to 'state sovereignty' subject to some recognition of international norms.[369] But, by a close vote, seventy-one to sixty-five, with twenty-one abstentions, Singapore's amendment was adopted.[370] Those voting in favour of the amendment were retentionist states, essentially from Africa, Asia and the Caribbean. But the amendment

[367] UN Doc. A/C.3/49/SR.43, paras. 74–76.
[368] UN Doc. A/C.3/49/L.73.   [369] UN Doc. A/C.3/49/L.74.
[370] *In favour*: Afghanistan, Algeria, Antigua-Barbuda, Bahamas, Bahrain, Bangladesh, Barbados, Belize, Bhutan, Brunei, Burkina Faso, Burundi, Cameroon, China, Côte d'Ivoire, Cuba, Korea, Egypt, Eritrea, Grenada, Guinea, Guyana, India, Indonesia, Iran, Iraq, Jamaica, Japan, Jordan, Kenya, Kuwait, Kyrgyzstan, Laos, Lebanon, Lesotho, Libya, Malaysia, Maldives, Mauritania, Mongolia, Morocco, Myanmar, Namibia, Nigeria, Oman, Pakistan, Papua New Guinea, Peru, Philippines, Qatar, Republic of Korea, Saudia Arabia, Senegal, Sierra Leone, Singapore, Sri Lanka, Sudan, Suriname, Swaziland, Syria,

made the resulting text unacceptable to many abolitionist States. It constituted a setback to efforts within the United Nations system, dating back to the 1950s, to consider capital punishment as an issue of international concern, and not merely a domestic matter. In the vote on the entire resolution, Italy continued to support the resolution, even with the Singapore amendment, but most of its co-sponsors had deserted the camp and abstained in the final vote (seventy-four States abstained). The remainder, essentially retentionist states, tended to divide: thirty-six voted in favour and forty-four voted against.[371]

It took a few years for the abolitionists to regroup after the 1994 setback in the General Assembly. A resolution was adopted at the fifth session of the Commission on Crime Prevention and Criminal Justice in 1996, following up on the quinquennial report of the Secretary-General.[372] The resolution was subsequently endorsed later that year by the Economic and Social Council.[373] In March 1997, a resolution on capital punishment was presented to the annual session of the Commission on Human Rights.[374] The resolution welcomed the

---

Tanzania, Thailand, Trinidad and Tobago, Tunisia, Uganda, United Arab Emirates, Uzbekistan, Vietnam, Yemen, Zambia, and Zimbabwe.
Against: Andorra, Angola, Argentina, Armenia, Australia, Austria, Belgium, Brazil, Bulgaria, Cambodia, Canada, Cape Verde, Chile, Colombia, Costa Rica, Cyprus, Czech Republic, Denmark, El Salvador, Estonia, Finland, France, Germany, Greece, Haiti, Honduras, Hungary, Iceland, Ireland, Israel, Italy, Latvia, Liechtenstein, Lithuania, Luxemburg, Macedonia, Malta, Marshall Islands, Micronesia, Monaco, Mozambique, Nepal, Netherlands, New Zealand, Nicaragua, Norway, Panama, Paraguay, Poland, Portugal, Moldova, Romania, Russian Federation, San Marino, Slovakia, Slovenia, Solomon Islands, South Africa, Spain, Sweden, United Kingdom, United States, Uruguay, Vanuatu and Venezuela.
Abstaining: Albania, Azerbaijan, Belarus, Benin, Bolivia, Croatia, Ecuador, Ethiopia, Fiji, Gabon, Gambia, Georgia, Ghana, Guatemala, Kazakhstan, Mali, Mauritius, Mexico, Niger, Togo and Ukraine.
[371] UN Doc. A/C.3/49/SR.61.
In favour: Argentina, Armenia, Cambodia, Cape Verde, Chile, Colombia, Costa Rica, Croatia, Cyprus, Ecuador, El Salvador, Fiji, Gambia, Georgia, Greece, Haiti, Ireland, Israel, Italy, Kyrgyzstan, Macedonia, Malta, Marshall Islands, Mexico, Mozambique, Namibia, Nepal, Nicaragua, Panama, Paraguay, Portugal, San Marino, Slovenia, Uruguay, Uzbekistan and Venezuela.
Against: Afghanistan, Algeria, Antigua-Barbuda, Bahamas, Bahrain, Bangladesh, Barbados, Belize, Brunei, Cameroon, China, Comoros, Egypt, Guinea, Guyana, India, Indonesia, Iran, Iraq, Jamaica, Japan, Jordan, Kuwait, Lebanon, Libya, Malaysia, Maldives, Morocco, Myanmar, Nigeria, Oman, Pakistan, Qatar, Republic of Korea, Saudi Arabia, Senegal, Sierra Leone, Singapore, Sudan, Syria, Trinidad and Tobago, United Arab Emirates, United States and Yemen.
Abstaining Albania, Andorra, Australia, Austria, Azerbaijan, Belarus, Belgium, Benin, Bolivia, Botswana, Brazil, Bulgaria, Burkina Faso, Burundi, Canada, Côte d'Ivoire, Cuba, Czech Republic, Denmark, Estonia, Ethiopia, Finland, France, Gabon, Germany, Grenada, Guatemala, Honduras, Hungary,Iceland, Kazakhstan, Kenya, Korea, Latvia, Lesotho, Liechtenstein, Lithuania, Luxemburg, Madagascar, Malawi, Mali, Mauritius, Micronesia, Moldova, Monaco, Mongolia, Netherlands, New Zealand, Niger, Norway, Papua New Guinea, Peru, Philippines, Poland, Romania, Russian Federation, Slovakia, South Africa, Spain, Sri Lanka, Suriname, Swaziland, Sweden, Tanzania, Thailand, Togo, Tunisia, Uganda, Ukraine, United Kingdom, Vanuatu, Vietnam, Zambia and Zimbabwe.
[372] UN Doc. E/CN.15/1996/19.   [373] UN Doc. E/RES/1996/15.
[374] In addition to the annual resolutions, which began in 1997, the Commission on Human Rights has also condemned the manner in which the death penalty is used in its geographic or country resolutions. For example, in 1998 it expressed its concern that use of the death penalty by military tribunals in the Democratic Republic of Congo was contrary to the provisions of the *International Covenant on*

exclusion of capital punishment from the statutes of the *ad hoc* international criminal tribunals, took note of the Human Rights Committee's General Comment noting that article 6 of the *International Covenant* refers to abolition of the death penalty in terms which strongly suggest that abolition is desirable, and said the Commission was '[c]onvinced that abolition of the death penalty contributes to the enhancement of human dignity and to the progressive development of human rights'. It called upon States parties to the *Covenant* that had not yet ratified or acceded to the *Second Optional Protocol* to consider doing so, urged States that still maintain the death penalty to comply fully with their international treaty obligations on the subject to observe the 'Safeguards' guaranteeing protection of the rights of those facing the death penalty, to restrict progressively the number of offences for which the death penalty may be imposed and to make available to the public information on imposition of the death penalty. It 'called upon' such States 'to consider suspending executions, with a view to completely abolishing the death penalty'.[375] The resolution was adopted by a roll-call vote of twenty-seven votes to eleven, with fourteen abstentions.[376]

The subject returned to the agenda of the Commission on Human Rights the following year.[377] The call for a moratorium was worded somewhat more robustly, 'urging' States that still maintain the death penalty '[t]o establish a moratorium on executions, with a view to completely abolishing the death penalty'.[378] The results of the voting were about the same: twenty-six to thirteen, with twelve abstentions, once again on a roll-call vote. The persistence of the abolitionist camp stirred its opponents into action. Fifty-one States filed a letter with the President of the Commission on Human Rights, on 31 March 1998, asserting that there was no international consensus calling for abolition of the death penalty, citing differences linked to religion and judicial systems in various countries.[379] The successful resolution in the Commission may also have helped provoke efforts a few months later to make the issue of the death penalty a

---

Civil and Political Rights. See: CHR Res. 1998/61, para. 2(b)(ii); also CHR Res. 1999/56, para. 2(b)(iv). Similarly, on death row conditions in Burundi: CHR Res. 1998/82, para. 12; on lapidation and public executions, and the scope of crimes for which the death penalty is imposed in Iran: CHR Res. 1998/80, para. 3(a), (j); CHR Res. 1999/13, para. 4(b); on arbitrary imposition of capital punishment in Iraq: CHR Res. 1999/14, para. 2(b).

[375] UN Doc. E/CN.4/1997/L.40.

[376] Retentionist States later complained to the Economic and Social Council: UN Doc. E/CN.4/ 1997/L.20, UN Doc. E/1997/196.

[377] UN Doc. E/CN.4/1998/L.12.   [378] 'The Question of the Death Penalty', E/CN.4/RES/1998/8.

[379] UN Doc. E/CN.4/1998/156. It was signed by: Algeria, Antigua and Barbuda, Bahamas, Bahrain, Bangladesh, Barbados, Bhutan, Brunei Darussalam, Burundi, China, Congo, Egypt, Ghana, Guyana, Indonesia, Iran, Iraq, Jamaica, Japan, Jordan, Kuwait, Lesotho, Lebanon, Liberia, Libya, Malaysia, Malawi, Maldives, Mauritania, Mongolia, Myanmar, Nigeria, Oman, Philippines, Qatar, Rwanda, St. Kitts and Nevis, St. Lucia, St. Vincent and the Grenadines, Saudi Arabia, Singapore, Sudan, Swaziland, Syria, Tajikistan, Tanzania, Trinidad and Tobago, United Arab Emirates, Vietnam, Yemen and Zimbabwe.

'deal breaker' during the Rome Diplomatic Conference where the *Statute of the International Criminal Court* was adopted.[380]

The 1999 resolution in the Commission on Human Rights was proposed by the fifteen-member European Union.[381] The preamble to the 1999 resolution 'welcomed' the exclusion of capital punishment from the *Rome Statute*, a jab at the retentionist States who, at the Rome Diplomatic Conference, had negotiated ambiguous statements that might suggest the *Statute* was neutral on the subject. The draft resolution went considerably further than the 1997 and 1998 version, calling upon States that still maintain the death penalty not to impose it 'for non-violent financial crimes or for non-violent religious practice or expression of conscience' or 'on a person suffering from any form or mental disorder', and '[n]ot to execute any person as long as any related legal procedure, at international or at national level, is pending'. The draft resolution also urged States not to enter any reservations to article 6 of the *Covenant*, and to withdraw any existing reservations (at the time, the only State with reservations to article 6 was the United States of America).[382] The addition of a reference to extradition, and a request for States to reserve explicitly the right to refuse extradition in the absence of effective assurances the death penalty would not be carried out, drove Canada, at least temporarily, off the list of the resolution's sponsors.[383] Compromise language was ultimately developed that managed to woo Canada back to the camp of those supporting the resolution. It was adopted in the final days of the Commission's annual session, on 28 April 1999, by a roll call vote of thirty votes to eleven, with twelve abstentions.[384]

The European Union was emboldened by this success in the Commission, and developed a strategy to conquer the General Assembly, where efforts had failed in 1994. Finland held the European Union presidency, and to it fell the initiative to submit the proposal. The Finnish delegation's draft, circulated on 7 October 1999, called on States to apply international safeguards in the application of death sentences, urged ratification of the *Second Optional Protocol* by States parties to the *International Covenant on Civil and Political Rights*,

---

[380] For the debate at the Rome Conference, see Chapter 6.
[381] UN Doc. E/CN.4/1999/L.91. There were seventy-two co-sponsors of the 1999 resolution, compared with sixty-five in 1998.
[382] UN Doc. E/CN.4/1999/L.91.   [383] UN Doc. E/CN.4/1999/SR.58, para. 40.
[384] CHR Res. 1999/61. See: UN Doc. E/CN.4/1999/SR.58, paras. 61–62. *In favour*: Argentina, Austria, Canada, Cape Verde, Chile, Colombia, Congo, Czech Republic, Ecuador, El Salvador, France, Germany, Ireland, Italy, Latvia, Luxemburg, Mauritius, Mexico, Mozambique, Nepal, Niger, Norway, Peru, Poland, Romania, Russian Federation, South Africa, United kingdom, Uruguay and Venezuela. *Against*: Bangladesh, Botswana, China, Indonesia, Japan, Korea (Republic of), Pakistan, Qatar, Rwanda, Sudan and United States. *Abstaining*: Bhutan, Congo (Democratic Republic), Cuba, Guatemala, India, Liberia, Madagascar, Morocco, Philippines, Senegal, Sri Lanka and Tunisia. A separate vote was held on paras. 3(f), 4(b) and 5, adopted by twenty-seven to thirteen with thirteen abstentions.

progressive restriction of the death penalty and establishment of a moratorium, all with a view to complete abolition.[385]

Opposition mobilized, with Egypt and Singapore – both of them subject to international criticism for death penalty practice[386] – in the lead. As in the past, the strategy was not to vote down the resolution but rather to use so-called 'wrecking amendments' to make it unpalatable for the abolitionists. Two draft amendments were submitted, adding language stating that the death penalty was not prohibited under international law, as there is no global consensus on the issue, invoking article 2§7 of the *Charter of the United Nations* ('Nothing contained in the present Charter shall authorize the United Nations to intervene in matters which are essentially within the domestic jurisdiction of any state . . .'), asserting that capital punishment is primarily a criminal justice issue, not a human rights one, 'in the context of the rights of victims and the community to live in peace', and recalling that not all rules are suitable for application in all places at all times because of diversity of socio-legal and economic conditions in each country.[387]

Humiliated, the European Union decided to withdraw the resolution rather than see it transformed beyond recognition. Speaking to the European Parliament some time afterwards, Commissioner Chris Patten said it had been necessary 'to freeze our resolution on the death penalty or risk the passing of a resolution that would have incorporated wholly unacceptable arguments that asserted that human rights are not universally applicable and valid'.[388] He said that 'following intensive negotiation, we decided at last year's General Assembly in November [1999] that no resolution was better than a fatally flawed text, and that therefore the EU should not pursue its initiative in [the General Assembly]'. Patten said that 'hardline retentionists' now seem resigned to resolutions in the Commission on Human Rights, but that they will continue to resist strongly any efforts to secure a General Assembly resolution. 'This would lead to further divisive debate', he noted. Consequently, the European Union decided

---

[385] UN Doc. A/C.3/54/L.8.

[386] On Singapore: UN Doc. E/CN.4/1997/60/Add.1, para. 438; on Egypt: UN Doc. E/CN.4/1999/39, para. 57.

[387] UN Docs. A/C.3/54/L.31 and A/C.3/54/L.32. These amending principles were signed by Afghanistan, Algeria, Antigua and Barbuda, Bahamas, Bahrain, Bangladesh, Barbados, Belize, Benin, Botswana, Brunei, Burkina Faso, Burundi, Cameroon, Chad, China, Comoros, Cuba, Congo, Dominica, Egypt, Equatorial Guinea, Eritrea, Ethiopia, Gabon, Ghana, Guatemala, Guyana, India, Indonesia, Iran, Jamaica, Japan, Jordan, Kazakhstan, Kenya, Kuwait, Kyrgyzstan, Laos, Lebanon, Lesotho, Liberia, Libya, Malawi, Malaysia, Maldives, Mauritania, Mongolia, Morocco, Myanmar, Niger, Nigeria, North Korea, Oman, Pakistan, Philippines, Qatar, South Korea, Rwanda, St. Kitts Nevis and Anguilla, St. Lucia, St. Vincent and Grenadines, Saudi Arabia, Sierra Leone, Somalia, Sudan, Suriname, Swaziland, Syria, Tajikistan, Tanzania, Thailand, Togo, Trinidad and Tobago, Tunisia, Turkey, Uganda, United Arab Emirates, Uzbekistan, Vietnam, Yemen, Yugoslavia, Zambia and Zimbabwe.

[388] Excerpts from a Statement Delivered by the Rt Hon. Christopher Patten, EU Commissioner for External Relations to the European Parliament, 16 February 2000.

'it would not be either advisable or timely to table a resolution on the death penalty' at the 2000 session of the General Assembly.[389]

Any nervousness that the setback in the General Assembly would ricochet on what had become a tradition in the Commission on Human Rights, with its progressively more exigent annual resolutions, proved to be misplaced. In 2000, the Commission resolution was adopted by twenty-seven votes to thirteen, with twelve abstentions, essentially comparable to the voting pattern in the previous three years.[390] It welcomed the fact that many countries were in fact applying a moratorium on executions, repeating the principles of the 1999 resolution.

In 2001, the result was twenty-seven votes to eighteen, with seven abstentions. The number in favour was once again quite comparable to results over the previous four resolutions, but the number against was the highest ever.[391] The resolution repeated its request to the Secretary-General to prepare annual updates to the quinquennial reports, a practice since the first Commission resolution in 1997. The resolution 'welcomed' a resolution adopted the previous August by the Sub-Commission on the Promotion and Protection of Human Rights, that had described the prohibition of juvenile executions as a norm of customary international law.[392]

The United Nations Sub-Commission on the Promotion and Protection of Human Rights, previously known as the Sub-Commission on Prevention of Discrimination and Protection of Minorities, had been responsible for the initial drafting of the *Second Optional Protocol*, in the early 1980s, but then did little on the subject for many years.[393] In 1999, it adopted a resolution by secret ballot condemning 'unequivocally the imposition and execution of the death penalty on those aged under eighteen at the time of the commission of the offence'. The resolution was adopted by fourteen votes in favour, with five opposed and five abstentions. Part of the controversy was due to the inclusion of reference to specific States in the preamble to the resolution. The resolution referred to executions of juvenile offenders in Iran, Nigeria, Pakistan, Saudi Arabia, the United States and Yemen. The resolution called upon States that still imposed capital punishment not to use it for refusal to serve in or desertion from the military when this was related to conscientious objections. The resolution called upon retentionist States that did not apply a moratorium

---

[389] Speech to European Parliament, 25 October 2000.

[390] 'The Question of the Death Penalty', E/CN.4/RES/2000/65. See Michael J. Dennis, 'The Fifty-Sixth Session of the UN Commission on Human Rights', (2001) 95 *AJIL* 213, at p. 214.

[391] 'The Question of the Death Penalty', UN Doc. E/CN.4/RES/2001/68, based on UN Doc. E/CN.4/2000/L.93. For the vote, see: UN Doc. E/CN.4/2001/SR.78, paras. 17–18.

[392] UN Doc. E/CN.4/Sub.2/RES/2000/17. The resolution is discussed below.

[393] The Sub-Commission and its sessional working group on the administration of justice have considered the evolution of capital punishment. See the working papers by El Hadji Guissé, e.g. UN Doc. E/CN.4/Sub.2/1998/WG.1/CRP.3; UN Doc. E/CN.4/Sub.2/1998/19, paras. 65–76.

'in order to mark the millennium, to commute the sentences of those under sentence of death on 31 December 1999 at least to sentences of life imprisonment and to commit themselves to a moratorium on the imposition of the death penalty throughout the year 2000'.[394] At the same session, the Sub-Commission also adopted a resolution expressing concern at denunciation of human rights treaties, referring specifically to the death-penalty related denunciation of the *Optional Protocol to the International Covenant on Civil and Political Rights* by Trinidad and Tobago and by Guyana.[395] The Sub-Commission returned to the issue in 2000, this time managing to achieve adoption of a resolution by consensus. The resolution claimed that execution for juvenile offences was contrary to customary international law. It adopted a draft decision for the Commission on Human Rights stating that 'international law concerning the imposition of the death penalty in relation to juveniles clearly establishes that the imposition of the death penalty on persons aged under 18 years at the time of the offence is in contravention of customary international law'.[396]

Much of the human rights monitoring work of the United Nations is carried out by special *rapporteurs* of the Commission on Human Rights or of its Sub-Commission, as well as by special representatives of the Secretary-General and by working groups. Capital punishment issues have arisen within the scope of the work of several of the thematic *rapporteurs*, including the Special *Rapporteur* on violence against women,[397] on religious intolerance[398] and on the independence of judges.[399] The Working Group on Arbitrary Detention has also considered death penalty cases.[400] Similarly, concerns about the death penalty have been expressed by the geographic *rapporteurs* with respect to Nigeria,[401] the Democratic Republic of Congo,[402] Myanmar,[403] Sudan,[404] Iraq,[405] Burundi[406]

---

[394] 'The Death Penalty, Particularly in Relation to Juvenile Offenders', UN Doc. E/CN.4/Sub.2/RES/1999/4.

[395] S-CHR Res. 1999/5.

[396] 'The Death Penalty in Relation to Juvenile Offenders', UN Doc. E/CN.4/Sub.2/RES/2000/17, para. 6.

[397] 'Report on the Mission to Rwanda on the Question of Violence Against Women in Situations of Armed Conflict', UN Doc. E/CN.4/1998/54/Add.1, para. 67; UN Doc. E/CN.4/1998/54, paras. 52, 139, 183.

[398] UN Doc. E/CN.4/1998/6, para. 62(A).

[399] UN Doc. E/CN.4/1998/39, paras. 96, 122, 170.

[400] 'Opinion No. 14/1997 (Russian Federation)', UN Doc. E/CN.4/1998/44/Add.1, para. 5, 'Visit to People's Republic of China', UN Doc. E/CN.4/1998/44/Add.2, para. 33.

[401] UN Doc. E/CN.4/1998/62, paras. 31, 81, 91, 109(g) and (x).

[402] UN Doc. E/CN.4/1998/65, paras. 102, 126.   [403] UN Doc. E/CN.4/1998/70, para. 24.

[404] UN Doc. E/CN.4/1998/66, paras. 7, 8, 9, 10, 11, 16.

[405] 'Report on the Situation of Human Rights in Iraq, Submitted by the Special Rapporteur, Mr. Max van der Stoel, in Accordance with Commission Resolution 1997/60', UN Doc. E/CN.4/1998/67, paras. 1–5, 12, 18, 32, 34, 37.

[406] UN Doc. E/CN.4/1998/72, paras. 45–46.

In his report on the mission, the Special *Rapporteur* condemned the reservations, declarations and understandings formulated by the United States at the time it ratified the *International Covenant*, saying they were 'incompatible with the object and purpose of the treaty and should therefore be considered void'.[421] Ndiaye noted the serious gap between federal and state governments on the subject of the death penalty, questioning the commitment of the federal government to enforce the international obligations it had assumed. He declared the practice of juvenile executions to violate international law, adding that reintroduction of the death penalty and extension of its scope contravened the spirit and purpose of article 6 of the *Covenant*. He also expressed concern about the execution of the mentally retarded and insane, saying this was 'in contravention of relevant international standards'.[422] Ndiaye said that '[d]espite the excellent reputation of the United States judiciary', imposition of death sentences was characterized by arbitrariness and a lack of objectivity and fairness.[423] He recommended that the United States impose a moratorium on executions, in accordance with recommendations made by the American Bar Association, that it discontinue the execution of mentally retarded persons, that it review the system of election of members of the judiciary and that it lift its reservations to the *International Covenant*.[424] The United States presented an answer to the Bacre report.[425]

The High Commissioner on Human Rights opposes capital punishment and regularly calls for its suspension, for a moratorium and for abolition.[426] A representative of the High Commissioner has noted that considering the death penalty within the United Nations exclusively as a human rights issue, rather than one of criminal justice, could be considered to be progress in promoting human rights.[427] In February 1998, the High Commissioner, Mary Robinson, condemned the execution of Carla Fay Tucker by the State of Texas.[428] In April 1998, she protested against Rwanda's execution of twenty-two persons convicted for their role in the 1994 genocide. Indeed, she has regularly issued statements condemning capital executions in various countries of the world.[429]

---

[421] 'Report of the Special Rapporteur on Extrajudicial, Summary or Arbitrary Executions, Mr. Bacre Waly Ndiaye, Submitted Pursuant to Commission Resolution 1997/61, Addendum, Mission to the United States of America', UN Doc. E/CN.4/1998/68/Add.3, para. 140.

[422] *Ibid.*, para. 145.   [423] *Ibid.*, paras. 148–150.

[424] *Ibid.*, para. 156. The resolution is annexed to his report.

[425] UN Doc. E/CN.4/1998/174.

[426] 'Field Operation for Rwanda', UN Doc. E/CN.4/1998/61, paras. 38, 81.

[427] UN Doc. E/CN.4/Sub.2/1998/19, para. 66.

[428] 'Statement by Mary Robinson, United Nations High Commissioner for Human Rights', UN Doc. HR/98/6, 4 February 1998.

[429] For example, 'Daily Press Briefing of Office of Spokesman for Secretary-General', 16 June 1999.

5

International humanitarian law

In time of war, use of the death penalty generally becomes more frequent and the safeguards surrounding its use less stringent. Even the most advanced international instruments dealing with the death penalty, the abolitionist protocols adopted by the United Nations, the Council of Europe and the Organization of American States, tolerate the death penalty during wartime.[1] In the case of *Protocol No. 6* to the *European Convention*, only abolition in time of peace is envisaged by the instrument, although a draft protocol is currently being prepared to provide for abolition in wartime as well. The other protocols outlaw the death penalty in all cases, although they permit States parties, at the time of ratification, to make reservation for the death penalty in time of war. At least seventy-four countries have abolished the death penalty for all crimes, even in exceptional circumstances such as wartime.[2] Of this group, forty-one have ratified the *Second Optional Protocol* without reservation and are therefore prohibited by international law from imposing the death penalty, even in time of war. Yet even citizens of fully abolitionist States remain exposed to the death penalty in time of war, if they have the misfortune to be confronted with a belligerent that retains capital punishment who is not bound by certain international norms, or if they fall into the hands of an organized group of combatants in the course of a non-international armed conflict. Two groups of individuals have been contemplated by the legal rules concerning the death penalty in time of war, combatants taken prisoner and non-combatant civilians in the hands of a belligerent.

---

[1] *Second Optional Protocol to the International Covenant on Civil and Political Rights Aiming at the Abolition of the Death Penalty*, GA Res. 44/128, art. 2 (see Appendix 4, pp. 397–401); *Protocol No. 6 to the Convention for the Protection of Human Rights and Fundamental Freedoms Concerning the Abolition of the Death Penalty*, ETS 114, art. 2 (see Appendix 15, pp. 424–429); *Additional Protocol to the American Convention on Human Rights to Abolish the Death Penalty*, OASTS 73, 29 *ILM* 1447, art. 2 (see Appendix 21, pp. 438–439).

[2] 'Capital punishment and implementation of the safeguards guaranteed protection of the rights of those facing the death penalty', UN Doc. E/2000/3, p. 10.

The protection of prisoners of war in international armed conflict is governed principally by the third *Geneva Convention* of 1949.[3] According to the *Convention*, prisoners of war are subject to the laws, regulations and orders in force in the armed forces of the detaining power.[4] If the death penalty is in force in the laws of the detaining power, then a prisoner of war may be exposed to the threat of capital punishment for behaviour not qualified as a lawful act of war. The third *Geneva Convention* specifically envisages this possibility in two articles whose aim is to mitigate the rigours of the death penalty and encourage commutation of the penalty or even exchange of prisoners.[5] These provisions are a more extensive version of an article in the earlier 1929 *Geneva Convention* protecting prisoners of war facing the death penalty.[6] As for prisoners taken during non-international armed conflict, they enjoy no particular legal status. They remain governed, however, by certain due process protections and a prohibition on juvenile executions set out in the second *Additional Protocol* to the *Geneva Conventions.*[7]

Civilians in the hands of a belligerent were slower to receive comprehensive protection in the international humanitarian conventions,[8] but the grave abuses of capital punishment, mainly by the Nazi occupying forces during the Second World War, compelled the elaboration of specific norms in the fourth *Geneva Convention.*[9] The *Convention* limits the nature of capital crimes *ratione materiae*, prohibits the execution of persons for crimes committed while under the age of eighteen, and establishes a six-month moratorium on execution after sentencing. It also provides that an occupying power may never impose the death penalty if this has been abolished under the laws of the occupied State prior to the hostilities.

The *Geneva Conventions* also contain a residual provision, common article 3, ostensibly applicable to non-international armed conflicts not otherwise governed by the conventions themselves, but now held to be applicable to international armed conflicts as well.[10] Common article 3 is a codification of

---

[3] *Geneva Convention of August 12, 1949 Relative to the Treatment of Prisoners of War,* (1950) 75 UNTS 135 (hereinafter the third *Convention*).
[4] *Ibid.,* art. 82.   [5] *Ibid.,* arts. 100, 101 (see Appendix 9, pp. 414–416).
[6] *International Convention Concerning the Treatment of Prisoners of War* (1932–33) 118 LNTS 343.
[7] *Protocol Additional II to the 1949 Geneva Conventions and Relating to The Protection of Victims of Non-International Armed Conflicts,* (1979) 1125 UNTS 609 (hereinafter *Protocol Additional II*).
[8] Some norms protecting civilians appear in the *Hague Regulations,* although none address the death penalty: *Convention Regulating the Laws and Customs of Land Warfare* (*Hague Convention No. IV*), *Regulations Concerning the Laws and Customs of Land War,* 3 Martens (3rd) 461, 2 *AJIL Supp.* 20, arts. 23, 25, 27, 28, 42–56.
[9] *Geneva Convention of August 12, 1949 Relative to the Protection of Civilians,* (1950) 75 UNTS 135, arts. 68, 75 (hereinafter the fourth *Convention*) (see Appendix 10, p. 416).
[10] *Prosecutor* v. *Delalic* et al. (Case no. IT-96-21-A), Judgment, 20 February 2001, para. 150.

customary international law.[11] It prohibits 'the passing of sentences and the carrying out of executions without previous judgment pronounced by a regularly constituted court, affording all the judicial guarantees which are recognized as indispensable by civilized peoples'. Although these 'judicial guarantees' are not defined in common article 3, such instruments as article 14 of the *International Covenant on Civil and Political Rights*,[12] the 'Safeguards Guaranteeing Protection of the Rights of Those Facing the Death Penalty',[13] and article 75§4 of *Additional Protocol I* to the *Geneva Conventions* provide an indication of what is 'recognized as indispensable by civilized peoples'.

There is a compelling argument by which humanitarian law provisions define the lowest common denominator of humane behaviour, a minimum standard below which no civilized society can descend, either in wartime or in peacetime. Thus, if the death penalty's application is limited in time of war, *a fortiori* an equivalent protection ought to avail in time of peace, even though humanitarian treaty law provisions are technically inapplicable. In that sense, they supplement the international human rights treaties, where these are in force, and in addition tend to confirm the existence of customary rules.[14] It should be borne in mind, however, that humanitarian law provisions protect specified categories of individuals, be they prisoners of war or civilians in occupied territories, who may be entitled to special standards that exceed those that apply within States in peacetime. There is an intriguing synergy between humanitarian norms in wartime and human rights in peacetime with respect to capital punishment. Because the fourth *Geneva Convention* declares that an occupying power cannot extend the scope of capital punishment under law applicable within the territory prior to the occupation, it incites States to abolish the death penalty in peacetime. Thereby, the *Convention* protects their own nationals from the death penalty in the eventuality of wartime occupation.[15] This humanitarian

---

[11] According to the International Court of Justice, common article 3 is a 'minimum yardstick' expressing 'elementary considerations of humanity': *Military and Paramilitary Activities in and Against Nicaragua (Nicaragua v. United States)*, [1986] ICJ Reports 14, para. 218. In the *Nicaragua* case, the International Court of Justice found a specific violation of article 3§1(d), which deals with summary executions (at paras. 255, 292(9)). Theodor Meron, who is critical of the decision, admits that 'at least the core due process principle' of art. 3§1(d) is a rule of customary international law: Theodor Meron, *Human Rights and Humanitarian Norms as Customary International Law*, Oxford: Clarendon Press, 1989, pp. 34–35.

[12] (1976) 999 UNTS 171.

[13] ESC Res. 1984/50 (See Appendix 8, p. 413). Subsequently endorsed by GA Res. 39/118.

[14] Professor Meron does not consider that all provisions of the *Geneva Conventions* deserve the status of customary law. In a list of some provisions that codify customary law, he does not include article 68 of the fourth *Convention*, dealing with the death penalty: Meron, *Human Rights and Humanitarian Norms*, pp. 46–50. Yet he also quotes a member of the United States Joint Chiefs of Staff who suggests that articles 76 and 77 of *Protocol Additional I*, which prohibit the death penalty for minors, pregnant women and mothers of dependent children, are 'likely candidates eventually to reflect general practice recognized as law' (at p. 66).

[15] Fourth *Geneva Convention*, art. 68.

law provision is consequently a powerful argument in favour of abolition in time of peace.

5.1 The third *Geneva Convention of 1949*

Some norms in the *Hague Convention* provided protection for prisoners of war.[16] Moreover, prisoners have also benefited from some customary norms, the most important being that they are not to be punished, by execution or otherwise, for 'lawful acts of war'. However, the first instrument exclusively devoted to establishing general rules treating them as non-combatants was the 1929 *Geneva Convention*.[17] The 1929 *Convention* has the distinction of containing the first international norm limiting application of the death penalty. It set out two principles with respect to the death penalty, notification of the sentence to the prisoner's government (via the protecting power) and a moratorium on execution of the sentence for the three months following sentencing, in order to permit political and diplomatic efforts at obtaining commutation or reprieve:[18]

> *Article 66*
> Section 1
> If sentence of death is passed on a prisoner of war, a communication setting forth in detail the nature and the circumstances of the offence shall be addressed as soon as possible to the representative of the Protecting Power, for transmission to the Power in whose armed forces the prisoner served.
>
> Section 2
> The sentence shall not be carried out before the expiration of a period of at least three months from the date of (the receipt of) this communication (by the protecting Power).[19]

[16] For example, the *Convention Regulating the Laws and Customs of Land Warfare* (*Hague Convention No. IV*), *Regulations Concerning the Laws and Customs of Land War*, art. 23§c, which codified the customary rule against killing prisoners of war. See also: *In re Heyer et al.* (*Essen Lynching Case*), (1946) 13 *Ann. Dig.* 287, 1 LRTWC 88 (British Military Court); *In re Dostler*, (1946) 13 *Ann. Dig.* 280, 2 LRTWC 18 (United States Military Commission); *In re Flesch*, 6 LRTWC 111; Norwegian Frostating Lagmannsrett (Court of Appeal), *Canada* v. *Meyer*, (1946) 13 *Ann. Dig.* 332, 4 LRTWC 97 (Canadian Military Court); Allan Rosas, *The Legal Status of Prisoners of War*, Helsinki: Suomalainen Tiedeakatemia, 1976, p. 439.

[17] *International Convention Concerning the Treatment of Prisoners of War*. The Nuremberg Military Tribunals held that 'most of the provisions' of the 1929 *Geneva Convention* were 'an expression of the accepted views of civilized nations' and therefore norms of customary international law: *US* v. *Von Leeb* (*The High Command Case*), (1948) 15 *Ann. Dig.* 37b, 11 LRTWC 462, at p. 535.

[18] International Committee of the Red Cross, *Report on the Work of the Conference of Government Experts for the Study of the Conventions for the Protection of War Victims (Geneva, April 14–26, 1947)*, Series I, no. 5b, Geneva, 1947, at p. 231.

[19] *International Convention Concerning the Treatment of Prisoners of War*. The words in brackets are added in the official British translation (*Manual of Military Law, 1929, Amendments (No. 13)*, London: His Majesty's Stationery Office, 1940, p. 84), and in the version included in the record of the 1949 conference

Within only a few years of its adoption, revision of the 1929 *Convention* was already being considered. A draft prepared following a meeting of international experts, convened by the International Committee of the Red Cross, was submitted to the Sixteenth International Red Cross Conference, held in London in 1938, and placed on the agenda of the Diplomatic Conference called by the Swiss government in 1940, which was adjourned because of the Second World War.[20] Study of the draft resumed in September 1945, when the International Committee of the Red Cross convened[21] a meeting of national Red Cross Societies, held the following summer.[22] At a conference of government experts in Geneva in the spring of 1947,[23] the provision dealing with capital punishment of prisoners of war was first considered. The experts recommended that the specific notification requirement found in article 66§1 of the 1929 *Convention* be eliminated, in favour of a notification rule applicable to all penal convictions, not only capital cases.[24] They also felt that the temporary stay of execution should be extended from three months to six months. The experts proposed some innovations that had not appeared in the 1929 instrument. Prisoners of war and the protecting power should be informed, in advance, of all offences which might involve the death penalty. Furthermore, the attention of the tribunal should be drawn to the fact that the prisoner is in the hands of the detaining power as a result of exceptional circumstances, beyond his or her control, and that he or she owes the detaining power no allegiance.[25]

The International Committee of the Red Cross also proposed that the number of crimes to which the death penalty applied should be limited.[26] However, a suggestion from one delegation that the death penalty be reserved for murder and rape was criticized by many experts, who pointed out the great differences existing in this field between national legislations. It was argued that provisions that were too progressive would discourage ratification by many States

---

(*Final Record of the Diplomatic Conference of Geneva of 1949*, Berne: Federal Political Department, p. 36) but do not appear in the French text or in the official American translation (USTS, no. 846). The official text is in French:

> Si la peine de mort est prononcée contre un prisonnier de guerre, une communication exposant en détail la nature et les circonstances de l'infraction sera adressée, au plus tôt, au représentant de la Puissance protectrice, pour être transmise à la Puissance dans les armées de laquelle le prisonnier a servi. Le jugement ne sera pas exécuté avant l'expiration d'un délai d'au moins trois mois á partir de cette communication.

[20] International Committee of the Red Cross (see n. 18 above), p. 7.

[21] A preliminary meeting was held in October 1945: 'Compte-rendu de la séance organisée par le Comité international de la Croix-rouge pour l'étude du programme de la réunion des Croix-Rouges de 1946', Geneva, 22 October 1945, ICRC Doc. M 1566.

[22] International Committee of the Red Cross, *Report on the Work of the Preliminary Conference of National Red Cross Societies for the Study of the Conventions and of Various Problems Relative to the Red Cross (Geneva, July 26–August 3, 1946)*, Series I, no. 3a, Geneva, 1947.

[23] International Committee of the Red Cross (see n. 18 above).   [24] *Ibid.*, p. 230.   [25] *Ibid.*

[26] Jean de Preux, *Commentary, III, Geneva Convention Relative to the Treatment of Prisoners of War*, Geneva: International Committee of the Red Cross, 1960, pp. 499–500.

or else provoke reservations to the convention. The amendment was rejected as was another suggestion that would effect a stay of execution of the death sentence until the close of hostilities.[27]

Basing itself on the recommendations of the Conference of Experts, the International Committee of the Red Cross prepared a detailed draft convention, which was examined at yet another conference, in Stockholm, in August 1948.[28] The provisions dealing with the death penalty received only the most summary attention at the 1949 Diplomatic Conference,[29] and the text adopted the previous year at Stockholm found its way virtually unchanged into the *Geneva Convention of August 12, 1949 Relative to the Treatment of Prisoners of War* or 'third' *Convention*.[30] As of 1 May 2001, the *Convention* had been ratified by 188 States. There are no reservations to the articles dealing with the death penalty. For this reason, there can be little doubt that its provisions concerning capital punishment reflect customary norms.

According to the *Convention*, prisoners of war are subject to the laws, regulations and orders in force in the armed forces of the detaining power, and any penal proceedings are taken before the military courts, unless the laws of the detaining power expressly permit such trial before the civil courts.[31] Prisoners of war are subject to the same penalties as those imposed on the members of the armed forces of the detaining power.[32] This general rule is

[27] International Committee of the Red Cross (see n. 18 above), p. 231.

[28] The Stockholm conference produced a new draft *Convention* (*Final Record of the Diplomatic Conference of Geneva of 1949, Vol. I*, Berne: Federal Political Department, pp. 93–94):

> *Article 91*
>> The prisoners of war and the Protecting Powers shall be informed, as soon as possible, of the offences which are punishable by death sentence under the laws of the Detaining Power.
>> Other offences shall not thereafter be made punishable by the death penalty without the concurrence of the Power upon which the prisoners of war depend.
>> The death sentence cannot be pronounced against a prisoner of war unless the attention of the court has, in accordance with Article 77, paragraph 2, been particularly drawn to the fact that the accused, not being a national of the Detaining Power, is not bound to it by any duty of allegiance, and that he is in its power as the result of circumstances independent of his own will.
> *Article 98*
>> If the death penalty is pronounced against a prisoner of war, the sentence shall not be executed before the expiration of a period of six months at least from the date of receipt by the Protecting Power, at the address fixed, of the detailed communication provided for in Article 96.

[29] *Final Record of the Diplomatic Conference of Geneva of 1949, Vol. IIA*, Berne: Federal Political Department, 1950 (Summary record of fourth meeting of Sub-Committee on Penal Sanctions, p. 495, Summary record of ninth meeting of Sub-Committee on Penal Sanctions, p. 508, Summary record of eleventh meeting of Sub-Committee on Penal Sanctions, p. 515, Summary record of seventeenth meeting of Committee II, pp. 311–312, Summary record of eighteenth meeting of Committee II, p. 318, Summary record of twenty-first meeting of Committee II, pp. 326–327, Report of Committee II, pp. 571–572, 595); *Final Record of the Diplomatic Conference of Geneva of 1949, Vol. IIB*, Berne: Federal Political Department, 1950 (Minutes of seventeenth meeting of Plenary, p. 312). In Committee II, article 100§1 was adopted by twenty-one votes to zero, 100§2 by twenty-seven votes to one, 100§3 by twenty-five votes to zero, and 100 as a whole by twenty-seven votes to zero. Committee II was unanimously approved by Committee II. Articles 100 and 101 were adopted in the plenary by consensus.

[30] *Geneva Convention of August 12, 1949 Relative to the Treatment of Prisoners of War.*

[31] *Ibid.*, arts. 82, 84.   [32] *Ibid.*, arts. 87, 102.

strengthened in capital cases by an obligation that the detaining power give prisoners of war and the protecting power notification 'as soon as possible' of all offences punishable by death. No other offences can be made punishable by death without the concurrence of the power upon which the prisoners of war depend.[33] Furthermore, the death sentence cannot be pronounced unless the court's attention has been called to the fact that, since the accused is not a national of the detaining power, he or she is not bound to it by any duty of allegiance and is in its power as a result of circumstances independent of his own will.[34] Even if the death penalty is mandatory, article 87 of the *Convention* provides that the courts, when pronouncing sentence, are not bound by a prescribed minimum penalty and that they are at liberty to impose a reduced sentence. In that sense, the death penalty can never be mandatory for a prisoner of war.

Article 101 establishes a moratorium of six months between imposition of the penalty and its execution, an increase from the three-month period provided for in the 1929 *Convention*. The moratorium exists in order to permit the prisoner's own government to be informed of the sentence, through the protecting power. Article 107 of the *Convention* sets out the requirements of this communication, which must include the precise wording of the finding of the sentence and a summary of the preliminary investigation and of the trial. Article 107 imposes the requirement in the case of all final convictions and in all cases where a death sentence is pronounced at first instance. Several other provisions of the *Convention* provide for the rights of the prisoner in judicial proceedings, and these are obviously applicable to capital cases.[35] Wilfully depriving a prisoner of war of a fair and regular trial is a grave breach of the *Convention*, and is recognised as a war crime within the jurisdiction of the International Criminal Court.[36]

5.2 The fourth *Geneva Convention of 1949*

The 1929 *Geneva Conventions* did not deal with civilians, but within a few years the International Committee of the Red Cross had turned its attention to their protection. The 'Tokyo draft', adopted at the Fifteenth International Red Cross Conference in 1934, proposed rules for protection of civilians. However, attempts to prepare a convention were delayed by the Second World War, and only in 1946 did the meeting of national red cross societies convened by the International Committee of the Red Cross address the matter.[37] Among the important issues was control of the imposition of death sentences on civilians by an

---

[33] *Ibid.*, art. 100.   [34] *Ibid.*, arts. 87, 100.

[35] *Ibid.*, art. 86 ('*non bis in idem*'), art. 99 (rule of law, protection against self-incrimination, right to full answer and defence), art. 103 (confinement awaiting trial), art. 104 (notification of proceedings), art. 105 (right to counsel, adequate time for preparation of the defence, right to be informed of the precise nature of the offence, right to a public trial), art. 106 (right to appeal).

[36] *Rome Statute of the International Criminal Court*, UN Doc. A/CONF.183/9, art. 8§2(a)vi).

[37] International Committee of the Red Cross (see n. 22 above), pp. 96–98.

occupying power. According to Claude Pilloud, of the International Committee of the Red Cross, 'After the second world war a very strong feeling arose against the numerous death sentences inflicted on inhabitants of occupied territories and there was a general desire that the possibility of inflicting capital punishment should be as restricted as possible.'[38] In this debate, the International Committee of the Red Cross made no secret of its real intention and ultimate objective: abolition of the death penalty.[39]

A draft convention of forty articles was submitted to the conference of government experts, held in Geneva in the spring of 1947.[40] Although the draft convention itself did not address the death penalty, annexed to it were a series of regulations, prepared by a drafting committee on the basis of texts framed by delegations.[41] Annex C, 'Regulations on judicial measures', stated:

> *Article 7*
> In the case of a death sentence, execution shall not take place before the expiration of a period of three months, as from the notification of the sentence and of its reception by the Protecting Power, or by the competent international body.
> The population of the occupied territory, all Civilian War Internees, the Protecting Power or the competent international body shall be informed previously of the facts entailing the death penalty under the laws, orders and regulations enacted by the occupying or detaining Power.
> Prior to any judgment liable to entail the death penalty, the attention of the court shall be drawn to the fact that the accused is in the hands of the Detaining Power following circumstances beyond his or her control, and that he or she owes no allegiance to the said Power.
> In no case shall the condemned be deprived of the right of appeal for mercy.[42]

These provisions were largely similar to those proposed and eventually adopted for prisoners of war. Considering that they were to protect civilians, they were modest indeed.

The 1948 conference held in Stockholm went much further towards protecting civilians from capital punishment, adding two important concepts, that the death penalty could not be imposed if it had been abolished in the occupied territory prior to occupation and that children under eighteen years of age could not be executed.[43] The Stockholm draft was incorporated, with

---

[38] Claude Pilloud, 'Reservations to the Geneva Conventions of 1949', [1976] *International Review of the Red Cross* 163, at pp. 184–185.
[39] International Committee of the Red Cross (see n. 18 above), p. 231.
[40] *Ibid.*   [41] *Ibid.*, pp. 269–331.   [42] *Ibid.*, p. 305.
[43] The 'Stockholm draft' provided (*Final Record of the Diplomatic Conference of Geneva of 1949, Vol. I*, pp. 123–124):
> *Article 59*
> Protected persons who commit an offence intended to harm the occupying Power, but which does not constitute an attempt on the life or limb of members of the occupying forces or administration, nor a grave collective danger, nor seriously damage the property of the occupying

minor changes, into the fourth *Geneva Convention*, adopted 12 August 1949 by the Diplomatic Conference. The *Convention* has been universally ratified, for all practical purposes, but not without some reservations to the death penalty provisions.

The general rule of the fourth *Convention* is that the penal laws of the occupied territory remain in force during the occupation.[44] However, the occupying power is entitled to modify this law to the extent necessary 'to maintain the orderly government of the territory, and to ensure the security of the occupying power, of the members and property of the occupying forces or administration, and likewise of the establishments and lines of communication used by them'.[45] The occupying power's freedom to modify penal legislation is limited by the *Convention*, however, in two respects in the case of the death penalty. The occupying power may only impose the death penalty for espionage, serious acts of sabotage against the military installations of the occupying power, or intentional offences that have caused death. 'Serious' acts of sabotage could include the destruction of an air base or a major line of communication but would not include such acts of resistance as a strike or work slowdown.[46] But, even in the case of these specific offences, the occupying power may only promulgate legislation imposing the death penalty if the legislation of the occupied territory contained similar provisions prior to the occupation.[47]

The International Committee of the Red Cross had hoped to limit the list of crimes still further, to 'the case of homicide, or any other willful offence directly

Power or the installations used by it, are liable to internment, according to Part III, Section IV, as the only penalty depriving them of liberty.

    The courts of the occupying Power shall not pass the death sentence on a protected person unless he is guilty of an offence which was punishable by the death penalty under the law of the occupied Power at the outbreak of hostilities.

    The death penalty may not be pronounced against a protected person unless the attention of the Court, has been particularly called to the fact that the accused, not being a national of the occupying Power, is not bound to it by any duty of allegiance and is in its power by reason of circumstances independent of his will.

    The three preceding paragraphs do not apply to the case of a protected person who is guilty of espionage to the detriment of the occupying Power.

    The death penalty may not be pronounced against a protected person under eighteen years of age for any offence whatsoever.

Article 65

    No death sentence shall be carried out before the expiration of a period of six months at least from the notification of judgment to the Protecting Power.

    In no case shall persons condemned to death be deprived of the right of petition for pardon or reprieve.

[44] *Geneva Convention of August 12, 1949 Relative to the Protection of Civilians*, art. 64§1.

[45] *Ibid.*, art. 64§2. Article 65 states that such provisions do not come into force until they have been published and brought to the knowledge of the inhabitants in their own language, and that they may not have retroactive effect.

[46] Oscar M. Uhler, Henri Coursier et al., *Commentary, IV, Geneva Convention Relative to the Protection of Civilian Persons in Time of War*, Geneva: International Committee of the Red Cross, 1958, p. 369.

[47] *Geneva Convention of August 12, 1949 Relative to the Protection of Civilians*, art. 68§2.

causing the death of a person or persons'.[48] An early version of the provision had referred to the law in force in the occupied territory 'at the outbreak of hostilities', an expression which the Red Cross experts insisted lacked clarity.[49] The danger would be that States would introduce more severe penal legislation after the outbreak of hostilities but prior to occupation. That the provision was aimed at abolition of the death penalty, in both peacetime and in wartime, is clear from remarks of the International Committee of the Red Cross submitted to the 1949 Conference: 'Where, for instance, the laws of the occupied Power do not provide for it, the death penalty might be totally barred – a solution which the ICRC could, of course, only regard with satisfaction.'[50]

These limitations on the power of an occupying power to promulgate capital offences provoked great controversy at the 1949 Diplomatic Conference. The provision in the Stockholm draft prohibiting the death penalty in an occupied territory if it had been abolished prior to the occupation was initially dropped by the Drafting Committee of Committee III.[51] Canada, the United Kingdom, the United States and Australia had argued vigorously for the elimination of the prohibition of the death penalty if it had been abolished in the occupied territory prior to the conflict. Among their arguments was the danger that, if the death penalty in an occupied territory were eliminated, it would only provoke soldiers in the occupying army to take matters into their own hands

---

[48] International Committee of the Red Cross, *Remarks and Proposals Submitted by the International Committee of the Red Cross, Document for the Consideration of Governments Invited by the Swiss Federal Council to Attend the Diplomatic Conference at Geneva (April 21, 1949)*, Geneva, 1949, p. 75.
[49] *Final Record of the Diplomatic Conference of Geneva of 1949, Vol. IIA* (Summary record of the nineteenth meeting of Committee III, p. 673).
[50] International Committee of the Red Cross (see n. 48 above).
[51] *Final Record of the Diplomatic Conference of Geneva of 1949, Vol. III*, Berne: Federal Political Department, pp. 140–141 (Annex 299):

> Protected persons who commit an offence solely intended to harm the Occupying Power, but which does not constitute an attempt on the life or limb of members of the occupying forces or administration, nor a grave collective danger, nor seriously damage the property of the occupying forces or administration or the installations used by them, are liable to internment or simple imprisonment, provided the duration of such internment or imprisonment is proportionate to the offence committed. Furthermore, internment or imprisonment for such offences shall be the only measure adopted for depriving protected persons of liberty. The courts provided for under Article 57 of the present Convention may at their discretion convert a sentence of imprisonment to one of internment for the same period.
>
> The penal provisions promulgated by the Occupying Power in conformity with Articles 55 and 56 may impose the death penalty on a protected person only in cases where the person is guilty of espionage, or of international offences which have caused the death of one or more persons, or serious injury to one or more members of the occupying forces or administration, or which constitute serious public danger, or which seriously damage the property of the occupying forces or administration or the installations or lines of communication used by them.
>
> The death penalty may not be pronounced against a protected person unless the attention of the court has been particularly called to the fact that since the accused not being a national of the Occupying Power he is not bound to it by any duty of allegiance.
>
> In any case, the death penalty may not be pronounced against a protected person who was under eighteen years of age at the time of the offence.

and summarily execute civilians rather than arrest them and turn them over to the judicial authorities.[52] The Soviet Union, which had been in the minority of the Drafting Committee, together with the representative of the International Committee of the Red Cross, challenged the Drafting Committee's amended draft.[53] During debate in Committee III, France proposed a new version:

> The penal provisions promulgated by the Occupying Power in conformity with Articles 55 and 56 may only impose the death penalty on a protected person in cases where the person is guilty of espionage, of serious acts of sabotage against the military installations of the Occupying Power and of international offences which have caused the death of one or more persons, provided that such cases were punishable by death under the law of the occupied territory in force before the occupation began.[54]

But when the matter was referred back to the Drafting Committee for further study, France retreated from this position and jointly authored, together with the United Kingdom, a new text that permitted an occupying power to impose capital punishment, even if it had been abolished in the occupied territory before the conflict. This new draft was endorsed by the Drafting Committee and resubmitted to Committee III.[55] However, other States had not abandoned the earlier French proposal, and it was adopted in Committee III by a narrow majority.[56]

In the Conference plenary, Australia, Burma, the Netherlands, the United Kingdom and the United States tried once again to change the provision, submitting a new amendment, identical to the second text which had been adopted by the Drafting Committee but rejected by Committee III.[57] Denmark,

---

[52] *Final Record of the Diplomatic Conference of Geneva of 1949, Vol. IIA* (Summary record of forty-second meeting of Committee III, pp. 767–768).

[53] *Ibid.* (Summary record of forty-first meeting of Committee III, p. 766). The Stockholm text was formally rejected in Committee III by fourteen votes to ten (Summary record of the forty-second meeting of Committee II, p. 768).

[54] *Ibid.* (Summary record of forty-second meeting of Committee III, p. 767).

[55] *Final Record of the Diplomatic Conference of Geneva of 1949, Vol. III*, pp. 140–141 (Annex 300):
> The penal provisions promulgated by the Occupying Power in conformity with Articles 55 and 56 may only impose the death penalty on a protected person only in cases where the person is guilty of espionage, or homicide or attempted homicide resulting in grave injury against the members of the occupying forces or administration or of grave acts of sabotage of installations having an essential military interest for the Occupying Power.

[56] *Final Record of the Diplomatic Conference of Geneva of 1949, Vol. IIA* (Summary record of forty-seventh meeting of Committee III, p. 790), by seventeen votes to thirteen. The entire article was then adopted by twenty-one votes to eleven. See also pp. 833–834.

[57] *Final Record of the Diplomatic Conference of Geneva of 1949, Vol. III*, pp. 140–141 (Annex 301):
> The penal provisions promulgated by the Occupying Power in conformity with Articles 55 and 56 may only impose the death penalty on a protected person only in cases where the person is guilty of
> (a) espionage;
> (b) homicide or attempted homicide resulting in grave injury, against the members of the occupying forces or administration;
> (c) grave acts of sabotage resulting in the destruction or severe damage to installations having an essential military interest for the Occupying Power.

Belgium, the Soviet Union, Bulgaria and Romania spoke against this attempt to change the text. The amendment was rejected by only two votes, and then the Committee text of article 67, based on the earlier French proposal, was adopted.[58]

International Committee official Claude Pilloud later argued that the fears of opponents of the measure were illusory, because 'there is no country, it appears, which in war-time does not have laws punishing with death the crimes listed in Article 68, especially when they are committed against military personnel or military property'.[59] Adoption of the provision was accompanied by identical reservations from the United States, Canada, the United Kingdom, New Zealand, Australia and the Netherlands,[60] protecting 'the right to impose the death penalty in accordance with the provisions of Article 68, paragraph 2, without regard to whether the offences referred to therein are punishable by death under the law of the occupied territory at the time the occupation begins'.[61] In addition, Australia specified that it interpreted the term 'military installations', as used in article 68§2, to mean installations having a military interest that were essential for the occupying power.[62] Canada's reservation was not maintained at the time of ratification,[63] and those of the United Kingdom and Australia were later withdrawn.[64]

Division on this question was, as a general rule, between those States that had not been occupied during the Second World War, and who feared any encroachment on their powers as an occupying army, and those who had been occupied, and who were anxious for any norms that would prevent the abuse of the death penalty that they had suffered during the conflict.[65] The scholar G. I. A. D. Draper charged that the United Kingdom's reservation 'reflects an anxiety to safeguard the lives of the military when in occupation of enemy territory' but shows 'rather less concern for our civil population in the event of this country being occupied'.[66]

---

[58] *Final Record of the Diplomatic Conference of Geneva of 1949, Vol. IIB* (Minutes of the twenty-seventh plenary meeting, p. 431).

[59] Claude Pilloud, 'Reservations to the 1949 Geneva Conventions', [1958] *Int'l Rev. Red Cross* 193, at p. 206. But if this were true in 1949, it is no longer the case today. Many States have now abolished the death penalty in wartime. Moreover, in ratifying the *Second Optional Protocol*, without reservations, they have affirmed this practice by subscribing to an international norm.

[60] See Appendix 10 for the text of the reservations.

[61] Pakistan ((1951) 95 UNTS 326), Australia ((1958) 314 UNTS 333–334), the Republic of Korea ((1966) 575 UNTS 286) and Suriname ((1979) 1151 UNTS 390) made the same reservation at the time of ratification of the fourth *Convention*. The International Committee of the Red Cross does not consider the reservations to article 68 to be 'incompatible with the aims and objects of the Convention': Pilloud, 'Reservations', at p. 208. Romania made an objection to the Korean reservation: ((1967) 609 UNTS 254).

[62] (1958) 314 UNTS 333–334.   [63] [1965] CTS 20.

[64] The United Kingdom's reservation was withdrawn on 2 February 1972 ((1972) 811 UNTS 377); Australia's reservation was withdrawn on 21 February 1974 ((1974) 949 UNTS 310).

[65] 'Brief on the Geneva Conventions of August 12, 1949 for the protection of war victims', unpublished document of the Canadian Red Cross Society, library of the Canadian Red Cross Society, Part IV.

[66] G. I. A. D. Draper, *The Red Cross Conventions*, London: Stevens & Sons, 1958, p. 44.

Like the prisoner of war *Convention*, the civilian *Convention* obliges the prosecutor who is seeking the death penalty to call the court's attention to the fact that the accused is not a national of the occupying power and owes it no duty of allegiance.[67] The corresponding provision in the third *Convention* notes that the prisoner is in the control of the detaining power 'as the result of circumstances independent of his own will'.[68] This phrase was eliminated from the text of the fourth *Convention* on the suggestion of the International Committee of the Red Cross, which explained that any person in an occupied territory who is guilty of an offence against the occupying power must expect arrest and punishment.[69]

Article 68§4 forbids the death penalty being pronounced against a protected person for crimes committed while under the age of eighteen. The measure resulted from a proposal at the Seventeenth International Conference of the Red Cross by the International Union for the Protection of Children and recognizes the principle that children are not fully responsible for their actions, either because of immaturity or coercion.[70] The addition of the provision created no real difficulty for the delegates at the Conference and was barely discussed.[71] The Drafting Committee of Committee III changed the wording to provide that the death penalty could not be applied for an individual under eighteen at the time of the offence,[72] thereby preventing the execution of eighteen year olds for crimes committed during their minority.

Article 75 of the fourth *Convention* grants a right to petition for pardon or reprieve to all persons condemned to death. The death sentence may not be carried out before expiration of a period of at least six months from the date the protecting power receives notification of the final judgment confirming the sentence or an order denying pardon or reprieve. The Diplomatic Conference modified the Stockholm draft somewhat, providing for a reduction of the six-month moratorium in individual cases, under circumstances of grave emergency involving the security of the occupying power or its forces.[73] However, even in

---

[67] Art. 68§3. [68] Arts. 87, 100.

[69] International Committee of the Red Cross (see n. 48 above), p. 75.

[70] Uhler, Coursier et al., *Commentary*, pp. 371–372.

[71] The United States delegate, during first reading of the provision in Committee III, said: 'The abolition of the death penalty in the case of protected persons under eighteen years of age (last paragraph) was a matter which called for very careful consideration before such a sweeping provision was adopted' (*Final Record of the Diplomatic Conference of Geneva of 1949*, *Vol. IIA* (Summary record of nineteenth meeting of Committee III, p. 673)).

[72] *Final Record of the Diplomatic Conference of Geneva of 1949*, *Vol. III*, p. 141 (Annex 299). See also: Letter of the International Union for Child Welfare, p. 131 (Annex 272).

[73] *Final Record of the Diplomatic Conference of Geneva of 1949*, *Vol. IIA* (Summary record of eighteenth meeting of Committee III, p. 675; Summary record of forty-third meeting of Committee III, p. 771; Report of Committee III, p. 835); *Final Record of the Diplomatic Conference of Geneva of 1949*, *Vol. III*, pp. 144–145 (Annex 310); *Final Record of the Diplomatic Conference of Geneva of 1949. Vol. IIB* (Minutes of the twenty-eighth plenary meeting, p. 439).

such cases, the protecting power must receive prior notification and be given reasonable time and opportunity to make representations on the subject.[74]

5.3 *Protocol Additional I* of 1977

Protocol Additional I to the 1949 Geneva Conventions and Relating to The Protection of Victims of International Armed Conflicts[75] deals with a wide range of legal issues addressed in other humanitarian law conventions, and only two articles concern the death penalty. These provisions appear in the human rights section of the *Protocol*, under the subheading 'Measures in Favour of Women and Children'. The first, article 76§3, prohibits the death penalty in the case of pregnant women or mothers having dependent infants, for an offence related to the armed conflict. The second, article 77§5, states that the death penalty for an offence related to the armed conflict shall not be executed on persons who had not attained the age of eighteen years at the time the offence was committed. The scope of these provisions is broader than those in the conventions in that they apply to all persons 'in the power of a party to the conflict', not only 'protected persons', providing that the offence is related to the armed conflict. Under *Protocol Additional I*, it is prohibited to execute a juvenile taken prisoner during the conflict, whereas the fourth *Convention* provides this protection only to civilians in an occupied territory.

In the original draft protocol, two distinct provisions dealt with 'mothers of infants' and pregnant women. The first stated that the death penalty 'shall not be pronounced on mothers of infants or on women responsible for their care', while the second stated: 'Pregnant women shall not be executed.'[76] One of the preparatory meetings for the 1974–1977 Diplomatic Conference, the 1972 Conference of Experts, recommended combining the two proposals[77] and raised questions about the meaning of the term 'infants'.[78] It was suggested that

---

[74] *Geneva Convention of August 12, 1949 Relative to the Protection of Civilians*, art. 75.

[75] UN Doc. A/32/144, Annex I.

[76] International Committee of the Red Cross, *Conference of Government Experts on the Reaffirmation and Development of International Humanitarian Law Applicable in Armed Conflicts, Geneva, 3 May–3 June 1972 (second session), Basic Texts I*, Geneva, 1972, p. 21; International Committee of the Red Cross, *Conference of Government Experts on the Reaffirmation and Development of International Humanitarian Law Applicable in Armed Conflicts, Geneva, 3 May–3 June 1972 (second session), Report on the Work of the Conference, II (Annexes)*, Geneva, 1972, p. 9:
> *Article 59 Mothers of infants.* The death penalty shall not be pronounced on mothers of infants or on women responsible for their care.
> *Article 60 – Death penalty.* In no case shall the death penalty be pronounced on civilians who are under eighteen years at the time of the offence. Pregnant women shall not be executed.

[77] ICRC Doc. CE/COM III/PC 28.

[78] International Committee of the Red Cross, *Conference of Government Experts on the Reaffirmation and Development of International Humanitarian Law Applicable in Armed Conflicts, Geneva, 3 May–3 June 1972 (second session), Report on the Work of the Conference, I*, Geneva, 1972, p. 159, paras. 3.249–3.254.

the term 'pronounced' be changed to 'carried out'[79] and that the age of infants be specified.[80] In a subsequent draft, prepared by the International Committee of the Red Cross prior to the 1974 Diplomatic Conference, the prohibition of the execution of pregnant women remained but the protection of mothers or persons responsible for the care of infants had been eliminated.[81] The Committee explained that its proposal was made in 'a spirit of realism', because of doubts that it could rally international consensus on a ban on the pronouncement of the death penalty on pregnant women. It expressed the desire that the ban on execution continue for a considerable time after birth of the child.[82]

The omission of mothers with dependent children was soon corrected by an amendment from the German Democratic Republic.[83] Poland proposed an amendment changing 'executed' to 'pronounced or executed'.[84] A corresponding provision in *Protocol Additional II*, which said that the death penalty shall not be 'carried out on pregnant women and mothers of young children', had been received by Committee III,[85] and delegates argued that *Protocol Additional I* should do no less.[86] Several delegations spoke on behalf of the German and Polish amendments,[87] others urging caution and supporting the more modest approach of the International Committee.[88] Committee III had no great problem with the

---

[79] ICRC Doc. CE/COM III/PC 14 (United States of America). See also: ICRC Doc. CE/COM III/PC 94 (German Democratic Republic).

[80] ICRC Doc. CE/COM III/PC 95.

[81] International Committee of the Red Cross, *Documents of the Diplomatic Conference*, Vol. I, Part III, p. 22:

> *Article 67. Protection of women*
> . . .
> 2. The death penalty for an offence related to a situation referred to in Article 2 common to the Conventions shall not be executed on pregnant women.

The 'Conventions' is defined, in article 2 of the draft protocol, as the four Geneva Conventions of 1949. Article 2 common to the *Geneva Conventions* defines the scope of international armed conflicts covered by the *Conventions*.

[82] ICRC Doc. CDDH/III/SR.44, paras. 59–60.

[83] ICRC Doc. CDDH/III/86, which was later replaced by ICRC Doc. CDDH/III/321:

> *Redraft* paragraph 2 as follows:
> 2. The death penalty shall not be pronounced on mothers of infants and on women or old persons responsible for their care. It shall not be pronounced and carried out on pregnant women.

See also: ICRC Doc. CDDH/III/SR.44, para. 61.

[84] ICRC Doc. CDDH/III/102, which was later replaced by ICRC Doc. CDDH/III/322:

> In paragraph 2, *replace* the words 'shall not be executed on pregnant women' by 'shall not be pronounced or executed on pregnant women.

See also: ICRC Doc. CDDH/III/SR.44, para. 62. Poland submitted a similar amendment to the corresponding provision in *Protocol Additional II*: ICRC Doc. CDDH/I/96.

[85] ICRC Doc. CDDH/I/GT/88, ICRC Doc. CDDH/I/317/Rev.2, art. 5.

[86] For example, Sweden (ICRC Doc. CDDH/SR.44, para. 67).

[87] Italy (ICRC Doc. CDDH/SR.44, para. 66), Sweden (ICRC Doc. CDDH/SR.44, para. 67), Union of Soviet Socialist Republics (ICRC Doc. CDDH/SR.44, para. 68), Republic of Korea (ICRC Doc. CDDH/SR.44, §69), Hungary (ICRC Doc. CDDH/SR.44, para. 70), Bulgaria (ICRC Doc. CDDH/SR.44, para. 72), Mongolia (ICRC Doc. CDDH/SR.44, para. 74), Holy See (ICRC Doc. CDDH/SR.44, para. 75).

[88] Canada (ICRC Doc. CDDH/SR.44, para. 71), Uruguay (ICRC Doc. CDDH/SR.44, para. 76).

prohibition with respect to pregnant women but considerable difficulty with the proposal to extend the protection to mothers of infants, problems it attributed to 'conflict with national laws and traditions'.[89] The result was a compromise provision that was quickly adopted by consensus[90] and included in the final instrument without further discussion.[91]

In its final version, the article distinguishes between 'pronouncement' of the death penalty and 'execution'. In the former case, several terms qualify the obligation, such as 'to the maximum extent feasible', 'shall endeavour' and 'avoid'. But, if there is no absolute prohibition on pronouncement of the death penalty, there is one on its execution, with respect to pregnant women and mothers with dependent children. The term 'mothers having dependent infants' is also used in article 76§2. During debate on that provision, the Committee had difficulty reaching agreement on an appropriate wording, realizing that it would differ from case to case and culture to culture. It rejected the term 'nursing mothers' in favour of the broader term used in the final version.[92] A very large scope is given to the term in the International Committee's *Commentary*: 'all infants are covered who require the presence and care of their mothers and have not yet acquired full independence'.[93] The prohibition of article 76§3 extends only to an 'offence related to the armed conflict'. Therefore, it is inapplicable to ordinary criminal offences unrelated to the conflict but committed during wartime.[94]

Article 77§5, the other death penalty provision in *Protocol Additional I*, prohibits execution of individuals for crimes committed while under the age of eighteen. It was first proposed in the International Committee draft for the 1972 Conference of Government Experts[95] and submitted without any substantive change at the outset of the 1974 Diplomatic Conference.[96] The representative of

---

[89] ICRC Doc. CDDH/407/Rev.1, para. 57.   [90] ICRC Doc. CDDH/III/SR.59, para. 16.
[91] ICRC Doc. CDDH/SR.43, paras. 54–55.   [92] ICRC Doc. CDDH/407/Rev.1, para. 56.
[93] Claude Pilloud, Jean Pictet, 'Article 76 – Protection of Women', in Yves Sandoz, Christophe Swinarski, Bruno Zimmermann, eds., *Commentary on the Additional Protocols of 8 June 1977 to the Geneva Conventions of 12 August 1949*, Geneva: Martinus Nijhoff, 1987, pp. 891–896, at p. 893.
[94] Claude Pilloud, Jean Pictet, 'Article 77 – Protection of Children', in Yves Sandoz, Christophe Swinarski, Bruno Zimmermann, eds., *ibid.*, pp. 897–905, at p. 904.
[95] International Committee of the Red Cross, *Conference of Government Experts on the Reaffirmation and Development of International Humanitarian Law Applicable in Armed Conflicts, Geneva, 3 May–3 June 1972 (second session), Basic Texts I*, Geneva, 1972, p. 21; International Committee of the Red Cross, *Conference of Government Experts on the Reaffirmation and Development of International Humanitarian Law Applicable in Armed Conflicts, Geneva, 3 May–3 June 1972 (second session), Report on the Work of the Conference, II (Annexes)*, Geneva, 1972, p. 9:
> *Article 60 Death penalty*   In no case shall the death penalty be pronounced on civilians who are under eighteen years at the time of the offence . . .
The United States experts wanted the age limit changed to fifteen: ICRC Doc. CE/COM III/PC 14.
[96] International Committee of the Red Cross, note 1 above, p. 22:
> *Article 68 Protection of children*
>   . . .
>   3.   The death penalty for an offence related to a situation referred to in Article 2 common to the Convention shall not be pronounced on persons who were under eighteen years at the time the offence was committed.

the International Committee of the Red Cross explained that it was a repetition of article 68§4 of the fourth *Geneva Convention* but that inclusion in the protocol would extend the prohibition because the category of protected persons was larger.[97] There were no amendments to the death penalty provision, although Brazil proposed adding a sentence that would prohibit any penal proceedings whatsoever being taken against persons under sixteen at the time of the offence.[98] The provision was studied by a Working Group of Committee III, which settled on the age of eighteen because this was also used in a corresponding provision of the second *Protocol*.[99] The original text had specified that the death penalty could not be 'pronounced', but this was changed to 'executed' upon the request of one delegate, who indicated that his country's legislation did not prohibit 'pronouncement' but did prohibit 'execution'.[100] The provision was adopted by consensus in Committee III[101] and in the plenary Conference.[102] According to the *Commentary* on article 77§5, 'it can be said that the death penalty for persons under eighteen years of age is ruled out completely'.[103] The *Commentary* adds:

> It is to be hoped that this provision will not be abused, especially urging young people under eighteen to perform highly perfidious or unscrupulous acts which would not carry the death penalty for their perpetrator because of his youth. Such practices could have damaging consequences if they occurred frequently and the authorities responsible might give up attempting to apprehend the perpetrators of such acts, seeking rather to eliminate them. The heavy responsibility upon those who ordered adolescents to commit such acts or tolerated them, should be underlined, for they jeopardize the safety of all young people. In addition, it should be recalled that they would have to account for their acts before the courts.[104]

5.4 *Protocol Additional II* of 1977

The death penalty provisions in *Protocol Additional II* were considerably more difficult to draft, partly because of the ambitions of the ICRC and partly because of bitter opposition from many States to what they deemed an attempt

---

The 'Conventions' is defined, in article 2 of the draft protocol, as the four Geneva Conventions of 1949. Article 2 common to the *Geneva Conventions* defines the scope of international armed conflicts covered by the *Conventions*.

[97] ICRC Doc. CDDH/III/SR.45, para. 8.
[98] ICRC Doc. CDDH/III/325:
   In paragraph 3, *add* the following sentence;
   Penal proceedings shall not be taken against, and sentence shall not be pronounced on, persons who were under sixteen years of age at the time the offence was committed.
A similarly unsuccessful proposal was submitted by Brazil in Committee I as an amendment to *Protocol Additional II*: ICRC Doc. CDDH/I/SR.34, para. 11.
[99] ICRC Doc. CDDH/407/Rev.1, para. 64.   [100] *Ibid.*; ICRC Doc. CDDH/III/SR.59, paras. 7–18.
[101] ICRC Doc. CDDH/III/SR.59, para. 18.   [102] ICRC Doc. CDDH/SR.43, para. 55.
[103] Claude Pilloud, Jean Pictet, 'Article 77 – Protection of Children', in Yves Sandoz, Christophe Swinarski, Bruno Zimmermann, eds., *Commentary on the Additional Protocols of 8 June 1977 to the Geneva Conventions of 12 August 1949*, Geneva: Martinus Nijhoff, 1987, pp. 897–905, at p. 904.
[104] Pilloud, Pictet, 'Article 77', p. 904.

to legislate on internal matters, an objection extending to the entire concept of an instrument regulating conduct during non-international armed conflict.[105] Article 6§4 prohibits the death penalty for crimes committed while under eighteen, for pregnant women and for mothers of young children.[106] The article was not particularly controversial and closely resembles obligations imposed by article 6§5 of the *International Covenant on Civil and Political Rights*, a non-derogable provision applicable during armed conflict.[107] But the drafters of *Protocol Additional II* had hoped to go even further than the *Covenant* with respect to the death penalty, providing for a moratorium on executions until the end of the conflict, in the hope that amnesty or some other form of reconciliation would intervene. The proposal survived debate in Committee only to be eliminated in a last minute compromise, and the most interesting story in the drafting of *Protocol Additional II* is not what was included but what was left out.

In preparation for a Conference of Government Experts, in 1971, the International Committee of the Red Cross suggested a provision that would defer executions until the conclusion of the armed conflict.[108] 'The purpose of this proposal', said the accompanying explanation, 'is to endeavour to eliminate summary executions which, on both sides, engender hate and provoke an endless spiral of reprisals. It is based on the recognition that crimes incurring the death penalty are far less numerous than they once were.'[109] The proposal met with a lukewarm reception from the experts, who considered that it would be difficult to put into practice. Such a provision would be feasible only if it were strictly respected by both parties, something which could not easily be guaranteed. Otherwise, said the experts, the party which carried out death sentences would have a far stronger grip on the civilian population, and eventually the other party would abandon its respect for the provision.[110]

However, for the 1972 Conference, the International Committee prepared a 'Draft Additional Protocol to Article 3 Common to the Four Geneva Conventions of August 12, 1949' that took its earlier proposal one step further. The provision specified that combatants, having fallen into the power of the

---

[105] *Protocol Additional II to the 1949 Geneva Conventions and Relating to the Protection of Victims of Non-International Armed Conflicts*, art. 1.
[106] *Protocol Additional II to the 1949 Geneva Conventions and Relating to the Protection of Victims of Non-International Armed Conflicts*, art. 6§4.
[107] *Legality of the Threat or Use of Nuclear Weapons, Advisory Opinion*, [1996] ICJ Reports 226, para. 25.
[108] ICRC Doc. CE/5b, p. 57. Canada had made a similar proposal along these lines: 'Canadian draft protocol to the Geneva Conventions of 1949 relative to conflicts not international in character', reprinted in (1971) *Canadian Defense Quarterly* 9, p. 11:

> *Article 18*
>
> (1) Death sentences imposed upon persons whose guilt arises only by reason of having participated as combatants in the conflict shall not be carried out until after hostilities have ceased.
>
> (2) Death sentences imposed on any person shall not, in any event, be carried out until the convicted person has exhausted all means of appeal and petition for pardon or reprieve.

[109] ICRC Doc. CE/5b, p. 58.   [110] *Ibid.*

adversary, could not be executed if their only crime was participating in the armed conflict and if they were sufficiently well identified as combatants, for example by bearing arms openly.[111] It is a provision that overlaps substantially with the prohibition of execution for political crimes that appears in some human rights instruments.[112] In effect, this radical provision gave a form of prisoner of war status to combatants in a 'non-international' armed conflict, guaranteeing them immunity from execution if not immunity from prosecution. In order to answer complaints, the International Committee came up with two less drastic alternatives, one urging courts to give such combatants the benefit of 'attenuating circumstances' and the other delaying the death penalty until after the hostilities.[113] At the Conference, Egypt rallied to the International Committee's proposal with a new amendment that abolished the death penalty for participants in the conflict.[114] Even the United States experts were favourable to the more modest proposal of postponement of the death sentence until the cessation of hostilities.[115]

In the draft protocol submitted to the Diplomatic Conference in 1974, the International Committee returned to its original idea of deferring execution until the end of hostilities.[116] Presenting the provision, the International Committee

---

[111] International Committee of the Red Cross, *Conference of Government Experts on the Reaffirmation and Development of International Humanitarian Law Applicable in Armed Conflicts, Geneva, 3 May–3 June 1972 (second session), Basic Texts I*, Geneva, 1972, pp. 41–42; International Committee of the Red Cross, *Conference of Government Experts on the Reaffirmation and Development of International Humanitarian Law Applicable in Armed Conflicts, Geneva, 3 May–3 June 1972 (second session), Report on the Work of the Conference, II (Annexes)*, Geneva, 1972, p. 19:

> Article 28 Penal prosecutions against combatants
> After having fallen into the power of the adversary, combatants who have fulfilled the conditions stipulated in Article 25 of the present Protocol [art. 4A(2) of Third Convention], as well as those combatants who, without having fulfilled the conditions stipulated in Article 4 A(2) of the Geneva Convention relative to the Treatment of Prisoners of War of August 12, 1949, will have at least, in the course of their operations, distinguished themselves from the civilian population by some distinctive sign or by any other means who had complied with the provisions of the present Protocol, shall not be punishable by death if they become the object of penal prosecutions only by reason of having taken part in hostilities or having been members of armed forces.

[112] E.g., *American Convention on Human Rights*, (1979) 1144 UNTS 123, OASTS 36, art. 4§3 (see Appendix 20, p. 436).

[113] International Committee of the Red Cross, *Conference of Government Experts on the Reaffirmation and Development of International Humanitarian Law Applicable in Armed Conflicts, Geneva, 3 May–3 June 1972 (second session), Commentaries, II*, Geneva, 1972, pp. 57–60.

[114] ICRC Doc. CE/COM II/39:

> No one shall incur death penalty solely for having taken part in hostilities or having been a member of armed forces, unless imperative security requirements make this necessary.

[115] ICRC Doc. CE/COM II/49.

[116] International Committee of the Red Cross (see n. 81 above), p. 22:

> Article 10 Penal prosecutions
>
> . . .
>
> 3. The death penalty pronounced on any person found guilty of an offence in relation to the armed conflict shall not be carried out until the hostilities have ceased.

of the Red Cross representative observed that experts had felt it was hardly possible to place a general prohibition on the death penalty. The Committee urged an 'attenuating clause' which would postpone execution until the end of hostilities, a point on which the Committee candidly admitted the government experts were not in agreement. However, according to the Committee, experts in penal law who had been consulted subsequently had supported the proposal, noting that it did not conflict with national laws because it did not prohibit pronouncement of the death penalty, merely deferring its being carried out.[117]

The draft article was only superficially discussed in 1975,[118] and then referred to a Working Group for detailed study. The Working Group modified the provision to provide that any death penalty pronounced against a person not be carried out until the end of the armed conflict, with the exception of a war crime or a crime against humanity.[119] In 1976, a compromise was worked out in order to eliminate the controversial mention of war crimes and crimes against humanity,[120] a mention that would, in effect, have recognized the legitimacy of the death penalty as a punishment for war crimes.[121] As amended, the draft article was adopted by consensus in Committee I,[122] with reservations being expressed by several States.[123]

Pakistan had opposed the proposal, saying that it executed insurgents and that any attempt by the *Protocol* to modify this point would be interference in

---

[117] ICRC Doc. CDDH/I/SR.34, §§4–5.

[118] ICRC Doc. CDDH/I/SR.34, ICRC Doc. CDDH/I/SR.41; 'Diplomatic Conference on the Reaffirmation and Development of International Humanitarian Law Applicable in Armed Conflicts, Summary of second session's work', [1975] *International Review of the Red Cross* 323, at p. 349. The *travaux préparatoires* of *Protocol Additional II* relating to article 6 and the death penalty have been integrally reprinted: Howard Levie, ed., *The Law of Non-international Armed Conflict*, Dordrecht/Boston/Lancaster: Martinus Nijhoff, 1988, pp. 245–303.

[119] ICRC Doc. CDDH/I/317/Rev.2, art, 10§4.

[120] The Soviet Union had urged such a provision, in an amendment sponsored by itself and several of its allies (ICRC Doc. CDDH/I/260):

Add a new paragraph 7:

7. Nothing in the present Protocol shall be invoked to prevent the prosecution and punishment of persons charged with crimes against humanity or who participate in the conflict as foreign mercenaries.

Even after the withdrawal of reference to war crimes and crimes against humanity, the Soviet Union said that it did not view the draft article as an obstacle to prosecution: ICRC Doc. CDDH/I/SR.64, para. 84.

[121] Italy said that had the reference to war crimes and crimes against humanity not been withdrawn, it would not have been able to join the consensus: ICRC Doc. CDDH/I/SR.64, para. 105.

[122] ICRC Doc. CDDH/I/SR.63, §71:

5. In case of prosecutions carried out against a person only by reason of his having taken part in hostilities, the court, when deciding upon the sentence, shall take into consideration, to the greatest possible extent, the fact that the accused respected the provisions of the present protocol. In no such case shall a death penalty be carried out until the end of the armed conflict.

[123] Indonesia (ICRC Doc. CDDH/I/SR.64, para. 31), United Kingdom (ICRC Doc. CDDH/I/SR.64, para. 40), Iraq (ICRC Doc. CDDH/I/SR.64, para. 50).

the sovereign rights of States.[124] Furthermore, Pakistan had argued that, under its internal law, a death penalty must be carried out within three months, because it was considered that to compel a prisoner to wait longer than that amounted to torture.[125] Pakistan returned to the matter in the plenary Conference, proposing a radical redrafting of the text that completely eliminated the controversial provision adopted in Committee.[126] The Swiss delegate, Bindschedler, wanted to retain the prohibition on execution until the end of the conflict.[127] Norway was also adamant, refusing to join the consensus for their deletion and insisting on a vote.[128] The provision was rejected by twenty-six votes to twelve with forty-nine abstentions,[129] many delegates explaining that they had abstained to make the *Protocol* acceptable to a larger number of countries, even if they did not oppose the provision.[130] Norway, Sweden and the Holy See explained why they had voted in favour.[131] The provision may well have been a sacrifice to preserve the entire *Protocol*, whose survival at times seemed threatened by States that claimed it veered dangerously close to a code of international penal procedure.

The death penalty provision that resulted from Pakistan's radical surgery upon the earlier draft became article 6§4, which protects juveniles, pregnant women and new mothers. The debates on this provision concerned essentially the age of eighteen and the extension of the prohibition on execution to new mothers. At the 1972 Conference of Government Experts, draft article 6 dealing with children was submitted in two versions, one stating 'fifteen' and the other stating 'eighteen',[132] and the age cut-off was in effect the only point in dispute in the Drafting Committee. The experts in the Drafting Committee, with the exception of the United States,[133] seemed virtually unanimous that eighteen should be the age.[134] The 1972 draft also prohibited the execution of 'mothers

---

[124] ICRC Doc. CDDH/I/SR.34, para. 17.
[125] ICRC Doc. CDDH/I/SR.34, para. 18. See also: ICRC Doc. CDDH/I/SR.34, para. 21 (Nigeria); ICRC Doc. CDDH/I/SR.34, para. 23 (Argentina); ICRC Doc. CDDH/I/SR.34, para. 34 (Mongolia).
[126] ICRC Doc. CDDH/SR.50, para. 56; ICRC Doc. CDDH/427 and Corr. 1.
[127] ICRC Doc. CDDH/SR.50, para. 63; supported by the Holy See (ICRC Doc. CDDH/SR.50, para. 65), Cyprus (ICRC Doc. CDDH/SR.50, para. 74), Italy (ICRC Doc. CDDH/SR.50, para. 67).
[128] ICRC Doc. CDDH/SR.50, paras. 77, 84.   [129] *Ibid.*, para. 86.
[130] *Ibid.*, para. 87 (Belgium), para. 88 (Switzerland), para. 89 (Federal Republic of Germany), para. 90 (Austria), para. 91 (Portugal), para. 92 (Finland, Denmark, Turkey, Ireland, Cyprus).
[131] *Ibid.*, para. 94 (Norway), para. 95 (Sweden), para. 96 (Holy See).
[132] International Committee of the Red Cross, *Conference of Government Experts on the Reaffirmation and Development of International Humanitarian Law Applicable in Armed Conflicts, Geneva, 3 May–3 June 1972 (second session), Report on the Work of the Conference, I*, Geneva, 1972, p. 77, para. 2.153. It had been submitted by the drafting committee.
[133] ICRC Doc. CE/COM II/26. International Committee of the Red Cross, *Conference of Government Experts on the Reaffirmation and Development of International Humanitarian Law Applicable in Armed Conflicts, Geneva, 3 May–3 June 1972 (second session), Report on the Work of the Conference, I*, Geneva, 1972, p. 76, para. 2.149.
[134] *Ibid.*, paras. 2.155–2.156.

of infants' and 'women responsible for their care'.[135] The proposal submitted to the Diplomatic Conference set the age at eighteen and prohibited the execution of pregnant women but made no mention of mothers.[136] The representative of the International Committee of the Red Cross explained that the experts consulted had been in general agreement that it was possible to prohibit or postpone the death penalty in these circumstances.[137] Sweden, unhappy with the limitations of this position, announced that it would submit an amendment calling for total abolition of the death penalty.[138] Pakistan provided one of the few opposition voices, arguing that a stipulation that the death penalty could not be pronounced on persons under eighteen would encourage rebels to force juveniles to participate in armed conflicts.[139]

Canada proposed addition of the phrase 'mothers of infants'.[140] A Working Group of Committee I considered reference to 'mothers of young children' as an option[141] but did not accept suggestions that the death penalty should be neither carried out nor pronounced on pregnant women.[142] After a separate vote,[143] Committee I decided to add the phrase 'mothers of young children', and then adopted the entire provision by consensus.[144] During explanations of vote, the United Kingdom expressed concern that the provision had departed from the text of article 6§5 of the *International Covenant*, notably because of uncertainty about

---

[135] International Committee of the Red Cross, *Conference of Government Experts on the Reaffirmation and Development of International Humanitarian Law Applicable in Armed Conflicts, Geneva, 3 May– 3 June 1972 (second session), Basic Texts I*, Geneva, 1972, p. 36 (eighteen years); International Committee of the Red Cross, *Conference of Government Experts on the Reaffirmation and Development of International Humanitarian Law Applicable in Armed Conflicts, Geneva, 3 May–3 June 1972 (second session), Report on the Work of the Conference, II (Annexes)*, Geneva, 1972, pp. 16–17 (fifteen years).
> *Article 6 Measures in favour of children*
>
> 3. The death penalty shall not be pronounced on civilians below [eighteen] [fifteen] years of age at the time when the offence was committed, nor on mothers of infants or on women responsible for their care. Pregnant women shall not be executed.

[136] International Committee of the Red Cross (see n. 81 above), p. 36:
> *Article 10 Penal prosecutions*
> . . .
> 4.   The death penalty shall not be pronounced for an offence in relation to the armed conflict committed by persons below eighteen years of age and shall not be carried out on pregnant women.

An amendment submitted by Canada renewed the option between eighteen and fifteen years of age: ICRC Doc. CDDH/I/259, art. 5.

[137]   ICRC Doc. CDDH/I/SR.34, para. 4.   [138]   *Ibid.*, para. 15; ICRC Doc. CDDH/I/261.

[139]   ICRC Doc. CDDH/I/SR.34, para. 19. This view was endorsed by Nigeria, which suggested the age limit be reduced to sixteen.

[140]   ICRC Doc. CDDH/I/259, art. 6.

[141]   ICRC Doc. CDDH/I/317/Rev.2, art. 10§5. The Working Group was not unanimous on this point however (ICRC Doc. CDDH/I/GT/88, Annex, para. 4):
> The death penalty shall not be pronounced on persons below eighteen years of age at the time of the offence and shall not be carried out on pregnant women [and mothers of young children].

[142]   See ICRC Doc. CDDH/I/GT/88, Annex, para. 4.

[143]   ICRC Doc. CDDH/I/SR.63, para. 74, by thirty-seven votes to two, with nine abstentions.

[144]   *Ibid.*

the meaning of the words 'young children'.[145] Furthermore, the United Kingdom delegation was not convinced of the humanitarian justification for protecting mothers of young children but not other persons who might have their care.[146]

In the plenary, the provision dealing with juveniles, pregnant women and mothers of young children was retained in the Pakistan delegation's revision, and it was adopted by consensus.[147] According to the *Commentary*, 'The results of the vote suggest that the concept will be broadly interpreted, and that in such special cases the death penalty will not be pronounced.'[148]

The final version of article 6 of *Protocol Additional II* is a compromise resulting from complex negotiations. Pakistan, for example, was equally opposed to any protection of minors, which it said would encourage rebels to force minors to take part in armed conflicts,[149] but went along with the amputated version of the article in order to eliminate the troubling moratorium on the death penalty during armed conflicts.

Article 6§5 of the *Protocol* refers to the possibility of amnesty but makes no mention of the death penalty. It is derived from earlier proposals that had echoed article 6§4 of the *International Covenant* and that had referred explicitly to capital punishment.[150] Article 6§5 had also been eliminated by Pakistan's amendment but was reinstated on a vote in the plenary,[151] at the insistence of the Soviet Union.[152]

The failure to include a moratorium on the death penalty during armed conflict was a setback for abolitionist lawmaking but one whose magnitude may tend to be exaggerated. The provision had been approved in Committee I and was abandoned in order to save other provisions of the *Protocol*. Pakistan and other opponents of the provision would have been happier to see the end of article 6 altogether. As a last-minute compromise, what could have been an important advance on international law and the death penalty was set aside. The additional protocols do mark progress in the abolition of the death penalty,

---

[145] ICRC Doc. CDDH/I/SR.64, para. 42. Similar views were expressed by Japan: ICRC Doc. CDDH/I/SR.64, para. 82. See also: Asbiorn Eide, 'The New Humanitarian Law in Non-International Armed Conflict', in A. Cassese (ed.), *The New Humanitarian Law of Armed Conflict*, Vol. I, Naples: Editoriale Scientifica, 1979, pp. 276–309, at p. 286. The International Committee of the Red Cross *Commentary* on *Protocol Additional II* suggests some guidance in construing the term can be obtained from the fourth *Convention*, art. 14§1, which refers to mothers of children under seven years old, and *Protocol Additional I*, art. 8, which uses the narrower term 'new-born babies': Sylvie Stoyanka-Junod, 'Article 6 – Fundamental guarantees', in Yves Sandoz, Christophe Swinarski, Bruno Zimmermann, eds., *Commentary on the Additional Protocols of 8 June 1977 to the Geneva Conventions of 12 August 1949*, Geneva: Martinus Nijhoff, 1987, pp. 1395–1402, at p. 1402.
[146] ICRC Doc. CDDH/I/SR.64, para. 43.   [147] ICRC Doc. CDDH/SR.50, para. 78.
[148] Junod, 'Article 6', p. 1402.   [149] ICRC Doc. CDDH/I/SR.34, para. 19.
[150] ICRC Doc. CDDH/I/317/Rev.2:
    7. Anyone sentenced shall have the right to seek pardon or commutation of the sentence. Amnesty, pardon or commutation of the sentence of death may be granted in all cases.
[151] ICRC Doc. CDDH/SR.50, para. 100, by thirty-seven votes to fifteen, with thirty-one abstentions.
[152] ICRC Doc. CDDH/SR.50, paras. 59–62.

however, in their extension of the prohibition on execution to 'mothers having dependent infants', in the case of *Protocol I*, and 'mothers of young children', in the case of *Protocol II*.[153] That the latter seems to go even farther than the former is a curious result, given the reluctance of States to extend norms for international armed conflict to non-international armed conflict. By adding yet another category to the enumeration of those who are immune from execution, the additional protocols represent a significant advance.

[153] Article 3 of the 'Safeguards Guaranteeing Protection of the Rights of Those Facing the Death Penalty', ESC Res. 1984/50 (see Appendix 8, p. 413), prohibits imposing the death penalty on 'new mothers.'

6

International criminal law

The adoption of the *Rome Statute of the International Criminal Court* crowns developments underway for many decades in the establishment of an international tribunal with jurisdiction over serious international crimes such as genocide, crimes against humanity, war crimes and aggression. Although the *Statute* excludes the death penalty, the question was vigorously debated during the 1998 Rome Conference where it was adopted. Earlier models of international justice considered capital punishment to be appropriate for crimes of such gravity. This chapter considers the evolution of the issue of capital punishment in the field of international criminal law.

There is some authority for the proposition that war crimes are punishable by death as a matter of international law. The *Lieber Code*, promulgated by President Abraham Lincoln to govern the conduct of the Union Army during the American Civil War and often held up as an early codification of the laws and customs of war, made frequent reference to the death penalty as an appropriate punishment.[1] More recently, in the commentary on war crimes trials held following the Second World War, the United Nations War Crimes Commission declared that '[i]nternational law lays down that a war criminal may be punished with death whatever crime he may have committed'.[2] A post-Second World War Norwegian court answered a defendant's plea that the death penalty did not apply to the offence as charged, because the death penalty had been abolished for such a crime in domestic law, by finding that violations of the laws and customs of war had always been punishable by death at international law.[3] There are even suggestions that international law governs the method of execution. In an early

[1] 'Instructions for the Government of Armies of the United States in the Field, Prepared by Francis Lieber, LLD, Originally Issued as General Orders No. 100', arts. 12, 47, 48, 58, 66, 71, 77, 83, 85, 89, 91, 92, 95, 97, 124, 127, 130.
[2] 'Punishment of Criminals', (1948) 15 LRTWC 200. The 1940 edition of the United States Army Manual *Rules of Land Warfare* declared that '[a]ll war crimes are subject to the death penalty, although a lesser penalty may be imposed': Field Manual 27-10, 1 October 1940, §357.
[3] *Public Prosecutor* v. *Klinge*, (1946) 13 *Ann. Dig.* 262 (Supreme Court, Norway).

235

case, the United States Supreme Court said that 'the custom of war' determined that spies and mutineers are traditionally hanged, whereas desertion and failure to obey orders compel shooting.[4]

Probably the earliest recorded international criminal trial is that of Peter van Hagenbach, who was convicted of violations of the laws and customs of war in the fourteenth century by a court of the Holy Roman Empire. He was indeed executed, but only after being subjected to various forms of torture and mutilation that were the customary accompaniments of capital punishment at the time.[5] The internationalization of prosecution for war crimes and similar offences really dates from the end of the First World War. The *Treaty of Versailles* contemplated prosecution of Kaiser Wilhelm II for 'a supreme offence against international morality and the sanctity of treaties', and of German soldiers charged with violations of the laws and customs of war. The Kaiser was to be tried by a five-judge tribunal, appointed by the victorious powers, whose duty it would be to 'fix the punishment which it considers should be imposed'. The German war criminals were to be tried by military tribunals of the victorious powers, and sentenced 'to punishments laid down by law'.[6] But the Kaiser was never apprehended. As for German soldiers, the Allies eventually agreed to suspend the war crimes provisions of the *Treaty of Versailles* so that the accused were tried by German courts. Only a handful of trials was actually held, and short prison terms were imposed.[7]

6.1 Post-Second World War prosecutions

The *Charter of the International Military Tribunal* authorized the Nuremberg court to impose upon a convicted war criminal 'death or such other punishment as shall be determined by it to be just'.[8] That capital punishment would be the likely result of conviction was so obvious that the drafters of the *Charter* did not even consider the matter.[9] Earlier, the Allies had questioned whether the leading Nazis should be tried at all, with many, including Churchill, favouring summary execution.[10] Of those accused at Nuremberg in the Trial of the Major

[4] *Wilkerson* v. *Utah*, 99 US 130, 134, 25 L.Ed. 345 (1878).
[5] M. Cherif Bassiouni, 'From Versailles to Rwanda in 75 Years: The Need to Establish a Permanent International Court', (1997) 10 *Harvard Human Rights Journal* 11.
[6] *Treaty of Peace Between the Allied and Associated Power and Germany* ('Treaty of Versailles'), [1919] TS 4, art. 228.
[7] *German War Trials, Report of Proceedings Before the Supreme Court in Leipzig,* Cmd 1450 (1921).
[8] *Agreement for the Prosecution and Punishment of Major War Criminals of the European Axis, and Establishing the Charter of the International Military Tribunal (IMT),* (1951) 82 UNTS 279, art. 27.
[9] *Report of Robert H. Jackson, United States Representative to the International Conference on Military Trials,* Washington: U.S. Government Printing Office, 1949.
[10] Arieh J. Kochavi, *Prelude to Nuremberg, Allied War Crimes Policy and the Question of Punishment,* Chapel Hill and London: University of North Carolina Press, 1998, pp. 63–91.

War Criminals, three were acquitted, seven were sentenced to prison terms, and twelve condemned to death by hanging. The four judges were deadlocked in the case of Albert Speer, but a last-minute change of heart by Francis Biddle saved his life and he was sentenced to twenty years.[11] Julius Streicher was found guilty of crimes against humanity for which he was sentenced to death.[12] All of the others who were condemned to death were found guilty of war crimes as well as of crimes against humanity. American prosecutor Robert Jackson, a lifelong abolitionist, believed imposing the death penalty on Nazi war criminals would only sanction violence, not condemn it. Uncomfortable with the provisions in the *Charter*, he decided simply to say nothing on the subject, and leave sentencing to the judges.[13]

No defendant at Nuremberg was sentenced to death for crimes against peace. Rudolf Hess, who was found guilty of crimes against peace but acquitted of war crimes and crimes against humanity, was condemned to life imprisonment.[14] Within weeks of the conviction, the executions were carried out in the Nuremberg prison gymnasium by an American hangman whose technical incompetence brought about superfluous suffering to the condemned criminals. Their heads struck the platform as the scaffold's trapdoor opened, and rather than breaking their necks, they probably died of slow strangulation.[15] Hermann Göring escaped execution by committing suicide in his cell the day before.

Subsequent prosecutions in post-war Germany by Allied military commissions and tribunals, as well as by German courts, were held pursuant to *Control Council Law No. 10*.[16] Like the *Charter of the International Military Tribunal*, *Control Council Law No. 10* provided that war crimes, crimes against peace and crimes against humanity could be punished by death.[17] In the twelve trials held by United States military tribunals at Nuremberg under *Control Council Law No. 10*, twenty-four of the 142 defendants were sentenced to capital punishment. *Ordinance No. 7* (art. XVIII) established that '[n]o sentence of death shall be carried into execution unless and until confirmed in writing by the Military Governor', but in only one case was a death sentence reduced to

---

[11] Joseph Persico, *Nuremberg, Infamy on Trial*, New York: Penguin Books, 1994, p. 404.

[12] *France et al. v. Göring et al.*, (1948) 22 IMT 547–549.

[13] Persico, *Nuremberg*, pp. 115–116. But Jackson refused to support commutation of the death sentences: Robert E. Conot, *Justice at Nuremberg*, New York: Harper and Row, 1983, p. 501.

[14] *Ibid.*, pp. 527–530. He served the sentence, apparently committing suicide in 1987 after regular but fruitless attempts at obtaining a pardon or conditional release.

[15] Telford Taylor, *The Anatomy of the Nuremberg Trials*, New York: Alfred A. Knopf, 1992, p. 611.

[16] *Control Council Law No. 10, Punishment of Persons Guilty of War Crimes, Crimes Against Peace and Against Humanity*, 20 December 1945, Official Gazette Control Council for Germany, art. 1(c).

[17] *Ibid.*, art. II(3). See also: *United States Zone Ordinance No. 7*, art. 16; *United Kingdom Royal Warrant*, §9; *Regulations Governing the Trial of Accused War Criminals*, Supreme Commander for the Allied Powers, art. 5(g).

one of life imprisonment.[18] Besides considering the fitness of the death penalty, the Clemency Board also considered a plea that because as much as five years had elapsed since the beginning of the proceedings, it would be wrong to impose capital punishment, something later known as the 'death row phenomenon':

> [W]e have not been moved by the argument that by remaining long under sentence of death, the defendant has suffered so much as to be entitled to consideration on that ground. Delays in executing the death sentences have been due to the defendants' efforts to have every possible review of their cases and to the time necessarily consumed in such reviews and extending to the defendants the fullest possible consideration of their cases. It always takes time in any civilized society to exhaust the salutary processes of the law for the individual's protection. Those defendants who will be spared execution by these processes will undoubtedly think the time so spent worthwhile, as obviously it is worthwhile in every case. It must follow, however, that in the cases remaining, where no consideration of clemency could possibly justify a change in sentence, there is no basis for making a change simply because the execution has been delayed in making doubly or triply sure that the judgment should be carried out.[19]

The twenty-four men condemned to death were all found guilty of war crimes as well as, in certain cases, the other punishable offences, namely crimes against peace, crimes against humanity and membership in a criminal organization.[20] Nobody was executed for committing crimes against humanity or crimes against peace in the absence of war crimes. In the 'Justice Trial', defendant Oswald Rothaug was convicted of crimes against humanity, and despite the fact that the court found there to be no mitigating circumstances, it also said there was 'no extenuation' and sentenced him to life imprisonment rather than death, the maximum provided by law at the time.[21]

The widespread use of the death penalty by Nazi courts within Germany and in occupied territories was the subject of prosecution in post-war proceedings. The Nuremberg trial of the major war criminals heard evidence of widespread use of capital punishment by the Nazi regime. The Soviet judge, I. T. Nikitchenko, cited Nazi abuse of capital punishment with respect to prisoner of war offences such as escaping from a camp. Under international law, he said, such offences did not carry any punishment. Nikitchenko noted the 'Night and Fog Decree', which said: 'Penalty for such offences, consisting of loss of freedom and even a life sentence is a sign of weakness. Only death sentences or measures which entail ignorance of the fate of the guilty by local population will achieve

---

[18] (1949) 15 TWC 1140–1147.

[19] 'Report of the Advisory Board on Clemency for War Criminals to the United States High Commissioner for Germany', 28 August 1950, (1949) 15 TWC 1157, p. 1164.

[20] 'Statistical Table of the 12 Nuernberg Trials Held Under the Authority of Control Council Law No. 10', (1949) 15 TWC 1149.

[21] *United States of America* v. *Alstötter et al.* ('Justice trial'), (1948) 3 TWC 1, 6 LRTWC 1, 14 *Ann. Dig.* 278 (United States Military Commission), p. 1201 (TWC).

real effectiveness.'[22] According to the Decree, as Wilhelm Keitel testified before the International Military Tribunal, Hitler had insisted that '[e]fficient and enduring intimidation can only be achieved either by capital punishment . . .'.[23]

The so-called 'Justice trial' (*United States* v. *Alstötter*), well known because it inspired the celebrated film *Judgment at Nuremberg*, convicted German judges, prosecutors and justice officials of crimes against humanity, in part for their resort to capital punishment. Documents filed with the court established that the death penalty was imposed by Nazi courts in thousands of cases. The court classified these into seven groups: cases against proven habitual criminals; cases of looting in the devastated areas of Germany, committed after air raids and under cover of blackout; crimes against the war economy such as hoarding; crimes undermining the defensive strength of the nation, such as defeatist remarks and criticisms of Hitler; crimes of treason and high treason; crimes committed under the 'Night and Fog' (*Nacht und Nebel*) Decree; and crimes of various types committed by Poles, Jews 'and other foreigners'.[24]

In *Alstötter*, the United States Military Tribunal discussed those 'instances where the death penalty might be considered justifiable'. It noted that sentences of life imprisonment can be imposed upon habitual criminals in 'many civilized states'. The Tribunal said it was 'unable to say in one breath that life imprisonment for habitual criminals is a salutary and reasonable punishment in America in peace time, but that the imposition of the death penalty was a crime against humanity here when the nation was in the throes of war'.[25] The Tribunal also recognized that the death penalty might be justifiable, or at least could not be deemed a crime against humanity, in cases of looting, hoarding and other offences against the war economy. Similarly, the Tribunal declared it was not prepared to rule that application of the death penalty for 'undermining military morale' constituted a crime against humanity.

The Tribunal made a distinction between capital punishment imposed within Germany and that carried out in occupied territories. Because the annexation of Poland was illegal, the Nazis were not entitled to loyalty from the Polish inhabitants, and as a result could not prosecute them for treason or high treason.[26] The imposition of the death penalty upon Poles for treason or high treason, when at the most the acts were those of insubordination, was therefore

---

[22] *France et al.* v. *Goering et al.*, Transcript, Afternoon Session, 25 January 1946. Nikitchenko used these examples to support his call for death sentences in the case of all convicted by the International Military Tribunal, a point upon which his colleagues did not agree.

[23] *United States* v. *Alstötter*, p. 55.

[24] *United States* v. *Alstotter*, pp. 50–51. Of course, it was incorrect to suggest that German Jews were 'foreigners'.

[25] *United States* v. *Alstotter*, p. 51.

[26] See *Convention Regulating the Laws and Customs of Land Warfare (Hague Convention No. IV), Regulations Concerning the Laws and Customs of War*, 3 Martens (3rd) 461, 2 *AJIL Supp.* 20, [1910] TS 9, arts. 44, 45.

unacceptable. The Tribunal reasoned that this violated a general prohibition upon the imposition of capital punishment for minor offences.[27] No positive law authority was given for this proposition, although the fourth *Geneva Convention*, adopted in 1949, codified by implication the prohibition upon capital punishment for treason.[28] As the Tribunal noted, the disappearances and deportation to Germany associated with *Nacht und Nebel* were used in the alternative, in cases where an offender was not likely to be condemned to death by the courts within the occupied territory.

Post-war Germany soon became a bastion of abolition, a position it has never relinquished.[29] The harshness of the death penalty in the post-war trials incited an unholy alliance in the post-war legislature of Nazi sympathizers, who were anxious to shelter their friends, and left-wing penal reformers. These rather different constituencies joined forces to prohibit capital punishment in the May 1949 German *Basic Law*, which formally abolished the death penalty.[30] A few years of uncertainty followed, because the occupying administrations did not consider that the *Basic Law* could overrule the application of *Control Council Law No. 10*, at least to the extent that it was administered by the Allies and where it was their desire to execute offenders.[31] Some of those sentenced to death by the Nuremberg courts unsuccessfully challenged the death penalty before the United States courts.[32] The last group of German war criminals was executed in 1951, and shortly afterwards the Allies agreed that the death penalty would cease within occupied Germany.[33] The Federal Republic of Germany was to become one of the most vigorous and devoted advocates of the abolition of the death penalty in international law.

The sentencing provisions of the *Charter of the International Military Tribunal for the Far East* (the 'Tokyo Tribunal') were similar to those adopted for the Nuremberg Trial of the Major War Criminals.[34] Of those accused, seven

---

[27] *United States* v. *Alstotter*, p. 53.

[28] *Geneva Convention (IV) Relative to the Protection of Civilians*, (1950) 75 U.N.T.S. 287, art. 68. For detailed discussion, see Chapter 5.

[29] The Federal Republic of Germany had the honour of first proposing to the United Nations General Assembly the adoption of an abolitionist protocol to the *International Covenant on Civil and Political Rights*: UN Doc. A/C.3/36/SR.27, §15.

[30] Richard J. Evans, *Rituals of Retribution, Capital Punishment in Germany 1600–1987*, Oxford: Clarendon Press, 1996, pp. 775–789.

[31] 'Statement of the High Commissioner for Germany, 31 January 1951, Upon Announcing His Final Decisions Concerning Requests for Clemency for War Criminals Convicted at Nuremberg', (1949) 15 TWC 1176, p. 1177.

[32] *Pohl et al.* v. *Acheson et al.*, *Schallmermair et al.* v. *Marshall et al.*, Memorandum of Court, D.C. District Court, 29 May 1951, 15 TWC 1192; *Pohl et al.* v. *Acheson et al.*, *Schallmermair et al.* v. *Marshall et al.*, Order, Supreme Court of the United States, 6 June 1951, 15 TWC 1198.

[33] Evans, *Rituals of Retribution*, pp. 775–789.

[34] *Special Proclamation by the Supreme Commander for the Allied Powers at Tokyo*, 4 Bevans 20, as amended, 4 Bevans 27 ('Charter of the Tokyo Tribunal'). 'Article 16. *Penalty*. The Tribunal shall have the power to

were sentenced to death and fifteen to life imprisonment. The President of the Tribunal penned a separate opinion, in which he examined sentencing practice at Nuremberg and found it to be equivocal on the issue of crimes against peace. He concluded that 'no Japanese accused should be sentenced to death for conspiring to wage, or planning and preparing, or initiating, or waging aggressive war'. As for those convicted of war crimes and crimes against humanity, he seemed to favour life imprisonment: 'It may well be that the punishment of imprisonment for life under sustained conditions of hardship in an isolated place or places outside Japan – the usual conditions in such cases – would be a greater deterrent to men like the accused than the speedy termination of existence on the scaffold or before a firing squad.'[35]

Prosecutions were also undertaken by national military tribunals in the Far East, and many death penalties were imposed. In the *Yamashita case*, which established the principle of command responsibility, it was argued unsuccessfully that the death sentence was 'disproportionate' to a crime that did not include any criminal intent, and that was no more than 'unintentional ordinary negligence'.[36] Yet in the *Abbaye Ardenne case*, where Nazi commander Kurt Meyer was held responsible on the basis of the command responsibility principle, his death sentence was overturned 'on the grounds that Meyer's degree of responsibility did not warrant the extreme penalty'.[37] The commentary of the United Nations War Crimes Commission notes that, in cases of failure to prevent crimes, like those of Yamashita and Meyer, the death penalty was not imposed as a general rule.

6.2 Towards an International Criminal Court and a Code of Crimes

In 1937, the League of Nations adopted a treaty providing for the creation of an international criminal court. It never came into force because of an insufficient number of ratifications. The instrument allowed for punishment of death.[38]

---

impose upon an accused, on conviction, death or such other punishment as shall be determined by it to be just.'
[35] *United States of America et al.* v. *Araki* et al., Judgment, 12 November 1948, in B. V. A. Röling and C. F. Rüter, eds., *The Tokyo Judgment*, Vol. II, Amsterdam: APA-University Press Amsterdam, 1977, p. 478.
[36] *United States of America* v. *Yamashita*, (1948) 4 LRTWC 1, pp. 36–37.
[37] *Canada* v. *Meyer*, (1946) 13 *Ann. Dig.* 332, 4 LRTWC 97 (Canadian Military Court), p. 109.
[38] *Convention for the Creation of an International Criminal Court*, League of Nations O.J. Spec. Supp. No. 156 (1936), LN Doc. C.547(I).M.384(I).1937.V (1938), arts. 39–42. The treaty was signed by thirteen States, but was never ratified. The proposed statute included a series of sentencing provisions that allowed for capital punishment, detention, confiscation and restoration of property, and, eventually, pardon. See: Antoine Sottile, 'Le terrorisme international', [1938] III *Recueil de cours de l'Académie de droit international* 89; H. Donnedieu de Vabres, 'La répression internationale du terrorisme: les Conventions de Genève (16 novembre 1937)', [1938] *Revue de droit international et de législation comparée* 37, which includes the text of the *Convention* as an appendix.

During the Second World War, the United Nations War Crimes Commission prepared a 'Draft Convention for the Establishment of a United Nations War Crimes Court'. It too authorized capital punishment.[39] In an annex to the initial draft of the *Genocide Convention*, the United Nations Secretary-General outlined two alternative statutes for an international tribunal with jurisdiction over genocide and, possibly, other international crimes. The texts were based on the 1937 League of Nations treaty, and included provision for the death penalty.[40] The draft statutes were eventually set aside in the final version of the *Convention*, adopted on 9 December 1948, in favour of a general pronouncement pointing to a yet-to-be-created international criminal court that, in practice, gave primary responsibility for genocide prosecutions to the State where the crime took place.[41] It only required that States parties establish 'effective' penalties for genocide within their domestic legal systems.[42] The following year, the *Geneva Conventions* created another category of international offence, labelled 'grave breaches', requiring States prosecuting such crimes to impose 'effective penal sanctions'.[43] Intentionally or otherwise, silence on the subject of capital punishment in these post-war treaties containing criminal law provisions was creating a window of opportunity for the exclusion of the death penalty as a sanction for war crimes and genocide.

When the *Genocide Convention* was adopted, the United Nations General Assembly invited the International Law Commission 'to study the desirability and possibility of establishing an international judicial organ for the trial of persons charged with genocide or other crimes'.[44] In 1950, the General Assembly created a Committee on International Criminal Jurisdiction, charged with preparing one or more draft conventions and proposals on the establishment of an international criminal court.[45] The Committee's proposal allowed the future tribunal to impose such penalties as it judged appropriate, without making specific reference to the death penalty. The draft provision read: 'The penalty for any offence defined in this Code shall be determined by the tribunal exercising jurisdiction over the individual accused, taking into account the gravity of the

---

[39] 'Draft Convention for the Establishment of a United Nations War Crimes Court', UNWCC Doc. C.50(1), 30 September 1944, NAC RG-25, Vol. 3033, 4060-40C, Part Four, art. 20.

[40] 'Establishment of a Permanent International Criminal Court for the Punishment of Act of Genocide', UN Doc. A/362, Annex, arts. 36–39.

[41] *Convention for the Prevention and Punishment of the Crime of Genocide*, (1951) 78 UNTS 277, art. VI. See: William A. Schabas, *Genocide in International Law*, Cambridge: Cambridge University Press, 2000.

[42] *Ibid.*, art. V.

[43] *Geneva Convention (I) for the Amelioration of the Condition of the Wounded and Sick in Armed Forces in the Field*, (1950) 75 U.N.T.S. 31, art. 49; *Geneva Convention (II) for the Amelioration of the Condition of the Wounded, Sick and Shipwrecked Members of the Armed Forces at Sea*, (1950) 75 U.N.T.S. 85, art. 50; *Geneva Convention (III) Relative to the Treatment of Prisoners of War*, (1950) 75 U.N.T.S. 135, art. 129; *Geneva Convention (IV) Relative to the Protection of Civilians*, (1950) 75 U.N.T.S. 287, art. 146.

[44] GA Res. 260B(III).   [45] GA Res. 489(V).

offence.' According to the report, '[t]he understanding was, that it would not be necessary for a convention defining a crime to specify the penalty for such crime'. Yet the Committee also felt that it might be appropriate for the convention to 'lay down limitations with respect to the penalty', giving the specific example that it might proclaim 'the death penalty should not be imposed'.[46] At a subsequent session of the Committee, in 1953, some delegates argued that 'according to present international law, penalties up to and including the death sentence could be imposed for crimes against humanity'.[47]

The question of fixed sentences in the statute of a future tribunal was also debated in the International Law Commission.[48] In the 'Draft Code of Offences Against the Peace and Security of Mankind', presented to the General Assembly in 1951, the Commission proposed the following text: 'The penalty for any offence defined in this Code shall be determined by the tribunal exercising jurisdiction over the individual accused, taking into account the gravity of the offence.'[49] In comments by governments to the draft *Code*, Yugoslavia insisted that it should be clearly stated that the tribunal be entitled to impose any sentence, including death.[50]

After two postponements in the General Assembly,[51] the international criminal court project was shelved for many years. Drafting of the Code of Offences was also suspended while a special committee of the General Assembly attempted to define the term 'aggression'.[52] Only in the early 1980s did the General Assembly decide to reactivate work by the International Law Commission on the Code of Offences (by then called the 'Code of Crimes').[53] At the end of that decade, the General Assembly also gave the Commission responsibility for drafting a statute for an international criminal court.[54] The issue of sentencing for crimes against humanity and other international crimes was considered in the 1990 session of the International Law Commission. It soon became apparent that there had been a sea change in thinking on the issue of the death penalty. The catalyst for this, quite obviously, was the presence and development of international human rights law and specifically its emerging focus on the abolition of capital punishment. Special *rapporteur* Doudou Thiam proposed three different

[46] 'Report of the Committee on International Criminal Jurisdiction on its Session Held from 1 to 31 August 1951', UN Doc. A/2136 (1952), §§110–111. See draft art. 32: 'The Court shall impose upon an accused, upon conviction, such penalty as the Court may determine, subject to any limitations prescribed in the instrument conferring jurisdiction upon the Court.'

[47] 'Report of the 1953 Committee on International Criminal Jurisdiction 27 July–20 August 1953', UN Doc. A/2136, §110.

[48] *Yearbook . . . 1954*, Vol. I, p. 139, paras. 45–52.

[49] *Yearbook . . . 1951*, Vol. II, pp. 134 *et seq.*, UN Doc. A/1858, para. 59. The Commission had been requested to prepare such a draft code in November 1947 (GA Res. 177 (II)), and in 1949 the Commission appointed Jean Spiropoulos as its special *rapporteur*.

[50] *Yearbook . . . 1954*, Vol. II, p. 121.   [51] G.A. Res. 898 (IX); GA Res. 1187 (XII).

[52] See: GA Res. 3314 (XXIX) (1974).   [53] G.A. Res. 36/106 (1981).   [54] G.A. Res. 44/89.

sentencing provisions to the International Law Commission, one which did not prohibit the death penalty, the other two expressly excluding the death penalty. Thiam said it seemed appropriate to provide for penalties 'on which there is the broadest agreement and whose underlying principle is generally accepted by the international community'.[55] The Report adopted by the Commission at the conclusion of its 1990 session said tersely: 'In the discussion of penalties, it was stated that a penalty should be proportionate to the gravity of the crime committed. The possibility of excluding the death penalty was also suggested.'[56]

The issue returned to the agenda of the International Law Commission in 1991, with special *rapporteur* Thiam then proposing that the *Code of Crimes Against the Peace and Security of Mankind* expressly exclude capital punishment.[57] Thiam explained that the establishment of a scale of penalties 'called for a uniform moral and philosophical approach that existed in domestic, but not in international, law', adding that '[p]enalties varied from country to country, according to the offences to be punished. In addition, there were penalties such as the death penalty and other afflictive punishments (for instance, physical mutilation) about which there was much controversy and which were not universally applied.' Thiam explained that he had endeavoured 'to avoid extremes and to find a middle way that might be acceptable to all States'.[58] Only a few members of the Commission disagreed with the special *rapporteur* on this point.[59] A handful of others were uncomfortable with addressing the matter at all, given what they deemed inconsistent State practice on the subject.[60] Several members saw the issue as an opportunity to promote the international trend towards abolition of the death penalty.[61] Many even expressed their reservations

---

[55] 'Eighth Report on the Draft Code of Crimes Against the Peace and Security of Mankind, by Mr. Doudou Thiam, Special Rapporteur', UN Doc. A/CN.4/430 and Add.1, §§101–105.

[56] 'Report of the International Law Commission on the Work of its Forty-Second Session', UN Doc. A/CN.4/SER.A/1990/Add.1 (Part 2), A/45/10 (1990), §149.

[57] UN Doc. A/CN.4/435 and Add.1, §29: 'Any defendant found guilty of any of the crimes defined in this Code shall be sentenced to life imprisonment. If there are extenuating circumstances, the defendant shall be sentenced to imprisonment for a term of ten to twenty years. [In addition, the defendant may, as appropriate, be sentenced to total or partial confiscation of stolen or misappropriated property. The Tribunal shall decide whether to entrust such property to a humanitarian organization.]' For the discussion of this proposal by the International Law Commission, see UN Doc. A/CN.4/SR.2207–2214; UN Doc. A/CN.4/Ser.A/1991/Add.1 (Part 2), UN Doc. A/46/10, §§70–105.

[58] UN Doc. A/CN.4/SR.2207, §6.

[59] Al-Khasawneh: UN Doc. A/CN.4/SR.2211, §15; UN Doc. A/CN.4/SR.2213, §55; Francis: UN Doc. A/CN.4/SR.2212, §28; Al-Baharna: UN Doc. A/CN.4/SR.2207, §24; Roucounos: UN Doc. A/CN.4/SR.2211, §28.

[60] Barsegov: UN Doc. A/CN.4/SR.2212, §51; Beesley: UN Doc. A/CN.4/SR.2210, §10.

[61] Tomuschat: UN Doc. A/CN.4/SR.2208, §15; Jiuyong Shi: UN Doc. A/CN.4/SR.2208, §2; Arangio-Ruiz: UN Doc. A/CN.4/SR.2210, §33; Illueca: UN Doc. A/CN.4/SR.2213, §12; Ogiso: UN Doc. A/CN.4/SR.2210, §25; Njenga: UN Doc. A/CN.4/SR.2210, §46; Razafindralambo: UN Doc. A/CN.4/SR.2211, §41; McCaffrey: UN Doc. A/CN.4/SR.2211, §50; Eiriksson: UN Doc. A/CN.4/SR.2213, §23; Pellet: UN Doc. A/CN.4/SR.2209, §5; Mahiou: UN Doc. A/CN.4/SR.2209, §29; Hayes: UN Doc. A/CN.4/SR.2207, §30; Graefrath: UN Doc. A/CN.4/SR.2208, §10.

about sentences of life imprisonment, which they said were also a form of cruel, inhuman and degrading punishment.[62] For example, Bernhard Graefrath of the German Democratic Republic not only opposed the death penalty, he considered that even life imprisonment 'was inhuman and contrary to human rights'.[63] The Commission's 1991 report contains the following description of the debate on capital punishment:

> 84. Many members of the Commission supported the Special Rapporteur's position that the death penalty should not be included among the penalties applicable to crimes against the peace and security of mankind. In that connection, it was indicated that the Commission should not seek to resist the world-wide trend towards the abolition of the death penalty, even for the most serious crimes, such as genocide. The move away from the death penalty had been evident in legal thinking since the Nürnberg and Tokyo trials. In the opinion of those members, the abolition of the death penalty was a step forward in moral terms that had to be consolidated. The death penalty was unnecessary and pointless and no one had the right to take another's life. In addition, that penalty had been eliminated long ago in many national legislations and the States which had abolished it would be reluctant to accede to an instrument which re-established it. In many of those countries, the abolition of the death penalty had become a constitutional principle and some international instruments, both universal and regional in scope, also provided for its abolition or for a prohibition on its reintroduction. The following instruments were cited: the Second Optional Protocol to the International Covenant on Civil and Political Right, aiming at the abolition of the death penalty (General Assembly resolution 44/128, annex), Additional Protocol No. 6 to the European Convention for the Protection of Human Rights and Fundamental Freedoms and the Protocol to the American Convention on Human Rights relating to the abolition of the death penalty.
>
> Some other members expressed reservations on that position, believing that it would be premature for the Commission, which was called upon to legislate for States which did not have the same ideas on the death penalty, to adopt a clear-cut opinion on the question instead of allowing the States concerned to exercise discretion. Many States still retained the death penalty in their internal law for particularly heinous crimes. Failure to include the death penalty in the draft Code was bound to give rise to discussion among those States and would risk rendering the Code less acceptable to them. Some members expressed the view that even certain regional instruments providing, in principle, for the abolition of the death penalty allowed for exceptions in certain circumstances. For example, Optional Protocol No. 6 to the European Convention referred to earlier, which provided for the abolition and non-restoration of the death penalty in peacetime, also contained a proviso for the case of war and for

---

[62] Calero Rodriguez; UN Doc. A/CN.4/SR.2208, §21; Barboza: UN Doc. A/CN.4/SR.2209, §20; Njenga: UN Doc. A/CN.4/SR.2210, §47; Solari Tudela: UN Doc. A/CN.4/SR.2212, §4; Pellet: UN Doc. A/CN.4/SR.2209, §9. See also the 'Report of the International Law Commission on the Work of its Forty-Third Session', UN Doc. A/CN.4/Ser.A/1991/Add.1 (Part 2), A/46/10, §88; Dirk van Zyl Smit, 'Life Imprisonment as an Ultimate Penalty in International Law: A Human Rights Perspective', (1998) 10 *Criminal Law Forum* 1.

[63] UN Doc. A/CN.4/SR.2208, §10.

the case of 'imminent threat of war', which in the view of some writers, the authorities of the State concerned would be free to determine. Moreover, the Second Optional Protocol to the International Covenant on Civil and Political Rights, adopted by the General Assembly, was, as its name indicated, optional and in no way mandatory. The draft Code dealt only with the most serious of crimes and should not be turned into an instrument for settling the question of capital punishment. In the view of those members, leaving the question to the discretion of States would in no way undermine the principle *nulla poena sine lege*. All that was needed was to include in the Code a general provision to the effect that such crimes should be punished in proportion to their gravity. One member in particular suggested that, in order to accommodate the sensibilities of States which had abolished the death penalty, the article of the Code providing for that penalty could be accompanied by a reservation entitling any State instituting proceedings to request the Court not to impose the death penalty in the event of a conviction.[64]

In 1993, the International Law Commission adopted a provisional draft statute of an international criminal court. Article 53 stated that a person convicted would be subject to imprisonment, up to and including life imprisonment, and a fine of any amount. In order to avoid any ambiguity, the Commentary prepared by the special rapporteur said: 'The Court would not be authorized to impose the death penalty.'[65] It added, somewhat equivocally: 'Various views were expressed on the Special Rapporteur's proposal that the death penalty should be ruled out.'[66] The Commentary reiterated: 'The Court is not authorized to impose the death penalty.'[67] Only two States offered comments on the sentencing provisions of the 1993 draft. Hungary reiterated its opposition to capital punishment being included in the draft statute;[68] the United States addressed the issue of sentencing, but said nothing about capital punishment.[69] The provision was somewhat reworked in the Commission's final 1994 draft, which was presented to the General Assembly, although the substance was not changed significantly. Penalties consisted of life imprisonment, imprisonment for a specified number of years, and a fine.[70]

The International Law Commission returned to the issue at its 1995 session, in the context of its still-unfinished work on the draft Code of Crimes.[71] The report said this on the death penalty:

> It was suggested that it would be sufficient to prescribe an upper limit for all the crimes, leaving it to the courts to determine the penalty in each particular case, following article 47 of the draft Statute which precluded the death penalty . . . However, questions

---

[64] UN Doc. A/CN.4/SER.A/Add.1 (Part 2), A/46/10, §§84–85.
[65] 'Report of the International Law Commission on the Work of its Forty-Fifth Session, 3 May–23 July 1993', UN Doc. A/48/10, at p. 318.
[66] *Ibid.*, p. 39, §85.   [67] *Ibid.*, pp. 123–125.   [68] UN Doc. A/CN.4/458/Add.7, p. 43, §28.
[69] *Ibid.*, p. 29.   [70] UN Doc. A/49/355, art. 47.
[71] 'Report of the International Law Commission on the Work of its Forty-Seventh Session', UN Doc. A/50/10, p. 183.

were raised regarding the legal basis for the absence of the death penalty from more recent instruments, whether that absence denoted significant progress in the human rights field, and the fate of the Second Optional Protocol to the International Covenant on Civil and Political Rights, aiming at the abolition of the death penalty. In this regard, attention was drawn to the discrepancy regarding the inclusion of the death penalty between the statutes of the ad hoc tribunals and the national legislation applicable in the former Yugoslavia and of Rwanda.[72]

The Code of Crimes Against the Peace and Security of Mankind was finally adopted in 1996, almost fifty years after the International Law Commission was given its first mandate on this matter. Ultimately, the final draft Code stated only that an individual responsible for a crime against the peace and security of mankind 'shall be liable to punishment', and that such punishment 'shall be commensurate with the character and gravity of the crime'. The Commission declined to specify precise penalties, noting in its commentary that 'everything depends on the legal system adopted to try the persons who commit crimes against the peace and security of humanity'.[73]

6.3 *Ad hoc* tribunals for Rwanda and Yugoslavia

While the debate on sentencing for international crimes by a permanent international criminal court was underway in the General Assembly and the International Law Commission, the Security Council addressed the issue of penalties when it set up the *ad hoc* tribunals for the former Yugoslavia and Rwanda. The statutes of the two tribunals contain brief provisions on sentencing, proposing essentially that sentences be limited to imprisonment (thereby tacitly excluding the death penalty, as well as corporal punishment, imprisonment with hard labour, and fines), and that they be established taking into account the 'general practice' of the criminal courts in the former Yugoslavia or Rwanda, as the case may be.[74] The Secretary-General's report to the Security Council proposing the draft statute for the Yugoslav tribunal states: 'The international tribunal should not be empowered to impose the death penalty.'[75]

The directive in the *Statutes* that judges of the tribunal have 'recourse to the general practice regarding prison sentences' in the former Yugoslavia or Rwanda, as the case may be, is a response to concerns about retroactive sentences. It was argued that the rule *nulla poena sine lege* required the international tribunals to

---

[72] *Yearbook . . . 1995*, Vol. I, p. 64, §124. See also the comments of Barboza, at p. 16, §19.

[73] 'Report of the International Law Commission on the Work of its Forty-Eighth Session, 6 May–26 July 1996', UN Doc. A/51/10, art. 3.

[74] *Statute of the International Criminal Tribunal for the Former Yugoslavia*, UN Doc. S/RES/827, annex (1993), art. 25; *Statute of the International Criminal Tribunal for Rwanda*, UN Doc. S/RES/955, annex (1994), art. 24.

[75] 'Report of the Secretary-General Pursuant to Paragraph 2 of Security Council Resolution 808 (1993)', UN Doc. S/25704 and Corr.1, §112.

harmonize their sentences with those in force in the territories where the crimes were committed.[76] The problem was first raised in a February 1993 proposal by the Conference on Security and Co-operation in Europe (now the Organization for Security and Co-operation in Europe) drafted by Hans Corell, Helmut Türk and Gro Hillestad Thune:

> According to the criminal law of the former Socialist Federal Republic of Yugoslavia the following punishments may be imposed: capital punishment, imprisonment and fines.
>
> Already in their report on Croatia the Rapporteurs concluded that it was in their opinion inconceivable that the CSCE should endorse the death penalty (cf. Section 7.1 of that report). The draft Convention therefore includes a provision to the effect that the Court shall not pass a sentence of capital punishment, although this punishment appears in provisions of the national law (Article 29, paragraph 2).
>
> Since capital punishment will be excluded, it is necessary to examine in more detail how imprisonment is imposed according to the pertinent national law. It appears that the general rule on imprisonment (Article 38 of the Penal Code) lays down that imprisonment may not be shorter than fifteen days, nor exceed fifteen years. However, for crimes for which capital punishment is prescribed, the Court may also impose the punishment of imprisonment for twenty years. The question is, therefore, if it is possible to lay down in the Convention the possibility of imposing imprisonment for life. A first look at the national law may indicate that this is not possible. On the other hand, it could be argued that, if capital punishment cannot be imposed, there would be a possibility of imposing imprisonment for more than twenty years, n.b. lifetime, according to the principle *maius includit minus*.[77]

The report insisted that it would be difficult to establish any concordance between sentences in effect in Yugoslavia at the time of the outbreak of the conflict and the provision of the statute because, in the former, the death penalty availed, whereas, in the latter, it did not. Significantly, although Yugoslavia still allowed for the death penalty, it considered life imprisonment to be cruel, inhuman and degrading treatment or punishment, and thus limited its maximum custodial sentence to fifteen or twenty years. Paragraph 2 of article 29 of the Corell–Türk–Thune draft declared: 'The Court shall not pass sentence of capital punishment.'[78]

A subsequent Italian proposal expressed the same sentiment.[79] The commentary on the Italian proposal for the tribunal stated: 'The death penalty has

---

[76] William A. Schabas, 'Perverse Effects of the Nulla Poena Principle: National Practice and the Ad Hoc Tribunals', (2000) 11 *European Journal of International Law* 521.

[77] Hans Corell, Helmut Türk & Gro Hillestad Thune, 'Proposal for an International War Crimes Tribunal for the Former Yugoslavia', in Virginia Morris & Michael Scharf, eds., *An Insider's Guide to The International Criminal Tribunal for the Former Yugoslavia*, Irvington-on-Hudson, NY: Transnational, 1995, pp. 211–310, at p. 264.

[78] *Ibid.*, p. 287.

[79] 'Letter from the Permanent Representative of Italy to the United Nations Addressed to the Secretary-General', UN Doc. S/25300, art. 7§§1–2.

been excluded, in line with a principle that is by now part of the European legal heritage, as shown by Additional Protocol No. 6 to the European Convention on Human Rights.' The Russian Federation's proposal, quite similar to that of Italy, also explicitly excluded capital punishment.[80] In a *note verbale*, Canada 'strongly oppose[d] the imposition of the death penalty, notwithstanding that the offence committed may be of a particularly heinous nature'.[81] The Committee of French Jurists was also against the death penalty.[82] The Netherlands stated that it 'agree[d] with the other proposals already submitted to the secretary-general that [capital punishment] should be ruled out'.[83] Two contributors to the debate who might have been expected to support the death penalty, the Organization of the Islamic Conference and the United States, avoided any direct confrontation. The Islamic Conference proposal left room for the death penalty, but made no explicit reference to it: 'Penalties shall be based on "general principles" of law as they exist in the world's major legal systems.'[84] The United States' proposal was similarly ambiguous on the issue of capital punishment: 'The Trial Court shall have the power to sentence convicted persons to imprisonment or other appropriate punishment.'[85]

There was no preparatory work of a comparable nature in the drafting of the *Statute of the International Criminal Tribunal for Rwanda*. The issue of capital punishment arose during debate in the Security Council when the draft statute was being adopted. In the Security Council, Rwanda claimed there would be a fundamental injustice in exposing criminals tried by its domestic courts with execution if those prosecuted by the international tribunal – presumably the masterminds of the genocide – would only be subject to life imprisonment. 'Since it is foreseeable that the Tribunal will be dealing with suspects who devised, planned and organized the genocide, these may escape capital punishment whereas those who simply carried out their plans would be subjected to the harshness of this sentence', said Rwanda's representative. 'That situation is not conducive to national reconciliation in Rwanda.' But to counter this argument, the representative of New Zealand reminded Rwanda that '[f]or over three decades the United Nations has been trying progressively to eliminate the death penalty. It would be

---

[80] 'Letter from the Permanent Representative of the Russian Federation to the United Nations Addressed to the Secretary-General (April 5, 1993)', UN Doc. S/25537, art. 22§3.
[81] 'Letter dated 13 April 1993 from the Permanent Representative of Canada to the United Nations Addressed to the Secretary-General', UN Doc. A/25594.
[82] 'Letter dated 10 February 1993 from the Permanent Representative of France to the United Nations Addressed to the Secretary-General', UN Doc. S/25266, §127(b).
[83] 'Letter dated 30 April 1993 from the Permanent Representative of The Netherlands to the United Nations Addressed to the Secretary-General', UN Doc. A/25716.
[84] 'Letter from the Representatives of Egypt, the Islamic Republic of Iran, Malaysia, Pakistan, Saudi Arabia, Senegal and Turkey to the United Nations Addressed to the Secretary-General (March 31, 1993)', UN Doc. A/47/920, UN Doc. S/25512.
[85] 'Letter from the Permanent Representative of the United States of America to the United Nations Addressed to the Secretary-General (April 5, 1993)', UN Doc. A/25575.

entirely unacceptable – and a dreadful step backwards – to introduce it here.'[86]
Prior to the 1994 genocide, Rwanda had become a *de facto* abolitionist State. The
death penalty has not been imposed since the early 1980s, and in 1992 President
Habyarimana systematically commuted all outstanding death sentences.[87] The
programme of the Rwandese Patriotic Front, which won military victory in
July 1994, called for the abolition of capital punishment. Furthermore, in the
1993 Arusha peace accords, which have constitutional force in Rwanda, the
government undertook to ratify the *Second Optional Protocol.*[88]

In August 1996, Rwanda's National Assembly enacted legislation aimed
at facilitating prosecutions of the more than 80,000 then detained for participation in genocide.[89] The new statute classified offenders and, in an extremely
generous gesture, excluded the death penalty for all but the instigators, planners
and organizers of the genocide. Thus, the many tens of thousands of 'followers'
who, pursuant to ordinary Rwandan criminal law, would be subject to the death
penalty, were spared the threat of capital punishment. The legislation has been
referred to by the International Criminal Tribunal for Rwanda in its discussion of appropriate sentences for those convicted of genocide.[90] Defendants
have argued that the relatively clement provisions should guide the Tribunal's
sentencing practice; in response, the judges have pointed to the possibility of
capital punishment for the instigators, planners and organizers. Although the
new Rwandan law is silent on the subject, presumably the death penalty now
ceases to apply for all other common law offenders who are not covered by the
special genocide legislation. It seems inconceivable that in the future Rwandan
courts will impose the death penalty for 'ordinary' murders, when they are now
forbidden to do so in the case of genocidal murders. On 24 April 1998, Rwanda
held public executions of twenty-two persons convicted of genocide, defying
appeals from the United Nations High Commission for Human Rights who indicated that due process standards might not have been respected and, moreover,
that 'the public nature of the proposed executions' will have a brutalizing effect

---

[86] UN Doc. S/PV.3453, p. 16. See: 'Report on the Mission to Rwanda on the Question of Violence
Against Women in Situations of Armed Conflict', UN Doc. E/CN.4/1998/54/Add.1, para. 40.

[87] *Arrêté présidentiel No. 103/105, Mesure de grâce, J.O.* 1992, p. 446, art. 1.

[88] 'Protocole d'Accord entre le Gouvernement de la République Rwandaise et le Front Patriotique
Rwandais portant sur les questions diverses et dispositions finales signé à Arusha', 3 August 1993, *Journal
officiel,* Year 32, No. 16, 15 August 1993, p. 1430, art. 15.

[89] 'Organic Law No. 8/96 of 30 August 1996', *Journal officiel,* Year 35, No. 17, 1 September 1996.

[90] *Prosecutor* v. *Kambanda* (Case No. ICTR 97-23-S), Judgment and Sentence, 4 September 1998,
paras. 18–22; *Prosecutor* v. *Serushago* (Case No. ICTR-98-39-S), Sentence, 5 February 1999, para. 17;
Prosecutor v. *Kayishema and Ruzindana* (Case no. ICTR-95-1-T), Sentence, 21 May 1999, para. 6;
Prosecutor v. *Rutaganda* (Case No. ICTR-96-3-T), Judgment and Sentence, 6 December 1999, para.
453; *Prosecutor* v. *Musema* (Case No. ICTR-96-13-T), Judgment and Sentence, 27 January 2000,
paras. 983–984; *Prosecutor* v. *Serushago* (Case No. ICTR-98-39-A), Reasons for Judgment, 6 April 2000;
Prosecutor v. *Ruggio* (Case No. ICTR-97-32-I), Judgment and Sentence, 1 June 2000, paras. 28–31.

on a population already traumatized by the genocide of 1994'.[91] Although many death sentences have been pronounced since then, none has been carried out.[92]

6.4 Drafting of the *Rome Statute*

The *Rome Statute of the International Criminal Court* was adopted on 17 July 1998, at the conclusion of a five-week-long diplomatic conference.[93] As of 31 December 2000, the cut-off date for deposit of signatures of the instrument, some 139 States had signed the instrument and nearly thirty had ratified. The *Statute* came into force on 1 July 2002, following deposit of the sixtieth ratification. Adoption of the *Statute* followed four years of negotiations within bodies established by the United Nations General Assembly, namely the *Ad Hoc* Committee, which met in 1995, the Preparatory Committee, which met several times from 1996 to 1998, and the Rome Conference itself. Although capital punishment seemed a marginal issue prior to 1998, it took on dramatic proportions in the final weeks of the Rome Conference and even threatened to undo consensus on the entire project.

The subject of penalties was first addressed during the August 1996 session of the Preparatory Committee. Some States with a predominantly Moslem population argued that if the statute were to be considered representative of all legal systems, it should include the death penalty, but these views were relatively isolated.[94] Citing the Islamic legal code of the *sharia*, the representative of Egypt said that the death penalty should be included as an option, perhaps applicable in cases where aggravating circumstances are present.[95] Malaysia also favoured the death penalty, which it said was provided for under many national legal

---

[91] The High Commissioner also called upon Rwanda to impose a moratorium on executions: UN Doc. E/CN.4/1998/61, para. 81.

[92] 'Report on the Situation of Human Rights in Rwanda Submitted by the Special Representative, M Michel Moussalli, Pursuant to Resolution 1998/9', UN Doc. E/CN.4/1999/33, para. 47.

[93] *Rome Statute of the International Criminal Court*, UN Doc. A/CONF.183/9. On the *Rome Statute* generally, see: William A. Schabas, *Introduction to the International Criminal Court*, Cambridge: Cambridge University Press, 2001. On its penalties provisions, see: Rolf Einer Fife, 'Article 80', in Otto Triffterer, ed., *Commentary on the Rome Statute of the International Criminal Court, Observers' Notes, Article by Article*, Baden-Baden: Nomos, 1999, pp. 1089–1014; Rolf Einer Fife, 'Penalties', in Roy Lee, ed., *The International Criminal Court, The Making of the Rome Statute*, Dordrecht/London/Boston: Kluwer Law, 1999, pp. 319–344; Faiza P. King & Anne-Marie La Rosa, 'Penalties under the ICC Statute', in Flavia Lattanzi & William A. Schabas, eds., *Essays on the Rome Statute of the ICC*, Rome: Editrice il Sirente, 2000, pp. 311–338; Daniel B. Pickard, 'Proposed Sentencing Guidelines for the International Criminal Court', (1997) 20 *Loyola of Los Angeles International and Comparative Law Journal* 123; William A. Schabas, 'Life, Death and the Crime of Crimes: Supreme Penalties and the ICC Statute', (2000) 2 *Punishment & Society* 263; William A. Schabas, 'Penalties', in Flavia Lattanzi, ed., *The International Criminal Court, Comments on the Draft Statute*, Naples: Editoriale Scientifica, 1998, pp. 273–299; William A. Schabas, 'Penalties', in Antonio Cassese, ed., *International Criminal Court, A Commentary on the Rome Statute for an International Criminal Court*, Oxford: Oxford University Press, 2002 (forthcoming).

[94] UN Doc. L/2805 (1996); also UN Doc. L/2813 (1996).   [95] UN Doc. L/2805.

jurisdictions.[96] Representatives of Italy, Portugal, Mexico, New Zealand and Denmark spoke against inclusion of the death penalty in the court statute.[97] The press release issued at the conclusion of the Preparatory Committee, on 30 August 1996, stated: 'Many insisted that the court should not provide for the death penalty, while others noted that if the statute was to be considered representative of all the legal systems of the world, it should allow capital punishment.'[98] The report of the Preparatory Committee to the 1996 General Assembly stated:

> Some delegations expressed their strong support for the exclusion of the death penalty from the penalties that the Court would be authorized to impose in accordance with article 47 of the draft statute. While the death penalty was ruled out by those delegations, others suggested that the death penalty should not be excluded a priori since it was provided for in many legal systems, especially in connection with serious crimes.[99]

When the Report was considered by the Sixth Committee of the General Assembly, in October and November 1996, Malaysia argued for the availability of the death penalty, to be imposed at the discretion of the court, noting that it was provided for in many national criminal justice systems. 'Exclusion of that option in the draft statute could give rise to serious difficulties', it said.[100] Romania[101] and Costa Rica[102] spoke in opposition to the death penalty. Although the vast majority of delegations appeared to consider the question of the exclusion of the death penalty to be settled, there was a lingering proposal to provide for the 'death penalty, as an option, in case of aggravating circumstances and when the Trial Chamber finds it necessary in light of the gravity of the crime, the number of victims and the severity of the damage'.[103]

In December 1997, the Preparatory Committee established a distinct Working Group on Penalties, chaired by Norwegian diplomat Rolf Einar Fife.[104] He deemed that no agreement could be reached on the issue of the death penalty and refused all consideration whatsoever of the question. There would be no point discussing it 'at the technical level', he said. The conference room paper that was adopted left several options in square brackets: life imprisonment; imprisonment for a specified number of years; imprisonment for a maximum term (thirty years was suggested); a definitive term of imprisonment (twenty to forty years was suggested), subject to a reduction in accordance with other provisions

---

[96] UN Doc. L/2806.   [97] *Ibid.*   [98] UN Doc. L/2813.

[99] 'Report of the Preparatory Committee on the Establishment of an International Criminal Court, Vol. I', UN Doc. A/51/22, §306.

[100] UN Doc. GA/L/3009.   [101] UN Doc. GA/L/3010.   [102] UN Doc. GA/L/3011.

[103] 'Proposals Relating to Article 47 of the Statute of an International Criminal Court', UN Doc. A/AC.249/CRP.13/Add.1. Also: 'Report of the Preparatory Committee on the Establishment of an International Criminal Court, Vol. II', UN Doc. A/51/22.

[104] 'Decisions Taken by the Preparatory Committee at its Session held from 1 to 12 Dec. 1997, Annex V, Report of the Working Group on Penalties', UN Doc. A/AC.249/1997/L.9/Rev.1, p. 18. For Fife's personal account of the negotiations, see: Fife, 'Penalties'.

of the statute.[105] An additional clause, also in square brackets, stated that the court could specify a minimum period to be served during which the convicted person would not be subject to provisional release or parole.[106]

At the Rome Diplomatic Conference, held from 15 June to 17 July 1998, a Working Group on Penalties was constituted, also chaired by Fife.[107] The Working Group met for the first time on 30 June 1998, expecting to wrap up its work in a few scheduled sessions over the next couple of days. However, while some concerns were disposed of quickly, it soon became apparent that it would be impossible to finalize the general provisions until debate on the death penalty had been completed. Because of the obstinacy of some States who were determined to make this an issue, the Working Group did not complete its report until the final days of the Diplomatic Conference.

During initial statements in the Working Group, many States expressed their opposition to a statute that provided for the death penalty.[108] Most of those who explained their position for this invoked human rights norms. Ukraine said it was obliged to take this view as a member of the Council of Europe. Some gave no reasons for this position. A few pointed to problems with the relationship between domestic criminal justice and the international scheme. Others said they had no firm position on the subject of capital punishment[109] or implied this by saying nothing on the subject and stating that they preferred imprisonment.[110] As for the chair, he made no secret of his personal preference by submitting a text 'proposed for consideration, in order to contribute to clarify as to a possible structure' that excluded the death penalty.[111]

Two geo-cultural blocs of States aggressively advocated the death penalty, those of the Arab and Islamic group, and those of the English-speaking Caribbean States. For the former, support was justified principally on religious and cultural considerations.[112] In the latter, domestic public opinion, enflamed by recent rulings prohibiting executions from the Judicial Committee of the Privy Council, the Inter-American Commission of Human Rights and the Human Rights Committee, was invoked. The death penalty proponents implied that they were not prepared to agree upon other issues related to penalties until they

---

[105] UN Doc. A/AC.249/1997/WG.6/CRP.2/Rev.1 (10 December 1997).

[106] The International Criminal Tribunal for the former Yugoslavia made such a recommendation in the *Tadic* case: *Prosecutor* v. *Tadic* (Case no. IT-94-1-S), Sentencing Judgment, 14 July 1997, (1999) 112 ILR 286, §76.

[107] There are no summary records of the Working Group on Penalties. Observations based on the debates in the Working Group are from the personal notes of the author, who attended the sessions.

[108] Argentina, Dominican Republic, France, Hungary, Israel, Mexico, Samoa, Spain, Uruguay; Andorra, Chile, Finland, Greece, Holy See, Philippines, Russian Federation, Sweden, Switzerland, Ukraine, Venezuela.

[109] Sierra Leone, Turkey.   [110] Congo (Democratic Republic), Cuba, Japan, Kenya, Senegal.

[111] 'Chairman's Working Paper on Article 75', UN Doc. A/CONF.183/C.1/WGP/L.3 (30 June 1998).

[112] Egypt.

had obtained some satisfaction with respect to capital punishment. Informally, they admitted that they never expected the death penalty to be included in the statute. Trinidad said it would prefer to include the death penalty, a matter which was 'of serious concern to us'. But, in a signal of conciliation, it added that 'we are conscious of the fact that no consensus can be reached, and would like to ensure that the concerns of death penalty states are adequately expressed, through declarations or understandings'. Some of the States that would later go to battle in the camp of the death penalty States were initially rather subdued, but became more insistent as the Conference plodded on and the tension mounted. Singapore, in its first speech in the Working Group, where it expressed its general views on the subject of penalties, did not even raise the issue. Later, it would become much more difficult, eventually insisting on having the last word of the entire Conference on the subject.

On 3 July 1998, a group of Arab and Islamic States presented what they described as an 'honest, genuine effort to bridge the gap'. It read:

> The Court may impose on a person convicted under this Statute one or more of the penalties provided for by the law of the State where the crime was committed.
> In cases where national law does not regulate a specific crime, the Court may apply one or more of the following penalties . . .[113]

The same day, the Caribbean States circulated a text that openly recognized the death penalty:

> The Court may impose upon a person convicted under this Statute one or more of the penalties:
> (a) The death penalty;
> (b) A term of life imprisonment;
> (c) A term of imprisonment not exceeding thirty (30) years.
> The Court may attach to any sentence of imprisonment a minimum period during which the convicted person may not be granted any [release under relevant provisions of the Statute].[114]

In parallel with the Caribbean proposal, and in keeping with its earlier promise of a compromise, Trinidad and Tobago circulated informally a document entitled: 'Sample Understanding/Declaration by Trinidad and Tobago in lieu of Article 75(e)':

> UNDERSTANDING. Trinidad and Tobago understands that International Law does not prohibit the death penalty, and that this Statute does not restrict the right of

---

[113] 'Proposal Submitted by Algeria, Bahrain, Comoros, Egypt, the Islamic Republic of Iran, Iraq, Kuwait, the Libyan Arab Jamahiriya, Nigeria, Oman, Qatar, Saudi Arabia, the Sudan, the Syrian Arab Republic, the United Arab Emirates and Yemen', UN Doc. A/CONF.183/C.1/WGP/L.11 & Corr.2 (3 July 1998).
[114] 'Proposal Submitted by Barbados, Dominica, Jamaica, Singapore and Trinidad and Tobago', UN Doc. A/CONF.183/C.1/WGP/L.13 (3 July 1998).

Trinidad and Tobago to apply the death penalty to persons duly convicted and sentenced to that penalty under the existing laws of Trinidad and Tobago. It also follows that under the principle of complementarity, recognized by the Statute of the International Criminal Court, Trinidad and Tobago retains the sovereign right to impose the death penalty on persons duly tried and convicted in Trinidad and Tobago, of international crimes potentially falling within the complementary jurisdiction of the International Criminal Court.

DECLARATION. Trinidad and Tobago declares that nothing in the Statute of the International Criminal Court and the Final Act of the Diplomatic Conference of Plenipotentiaries on the Establishment of an International Criminal Court affects the right of Trinidad and Tobago or of other States to impose the death penalty under their domestic law.

The subject was aired at an informal session of the Working Group on the afternoon of 3 July 1998. The Chair of the Working Group explained that under the principle of complementarity with domestic jurisdictions, the penalties regime chosen for the international court would have no impact on the scheme in force within national courts. Complementarity recognizes that priority of prosecution belongs with domestic justice systems. Under the principle of complementarity, prosecutions can only be undertaken when States with jurisdiction over the crime are either unwilling or unable to proceed. Fife told the Working Group that including the death penalty in the statute, either directly, as in the Caribbean States' proposal, or implicitly, as in the Arab and Islamic States' proposal, would make it impossible for a huge number of States to accede to the treaty. Many States spoke in support of the chair, some of them predictable, such as Chile, Costa Rica, Greece, France, Namibia and New Zealand, others perhaps not so, such as Kenya. Slovenia and Colombia pointed to constitutional problems if capital punishment were to be included.

The United States, many of whose national jurisdictions are keen supporters of capital punishment, took the floor at the formal, public session of the Working Group on the evening of 3 July 1998. It was a sincere effort to assist the chair in his search for a workable solution. Ambassador David Scheffer focused on the concept of complementarity, noting that 'we know the death penalty very well in the United States, where it is imposed in many jurisdictions including by the federal system, and where it is supported by the executive'. He said he was confident that federal prosecutors would seek the death penalty in appropriate cases where genocide, crimes against humanity and war crimes were charged, citing relevant United States legislation. Scheffer said that the international criminal court should encourage national judicial systems to prosecute and punish the crimes within its jurisdiction, 'and this will include the death penalty'. But, said Scheffer, a second principle was the need to create a uniform penalty regime for the court, failing which the operation of the court would be diverse and unpredictable. 'The United States believes that the language proposed by the chair achieves the goal of just and severe punishment on an international level', he concluded.

Three days later, on 6 July 1998, the chair of the Working Group issued a 'position paper' containing a detailed assessment of the death penalty debate:

> 2. The Coordinator would like to stress the following:
>
> Extensive consultations, as well as statements in the Plenary of the Conference and in the Working Group on Penalties, have shown that a number of delegations strongly favor an inclusion of the death penalty as one of the penalties to be applied by the Court. On the other hand, the consultations as well as statements in the Plenary and in the Working Group have also shown that a number of other delegations are strongly opposed to such an inclusion. In this context, a number of delegations have stressed that cooperation between States and the Court would effectively be hindered should the Statute provide either directly or indirectly for an inclusion of the death penalty.
>
> On the basis of these consultations it is the opinion of the Coordinator that there are no grounds for establishing a consensus on this issue. At the same time, a very substantial number of interventions of delegations in the course of the work of the Working Group have indicated a strong desire to achieve a balanced compromise on the main penalties to be included in the Statute. All delegations have indicated a willingness to find solutions which may be conducive to the shared goal of an early establishment of an International Criminal Court with a broad basis of support from the international community.
>
> It should be noted that not including the death penalty in the Statute would have no bearing on national legislations and practices in this field. States have the primary responsibility for prosecuting and punishing individuals for crimes falling under the subject-matter jurisdiction of the Court. In accordance with the principle of complementarity between the Court and national jurisdictions, the Court would clearly have no say on national practices in this field.[115]

The Working Group reconvened on 16 July 1998, just one day before the end of the Diplomatic Conference, with the death penalty issue still on the table. Fife referred to 'intense consultations' on the subject, citing an informal consultation held on 11 July 1998 where he was mandated to prepare a compromise position. It had three constituent elements. The first was deletion of any reference to the death penalty in the statute, accompanied by a footnote in the report of the Working Group that said '[s]ome delegations do not agree with the decision to exclude the death penalty but they have decided to permit the Conference to proceed on the basis of the Chairman's proposal while reserving the right to put their views on record at appropriate stages of the Conference'.[116]

---

[115] 'Chairman's Working Paper on Article 75, Paragraph 1', UN Doc. A/CONF.183/C.1/WGP/L.3/Rev.1 (6 July 1998), pp. 2–3.
[116] 'Report of the Working Group on Penalties', UN Doc. A/CONF.183/C.1/WGP/L.14/Add.3/Rev.1 (17 July 1998), p. 2.

The second was the addition of a provision which would later be numbered article 80 of the *Rome Statute*:

Non-prejudice to national application of penalties and national laws
Nothing in this Part of the Statute affects the application by States of penalties prescribed by their national law, nor the law of States which do not provide for penalties prescribed in this Part.

The third element was a statement which the Working Group was to recommend be read by the President of the Conference, and that would be included in the official records of the conference:

The debate at this Conference on the issue of which penalties should be applied by the Court has shown that there is no international consensus on the inclusion or non-inclusion of the death penalty. However, in accordance with the principles of complementarity between the Court and national jurisdictions, national justice systems have the primary responsibility for investigating, prosecuting and punishing individuals, in accordance with their national laws, for crimes falling under the jurisdiction of the International Criminal Court. In this regard, the Court would clearly not be able to affect national policies in this field. It should be noted that not including the death penalty in the Statute would not in any way have a legal bearing on national legislations and practices with regard to the death penalty. Nor shall it be considered as influencing, in the development of customary international law or in any other way, the legality of penalties imposed by national systems for serious crimes.[117]

There were statements from some of the concerned delegations. The Minister of Justice of the Sudan, who was present, took the floor:

On behalf of the Arab group, which we chair, I thank you for your efforts. We accept, on behalf of our group, this compromise; we do not want this issue to be a stumbling block to the advancement of this conference; we should like to express clearly and unequivocally our views. This must not be interpreted as proof that it is an acceptance of worldwide abolition of the death penalty.

Trinidad and Tobago's Attorney General also made a statement:

We cannot agree with the decision to exclude the death penalty. But in order to permit the conference to proceed, we will not oppose this. We want to make it quite clear that we do not consider the death penalty to be a human rights issue.

His remarks were endorsed in brief comments by the delegations of Dominica, Ethiopia, Barbados and Jamaica.

The same afternoon, the Working Group's report was presented to the Committee of the Whole. Singapore had reserved its right to intervene during the morning session, and had a prepared statement to deliver:

---

[117] *Ibid.*

Penalties must be commensurate with the gravity of the crime. We co-sponsored the proposal to introduce the death penalty. No delegation made the mistaken assertion that the death penalty is prohibited under international law. Even the Second Optional Protocol allows the death penalty. It has been characterised by some as a human rights question. We should not overplay the right to life of the convicted person *vis à vis* the right to security of the victim. We do not want to impose our system of criminal justice on others. The decision not to include the death penalty would not impede the sovereign right of states to impose the death penalty. The record of this conference shows that there is no international consensus as to the abolition of the death penalty.

Trinidad and Tobago, Ethiopia, Lebanon, Saudi Arabia and Rwanda also made declarations expressing their preference for the death penalty.

The next evening, when the final draft statute was presented in the plenary committee of the conference, President Giovanni Conso dutifully – and surely without a degree of personal anguish – read the statement that had been agreed upon. Singapore again took the floor to affirm that 'the debate in the conference clearly demonstrates that there is no international consensus on abolition of the death penalty'. In fact, what the debate in the Working Group showed is that a relatively small number of States favoured retention of the death penalty and a very large number were opposed. This is a dramatic development when viewed from an historical perspective. Half a century earlier, when the international military tribunals were established to try criminals from the Second World War, the death penalty was not a source of controversy and was, in fact, carried out with enthusiasm by international justice. The exclusion of the death penalty from the *Rome Statute* is a significant benchmark in an unquestionable trend towards universal abolition of capital punishment, although it shows that a few regions of the world continue to resist progress in this respect.

Despite, then, the efforts of some retentionist countries to assert that exclusion of the death penalty from the Rome Statute is 'neutral', and does not testify to any trend or evolution in customary law, this is not how the provision has been interpreted. For example, the quinquennial report of the Secretary-General of the United Nations on capital punishment noted the exclusion of capital punishment from the Rome Statute as a significant international development.[118] Similarly, the European Union, in its 2000 annual report on human rights, cites exclusion of the death penalty from the *Rome Statute* as evidence of growing international consensus on the subject.[119]

[118] UN Doc. E/2000/3, para. 66.
[119] 'EU Memorandum on the Death Penalty', European Union Annual Report on Human Rights, 11317/00, p. 81.

7

European human rights law

The European regional system of human rights emerged following the Second World War, and many of its instruments were drafted at the same time as those of the United Nations, indeed, often by the same individuals. One of the European system's exceptional features is its highly developed implementation mechanism built around the European Court of Human Rights. This body interprets and applies the *Convention for the Protection of Human Rights and Fundamental Freedoms*, known as the *European Convention on Human Rights*, and its protocols.[1] Several Western European States – Austria, Germany, the Netherlands, the Scandinavian countries, Spain, Portugal and Italy – have played a pivotal role in advancing the abolition of the death penalty within the United Nations system. The sponsors of numerous resolutions within the General Assembly, they also take credit for proposing and promoting the *Second Optional Protocol to the International Covenant on Civil and Political Rights Aiming at the Abolition of the Death Penalty*.[2] Not surprisingly, it is within the regional system of these same States that the death penalty debate has been the most advanced. *Protocol No. 6* to the *European Convention*,[3] abolishing the death penalty in peacetime, was adopted in April 1983, many years before the corresponding instruments in the United Nations and Inter-American systems.

The *European Convention on Human Rights* was signed at Rome on 4 November 1950, and entered into force on 3 September 1953. The result of a relatively brief drafting period which only began in 1949, the *Convention* provided a model for subsequent instruments in other human rights systems, notably the *International Covenant on Civil and Political Rights*[4] and the

---

[1] *Convention for the Protection of Human Rights and Fundamental Freedoms*, (1955) 213 UNTS 221, ETS 5 (see Appendix 14, p. 423). Prior to recent amendments, the now abolished European Commission of Human Rights was also involved in implementation of the *Convention*.
[2] GA Res. 44/128, (1990) 29 *ILM* 1464.
[3] *Protocol No. 6 to the Convention for the Protection of Human Rights and Fundamental Freedoms Concerning the Abolition of the Death Penalty*, ETS no. 114 (see Appendix 15, pp. 424–429).
[4] (1976) 999 UNTS 171 (See Appendix 2, p. 380).

American Convention on Human Rights,[5] instruments which adopted many concepts from the European text while at the same time adapting them to the progressive development of international legal thinking on the scope of human rights and freedoms.

Nowhere is this more evident than in the *European Convention*'s provisions dealing with capital punishment, which were drafted at a time when many European States still applied the death penalty and when the execution of Nazi war criminals was fresh in the collective memory.[6] Paradoxically, although the European continent has progressed furthest towards abolition of the death penalty, the provisions of the *European Convention* concerning capital punishment are the most conservative and anachronistic.[7]

The *European Convention* presents the death penalty as an exception to the right to life, but without most of the limitations or safeguards found in other instruments:

> *Article 2*
> 1. Everyone's right to life shall be protected by law. No one shall be deprived of his life intentionally save in the execution of a sentence of a court following his conviction of a crime for which this penalty is provided by law.

Paragraph 2 of the right to life article enumerates other exceptions to the right to life: defence of any person from unlawful violence, effecting a lawful arrest or preventing an escape from custody, and lawful action taken to suppress a riot or an insurrection. The *European Convention* is the only human rights treaty to set out expressly any exceptions to the right to life, other than capital punishment.

The shortcomings of the *Convention*'s provisions on the death penalty have posed no serious problem, because capital punishment has been only rarely employed since 1950 in the States parties to the *Convention*, and never has its actual imposition within a State party resulted in litigation before the European Commission of Human Rights or European Court of Human Rights. In *Soering* v. *United Kingdom and Germany*, the European Court stated that the

---

[5] (1979) 1144 UNTS 123, OASTS 36 (see Appendix 20, p. 436). See also: Thomas Buergenthal, 'The American and European Conventions on Human Rights: Similarities and Differences', (1980) 30 *American University Law Review* 155; J. A. Frowein, 'The European and the American Conventions on Human Rights – A Comparison', (1980) 1 *HRLJ* 44.

[6] See, for example, *Public Prosecutor* v. *Klinge*, (1946) 13 *Ann. Dig.* 262 (Supreme Court, Norway), in which Norway's courts declared the death penalty to be actually provided for by customary international law in the case of war crimes.

[7] See the concurring opinion of Judge De Meyer in *Soering* v. *United Kingdom and Germany*, 7 July 1989, Series A, Vol. 161, 11 EHRR 439, p. 51: 'The second sentence of Article 2§1 of the Convention [which permits the death penalty as an exception to the right to life] was adopted nearly forty years ago, in particular historical circumstances, shortly after the Second World War. In so far as it still may seem to permit, under certain conditions, capital punishment in time of peace, it does not reflect the contemporary situation, and is now overridden by the development of legal conscience and practice.'

death penalty no longer exists *de facto* in any of the contracting states of the *European Convention.*[9] Nevertheless, one State party to the *Convention*, Turkey,[10] still continues to pronounce the death penalty, although it has not imposed it for many years. As a condition of admission, all new Member States in the Council of Europe must undertake to abolish the death penalty.

Article 2§1 of the *Convention* soon found itself out of step with social progress in Western Europe, and by the early 1970s initiatives in the Council of Europe were afoot that eventually led, in 1983, to adoption of *Protocol No. 6.* Europe now exports its philosophy, by refusing extradition to States on other continents where capital punishment still exists.[11] Although the study of European human rights law represents a modest portion of the present work, the progressive abolition of the death penalty in international human rights law cannot be better demonstrated than with reference to the European system. From a Europe that only fifty years ago recognized the legitimacy of the death penalty with only the most minimal limitations on its use, the entire continent has virtually abolished the death penalty. International law has played a central role in this process of abolition.

7.1 The *European Convention on Human Rights*

7.1.1 *Drafting of the* Convention

The drafters of the *European Convention on Human Rights* drew heavily on the early work of the United Nations Commission on Human Rights on the draft *International Covenant on Civil and Political Rights.* At the time, the debate in the Commission on the right to life provisions focused principally on the choice of the terms 'arbitrarily' or 'intentionally' to qualify the circumstances under which the State may deprive an individual of his or her life and on whether or not the draft article should enumerate exceptions to the right to life or simply leave these to subsequent interpretation. The United States, the Soviet Union and several

---

[8] *Ibid.*, §102.   [9] *Ibid.*, para. 102.
[10] Turkey's last execution dates to 1984. Turkey was strongly criticized earlier in the 1980s by the Freedom of Association Committee of the International Labour Organization for death sentences imposed against trade unionists in the early 1980s: Case Nos. 997, 999 and 1029, *Official Bulletin*, Vol. LXIV, Series B, no. 3, para. 485.
[11] *Fidan,* (1987) II *Recueil Dalloz-Sirey* 305 (Conseil d'État); *Gacem,* (1988) I *Semaine juridique* IV–86 (Conseil d'État), 14 December 1987; *Short* v. *Netherlands,* Supreme Court of the Netherlands, 30 March 1990, (1990) 76 *Rechtspraak van de Week* 358, (1990) 29 *ILM* 1378. For a discussion of *Short*: John E. Parkerson Jr, Steven J. Lepper, 'Commentary on *Short* vs *Netherlands*', (1991) 85 *AJIL* 698; J. E. Parkerson Jr, C. S. Stoehr, 'The US Military Death Penalty in Europe: Threats From Recent European Human Rights Developments', (1990) 129 *Military Law Review* 41; S. J. Lepper, 'Short v. The Kingdom of the Netherlands: Is It Time to Renegotiate the NATO Status of Forces Agreement?', (1991) 24 *Vanderbilt Journalist Transnational Law* 867. The case of *Soering* v. *United Kingdom and Germany*, is discussed later in this chapter.

Latin American countries generally favoured the term 'arbitrarily', but the United Kingdom and France preferred 'intentionally'. The United Kingdom also led the campaign for an exhaustive enumeration of limitations on the right to life. Although 'arbitrarily' would eventually prevail in the *International Covenant*, the United Kingdom and France found little opposition within the Council of Europe to the term 'intentionally' and to a purportedly exhaustive list of exceptions.

Work on the drafting of the Council of Europe's human rights convention began with a motion tabled in the organization's Consultative Assembly by H. Teitgen and Sir David Maxwell-Fyfe on 19 August 1949.[12] Appended to the resolution was a draft declaration, of which article 1 read as follows:

> Every State party . . . shall guarantee to all persons within its territory the following rights:
> (a) Security of life and limb . . .[13]

In September, the Consultative Assembly submitted a draft instrument whose article 2 provided that Member States of the Council of Europe would undertake to guarantee 'security of the person' in accordance with articles 3, 5 and 8 of the *Universal Declaration of Human Rights*.[14] Article 3 of the *Universal Declaration* ensures that 'Everyone has the right to life, liberty and security of the person'.

Later that year, a Committee of Government Experts was convoked by the Secretary-General. By this time, the United Kingdom had proposed a more thorough instrument, which included an autonomous right to life provision providing for the death penalty 'in those States where capital punishment is lawful' (an implied reference to the possibility of abolition), and 'in accordance with the sentence of a court'.[15] A preparatory document for the meeting of

---

[12] On the drafting history of the right to life provision of the *European Convention*, see: Bertrand G. Ramcharan, 'The Drafting History of Article 2 of the European Convention on Human Rights', in Bertrand G. Ramcharan, ed., *The Right to Life in International Law*, Dordrecht/Boston/Lancaster: Martinus Nijhoff 1985, pp. 57–61; Jacques Velu, Rusen Ergec, *La Convention européenne des droits de l'homme*, Brussels: Bruylant, 1990, pp. 37–39, 169–171, Alphonse Spielman, 'La Convention européenne des droits de l'homme et la peine de mort', in *Présence du droit public et les droits de l'homme, Mélanges offerts à Jacques Vélu*, Brussels: Bruylant, 1992, pp. 1503–1527.

[13] *Collected Edition of the 'Travaux préparatoires' of the European Convention on Human Rights, Vol. III*, Dordrecht: Martinus Nijhoff, 1985, p. 28.

[14] *Collected Edition of the 'Travaux préparatoires' of the European Convention on Human Rights, Vol. I*, Dordrecht: Martinus Nijhoff, 1985, pp. 223–227.

[15] *Collected Edition, Vol. III*, p. 296; *Collected Edition of the 'Travaux préparatoires' of the European Convention on Human Rights, Vol. II*, Dordrecht: Martinus Nijhoff, 1985, p. 352:

> 1   No one shall be deprived of his life intentionally.
> 2   There shall be no exception to this rule save where death results, in those States where capital punishment is lawful, from the execution of such a penalty in accordance with the sentence of a court.
> 3   Deprivation of life shall not be regarded as intentional when it results from the use of force which is no more than absolutely necessary:

experts from the Secretary-General compared the European draft with the draft United Nations covenant. In the Committee of Experts, Sir Oscar Dowson of the United Kingdom urged that the convention borrow certain provisions from the United Nations draft, but the right to life provision, which he described as referring 'to punishment of offenders, including deprivation of life', was not one of these. In the United Kingdom draft, life could not be taken 'intentionally', capital punishment was an exception to the right to life, and several other exceptions were also enumerated.[16] The draft article was almost identical to a proposal for the right to life provision of the covenant that had been submitted by the United Kingdom to the United Nations Commission on Human Rights.[17]

There was some opposition to the United Kingdom's insistence upon a precise and complete enumeration of exceptions.[18] Two drafts, reflecting the different approaches, were submitted to the Committee of Ministers. The first, 'Alternative A', echoed article 3 of the *Universal Declaration of Human Rights*.[19] The second, 'Alternative B', was the United Kingdom draft.[20]

A. H. Robertson analysed the debate in an article published that year in the *British Yearbook of International Law*:

> Article 3 of the United Nations Declaration reads 'Everyone has the right to life, liberty and security of person'. The civilians were content to incorporate the words textually in the draft Convention. The common lawyers, on the other hand, thought that a statement of the 'right to life' necessitated a statement of the circumstances in which someone may be legally deprived of his life . . . The results of this method of definition are to be found in article 2 of the Convention.
>
> . . . any attempt at exhaustive definition always carries with it the danger of unintentional omissions which may later be constructed as deliberate exclusions. Only the future will show whether the pitfall has been successfully avoided.[21]

(i)   in defence of any person from unlawful violence;
(ii)   in order to effect a lawful arrest or to prevent an escape from custody; or
(iii)   an action lawfully taken for the purpose of quelling a riot or insurrection, or for prohibiting entry to a clearly defined place to which such access is forbidden on grounds of national security.

[16] *Collected Edition, Vol. III*, p. 186:
> 1.   No one shall be deprived of his life intentionally save in the execution of the sentence of a court following his conviction of a crime for which this penalty is defined by law.
> 2.   Deprivation of life shall not be regarded as intentional when it results from the use of force, which is not more than absolutely necessary:
> (a)   in defence of any person from unlawful violence;
> (b)   in order to effect lawful arrest or to prevent an escape from lawful custody;
> (c)   any action lawfully taken for the purpose of quelling a riot or insurrection or for prohibiting entry to clearly defined places to which access is forbidden on grounds of national security.

[17] UN Doc. E/CN.4/188; UN Doc. E/CN.4/204; UN Doc. E/CN.4/353/Add.2, UN Doc. E/CN.4/365, p. 23.
[18] Ramcharan, 'The Drafting History', p. 60.
[19] GA Res. 217 A (III), UN Doc. A/810 (see Appendix 1, p. 000).
[20] *Collected Edition, Vol. III*, p. 58.
[21] A. H. Robertson, 'The European Convention for the Protection of Human Rights', (1950) 25 *BYIL* 145, pp. 151–152.

The debate about whether the convention should declare rights in a detailed or merely general fashion was renewed at the Conference of Senior Officials, which met in June 1950. An effort was made to reconcile the two approaches by taking 'Alternative B' and including in it some of the general formulations found in 'Alternative A'. The Conference of Senior Officials proposed a draft provision that closely resembled the United Kingdom proposal. Addition of the first sentence, from 'Alternative A', brought the text closer to that of article 3 of the *Universal Declaration of Human Rights.*[22] This text became the final version of the right to life provision in the *European Convention*, adopted by the Committee of Ministers on 7 August 1950.[23] A proposal to include a cross-reference to the *Convention for the Prevention and Punishment of the Crime of Genocide*,[24] similar to the provision eventually included in article 6§3 of the *International Covenant*, was not pursued.[25] No commentary of any kind on article 2 appears in the report, and the *travaux préparatoires* that have been published by the Council of Europe are of little assistance in the interpretation of the provision.[26]

The *European Convention* came into force on 3 September 1953 and as of 1 May 2001 had been ratified by forty-one States. There have been no reservations to article 2§1.[27]

7.1.2 *Interpretation of the* Convention

As the European Court of Human Rights stated in a 1995 judgment, *McCann et al.* v. *United Kingdom*, article 2 of the *Convention* must be interpreted and applied 'so as to make its safeguards practical and effective'.[28] The text is to be strictly construed. The Court continued: 'as a provision which not only safeguards the right to life but sets out the circumstances when the deprivation of life

---

[22] Ramcharan, 'The Drafting History', p. 60

[23] *Collected Edition of the 'Travaux préparatoires' of the European Convention on Human Rights, Vol. V,* Dordrecht: Martinus Nijhoff, 1985, pp. 120–122, 146.

[24] (1951) 78 UNTS 277.   [25] *Collected Edition, Vol. V,* pp. 258–261.

[26] 'There is almost no reported discussion of the drafts,' notes James Fawcett, *The Application of the European Convention on Human Rights*, 2nd edn, Oxford: Clarendon Press, 1987, p. 34. 'Les travaux préparatoires de l'article 2 ne sont pas d'un grand secours pour éclairer la portée due texte', state Velu, Ergec, *La Convention européenne,* at p. 169. See also: Ramcharan, 'The Drafting History', pp. 57–61; Gilbert Guillaume, 'Article 2', in L. E. Pettiti, E. Decaux and P.-H. Imbert, eds., *La Convention européenne des droits de l'homme, commentaire article par article,* Paris: Economica, 1995, pp. 143–154, at p. 143. Aside from the published volumes of *travaux préparatoires,* all other documentation is sealed.

[27] Malta made a reservation to article 2§2 to the effect that the right to self-defence also includes defence of property: 'The Government of Malta, having regard to article 64 of the *Convention,* declares that the principle of lawful defence admitted under subparagraph 2(a) of Art. 2 of the Convention shall apply in Malta also to the defence of property to the extent required by the provisions of pars. (a) and (b) of Sect. 238 of the Criminal Code of Malta': (1966) 590 UNTS 301, 10 *YECHR* 24.

[28] *McCann et al.* v. *United Kingdom,* 27 September 1995, Series A, Vol. 324, 16 *HRLJ* 260, para. 146.

may be justified, article 2 ranks as one of the most fundamental provisions in the Convention – indeed one which in peacetime, admits of no derogation under Article 15. Together with Article 3 of the Convention, it also enshrines one of the basic values of the democratic societies making up the Council of Europe.'[29]

Article 2§1 of the European *Convention* does not provide the detailed guarantees and limitations that appear in other international instruments concerning the death penalty, for example, prohibition of the execution of minors, pregnant women and the elderly or confinement of the death penalty to the 'most serious crimes'.[30] This may be largely due to the fact that in 1950, when the *European Convention* text was finalized, there had been little consideration in international institutions to the elaboration of such safeguards. Much of the detailed wording used in the *International Covenant on Civil and Political Rights* evolved during the lengthy and complex drafting procedure of that instrument subsequent to 1950, the result of suggestion, reflection and consensus rather than of controversy and conflict. For example, the prohibition of the death penalty for crimes committed while under eighteen years of age was not seriously considered for insertion in the *Covenant* until 1957, at the twelfth session of the Third Committee.[31] Reference to pregnant women was first suggested in 1952, at the eighth session of the Commission on Human Rights.[32] As for the elderly, they were only mentioned in the *American Convention on Human Rights*,[33] not having even been considered at the time of drafting of the *Covenant*.

The failure of the *European Convention* to limit the death penalty to 'the most serious crimes' may have been more intentional. By 1949, this limitation already appeared in the draft covenant of the United Nations,[34] but the United Kingdom was consistently opposed to such a term, which it qualified as lacking precision.[35] Recognition of the right to seek amnesty, pardon or commutation also appeared in the 1949 draft covenant[36] but was never added to the *Convention*, an omission that is more difficult to explain because this provision was not particularly controversial.[37] Were these intentional omissions

---

[29] *Ibid.*, para. 147.

[30] *International Covenant on Civil and Political Rights*, art. 6§2; *American Convention on Human Rights*, art. 4§2.

[31] UN Doc. A/C.3/L.647; UN Doc. A/C.3/L.650. Although the prohibition of execution of juveniles was certainly well known at international law, having been included in the *Geneva Convention of August 12, 1949 Relative to the Protection of Civilians*, (1950) 75 UNTS 135, art. 68§4 (see Appendix. 10, p. 416).

[32] UN Doc. E/CN.4/SR.309, p. 3.   [33] *American Convention on Human Rights*, art. 4§5.

[34] UN Doc. E/1371. As early as 1948, a version of the draft covenant suggested the wording 'gravest of crimes' (UN Doc. E/CN.4/AC.1/8).

[35] UN Doc. E/CN.4/AC.1/SR.3, p. 12 (on the term 'gravest of crimes'); UN Doc. E/CN.4/SR.149, para. 35.

[36] UN Doc. E/1371, UN Doc. E/CN.4/350; see also UN Doc. E/CN.4/SR.98, p. 121.

[37] UN Doc. E/CN.4/SR.98. It was adopted by nine votes to one, with five abstentions (UN Doc. E/CN.4/SR.98, p. 12).

or merely decisions by harried drafters preoccupied as much by form as by content and anxious not to burden the text with exceptions that were in any case in accordance with State practice of the members of the Council? In the absence of more information from the *travaux préparatoires*, much of which remains confidential to this date, it would be hazardous to attempt an answer to this question.

Unfortunately, the concern of the English experts with precise norms that would leave little room for interpretation meant that the one word which might have given the *European Convention* some flexibility in this respect, 'arbitrarily', was not included in article 2§1. In its stead is the term 'intentionally', whose only purpose appears to be to indicate that article 2§1 refers exclusively to the death penalty.[38] As a result, the text of article 2§1 of the *European Convention* seems woefully inadequate in terms of limiting use of the death penalty, at least when set alongside the equivalent provisions in the *Covenant* and the *American Convention*.[39]

In a comparative study of the *Convention* and the *International Covenant on Civil and Political Rights*, a Committee of Experts on Human Rights appointed by the Council of Europe implied that article 2 of the *Convention* provides essentially the same protections in death penalty cases as article 6 of the *Covenant*,[40] but a close reading of the study indicates that the only real conclusion was that there was no incompatibility between the instruments. There may be no incompatibility or contradiction, but there is little doubt that the *Covenant* more thoroughly restricts use of the death penalty.[41]

The European Court of Human Rights has left open the possibility that the limitations in the other instruments, such as the prohibition of execution for crimes committed while under the age of eighteen, are implicit in the wording of article 2 of the *Convention*.[42] Such limitations could readily be added to article 2 in a dynamic interpretation of the *Convention*. This approach would find support

---

[38] The exceptions in article 2§2 are not truly 'intentional' cases of deprival of life. See: Velu, Ergec, *La Convention européenne*, at p. 242; see also P. Van Dijk, G. J. H. VanHoof, *Theory and Practice of the European Convention* on *Human Rights*. Deventer: Kluwer, 1984, p. 189; C. Warbrick, 'The European Convention on Human Rights and the Prevention of Terrorism', (1983) 32 *ICLQ* 82, at p. 104. See also: *Stewart* v. *United Kingdom* (App. No. 10044/82), (1985) 7 EHRR 453, at p. 458.

[39] The inadequacies of the provision were recognized relatively early: K. Vasak, *La Convention européenne des droits de l'homme*, Paris: Librairie générale de droit et de jurisprudence, 1964, p. 17. See also, Gérard Cohen-Jonathan, *La Convention européenne des droits de l'homme*, Paris: Economica-PUAM, 1989, p. 279.

[40] 'Corresponding provisions [to article 6§2 of the *Covenant*] appear in different places of the European Convention (in particular in Articles 3, 6§1, 7 and 13) so that the adoption of the Covenant text should not, in this respect, impose any additional obligations on the States bound by the European Convention': C. of E. Doc. H(70)7, para. 91 See also: Marc-André Eissen, 'European Convention on Human Rights and the United Nations Covenant on Civil and Political Rights: Problems of Coexistence', (1972) 22 *Buffalo Law Review* 18.

[41] The reasons of Judge De Meyer in *Soering* v. *United Kingdom and Germany*, confirm this view.

[42] *Soering* v. *United Kingdom and Germany*, para. 108.

in the universal acceptance of the more advanced norms found in the *Civil Rights Covenant* by the parties to the *Convention*. The requirement that capital punishment be imposed only for the 'most serious crimes' is even recognized in documents of the Organization for Security and Cooperation in Europe.[43] Therefore, it may be contended that the limits on use of the death penalty found within article 6 of the *Covenant* and even more recent pronouncements on the death penalty, such as the 'Safeguards Guaranteeing the Protection of Rights of Those Facing the Death Penalty',[44] are implicit within article 2§1 of the *Convention*.

Two explicit limitations to the death penalty are included within article 2 of the *Convention*: sentence of death must be pronounced by a 'court' and it must be 'provided for by law'. 'Courts' are often qualified, in international human rights law, with such adjectives as 'independent', 'competent' and 'impartial', but in article 2§1 of the *Convention* the term stands alone. The word 'court' appears elsewhere in the *Convention*,[45] where it has been interpreted as implying a body independent of the executive branch of government and offering the guarantees of a judicial procedure.[46] The Human Rights Chamber of Bosnia and Herzegovina, applying article 2§1 of the *Convention*,[47] concluded: '[A] death sentence cannot be carried out under Article 2(1) of the Convention unless it was imposed by a "court" which was independent of the executive and the parties to the case and which offered procedural guarantees appropriate to the circumstances. In relation to the latter requirement the Chamber considers that the guarantees required in a case involving the imposition of the death penalty must be of the highest order.'[48]

The term 'provided by law' imposes an obligation on any State that wishes to impose the death penalty to ensure that this is in fact authorized by a positive legal provision.[49] The publicists Velu and Ergec consider that the term is another

[43] On the issue of the death penalty within the Organization on Security and Cooperation in Europe, see pp. 299–302 below.

[44] ESC Res. 1984/50 (see Appendix 8, p. 413). Subsequently endorsed by GA Res. 39/118.

[45] Art. 5§1(a) ('competent court'), art. 5§1(b) ('court'), art 5§4 ('court'), art. 6§1 ('independent and impartial court').

[46] *De Wilde, Ooms and Versyp* v. *Belgium*, 18 June 1971, Series A, Vol. 12, 1 EHRR 373, 56 ILR 351, 11 *ILM*. 690n, para. 78; *Ringeisen* v. *Austria*, 16 July 1971, Series A, Vol. 84, 1 EHRR 455, 56 ILR 442, para. 36; *X.* v. *United Kingdom*, 15 November 1981, Series A, Vol. 46, 4 EHRR 188, 67 ILR 466, para. 39; Francis G. Jacobs, *The European Convention on Human Rights*, Oxford: Clarendon Press, 1975, p. 104.

[47] The *European Convention on Human Rights* is incorporated in the Constitution of Bosnia and Herzegovina, although the State is not yet a member of the Council of Europe and cannot therefore sign or ratify the instrument.

[48] *Damjanovic* v. *Federation of Bosnia and Herzegovina* (Case no. CH/96/30), 5 September 1997, Decisions on Admissibility and Merits 1996–1997, p. 147, para. 38.

[49] In another context, the European Court was prepared to extend the scope of the word 'law' to the unwritten common law of the English system: see *Sunday Times* v. *United Kingdom*, 26 April 1979, Series A, Vol. 30, 2 EHRR 245, 58 ILR 491.

expression of the principle expressed in article 7 of the *Convention*, which protects against retroactive penalties and assures the least severe sentence.[50] In any case, these matters are specifically addressed in article 7, which is a non-derogable provision.[51]

Some scholars have questioned whether a breach of the procedural safeguards contained in article 6 of the *Convention* is also a breach of article 2 in death penalty cases.[52] This would imply a restriction on the right of derogation found in article 15 of the *Convention*, because States parties that can otherwise derogate from article 6 would find themselves foreclosed from doing this in capital cases.[53] This argument is supported by use of the word 'court' in article 2, which may implicitly incorporate the procedural guarantees found in article 6. The question is far from moot because, although the death penalty may now be abolished in peacetime throughout most of Europe, its spectre remains in time of war. At the time of the last world war, even the most enlightened of European countries were occasionally somewhat cavalier, on a procedural level, during the summary trials and executions that followed the German surrender.

There can be no derogation from the rather limited provisions dealing with capital punishment in the *European Convention*, unless of course a State actually denounces the *Convention*. Article 15 of the *Convention* permits derogation 'in time of war or other public emergency threatening the life of the nation', but paragraph 2 of the article makes it very clear that no derogation from article 2 is permitted 'except in respect of deaths resulting from lawful acts of war'.[54] Use of the death penalty in wartime is already regulated by the *Geneva Conventions* and their additional protocols.[55] In any case, it seems far-fetched to stretch the meaning of the term 'act of war' to include imposition of the death penalty. Consequently, there can be no derogation to article 2§1 of the *Convention* with respect to the death penalty.

In *Kirkwood* v. *United Kingdom*, the European Commission first considered the possibility that the death penalty, although ostensibly permitted by article 2§1 of the *Convention*, might raise issues under article 3, which is the prohibition of inhuman and degrading treatment. According to the Commission's report:

---

[50] Velu, Ergec, *La Convention européenne*, p. 183.   [51] Art. 15§2.

[52] Velu, Ergec, *La Convention européenne*, pp. 183–184. Velu and Ergec note that the majority of scholars consider that article 6 does indeed apply to article 2. A similar approach has been taken by the Human Rights Committee to construction of the *International Covenant on Civil and Political Rights*: see our discussion of this point, pp. 112–131 above. For a decision of the European Commission of Human Rights where this matter is addressed with regard to a capital trial held in Belgium following the Second World War, see: *Byttebier* v. *Belgium* (App. No. 14505/89), (1991) 68 DR 200.

[53] Rusen Ergec, *Les droits de l'homme à l'épreuve des circonstances exceptionelles*, Brussels: Éditions Bruylant, 1987, p. 246.

[54] For an exhaustive analysis of article 15 of the *Convention*, see: Ergec, *ibid.*

[55] See Chapter 5.

Whilst it acknowledges that the Convention must be read as one document, its respective provisions must be given appropriate weight where there may be implicit overlap, and the Convention organs must be reluctant to draw inferences from one text which would restrict the express terms of another.

As both the Court and the Commission have recognized, Article 3 is not subject to any qualification. Its terms are bald and absolute. This fundamental aspect of Article 3 reflects its key position in the structure and rights of the Convention, and is further illustrated by the terms of Article 15§2 which permit no derogation from it even in time of war or other public emergency threatening the life of the nation.

In these circumstances the Commission considers that notwithstanding the terms of Article 2§1, it cannot be excluded that the circumstances surrounding the protection of one of the other rights contained in the Convention might give rise to an issue under Article 3.[56]

Kirkwood's application was declared inadmissible, because he had not demonstrated that detention on 'death row' was inhuman and degrading treatment, within the meaning of article 3. After *Kirkwood,* another United Kingdom case came before the Commission, this one involving extradition to Florida. The applicant said that the issues could be distinguished from those in California, the state to which Kirkwood was extradited. Also, he raised the intriguing issue of the compatibility of the electric chair – the method of execution used in Florida – with article 3 of the *European Convention.* At the applicant's request, the case was discontinued.[57] The same issue returned to the Commission several years later in the case of Jens Soering, who had been arrested in the United Kingdom under an extradition warrant issued at the request of the United States. Soering was a national of the Federal Republic of Germany, although he had lived in the United States since the age of eleven. In 1985, when he was eighteen years old, Soering had murdered his girlfriend's parents in Bedford, Virginia. After the killing, he fled to the United Kingdom, where he was arrested in 1986. The United States government promptly sought his extradition but, a year later, the German government also requested his extradition so that he could stand trial in Germany for the murder. Germany had of course abolished the death penalty, whereas in Virginia the death penalty was still very much in force.

The United Kingdom decided to comply with the extradition request from the United States. It sought an undertaking, pursuant to its extradition treaty, that Virginia not impose the death penalty. The United Kingdom was empowered to refuse Soering's extradition to the United States because of a

---

[56] *Kirkwood* v. *United Kingdom* (App. No. 10308/83), (1985) 37 DR 158, p. 184.

[57] *N.E.* v. *United Kingdom* (App. No. 12553/86), 7 July 1987. The records of the Commission reveal yet another United Kingdom case involving capital punishment, *Amekrane* v. *United Kingdom* (App. No. 5961/72) 44 *Coll.* 101. Amekrane had fled to Gibraltar following an aborted *coup d'état* in his native Morocco. He was returned to Morocco the following day, tried and executed. In 1974, the United Kingdom and Amekrane's widow reached a friendly settlement involving a payment of £35,000.

provision in the extradition treaty between the two countries entitling either contracting party to insist upon an undertaking from the other that the death penalty would not be imposed.[58] The provision is drawn from article 11 of the *European Convention on Extradition*, which states that, when the offence is punishable by death under the law of the requesting party but not that of the requested party, or the death penalty is not normally carried out by the latter party, 'extradition may be refused unless the requesting Party gives such assurance as the requested Party considers sufficient that the death-penalty will not be carried out'.[59] The prosecutor in Virginia agreed to make representations before the judge to the effect that the United Kingdom did not want the death penalty to be imposed, but also confirmed that he personally would request the court to impose the ultimate sanction. Soering was unsuccessful in challenging the extradition before the courts in the United Kingdom, but after exhausting his remedies, he applied to Strasbourg and obtained a request by the Commission for provisional measures pending determination of his rights under the *Convention*.[60]

The European Commission of Human Rights followed its case law in *Kirkwood*, declaring the argument based on article 3 of the *Convention* to be inadmissible (by six votes to five), although it found a breach of article 13 (by seven votes to four), which ensures the right to an effective remedy.[61] The case was then taken before the European Court of Human Rights. As a preliminary

---

[58] *Extradition Treaty Between the Government of the United Kingdom of Great Britain and Northern Ireland and the Government of the United States of America*, (1977) 1049 UNTS 167, art. IV:

> If the offence for which extradition is requested is punishable by death under the relevant law of the requesting Party, but the relevant law of the requested Party does not provide for the death penalty in a similar case, extradition may be refused unless the requesting Party gives assurances satisfactory to the requested Party that the death penalty will not be carried out.

[59] *European Convention on Extradition*, (1960) 359 UNTS 273, ETS 24. Similar provisions can be found as early as 1889, in the *South American Convention*, in the 1892 extradition treaty between the United Kingdom and Portugal, in the 1908 extradition treaty between the United States and Portugal, and in the 1912 treaty prepared by the International Commission of Jurists. On these early versions, see: J. S. Reeves, 'Extradition Treaties and the Death Penalty', (1924) 18 *AJIL* 290; 'American Institute of International Law, Project No. 17', (1926) 20 *AJIL Supp.* 331; 'Harvard Law School Draft Extradition Treaty', (1935) 29 *AJIL* 228. The Italian Constitutional Court has ruled that article 11 of the *European Convention on Extradition* does not codify a customary rule of international law: *Re Cuillier, Ciamborrani and Vallon*, (1988) 78 ILR 93. A similar provision is found in the *Inter-American Convention on Extradition*, (1981) 20 *ILM* 723, art. 9. The 'Model Treaty on Extradition' proposed by the Eighth United Nations Congress on the Prevention of Crime and Treatment of Offenders, 1990, contains the following: 'Article 4. Extradition may be refused in any of the following circumstances: ... (c) If the offence for which extradition is requested carries the death penalty under the law of the requesting State, unless that State gives such assurance as the requested State considers sufficient that the death penalty will not be imposed or, if imposed, will not be carried out' (UN Doc. A/CONF. 14/28/Rev.1, p. 68).

[60] C. Warbrick, 'Coherence and the European Court of Human Rights: the Adjudicative Background to the Soering Case', (1989–90) 11 *Michigan Journal of International Law* 1073; Vincent Berger, *Jurisprudence de la Cour européenne des droits de l'homme*, 4th edn, Paris: Sirey, 1994, pp. 12–13.

[61] *Soering* v. *United Kingdom* (App. No. 14038/88), Series A, Vol. 161, pp. 53–83.

matter, the European Court unanimously endorsed the established case law of the European Commission[62] by which extradition to a State where torture or inhuman or degrading treatment might be imposed may involve a breach of article 3 of the *Convention*.[63]

In a judgment issued on 7 July 1989,[64] the Court acknowledged the idea that capital punishment as such is accepted under the *European Convention*. It noted that in light of the wording of article 2§1, neither Soering nor the two Government parties had taken the position that the death penalty *per se* violated article 3 of the *Convention*. However, the prominent non-governmental organization Amnesty International, which intervened in the litigation,[65] had argued before the Court that evolving standards of interpretation of the *Convention* meant that the death penalty should now be considered to breach article 3. The Court observed, in this respect, that '[d]*e facto* the death penalty no longer exists in time of peace in the contracting States of the Convention. In the few contracting States which retain the death penalty in law for some peacetime offences, death sentences, if ever imposed, are nowadays not carried out.'[66]

But the Court rejected the argument that the interpretation of the *Convention* could be extended in this way, so that article 3, in effect, rendered inoperative a portion of article 2§1. In light of the mention of the death penalty in article 2 of the *Convention*, the European Court of Human Rights was not prepared to consider that the death penalty *per se* constitutes inhuman treatment. As the scholar Francis Jacobs stated presciently, many years before the judgment

---

[62] *Kerkoub* v. *Belgium* (App. No. 5012/71), 40 *Coll.* 62; *Altun* v. *Federal Republic of Germany* (App. No. 10308/82), (1983) 5 EHRR 651. See also: Cohen-Jonathan, *La Convention européenne*, pp. 304–310.

[63] *Soering* v. *United Kingdom and Germany*, paras. 81–91.

[64] *Ibid*. For scholarly comment on the *Soering* case, see: W. Ganshof van der Meersch, 'L'extradition et la Convention européenne des droits de l'homme. L'affaire Soering', (1990) *Revue trimestrielle des droits de l'homme* 5; Frédéric Sudre, 'Extradition et peine de mort – arrêt Soering de la Cour européenne des droits de l'homme du 7 juillet 1989', (1990) *RGDIP* 103; Richard B. Lillich, 'The *Soering* Case', (1991) 85 *AJIL* 128; Michael O'Boyle, 'Extradition and Expulsion under the European Convention on Human Rights, Reflections on the *Soering* Case', in James O'Reilly, ed., *Human Rights and Constitutional Law, Essays in Honour of Brian Walsh*, Dublin: The Round Hall Press, 1992, p. 93; Ann Sherlock, 'Extradition, Death Row and the Convention', (1990) 15 *European Law Review* 87; David L. Gappa, 'European Court of Human Rights – Extradition – Inhuman or Degrading Treatment or Punishment, Soering Case, 161 Eur.Ct.H.R. (Ser.A) 1989)', (1990) 20 *Georgia Journal of International and Comparative Law* 463; H. Wattendorff, E. du Perron, 'Human Rights v. Extradition: the Soering case', (1990) 11 *Michigan Journal of International Law* 845; John Quigley, J. Shank, 'Death Row as a Violation of Human Rights: Is it Illegal to Extradite to Virginia?', (1989) 30 *Virginia International Law Journal* 251; Richard B. Lillich, 'The *Soering* case', (1991) 85 *AJIL* 128; Christine van den Wyngaert, 'Applying the European Convention on Human Rights to Extradition: Opening Pandora's Box?', (1990) 39 *ICLQ* 757; Susan Marks, 'Yes, Virginia, Extradition May Breach the European Convention on Human Rights', (1990) 49 *Cambridge Law Journal* 194; Henri Labayle, 'Droits de l'homme, traitement inhumain et peine capitale: Réflexions sur l'édification d'un ordre public européen en matiére d'extradition par la Cour européenne des droits de l'homme', (1990) 64 *Semaine juridique* 3452; L. E. Pettiti, 'Arrêt Soering c./Grande-Bretagne du 8 juillet 1989', [1989] *Revue de science criminelle et de droit pénal comparé* 786.

[65] *Soering* v. *United Kingdom and Germany*, para. 8.   [66] *Ibid*., para. 102.

in *Soering*, punishment could be contrary to article 3 of the *Convention* 'only if it did not involve the ultimate penalty'.[67] The Court declared:

> Whether these marked changes have the effect of bringing the death penalty *per se* within the prohibition of ill-treatment under article 3 must be determined on the principles governing the interpretation of the Convention.
>
> The Convention is to be read as a whole and article 3 should therefore be construed in harmony with the provisions of article 2. On this basis article 3 evidently cannot have been intended by the drafters of the Convention to include a general prohibition of the death penalty since that would nullify the clear working of article 2§1.
>
> Subsequent practice in national penal policy, in the form of a generalized abolition of capital punishment, could be taken as establishing the agreement of the Contracting States to abrogate the exception provided for under article 2§1 and hence to remove a textual limit on the scope for evolutive interpretation of article 3. However, Protocol No. 6, as a subsequent written agreement, shows that the intention of the Contracting Parties as recently as 1983 was to adopt the normal method of amendment of the text in order to introduce a new obligation to abolish capital punishment in time of peace and, what is more, to do so by an optional instrument allowing each State to choose the moment when to undertake such an engagement. In these conditions, notwithstanding the special character of the Convention, article 3 cannot be interpreted as generally prohibiting the death penalty.[68]

In fact, in 1979 when the issue of amending article 2 of the *Convention* arose so as to bring it into step with the more advanced norms of the *American Convention on Human Rights*, the Steering Committee on Human Rights of the Council of Europe felt that any such amendment would imply acceptance of the death penalty at a time when there was a general trend towards abolition.[69] Amendment of the *Convention* might only legitimize the death penalty and, for this reason, the lawmakers of the Council of Europe chose the route of an optional protocol, updating the *Convention* and abolishing the death penalty. Consequently, the current inadequacies, indeed the obsolescence, of article 2§1 of the *Covenant* can only be properly appreciated in the light of *Protocol No. 6*.

The suggestion that the *Convention*'s recognition of the death penalty as an exception to the right to life is now obsolete and incompatible with the legal conscience and practice of contemporary Europe was advanced by a single member of the Court, Judge De Meyer, in a concurring opinion.[70] Judge De Meyer held

---

[67] Francis G. Jacobs, *The European Convention*, at p. 23. The Turkish courts have upheld the constitutionality of that country's death penalty, provided in article 11 of its penal code, with reference to article 2§1 of the *European Convention*: (1963) 4 YECHR 821.

[68] *Soering* v. *United Kingdom and Germany*, §§102–104 (references omitted).

[69] 'Opinion of the Steering Committee on Human Rights', 12–16 November 1979.

[70] This view was advanced by Judge De Meyer in his concurring opinion in *Soering* v. *United Kingdom and Germany*, pp. 51–52. Note that at least one commentator has suggested that 'there is a general practice amounting to customary international law, in the conditional and presumptive sense indicated, that when a State (like the US) which has not abolished capital punishment seeks extradition from a State which has

that extradition of Soering would breach article 2 of the *Convention*. Because article 2§1 permits imposition of the death penalty only where this 'is provided by law' and because the death penalty is not 'provided by law' in the United Kingdom, the fact that it is allowed in Virginia is irrelevant, he wrote.[71] 'When a person's right to life is involved, no requested State can be entitled to allow a requesting State to do what the requested State is not itself allowed to do.'[72] Judge De Meyer added that the unlawfulness of the death penalty in Europe was recognized by the Committee of Ministers when it adopted *Protocol No. 6* in December 1982:

> No State party to the Convention can in that context, even if it has not yet ratified the Sixth Protocol, be allowed to extradite any person if that person thereby incurs the risk of being put to death in the requesting State. Extraditing somebody in such circumstances would be repugnant to European standards of justice, and contrary to the public order of Europe.[73]

Although it refused to follow such a radical view of article 3, the Court confirmed that circumstances relating to a death sentence could give rise to issues respecting the prohibition of inhuman and degrading treatment or punishment, pursuant to article 3 of the *Convention*. It addressed four of them: length of detention prior to execution; conditions on death row; age and mental state of the applicant; and the competing extradition request from Germany.

The Court noted that a condemned prisoner could expect to spend six to eight years on death row before being executed. The Court agreed that this was 'largely of the prisoner's own making', in that it was the result of systematic appellate review and various collateral attacks by means of *habeas corpus*. 'Nevertheless,' said the Court, 'just as some lapse of time between sentence and execution is inevitable if appeal safeguards are to be provided to the condemned person, so it is equally part of human nature that the person will cling to life by exploiting those safeguards to the full. However well-intentioned and even potentially beneficial is the provision of the complex of post-sentence procedures in Virginia, the consequence is that the condemned prisoner has to endure for many years the conditions on death row and the anguish and mounting tension

(like the U.K.), the requesting State must guarantee that the extraditee would not be executed': Yoram Dinstein, 'General Report', (1991) 62 *International Review of Penal Law 31*, p. 36.
[71] It is clear from the judgment that the argument had been made that the United Kingdom had not rejected capital punishment unequivocally because it had failed to ratify *Protocol No. 6* to the *Convention*. The European Commission, in the same case, held that the *Protocol* had 'no relevance' to the obligations of the United Kingdom under the *Convention* because it had neither signed nor ratified the *Protocol* (at p. 56 in Series A). In his concurring view, Judge De Meyer observed that the failure to ratify *Protocol No. 6* was not in any way decisive, because the 'unlawfulness' of capital punishment had already been recognized by the Committee of Ministers of the Council of Europe in opening the instrument for signature.
[72] *Soering* v. *United Kingdom and Germany*, p. 51.   [73] *Ibid.*, p. 52.

of living in the ever-present shadow of death.'[74] The Court took note of the exceptionally severe regime in effect on death row, adding that it was 'compounded by the fact of inmates being subject to it for a protracted period lasting on average six to eight years'.[75] What the Court had described is often labelled the 'death row phenomenon'.[76]

The Court also considered Soering's age and mental state as 'particular circumstances'. It noted that the norm prohibiting execution of juveniles, found in 'other, later international instruments, the former of which [the *International Covenant on Civil and Political Rights*] has been ratified by a large number of States parties to the European Convention, at the very least indicates that as a general principle the youth of the person concerned is a circumstance which is liable, with others, to put in question the compatibility with article 3 of measures connected with the death sentence'.[77] It added that 'disturbed mental health' could also be considered an attenuating factor in terms of the assessment of whether treatment was inhuman or degrading, within the meaning of article 3 of the *Convention*.[78] Finally, the Court also considered that the competing demand by Germany for Soering was a relevant factor in the overall assessment of 'the requisite fair balance of interests' and the 'proportionality of the contested extradition decision' within the context of article 3.

The European Court of Human Rights cited these factors in finding a breach of article 3 of the *Convention*. '[I]n the Court's view, having regard to the very long period of time spent on death row in such extreme conditions, with the ever present and mounting anguish of awaiting execution of the death penalty, and to the personal circumstances of the appellant, especially his age and mental state at the time of the offence, the applicant's extradition to the United States would expose him to a real risk of treatment going beyond the threshold set by Article 3. A further consideration of relevance is that in the particular instance the legitimate purpose of extradition could be achieved by another means which would not involve suffering of such exceptional intensity or duration.'[79] The Court also said that 'the applicant's youth at the time of the offence and his then mental state, on the psychiatric evidence as it stands, are therefore to be taken into consideration as contributory factors tending, in his case, to bring the treatment on death row within the terms of Article 3'.[80]

The *Soering* decision was submitted to the Committee of Ministers of the Council of Europe, which oversees implementation of Court rulings, pursuant to the terms of article 54 of the *Convention*. The United Kingdom reported

---

[74] *Ibid.*, para. 106.   [75] *Ibid.*, para. 107.

[76] The issue of the 'death row phenomenon' has been litigated before many domestic courts. See William A. Schabas, *The Death Penalty as Cruel Treatment and Torture*, Boston: Northeastern University Press, 1996, pp. 96–115.

[77] *Soering* v. *United Kingdom and Germany*, para. 108.

[78] *Ibid.*   [79] *Ibid.*, para. 111.   [80] *Ibid.*, para. 109.

to the Committee that on 28 July 1989 it had informed the United States authorities that extradition for an offence that might include imposition of the death penalty was refused. Three days later the United States answered that 'in the light of the applicable provisions of the 1972 extradition treaty, United States law would prohibit the applicant's prosecution in Virginia for the offence of capital murder'.[81] The Committee said it was satisfied that the United Kingdom had paid Soering the sums provided for in the judgment, and concluded that it had exercised its functions under the *Convention*.[82] Soering was subsequently extradited to Virginia where he pleaded guilty to two charges of murder, for which he was sentenced to terms of ninety-nine years.

The European Court's judgment in *Soering* has since been discussed, and interpreted, by both domestic and international courts. Some courts have given the decision a narrow construction, insisting upon the various extenuating factors in asserting that prolonged detention on death row *per se* does not constitute inhuman or degrading treatment or punishment. The majority of the United Nations Human Rights Committee has taken the view that delay must be accompanied by other extenuating circumstances. Moreover, it has expressed the concern that the 'death row phenomenon' argument may actually incite States to execute offenders more rapidly.[83] Christine Chanet has led the dissenters on the Committee who, relying upon *Soering*, have considered prolonged detention without other factors to breach fundamental rights.[84] The Zimbabwe Supreme Court endorsed *Soering* in a 1993 ruling, adding that Chanet's dissenting views in the Human Rights Committee were 'more plausible and persuasive' than those of the majority.[85] Citing *Soering*, the Judicial Committee of the Privy Council also held that inordinate delay is itself sufficient for there to be a breach of the norm prohibiting inhuman or degrading treatment, and that no extenuating circumstance such as age or mental state are necessary.[86] Justice Gerald La Forest of the Supreme Court of Canada, in *Kindler* v. *Canada*, dismissed an argument based on the length of detention on death row adding, with reference to *Soering*, that 'there may be situations where the age or mental capacity of the fugitive may affect the matter, but again that is not this case'.[87] But some ten

---

[81] Resolution DH (90) 8, appendix. [82] Resolution DH (90) 8.

[83] See, for example: *Errol Johnson* v. *Jamaica* (No. 588/1994), UN Doc. CCPR/C/56/D/588/1994, para. 8.2. The Human Rights Committee's case law on the 'death row phenomenon' is discussed in detail in Chapter 3, at pp. 141–151.

[84] *Barrett and Sutcliffe* v. *Jamaica* (Nos 270/1988 and 271/1988), UN Doc. A/47/40, p. 254 (*per* Chanet).

[85] *Catholic Commission for Justice and Peace in Zimbabwe* v. *Attorney-General, Zimbabwe, et al.*, [1993] 4 SA 239 (ZSC), [1993] 1 ZLR 242 (S), 14 *HRLJ* 323.

[86] *Pratt* et al. v. *Attorney General for Jamaica* et al., [1993] 4 All ER 769, [1993] 2 LRC 349, [1994] 2 AC 1, [1993] 3 WLR 995, 43 WIR 340, 14 *HRLJ* 338, 33 ILM 364 (JCPC), para. 57. See also: *Fisher* v. *Minister of Public Safety and Immigration*, [1998] AC 673; [1998] 3 WLR 201 (JCPC), paras. 31–32; *Guerra* v. *Baptiste and others*, [1996] AC 1997; [1995] 3 WLR 891; [1995] 4 All ER 583 (JCPC).

[87] *Kindler* v. *Canada*, [1991] 2 SCR 779, 67 CCC (3d) 1, 84 DLR (4th) 438, 6 CRR (2d) 193.

years later, after noting that the 'death row phenomenon' issue had not been 'definitively settled' in *Kindler*, the Supreme Court of Canada unanimously recognized the relevance of the psychological trauma associated with prolonged detention while awaiting capital punishment.[88]

Since *Soering* in 1989, the European Commission on Human Rights has returned on numerous occasions to death-penalty-related matters. In January 1994, it ruled an application from an individual subject to extradition to the United States for a capital offence to be inadmissible. The Commission considered the guarantees that had been provided by the Dallas County prosecutor to the French Government, to the effect that, if extradition were granted, 'the State of Texas [would] not seek the death penalty', to be sufficient. Texas law stated that the death penalty could only be pronounced if requested by the prosecution. Aylor-Davis had claimed that the undertaking was 'vague and imprecise'. Furthermore, she argued that it had been furnished by the federal authorities through diplomatic channels, and did not bind the executive or judicial authorities of the State of Texas. The Commission compared the facts with those in *Soering*, where the prosecutor had made clear an intention to seek the death penalty.[89] The Commission found the Texas prosecutor's attitude to be fundamentally different, and concurred with an earlier decision of the French Conseil d'État holding the undertaking to be satisfactory.[90]

In *Çinar* v. *Turkey*, the applicant was sentenced to death in 1984, and the judgment maintained on appeal in 1987. In 1991, he was released on parole, pursuant to legislation that also declared that all death sentences were to be commuted. The Commission recalled that article 3 of the *Convention* could not be interpreted as prohibiting the death penalty. Moreover, it held that a certain period of time between pronouncement of the sentence and its execution was inevitable. The Commission added that article 3 would only be breached where an individual passed a very long time on death row, under extreme conditions, and with the constant anxiety of execution. Thus, the Commission adopted a large view of *Soering*, in that it did not insist upon the various extenuating factors, such as young age and mental instability, which had been referred to by the Court.[91] Furthermore, the Commission concluded that in Turkey during the period Çinar was on death row there was no serious danger of his death sentence

---

[88] The Supreme Court of Canada revisited the matter ten years later in *United States* v. *Burns*, [2001] 1 SCR 283, paras. 122–123.

[89] *Aylor-Davis* v. *France* (App. No. 22742/93), (1994) 76B DR 164. See also *Nivette* v. *France* (App. No. 44190/98), Interim Measures, November 1999, in which the Court refused interim measures under Rule 39 in a case of extradition to the United States where specific and renewed assurances had been given by United States authorities that the death penalty would not be imposed.

[90] *Dame Joy Davis-Aylor*, CE, Req. No. 144590, 15/10/93, D. 1993, IR, 238; JCP 1993, Actualités No. 43, [1993] *Revue française de droit administratif* 1166, conclusions C. Vigoreux.

[91] *Çinar* v. *Turkey* (App. No. 17864/91), (1994) 79A DR 5, pp. 8–9.

actually being carried out. Referring to the Court's judgment in *Soering*, which observed that the death penalty no longer existed in the States parties to the *Convention*, the Commission described the threat of execution as 'illusory'.[92]

The Commission has made similar findings in several cases where applicants have alleged the possibility of execution in the event of expulsion or extradition. These have all been dismissed because of the sufficiency of assurances that the death penalty would not be imposed, the relatively minor nature of the offence in question,[93] or the unlikelihood of capital punishment actually being imposed in the receiving State. In a case involving Turkey, the Commission noted that the death penalty had not been imposed for the crimes in question since 1960, that there had been no death penalties imposed whatsoever since 1984, and that 'in legal writing in Turkey the opinion prevails that the death penalty should be abolished'.[94] Some applications have been rendered moot when constitutional courts or government authorities intervened to protect the applicants while the case was pending before the Commission.[95] Others have been resolved with a friendly settlement.[96]

An anomaly resulting from the recent expansion of the Council of Europe is that occasional applications are still filed against States parties to the *Convention* with respect to the death penalty on their own territory. Two pending applications, filed in 1998 against Bulgaria, concern persons sentenced to death in 1989. Bulgaria has since abolished the death penalty, of course. The petitions invoke articles 2 and 3 of the Convention, and challenge the death penalty as such as well as the prolonged wait on death row since sentence was pronounced.[97] Poor conditions on death row in the Ukraine have been invoked in several applications.[98]

The most significant application concerning the threat of imposition of the death penalty by a State party was filed by Kurdish rebel leader Abdullah Öcalan, on 16 February 1999, while his trial was still pending before Turkish courts. The Court issued provisional measures on 4 March 1999, applying Rule 39 of its Rules of Procedure, to ensure that proceedings conducted by the National Security Court complied with article 6 of the *Convention*. On 29 June 1999, Öcalan was sentenced to death by the Second State Security Court, pursuant to article 125 of the Turkish Penal Code. The Court was then

---

[92] *Ibid.*, p. 9.   [93] *H. v. Sweden* (App. No. 22408/93), (1994) 79A DR 85, p. 96.

[94] *Z.Y. v. Germany* (App. No. 16846/90), Admissibility Decision, 13 July 1990.

[95] *Lei Ch'an Wa v. Portugal* (App. No. 25410/94), unreported decision of 27 November 1995. See also: *Yenng Yuk Leung v. Portugal* (App. No. 24464/94), unreported decision of 27 November 1995; *Venezia v. Italy* (App. no. 29966/96), (1996) 87-A DR 140; *Cheong Meng v. Portugal* (App. No. 25862/94), (1995) 83-A DR 88.

[96] *Dehwari v. Netherlands* (App. No. 34014/97), 27 April 2000.

[97] *Iorgov v. Bulgaria* (App. No. 40653/98); *Belchinov v. Bulgaria* (App. No. 42346/98).

[98] For example: *Poltoratskiy v. Ukraine* (App. No. 38812/97).

asked to issue provisional measures suspending the execution until the case had been adjudicated on the merits, but decided instead to await determination of the appeal. The death sentence was confirmed on 25 November 1999 by the Court of Cassation.[99] On 30 November 1999, the European Court of Human Rights requested Turkey 'to take all necessary measures to ensure that the death penalty is not carried out so as to enable the Court to proceed effectively with the examination of the admissibility and merits of the applicant's complaints under the Convention'.[100]

The Court is now faced once again with the death penalty issue that it so adroitly sidestepped in *Soering* in 1989. This time, the threat of the death penalty exists in a Member State and not a third State. The argument that article 2§1 of the *Convention* is implicitly repealed by article 3, advanced by the *amicus curiae* Amnesty International in *Soering*, has been resubmitted by counsel for Öcalan.[101] The Court will be reminded that the 'the Convention is a living instrument which must be interpreted in the light of present day conditions [and] the increasingly high standard being required in the area of the protection of human rights and fundamental liberties'.[102] When *Soering* was issued, *Protocol No. 6* was still quite far from universal ratification among Council of Europe members, many of whom, including the United Kingdom, appeared unlikely to accept the instrument within the near future. That hesitant position seems almost unthinkable in 2001, given the strengthened and unequivocal commitments of the Council of Europe on the subject of capital punishment in the decade since *Soering*. The Council of Europe now boasts that its territory is a death-penalty-free zone, and that capital punishment has no place in a civilized society. The European Court of Human Rights will be challenged to revisit *Soering* and see that these universal European values are now translated into its jurisprudence.

Aside from reconsidering whether article 3 of the Convention 'trumps' article 2§1, the Court might also examine whether the exception to the right to life in the latter provision is now contrary to a regional customary norm.[103] This would involve a determination that a new rule of customary international law can have the effect of repealing a human rights treaty provision that has become manifestly anachronistic.

---

[99] An observer mission from the Parliamentary Assembly of the Council of Europe found the procedure to be compatible with norms of the Council of Europe, but condemned the sentence of death that was imposed: 'Ad Hoc Committee to Ensure the Presence of the Assembly at the Trial of Abdullah Öcalan', Doc. 8596, 15 December 1999. On 30 November 1998, the Parliamentary Assembly applauded Italy's refusal to extradite Öcalan to Turkey because he would face capital punishment.

[100] *Öcalan v. Turkey* (No. 46221/99), Interim Measures, 30 November 1999.

[101] *Öcalan v. Turkey* (No. 46221/99), Applicant's Final Submissions.

[102] *Selmouni v. France* (App. No. 25803/94), Judgment, 28 July 1999, para. 101.

[103] *Asylum Case (Columbia v. Peru)*, [1950] ICJ Reports 266, pp. 276–277; *Anglo-Norwegian Fisheries Case (United Kingdom v. Norway)*, [1951] ICJ Reports 116, pp. 136–139; *Rights of US Nationals in Morocco Case (United States v. France)*, [1952] ICJ Reports 176, p. 200.

Öcalan has also argued that there is a violation of article 2 because he was not sentenced by 'a court', and because the death sentence was imposed following criminal proceedings that breached articles 5 and 6 in several respects. Because he is subject to death by hanging, Öcalan is claiming that the method of execution violates article 3, a question that has yet to be adjudicated by an international human rights body. The United Nations Human Rights Committee has deemed execution in a gas chamber to be cruel, inhuman and degrading treatment or punishment,[104] but rejected a similar claim in a case involving lethal injection.[105] There is considerable case law supporting the inhumanity of execution by hanging.[106] Finally, Öcalan has invoked article 14 of the *Convention*, dealing with non-discrimination, in conjunction with article 2, on the grounds that the death penalty is discriminatory because it is no longer Turkish Government policy to carry out death sentences.

Turkey challenged the admissibility of Öcalan's application, noting that an interpretation holding the death penalty contrary to article 3 of the Convention was untenable. It observed that even article 2 of *Protocol No. 6*, in allowing the death penalty in time of war or of imminent threat of war, indicates that capital punishment is not considered to be inhuman or degrading punishment. After all, the imminence or existence of war cannot make a punishment less inhuman or degrading. On 14 December 2000, after a preliminary assessment of these points, the Court declared that the arguments 'raise complex legal and factual issues which cannot be determined at [the admissibility] stage of the examination of the application but require an examination of the merits'.[107] The case is expected to be heard on the merits in 2002 by a Grand Chamber of the European Court of Human Rights.

7.2 Protocol No. 6 to the *European Convention*

7.2.1 *Drafting of the* Protocol

The issue of capital punishment appeared on the first agenda of the newly created European Committee on Crime Problems, an institution of the Council of Europe, in 1957.[108] In 1962, the Committee created a special sub-committee on the death penalty and named French jurist Marc Ancel as *rapporteur*, with the

---

[104] *Ng* v. *Canada* (No. 469/1991), UN Doc. A/49/40, Vol. II, p. 189, 15 *HRLJ* 149, paras. 16.3–16.5.
[105] *Cox* v. *Canada* (No. 539/1993), UN Doc. CCPR/C/52/D/539/1993, (1995) 15 *HRLJ* 410.
[106] *Republic* v. *Mbushuu et al.*, [1994] 2 LRC 335 (High Court of Tanzania); *Campbell* v. *Wood*, 18 F.3d 662, 695 (9th Cir.1994), *cert. denied*, 114 S.Ct. 2125 (1994).
[107] *Öcalan* v. *Turkey* (No. 46221/99), Admissibility, 14 December 2000.
[108] 'Les activités du Comité européen pour les problèmes criminels du Conseil de l'Europe', (1961) 16 *Revue de science criminelle et de droit pénal comparé* n.s. 646, pp. 646–647.

mandate to prepare a study on capital punishment in Europe.[109] The European Committee also asked the Centre français de droit comparé to conduct an inquiry on the subject, and it created a scientific commission for this purpose. It was understood that the investigation would concern only common law crimes and exclude political and military crimes.

Ancel's report concerned the status of capital punishment in the Member States of the Council of Europe, as well as Finland, Monaco, Portugal, San Marino and Spain. Ancel's study noted that, because of political developments in Europe earlier in the century, some abolitionist countries had revived the death penalty, but that it would be an error to consider this as a renunciation of their commitment to abolition.[110]

Following publication of Ancel's report, the European Committee on Crime Problems continued to work on a study of crimes for which the death penalty existed but for which it was never imposed, examining the possibility of drafting a resolution demanding the repeal of the death penalty in such cases.[111] In 1966, the Committee of Ministers decided to discontinue any further study of the consequences of the abolition of the death penalty.[112]

Interest in the death penalty revived in 1973, when the Consultative Assembly of the Council of Europe sent a draft resolution[113] on the abolition of capital punishment to the Committee on Legal Affairs.[114] The resolution took note of the recent decision of the United Kingdom's House of Commons not to reintroduce capital punishment and affirmed that capital punishment 'must now be seen to be inhuman and degrading within the meaning of article 3 of the European Convention on Human Rights'. It called upon governments of Member States that still retained the death penalty for certain crimes to abolish it as a legal sanction.[115]

The resolution was referred to the Committee on Legal Affairs for further study.[116] Bertil Lidgard, a Swedish Conservative, was appointed *rapporteur* of the Committee on Legal Affairs. Lidgard's report, submitted in the summer of 1974, was staunchly abolitionist, and it met with vigorous opposition within the Committee, inspired largely by Conservative English delegates. Even the

---

[109] Marc Ancel, *The Death Penalty in European Countries*, Strasbourg: Council of Europe, 1962. At the same time Ancel prepared a study on capital punishment on a world scale at the request of the United Nations: *Capital Punishment*, UN Doc. ST/SOA/SD/9, Sales No. 62.IV.2.
[110] Ancel, *The Death Penalty*, p. 1.
[111] Norman Bishop, 'L'activité du Comité européen pour les problèmes criminels du Conseil de l'Europe', (1966) 21 *Revue de science criminelle et de droit pénal comparé* n.s. 427, at p. 428.
[112] Erik Harremoes, 'L'activité du Comité européen pour les problèmes criminels du Conseil de l'Europe 1966–1974', (1975) 30 *Revue de science criminelle et de droit pénal comparé* 327.
[113] Council of Europe, Consultative Assembly, Doc. 3297. Proposed by Bergegren, Wiklund, Aasen, Stewart, Dankert, Radinger, Renschler, Bohman, Sjönell, Wääg and Hansen.
[114] Council of Europe, Consultative Assembly, Debates, 18 May 1973, p. 246.
[115] C. of E. Doc. 3297.   [116] Reference No. 975 (8th sitting, 18 May 1973).

Committee's chairman said that he supported capital punishment in certain circumstances. The retentionist camp invoked growing problems with terrorism and argued that the death penalty was still essential as a deterrent to such 'new crimes'. The Committee was bitterly divided between abolitionist and retentionist camps. At a subsequent meeting, Lidgard suggested that opposition might have been due to his failure to distinguish between capital punishment in wartime or under military law and capital punishment in peacetime, indicating that his report had only contemplated the latter. But even this concession was not enough to appease the proponents of the death penalty. Faced with an impasse, the Committee decided, by nine votes to seven with two abstentions, not to submit Lidgard's report to the Parliamentary Assembly and to propose that the issue be struck from the Assembly's register.[117] The Parliamentary Assembly, however, refused to adopt such a course, and by fifty votes to twenty-nine it decided not to remove the question from its register but instead to refer the matter back to the Committee on Legal Affairs for further examination.[118]

The Committee on Legal Affairs met in July 1975 and instructed Lidgard to present a revised report, which was to be presented to the Assembly in January 1976. That report began:

> The abolition of the death penalty is one of those problems that involve the very principles of moral, philosophical, legal and criminological, political and other sciences, and yet the various questions it raises may ultimately be reduced to a single fundamental question, to that direct, crucial, blunt question which Cesare Beccaria asked more than two centuries ago: 'What is this right whereby men presume to slaughter their fellows?'[119]

Lidgard noted that the position of the United Nations on the death penalty had evolved considerably, from one that was originally neutral to one that now favoured abolition.[120] The revised report referred to executions in Spain that had taken place in September 1975 and that had provoked a debate in the Parliamentary Assembly and worldwide appeals for clemency.[121] Lidgard also recognized that abolition would not extend to wartime, thereby giving some credence to the argument of the death penalty's deterrent effect, at least in the case of war criminals. He said that the death penalty should be maintained for the most serious war crimes, such as genocide. Lidgard argued that the Parliamentary Assembly should appeal to States that maintain the death penalty in the case of common law crimes, including so-called 'new crimes' such as terrorism, to suppress this in their penal systems. States that maintain the death

---

[117] See the comments of Stoffelen of the Netherlands on this debate: Council of Europe, Parliamentary Assembly, 22 April 1980, p. 60 (Stoffelen was a member of the Legal Affairs Committee at the time).
[118] 27th Session, 3rd sitting, 22 April 1975, pp. 77–78.   [119] Quoted in C. of E. Doc. 4509, para. 1.
[120] Note particularly UN Doc. E/2342, para. 16.   [121] They were the last executions in Spain.

penalty in wartime or for military crimes should be encouraged 'to examine the possibility' of the suppression of the death penalty. Lidgard's report noted that capital punishment could also be regarded as 'inhuman' within the meaning of article 3 of the *European Convention.*

The Committee considered Lidgard's revised report at its January 1976 session, but again, intransigent English delegates said it was not an appropriate time to talk of capital punishment. A bitter and frustrated Lidgard announced that he was resigning as *rapporteur.* The Committee then decided that the report should again be deferred. The question of capital punishment remained dormant for a few years, during which there were developments within the Council of Europe that changed the balance within the Committee. Three abolitionist States joined the Council of Europe, Spain, Portugal and Liechtenstein.[122] An attempt to reintroduce the death penalty in the United Kingdom failed. The prominent non-governmental organization, Amnesty International, held a conference in Stockholm, in December 1977, which resulted in an important declaration calling for abolition of the death penalty.[123]

In June 1978 at a meeting of the European Ministers of Justice, the issue of capital punishment was addressed in light of a report presented by Christian Broda, the Austrian Minister of Justice and a well-known abolitionist.[124] The meeting recommended: 'that the Committee of Ministers of the Council of Europe refer questions concerning the death penalty to the appropriate Council of Europe bodies for study as part of the Council's work programme, especially in the light of the Austrian memorandum and the exchange of views at the present conference'.[125] Pursuant to this resolution, the issue was then taken up by the European Committee on Crime Problems and by the Steering Committee on Human Rights, which sent a questionnaire on the subject to governments of the Member States.

---

[122] Portugal abolished the death penalty in 1976. Liechtenstein, which did not abolish the death penalty until 1987, had executed nobody since 1785. Spain abolished the death penalty in 1978. See: M. Barbero Santos, 'La peine de mort en Espagne: histoire de son abolition, in *Mélanges en l'honneur de Doyen Pierre Bouzat*, Paris: Pedone, 1980, p. 103; A. Beristain, 'La sanction capitale en Espagne. Référence spéciale à la dimension religieuse Chrétienne', (1987) 58 *Revue internationale de droit pénal* 613.

[123] Nigel Rodley, *The Treatment of Prisoners Under International Law*, Paris: Unesco, Oxford: Clarendon Press, 1987, p. 170. The declaration can be found in UN Doc. E/AC.57/30; C. of E. Doc. 5409, pp. 22–23; (1978) 33 *Revue de science criminelle et de droit pénal comparé* n.s. 469 (French only). The Stockholm declaration described the death penalty as 'the ultimate cruel, inhuman and degrading punishment' that 'violates the right to life'. It called upon non-governmental organizations, both national and international, to work collectively and individually to provide informational materials directed towards the abolition of the death penalty, demanded that all governments bring about the immediate and total abolition of the death penalty, and insisted that the United Nations unambiguously declare that the death penalty is contrary to international law. The Stockholm conference assembled more than 200 delegates and participants from Africa, Asia, Europe, the Middle East, North and South America, and the Caribbean region.

[124] See a speech by Broda to a meeting of European death penalty coordinators of Amnesty International, Stockholm, 30 March 1985, AI Index: EUR/01/01/85.

[125] C. of E. Doc. 4509, Appendix III.

The European Committee on Crime Problems prepared an opinion that noted the widespread abolition of the death penalty *de jure* and recommended that new norms be adopted with a view to abolition. It proposed that, while these norms were being prepared, use of the death penalty should be suspended. The Steering Committee on Human Rights also drafted an opinion, stating that the time had come for the Council of Europe to consider either aligning article 2 of the *Convention* with the more recent article 4 of the *American Convention on Human Rights* or simply abolishing the death penalty. A third suggestion was that the Committee of Ministers make a recommendation to governments concerning abolition.

In May 1980, spurred by an announcement the previous year from the Austrian and West German Ministers of Justice, the Conference of European Ministers of Justice took up the question of abolition. The Ministers noted that article 2 of the *European Convention* 'does not adequately reflect the situation actually attained in regard to the death penalty in Europe' and recommended that the Committee of Ministers study the possibility of establishing new norms in Europe that would contemplate abolition of the death penalty. The meeting suggested two solutions: amendment of article 2 of the *European Convention*, along the lines of similar 'amending' protocols, notably numbers 3 and 5,[126] or alternatively, adoption of an optional protocol requiring a certain number of ratifications before it would come into force. Following an informal meeting in September, the Ministers of Justice expressed great interest in any domestic plans for abolition and at efforts undertaken to that effect on an international scale, notably within the Council of Europe.

Parallel to this activity, the Committee on Legal Affairs, which had quietly abandoned the issue in January 1976 following the resignation of Lidgard, also revived the question in 1979. It assigned another Swede, this time a Social Democrat named Lidbom, to prepare a new report. Lidbom's draft report was confined to the death penalty in peacetime and was discussed at a number of sessions of the Committee during 1979. The Committee's draft recommendation was adopted by twelve votes to six with two abstentions and then submitted, with the Lidbom report, to the Parliamentary Assembly in early 1980.[127] The report noted that the death penalty was 'inconsistent with the new trends in criminology and criminal law', and that furthermore it was also contrary to human rights law,[128] notably the right to be protected from inhuman and degrading treatment or punishment, as provided by article 3 of the *European Convention*.[129] The

---

[126] *Protocol No. 3 to the Convention for the Protection of Human Rights and Fundamental Freedoms, amending Articles 29, 30 and 34 of the Convention*, ETS 45; *Protocol No. 5 to the Convention for the Protection of Human Rights and Fundamental Freedoms, amending Articles 22 and 40 of the Convention*, ETS 55.
[127] C. of E. Doc. 4509.   [128] *Ibid.*, para. 23, p. 12.
[129] The report said that the death penalty was 'undoubtedly' contrary to article 3 of the *Convention*. C. of E. Doc. 4509, para. 4, p. 14. In support of this rather bold interpretation, it noted that the European

report noted that: 'Legally speaking, however, the European Convention on Human Rights does not preclude capital punishment. Article 2 even allows it *expressis verbis.*'[130] The report concluded that article 2 of the *European Convention on Human Rights* should be amended in order to abolish capital punishment.[131]

The Committee on Legal Affairs presented draft Resolution 727 to the Council of Europe's Parliamentary Assembly, appealing to parliaments of European Member States to abolish the death penalty for crimes committed in times of peace.[132] It also submitted a Recommendation, calling on the Committee of Ministers to amend article 2 of the *European Convention.*[133] The proposals were introduced in the Assembly by *rapporteur* Lidbom, who noted that the Committee had dealt only with the death penalty in peacetime, not because of principle but out of a concern to proceed in stages, so as to be certain to reach a positive result.[134] Lidbom said it was illusory to think that all forms of barbarism could be outlawed, and for that reason, on his suggestion, the Committee had not considered the death penalty in wartime in its resolution. He noted that the draft recommendation sought to focus attention on an 'inherent contradiction' in the *European Convention*: article 3 prohibits torture and inhuman or degrading treatment, yet article 2 explicitly permits the death penalty. Abolition of the death penalty would resolve this contradiction, said Lidbom, and the Committee proposed, therefore, that the Committee of Ministers of the Council of Europe proceed with a 'revision' of the *Convention.*[135]

Lidbom explained to the Assembly that although the death penalty still existed on the statute books of seven of the twenty-one members of the Council of Europe, in virtually all of those seven countries it had not been applied in practice for many years. France was the only exception, with three executions

---

Court of Human Rights had decided that even corporal punishment was a violation of the *Convention*: *Tyrer* v. *United Kingdom*, 25 April 1978, Series A, Vol. 26, 2 EHRR 1, 59 ILR 339. However, the European Court has since ruled out such an interpretation of article 3 of the *Convention*: *Soering* v. *United Kingdom*.

[130] C. of E. Doc. 4509, para. 25, p. 13.   [131] *Ibid.*, para. 5, p. 22.

[132] *Ibid.*, p. 1:

The Assembly

1. Considering that capital punishment is inhuman,

2. Appeals to the parliaments of those member states of the Council of Europe which have retained capital punishment for crimes committed in times of peace, to abolish it from their penal systems.

[133] C. of E. Doc. 4509, pp. 1–2:

The Assembly

1. Referring to its Resolution 727 (1980) on the abolition of capital punishment,

2. Considering that Article 2 of the European Convention on Human Rights recognizes everyone's right to life, but provides that a person may be deprived of his life intentionally in the execution of a sentence of a court following his conviction of a crime for which this penalty is provided by law.

3. Recommends that the Committee of Ministers amend Article 2 of the European Convention on Human Rights to bring it into line with Assembly Resolution 727 (1980).'

[134] Council of Europe, Parliamentary Assembly, 22 April 1980, pp. 52–53.   [135] *Ibid.*, p. 53.

since the election of Giscard d'Estaing as President in 1974,[136] and for that reason Lidbom addressed a special appeal.[137]

Lidbom was supported by a number of speakers, including a French representative, Mercier.[138] The entire delegations of Switzerland,[139] Denmark,[140] Germany[141] and Spain backed the draft resolution and recommendation.[142] However, Smith of the United Kingdom said the Council had no business addressing an issue which related to political problems of Member States. He said that in most countries that had abolished the death penalty, a majority of the population was opposed to such a measure.[143] A Turkish member of the Assembly, Aksoy, said that he supported the report and the recommendation 'in principle', but that it did not take sufficient account of the particular situation of certain Member States. He suggested that because of differing economic, social and political structures it was not possible to apply identical sentences in all countries. Were he Swedish, Swiss, Norwegian, Austrian or German, he would most certainly support total abolition of the death penalty, said Aksoy. Yet it would be a grave error to recommend abolition in countries where political assassination and terrorism are organized on a systematic scale.[144] Aksoy submitted an amendment to the recommendation which gave effect to these comments.[145] Aksoy was, however, not present at the time of the voting. As no other member desired to speak in defence of the amendment, the chairman declared it withdrawn.[146]

The Parliamentary Assembly adopted Resolution 727[147] and Recommendation 891,[148] decisions which were endorsed shortly afterwards by the Committee of Ministers. Later that year, the Committee asked the Steering Committee

---

[136] The last execution in France took place in 1977. See: Robert Badinter, 'France: The Abolition of Capital Punishment: The French Experience', (1984) 11 *United Nations Crime Prevention and Criminal Justice Newsletter* 17; Jean Bloch-Michel, 'La peine de mort en France', in Albert Camus, Arthur Koestler, eds., *Réflexions sur la peine capitale*, Paris: Clamann-Lévy, 1957.

[137] Council of Europe, Parliamentary Assembly, 22 April 1980, p. 54.

[138] *Ibid.*, p. 55. [138] *Ibid.*, p. 60. [139] *Ibid.*, p. 66. [140] *Ibid.*, p. 65. [141] *Ibid.*, p. 60.

[143] *Ibid.*, pp. 58–59. See also Banks of the United Kingdom at pp. 78–79; Beith of the United Kingdom at pp. 80–81; Grieve of the United Kingdom at pp. 86–87; Michel of Belgium at p. 59.

[144] *Ibid.*, pp. 57–58. Turkish representative Karamollaoglu declared he would vote against the proposition: p. 68.

[145] C. of E. Doc. 4509, Amendment No. 2:

    3. Recommends that the Committee of Ministers amend Article 2 of the European Convention on Human Rights to the following effect:

    i. The death penalty shall be abolished in the member states of the Council of Europe.

    ii. The death penalty may, however, be kept during peacetime for organized murder in those member states in which people are frequently assassinated by terrorist acts because of their political opinions and where the right to life of all people is thus seriously threatened.'

[146] Council of Europe, Parliamentary Assembly, 22 April 1980, p. 88. An amendment by Cavaliere of Italy adding the words 'at least for political offences and for all other offences which have not intentionally resulted in the death of one or more persons' to paragraph 2 was also withdrawn: C. of E. Doc. 4509, Amendment No. 1; Council of Europe, Parliamentary Assembly, 22 April 1980, pp. 63–64, 87.

[147] *Ibid.*, p. 87, by show of hands, no roll-call vote being requested. It was identified as Resolution 727.

[148] *Ibid.*, p. 89, by ninety-eight in favour, twenty-five opposed and no abstentions.

on Human Rights and the European Committee on Crime Problems to prepare an opinion on action to be taken with the aim of abolition of the death penalty, referring directly to the idea of an 'additional protocol'. The two Committees drafted a joint opinion, concluding that it would be difficult to adopt an amending protocol, because it seemed very unlikely to rally the support of all parties to the *Convention*, and recommending instead that an additional or optional protocol be considered. The two Committees observed that they had no mandate to draft such an instrument. During these meetings both the United Kingdom and Turkey manifested their opposition to the idea of any protocol, the United Kingdom because this was a matter for the conscience of individual parliamentarians, and Turkey because it simply did not feel it was in a position to abolish the death penalty.

In light of these reports, in September 1981, the Committee of Ministers mandated the Steering Committee on Human Rights to prepare a draft protocol concerning abolition of the death penalty 'in time of peace',[149] fixing a deadline of June 1982. The Steering Committee met in November 1981 and again in April 1982, when it completed its report, together with a draft additional protocol, for submission to the Committee of Ministers.[150]

At a meeting of Deputies in September 1982, the Steering Committee's draft additional protocol to the *Convention* was discussed and approved. The Secretariat was asked to prepare a synoptic report for the Committee of Ministers meeting in December 1982. The Committee of Ministers made no changes to the draft that had been accepted by the Deputies in September and formally adopted the text of the protocol at its 354th meeting, held from 6–10 December 1982.[151] On 28 April 1983 *Protocol No. 6* was signed by

---

[149] 'Explanatory Report on Protocol No. 6', C. of E. Doc. H(83) 3, (1982) 25 *YECHR* Part I, Chapter 4, p. 24, 5 *HRLJ* 78.

[150] C. of E. Doc. H/INF (82) 1, p. 20. On 27 April 1982, the Committee of Ministers was asked by a member of the Parliamentary Assembly to provide a progress report on the Protocol, and it replied: 'In its provisional reply to Recommendation 891 (Doc. 4659), to which Mr Flanagan refers, the Committee of Ministers pointed out that it had instructed the European Committee on Crime Problems (CDPC) and the Steering Committee for Human Rights (CDDH) to draw up an opinion on action which would be taken with a view to the abolition of the death penalty in time of peace, including the possibility of elaborating an additional protocol to the European Convention on Human Rights or a recommendation to member states. In their joint opinion, the two steering committees reached the conclusion that 'the adoption of an additional protocol to the European convention on human rights, modelled on protocols 1 and 4, would be a possible solution'. In the light of this opinion, the Committee of Ministers instructed the CDDH to prepare a draft additional protocol to the European Convention on Human Rights abolishing the death penalty in peacetime. The Committee of Ministers, which has recently received this draft, will naturally inform the Assembly of the outcome of its examination.'

[151] Announced in the Parliamentary Assembly on 26 January 1983. See also Press Release I (83) 5 of 26 January 1983. Several brief articles have been written on the *Protocol*: A. Adinolfi, 'Premier instrument international sur l'abolition de la peine de mort', (1987) 58 *Revue internationale de droit pénal* 321; Peter Leuprecht, 'The First International Instrument for the Abolition of the Death Penalty', (1983) 2 *Forum* 2; Erik Harremoes, 'The Council of Europe and Its Efforts to Promote the Abolition of the Death Penalty',

representatives of Austria, Belgium, Denmark, France,[152] Germany, Luxemburg, the Netherlands, Norway, Portugal, Spain, Sweden and Switzerland. The *Protocol* entered into force on 1 March 1985.

7.2.2 *Interpretation of the* Protocol

The instructions from the Committee of Ministers to the Steering Committee on Human Rights had been to draft a protocol providing for abolition of the death penalty 'in peacetime'. However, this term does not appear in the title of the instrument. During the drafting, it was argued that the title should specify this point, but it was decided this was unnecessary. There is no mention of 'peacetime' in article 1 either, despite the instructions from the Committee of Ministers and numerous proposals to this effect during the drafting process. The intention of the drafters was apparently to avoid drawing attention to the wartime exception. Although mention of wartime could not be totally avoided, it was considered important to stress that the goal of the *Protocol* was abolition purely and simply.

The preamble is succinct and makes no reference whatsoever to any substantive law. It does not, for example, refer to articles 2§1 or 3 of the *Convention* or suggest the relationship between that provision and the *Protocol*. During the drafting, there had been suggestions that the preamble be more extensive and that it include reference both to article 2§1 of the *Convention* and to the right to life, similar to the approach followed in the preamble to the *Second Optional Protocol*.[153] Nor does the preamble refer either to the right to life or to the issue of inhuman treatment, obviously a compromise that avoided irritating those members of the Council of Europe that had not yet abolished the death penalty. Furthermore, a reference to the prohibition of inhuman treatment might be difficult to explain in an instrument that only partially abolished the death penalty.

Article 1 of *Protocol No. 6* establishes three principles: the death penalty shall be abolished, no one may be condemned to death and no one may be

---

(1986) 12–13 *United Nations Crime Prevention and Criminal Justice Newsletter* 62; Gilbert Guillaume, 'Protocole no 6, article 1–4', in Pettiti, Decaux, Imbert, *La Convention européenne*, pp. 1067–1072.

[152] In France, ratification of *Protocol No. 6* provoked a debate in the National Assembly on the grounds that it would impinge on its sovereignty (*Journal officiel des débats parlementaires, Assemblée nationale*, 4 July 1983, p. 2938; *Journal officiel des débats parlementaires, Assemblée nationale*, 21 June 1985, pp. 1867–1889) and violate article 16 of the *Constitution*. The matter was submitted to the Conseil constitutionnel, which noted that it was constitutionally permissible to ratify the *Protocol*, and which stressed the fact that the *Protocol* could always be denounced, under the terms of article 65 of the *Convention*; see also Louis Favoreu, 'La décision du conseil constitutionnel du 22 mai 1985 relative au protocole no 6 additionnel à la Convention européenne des droits de l'homme', [1985] *AFDI* 868; Cohen-Jonathan, *La Convention européenne*, pp. 279–280.

[153] The draft second optional protocol *which* had been proposed by a number of European States in 1980 left room for preambular paragraphs, but did not spell out their content: UN Doc. A/C.3/35/L.75.

executed. The English version declares 'the death penalty shall be abolished', imposing an obligation on States parties to abolish the death penalty.[154] The French version states 'La peine de mort est abolie', a formulation that is more clearly self-executing, in countries whose constitution provides for such immediate effect of ratification of international treaties.[155] No explanation for the discrepancy is provided in the 'Explanatory Report to the Protocol' accompanying the *Protocol*. The 'Explanatory Report' was drafted by the Steering Committee on Human Rights and adopted by the Committee of Ministers, and as such it represents a form of official interpretation or commentary on the *Protocol*.

The second sentence of article 1 prohibits execution, even in the case of an individual condemned to death prior to the entry into force of the *Protocol*. The death penalty may be neither pronounced nor carried out by States parties to the *Protocol*. According to the 'Explanatory Report', '[t]he second sentence of [article 1] aims to underline the fact that the right guaranteed is a subjective right of the individual'.[156] As an individual right, rather than merely an obligation upon States parties, it becomes subject to the petition mechanisms of the *European Convention*.

Article 2 sets out the sole exception to the principle of abolition, that a State may make provision in its law for the death penalty in respect of acts committed in time of war or of imminent threat of war. The principal effect of article 2 is to confirm that the *Protocol* applies only in time of peace. Consequently, the abolitionist scope of the *Protocol* is not as extensive as the corresponding protocols in the United Nations and Inter-American systems, the latter instruments abolishing the death penalty in wartime as well, although they permit States parties to make reservations on this point.[157] The only condition for the application of article 2 is that the State party must notify the Secretary-General of the Council of Europe as to the relevant provisions of such laws. The language of article 2 suggests that such notification may be made at any time and that it may also be changed.

The drafters had considerable difficulty agreeing upon the text of article 2, and the result is an attempt to satisfy different perspectives. Some would have preferred a general declaration abolishing the death penalty, but allowing reservations in wartime as in the *Second Optional Protocol to the International Covenant on Civil and Political Rights*. Another proposal was a text declaring the death penalty abolished 'in peacetime', an approach which would have necessitated some definition of the term 'peacetime'. The result is a compromise, a principle accompanied by an exception but with no possibility of reservation.[158]

---

[154] Harremoes, 'The Council of Europe', at p. 63.
[155] Guillaume, 'Protocole no 6, article 1–4', at p. 1068.   [156] C. of E. Doc. H(83)3.
[157] The Council of Europe is now attempting to correct the situation with yet another protocol, discussed later in this Chapter.
[158] Guillaume, 'Protocole no 6, article 1–4', at p. 1069.

During the drafting, there were suggestions that the terms 'time of war or of imminent threat of war' be replaced by 'international armed conflict', which is the expression used in *Protocol Additional I to the 1949 Geneva Conventions.* However, the term 'time of war' was retained because the same expression is used in article 15 of the *European Convention*, a provision which permits derogation from the provisions of the *Convention* 'in time of war or other public emergency threatening the life of the nation'.[159]

Would it be possible, in accordance with article 1 of the *Protocol*, for a State party to impose the death penalty in a time of internal armed conflict or civil war? The fact that the drafters of the *Protocol* did not copy the wording of article 15, dropping the phrase 'other public emergency threatening the life of the nation', suggests that internal strife is not the same as 'time of war'. Had the proposal to refer to 'international armed conflict' been followed, it would have dispelled any doubt about the scope of article 2, in effect referring to the definition of 'international armed conflict' in article 1 of *Protocol Additional I*. Scholars have maintained that the reference to 'war' excludes civil war on the premise that, had this been the intention, it would have been mentioned expressly.[160]

At international law, a 'state of war' may exist in the absence of hostilities.[161] Sir Nigel Rodley argues, however, that a 'state of war' is a legal status requiring a declaration by at least one of the parties and that armed conflict falling short of this standard is not envisaged by the *Protocol.*[162] Because the *Protocol* uses the phrase 'or imminent threat of war', it would seem that the intention of the drafters was to avoid technical debates about when a war was formally declared. The purpose of adding the latter term is to eliminate formalism concerning the beginning of a war and to disallow States parties to extend the death penalty to a variety of crises on the pretext that war is remotely foreseeable. It should be noted that the companion to the *European Convention*, the *European Social Charter*, states that 'time of war' also means '*threat* of war'.[163]

According to Rusen Ergec, war as it is contemplated by article 15 of the *European Convention* 'peut être définie comme un affrontement armé d'une certaine envergure et d'une certaine durée conduite par des armées organisées sous la responsabilité des gouvernements respectifs dont elles relèvent'.[164] However, not

---

[159] According to Velu and Ergec, the reference is to war in a material sense and not just a formal one: Velu, Ergec, *La Convention européenne*, p. 185.

[160] Rodley, *The Treatment of Prisoners*, p. 173. Also: Velu, Ergec, *La Convention européenne*, p. 185. See our comments on this subject in Chapter 4, with respect to the *Second Optional Protocol to the International Covenant on Civil and Political Rights Aiming at Abolition of the Death Penalty*, above at pp. 183–186.

[161] O. Wright, 'When Does War Exist?', (1932) 26 *AJIL* 363; L. Delbaz, 'La notion juridique de guerre', (1953) 62 *RGDIP* 193.

[162] Rodley, *The Treatment of Prisoners*, at p. 172.

[163] (1965) 529 UNTS 89, ETS 35, Appendix, Part V (my italics).

[164] Ergec, *Les droits de l'homme*, p. 125. See also K. J. Parsch, 'Experiences Regarding the War and Emergency Clause (art. 15) of the European Convention on Human Rights', (1971) 1 *Israel Yearbook on Human Rights* 327.

any 'war' will be sufficient to allow exceptions to the *Protocol*. Again, by way of analogy with the scope of the term 'war' in article 15 of the *Convention*, it is very significant that the provision refers to 'time of war or *other* emergency threatening the life of the nation', indicating that a war must at the same time constitute an 'emergency threatening the life of the nation'.[165] Recent wars in which European States were involved, such as the Malvinas/Falklands war between the United Kingdom and Argentina, and the Gulf War of 1991, probably do not meet this standard.

'Time of war' should not be confused with the military death penalty. Many States provide for capital punishment in their military code but not in their general criminal law.[166] The military death penalty is proscribed by *Protocol No. 6*, except of course in time of war. Unlike the *Second Optional Protocol*, which only permits the death penalty for military crimes of a serious nature, *Protocol No. 6* establishes no limit *ratione materiae* on use of the death penalty during wartime. During the drafting of the *Protocol*, suggestions were made that the instrument restrict the death penalty in wartime to the 'most serious crimes', but these were rejected.[167] In any case, the *European Convention* continues to apply, and an execution imposed in wartime for a crime that was not very serious could violate articles 2 and 3 of the *Convention*. Furthermore, in time of war, the provisions of international humanitarian law take effect, although they are not applicable in time of 'imminent threat of war'.

Declarations have been made pursuant to article 2, by Switzerland, the Netherlands, Cyprus and Ukraine.[168] These States have legislation allowing for the death penalty in time of war, but none of them confines this to cases of 'an emergency threatening the life of the nation'. The Human Rights Chamber for Bosnia and Herzegovina, interpreting article 2 of *Protocol No. 6*,[169] has considered it insufficient that existing legislation providing for the death penalty be applied in time of war or imminent threat thereof. It is essential that the legislator actually contemplate the possibility of imposing capital punishment under such circumstances.

> the Chamber considers that before Article 2 of Protocol No. 6 can apply there must be specific provision in domestic law authorising the use of the death penalty in respect of defined acts committed in time of war or of imminent threat of war. The law must define with adequate precision the acts in respect of which the death penalty may be

---

[165] The European Court of Human Rights has amplified the term, explaining that it refers to an 'exceptional and imminent situation of crisis and emergency which affects the whole population and constitutes a threat to the organized life of the community of which a state is composed': *Lawless* v. *United Kingdom*, 1 July 1961, Series A, Vol. 2, para. 28.

[166] Christine van den Wyngaert, 'Military Offences, International Crimes and the Death Penalty', (1987) 58 *Revue internationale de droit pénal* 737.

[167] Guillaume, 'Protocole no 6, article 1–4', at p. 1069.

[168] See Appendix 15, at pp. 424–429, for the texts of the declarations.

[169] *Protocol No. 6* is incorporated in the Constitution of Bosnia and Herzegovina, although the State is not yet a member of the Council of Europe and cannot therefore sign or ratify the instrument.

applied, the circumstances in which it may be applied, and the concepts of 'time of war or of imminent threat of war'. Article 2 requires that before it can apply the legislature should have considered and defined the circumstances in which, exceptionally in the context of a legal system where the death penalty has been abolished, such penalty may nevertheless be applied in respect of acts committed in time of war or imminent threat thereof.[170]

There is no provision for renewal or withdrawal of the declaration envisaged in article 2, and no indication either of the consequence of the failure to make such a declaration. Some States whose legislation has allowed for the death penalty in wartime – Spain,[171] Italy[172] and Malta[173] – have ratified the *Protocol* without making any declaration under article 2. The text is looser and more permissive than typical 'derogation' clauses, which imply that in the absence of formal notice of derogation there is clear violation of the substantive clauses of the instrument. Failure to notify the Council of legislation concerning the death penalty in wartime is a breach article 2 of the *Protocol* but may not foreclose a State from actually employing the death penalty in time of war or imminent danger of war. A suggestion that the wartime exception be formulated as a possibility of reservation, an approach subsequently adopted in the United Nations and Inter-American protocols, was rejected by the drafters.

Article 3 of the *Protocol* prohibits any derogation by virtue of article 15 of the *European Convention*. Ordinarily article 15 would apply to an additional protocol to the *Convention*, permitting States parties to derogate in time of war or public emergency threatening the life of the nation. The *Protocol* does not apply in time of war, where there is a clear overlap between its article 2 and article 15 of the *Convention*. However, without such a provision, it would have been possible for States to avoid the provisions of the *Protocol* in time of 'other public emergency threatening the life of the nation', by making a formal derogation.

Although reservations to the *Protocol* are excluded by article 4, it would seem possible to make interpretative declarations.[174] Germany made an interpretative declaration to the effect that its non-criminal legislation is not affected

---

[170] *Damjanovic* v. *Federation of Bosnia and Herzegovina*, para. 32.

[171] The death penalty in wartime in Spain was also discussed in the Human Rights Committee: 'Third Periodic Report of Spain', UN Doc. CCPR/C/58/Add. 1 and 3, UN Doc. CCPR/C/SR.1018–1021, UN Doc. A/46/40, pp. 35–45. Note that Spain made a reservation to this effect when it ratified the *Second Optional Protocol* (for the text of Spain's reservation, see Appendix 4, p. 399). The reservation was withdrawn on 13 January 1998.

[172] Italy was challenged about its maintenance of the death penalty in wartime by Sir Vincent Evans in the Human Rights Committee: UN Doc. CCPR/C/SR.257, §37. In 1994, Italy abolished the death penalty in wartime as well as in peacetime.

[173] Malta ratified the *Protocol* on 26 March 1991 and it came into force on 1 April 1991. Note that Malta made a reservation to this effect when it ratified the *Second Optional Protocol* (for the text of Malta's reservation, see Appendix 4, p. 400). Malta's reservation was withdrawn on 15 June 2000.

[174] *Ibid.* For the distinction between reservations and interpretative declarations, see: *Belilos* v. *Switzerland*, 29 April 1988, Series A, Vol. 132, 10 EHRR 466, 88 ILR 635. The same rule has been accepted by the Human Rights Committee: 'General Comment No. 24 (52)', UN Doc. CCPR/C/21/Rev.1/Add.6 at §3; *T.K.* v. *France* (No. 220/1987), UN Doc. A/45/40, Vol. II, p. 118,

by the *Protocol*. Furthermore, according to article 5, a State may specify the territory or territories to which the *Protocol* shall apply.[175] The German declaration states that its government considers the *Protocol* to contain no other obligation than to abolish the death penalty in its domestic legislation, something it points out Germany has already done. Unlike the declaration under article 2, an 'interpretative declaration' must be made at the time of ratification, acceptance or approval.

A State may extend the protection of the *Protocol* to territories excluded in the initial declaration but may not do the opposite, that is, withdraw the protection of the *Protocol* from specified territories. The declaration by the Netherlands extended the protection of the *Protocol* to its Caribbean territories. The declaration by Germany extended the protection of the *Protocol* to Berlin, something which became quickly obsolete with the reunification of Germany and the extension of the *Protocol's* scope to the entire German territory. In a *Protocol No. 6* application against Portugal by a Chinese national threatened with deportation from Macao, the European Court of Human Rights found it was without jurisdiction *ratione loci* because of the absence of such a declaration.[176]

Article 6 of the *Protocol* explains that its provisions shall be considered to be additional articles to the *Convention*, with the consequence that the protection mechanisms established by the *Convention* applies. It also ensures that article 2§1 of the *Convention* continues to apply in cases where the death penalty is imposed in time of war or imminent threat of war. According to Pierre-Henri Imbert, the fact that States parties to *Protocol No. 6* are automatically subject to the jurisdiction of the Commission of the Court is further evidence of the absolute character of abolition of the death penalty, which was the objective of the drafters of the *Protocol*.[177]

The *Protocol* provides that it comes into force with five ratifications. There were suggestions that this be increased to seven and even ten, but the drafters eventually returned to the original proposal of the Steering Committee on Human Rights back in 1979. The *Protocol* can only be denounced pursuant to the conditions set out in the *European Convention*, which states that such action may not be taken until five years have elapsed since ratification. Moreover, notice of six months must be provided before denunciation is legally effective. During the drafting of the *Protocol*, it was proposed that the terms of

para. 8.6. See: Donald McRae, 'The Legal Effect of Interpretative Declarations', (1978) 49 *BYIL* 160; Gérald Cohen-Jonathan, 'Les réserves à la Convention européenne des droits de l'homme (à propos de l'arrêt Belilos du 29 avril 1988)', (1989) 93 *RGDIP* 273.

[175] Michael Wood, 'Protocole no 6, article 5', in Pettiti, Decaux, Imbert, *La Convention européenne*, p. 1073.

[176] *Yonghong* v. *Portugal* (No. 50887/99), Decision, 15 November 1999.

[177] Pierre-Henri Imbert, 'Protocole no 6, article 6', in Pettiti, Decaux, Imbert, *La Convention européenne*, p. 1075.

denunciation be made less onerous, for example, by providing for a notice period of six months but no minimum period of application of the *Protocol*. The drafters opted for a mechanism that mirrored that of the other additional protocols to the *Convention*.[178]

Protocol No. 6 has been invoked in cases before the Court and, prior to its abolition, the European Commission. Several applications have been lodged against the Netherlands by drug traffickers threatened with deportation to Malaysia, where they might be exposed to the mandatory death sentence. The applicants maintained that this was contrary to both article 3 of the *Convention* and article 1 of *Protocol No. 6*. The Commission recalled authorities under the *Convention*, notably *Soering* v. *United Kingdom*, by which the decision to deport a person may give rise to an issue under article 3 and engage the responsibility of the State:

> The question arises whether analogous considerations apply to Article 1 of Protocol No. 6 to the Convention, in particular whether this provision equally engages the responsibility of a Contracting State where, upon deportation, the person concerned faces a real risk of being subjected to the death penalty in the receiving state. The question also arises whether if Article 1 of Protocol No. 6 cannot engage the responsibility of a Contracting State in such circumstances, Article 3 of the Convention may serve to prohibit deportation to a country where the person concerned may be subjected to the treatment complained of.[179]

The Commission concluded that the evidence submitted by the applicant that he would be subject to prosecution for drug trafficking was insufficiently substantiated. As a result, the applications were declared inadmissible. In another case, involving extradition from Austria to the Russian Federation to stand trial for murder, the Commission noted a maximum sentence of ten years in the Penal Code of the Russian Federation and the fact that two accomplices had been sentenced to nine years, concluding that 'there are no substantial grounds for believing that the applicant faces a real risk of being subjected to the death penalty in the Russian Federation'.

Protocol No. 6 has also been cited in domestic law in cases concerning extradition of fugitives to States imposing the death penalty. On two occasions, the French Conseil d'État has refused to extradite, expressing the view that *Protocol No. 6* establishes a European *ordre public* that prohibits extradition in capital cases.[180] The Supreme Court of the Netherlands took a similar

---

[178] Guillaume, 'Protocole no 6, article 1–4'.

[179] *App. No. 15216/89* v. *Netherlands*, unreported decision on admissibility of 16 January 1991; *Y.* v. *Netherlands* (App. No. 16531/90), (1991) 68 DR 299.

[180] *Fidan*, *Gacem*. *Fidan* was cited by Judge De Meyer in his concurring opinion in *Soering* v. *United Kingdom*, at p. 51.

view, invoking the *Protocol* in refusing to return a United States serviceman,[181] although required to do so by the *NATO Status of Forces Agreement*.[182] The Court considered that the *European Convention* and its *Protocol No. 6* took precedence over the other treaty.

Protocol No. 6 has even been cited before domestic courts of non-European states as a demonstration of the breadth of international sentiment in favour of the abolition of the death penalty.[183] In *United States* v. *Burns*, decided on 15 February 2001, the Supreme Court of Canada noted that 'a significant number of countries' had either signed or ratified *Protocol No. 6* since the Court had last examined the issue of capital punishment, a decade earlier. This was taken as evidence of the international trend towards the abolition of capital punishment.[184] Its influence has even been felt deep within the United States, in the death-penalty state of Ohio. In the Dayton Peace Agreement, signed at Paris on 14 December 1995, the new state of Bosnia and Herzegovina was held to the highest standard of compliance with contemporary human rights norms. The country's Constitution, which is also Annex IV of the Dayton Agreement, declares: 'The rights and freedoms set forth in the European Convention for the Protection of Human Rights and Fundamental Freedoms and its Protocols shall apply directly in Bosnia and Herzegovina. These shall have priority over all other law.'[185] Accordingly, capital punishment is abolished because *Protocol No. 6* is directly incorporated into the laws of Bosnia and Herzegovina.[186]

In 1994, the Parliamentary Assembly of the Council of Europe adopted a resolution calling upon Member States that had not yet done so to ratify *Protocol No. 6*. The resolution praised Greece, which in 1993 had abolished the death penalty for crimes committed in wartime as well as in peacetime. It stated: 'In view of the irrefutable arguments against the imposition of capital punishment, it calls on the parliaments of all Member States of the Council of Europe, and of all states whose legislative assemblies enjoy special guest status at the Assembly,

---

[181] *Short* v. *The Netherlands*.

[182] *Agreement Between the Parties to the 1949 North Atlantic Treaty Regarding the Status of Their Forces*, (1951) 199 UNTS 67. Note that on 19 June 1995, the States parties to the NATO treaty finalized the *Agreement among the States Parties to the North Atlantic Treaty and the Other States Participating in the Partnership for Peace Regarding the Status of Their Forces* together with an *Additional Protocol*. Article 1 of the *Additional Protocol* states: 'Insofar as it has jurisdiction according to the provisions of the agreement, each State party to the present additional protocol shall not carry out a death sentence with regard to any member of a force and its civilian component, and their dependents from any other State party to the present additional protocol.'

[183] *Kindler* v. *Canada*; *S.* v. *Makwanyane*, 1995 (3) SA 391, (1995) 16 *HRLJ* 154; *Catholic Commission for Justice and Peace in Zimbabwe* v. *Attorney-General et al.*

[184] *United States* v. *Burns*, para. 87.

[185] *General Framework Agreement for Peace in Bosnia and Herzegovina*, Annex 4: Constitution of Bosnia and Herzegovina, art. II§2. Also: *Ibid.*, Annex I, para. 7; *General Framework Agreement for Peace in Bosnia and Herzegovina*, Annex 6: Agreement on Human Rights, art. 1.

[186] *Damjanovic* v. *Federation of Bosnia and Herzegovina*.

which retain capital punishment for crimes committed in peacetime and/or in wartime, to strike it from their statute books completely.' It also affirmed that willingness to ratify *Protocol No. 6* be made a prerequisite for membership of the Council of Europe. It concluded by urging all heads of state and all parliaments in whose countries death sentences are passed to grant clemency to the convicted.[187]

On the same date, the Parliamentary Assembly also adopted a Recommendation that deplored the fact that the death penalty was still provided by law in eleven Council of Europe Member States and seven States whose legislative assemblies had special status with respect to the organization.[188] The Assembly expressed shock that fifty-nine people were legally put to death in Europe in 1993, and that at least 575 prisoners were known to be awaiting their execution. The Assembly said that application of the death penalty 'may well be compared with torture and be seen as inhuman and degrading punishment within the meaning of Article 3 of the *European Convention on Human Rights*'. The Recommendation urged the Committee of Ministers to draft an additional protocol to the *European Convention on Human Rights*, abolishing the death penalty both in peace- and wartime, and obliging the parties not to reintroduce it under any circumstances. The recommendation also proposed establishing a control mechanism that would oblige States where the death penalty was still provided by law to set up a commission with a view to abolishing capital punishment. A moratorium would be declared on all executions while the commissions fulfilled their tasks. The commissions would be required to notify the Secretary General of the Council of Europe of any death sentences passed and any executions scheduled without delay. Any country that had scheduled an execution would be required to halt it for a period of six months from the time of notification of the Secretary General. During this time the Secretary General would be empowered to send a delegation to conduct an investigation and make a recommendation to the country concerned. Finally, all States would be bound not to allow the extradition of any person to a country in which he or she risked being sentenced to death and subjected to the extreme conditions on 'death row'.

The Parliamentary Assembly's 1994 recommendation that a new protocol be adopted, abolishing the death penalty in wartime, was greeted favourably by the Council of Europe's Steering Committee for Human Rights. However, the Committee of Ministers, in its decision of 16 January 1996, considered that the political priority was moratoria on executions, to be consolidated by complete abolition of the death penalty.[189] The idea of a new protocol lingered until the

---

[187] Resolution 1044 (1994) on the abolition of capital punishment, 4 October 1994, para. 6.i.
[188] Recommendation 1246 (1994) on the abolition of capital punishment, 4 October 1994.
[189] This point was soon taken up by the Parliamentary Assembly in Recommendation 1302 (1996) on the abolition of the death penalty in Europe, 28 June 1996.

Ministerial Conference, held in Rome on 3–4 November 2000, to commemorate the fiftieth anniversary of the adoption of the *European Convention on Human Rights*. A resolution adopted at that meeting invited the Committee of Ministers 'to consider the feasibility of a new additional protocol to the Convention which would exclude the possibility of maintaining the death penalty in respect of acts committed in time of war or of imminent threat of war'.[190] A week later, the Committee of Ministers adopted a 'Declaration for a European Death Penalty-Free Area' that declared the achievement of the abolition of the death penalty in all Member States to be 'our common goal'. Sweden then took the initiative to prepare the text of a draft 'Protocol No. 13' whose legal effect would be to neutralize article 2 of *Protocol No. 6*, somewhat in the same way as *Protocol No. 6* neutralizes article 2§1 of the *Convention*. Sweden's proposal was presented to the 7 December 2000 meeting of Ministers' Deputies and, a month later, that body instructed the Steering Committee for Human Rights 'to study the Swedish proposal for a new protocol to the Convention . . . and submit its views on the feasibility of a new protocol on this matter'. Using the Swedish proposal as a basis, the Committee asked its Committee of Experts for the Development of Human Rights to finalize a draft protocol and an explanatory report.

The Committee of Experts for the Development of Human Rights addressed this mandate at its June 2001 meeting. There was little disagreement about the substantive and procedural provisions of the Swedish proposal, which essentially replicate *Protocol No. 6* except that article 2, which allows for capital punishment in time of war and imminent threat of war, has been eliminated. Most of the attention at the expert meeting was directed to the terms of the preamble. The proposed draft has a short preamble that refers to the *European Convention* and *Protocol No. 6*, noting that 'the abolition of the death penalty is essential for the full recognition of the inherent dignity of all human beings' and stressing that protection of the right to life 'is a basic value in a democratic society'. The draft explanatory report traces post-*Protocol No. 6* developments within the Council of Europe, such as the October 1997 Final Declaration at the Second Summit of Heads of State and Government of Member States of the Council of Europe, calling for 'universal abolition of the death penalty' and insisting upon 'the maintenance, in the meantime, of existing moratoria on executions in Europe'. The draft report also takes note of parallel developments within the European Union, and of the exclusion of the death penalty from the *Rome Statute of the International Criminal Court.*

Aside from the development of new normative instruments like *Protocol No. 6* and the new draft protocol, since the mid-1990s the political institutions

---

[190] Paragraph 14(ii) of Resolution IIB.

of the Council of Europe have aggressively pursued an abolitionist agenda, both within and without Member States. The Council was in a phase of rapid expansion, and several new members in Central and Eastern Europe that still had legislation allowing for the death penalty and, in some cases, still imposed it, had been admitted by the Committee of Ministers. What only a few years earlier had seemed an emerging abolitionist consensus within the organization was in danger of being dramatically diluted. Accordingly, on 18 June 1996, the Parliamentary Assembly requested that three new members of the Council of Europe, Russia, Ukraine and Latvia, abolish capital punishment, threatening them with exclusion if they did not. The Assembly rebuked the Committee of Ministers, urging it to pay more attention to the issue of the death penalty in admitting members to the Council.[191]

Capital punishment is one of six themes comprising the monitoring procedure of the Committee of Ministers, set up as a consequence of the first Summit of Heads of State and Government held in Vienna in 1993.[192] States have been requested to submit information on capital punishment.[193] This has led to exchanges in meetings of Ministers' Deputies, some of which have been made public.[194]

The relationship between the Council of Europe and Ukraine has been particularly difficult. On joining the Council in November 1995, Ukraine pledged a moratorium on the use of capital punishment. The Parliamentary Assembly had only pronounced itself in favour of admission after Ukraine committed itself to 'put into place, with immediate effect from the day of accession, a moratorium on executions'.[195] But in its 1996 resolution on capital punishment, the Assembly condemned Ukraine for not honouring this commitment, and spoke of consequences if there were further breaches.[196] On 29 January 1997, the Assembly warned the Ukrainian authorities 'that it will take all necessary steps to ensure compliance with commitments entered into', including, if necessary, the non-ratification of the credentials of the Ukrainian parliamentary delegation, at its next session in January 1998.[197] Following reports that thirteen executions had taken place in Ukraine in 1997, and a report by *rapporteur* Renate Wohlwend

---

[191] Resolution 1097 (1996).

[192] The procedure is outlined in detail in a memorandum prepared by the Secretary General's Monitoring Unit: 'Monitoring Procedure of the Committee of Ministers on the Theme Capital Punishment: Collection of Materials Declassified in February 2000', CM/Monitor (2000)3, AS/Inf (2000) 2.

[193] 'Capital Punishment: Information Submitted by Member States', AS/Inf (1999) 2 and CM/Monitor (99)2 rev., Addendum, AS/Inf (1999) 2 Addendum.

[194] Summary Records, 673rd Meeting of the Ministers' Deputies, 1 June 1999, CM/Del/Act(99)673, paras. 28–56; Summary Records, 683rd Meeting of the Ministers' Deputies, 13 and 17 November 1999, CM/Del/Act(99)683, paras. 11–12

[195] Opinion No. 190 on the Application by Ukraine for Membership of the Council of Europe.

[196] Resolution 1097 (1996), para. 2.   [197] Resolution 1112 (1997).

who said she could no longer trust the promises of the Ukrainian authorities,[198] the Parliamentary Assembly declared that '[w]hen the credentials of the delegation are examined at one of the next sittings of the Assembly or the Standing Committee, it should be taken into account whether the Ukrainian authorities have lifted the secrecy surrounding executions and have furnished documentary and undeniable proof that a moratorium on executions has been established in Ukraine'.[199] In January 1999, the Assembly adopted a resolution threatening to annul the credentials of the Ukrainian parliamentary delegation if substantial progress towards abolition was not made promptly.[200] In May 1999, the Council's Committee on the Honouring of Obligations and Commitments of Member States recommended that Ukraine be suspended from the Council. In June 1999, the Parliamentary Assembly granted that, although certain progress had been made, the process of suspending the Ukrainian delegation's rights should be initiated. The issue was finally resolved on 29 December 1999, when Ukraine's Constitutional Court ruled the death penalty to be contrary to the Constitution and ordered the Parliament to enact legislation abolishing capital punishment. The Constitutional Court invoked the right to life provision of the Constitution, noting that there was no exception allowed for using the death penalty. On 22 February 2000, Ukraine's Criminal Code was amended, replacing the death penalty with life imprisonment.

Belarus, the Russian Federation and Albania have also been challenged by the Parliamentary Assembly. In January 1997, the Parliamentary Assembly of the Council of Europe suspended the Belarus Parliament's special guest status following the constitutional changes introduced by President Lukashenko. At the same time, the Assembly also adopted Resolution 1111 (1997) addressing reports of continuing executions in Russia. The Parliamentary Assembly took action in 1999 against Albania, in a resolution expressing concern at statements by local politicians suggesting its moratorium on capital punishment might be terminated. The Assembly reminded Albania that any retreat on its commitment to introduce an immediate moratorium and to ratify *Protocol No. 6* within three years would have serious consequences for its membership of the Council of Europe. Albania's Constitutional Court, in a judgment of 10 December 1999, declared capital punishment in peacetime to be contrary to the country's new constitution. The abolitionist agenda of the Parliamentary Assembly was also reaffirmed in Resolution 1187 (1999), entitled 'Europe: A Death Penalty-Free Continent', adopted on 26 May 1999.

---

[198] Honouring of the Commitments by Ukraine to Introduce a Moratorium on Executions and Abolish the Death Penalty, Doc. 7974, 23 December 1997.
[199] Resolution 1145 (1998) Executions in Ukraine, para. 13. See also: Order No. 538 (1998) Executions in Ukraine.
[200] Resolution 1194 (1999).

By then, the death penalty had been essentially eradicated within the forty-three Member States of the Council of Europe, comprising a population of 800 million, with the exception of rebel-held parts of Chechnya in the Russian Federation, described by the Parliamentary Assembly as 'a consequence of a fundamentalist interpretation of the Sharia'.[201] The Parliamentary Assembly has now set its sights on States with observer status. Two of them, Japan and the United States, continue to impose capital punishment. In the two others, Canada and Mexico, the death penalty has been abolished. In June 2001, *rapporteur* Renate Wohlwend submitted a report to the Parliamentary Assembly recalling that observer States have to accept the principles of democracy, the rule of law and the enjoyment by all persons within its jurisdiction of human rights and fundamental freedoms, pursuant to Statutory Resolution (93) 26 on observer status.[202] On 25 June 2001, the Parliamentary Assembly adopted a resolution requiring Japan and the United States to put a moratorium on executions without delay, and to take steps towards abolition. The Parliamentary Assembly has set a deadline of January 2003.

7.3 Organization for Security and Cooperation in Europe

European States have brought the death penalty debate to the Organization (formerly the Conference) for Security and Cooperation in Europe (OSCE), but with only rather modest results. Historically, this was explained by the presence of a large number of retentionist States within the organization, including the United States and, until recently, the former republics of the Soviet Union and the States of Central and Eastern Europe. The OSCE is almost certainly the international organization in which the trend towards abolition of the death penalty is the most apparent. In 1998 and 1999 alone, seven participating States abolished the death penalty completely. Now, only the United States and a handful of Asian members of the organization actually impose the death penalty.[203] Capital punishment also remains in force in some separatist, internationally unrecognized entities within the OSCE region: Abkhazia and South-Ossetia (both within Georgia), Chechnya (within the Russian Federation), Nagorno-Karabakh (within Azerbaijan), and Transdniestria (within Moldova).

The question of capital punishment had not been addressed in the documents of the OSCE prior to 1989. That year, in the concluding document of the Vienna Follow-Up Meeting, the participating States simply 'note[d]' that capital punishment had been abolished 'in a number of them'. Participating States that

---

[201] See: Doc. 8340, para. 44.
[202] Abolition of the Death Penalty in Council of Europe Observer States, Doc. 9115, 7 June 2001.
[203] Belarus, Kazakhstan, Kyrgystan, Turkmenistan, United States and Uzbekistan.

had not abolished the death penalty committed themselves to imposing it 'only for the most serious crimes in accordance with the law in force at the time of the commission of the crime and not contrary to their international commitments', a provision that echoes article 6§1 of the *International Covenant on Civil and Political Rights*. Furthermore, participating States agreed to keep the question of capital punishment under consideration, and to co-operate on the issue within relevant international organizations.[204]

The issue returned almost immediately within the context of OSCE initiatives on the human dimension, as abolitionist States attempted to build on the cautious statement in the Vienna Document. A proposal from Portugal, Austria, Cyprus, France, the Federal Republic of Germany, Greece, Italy, Liechtenstein, Luxemburg, the Netherlands, San Marino, Spain and Switzerland noted that the death penalty was being abolished in 'most of the legal systems of the participating States within the context of an international human rights movement' and called for 'progressive abolition in peacetime' of the death penalty where it still exists.[205] However, the text was never adopted. In 1990, at the Copenhagen meeting of the Conference on the Human Dimension, there was a similar initiative. Reflecting recent political changes within Europe, the resolution was supported not only by its traditional Western European sponsors, but also by Czechoslovakia, the German Democratic Republic and Romania.[206] It took note of the adoption by the United Nations General Assembly, in December 1989, of the *Second Optional Protocol to the International Covenant on Civil and Political Rights*, called upon participating States to exchange information on national measures taken towards the abolition of the death penalty, and affirmed the principle of progressive abolition of the death penalty in peacetime where it still existed. A competing proposal, from Austria and the Scandinavian States, also called for an exchange of information, but eliminated reference to the desirability of progressive abolition.[207] This second text appears to have been the basis of the tame provisions that were finally incorporated into the *Document of the Copenhagen Meeting*.[208] Similar pronouncements have appeared in the document of the 1991

---

[204] *A Frame Work for Europe's Future, Concluding Document of the Vienna Follow-Up Meeting, 1989*, para. 24 (see Appendix 18, p. 433).
[205] 'Abolition of the Death Penalty, Proposal Submitted by Portugal, Austria, Cyprus, France, the FRG, Greece, Italy, Liechtenstein, Luxemburg, the Netherlands, San Marino, Spain and Switzerland', OSCE Doc. CSCE/CDHP.28, 19 June 1989.
[206] 'Abolition of the Death Penalty, Proposal Submitted by the Delegation of Portugal, and Those of Belgium, Cyprus, Czechoslovakia, France, the GDR, the FRG, Greece, Ireland, Italy, Liechtenstein, Luxemburg, the Netherlands, Romania, San Marino, Spain and Switzerland', OSCE Doc. CSCE/CHDC.18, 6 June 1990.
[207] 'Abolition of the Death Penalty, Proposal Submitted by the Delegations of Austria, Denmark, Finland, Iceland, Norway and Sweden', OSCE Doc. CSCE/CHDC.13, 8 June 1990.
[208] *Document of the Copenhagen Meeting of the Conference on the Human Dimension of the CSCE*, art. 17 (see Appendix 18, p. 433).

Moscow Meeting on the Human Dimension,[209] and they were reaffirmed at the 1992 Helsinki Summit and the 1994 Budapest Summit.[210]

Paragraph 17.7 of the *Copenhagen Document* declares that the participating States 'will exchange information within the framework of the Conference on the Human Dimension on the question of the abolition of the death penalty and keep that question under consideration'. Under paragraph 17.8, they are to make information on the death penalty available to the public. In this context, the OSCE's Office for Democratic Institutions and Human Rights (ODIHR) has been asked to act as a clearing house. However, some of the participating States have refused to disclose information regarding capital punishment, in violation of their commitments. A recent publication of the OSCE noted that '[s]everal governments, including the governments of Belarus, Kazakhstan, Tajikistan, Turkmenistan, and Uzbekistan, regard information related to capital punishment as a state secret and refuse to disclose relevant material – a practice that is in clear contradiction to paragraph 17.8 of the Copenhagen Document'.[211]

Abolition of the death penalty has been regularly addressed at the Supplementary Human Dimension Meetings, which are organized jointly by the OSCE Chairman-in-Office and ODIHR. It was considered at the Implementation Meeting on the Human Dimension, held in Warsaw in late 1993, under the agenda item 'Exchange of information on the question of the abolition of the death penalty'. The question returned at the 1995 Implementation Meeting on the Human Dimension, but again there was no significant evolution in the Organization's position. However, at the November 1997 Implementation Meeting on Human Dimension Issues, held in Warsaw, a recommendation on abolition of the death penalty was adopted. It states: 'The OSCE participating States should consider introducing measures aimed at facilitating the exchange of information on the question of the abolition of capital punishment to which they are already committed under existing OSCE provisions.' The recommendation slightly strengthened the effort of the OSCE's Office for Democratic Institutions and Human Rights as a clearing-house of information on the abolition of capital punishment in participating States. At the 1998 Implementation Meeting, the fact that some of the participating States did not disclose details about their use of capital punishment and had not made basic information public, in violation of OSCE commitments, was also noted. Recommendations from the discussion included: urging all OSCE countries to abolish the death penalty as soon as possible (specific concerns were raised regarding the execution

---

[209] *Document of the 1991 Moscow Meeting of the Conference on the Human Dimension of the CSCE*, para. 36 (see Appendix 18, p. 434).

[210] *Budapest Document 1994, Towards a Genuine Partnership in a New Era, Budapest Decisions*, VIII, §19 (see Appendix 18, p. 434).

[211] 'The Death Penalty in the OSCE Area', ODIHR background paper prepared for the seminar on 27 March 2000, 'Human Rights and Inhuman Treatment or Punishment'.

of juvenile or mentally impaired offenders), asking the OSCE to consider introducing concrete measures designed to facilitate the exchange of information on the question of the abolition of the capital punishment, and having participating States 'encourage ODIHR and OSCE Missions, in cooperation with the Council of Europe, to develop activities aimed at raising awareness against recourse to the death penalty, particularly with media circles, law enforcement officials, policy-makers, and the general public'.

During the 1999 Review Conference, held in Vienna and Istanbul, steps towards the abolition of the death penalty taken by several OSCE participating States were mentioned. Many at the Conference called for the abolition of the death penalty, or at least for the establishment of a moratorium. The conference called upon the OSCE participating States that still retain the death penalty 'to provide information at each human dimension implementation meeting on its use, comprising the scope of capital crimes, the respect for due process, possibilities for appeal, the number of persons executed in the previous year, and other relevant data'.[212]

The OSCE held a Supplementary Human Dimension Meeting on Human Rights and Inhuman Treatment or Punishment, in March 2000 in Vienna, that included a session entitled 'Exchange of Information on Capital Punishment in the OSCE Region'. A number of recommendations emerged along the lines of previous OSCE commitments, with retentionist States being urged to ratify the abolitionist protocols, to consider imposing a moratorium, and to publish detailed information on a regular basis. There was a particular focus on the need to raise public awareness on the subject, for example by encouraging respected public figures to take positions in favour of abolition. The OSCE itself was urged to 'consider stability and security aspects of the use of the death penalty especially in political cases, for example in Central Asia'. These points were reaffirmed at the Implementation Meeting on Human Dimension Issues held in October 2000, in Warsaw.

7.4 European Union

The European Union is currently composed of fifteen Member States essentially from Western and Southern Europe, although expansion into Eastern Europe is to be expected within the early years of the twenty-first century. It is the direct descendant of efforts that date to the 1950s to promote greater economic and, later, political integration among its members. Although this was not always the case, the death penalty has been abolished by all members of the European

---

[212] 'The Death Penalty in the OSCE Area'.

Union, and is a condition of admission for any new members.[213] For many years, the European Union did not particularly concern itself with human rights issues such as the death penalty, leaving these to the Council of Europe whose composition was similar though far from identical. More recently, though, the European Union, through its three main component parts, the European Parliament, the European Commission and the European Council, has taken an increasingly dynamic role in efforts to abolish capital punishment internationally. The question has become a pillar in its foreign policy.

Death penalty issues were first raised in the early 1980s in the European Parliament, when a resolution called for abolition of the death penalty in the European Community.[214] In 1986, the European Parliament called upon its Member States to ratify *Protocol No. 6 to the European Convention on Human Rights*.[215] In 1989, the European Parliament adopted the 'Declaration of Fundamental Rights and Freedoms', which proclaimed the abolition of the death penalty.[216] In 1990, the President of the European Parliament announced that he had forwarded a motion for a resolution on abolition of the death penalty in the United States.[217] Subsequently, the Political Affairs Committee appointed a rapporteur on the subject, Maria Adelaide Aglietta. A 1992 resolution of the European Parliament called upon those Member States whose legislation still provided for the death penalty, namely Greece, Belgium, Italy, Spain and the United Kingdom, to abolish it altogether. It also urged all Member States that had not yet done so to ratify *Protocol No. 6* as well as the *Second Optional Protocol to the International Covenant on Civil and Political Rights*. Member States were to refuse extradition to States where capital punishment still exists, unless sufficient guarantees that it will not be provided were obtained. The resolution also stated that the European Parliament '[h]opes that those countries which are members of the Council of Europe, and have not done so, will undertake to abolish the death penalty (in the case of exceptional crimes, this applies to Cyprus, Malta and

---

[213] 'Communication from the Commission to the Council and the European Parliament, the European Union's Role in Promoting Human Rights and Democratisation in Third Countries', COM (2001) 252 final (8 May 2001), p. 16. In a speech to the European Parliament on 24 October 2000, the European Commissioner for External Relations, Chris Patten, stated that all candidate members for the European Union have abolished the death penalty.
[214] E.C. Doc. 1-20/80, 13 March 1980; E.C. Doc. 1-65/81; *Official Journal of the European Communities, Debates of the European Parliament*, No. 1-272, Annex, pp. 116–129. The Irish extremist Ian Paisley spoke against the proposal, as did some Greek members. The Report was adopted on 18 June 1981: *Official Journal of the European Communities, Debates of the European Parliament*, No. 1-272, Annex, pp. 225–228; E.C. Doc. A 2-167/85, Doc. B 2-220/85; *Official Journal of the European Communities, Debates of the European Parliament*, No. 2-334, Annex, pp. 300–303.
[215] E.C. Doc. A2-0187/85; *Official Journal of the European Communities, Debates of the European Parliament*, C 36, 17 February 1986, p. 214.
[216] *Official Journal of the European Communities, Debates of the European Parliament*, Annex, No. 2-377, pp. 56–58, 74–79, 151–155; E.C. Doc. A 2-3/89.
[217] E.C. Doc. B3-0605/89. See also: E.C. Doc. B3-0682/90; E.C. Doc. B3-1915/90.

Switzerland, and in the case of both ordinary and exceptional crimes, to Turkey and Poland), together with those countries which are members of the CSCE, in which the death penalty still exists (Bulgaria, United States of America, Commonwealth of Independent States, Yugoslavia, Lithuania, Estonia, Latvia, and Albania)'. It urged the United Nations to adopt a 'binding decision imposing a general moratorium on the death penalty'.

The *Amsterdam Treaty*, which was adopted on 2 October 1997 and came into force on 1 May 1999, was the first of the legal instruments that underpin the European Union to speak of the death penalty. It provides the organization as a whole with a mandate to promote abolition. In addition to a general affirmation that '[t]he Union is founded on the principles of liberty, democracy, respect for human rights and fundamental freedoms, and the rule of law, principles which are common to the Member States',[218] the Final Act includes a number of declarations, of which the first is a 'Declaration on the Abolition of the Death Penalty':

> With reference to Article F(2) of the Treaty on European Union, the Conference recalls that Protocol No. 6 to the European Convention for the Protection of Human Rights and Fundamental Freedoms signed in Rome on 4 November 1950, and which has been signed and ratified by a large majority of Member States, provides for the abolition of the death penalty.
> In this context, the Conference notes the fact that since the signature of the abovementioned Protocol on 28 April 1983, the death penalty has been abolished in most of the Member States of the Union and has not been applied in any of them.

The *Charter of Fundamental Rights* of the European Union was adopted at Nice in December 2000, following a decision to prepare such an instrument taken at the European Council of Cologne, in June 1999. The *Charter* was intended to reflect the fundamental rights guaranteed by the *European Convention on Human Rights*, as well as those derived from constitutional traditions common to Member States and general principles of community law. The *Charter* is not a treaty and is without binding effect, although there would be little quarrel among Member States with a claim that it codifies European human rights norms dealing with capital punishment. Article 2, entitled 'Right to Life', states;

1. Everyone has the right to life.
2. No one shall be condemned to the death penalty, or executed.

Additionally, article 19§2 declares: 'No one may be removed, expelled or extradited to a State where there is a serious risk that he or she would be subjected

---

[218] *Treaty of Amsterdam Amending the Treaty on European Union, the Treaties Establishing the European Communities and Certain Related Acts*, OJ C 340, 10 November 1997, art. F(a)(1).

to the death penalty, torture or other inhuman or degrading treatment or punishment.[219]

The *Amsterdam Treaty* and its declaration on capital punishment was the impetus for the General Affairs Council of the European Union to adopt, on 29 June 1998, the 'Guidelines to EU Policy Towards Third Countries on the Death Penalty'.[220] The EU's objectives, according to the Guidelines, are 'to work towards universal abolition of the death penalty as a strongly held policy view agreed by all EU Member States' and 'where the death penalty still exists, to call for its use to be progressively restricted and to insist that it be carried out according to minimum standards'. The 1998 Guidelines include a list of 'minimum standards' to be used in auditing third States that still maintain capital punishment. In a general sense, these follow the classic statements of limitations on capital punishment that are found in article 6 of the *International Covenant on Civil and Political Rights* as well as in the 1984 resolution of the Economic and Social Council entitled 'Safeguards Guaranteeing Protection of those Facing the Death Penalty'.[221] In some respects, they attempt to push the law somewhat further, although they do not attempt to expand the categories of persons upon whom the death penalty may be imposed. Thus, they determine that the death penalty may not be imposed for juvenile offences, upon pregnant women and young mothers, and upon the insane, but they do not extend the list to cover the mentally disabled,[222] a category recognized by the Economic and Social Council in its 1988 resolution,[223] and the elderly, a prohibited category according to article 4 of the *American Convention on Human Rights*.[224]

The European Union Guidelines declare that '[t]he death penalty should not be imposed for non-violent financial crimes or for non-violent religious practice or expression of conscience'. They also affirm that anyone sentenced to death shall be entitled to submit an individual complaint under international procedures; the death sentence is not to be carried out while the complaint remains under consideration. It is not to be imposed in violation of a State's international commitments. The Guidelines state that '[t]he length of time spent

---

[219] *Charter of Fundamental Rights*, OJ C 364/1, 18 December 2000.

[220] 'Guidelines for EU Policy Towards Third Countries on the Death Penalty', in European Union Annual Report on Human Rights, 11317/00, p. 87.

[221] ESC Res. 1984/50. These are discussed in Chapter 4, at pp. 168–173.

[222] The 1998 document refers to the 'insane', which is the same language employed in the 1984 Safeguards. But in a 2000 publication of the Commission, this is changed to the 'mentally ill', which is clearly a broader term than 'insane' although a narrower one than 'mentally disabled' (European Union Annual Report on Human Rights, 11317/00, p. 29). The EU Memorandum on the Death Penalty, in European Union Annual Report on Human Rights, 11317/00, p. 84, says it is concerned about the execution of 'persons suffering from any form of mental disorder'. In 2001, the European Union intervened in a case before the United States Supreme Court as *amicus curiae* in support of a defendant arguing that it was illegal to execute the mentally disabled.

[223] ESC Res. 1989/64.

[224] *American Convention on Human Rights*, (1979) 1144 UNTS 123, OASTS 3, art. 4§5.

after having been sentenced to death may also be a factor' in determining whether or not to impose capital punishment. With respect to manner of execution, the Guidelines declare that the death penalty should be carried out 'so as to inflict the minimum possible suffering', and that it may not be carried out in public or in any other degrading manner. Finally, '[t]he death penalty shall not be imposed as an act of political revenge in contravention of the minimum standards, e.g. against coup plotters'.

Pursuant to the Guidelines, the EU has adopted a practice of communicating with third governments (*démarches*) with the goal of achieving formal or *de facto* moratoriums on executions and the eventual abolition of the death penalty. For example, on 10 May 2001, the EU sent a *démarche* to the United States reiterating its opposition to the use of the death penalty under any circumstances and expressing concern about the relatively high number of executions.[225] In December 1999, the European Union embassies in Washington drew up a document entitled 'Common EU Embassy Actions on Death Penalty in the US'. In addition to the United States, the EU has addressed the use of the death penalty with numerous other countries in recent years.[226] China, in particular, has been the focus of several initiatives, including the organization of seminars with Chinese academics and officials on the subject.[227] The European Union says it is 'particularly concerned about those countries which execute large numbers of prisoners (e.g., China, Democratic Republic of Congo, Iran, Iraq and United States of America), as well as cases where countries have resumed executions or which have withdrawn from international safeguards aimed at preventing miscarriages of justice, such as Trinidad and Tobago and Peru'.[228]

In addition to these general *démarches*, the EU has protested the death sentences of individual prisoners where execution violates the minimum standards set forth in its Guidelines. In the case of the United States alone, it has taken such initiatives by writing to governors and other officials in Arizona, Illinois, Georgia, Nevada, New Hampshire, Missouri, Ohio, Oklahoma, Tennessee, Texas and Virginia. The European Union has also intervened in proceedings

---

[225] See 'EU Policy on the Death Penalty', Press Release, Embassy of Sweden, Washington, 10 May 2001. A similar demarche was issued in February 2000 (European Union Annual Report on Human Rights, 11317/00, p. 30).

[226] The European Union has raised the issue of capital punishment with the governments of Antigua and Barbuda, Benin, Burundi, the Bahamas, China, Cuba, Guyana, India, Iran, Kyrgystan, the Palestinian Authority, Jamaica, Pakistan, the Philippines, Uganda, Tajikistan, Thailand, Trinidad and Tobago, Turkey, the United Arab Emirates, the United States, Uganda, Uzbekistan, Vietnam, Yemen and Zimbabwe.

[227] See, for example: Communique on China at 2000 Commission on Human Rights, adopted at 2249th Meeting of Council (General Affairs), Brussels, 20 March 2000, which noted 'with distress the frequent use of the death penalty in China', and the 'use of death penalty for non-violent crimes, including those of an economic nature' (p. 126, para. 5).

[228] European Union Annual Report on Human Rights, 11317/00, p. 49.

in the Supreme Court of the United States as an *amicus curiae*, supporting the appeal of Ernest Paul McCarver in arguing that execution of the mentally disabled is contrary to international law.[229]

European Council directives concerning development cooperation support initiatives to abolish the death penalty.[230] The European Commission has provided substantial funding to non-governmental organizations in their efforts to promote abolition of capital punishment throughout the world. As part of the €100 million budget of the European Initiative for Democracy and Human Rights (EIDHR), the European Commission has backed projects aimed at reducing the use of the death penalty, such as publicizing the ineffectiveness of capital punishment as a mechanism to reduce crime.[231] For example, in 2000 the Free Legal Assistance Group (FLAG) Human Rights Foundation, based in the Philippines, was awarded a grant of €200,205 to provide legal services for capital prisoners. The London-based NGO Penal Reform International has received €512,952 to provide legal assistance for death row prisoners in the Caribbean. The Centre for Studies of Capital Punishment at the University of Westminster, in London, has received €675,859 for a range of projects focused on the death penalty in the United States.[232]

The European Parliament, which initiated European Union interest in the subject of capital punishment, has accelerated its activities in recent years. In February 1999, the European Parliament criticized the failure of the United States to abide by its commitments under the *Vienna Convention on Consular Relations*.[233] On 6 May 1999, the Parliament welcomed the adoption of a resolution by the Commission on Human Rights and requested that the issue of a moratorium on capital punishment be introduced on the agenda of the United Nations General Assembly later in 1999.[234] The European Union's Council subsequently decided to submit a resolution. The decision was again endorsed by the European Parliament, which added the suggestion that a *rapporteur* be

---

[229] *McCarver v. North Carolina*, Brief of *amicus curiae*, the European Union in Support of the Petitioner, 10 June 2001.

[230] Council Regulation (EC) no. 975/1999 of 29 April 1999 laying down the requirements for the implementation of development cooperation operations which contribute to the general objective of developing and consolidating democracy and the rule of law and to that of respecting human rights and fundamental freedoms', art. 2(2), Council Regulation (EC) No. 976/1999 of 29 April 1999 laying down the requirements for the implementation of Community operations, other than those of development cooperation, which, within the framework of Community cooperation policy contribute to the general objective of developing and consolidating democracy and the rule of law and to that of respecting human rights and fundamental freedoms in third countries', art. 3(2)(a).

[231] See Communication from the Commission to the Council and the European Parliament: The European Union's Role in Promoting Human Rights and Democratisation in Third Countries, 8 May 2001, p. 13.

[232] Commission Staff Working Document: Report on the Implementation of the European Initiative for Democracy and Human Rights in 2000, pp. 14–15.

[233] Resolution B4-0188/99.   [234] Resolution B4-0461, 0473, 0475, 0480, 0496, 0502/99.

appointed to ensure implementation of the draft resolution.[235] When the resolution floundered, the Parliament deplored this development.[236]

In July 1999, the European Parliament called upon Turkey to commute the death sentence imposed upon Abdullah Öcalan, noting that the execution could impede Turkey's admission into the European Union. It also called upon the Turkish Government to change its *de facto* moratorium on capital punishment into formal, legal abolition.[237] An *ad hoc* committee of the Parliament attended proceedings in the Öcalan case, concluding that he was given a fair hearing by the Court of Cassation but that 'the death penalty was unacceptable as contrary to the norms and standards of the Council of Europe'.[238] The European Parliament also condemned use of the death penalty for persons convicted of espionage by Iran.[239] It urged Jamaica to reverse its decision to withdraw from the *Optional Protocol to the International Covenant on Civil and Political Rights*, and appealed to Trinidad and Tobago and Barbados not to follow Jamaica's example.[240] It urged El Salvador not to extend the scope of capital punishment to rape and violent killings, something that would violate the country's obligations under the *American Convention on Human Rights*.[241] The European Parliament has denounced the death sentences imposed in the United States upon Joaquin José Martinez, Mumia Abu Jamal, Larry Robinson,[242] Derek Rocco Barnabei[243] and Juan Raul Garza.[244] In a resolution of October 2000, the European Parliament reiterated its belief that the abolition of capital punishment constitutes part of the *acquis éthique* of the European Union. It called on the Commission to report on the initiatives it supports aimed at the abolition of the death penalty and the promotion of a universal moratorium on capital punishment.[245]

7.5 Conclusion

The day appears not far off when capital punishment will be eradicated from the European continent. Abolition of the death penalty has become indispensable for full participation in such organizations as the Council of Europe and the European Union. In this way, Europe signals that prohibition of capital

---

[235] Approved by Resolution B5-0144, 0155, 0159, 0169, 0171/1999, 7 October 1999.

[236] Resolution B5-0272, 0274, 0282, 0283, 0284, 0287, 0297, 0306/1999. For the discouraging results of this initiative in the United Nations General Assembly, see pp. 000–000.

[237] 'Resolution on the Death Sentence of A. Ocalan and the Future of the Kurdish Question in Turkey', B5–0006, 0012, 0018, 0023, 0026/99, 22 July 1999.

[238] 'Ad Hoc Committee to Ensure the Presence of the Assembly at the Trial of Abdullah Öcalan', Doc. 8596, 15 December 1999, para. l4.

[239] Resolution B5-0079, 0093, 0098, 0107/1999, 16 September 1999.

[240] Resolution B4-0340/98, 12 March 1998.   [241] Resolution B4-0821/98, 17 September 1998.

[242] Resolution B5-0272, 0274, 0282, 0283, 0284, 0287, 0297, 0306/1999, 18 November 1999.

[243] Resolution B5-0613, 0624, 0631, 0638/2000, 6 July 2000.

[244] Resolution B5-0341, 0359, 0370, 0376/2000, 13 April 2000.

[245] Resolution B5-0804/2000, 26 October 2000.

punishment forms part of the central core of human rights. It now seems appropriate to consider abolition of the death penalty to be such a customary norm, at least within Europe. The rapid emergence of this customary norm prohibiting the death penalty within Europe itself, where capital punishment was still being practised in France, Spain and Portugal as late as the 1970s, also indicates how quickly the principle may progress elsewhere in the world. Nobel prize-winning French philosopher Albert Camus, an outspoken abolitionist, was indeed prophetic when he wrote: 'Dans l'Europe unie de demain . . . l'abolition solennelle de la peine de mort devrait être le premier article du Code européen que nous espérons tous.'[246]

---

[246] Albert Camus, 'Réflexions sur la guillotine', in Arthur Koestler and, Albert Camus, *Réflexions sur la peine capitale*, Paris: Pluriel, 1979, p. 176.

8

Inter-American human rights law

The Inter-American human rights system of the Organization of American States, encompassing the Western hemisphere, is one of two regional systems with a convention abolishing the death penalty.[1] Several years behind the European system in adopting this protocol, the Inter-American instrument only came into force in 1991. Yet Latin American countries such as Uruguay and Venezuela played a pivotal role within the United Nations in promoting abolition of the death penalty. Several Latin American States abolished the death penalty in the nineteenth century or early in the twentieth century.[2] Many Latin American constitutions contain references to the death penalty, usually limiting its scope, or providing for due process in capital cases, or, in some cases, declaring it to be abolished.[3] According to Roger Hood's study, '[t]he hundred year tradition of abolition in South America now holds sway over almost all of the region . . . However, history shows that, in this region at times of political instability, military governments may reinstate the death penalty for a variety of offences against the state and public order'.[4] On the other hand, the membership of the Organisation of American States also includes some of the most enthusiastic retentionist States, including Jamaica, Trinidad and Tobago, and the United States.

[1] *Additional Protocol to the American Convention on Human Rights to Abolish the Death Penalty*, OASTS 73, 29 *ILM* 1447.
[2] Brazil (1882), Colombia (1910), Costa Rica (1877), Ecuador (1906), Panama (1903), Uruguay (1907), Venezuela (1863). See: Ricardo Ulate, 'The Death Penalty: Some Observations on Latin America', (1986) 12–13 *Crime Prevention and Criminal Justice Newsletter* 27.
[3] Colombia (1886), art. 29: 'The legislature may not impose capital punishment in any case'; Costa Rica (1871), art. 45: 'Human life is inviolable in Costa Rica'; Ecuador (1946), art. 187: 'The State shall guarantee to the inhabitants of Ecuador: (1) the sanctity of human life: there shall be no death penalty'; Panama (1946), art. 30: 'There is no penalty of death, expatriation, or confiscation of property'; Uruguay (1934), art. 25: 'The penalty of death shall not be inflicted on any person.'
[4] Roger Hood, *The Death Penalty, A World-wide Perspective*, 2nd ed., Oxford: Clarendon Press, 1996, pp. 43–44.

Inter-American human rights law has drawn on both the United Nations and European human rights traditions. Like the United Nations system, it began with a declaration in 1948, the *American Declaration of the Rights and Duties of Man*,[5] and completed this with a convention in the late 1960s, the *American Convention on Human Rights*.[6] The right to life provisions in the Inter-American instruments are very similar to those in their United Nations counterparts. The protocols abolishing the death penalty were adopted by the United Nations and the Organisation of American States at the end of the 1980s and the contents of the two are also comparable. From the European system, Inter-American human rights law has drawn its organs of implementation, the Inter-American Commission and Court of Human Rights.[7] Because use of the death penalty is relatively more widespread in the Americas than in Europe, the two Inter-American institutions now have a rather abundant body of case law dealing with the death penalty.

Efforts at codifying international human rights law in the Western hemisphere date to the early years of the twentieth century.[8] At the 1936 Inter-American Conference for the Maintenance of Peace, Chile submitted a draft declaration of human rights that recognized the right to life.[9] The proposal was rejected because it violated the non-interventionist principle of international law. Delegates to the Conference considered that humanitarian intervention in international law was allowed only in the most extreme cases. The Second World War changed thinking on this question, and at its close, the States of the Western hemisphere began to examine more closely the development of a regional human rights system.

8.1 The *American Declaration of the Rights and Duties of Man*

8.1.1 *Drafting of the* Declaration

The Inter-American Conference on the Problems of War and Peace, held at Chapultepec, near Mexico City, in 1945, entrusted the Inter-American Council

---

[5] *American Declaration on the Rights and Duties of Man*, OAS Doc. OEA/Ser.L./V/I.4.

[6] *American Convention on Human Rights*, (1979) 1144 UNTS 123, OASTS 36.

[7] Thomas Buergenthal, 'The American and European Conventions on Human Rights: Similarities and Differences', (1980) 30 *American University Law Review* 155; Jochen Abr. Frowein, 'The European and the American Conventions on Human Rights – A Comparison', (1980) 1 *HRLJ* 44.

[8] Francisco José Aguilar-Urbina, 'An Overview of the Main Differences Between the Systems Established by the Optional Protocol to the ICCPR and the ACHR as Regards Individual Communications', [1991–92] *CHRY* 127.

[9] M. Margaret Ball, *The OAS in Transition*, Durham, NC: Duke University Press, 1969, pp. 512–513: 'the right of every individual to life, liberty, and the free exercise of his religion, the practice of which does not conflict with the public order and that each country grant protection of these rights to every person within its territory, without distinction of race, sex, nationality or religion.'

of Jurists with the mission of drafting a 'Declaration on the Fundamental Rights and Duties of Man',[10] to be completed by the end of 1945. Authored by Francisco Campos, F. Nieto del Rio, Charles G. Fenwick and A. Gómez Robledo, article I affirmed the right to life, but expressly admitted the death penalty as an exception.[11] A new draft, which also contemplated capital punishment as an exception to the right to life, was submitted to the Council of Jurists at a meeting in December 1946.[12] In this draft, however, the death penalty could only be imposed 'for crimes of exceptional gravity'. In explanatory notes accompanying the text, the Council of Jurists observed that a number of States considered that the imposition of the death penalty involves an element of moral degradation on the part of the State itself. The Council expressed no opinion on the matter of capital punishment, commenting only that 'the right to life does not protect a person against punishment prescribed for the gravest of crimes'.[13]

The 1945 Resolution had contemplated the convening of a Conference of American Jurists where the 'Declaration' would be adopted as a convention. However, the conference was never held, and the draft declaration was instead considered by the Ninth International Conference of American States, held in Bogotá in 1948.[14] A slightly modified version of the Council of Jurists' right to life article was submitted to the Conference by the Inter-American Juridical Committee.[15] The Committee said that, in recognition of the authority of each

[10] Resolution XL, 'International Protection of the Essential Rights of Man', Inter-American Commission on Human Rights, *Diez Años de Actividades, 1971–1981*, Washington: Organization of American States, 1982, p. 4. The resolution is reported in Francisco Campos, F. Nieto del Rio, Charles G. Fenwick and A. Gómez Robledo, 'Report to Accompany the Draft Declaration of the International Rights and Duties of Man', (1946) 40 *AJIL Supplement* 100. For a discussion of the preparatory work of the *Declaration*, see Karl Vasak, *La Commission Interaméricaine des droits de l'homme*, Paris: Bibliothèque constitutionnelle et de science politique, 1968, pp. 25–27.

[11] 'Draft Declaration of the International Rights and Duties of Man, December 31, 1945', (1946) 40 *AJIL Supplement* 93: 'Every person has the right to life. This right extends to the right to life from the moment of conception; to the right to life of incurables, imbeciles and the insane. It includes the right to sustenance and support in the case of those unable to support themselves by their own efforts; and it implies a duty of the state to see to it that such support is made available. The right to life may be denied by the state only on the ground of a conviction of the gravest of crimes, to which the death penalty has been attached.'

[12] Novena Conferencia Internacional American, *Actas y Documentos*, vol. V, p. 449; also Resolution 40 in *International Conferences of American States, Second Supplement, 1942–1954*, Washington: Pan American Union, 1958, pp. 93–94: 'Every person has the right to life. This right extends to the right to life from the moment of conception; to the right to life of incurables, imbeciles and the insane. Capital punishment may only be applied in cases in which it has been prescribed by pre-existing law for crimes of exceptional gravity.'

[13] Inter-American Council of Jurists, *Recommendaciones e Informes, Documentos Oficiales, 1945–1947*, Washington: Organization of American States, 1948, pp. 22–23. A slightly different unofficial translation appears in J. Colon-Collazo, 'A Legislative History of the Right to Life in the Inter-American Legal System', in Bertrand G. Ramcharan, ed., *The Right to Life in International Law*, Dordrecht/Boston/Lancaster: Martinus Nijhoff Publishers, 1985, pp. 33–41, at p. 35.

[14] 'The Draft Inter-American Convention on Protection of Human Rights', *Inter-American Yearbook on Human Rights 1968*, Washington: Organization of American States, 1973, p. 65.

[15] OAS Doc. CB-7-E, p. 2; Novena Conferencia Internacional American, *Actas y Documentos*, p. 456: 'Every person has the right to life. This right extends to the right to life from the moment of conception;

State to regulate the question, it had modified the final portion of the provision, dealing with the death penalty, 'in order to emphasize that the Committee is not taking sides in favour of the death penalty but rather admitting the fact that there is a diversity of legislation in this respect'. The report added that the constitutions of Colombia, Panama, Uruguay, Brazil and Venezuela, based on 'generous humanitarian considerations', prohibited imposition of the death penalty.[16] Haiti proposed an amendment to the right to life article aimed at imposing a further limit on capital punishment by controlling its use in political offences.[17]

A Working Group at the Ninth International Conference attempted to reconcile the draft article proposed by the Council of Jurists with the legislation in force in a number of American States, including the United States. It considered the draft prepared by the Judicial Committee, as well as the draft of the *Universal Declaration of Human Rights* that had been adopted by the Commission on Human Rights at its session in Geneva in December 1947[18] together with the amendments proposed by various States.[19] The Working Group was therefore aware that the Commission on Human Rights of the United Nations had decided to work on two distinct instruments, one a declaration or manifesto, expressed in relatively succinct and general terms, and the other a binding convention, worded in a more precise fashion. Given that the idea of drafting a convention had been temporarily abandoned within the Inter-American system,[20] the Working Group report came up with a new right to life provision in an abbreviated form that was similar to article 3 of the *Universal Declaration of Human Rights* and where any reference to the death penalty had been removed.[21] The deletion was in the interest of succinctness, and the qualifications found in earlier drafts, namely that the death penalty can only be permitted as an exception to the right to life where provided by pre-existing law for crimes of exceptional gravity, must nevertheless be considered to be implicit in the text.

The word 'integrity' was removed from the Working Group's draft provision, leaving what became the final version of article I of the *American Declaration of the Rights and Duties of Man*:

to the right to life of incurables, imbeciles and the insane. Capital punishment may only be applied in cases in which it has been prescribed by pre-existing law for crimes of exceptional gravity.'

[16] OAS Doc. CB-7-E, pp. 5–6; Novena Conferencia Internacional American, *Actas y Documentos*, pp. 456–457.

[17] OAS Doc. CB-328-E/C.VI-19, CB-420/C.VI-34; Novena Conferencia Internacional American, *Actas y Documentos*, p. 485: 'Capital punishment may be applied only in cases where it has been previously prescribed by law, and in political matters this penalty shall be imposed only for the punishment of crimes of high treason or an attempt against the life of a chief of state.'

[18] UN Doc. E/CN.4/77, Annex A; UN Doc. E/600, Annex A.

[19] Novena Conferencia Internacional American, *Actas y Documentos*, p. 475.

[20] J. Colon-Collazo, 'A Legislative History', p. 36.

[21] OAS Doc. CB-310/CIN-41: 'Every human being has the right to life, liberty, security and integrity of his person.'

> Every human being has the right to life, liberty and the security of his person.

The provision was adopted by the Sixth Committee of the Conference at its fifth session, on 22 April 1948,[22] and by the plenary, on 2 May 1948.

8.1.2 Interpretation of article I of the Declaration

Although the *American Declaration of the Rights and Duties of Man* was originally intended as a non-binding declaration, similar to the *Universal Declaration of Human Rights*, amendments to the *Charter of the Organization of American States*[23] in 1967 made the *American Declaration* mandatory.[24] Member States of the Organisation of American States are now legally bound to respect the provisions of the *Declaration*, including of course article I. Those that have not yet ratified the *American Convention on Human Rights* are also subject to a petition procedure before the Inter-American Commission on Human Rights.[25]

Several petitions dealing with capital punishment and the application of article I of the *Declaration* have come before the Inter-American Commission which is, for all practical purposes, the instrument's interpreter. Most of these petitions have concerned the United States, which has not ratified the *Convention*. The United States does not contest the legitimacy of the petition procedure before the Commission, but continues to insist that the *American Declaration* is a non-binding instrument.[26] The United States has regularly defied 'precautionary measures' requests from the Inter-American Commission in cases involving application of capital punishment.[27] As a result, the Commission's findings in

---

[22] OAS Doc. CB-455/C.VI-36; Novena Conferencia Internacional American, *Actas y Documentos*, p. 578.

[23] (1952) 119 UNTS 4.

[24] *Protocol of Buenos Aires*, (1970) 721 UNTS 324, arts. 3j, 16, 51e, 112 and 150.

[25] *Interpretation of the American Declaration of the Rights and Duties of Man Within the Framework of Article 64 of the American Convention on Human Rights*, Advisory Opinion OC-10/89 of 14 July 1989, OAS Doc. OAS/Ser.L/V/III.21, doc. 14, Appendix IV, p. 109, paras. 42–47; *Baptiste* v. *Grenada* (Case No. 11.743), Report No. 38/00, 13 April 2000, para. 57. The petition procedure is created by article 20(b) of the *Statute of the Inter-American Commission of Human Rights*, OAS Doc. OEA/Ser.L.V/II.71, Doc. 6 rev.1, p. 65 and by article 51 of the *Regulations of the Inter-American Commission of Human Rights*, OAS Doc. OEA/Ser.L.V/II.71, Doc. 6 rev.1, p. 75. See also: Thomas Buergenthal, 'The Revised OAS Charter and the Protection of Human Rights', (1975) 69 *AJIL* 828.

[26] *Andrews* v. *United States* (Case No. 11.139), Report No. 57/96, 6 December 1996, para. 59.

[27] For example: *Andrews* v. *United States* (Case No. 11.139), Precautionary Measures Decision of 28 July 1992; *Faulder* v. *United States*, Precautionary Measures Decision of 9 June 1999; *Graham* v. *United States* (Case No. 11.193), Precautionary Measures Decisions of 27 October 1993 and 29 October 1993. Since its earliest death penalty petitions, the Inter-American Commission has had a practice of requesting a stay of execution pending its consideration of the matter. Although nothing explicitly supports such a power in the *Convention*, the Commission makes such 'precautionary measures' orders, in 'serious and urgent' cases, pursuant to article 25 of its Rules of Procedure. According to the Commission:

> its ability to effectively investigate and determine capital cases has frequently been undermined when states have scheduled and proceeded with the execution of condemned persons, despite

particular cases are rather frequently delivered after the execution. In *Andrews* v. *United States*, the Commission concluded there had been a violation of article I of the *Declaration* after the petitioner's execution, despite a precautionary measures request. It recommended that the United States compensate the victim's next of kin. The United States replied that it 'cannot agree with the Commission's findings, or carry out its recommendations'.[28] On 18 June 2001, the United States Government executed Juan Raul Garza despite a finding some weeks earlier by the Commission that this would violate its obligations under the *American Declaration*.[29]

The Inter-American Commission has expressed the view, but only in its most recent decisions, that in death penalty cases there is a 'heightened level of scrutiny'. It has noted that such a test is consistent with the restrictive approach to the death penalty provisions of human rights treaties advocated by other international authorities.[30] Echoing statements of United States judges, it considers that, for the purposes of interpretation of article I, death is qualitatively different from other penalties and procedures.[31] In this context, it has noted the 'demonstrable international trend towards more restrictive application of the death penalty', something germane to an analysis of 'the spirit and purposes underlying the American Declaration'.[32]

The laconic text of article I could, on a literal reading, be construed as a total prohibition on capital punishment. The *travaux préparatoires* do not confirm this, of course, but they ought not to be decisive in assessing the content of article I. Above all, the right to life provision of the *American Declaration* should be subject to a dynamic interpretation, taking into account the evolving values within the region as well as universally. As recently as 2001, the Inter-American Commission reaffirmed its resistance to such a bold and innovative interpretation.[33]

---

the fact that those individuals have proceedings pending before the Commission. It is for this reason that in capital cases the Commission requests precautionary measures from states to stay a condemned prisoner's execution until the Commission has had an opportunity to investigate his or her claims. Moreover, in the Commission's view, OAS member states, by creating the Commission and mandating it through the OAS Charter and the Commission's Statute to promote the observance and protection of human rights of the American peoples, have implicitly undertaken to implement measures of this nature where they are essential to preserving the Commission's mandate. Particularly in capital cases, the failure of a member state to preserve a condemned prisoner's life pending review by the Commission of his or her complaint emasculates the efficacy of the Commission's process, deprives condemned persons of their right to petition in the inter-American human rights system and results in serious and irreparable harm to those individuals, and accordingly is inconsistent with the state's human rights obligations. *Garza* v. *United States* (Case No. 12.243), Report No. 52/01, 4 April 2001, para. 117.

[28] *Andrews* v. *United States*, para. 190.   [29] *Garza* v. *United States*.

[30] *Edwards* et al. v. *Bahamas* (Case nos. 12.067, 12.068, 12.086), Report No. 48/01, 4 April 2001, para. 109; *Garza* v. *United States*, para. 71. These statements essentially reproduce similar pronouncements in cases where the Commission interprets the *American Convention* in death penalty cases.

[31] *Edwards* et al. v. *Bahamas*, para. 132.   [32] *Garza* v. *United States*, para. 94.   [33] *Ibid.*, para. 90

One of its members, Hélio Bicudo, has espoused this unequivocally abolitionist view in individual opinions.[34]

However, the Commission has consistently refused to go to the other extreme, and take the silence on the subject to mean that the *Declaration* simply fails to regulate the issue in any way.[35] Such a conservative interpretation has been defended more or less consistently by the United States during litigation before the Commission. In *Roach and Pinkerton*, the United States insisted that 'the Declaration is deliberately silent on the issue of capital punishment', because the drafters wished to leave States with the discretion to legislate on the subject as they saw fit.[36] In *Garza*, it argued 'a state cannot be bound to legal obligations, either under treaties or under customary international law, that it has not explicitly accepted, and contends that the Petitioner's representatives cannot claim that general language in an instrument negotiated in 1948 has taken on a different meaning fifty years later so as to prohibit the United States from employing the death penalty'.[37] In *Roach and Pinkerton* v. *United States*, counsel for the applicants responded that deletion of any reference to capital punishment in the draft *Declaration* meant only that 'the drafters were simply unable or unwilling to delineate each and every instance when capital punishment would be prohibited as they did not want to authorize it necessarily in every context'.[38]

Actually, it was abortion, not capital punishment, that preoccupied the drafters of the *American Declaration*. The Working Group quite unequivocally omitted reference to the right to life 'from conception' because this would be incompatible with the legislation in several American countries.[39] Yet the same conclusion cannot be made with respect to capital punishment,[40] where there was clearly no obstacle to a provision preventing capital punishment except for grave crimes under pre-existing law. Nor should the international context be lost sight of, for at the same time as the drafting of the *Declaration* was proceeding, the Commission on Human Rights of the United Nations had more or less settled on a right to life provision of the *Universal Declaration of Human Rights* that made

---

[34] For example: *Garza* v. *United States* (Case No. 12.243), Report No. 52/01, 4 April 2001, Concurring Opinion of Commissioner Hélio Bicudo.

[35] But see the dissent in *Roach and Pinkerton* v. *United States* by Commissioner Marco Gerardo Monroy Cabra.

[36] *Roach and Pinkerton* v. *United States* (Case No. 9647), Resolution No. 3/87, reported in OAS Doc. OEA/Ser.L/V/II.71 doc. 9 rev.1, p. 147, *Inter-American Yearbook on Human Rights, 1987*, Dordrecht/Boston/London: Martinus Nijhoff, 1990, p. 328, 8 *HRLJ* 345, para. 38(b), (c). See also the dissent in *Roach and Pinkerton* by Commissioner Marco Gerardo Monroy Cabra.

[37] *Garza* v. *United* States, para. 55.   [38] *Roach and Pinkerton* v. *United States*, para. 37(j).

[39] *White and Potter* v. *United States* (Case No. 2141), Resolution No. 23/81, OAS Doc. OEA/Ser.L/V/II.52 doc. 48, OAS Doc. OEA/Ser.L/V/II.54 doc. 9 rev.1, pp. 25–54, Inter-American Commission on Human Rights, *Ten Years of Activities, 1971–1981*, Washington: Organization of American States, 1982, pp. 186–209, (1981) 1 *HRLJ* 110, para. 19 (d), (e).

[40] Despite the comment to this effect in *White and Potter* v. *United States*, ibid., *in fine*.

no mention of the death penalty but that undoubtedly encompassed limits upon capital punishment.[41] The *travaux préparatoires* do not therefore support the interpretation given by the United States and Commissioner Cabra to the deletion of any reference to capital punishment in article I of the *American Declaration*.

The Commission has developed an interpretation of article I of the *Declaration* whereby it has an 'inherent content' that limits but does not prohibit the death penalty:

> Thus, the construction of Article I of the Right to Life of the American Declaration does not define nor sanction capital punishment by a member State of the OAS. However, it provides that a member State can impose capital punishment if it is prescribed by pre-existing law for crimes of exceptional gravity. Therefore, inherent in the construction of Article I, is a requirement that before the death penalty can be imposed and before the death sentence can be executed, the accused person must be given all the guarantees established by pre-existing laws, which includes guarantees contained in its Constitution, and its international obligations, including those rights and freedoms enshrined in the American Declaration. These guarantees include, the right to life, and not to be arbitrarily deprived of one's life, the right to due process of law, the right to an impartial and public hearing, the right not to receive cruel, infamous, or unusual punishment, and the right to equality at law.[42]

Returning once again to the *travaux préparatoires* of article I, the Commission has proposed an even more demanding and rigorous formulation:

> despite the omission of the original paragraph 2 in the final draft of the Declaration [allowing for the death penalty], the Commission is of the opinion that the founding fathers of the Declaration intended that the states in issuing legislation in respect of capital punishment uphold the sanctity of life as being *sacrosanct* with all the due process guarantees found in other Articles of the Declaration before the imposition and implementation of capital punishment.[43]

But how is this 'implicit content' to be identified. Recently, the Commission appears to have been guided by its case law applying article 4 of the *American Convention on Human Rights*, saying that 'in many instances' it may be considered to represent 'an authoritative expression of the fundamental principles set forth in the American Declaration'.[44] The key word here is 'arbitrarily', employed in article 4§1 of the *Convention* and article 6§1 of the *International Covenant on Civil and Political Rights*, and read into the text of article I of the *Declaration* by the Commission. The scope of the term 'arbitrarily' is large enough to enable interpreters to expand the limitations upon the death penalty in those treaty provisions. Thus, by deeming 'arbitrarily' to be implied within the text of article I, the logic of the Commission's approach would suggest that the

---

[41] This is discussed in Chapter 1.   [42] *Andrews* v. *United States*, para. 177.
[43] *Edwards* et al. v. *Bahamas*, para. 128.   [44] *Garza* v. *United States*, paras. 89–90.

Declaration, at a minimum, provides at least the same restrictions and limitations on capital punishment as article 4 of the *Convention*.

But this is a relatively recent formulation. Indeed, in its early decisions, the Commission rejected the idea that article I of the *Declaration* was to be construed as if it incorporated the language of article 4 of the *American Convention*. For example, it refused to interpret article I as if it included the words 'generally from the moment of conception', found in article 4§1 of the *Convention*, so as to support an application challenging liberal abortion laws in the United States.[45] In the same manner, in *Roach and Pinkerton*, it declined to imply a prohibition upon executions for crimes committed under the age of eighteen. Although counsel for Roach and Pinkerton referred to article 4§5 of the *Convention*, which prohibits execution of juvenile offenders, they argued that it and similar norms found in other international human rights and humanitarian law instruments merely codified a customary norm.[46] In their view, it was customary law, not the *American Convention*, that furnished the implied content for article I of the *Declaration*.[47]

The Inter-American Commission held that there was no rule of customary international law establishing eighteen to be the minimum age for imposition of the death penalty.[48] Nevertheless, the Commission recognized that there was a relevant norm applicable to the Member States of the Organization of American States, that it went so far as to qualify as *jus cogens*, within the meaning of article 53 of the *Vienna Convention on the Law of Treaties*.[49] The Commission said that this norm prohibited execution of juveniles, but it fixed an age of majority at some unspecified point below eighteen.[50] On this point, it expressed 'shock' at Indiana's statute, which theoretically permitted a ten-year-old to be executed, but did not suggest at what point between ten and eighteen its shock would diminish to a threshold of tolerance.[51] Referring to the widespread ratification of the *American Convention* and the *International Covenant on Civil and Political*

---

[45] *White and Potter* v. *United States*.

[46] *American Convention on Human Rights*, art. 4§5; *International Covenant on Civil and Political Rights*, (1976) 999 UNTS 171, art. 6§5; *Geneva Convention of August 12, 1949 Relative to the Treatment of Civilians*, (1950) 75 UNTS 287, art. 68§4. Interestingly, they do not appear to have invoked similar provisions in the *Additional Protocols* to the *Geneva Conventions* that were adopted in 1977, perhaps because they considered levels of ratification of these instruments to be insufficient for evidence that they codified customary norms.

[47] The United States Supreme Court has decided that there is no such rule of customary international law, nor is such an execution a violation of the Eighth Amendment protection against cruel and unusual treatment or punishment: *Thompson* v. *Oklahoma*, 487 US 815, 108 S.Ct. 2687, 101 L.Ed.2d 702 (1988). See: David Weissbrodt, 'Execution of Juvenile Offenders by the United States Violates International Human Rights Law', (1988) 3 *American University Journal of International Law and Policy* 339; Christina M. Cerna, 'US Death Penalty Tested Before the Inter-American Commission on Human Rights', (1992) 10 *Netherlands Quarterly of Human Rights* 155.

[48] *Roach and Pinkerton* v. *United States*, para. 60.   [49] *Ibid.*, paras. 55–56.   [50] *Ibid.*, para. 57.
[51] *Ibid.*, para. 58.

Rights, as well as the practice of many States, including various jurisdictions within the United States, the Commission was only prepared to say that a norm prohibiting executions for crimes committed under the age of eighteen was 'emerging'.[52]

In any case, the Inter-American Commission said that, even if a customary norm were to exist, it would not bind a State that had protested the norm.[53] Because the United States Government had proposed to ratify the *American Convention on Human Rights* with a reservation to article 4§5 stating that the United States 'reserves the right in appropriate cases to subject minors to procedures and penalties applicable to adults', the Commission considered that it had protested the norm.[54] But under international law, a State seeking to block application of a customary norm must do so persistently.[55] The Commission did not consider in detail the behaviour of the United States, whose objections to international prohibition of juvenile executions have not been entirely constant and unequivocal. For example, the United States ratified the fourth *Geneva Convention* without any objection to article 68§4.[56] Roach and Pinkerton pointed out that 'if nearly all the nations of the world, including the United States, have agreed to such a norm for periods of international armed conflict, the norm protecting juvenile offenders from execution ought to apply with even greater force for periods of peace'.[57]

The Commission went on, however, to address the 'patchwork scheme of legislation' in the United States which resulted in startling variations in the juvenile death penalty from state to state. In leaving the issue of 'this most fundamental right – the right to life' to its states, with the ensuing 'pattern of legislative arbitrariness', the United States had created a situation of 'arbitrary deprivation of life and inequality before the law', contrary to articles I and II of the *American Declaration*, said the Commission.[58] This unlikely conclusion is intriguing, because it would seem applicable not only to the juvenile death penalty but to the death penalty as a whole. The apparent logic of the Commission's position is that if the application of the death penalty is arbitrary, and depends only upon the state in which the crime is committed, then it is arbitrary for adults, women, African-Americans, the mentally disabled and children alike. It has never extended the conclusion, however. Nevertheless, *Roach and Pinkerton*

---

[52] *Ibid.*, para. 60.   [53] *Ibid.*, para. 52.   [54] *Ibid.*, para. 53.

[55] *Anglo Norwegian Fisheries Case (United Kingdom v. Norway)*, [1951] ICJ Reports 116.

[56] More recently, it signed the *Convention on the Rights of the Child* without objection or reservation concerning article 37§a.

[57] *Ibid.*, para. 37. On this point, Commissioner Cabra, in his dissenting opinion, observed that the norm only applies to armed conflicts and that it cannot be considered a demonstration of a custom in time of peace (at p. 179). This reasonable observation is confirmed by the fact that many death penalty States accept humanitarian law norms obliging them to respect restrictions on the use of capital punishment for civilians in occupied territories that they do not observe at home.

[58] *Ibid.*, para. 63.

first established that arbitrariness would be the standard for examining the compatibility of the death penalty with article I's protection of the right to life.

In 2000, the Commission ruled that a petition from the United States raising this issue was admissible, suggesting that it will revisit the issue of juvenile executions.[59] Developments in international human rights law since 1987, such as the virtually universal ratification of the *Convention on the Rights of the Child*, combined with the Commission's recent interpretative approach that relies on article 4 of the *American Convention*, make it likely that the Commission will reverse its previous position and declare execution for crimes committed under the age of eighteen to be contrary to article I of the *American Declaration*

In *Celestine v. United States*, an impoverished young black man with a far below normal IQ was convicted of the rape and murder of an elderly woman while under the influence of drugs and alcohol and was sentenced to death in Louisiana.[60] In the words of the Commission, it was 'a poor case upon which to recommend the reversal of the U.S. criminal justice practice'.[61] Celestine alleged the unfairness of his conviction by a 'death qualified jury', in which potential members had been screened for their opinions of capital punishment in order to discharge those with abolitionist views.[62] Dismissing the argument, the Commission was equally impressed by the United States Supreme Court's case law on the matter of 'death qualified juries'.[63]

But the heart of Celestine's petition was the claim that in Louisiana the death penalty was imposed in a racially discriminatory manner. He invoked studies showing that the race of the defendant is a significant factor at all stages of the criminal justice system, from the decision to file a first-degree murder charge to the decision to submit the case to a jury trial. The studies also showed that, in Louisiana, whites who kill blacks virtually never receive the death sentence, whereas the opposite is not the case. The Commission relied heavily on a recent United States Supreme Court case, *McCleskey v. Kemp*,[64] in which much of the same statistical evidence had been produced. In that case, the Supreme Court, by a single vote, had rejected McCleskey's claim that Georgia's capital

---

[59] *Graham (Shaka Sankofa) v. United States* (Case No. 11.193), Report No. 51/00, 15 June 2000.
[60] *Celestine v. United States* (Case No. 10.031), Resolution No. 23/89, reported in OAS Doc. A/Ser.L./V/II.76, doc. 44, OAS Doc. A/Ser.L/V/II.77 rev.1, doc. 7, p. 62.
[61] *Ibid.*, para. 45.
[62] See: Welsh S. White, *The Death Penalty in the Nineties*, Ann Arbor: University of Michigan, 1991, pp. 186–218.
[63] *Witherspoon v. Illinois*, 391 US 510, 88 S.Ct. 1770, 20 L.Ed.2d 776 (1968); *Wainwright v. Witt*, 469 US 412 (1985).
[64] *McCleskey v. Kemp*, 481 US 279, 107 S.Ct. 1756, 95 L.Ed.2d 262 (1987). See: Samuel R. Gross, Robert Mauro, *Death and Discrimination, Racial Disparities in Capital Sentencing*, Boston: Northeastern, 1989; R. L. Kennedy, 'McCleskey v. Kemp: Race, Capital Punishment and the Supreme Court', (1988) 101 *Harvard Law Review* 1388; D. C. Baldus, C. Pulaski and G. Woodworth, 'Arbitrariness and Discrimination in the Administration of the Death Penalty', (1986) 15 *Stetson Law Review* 133.

sentencing process was racially discriminatory, although the majority admitted that 'Black defendants, such as McCleskey, have the greatest likelihood of receiving the death penalty'.[65] For the United States Supreme Court, statistical likelihoods are insufficient to prove racial discrimination.[66] The Inter-American Commission agreed that the statistical evidence demonstrating that the death penalty is applied in a racially discriminatory manner was insufficient.[67] It ruled that Celestine had not even set out a *prima facie* case of racial discrimination, thereby going somewhat further than the Supreme Court, which had held the statistical evidence to be insufficient. The Commission was impressed by the fact that in more than 100 subsequent decisions of federal and state courts, *McCleskey* had been neither overturned nor distinguished.[68]

The Inter-American Commission revisited the issue of racism in capital punishment in the application of another African-American, William Andrews. During trial, a note was found in the jury room with the notation 'Hang the Nigger's' [*sic*]. The jury was not only all-white, it included several Mormons, members of a religious group that believes in white supremacy. Because the judge lectured the jury on the subject of racial discrimination after the racist note was discovered, the United States Supreme Court considered that any possible damage had been corrected, and that the conviction and sentence of death could stand. Dissenting Justices Marshall and Brennan described the note as 'a vulgar incident of lynch-mob racism reminiscent of Reconstruction days'.[69]

The Inter-American Commission readily concluded that there had been a breach of article XXVI(2) of the *Declaration*, which ensures the right to a fair trial. Echoing the case law of the United Nations Human Rights Committee, it said that '[i]n capital punishment cases, the States Parties have an obligation to observe rigorously all the guarantees for an impartial trial'.[70] Among the due process violations, it held that Andrews should not have been sentenced to death by the same jury that had earlier convicted him.[71] The Inter-American Commission also ruled that Andrews had not received equal treatment, in violation of article II of the *American Declaration*, and that he had been subject to 'cruel, infamous or unusual punishment', contrary to article XXVI. On this point, it noted he had spent eighteen years on death row and had not been allowed to leave his cell for more than a few hours a week. Moreover, he had received notice of at least eight execution dates before being executed in July 1992, while his application to the Inter-American Commission was still pending.[72]

---

[65] *McCleskey* v. *Kemp*, p. 1764 (S.Ct.).　　[66] *Ibid.*, p. 1765.

[67] *Celestine* v. *United States*, para. 41.　　[68] *Ibid.*, para. 35.

[69] *Andrews* v. *Shulsen*, 485 US 919, 920 (1988) (dissent from denial of certiorari).

[70] *Andrews* v. *United States*, para. 172.

[71] *Ibid.*, para. 178. However, this point appears in a portion of the decision dealing with cruel treatment, not procedural fairness.

[72] *Ibid.*, para. 178.

The Commission has surely not said its last word on the subject of racism with respect to death penalty practice in the United States. In *Andrews*, it took some pains to distinguish the case from *Celestine*, noting that it applied to the specific facts of the case.[73] In 2001, the issue of racism returned when petitioner Juan Raul Garza invoked a report prepared by the Attorney General of the United States that described endemic racism in the implementation of capital punishment by federal authorities. The United States government dismissed the significance of its own report, arguing it was based on 'mere statistical studies' that were insufficient to support such a claim.[74] Unfortunately, the Commission declined to consider the issue because of failure to exhaust domestic remedies.[75]

The Commission has held that executions are arbitrary, and therefore contrary to article I of the *Declaration*, when a State fails to limit the death penalty to crimes of exceptional gravity prescribed by pre-existing law, when it denies an accused strict and rigorous judicial guarantees of a fair trial, and when there is a notorious and demonstrable diversity of practice within a Member State that results in inconsistent application of the death penalty for the same crimes.[76] In *Garza* v. *United States*, it examined a practice whereby alleged crimes for which a person has never been convicted may be taken into account in the decision to impose a death sentence for another offence. Garza was allegedly involved in four other murders committed in Mexico and over which the United States justice system could not even purport to exercise jurisdiction. The Inter-American Commission considered that it was 'prejudicial and improper' to consider the four unadjudicated murders in the sentencing phase, especially because evidence of the crimes was admissible according to a lower standard of evidence than would be allowed during the trial proper. 'Inasmuch as the jury's death sentence was influenced by the "aggravating factor" of the unadjudicated murders, the sentence constituted a violation of Mr. Garza's rights under Articles I, XVIII, and XXVI of the American Declaration', the Commission concluded.[77]

The Inter-American Commission has found, in an application lodged against the Bahamas, that the 'implicit content' of article I also prohibits mandatory death sentences. The United States Supreme Court has long considered mandatory sentencing to be unconstitutional, so the question has not arisen in the American cases. Indeed, the ruling of the United States Supreme Court in *Woodson* v. *North Carolina*,[78] as well as similar pronouncements by the Supreme Court of India[79] and the South African Constitutional Court,[80] have been invoked to support the Commission's conclusion that mandatory death

---

[73] *Andrews* v. *United States*, paras. 117, 180, 182   [74] *Ibid.*, para. 51.
[75] *Garza* v. *United States*, para. 68.   [76] *Garza* v. *United States*, para. 91.   [77] *Ibid.*
[78] *Woodson* v. *North Carolina*, 428 US 280 (1976).
[79] *Bachan Singh* v. *State of Punjab*, AIR 1980 SC 898.   [80] *S.* v. *Makwanyane*, 1995 (3) SA 391.

sentences are prohibited by article I of the *American Declaration*. It has held that mandatory sentencing 'leads to the arbitrary deprivation of life within the meaning of Article I of the Declaration' according to 'accepted principles of treaty interpretation'.[81] The Commission has also suggested that mandatory sentencing, by eliminating any individual determination of an appropriate sentence, may impact upon the right to an appeal, by precluding any consideration of factual issues at that stage, and upon the prohibition of the death penalty except for the 'most serious offences'.[82] The Commission's case law with respect to mandatory sentencing received a stunning endorsement from the Eastern Caribbean Court of Appeal on 2 April 2001, which ruled the mandatory imposition of the death penalty in St. Vincent and the Grenadines and St. Lucia to violate constitutional prohibitions of torture or inhuman or degrading punishment or other treatment.[83] Referring to the Commission's rulings in *McKenzie et al.* v. *Jamaica* and *Baptiste* v. *Grenada*, Chief Justice Byron concluded that 'the requirement of humanity in our Constitution does impose a duty for consideration of the individual circumstances of the offence and the offender before a sentence of death could be imposed in accordance with its provisions'.[84]

The case law of the Commission has also dealt with amnesty, pardon and commutation as part of Article I's implicit content. Article 4§6 of the *American Convention* and article 6§4 of the *International Covenant on Civil and Political Rights* make this explicit. For the Commission, article I of the *Declaration* includes the right to apply for amnesty, pardon or commutation of sentence, to be informed of when the competent authority will consider the offender's case, to make representations, in person or by counsel, to the competent authority, and to receive a decision from that authority within a reasonable period of time prior to execution. It also entails the right not to have capital punishment imposed while such a petition is pending before the competent authority. The Commission requires that States establish a procedure for such applications so that condemned persons have an effective opportunity to exercise this right, a remedy.[85]

Article 4 of the *Convention* prohibits States from reintroducing the death penalty if it has already been abolished, and from extending it to other crimes for which it was not previously available. The Commission has regularly complained about re-enactment of the death penalty, where it has already been abolished.[86]

---

[81] *Edwards* et al. v. *Bahamas*, para. 139.   [82] *Ibid.*, para. 139.
[83] *Spence v. The Queen, Hughes v. The Queen*, Criminal Appeal Nos. 20 of 1998 and 14 of 1997, Judgment of 2 April 2001 (Eastern Caribbean Court of Appeal).
[84] *Ibid.*, para. 46.   [85] *Edwards* et al. v. *Bahamas*, para. 170.
[86] 'Annual Report of the Inter-American Commission on Human Rights, 1971', OAS Doc. OEA/Ser.L/V/II.25, doc. 9, p. 33; Inter-American Commission on Human Rights, *Ten Years of Activities, 1971–1981*, Washington: Organization of American States, 1982, at p. 316; 'Report on the Situation of Human Rights in Argentina, 1982', OAS Doc. OEA/Ser.L/V/II.49, doc. 19 corr.1, p. 29; 'Annual Report

However, it balked at holding that the United States had breached article I of the *Declaration* when new legislation reinstated and extended the death penalty following the 1972 judgment of the Supreme Court of the United States in *Furman* v. *Georgia*.[87] In that decision, the Court ruled that procedures in capital cases were unconstitutional, forcing United States legislators to introduce new legislation that, by and large, was then upheld by national courts as consistent with the Constitution.[88] The Inter-American Commission said it had no evidence that the United States had abolished the death penalty under its law so as to preclude it from applying it in the applicant's case.

With respect to the requirement that capital punishment only be imposed for the 'most serious crimes', the Commission would also appear to consider this to be a part of article I's implicit content. In *Garza*, which concerned a drug trafficking-related murder, the Commission wrote:

> Further, the Commission is not satisfied based upon the information available that the norms of international law under Article I of the Declaration, as informed by current developments in international human rights law, prevented the State from prescribing the penalty for the crimes for which Mr. Garza was tried and convicted. In particular, the Commission does not find before it sufficient evidence establishing the existence of an international legal norm binding upon the United States, under Article I of the Declaration or under customary international law, that prohibited the extension of the death penalty to Mr. Garza's crimes, provided that they are properly considered to be of a 'most serious' nature.[89]

Use of the death penalty in Cuba for politically related crimes has been a frequent cause for censure by the Commission.[90] In its 1988–1989 Report, the Commission took note of the execution of four officers in Cuba, following sentencing for crimes of drug trafficking and the commission of hostile acts against third countries. The Commission observed that the crimes were not capital crimes, and that 'the celerity with which the trials were conducted, the publicity they received, and the lack of outside observers at the trial raise well-founded doubts as to compliance with fundamental guarantees of due process'.[91]

---

of the Inter-American Commission on Human Rights, 1981–1980', OAS Doc. OEA/Ser.L/V/II.57 doc. 6 rev.1, p. 106; 'Report on the Situation of Human Rights in Chile, 1985', OAS Doc. OAS/Ser.L/V/II.66 doc. 17, pp. 48–50.

[87] *Furman* v. *Georgia*, 408 US 238, 92 S.Ct. 2726, 33 L.Ed.2d 346 (1972).

[88] *Gregg* v. *Georgia*, 428 US 153, 96 S.Ct. 2909, 49 L.Ed.2d 859 (1976).

[89] *Garza* v. *United States*, para. 95.

[90] 'Sixth Report on the Situation of Political Prisoners in Cuba', OAS Doc. OEA/Ser.L/V/II.48 doc. 7, pp. 10–11; 'The Situation of Human Rights in Cuba, Seventh Report', OAS Doc. OEA/Ser.L/V/II.61 doc. 29 rev.1, pp. 71–72; 'Annual Report of the Inter-American Commission on Human Rights, 1991', OAS Doc. OEA/Ser.L/V/II.81 rev.1 doc. 6, pp. 196–197.

[91] 'Annual Report of the Inter-American Commission on Human Rights, 1988–1989', OAS Doc. OEA/Ser.L/V/II.76 doc. 10, p. 158. Also: 'Annual Report of the Inter-American Commission on Human Rights, 1999', OAS Doc. OEA/Ser.L/V/II.106 doc. 6 rev., para. 48.

8.2 The *American Convention on Human Rights*

8.2.1 *Drafting of the* Convention

At the Fifth Meeting of Consultation of the Ministers of Foreign Affairs, held in Santiago, Chile, in August–September 1959, agreement was reached to advance the protection of human rights in the Western hemisphere with a convention, in keeping with a suggestion from the Inter-American Juridical Committee.[92] The Inter-American Council of Jurists was mandated to prepare a draft, and this body met in Santiago during August and September. Only two years earlier, during debate in the Third Committee of the General Assembly on the text of article 6 of the *International Covenant on Civil and Political Rights*, Uruguay had been uncompromisingly abolitionist. Now it presented a draft right to life provision that was inspired by article 6 of the draft *International Covenant*, admitting the death penalty as an exception, adding that it could only be applied 'in those countries where capital punishment exists' for 'the most serious crimes',[93] pursuant to the sentence of a competent court, in accordance with previous law, and not for reasons of a political nature.

A Working Group considered the Uruguayan proposal and prepared a revised draft, based on a comparative study of the *American Declaration*, the *European Convention on Human Rights*, and the draft *International Covenant on Civil and Political Rights*.[94] Upon the suggestion of the Mexican representative, the phrase 'reasons of a political nature' in paragraph 3 was replaced with 'political offences'. A final paragraph, dealing with juveniles and pregnant women, in language similar to that of paragraph 6§5 of the draft *Covenant*, was added. The Venezuelan representative suggested a change that would forbid execution of persons under eighteen yet make no reference to the moment when the crime was committed, but the final version, proposed by Haiti, mirrored the United

---

[92] *Inter-American Yearbook on Human Rights 1968*, Washington: Organisation of American States, 1973, p. 67.

[93] OAS Doc. OEA/ser.I/ENG/CIJ-47, doc. 21:

    1.　No one shall be arbitrarily deprived of their life. Every individual's right to life shall be protected by law.

    2.　In those countries where capital punishment exists, sentence of death may be imposed only as a penalty for the most serious crimes pursuant to the sentence of a competent court and in accordance with a previous law that establishes such punishment.

    3.　In no case shall capital punishment be applied for reasons of a political nature.'

[94] 'Report of the Work Group Appointed by the Special Committee to Study and Propose Articles on Human, Civil and Political Rights to be Inserted in the Convention', OAS Doc. OEA/ser.I/ENG/CIJ-47, doc. 52 (Eng.) Rev., p. 1. The report of the Work Group says it examined 'the project of the Commission on Human Rights', presumably an error, because the final text referred to the draft covenant approved by the Third Committee of the General Assembly in 1957, at least with respect to those articles, such as the right to life article, which had already been adopted.

Nations text.[95] The draft right to life provision was adopted by the Working Group and subsequently approved by the Council of Jurists.[96]

This draft was submitted to governments for consideration at the Eleventh Inter-American Conference, scheduled for 1961 but postponed.[97] It was eventually considered by the Second Special Inter-American Conference, held in Rio de Janeiro in November 1965. To the Council of Jurists draft were added two additional proposals, one from Chile and one from Uruguay. The Chilean proposal confined itself to the addition of a fifth paragraph dealing with amnesty and pardon, borrowed from article 6§4 of the draft *International Covenant on Civil and Political Rights*.[98] The Uruguayan delegation transformed the text into a thoroughly abolitionist provision. In substance, the contents of the Council of Jurists draft with the addition of the Chilean amendment were repeated, except that paragraph 2 called on States to abolish the death penalty. In an attempt to appease retentionist sentiment and thereby effect a compromise, Uruguay suggested that States be permitted to retain the death penalty by making a reservation to the *Convention*.[99] The Fourth Committee of the Rio Conference[100] considered

---

[95] Inter-American Council of Jurists, Fourth meeting, August–September, 1959, Doc. 81 (Summary Record of the Fourth Session of the Special Committee, 1 September 1959), p. 4: 'Capital punishment shall not be imposed on persons who, at the time of the commission of the crime, were under 18 years of age; nor shall it be applied to pregnant women.'

[96] OAS Doc. OEA/ser.I/ENG/CIJ-47, doc. 128 (Eng.) rev., OEA/ser.I/ENG/CIJ-47, doc. 101 (Eng.); OAS Doc. OEA/ser.I/ENG/CIJ-47, doc. 119 (Eng.), p. 63:
> 1. The right to life is inherent in the human person. The right shall be protected by law starting with the moment of conception. No one shall be arbitrarily deprived of his life.
> 2. In countries where capital punishment has not been abolished, sentence of death may be imposed only as a penalty for the most serious crimes and pursuant to the final judgment of a competent court, and in accordance with a law establishing such punishment, enacted before the commission of the crime.
> 3. In no case shall capital punishment be applied for political offences.
> 4. Capital punishment shall not be imposed on persons who, at the time of the commission of the crime, were under 18 years of age; nor shall it be applied to pregnant women.

[97] Resolution XX of the Fourth Meeting of the Inter-American Council of Jurists.

[98] OAS Doc. OEA/Ser.L/V/II.14 Doc. 7 (Eng.) Corr., p. 4; OAS Doc. OEA/Ser.E/XI.1 Doc. 35:
> 5. Every person condemned to death shall have the right to request pardon or commutation of sentence. Amnesty, pardon or commutation of capital punishment may be granted in all cases.

[99] OAS Doc. OEA/Ser.L/V/II.14 Doc. 7 (Eng.) Corr., pp. 3–4; OAS Doc. OEA/Ser.E/XI.1 Doc. 49:
> 1. Every person has the right to have his life respected. This right shall be protected by law from the moment of conception. No one shall be arbitrarily deprived of his life.
> 2. The States Parties to this Convention shall abolish capital punishment. Reservations to this provision shall be admitted solely on condition that sentence of death may be imposed only as a penalty for the most serious crimes and pursuant to the final judgment of an independent and impartial regular court, which will satisfy due process of law, and in accordance with a law establishing such punishment enacted prior to the commission of the crime.
> 3. In no case shall capital punishment be inflicted for political offences.
> 4. Capital punishment shall not be imposed upon persons who, at the time the crime was committed, were under 18 years of age; nor shall it be applied to pregnant women.
> 5. Amnesty, pardon or commutation of sentence of death may be granted in all cases.

[100] OAS Doc. OEA/Ser.E/XIII.1 Doc. 144–148.

the three drafts, referring them to the Permanent Council of the Organisation of American States for study by the Inter-American Commission on Human Rights and other organs and bodies of the Organisation of American States.[101] The Council sent the three drafts to the Committee on Juridical Political Affairs and to the Inter-American Commission on Human Rights.

The Commission began considering the draft convention at its thirteenth session, in April 1966, assigning one of its members, Carlos A. Dunshee de Abranches, as rapporteur. The Commission studied the drafts in more detail at its Fourteenth Session, in October 1966, completing a thorough examination of the first nineteen articles, dealing with civil and political rights. The Commission had opted in favour of the Uruguayan draft, with its abolitionist provisions, which it called more 'complete and precise'. There were some minor changes: the right to life was to be protected from the moment of conception 'in general';[102] the expression 'most serious crimes' was substituted for 'exceptionally serious crimes'; and the words 'or more than seventy years' were added to paragraph 4, introducing a prohibition of execution of the elderly.[103] To paragraph 5, the Commission added a sentence: 'Capital punishment shall not be imposed while such a petition is pending decision by competent authority.'[104] The Commission also decided to examine in greater depth the question of capital punishment by commissioning Angela Acuña de Chacón to prepare a study on 'The Right to Life', which it considered the following year.[105] The study included extensive documentation on the laws in American countries concerning the death penalty and reviewed the reasons for its abolition.[106]

[101] Resolution XXIV: 'Final Act of the Second Special Inter-American Conference', OAS Doc. OEA/ Ser.E/XIII.1 Doc. 150, pp. 59–60.
[102] The addition of these two words tempered the anti-abortionism of the *Convention*. See: *White and Potter* v. *United States*.
[103] OAS Doc. OEA/Ser.L/V/II.15 doc. 29 (esp.), p. 25.
[104] *Ibid.*, p. 26; OAS Doc. OEA/Ser.L/V/II.19 Doc. 4 (Eng.) rev., pp. 11–12.
  1. Every person has the right to have his life respected. This right shall be protected by law, in general, from the moment of conception. No one shall be arbitrarily deprived of his life.
  2. The Contracting Parties shall abolish capital punishment. Reservations to this provision shall be admitted solely on condition that sentence of death may be imposed only as a penalty for exceptionally serious crimes and pursuant to the final judgment of an independent and impartial regular court, which will satisfy due process of law, and in accordance with a law establishing such punishment, enacted prior to the commission of the crime.
  3. In no case shall capital punishment be inflicted for political offences.
  4. Capital punishment shall not be imposed upon persons who, at the time the crime was committed, were under 18 years of age or over 70 years of age; nor shall it be applied to pregnant women.
  5. Every person condemned to death shall have the right to request pardon or commutation of sentence. Amnesty, pardon or commutation of capital punishment may be granted in all cases. Capital punishment shall not be imposed while a decision is pending on the first petition for commutation presented to the competent authority.
[105] OAS Doc. OEA/Ser.L./V/II.15 Doc. 29, paras. 71–72; OAS Doc. OEA/Ser.L/V/II/17 Doc. 24, paras. 65–67.
[106] OAS Doc. OEA/Ser.L/V/II/17 Doc. 24, para. 67.

The Commission's report was referred to the Committee on Juridical-Political Affairs, which focused its energies on the advisability of creating a regional human rights system, given the recent adoption by the General Assembly of the United Nations of the *International Covenants* and the *Optional Protocol.*[107] A consultation with Member States on this subject followed. However, the substantive rights of the draft convention were not considered in this process.

The Commission returned to the draft convention at its seventeenth session, in October 1967. It appointed Carlos A. Dunshee de Abranches to make a comparative study of the Commission text, the relevant provision in the *International Covenant on Civil and Political Rights*, and the original Commission of Jurists text.[108] Dunshee's report noted that, in contrast with the other instruments, the Commission text 'obliged' States parties to abolish the death penalty. He also observed that, unlike the *International Covenant on Civil and Political Rights*, the Commission draft did not refer to the *Genocide Convention.*[109] The report concluded that this was unnecessary, as it was a limitation of a general character that would be applicable in any case, by virtue of other provisions of the convention.[110] The report on the Commission draft added a procedural limitation, that the death penalty could only be imposed by a 'regular Court', thus eliminating the competence of *ad hoc* or special courts. Finally, the text extended the prohibition of the death penalty to persons over seventy years of age,[111] in distinction with the *Covenant*, which imposed no upper age limit.

The Council of the Organization of American States took note of the work of the Commission, and asked it to draw up a revised and complete draft convention. The Council was quite clear in ordering the Commission to retain the amendments and changes that it had suggested to the Council of Jurists draft.[112] The Council made specific comments on the substantive articles and, with respect to the right to life, it indicated that it had no disagreement with the abolitionist paragraph 2 of the draft article, although it suggested that the provision be reconciled with the general draft article concerning reservations to the convention.[113]

In keeping with the mandate from the Council, a special session of the Inter-American Commission on Human Rights was held in July 1968, at which a new study of the substantive provisions fo the draft convention was carried out. The Commission decided to reconsider the earlier changes it had recommended and again modified the right to life article so that it corresponded far more closely to the text of the *International Covenant on Civil and Political Rights*.

[107] OAS Doc. OEA/Ser.G/IV/C-i-787 Rev.

[108] OAS Doc. OEA/Ser.L/V/II.18 Doc. 25, paras. 50, 52.

[109] *Convention for the Prevention and Punishment of the Crime of Genocide*, (1951) 78 UNTS 277.

[110] OAS Doc. OEA/Ser.L/V/II.19 Doc. 4 (Eng.) Rev., p. 13.   [111] *Ibid.*, pp. 14–15.

[112] OAS Doc. OEA/Ser.G/IV-C-i-837 Rev.3.

[113] OAS Doc. OEA/Ser.L/V/II.19 Doc. 51 (Eng.), p. 19.

In so doing, the openly abolitionist provision that had derived from the Uruguayan draft disappeared, in apparent violation of the instructions from the Council. The only major differences with article 6 of the *Covenant* were the upper age limit of seventy years and the political offence exclusion.[114] The Inter-American Commission transmitted this revised draft to the Permanent Council, which in turn referred to it the Specialized Inter-American Conference on Human Rights, to be held in San Jose de Costa Rica, from 7 to 22 November 1969.[115]

Uruguay, whose abolitionist provision had originally been accepted by the Commission and then subsequently removed, said that the existing version deviated from its convictions and traditions. Uruguay admitted that the revised Commission draft was, however, a result of 'unavoidable compromises' and that there did not seem to be 'a climate of opinion favouring the elimination of the death penalty'.[116] That being the case, Uruguay felt it useful to 'refine' the draft by adding an additional paragraph: 'The death penalty shall not be established in States that have abolished it, nor shall its application be extended to crimes with respect to which it does not presently apply.'[117] Ecuador proposed adding a similar paragraph, foreclosing the return of capital punishment where it had already been abolished. Ecuador also suggested a rewording of paragraph 2 of the article.[118] The effect of these changes was to make the convention an abolitionist instrument, at least for those States that have already abolished the death penalty at the time of ratification or subsequently.

---

[114] *Ibid.*, p. 20; OAS Doc. OEA/Ser.L/V/II.19 Doc. 48 Rev.1:

1.   Every person has the right to have his life respected. This right shall be protected by law, in general, from the moment of conception. No one shall be arbitrarily deprived of his life.

2.   In countries which have not abolished the death penalty, sentence of death may be imposed only for the most serious crimes and pursuant to a final judgment rendered by a competent court, and in accordance with a law establishing such punishment, enacted prior to the commission of the crime.

3.   In no case shall capital punishment be inflicted for political offences.

4.   Capital punishment shall not be imposed upon persons who, at the time the crime was committed, were under 18 years of age or over 70 years of age; nor shall it be applied to pregnant women.

5.   Every person condemned to death shall have the right to request pardon or commutation of sentence. Amnesty, pardon or commutation of capital punishment may be granted in all cases. Capital punishment shall not be imposed while a decision is pending on the first application for commutation, presented to the competent authority.

[115] OAS Doc. OEA/Ser.G/V-C-d-1631. Annotations of the draft were prepared for the Conference by the Commission. For the brief comments on the right to life provision, see: OAS Doc. OEA/Ser.L/V/II.19 Doc. 53 (Eng.), pp. 9–10; OAS Doc. OEA/Ser.K/XVI/1.1 Doc. 12 (Eng.), pp. 9–10.

[116] OAS Doc. OEA/Ser.K/XVI/1.1 Doc. 6 (Eng.), p. 2; OAS Doc. OEA/Ser.L/V/II.22 Doc. 10.

[117] *Ibid.*

[118] OAS Doc. OEA/Ser.K/XVI/1.1 Doc. 23 (Eng.), p. 2:

In the countries that maintain the death penalty, sentence of death may be imposed only for the most serious crimes and pursuant to a final judgment rendered by a competent court, and in accordance with a law specifying the crime and establishing that penalty therefor, enacted prior to the commission of the crime.

The Uruguayan and Ecuadorean proposals were considered briefly in Committee I of the San Jose Conference and were by and large accepted. The United States delegate, Richard D. Kearney, expressed concern about the value of the amendment, suggesting it might lead to results that were very different from those intended by the *Convention* in general.[119] The Salvadorean representative said that, although he was in sympathy with the Uruguayan amendment, he wondered about the effect this might have on the elaboration of modern penal legislation in the hemisphere.[120] Costa Rica abstained in the vote because it sought total abolition of the death penalty.[121] The *rapporteur* later described the Uruguayan amendment as a 'conciliatory formula, taking into account the trend in the Americas toward eliminating this form of punishment', adding that 'the Committee reflected this trend' by adopting the second paragraph.[122]

The United States urged deletion of the paragraph dealing with political offences.[123] The United States observed that the assassination of a president might be deemed to fall within the political offence exception. Brazil agreed with the comments of the United States, supporting the proposed deletion of the third paragraph.[124] During the debate in Committee I, El Salvador proposed that a definition of political offence be provided in the instrument.[125] However, delegations felt that, while it was important to have such a definition, this matter fell within the province of other organizations in the Inter-American system, and the Salvadorean text was transmitted to the Council of the Organization of American States with a resolution intended to effect the legal work necessary in defining the term political offence.[126]

The United States also urged deletion of paragraph 4, because it said 'the proscription of capital punishment within arbitrary age limits presents various difficulties in law'. However, the United States couched its proposal in abolitionist terms, noting that such a provision weakened the text, given 'the general trend, already apparent, for the gradual abolition of the death penalty'.[127] The United

---

[119] OAS Doc. OEA/Ser.K/XVI/1.1 Doc. 36, p. 161.   [120] *Ibid.*   [121] *Ibid.*, p. 162.

[122] OAS Doc. OEA/Ser.K/XVI/1.1 Doc. 60 (Eng.), p. 4.

[123] *Ibid.*, p. 9; OAS Doc. OEA/Ser.L/V/II.22 Doc. 10.

[124] OAS Doc. OEA/Ser.K/XVI/1.1 Doc. 31 (Eng.), pp. 1–2.

[125] OAS Doc. OEA/Ser.K/XVI/1.1 Doc. 38 Corr. 1, p. 165.

[126] OAS Doc. OEA/Ser.K/XVI/1.1 Doc. 55 (Eng.); OAS Doc. OEA/Ser.K/XVI/1.1 Doc. 59 (Eng.). See also the 'Report of the Rapporteur of Committee I', OAS Doc. OEA/Ser.L/XVI/1.1 Doc. 60 (Eng.), p. 5. This was approved at the Second Plenary Session of the Conference: OAS Doc. OEA/Ser.K/XVI/1.1 Doc. 59 (Eng.) Rev.1. Definition of the term 'political offence' arises frequently in matters of extradition and asylum, and the law on this point is, to say the least, unsettled. See the definition given by dissenting Judge Alvarez in the *Asylum Case (Colombia v. Peru)*, [1950] ICJ Reports 266, at p. 298: 'International law contains no precise rules on the subject, but the numerous precedents in existence may serve to provide general directives. It may be said that any act which purports to overthrow the domestic political order of a country must be regarded as political; in that sense even murder may sometimes be termed a political offence. This consequently also applies to military rebellion.'

[127] OAS Doc. OEA/Ser.K/XVI/1.1 Doc. 10 (Eng.), p. 9.

States delegate subsequently withdrew this proposal during debate in Committee I.[128] Almost two decades later, in an effort to claim it was a 'persistent objector' to the developing norm prohibiting execution for crimes committed while under the age of eighteen, the United States contended that 'the United States delegate at the drafting of the *American Convention* pointed out that the United States had problems with Article 4§5's arbitrary age limit of eighteen conflicting with its federal structure'.[129] But the 1969 debates at the time the *Convention* was being adopted do not tend to bear out this claim.

The final version of the *American Convention on Human Rights* was approved by the Conference and opened for signature, ratification and accession.[130] But, in order to register their commitment to abolition, fourteen of the nineteen delegations at the Conference made the following declaration in the final plenary session:

> The undersigned Delegations, participants in the Specialized Inter-American Conference on Human Rights, in response to the majority sentiment expressed in the course of the debates on the prohibition of the death penalty, in agreement with the most pure humanistic traditions of our peoples, solemnly declare our firm hope of seeing the application of the death penalty eradicated from the American environment as of the present and our unwavering goal of making all possible efforts so that, in a short time, an additional protocol to the American Convention on Human Rights – Pact of San José, Costa Rica – may consecrate the final abolition of the death penalty and place America once again in the vanguard of the defence of the fundamental rights of man.[131]

In an advisory opinion issued in 1984, the Inter-American Court of Human Rights referred to this declaration, describing it as '[t]he prevailing attitude, and clearly the majority view in the Conference'.[132]

Signed on 22 November 1969, it came into force on 18 July 1978 following its ratification by eleven States. As of 1 May 2001, twenty-five States had ratified the *American Convention*. Seventeen of the States parties to the *Convention* have abolished the death penalty in their domestic law,[133] and therefore, by virtue of article 4§3 of the *Convention*, which prevents States that have abolished the death penalty from reintroducing it, they are also abolitionist at international law.

---

[128] OAS Doc. OEA/Ser.K/XVI/1.1 Doc. 40 Corr.1, p. 170. In *Roach and Pinkerton* v. *United States*, as evidence of its rejection of the norm concerning execution of juveniles, the United States contended that 'the United States delegate at the drafting of the *American Convention* pointed out that the United States had problems with Article 4§5's arbitrary age limit of eighteen conflicting with its federal structure' (at para. 38(f)).

[129] *Roach and Pinkerton* v. *United States*, para. 38(f).

[130] For the text, see Appendix 20, at pp. 436–437.　　[131] OAS Doc. OEA/Ser.K/XVI/1.2, p. 467.

[132] *Restrictions to the Death Penalty (Arts. 4§2 and 4§4 American Convention on Human Rights)*, Advisory Opinion OC-3/83 of 8 September 1983, Series B, No. 3, para. 58.

[133] Argentina, Bolivia, Brazil, Colombia, Costa Rica, Dominican Republic, Ecuador, El Salvador, Guatemala, Haiti, Honduras, Mexico, Nicaragua, Panama, Paraguay, Peru, Uruguay, Venezuela.

8.2.2 *Reservations to the* Convention

The Dominican Republic ratified the American Convention on Human Rights on 19 April 1978, making at the time a declaration reinforcing its commitment to abolition of the death penalty and setting out its aspiration that the principle of abolition would come to have general application within the hemisphere.[134] Three States, Barbados, Trinidad and Tobago and Dominica, have made reservations with respect to specific limitations on use of the death penalty.[135] When Barbados ratified the *Convention* in 1982, it made a reservation with respect to article 4§4, noting that, under its criminal law, treason was punishable by death, although the whole matter of the death penalty was under review.[136] A second reservation to article 4§5 noted that while youth or old age may be factors to be considered by the Privy Council in deciding whether the death penalty should be carried out, Barbadian legislation allowed the execution of persons over sixteen and set no upper age limit.[137] Trinidad and Tobago ratified the *Convention* in 1991, with a reservation noting that its laws did not prohibit execution of a person over seventy years of age.[138] Dominica ratified the *Convention* with a reservation to the phrase 'or related crimes' which appears in article 4§4.[139]

Guatemala's reservation specified that article 54 of its *Constitution* only excluded the application of the death penalty to political crimes and not to common crimes related to political crimes. In the early 1980s, four politically related death sentences handed down in Guatemala provoked individual petitions to the Inter-American Commission of Human Rights.[140] The four condemned men were executed by firing squad, after being sentenced by 'Courts of Special Jurisdiction'. The Commission noted 'the innumerable procedural nullities' in the judicial proceedings, including lack of independence and impartiality of the court, refusal to grant the accused adequate means to prepare their defence, denial of the right to be assisted by defence counsel of their choice and to communicate with them freely and privately, denial of the right to examine witnesses

---

[134] (1979) 1144 UNTS 208, OAS Doc. OEA/Ser.L.V/II.71, Doc. 6 rev.1, at p. 56 (for the text of its declaration, see Appendix 20, p. 437).

[135] There do not appear to have been any objections by States parties to reservations formulated with respect to article 4 and the death penalty.

[136] (1983) 1298 UNTS 441, OAS Doc. OEA/Ser.L.V/II.71, Doc. 6 rev.1, at p. 58 (for the text of its reservation, see Appendix 20, p. 437).

[137] *Ibid.* No similar reservation was made by Barbados when it ratified the *International Covenant on Civil and Political Rights*, which has an identical provision. In 1982, Martin Marsh, who was convicted of murder committed while seventeen years of age, was executed by Barbados.

[138] (1979) 1144 UNTS 210, OAS Doc. OEA/Ser.L/V/II.81 rev.1 Doc. 6, p. 335 (for the text of its reservation, see Appendix 20, p. 437).

[139] OAS Doc. OEA/Ser.L/V/II.88 Doc. 9 rev., at p. 243 (for the text of its reservation, see Appendix 20, p. 437).

[140] *Marcelino Marroquín* et al. v. *Guatemala* (Case No. 8094), *Walter Vinicio Marroquín González* et al. v. *Guatemala* (Case No. 9038), Resolution No. 15/84, reported in OAS Doc. OEA/Ser.L/V/II.66 Doc. 10 rev.1, at pp. 81–84.

or experts, and being compelled in several cases to declare themselves guilty and incriminate themselves. In some of the trials, the right to appeal was denied. The right to a public trial was also denied; the proceedings were inquisitorial and held in private. But the heart of the issue was the fact that the death sentence was imposed for crimes that were not punishable by death at the time of Guatemala's ratification of the *American Convention*, in violation of article 4§2. In an exchange of notes with the Inter-American Commission, Guatemala had argued that its reservation to article 4§4 permitted it to regulate and legislate with respect to the death penalty for common crimes related to political offences.[141] The only reasonable interpretation that could be given to its reservation, argued Guatemala, was one that permitted it to enact new legislation imposing the death penalty for common crimes related to political offences.

The Commission sought an opinion from the Inter-American Court of Human Rights in exercise of its advisory jurisdiction.[142] The Court discussed the relationship between paragraphs 2 and 4 of article 4, noting that a reservation to paragraph 4 could not undermine the 'absolute prohibition' upon the expansion of the scope of the death penalty set out in paragraph 2. Referring to Guatemala's reservation to paragraph 4, the Court concluded that 'the only subject reserved is the right to continue the application of the death penalty to political offences or related common crimes to which that penalty applied previously'.[143] Speculating on the behaviour of future parties to the *Convention*, the Court said 'a reservation made to paragraph 2, but not to paragraph 4, would permit the reserving State to punish new offences with the death penalty in the future provided, however, that the offences in question are mere common crimes not related to political offences'.[144] In other words, in order to protect the possibility of enlarging the scope of the death penalty to political crimes and related common crimes, Guatemala would have had to make a reservation to both paragraphs 2 and 4 of article 4. But the Court said there was 'no reason for assuming either as a matter of logic or law' that Guatemala had meant such a result, and that its reservation to paragraph 4 should be taken to imply a reservation to paragraph 2 as well.[145]

In its advisory opinion on the Guatemalan reservations, the Court confirmed that blanket reservations to the right to life, as a non-derogable provision, were incompatible with the object and purpose of the *Convention*.[146] However, reservations seeking only to restrict certain aspects of a non-derogable right, such as that made by Guatemala, could not be presumed contrary to the *Convention*,

---

[141] *Restrictions to the Death Penalty (Arts. 4§2 and 4§4 American Convention on Human Rights)*, p. 10.
[142] *American Convention on Human Rights*, art. 64§1. See also: Thomas Buergenthal, 'The Advisory Practice of the Inter-American Human Rights Court', (1985) 79 *AJIL* 1.
[143] *Restrictions to the Death Penalty (Arts. 4§2 and 4§4 American Convention on Human Rights)*, para. 70.
[144] *Ibid.*   [145] *Ibid.*, para. 71.
[146] *Vienna Convention on the Law of Treaties*, (1979) 1155 UNTS 331, art. 20§1.

providing they did not deprive the right to life as a whole of its basic purpose.[147] The point may eventually merit some interest, if the United States ever ratifies the *Convention*. In December 1977, President Jimmy Carter submitted the *American Convention on Human Rights* to the United States Senate for advice and consent, accompanied by a draft reservation to article 4 which noted that its provisions on capital punishment might be in conflict with the 'unsettled' state of domestic legislation, and that: 'United States adherence to Article 4 is subject to the Constitution and other law of the United States.'[148] In light of the Court's *dictum*, such a reservation is probably illegal.

Acceptance of the compulsory jurisdiction of the Inter-American Court of Human Rights is effected by making a distinct declaration. In so doing, Trinidad and Tobago formulated a reservation stating that the Court can only have jurisdiction to the extent that it is consistent with the Constitution of Trinidad and Tobago. At the request of the Inter-American Commission on Human Rights, the Inter-American Court has issued provisional measures orders against Trinidad and Tobago, in accordance with article 63§2 of the *Convention*. Trinidad and Tobago now claims that, because of this reservation, the Commission is without jurisdiction to prevent a sentence that is authorized by the country's Constitution and laws and pronounced by a court of competent jurisdiction from being carried into effect. According to Trinidad and Tobago, it may accordingly carry out a death sentence while a case is pending before the Commission, despite an order from the Court.[149] Sadly, on 4 June 1999, Trinidad and Tobago executed Joey

---

[147] *Restrictions to the Death Penalty (Arts. 4§2 and 4§4 American Convention on Human Rights)*, para. 61.

[148] US Department of State Publication 8961, General Foreign Policy Series 310, Letters of Transmittal and Submittal, with Suggested Reservations, Understandings, and Declarations (November 1978):

> Article 4 deals with the right to life generally, and includes provisions on capital punishment. Many of the provisions of article 4 are not in accord with United States law and policy, or deal with matters in which the law is unsettled. The Senate may wish to enter a reservation as follows: 'United States adherence to Article 4 is subject to the Constitution and other law of the United States.
>
> [Article 5], [p]aragraph 5 requires that minors subject to criminal proceedings are to be separated from adults and brought before specialized tribunals as speedily as possible... With respect to paragraph 5, the law reserves the right to try minors as adults in certain cases and there is no present intent to revise these laws.
>
> The following statement is recommended.
>
> 'The United States ... with respect to paragraph 5, reserves the right in appropriate cases to subject minors "to procedures and penalties applicable to adults".'

[149] *Hilaire* v. *Trinidad and Tobago* (Case No. 11.816), Report No. 43/98, Admissibility, 25 September 1998, para. 7; *Noel* v. *Trinidad and Tobago* (Case No. 11.854), Report No. 44/98, 25 September 1998, Admissibility, para. 7; *Garcia* v. *Trinidad and Tobago* (Case No. 11.855), Report No. 45/98, Admissibility, 25 September 1998, para 6; *Baptiste* v. *Trinidad and Tobago* (Case No. 11.840), Report No. 91/98, 3 November 1998, para. 7. Because Trinidad and Tobago has been the only death penalty State to have ratified the Convention and accepted the compulsory jurisdiction of the Inter-American Court, it has been subject to 'provisional measures' orders, in accordance with article 63§2 of the *Convention*: 'In cases of extreme gravity and urgency, and when necessary to avoid irreparable damage to persons, the Court shall adopt such provisional measures as it deems pertinent in matters it has under consideration. With respect to a case not yet submitted to the Court, it may act at the request of the Commission.'

Ramiah, and on 28 July 1999 it executed Anthony Briggs, despite provisional measures orders by the Court.[150]

The Inter-American Court addressed the issue when Trinidad and Tobago invoked its reservation as a preliminary objection in the *Hilaire* case.[151] Trinidad and Tobago argued that the reservation was a bar to the Court exercising jurisdiction in the case. Alternatively, it argued that, if the reservation were judged incompatible with the object and purpose of the *Convention*, then the original declaration recognizing the jurisdiction of the Court (subject to limitations) would be null and void *ab initio* and therefore frustrate the Court's jurisdiction. The Court relied on earlier decisions in two Peruvian cases, holding that a court cannot be deprived of its jurisdiction by a unilateral act of a State once such jurisdiction has been accepted. The Court said that 'accepting said declaration in the manner proposed by the State would lead to a situation in which the Court would have the State's Constitution as its first point of reference, and the American Convention only as a subsidiary parameter, a situation which would cause a fragmentation of the international legal order for the protection of human rights, and which would render illusory the object and purpose of the Convention'.[152]

The Inter-American Court held the reservation to be invalid: '[I]t completely subordinates the application of the American Convention to the internal legislation of Trinidad and Tobago as decided by its courts. This implies that the instrument of acceptance is manifestly incompatible with the object and purpose of the Convention.'[153] The argument whereby a finding of invalidity of the reservation would in effect render the declaration null and void and thereby deprive the Court of jurisdiction was not considered. The ruling in *Hilaire* has been reiterated in Court decisions on preliminary objections in two other cases pending against Trinidad and Tobago, *Constantine* et al. and *Benjamin* et al.

8.2.3 *Denunciation of the* Convention

Pursuant to article 78 of the *Convention*, a State party may denounce it at any time following five years from the time it has entered into force. The State party must provide notice of one year of such denunciation, which is communicated to the other States parties by the Secretary General of the Organization. Of course, the State remains responsible under the *Convention* for any violation committed during the period when it was in force for that country.

---

[150] 'Annual Report of the Inter-American Commission on Human Rights, 1999', para. 90.
[151] *Hilaire* v. *Trinidad and Tobago*, Preliminary Objections, 1 September 2001.
[152] *Constitutional Court* v. *Peru*, Competence, 24 September 1999, Series C, No. 54, para. 93; *Ivcher Bronstein* v. *Peru*, Competence, 24 September 1999, Series C, No. 55, para. 93.
[153] *Ibid.*, para. 88.

There has been only one denunciation of the *Convention*, by Trinidad and Tobago on 26 May 1998. The denunciation is intimately associated with that country's death penalty practice and with its complaints about the petition system before the Inter-American Commission on Human Rights. Trinidad and Tobago tried something similar with the *International Covenant on Civil and Political Rights*. But in that case, it could exclude death penalty litigation before the Human Rights Committee by denouncing the *Optional Protocol* and not the *Covenant* as such. However, with respect to the *American Convention*, where the individual petition procedure is an automatic feature of the treaty regime, this alternative was not available.

The denunciation was accompanied by a lengthy statement explaining that the Judicial Committee of the Privy Council, in *Pratt and Morgan*, had ruled that strict guidelines were to be followed in deciding appeals by persons condemned to death, in order to minimize the delay between sentence and execution.[154] In its celebrated 1993 decision, the Privy Council dictated that no more than five years could elapse, and that this period was to comprise not only domestic appeals but also subsequent applications to international human rights bodies like the Inter-American Commission on Human Rights. The denunciation statement explains that representatives of Trinidad and Tobago had met with officials of the Organization of American States in order to find means of expediting applications before the Commission. According to the statement, '[t]he Commission indicated that whilst it was sympathetic to the problem facing Trinidad and Tobago, the Commission had its own established procedures for the termination of Petitions. Accordingly for reasons which the Government of Trinidad and Tobago respects, the Commission was unable to give any assurances that capital cases would be completed within the timeframe sought.' Trinidad and Tobago said it was 'unable to allow the inability of the Commission to deal with applications in respect of capital cases expeditiously to frustrate the implementation of the lawful penalty for the crime of murder'.

Despite denunciation of the *Convention*, Trinidad and Tobago remains a member of the Organization of American States. Consequently, it continues to be subject to the petition procedure before the Commission for violations of the *American Declaration of the Rights and Duties of Man*. Several applications against Trinidad and Tobago are still pending before the Inter-American Court of Human Rights alleging violations of the *Convention* prior to the denunciation.[155]

---

[154] *Pratt* et al. v. *Attorney General for Jamaica* et al., [1993] 4 All ER 769, [1993] 2 LRC 349, [1994] 2 AC 1, [1993] 3 WLR 995, 43 WIR 340, 14 *HRLJ* 338, 33 ILM 364 (JCPC).

[155] *Hilaire* v. *Trinidad and Tobago* (Case No. 11.816); *Constantine* et al. v. *Trinidad and Tobago* (Case nos. 11.787, 11.814, 11.840, 11.851, 11.853, 11.855, 12.005, 12.021, 12.042, 12.043, 12.052, 12.072, 12.073, 12.075, 12.076, 12.082, 12.093, 12.111, 12.112, 12.129, 12.137, 12.140 and 12.141); *Benjamin* et al. v. *Trinidad and Tobago* (Case No. 12.149).

8.2.4 *Interpretation of the* Convention

Discussing the interpretation of article 4 in general, the Inter-American Court of Human Rights has said:

> The purpose of Article 4 of the Convention is to protect the right to life. But this article, after proclaiming the objective in general terms in its first paragraph, devotes the next five paragraphs to the application of the death penalty. The text of the article as a whole reveals a clear tendency to restrict the scope of this penalty both as far as its imposition and its application are concerned.[156]

Furthermore, death penalty cases require a 'heightened level of scrutiny'.[157] According to the Inter-American Commission on Human Rights, '[t]his "heightened scrutiny" test is consistent with the restrictive approach to the death penalty provisions of human rights treaties advocated by other international authorities'.[158] Relying on the jurisprudence of human rights monitoring bodies, the Commission has held that the right to life provisions of human rights treaties, to the extent they allow for the death penalty, are subject to rules of strict or restrictive interpretation.[159] The Commission considers it relevant, for purposes of interpretation of article 4, to note that death is qualitatively different from other forms of punishment.[160]

Although paragraph 1 of article 4 makes no explicit reference to capital punishment, it does prohibit the taking of life arbitrarily. In the view of the Court, the paragraph governs capital punishment by 'a substantive principle laid down in the first paragraph, which proclaims that "every person has the right to have his life respected", and by the procedural principle that "no one shall be arbitrarily deprived of his life"'.[161] For the Inter-American Commission, '[t]he ordinary meaning of the term "arbitrary" connotes an action or decision that is based on random or convenient selection or choice rather than on reason or nature'.[162] An arbitrary decision 'includes one that is taken in the absence of a reasoned consideration of the circumstances of the case in respect of which the

---

[156] *Restrictions to the Death Penalty (Arts. 4§2 and 4§4 American Convention on Human Rights)*, para. 52.
[157] *Baptiste* v. *Grenada*, para. 64; *Lamey et al.* v. *Jamaica* (Case Nos. 11.826, 11.843, 11.846, 11.847), Report No. 49/01, 4 April 2001, para. 103; *McKenzie* et al. v. *Jamaica* (Case Nos. 12.023, 12.044, 12.107, 12.126, 12.146), Report No 41/00, 13 April 2000, para. 169; *Knights* v. *Grenada* (Case No. 12.028), Report No. 47/01, 4 April 2001, para. 57.
[158] *Ibid.*
[159] *Baptiste* v. *Grenada*, paras. 74–75; *Lamey et al.* v. *Jamaica*, paras. 118–119; *Knights* v. *Grenada*, paras. 66–67; *McKenzie* et al. v. *Jamaica*, paras. 186–187.
[160] *Baptiste* v. *Grenada*, para. 76; *Lamey et al.* v. *Jamaica*, para. 120; *McKenzie* et al. v. *Jamaica*, para. 188; *Knights* v. *Grenada*, para. 68.
[161] *Restrictions to the Death Penalty (Arts. 4§2 and 4§4 American Convention on Human Rights)*, para. 53.
[162] *Baptiste* v. *Grenada*, para. 84; *Lamey et al.* v. *Jamaica*, para. 129. The Commission notes that this is similar to the approach taken by the Human Rights Committee in *Kindler* v. *Canada* (No. 470/1991), UN Doc. A/48/40, Vol. II, p. 138, UN Doc. CCPR/C/45/D/470/1991, 14 *HRLJ* 307, 6 RUDH 165.

decision is made'.[163] Applying this prohibition on the arbitrary deprivation of life, the Commission has held mandatory death sentences to be contrary to article 4: 'Accepted principles of treaty interpretation suggest that sentencing individuals to the death penalty through mandatory sentencing and absent consideration of the individual circumstances of each offender and offence leads to the arbitrary deprivation of life within the meaning of Article 4§1 of the Convention.'[164] Furthermore:

> In this respect, the mandatory death penalty can be regarded as arbitrary within the ordinary meaning of that term. The decision to sentence a person to death is not based upon a reasoned consideration of a particular defendant's case, or upon objective standards that guide courts in identifying circumstances in which the death penalty may or may not be an appropriate punishment. Rather, the penalty flows automatically once the elements of the offence of murder have been established, regardless of the relative degree of gravity of the offence or culpability of the offender.[165]

The text of article 4 of the *American Convention* is in many respects similar to that of article 6 of the *International Covenant on Civil and Political Rights*. For example, although the wording varies slightly, there are no significant legal distinctions between paragraphs 1 of the two instruments, at least as far as the death penalty is concerned.[166] An obvious difference between the two instruments in paragraph 2 is the cross-reference in the *International Covenant* to other provisions of the *Covenant* and to the *Genocide Convention*, something absent in the *American Convention*. The right to life provision of the *American Convention* does not insist that application of the death penalty not be 'contrary to the provisions of the present [Convention]'. In interpretation of the *Covenant*, this cross-reference has been used to support the idea that a breach of any other provision, notably article 14, which concerns procedural rights, is also a breach of the right to life in a capital case. Indeed, in a dissenting opinion on the subject, Human Rights Committee member Bertil Wennergren noted the absence of such a provision in article 4§2 of the *American Convention*.[167] If the procedural guarantees of article 8 are not incorporated by reference within article 4 of the *Convention*, then it would be possible to suspend these procedural guarantees in time of war or other serious crisis, in accordance with article 27§1

---

[163] *Knights* v. *Grenada*, para. 77.

[164] *Lamey et al.* v. *Jamaica*, paras. 140–149. Also: *Baptiste* v. *Grenada*, paras. 86, 95–106; *McKenzie et al.* v. *Jamaica*, paras. 208, 211–219; *Knights* v. *Grenada*, paras. 87, 90–99.

[165] *Baptiste* v. *Grenada*, para. 85; *Lamey et al.* v. *Jamaica*, para. 130.

[166] The *Covenant* speaks of the 'inherent' right to life, a concept absent in the *Convention* text. The *Covenant* guarantees the right to life to 'every human being' whereas the *Convention* grants it to 'every person'. The *Convention* also insists that the right to life is to be protected by law 'in general, from the moment of conception'. Otherwise, the two provisions are essentially identical.

[167] *Pinto* v. *Trinidad and Tobago* (No. 232/1987), UN Doc. A/45/40, Vol. II, p. 69, at pp. 75–76; *Reid* v. *Jamaica* (No. 250/1987), UN Doc. A/45/40, Vol. II, p. 85, at pp. 94–95.

of the *Convention*. Yet capital punishment without the procedural safeguards of article 8 would amount to summary execution. It would be arbitrary, and therefore in breach of article 4§1 of the *Convention*.

Accordingly, in interpreting article 4, the Inter-American Court and Inter-American Commission have considered that the imposition of capital punishment without respect for due process constitutes the deprivation of life 'arbitrarily'.[168] Due process requirements include, for example, the availability of legal aid for indigent defendants.[169] In Advisory Opinion 16, the Inter-American Court of Human Rights declared:

> That failure to observe a detained foreign national's right to information, recognized in Article 36§1(b) of the Vienna Convention on Consular Relations, is prejudicial to the due process of law and, in such circumstances, imposition of the death penalty is a violation of the right not to be deprived of life 'arbitrarily', as stipulated in the relevant provisions of the human rights treaties (*e.g.* American Convention on Human Rights, Article 4; International Covenant on Civil and Political Rights, Article 6), with the juridical consequences that a violation of this nature carries, in other words, those pertaining to the State's international responsibility and the duty to make reparation.[170]

Advisory Opinion 16 had been requested by Mexico and was quite obviously aimed at the widespread phenomenon of execution in the United States of America of foreign nationals who had not received information about their right to consular assistance at the time of arrest.[171] The United States actually sent a letter to the Court complaining that 'Mexico has presented a contentious case in guise of a request for an advisory opinion'.

The Court spoke of an internationally recognized principle by which States that still maintain the death penalty must only impose it after the strictest observance of procedural safeguards.[172] The Court noted that the right to be informed of the right to consular assistance is a right that affects the legal guarantees available to the defence. The Court noted that both the *International Covenant on Civil and Political Rights* and the *American Convention on Human Rights* limit application of the death penalty to 'the most serious crimes' and point towards abolition. It referred to General Comment 6(16) and to the views of the Human Rights Committee on the necessity of observing strict procedural guarantees in death penalty cases.[173] The Court's advisory opinion was endorsed by the

---

[168] *Baptiste* v. *Granada*, para. 87.   [169] *Lamey* et al. v. *Jamaica*, paras. 222–226.

[170] *The Right to Information on Consular Assistance in the Context of the Guarantees of Due Process of Law*, Advisory Opinion OC-16/99 of 1 October 1999, para. 141(7).

[171] See also: *LaGrand (Germany v. United States of America)*, 27 June 2001.

[172] *The Right to Information on Consular Assistance in the Context of the Guarantees of Due Process of Law*, paras. 135–136.

[173] *Ibid.*, paras. 131–133. The Court referred to: *Mbenge* v. *Zaire* (No. 16/1977), UN Doc. CCPR/C/OP/2, p. 76; *Reid* v. *Jamaica* (No. 250/1987), UN Doc. A/45/40, Vol. II, p. 85, 11 *HRLJ* 319; *Wright* v. *Jamaica* (No. 349/1989), UN Doc. A/47/40, p. 300, 13 *HRLJ* 348.

United Nations General Assembly in December 1999 resolution on protection of migrants, in a preambular paragraph that was proposed by Mexico.[174]

The existence of a requirement that any death sentence be imposed following the strictest respect for due process norms, whether it be found in article 4§1 of the *Convention* ('arbitrarily') or article 6§2 of the *International Covenant* ('contrary to the provisions of the present Covenant') does not mean that the organs charged with implementation of the two treaties will never differ in their appreciation of the scope of these procedural guarantees.[175] Earl Pratt's case is of considerable interest in this respect, because at various times it has been considered by both the Inter-American Commission and the Human Rights Committee. Pratt and his accomplice, Ivan Morgan, had been sentenced to hang following conviction for first degree murder in January 1979. In December 1980, their appeals were dismissed by the Jamaican Court of Appeal. In June 1981, Pratt petitioned the Inter-American Commission on Human Rights, complaining that various procedural difficulties during the trial and the appeal breached the *American Convention on Human Rights*. The Inter-American Commission, in a resolution dated 3 October 1984, concluded that the requirements of due process had been fulfilled by Jamaica during Pratt's trial and appeal. Nevertheless, the Commission recommended 'that the Government of Jamaica suspend the execution of those persons sentenced to death, commute the sentence of Earl Pratt and request, in accordance with its Regulations and the spirit of Article 4§3 of the American Convention on Human Rights as well as for humanitarian reasons, that the Government take definite steps to abolish the death penalty as has been done in various countries'.[176]

Only days prior to the Inter-American Commission's resolution, the Jamaican Court of Appeal had finally issued its reasons for judgment, almost four years after it had verbally dismissed their appeal of conviction. However, Jamaica did not proceed with execution, and Pratt took no steps to reactivate the file until January 1986, when he filed a communication with the Human Rights Committee (his accomplice Morgan later filed a related petition and the two cases were joined), alleging violations of articles 6, 7 and 14 of the *International Covenant on Civil and Political Rights*.[177] Specifically, he claimed that the Court of Appeal's four-year delay in issuing its reasons for judgment

[174] 'Protection of Migrants', UN Doc. A/RES/54/166.

[175] On problems with the co-existence of petition mechanisms in the United Nations and Inter-American systems, see: M. Tardu, 'The Protocol to the United Nations Covenant on Civil and Political Rights and the Inter-American System: A Study of Coexisting Petition Procedures', (1976) 70 *AJIL* 778; A. A. Cançado Trindade, 'Co-existence and Co-ordination of Mechanisms of International Protection of Human Rights (At Global and Regional Levels)', (1987) 202 *RCADI* 9.

[176] *Pratt v. Jamaica* (Case No. 9054), Resolution No. 13/84, reported in OAS Doc. OEA/Ser.L/V/II.66 Doc. 10 rev.1, pp. 111–113.

[177] *Pratt and Morgan v. Jamaica* (Nos. 210/1986, 225/1987), UN Doc. A/44/40, p. 222, 11 *HRLJ* 150, paras. 14–15.

constituted cruel and inhuman treatment. He alleged, apparently erroneously,[178] that the absence of written reasons had prevented him from applying to the Privy Council for special leave. During the four years, Pratt was detained on death row.

But while written reasons for the appeal judgment had been issued in September 1984, it was not until March 1986 that Pratt and Morgan actually lodged a notice of intention to file for special leave to appeal to the Judicial Committee of the Privy Council.[179] On 17 July 1986, the Privy Council dismissed the application, although Lord Templeman expressed concern about the nearly four-year delay between the appeal ruling and delivery of a written judgment. According to Lord Templeman, '[d]uring the whole of that period the appellant had sentence of death hanging over him and, of course, no action could be taken on his behalf, or on behalf of the authorities, pending the possibility of an appeal to this Board which could only be considered when those reasons had been delivered'.[180] A few days later, the United Nations Human Rights Committee issued an interim decision requesting that execution of Pratt be stayed until it had time to consider the admissibility of the application.[181]

The Jamaican Privy Council examined the cases of Pratt and Morgan in November 1986, but refused to accede to the Human Rights Committee's request for a stay. In February 1987, a warrant of execution was issued. On 23 February 1987, the Governor-General of Jamaica issued a stay, possibly the result of his being informed that the matter was due to be considered not only by the Human Rights Committee at its March 1987 session but also by the Inter-American Commission on Human Rights, also in March.[182]

Neither the Human Rights Committee nor the Inter-American Commission permit concurrent applications,[183] but this did not stop both bodies from pursuing Pratt and Morgan's case. On 9 July 1987, the Inter-American Commission communicated the following to the Jamaican Government:

> Pratt and Morgan suffered a denial of justice during the period 1980–1984 violative of Article 5(2) of the American Convention on Human Rights. The Commission found that the fact that the Jamaican Court of Appeal issued its decision on December 5, 1980 but did not issue the reasons for that decision until four years later, September 24, 1984, was tantamount to cruel, inhuman and degrading treatment because during that four year delay the petitioners could not appeal to the Privy Council and had to

---

[178] *Pratt* et al. v. *Attorney General for Jamaica* et al., para. 24.   [179] *Ibid.*, para. 22.

[180] *Pratt* v. *Attorney General for Jamaica*, unreported judgment of the Judicial Committee of the Privy Council, 17 July 1986, quoted in *Pratt* et al. v. *Attorney General for Jamaica* et al., para. 23.

[181] *Pratt and Morgan* v. *Jamaica* (Nos. 210/1986, 225/1987), para. 3.

[182] *Pratt* et al. v. *Attorney General for Jamaica* et al., para. 27.

[183] *Regulations of the Inter-American Commission on Human Rights*, art. 39§1(a); *Optional Protocol to the International Covenant on Civil and Political Rights*, (1976) 999 UNTS 171, art. 5§2(a). See: *Blaine* v. *Jamaica* (Case No. 11.827), Report No. 96/98, Admissibility, 17 December 1998.

suffer four years on death row awaiting execution. The Inter-American Commission on Human Rights, pursuant to its cable of July 7, 1987 requests that the execution of Messrs. Pratt and Morgan be commuted for humanitarian reasons.[184]

Interestingly, this 'decision' was never published in the Commission's annual reports, and only came to public attention when it was referred to by the Judicial Committee of the Privy Council in its November 1993 judgment in *Pratt and Morgan*. It is striking because not only was there an apparent violation of the rule preventing the Commission from considering cases pending before another international body, it is also in apparent contradiction with the October 1984 report of the Commission. Moreover, the Commission's own *Regulations* prevent it from considering a petition where the subject of the petition 'essentially duplicates a petition pending or already examined and settled by the Commission'.[185] The July 1987 comment by the Commission was apparently little more than a manifestation that the body was disturbed by the cases of Pratt and Morgan, and no further action appears to have been taken. Subsequently, in April 1989, the Human Rights Committee found there had been a violation of the *International Covenant* and recommended that Jamaica commute their sentences.[186] But Jamaica did not heed this suggestion until the matter had once again been presented to the Judicial Committee of the Privy Council which ordered, in November 1993, commutation of sentence to life imprisonment.[187]

In another Jamaican death row case, *Wright* v. *Jamaica*, a death row petitioner explained that he had only had the most summary of hearings and that he was represented by a court-appointed attorney who had met with him only a few weeks before the trial. He alleged an almost invincible alibi defence, namely, that at the time the crime was committed, he was in police custody.[188] The issue had not been raised at trial or on appeal, because it had apparently been unnoticed, but there was no reason to question the fact because it had been part of the prosecution's own case. Wright argued this matter on appeal to the Judicial Committee of the Privy Council in London, but his application for leave was dismissed, the Law Lords citing judicial restraint in any review of criminal proceedings.[189] The Inter-American Commission said that it was not its function 'to act as a quasi-judicial fourth instance and to review the holdings of the domestic courts of the OAS member States'. Yet it concluded that, because the conviction and sentence were undermined by the record in this case, with the appeals process helpless to permit correction, Jamaica had violated article 25 of

---

[184] *Pratt* et al. v. *Attorney General for Jamaica* et al., para. 32.
[185] *Regulations of the Inter-American Commission on Human Rights*, art. 39§1(b).
[186] *Pratt and Morgan* v. *Jamaica* (Nos. 210/1986, 225/1987), para. 15.
[187] *Pratt* et al. v. *Attorney General for Jamaica* et al., para. 69.
[188] *Wright* v. *Jamaica* (Case No. 9260), Resolution No. 29/88, reported in OAS Doc. OEA/Ser.L/V/II.74 Doc. 10 rev.1, p. 154. Discussed by the Commission in *Baptiste* v. *Grenada*, para. 65.
[189] *Wright* v. *Jamaica*, pp. 157–158.

the *Convention*, which recognizes a right to effective remedy or recourse.[190] Nevertheless the Commission remained silent on the subject of article 4 of the *Convention*. Wright subsequently petitioned the Human Rights Committee. Taking note of the proceedings before the Inter-American Commission,[191] the Committee concluded that the failure of the trial court to inform the jury of Wright's alibi defence, even though this had not been raised by his own counsel, constituted a violation of article 14§1 of the *Covenant*.[192] In other words, unlike the Inter-American Commission, the Human Rights Committee was prepared to act as 'a quasi-judicial fourth instance' in order to challenge a clear denial of justice and the threat of execution of an innocent man. The Committee held that the breach of article 14 also amounted to a breach of article 6 because this was a death penalty case, and held that Wright was entitled to an effective remedy entailing his release.

In addition to prohibiting application of the death penalty where this is done 'arbitrarily', article 4 of the *Convention* also provides a list of specific limitations, set out in paragraphs 2 to 6. According to the Inter-American Court, 'the Convention adopts an approach that is clearly incremental in character. That is, without going so far as to abolish the death penalty, the Convention imposes restrictions designed to delimit strictly its application and scope, in order to reduce the application of the penalty to bring about its gradual disappearance.'[193]

The text of paragraph 2 is clearly modelled on paragraph 2 of article 6 of the *International Covenant on Civil and Political Rights*. Applicable only to countries 'that have not abolished the death penalty', it confines use of the death penalty to cases of 'the most serious crimes', adding that this must be pursuant to a final judgment of a competent court in accordance with pre-existing law. Referring to paragraph 2, the Inter-American Court has said: 'The fact that these guarantees are envisaged in addition to those stipulated in Articles 8 [right to a fair trial] and 9 [principle of legality] clearly indicates that the Convention sought to define narrowly the conditions under which the application of the death penalty would not violate the Convention in those countries that had not abolished it.'[194] Although these limitations have not really been explored in the case law of the Inter-American Commission or Court, it would seem likely that interpreters of the provision seek guidance from the jurisprudence of the Human Rights Committee and other bodies that have considered and applied article 6§2 of the *International Covenant on Civil and Political Rights*.

Article 4§2 of the *Convention* concludes with the sentence: 'The application of such punishment shall not be extended to crimes to which it does not

---

[190] *Ibid.*, pp. 161–162.   [191] *Wright* v. *Jamaica* (No. 349/1989), paras. 2.8, 5.2, 7.5.
[192] *Ibid.*, para. 8.3.
[193] *Restrictions to the Death Penalty (Arts. 4§2 and 4§4 American Convention on Human Rights)*, para. 57.
[194] *Ibid.*, para. 53.

presently apply'. There is no similar provision in the *International Covenant on Civil and Political Rights.* Clearly, the text only applies to States that have not abolished the death penalty. For States that have, article 4§3 of the *Convention* prevents any re-imposition of capital punishment. According to the Court, '[h]ere it is no longer a question of imposing strict conditions on the exceptional application or execution of the death penalty, but rather of establishing a cut off as far as the penalty is concerned and doing so by means of a progressive and irreversible process applicable to countries which have not decided to abolish the death penalty altogether as well as to those countries which have done so'.[195]

Accordingly, article 4§2 prevents 'any expansion of the list of offenses subject to the death penalty'.[196] In the opinion of the Court:

> It follows that, in interpreting the last sentence of Article 4§2 'in good faith in accordance with the ordinary meaning to be given to the terms of the treaty in their context and in the light of its object and purpose' [Vienna Convention, art. 31§1], there cannot be the slightest doubt that Article 4§2 contains an absolute prohibition that no State Party may apply the death penalty to crimes for which it was not provided previously under the domestic law of that State. No provision of the Convention can be relied upon to give a different meaning to the very clear text of Article 4§2, in fine. The only way to achieve a different result would be by means of a timely reservation designed to exclude in some fashion the application of the aforementioned provision in relation to the State making the reservation. Such a reservation, of course, would have to be compatible with the object and purpose of the treaty.[197]

The Court was referring to an argument invoked by Guatemala to justify extending the death penalty to certain political offences. Although article 4§4 prohibits the death penalty for political offences, Guatemala had formulated a reservation in this respect. Accordingly, it argued that the reservation to article 4§4 authorized it to extend the death penalty to political offences, even if this appeared to contradict article 4§2. The Court considered that article 4§4 only added a further prohibition on use of the death penalty, and did not in any way restrict the scope of article 4§2. It said that article 4§4 'obviously refers to those offences which prior thereto were subject to capital punishment, since for the future the prohibition set forth in paragraph 2 would have been sufficient'.[198] The Court continued: 'It follows that a State which has not made a reservation to paragraph 2 is bound by the prohibition not to apply the death penalty to new offences, be they political offences, related common crimes or mere common crimes.'[199]

Because the Court was exercising its advisory jurisdiction, it did not formally find Guatemala in breach of the *Convention.*[200] By the date of the hearing before the Court, Guatemala had already suspended use of capital punishment,

---

[195] *Ibid.,* para. 57. [196] *Ibid.,* para. 57. [197] *Ibid.,* para. 59.
[198] *Ibid.,* para. 68. [199] *Ibid.,* para. 70. [200] *Ibid.,* para. 74.

and it eventually withdrew its reservation to article 4 of the *Convention*.[201] Relying upon the advisory opinion of the Court that addressed the Guatemalan reservation to article 4§4, the Commission concluded there had been a violation of the *Convention* in three contentious cases.[202] In the mid-1990s, Guatemala again attempted to extend the scope of the death penalty, this time to cover kidnapping even where there is no death of the victim. Earlier legislation authorized capital punishment in the case of kidnapping that led to the death of the victim. On 30 January 1997, the Ninth Chamber of the Court of Appeals of Guatemala, relying upon article 4§2 of the *American Convention*, commuted three death sentences that had been imposed for kidnapping.[203] The Inter-American Commission congratulated Guatemala's domestic courts for decisions that properly respect and reflect the international human rights obligations which the State has undertaken.[204] Referring to the Court's 1984 advisory opinion, the Commission noted that such an interpretation was '[i]n accordance with the principle of irreversibility of rights'.[205] Four petitions are currently pending before the Inter-American Commission,[206] although all but one of the applicants has already been executed, in at least one case in defiance of precautionary measures orders from the Commission.[207] The Commission repeated its many concerns about Guatemala in its 2001 Annual Report.

Application of article 4§2 was again considered by the Inter-American Court in an advisory opinion issued on 9 December 1994. The opinion was requested by the Inter-American Commission after Peru included a provision in its new *Constitution* extending the death penalty to crimes which were not previously subject to capital punishment. Under the earlier 1979 Constitution, the death penalty was applicable exclusively to the crime of treason against the State in time of external war.[208] The new *Constitution* stated: 'The death penalty shall only be imposed for the crime of treason against the state in time of war, and for the crime of terrorism, in accordance with the laws and treaties to which Peru is a party.'[209] The *Constitution* had been amended following a national

---

[201] 'Annual Report of the Inter-American Commission on Human Rights, 1985–1986', OAS Doc. OEA/Ser.L/V/II.68 Doc. 8 rev.1, p. 158.

[202] *Marcelino Marroquín* et al. v. *Guatemala* (Case No. 8094), *Walter Vinicio Marroquín González* et al. v. *Guatemala* (Case No. 9038).

[203] 'Annual Report of the Inter-American Commission on Human Rights, 1997', Chapter V, para. 39.

[204] *Ibid.*, para. 27.

[205] 'Annual Report of the Inter-American Commission on Human Rights, 1996', Chapter V, para. 41.

[206] *Giron and Castillo* v. *Guatemala* (Case No. 11.686); *Rodriguez* v. *Guatemala* (Case No. 11.782); *Martinez* v. *Guatemala* (Case No. 11.834); *Ramirez* v. *Guatemala*.

[207] *Martinez* v. *Guatemala* (Case No. 11.834), Precautionary Measures, 18 November 1997; *Martinez* v. *Guatemala* (Case No. 11.834), Precautionary Measures, 24 November 1997; *Martinez* v. *Guatemala* (Case No. 11.834), Precautionary Measures, 9 February 1998.

[208] *Political Constitution of 1979*, art. 235: 'There shall be no death penalty, except for treason against the state in time of external war.'

[209] *Peruvian Constitution*, art. 140.

referendum, although no changes were made to criminal legislation as a result.[210] The Commission considered that Peru had breached articles 4§2 and 4§3, and sought an opinion from the Court on the legal effects of legislation contrary to the *Convention*, duties and responsibilities of the agents or officials of a State party to the *Convention* which promulgates a law whose enforcement would constitute 'a manifest violation of the Convention'. But despite the particular circumstances giving rise to the request, the Court decided to consider the matter in the abstract, and not to examine the Peruvian legislation or to interpret article 4 of the *Convention*. The Court held that 'the promulgation of a law that manifestly violates the obligations assumed by a State upon ratifying or acceding to the Convention constitutes a violation of the treaty and, if such violation affects the guaranteed rights and liberties of specific individuals, gives rise to international responsibility for the State in question'. The Court found that individual liability would be incurred if enforcement of such a law constituted an international crime.[211] The impugned legislation was never actually invoked, despite rumours that the government intends to use it in terrorist cases. It is currently under review, with the expectation that the provision will be repealed.

In 1996, the Inter-American Commission sent a note to El Salvador informing it that proposed constitutional amendments extending the death penalty to crimes for which it did not previously apply would violate the Convention.[212]

Article 4§3 states that the death penalty shall not be re-established in States that have abolished it. This makes explicit what may in any event be implied from the text of article 4§2. According to the Inter-American Court of Human Rights, in an interpretation of these provisions, 'a decision by a State Party to the Convention to abolish the death penalty, whenever made, becomes, *ipso jure*, a final and irrevocable decision'.[213]

Article 4§4 prohibits the death penalty for political offences or related common crimes. The language resembles the terminology of extradition treaties. Latin America has traditionally been hospitable to the notion of political asylum and of refusal to extradite where the motivation is political. Nevertheless, even in Latin America there is no consensus on the term's definition.[214] At the time the *Convention* was adopted, at the San José conference, this was frankly admitted by the participants. Because neither the *International Covenant on Civil and Political Rights* nor the *European Convention* make any similar exception,

---

[210] U.N. Doc. E/1995/78, para. 14.
[211] *International Responsibility for the Promulgation and Enforcement of Laws in Violation of the Convention (Arts. 1 and 2 of the American Convention on Human Rights)*, Advisory Opinion OC-14/94 of 9 December 1994.
[212] 'Annual Report of the Inter-American Commission on Human Rights, 1996', Chapter II.
[213] *Restrictions to the Death Penalty (Arts. 4§2 and 4§4 American Convention on Human Rights)*, para. 56.
[214] Nigel Rodley, *The Treatment of Prisoners Under International Law*, Paris: Unesco, Oxford: Clarendon Press, 1987, pp. 176–177.

their jurisprudence is of no assistance in interpreting the provision. The Inter-American Court considered that because Guatemala's reservation to article 4§4 did not appear 'to be of a type that is designed to deny the right to life as such, the Court concludes that to that extent it can be considered, in principle, as not being incompatible with the object and purpose of the Convention'.[215]

The prohibition of execution of juveniles and pregnant women appears in article 4§5 of the *Convention* and article 6§5 of the *International Covenant on Civil and Political Rights*. The *Convention* adds to this group of protected persons anyone over the age of seventy. The provision was added without debate, and no explanation is provided for its *raison d'être*, although this is presumably a humanitarian gesture. Finally, the *Convention* not only provides for the possibility of amnesty, pardon or commutation, but also specifies that the death penalty may not be carried out until such procedures have been exhausted. This condition seems implicit, in any case, but by stating this clearly the *Convention* avoids any misunderstanding on the point.

Article 4§6 of the *Convention* corresponds to article 6§4 of the *International Covenant on Civil and Political Rights* although, once again, there are minor differences in the wording. The *Convention* essentially covers the same ground as the *Covenant*, but adds that '[c]apital punishment shall not be imposed while such a petition is pending decision by the competent authority'. The Inter-American Commission has held that the prerogative of mercy is not an effective remedy within the meaning of article 4§6.[216] According to the Commission:

> [T]he right to apply for amnesty, pardon or commutation of sentence under Article 4§6 of the Convention, when read together with the State's obligations under Article 1§1 of the Convention, must be read to encompass certain minimum procedural protections for condemned prisoners, if the right is to be effectively respected and enjoyed. These protections include the right on the part of condemned prisoners to apply for amnesty, pardon or commutation of sentence, to be informed of when the competent authority will consider the offender's case, to make representations, in person or by counsel, to the competent authority, and to receive a decision from that authority within a reasonable period of time prior to his or her execution. It also entails the right not to have capital punishment imposed while such a petition is pending decision by the competent authority. In order to provide condemned prisoners with an effective opportunity to exercise this right, a procedure should be prescribed and made available by the State through which prisoners may file an application for amnesty, pardon or commutation of sentence, and submit representations in support of his or her application. In the absence of minimal protections and procedures of this nature, Article 4§6 of the American Convention is rendered meaningless, a right without a remedy. Such an interpretation cannot be sustained in light of the object and purpose of the American Convention.[217]

---

[215] *Restrictions to the Death Penalty (Arts. 4§2 and 4§4 American Convention on Human Rights)*, para. 61.

[216] *Baptiste* v. *Grenada*, para. 117; *Lamey et al.* v. *Jamaica*, para. 157.

[217] *Baptiste* v. *Grenada*, para. 121; *Lamey et al.* v. *Jamaica*, para. 159; *McKenzie* et al. v. *Jamaica*, para. 228; *Knights* v. *Grenada*, para. 110.

In *Constantine* et al., a case now pending before the Inter-American Court, the Inter-American Commission is arguing that, by mandatory sentencing in capital cases, Trinidad and Tobago has failed to ensure an effective opportunity to apply for granting amnesty, pardon or commutation of sentence, in breach of article 4§6 of the *Convention*.[218]

The *Convention* provision dealing with cruel, inhuman or degrading treatment or punishment, article 5, is also relevant to death penalty litigation. The Commission has held that, besides being an arbitrary violation of the right to life, mandatory death sentences are also prohibited by article 5 of the *Convention*.[219] It has also condemned a failure of authorities to turn over the remains of the victims to their families, something which was 'offensive to elementary humanitarian sentiments'.[220] The Commission has not pronounced itself clearly on the 'death row phenomenon'. In *Lamey*, where a lengthy period of detention prior to execution was alleged to violate article 5, the Commission found violations of other provisions and did not consider it necessary to rule on whether the delay itself also rendered the executions to be unlawful.[221] But in *Andrews*, an *American Declaration* case filed against the United States, it found that a prisoner who had spent eighteen years on death row, who was not allowed to leave his cell for more than a few hours every week, who had received notice of at least eight execution dates, and who was executed on the basis of a jury decision tainted with racial bias, had received cruel, infamous or unusual punishment pursuant to article XXVI of the *American Declaration*.[222] The Commission has declined ruling on whether the method of execution, namely hanging, is a breach of article 5.[223] Conditions on death row, particularly the notorious situation at the St. Catherine's Prison in Jamaica, have been found contrary to article 5.[224] The Inter-American Commission has taken the view that conditions of detention must respect the United Nations *Standard Minimum Rules*,[225] in accordance with the case law of the Human Rights Committee.[226]

One member of the Inter-American Commission, Hélio Bicudo, has espoused the radical view that article 5's prohibition of cruel punishment means the death penalty is now forbidden, despite the fact that article 4 tolerates its imposition in certain cases.[227] Bicudo's view is similar to the one taken by Judge De

---

[218] 'Annual Report of the Inter-American Commission on Human Rights, 1999', OAS Doc. OEA/Ser.L/V/II.106 Doc. 6 rev., para. 126.
[219] *Baptiste* v. *Grenada*, para. 90; *Lamey et al.* v. *Jamaica*, para. 133; *McKenzie* et al. v. *Jamaica*, paras. 201–203; *Knights* v. *Grenada*, paras. 80–82.
[220] *Ibid.*   [221] *Lamey et al.* v. *Jamaica*, para. 189; also para. 207.
[222] *Andrews* v. *United States*, para. 178.   [223] *McKenzie* et al. v. *Jamaica*, para. 294.
[224] *Baptiste* v. *Grenada*, para. 138; *McKenzie* et al. v. *Jamaica*, para. 287; *Lamey et al.* v. *Jamaica*, paras. 199–206.
[225] *Edwards* et al. v. *Bahamas*, para. 195; *Knights* v. *Grenada*, para. 127.
[226] *Mukong* v. *Cameroon* (No. 458/1991), UN Doc CCPR/C/51/D/458/1991, para. 9.3.
[227] *Lamey et al.* v. *Jamaica* (Cases Nos. 11.826, 11.843, 11.846, 11.847), Report No. 49/01, 4 April 2001, Concurring Opinion of Commissioner Hélio Bicudo; *Knights* v. *Grenada* (Case No. 12.028), Report No. 47/01, 4 April 2001, Concurring Opinion of Commissioner Hélio Bicudo.

Meyer of the European Court of Human Rights in the *Soering* case.[228] According to Commissioner Bicudo, provisions such as Article 4(2) of the American Convention on Human Rights should be disregarded, in favour of legal instruments that better protect the interests of the victims of violations of human rights'.[229] Commissioner Bicudo has made the interesting assertion that the 1994 *Inter-American Convention on the Prevention, Punishment and Eradication of Violence against Women* does not allow the imposition of the death penalty on women. In effect, article 3 states that '[e]very woman has the right to be free from violence in both the public and private spheres', while article 4 declares that '[e]very woman has the right to have her life respected'.[230]

The norms of the *American Convention* are more advanced, with respect to the death penalty, than their counterparts in the European and United Nations systems. By the inclusion of article 4§3, the *Convention* is in fact abolitionist for those States parties – and they are the majority in the Organization of American States – that have abolished the death penalty in their internal legislation. Yet what is apparently a progressive provision was considered, by its authors, to be a timid compromise, made in the interests of consensus and widespread ratification. The drafters of the *Convention*, in 1969, were the first in any of the human rights systems to evoke the possibility of a future protocol, one that would abolish the death penalty altogether. Their declaration at San José in 1969 called for an additional protocol 'in a short time' that would 'consecrate the final abolition of the death penalty', putting the American continent once again in the vanguard of human rights. The declaration may have inspired law-makers at the United Nations and the Council of Europe to proceed with revision of their instruments. Perhaps because of political turmoil in Latin America during the 1970s and the rise of reactionary regimes in several States, efforts aimed at an abolitionist protocol were rather slow to begin.

8.2.5 *The* Protocol *to the* American Convention *abolishing the death penalty*

In 1984, the Inter-American Commission of Human Rights, troubled by the conduct of some States in extending the application of the death penalty, called upon all American governments that had not yet done so to abolish the death penalty in accordance with the spirit of article 4 of the *American Convention* and with 'the universal trend favourable to the abolition of the death penalty'.[231] In

---

[228] *Soering* v. *United Kingdom and Germany,* 7 July 1989, Series A, No. 161, 11 EHRR 439, p. 51.
[229] *Lamey et al.* v. *Jamaica* (Cases Nos. 11.826, 11.843, 11.846, 11.847), Report No. 49/01, Concurring opinion of Commisioner Hélio Bicudo, 4 April 2001, para. 68.
[230] *Ibid.,* para. 14.
[231] Resolution adopted by the sixty-third regular session of the Inter-American Commission of Human Rights.

its 1986–87 Annual Report, the Inter-American Commission broached the idea of an additional protocol to the *American Convention* on the abolition of the death penalty, the result of a proposal from Uruguay. The idea had originally been raised in a declaration by fifteen States at the close of the San José Conference, in 1969.[232] A draft instrument was presented at the 1986 meeting of States parties to the *Convention*, held on the occasion of the Organization of American States General Assembly.[233] The Commission said that, in 1969 when the *Convention* was adopted, prevailing conditions would not have permitted abolition, but that there had been an evolution since then. It noted the abolitionist provisions in the new constitutions of Haiti[234] and Nicaragua[235] and said that 'conditions are now ripe for adopting an instrument to abolish the death penalty'.[236] It observed that, of the nineteen States parties to the *Convention*, only four retained the death penalty.[237] The Commission cited the abolitionist trend in other jurisdictions, specifically *Protocol No. 6* to the *European Convention* and the draft optional protocol to the *International Covenant on Civil and Political Rights* then being prepared within the United Nations.[238] The Commission said it agreed with the approach in those instruments, namely of permitting the imposition of the death penalty for specified military offences committed in wartime, in order to obtain the largest number of ratifications or adhesions possible.[239]

[232] OAS Doc. OEA/Ser.K/XVI/1.2, p. 467.
[233] 'Annual Report of the Inter-American Commission on Human Rights, 1986–1987', pp. 272–277. The proposed text consisted of three articles:
> *Article 1*
> The States Parties to this Protocol shall not impose the death penalty on any person under their jurisdiction. Accordingly, no one may be punished by the death penalty or executed.
> *Article 2*
> 1. Reservations may not be made to this Protocol except for the sole purpose of excluding from application of the Protocol especially severe military offences that were committed during a foreign war.
> 2. A State making the reservation authorized by the previous paragraph may, at the time of deposition of its instrument of ratification or adhesion, inform the Secretary General of the Organization of American States as to what military offences are subject to the death penalty under that country's domestic law.
> *Article 3*
> 1. This Protocol shall be open to the signature and to the ratification or adhesion of any State Party to the American Convention on Human Rights.
> 2. Ratification of this Protocol or adhesion to it shall be made through deposit of an instrument of ratification or adhesion at the General Secretariat of the Organization of American States.

[234] Article 20 of Haiti's 1987 Constitution, which was approved by referendum, states: 'The death penalty is abolished in all cases.' It was repealed in 1988 following a military coup, but the abolition of the death penalty was reaffirmed in a decree by President Namphy. See: 'Report on the Situation of Human Rights in Haiti, 1990', OAS Doc. OEA/Ser.L/V/II.77, rev.1, p. 31; Amnesty International, *When the State Kills* ..., p. 144.
[235] Abolished in 1979 by decree, this was confirmed in the 1987 *Constitution*: 'Report on the Situation of Human Rights in the Republic of Nicaragua', 1981, OAS Doc. OEA/Ser.L/V/II.53, doc. 25, at p. 40.
[236] 'Annual Report of the Inter-American Commission on Human Rights, 1986–1987', pp. 272–273.
[237] Barbados, Guatemala, Jamaica, Suriname.
[238] 'Annual Report of the Inter-American Commission on Human Rights, 1986–1987', p. 275.
[239] *Ibid.*, p. 276.

In 1987, the General Assembly of the Organization of American States instructed the Inter-American Commission to study the draft protocol[240] and the following year confirmed that the Organization's Permanent Council should submit a draft protocol.[241] The Permanent Council subsequently prepared a report[242] which was acted upon at the 1989 meeting of the General Assembly.[243] The *Protocol to the American Convention on Human Rights to Abolish the Death Penalty* was adopted by the General Assembly of the Organisation of American States at its Twentieth Regular Session, by Resolution 1042 of 8 June 1990.

The *Protocol* is shorter than its United Nations and European counterparts, consisting of a preamble and four articles. The preamble begins by citing article 4 of the *American Convention*, which 'recognized the right to life and restricts the application of the death penalty'. It notes that the right to life is inalienable, that it cannot be suspended for any reason, and that there is a tendency towards its abolition among the American States. Furthermore, it notes the irrevocable consequences of the death penalty, that it forecloses the correction of judicial error, and precludes any possibility of changing or rehabilitating those convicted.

Article 1 declares that the death penalty shall not be applied by States parties, 'in their territory to any person subject to their jurisdiction'. It does not, unlike the United Nations and European instruments, impose an obligation on States parties to abolish the death penalty. States that are *de facto* abolitionist may therefore ratify the *Protocol* without any change to their domestic legislation.

The United Nations and European instruments differ in their approach to the death penalty in time of war. The latter applies only in time of peace, whereas the former applies at all times but permits States parties to make reservations respecting use of the death penalty during time of war. The Inter-American *Protocol* follows the United Nations approach, which is more fully abolitionist than the European instrument. The drafters of the *Protocol* provided for reservation in terms that are similar to the *Second Optional Protocol to the International Covenant on Civil and Political Rights*, but with some significant differences. In the Inter-American *Protocol*, States parties may 'apply the death penalty in wartime in accordance with international law, for extremely serious crimes of a military nature'. The reference to international law, which incorporates the death penalty provisions of the *Geneva Conventions*[244] as well as the additional protocols,[245]

---

[240] OAS Doc. AG/RES.889/XVII-O/87, reprinted in *Inter-American Yearbook on Human Rights, 1987*, Dordrecht/Boston/London: Martinus Nijhoff, 1990, pp. 906–907.
[241] OAS Doc. AG/RES/943 (XVIII-O/88), reprinted in *Inter-American Yearbook on Human Rights, 1988*, p. 1042.
[242] OAS Doc. AG/doc.2428/89.   [243] OAS Doc. AG/RES.1013 (XIX-O/89).
[244] *Geneva Convention of August 12, 1949 Relative to the Protection of Civilians*, (1950) 75 UNTS 287 (see Appendix 10, p. 416); *Geneva Convention of August 12, 1949 Relative to the Treatment of Prisoners of War* (see Appendix 9, p. 414).
[245] *Protocol Additional I to the 1949 Geneva Conventions and Relating to the Protection of Victims of International Armed Conflicts*, (1979) 1125 UNTS 3 (see Appendix 11, p. 420); *Protocol Additional II to*

does not appear in the *Second Optional Protocol.* However, a distinction in the *Second Optional Protocol* clarifying the fact that crimes must have been committed during wartime and precluding the possibility of capital punishment during wartime but for offences prior to the conflict is absent in the Inter-American *Protocol.* The formalities of reservation are the same and require that any reserved legislation be annexed to the declaration at the time of ratification, thereby prohibiting subsequent modification of the reservation by a simple change in domestic legislation.

Article 4 specifies that the *Protocol* 'shall enter into force among the States that ratify or accede to it when they deposit their respective instruments of ratification or accession with the General Secretariat of the Organisation of American States'. The *Protocol* came into force with the deposit of the second instrument of ratification, on 28 August 1991.

8.3 Conclusion

Since the nineteenth century, the Western hemisphere has been in the forefront on the subject of abolition, a situation that was confirmed in 1969 with the adoption of the *American Convention on Human Rights.* In accordance with article 4§3 of the *Convention,* sixteen Central and South American governments are bound at international law not to impose the death penalty. Furthermore, eight of them have also ratified the *Optional Protocol* to the *Convention.* Canada, although not a party or even a signatory to the *Convention*,[246] has nevertheless abolished capital punishment in its national law and would seem to have a constitutional prohibition of reinstating it.[247]

But there is a dark side to the subject. Several Member States of the Organization of American States continue to impose the death penalty, and often in violation of the norms set out in article 4 of the *Convention* and other international instruments. For example, the United States is among the very few States in the world to continue to execute individuals for crimes committed while under the age of eighteen. Cuba continues to impose the death penalty for political offences. The sorry record of Jamaica, Grenada, Trinidad and Tobago and other English-speaking Caribbean States have been frequently condemned by the Inter-American Commission on Human Rights. Precautionary measures requests, some of them endorsed by the Court, have been disregarded in some cases. Some States have indicated their desire to reinstate the death penalty, or to increase its scope.

---

the 1949 Geneva Conventions and Relating to the Protection of Victims of Non-International Armed Conflicts, (1979) 1125 UNTS 609 (see Appendix 12, p. 421).
[246] See: William A. Schabas, 'Canadian Ratification of the American Convention on Human Rights', (1998) 16 *Netherlands Quarterly of Human Rights* 315.
[247] *United States* v. *Burns,* [2001] 1 SCR 283, reversing *Kindler* v. *Canada,* [1991] 2 SCR 779.

In 1969, when the *Convention* was adopted, the Western hemisphere was somewhat more advanced than Europe in terms of its trend towards abolition. The chapter on European law tracks this inexorable momentum. But no similar generalization can be made of the members of the Organization of American States. Undoubtedly, the imposing shadow of the United States is the decisive factor. Recent developments within that country are encouraging[248] and may inspire others within the hemisphere.

[248] Michael L. Radelet & Marian J. Borg, 'The Changing Nature of Death Penalty Debates', (2000) 26 *Annual Review of Sociology* 43.

9

African human rights law

The *African Charter on Human and Peoples' Rights*, adopted in 1981 by the Organization of African Unity, makes no mention of the death penalty, in contrast with the regional conventions of the European and American systems. Whether the drafters of the *African Charter* intentionally omitted reference to the death penalty and what conclusions are to be drawn from such an omission are questions to which we cannot provide a thorough answer, because of the paucity of available materials on the drafting history. Like the other instruments, of course, the *African Charter* provides for a right to life, for a protection against inhuman treatment, and for procedural safeguards in criminal proceedings.[1] According to article 4 of the *Charter*, no individual may be deprived 'arbitrarily' of life. It declares:

> Human beings are inviolable. Every human being shall be entitled to respect for his life and the integrity of his person. No one may be arbitrarily deprived of this right.

One scholar, Etienne-Richard Mbaya, has written that article 4 of the *African Charter* permits the death penalty, which is widespread in Africa, providing it is imposed in accordance with the law.[2] It would be wrong to exaggerate the

[1] *African Charter on Human and People's Rights*, OAU Doc. CAB/LEG/67/3 rev.5, 4 EHRR 417, 21 *ILM* 58. For a comment on the right to life provision in the *African Charter*, see Johannes G. C. van Aggelen, *Le rôle des organisations internationales dans la protection du droit à la vie*, Brussels: E. Story-Scientia, 1986, p. 41. On the *African Charter* generally, see: Fatsah Ouguergouz, *La Charte africaine des droits de l'homme et des peuples*, Geneva: Presses universitaires de France, 1993; Keba Mbaye, *Les droits de l'homme en Afrique*, Paris: Pedone, 1992; René Degni-Segui, 'L'apport de la Charte africaine des droits de l'homme et des peuples au droit international de l'homme', (1991) 3 *African Journal of International and Comparative Law* 699.
[2] Etienne-Richard Mbaya, 'A la recherche du noyau intangible dans la Charte africaine', in *Le noyau intangible des droits de l'homme*, Fribourg: Éditions universitaires Fribourg Suisse, 1991, pp. 207–226, at p. 221. See also: Keba Mbaye, *Les droits de l'homme en Afrique*, Paris: Pedone, 1992, p. 197. Since 1990, abolition has made considerable progress on the African continent. Nineteen African States are now abolitionist, either *de jure* or *de facto*. Mozambique, Namibia and Seychelles have ratified the *Second Optional Protocol to the International Covenant on Civil and Political Rights Aimed at Abolition of the Death Penalty*, GA Res. 44/128. If the Arab States of northern Africa are excluded, a majority of African States

355

scope of capital punishment in Africa, however. Leaving aside the Arab States north of the Sahara, nearly half of African States have stopped using the death penalty and many have abolished it *de jure*. South Africa set the tone when its Constitutional Court, in 1995, declared capital punishment to be contrary to the country's interim constitution.[3] Even Rwanda, in legislation designed to facilitate genocide prosecutions adopted by the country's National Assembly in August 1996, has actually reduced the scope of the death penalty with respect to the previous provisions of the *Penal Code*.[4] Perhaps the most dramatic international abolitionist initiative in Africa in recent years is the exclusion of the death penalty in the *Statute of the International Criminal Tribunal for Rwanda*.[5]

The language of article 4 of the *African Charter*, with its reference to 'arbitrary' deprivation of life, echoes article 6§1 of the *International Covenant on Civil and Political Rights*, and most certainly indicates a prohibition of the arbitrary use of capital punishment.[6] Furthermore, the *African Charter* invites recourse to 'international law on human and peoples' rights', including the *Universal Declaration of Human Rights* and 'other instruments adopted by the United Nations'.[7] To this extent, an analysis of the death penalty in light of article 3 of the *Universal Declaration* may be useful for the purposes of interpreting article 4 of the *African Charter*.[8] The analysis of the right to life provision of the *Universal Declaration* in Chapter 1 of this book points towards abolition as a goal, relying in part upon the drafting history but also upon subsequent developments in State practice including 'soft law' principles adopted by United Nations organs. In this respect, it would seem reasonable that article 4 of the *African Charter* be interpreted in such a way as to incorporate norms such as those set out in the 'Safeguards Guaranteeing the Rights of Those Facing the Death Penalty'.[9] Going even further, under a dynamic interpretation of the *African Charter*, one informed by jurisprudential developments such as the judgment of the South African Constitutional Court abolishing the death penalty, it is argued that the *African Charter* should be construed in the same manner as the Constitution

---

no longer employ the death penalty. See: John Hatchard and Simon Coldham, 'Commonwealth Africa', in Peter Hodgkinson and Andrew Rutherford, *Capital Punishment: Global Issues and Prospects*, London: Waterside Press, 1996, pp. 155–191; William A. Schabas, 'Abolition of the Death Penalty in Africa', in William A. Schabas, ed., *Sourcebook on the Abolition of the Death Penalty*, Boston: Northeastern University Press, 1997, pp. 30–65.

[3] S. v. *Makwanyane*, 1995 (3) SA 391.

[4] 'Organic Law No. 8/96 of 30 August 1996', *Journal officiel*, Year 35, No. 17, 1 September 1996.

[5] UN Doc. S/RES/955 (1994), annex. This is discussed in detail in Chapter 6.

[6] Tunguru Huaraka, 'The African Charter on Human and Peoples' Rights: A Significant Contribution to the Development of International Human Rights Law', in Daniel Prémont, ed., *Essais sur le concept de 'droit de vivre' en mémoire de Yougindra Khushalani*, Brussels: Bruylant, 1988, pp. 193–211, at p. 203.

[7] *African Charter on Human and Peoples' Rights*, art. 60.

[8] Amos Wako, 'Comparison of the African Charter of Human and Peoples' Rights and the Optional Protocol to the International Covenant on Civil and Political Rights', [1991–92] *CHRY* 145.

[9] ESC Res. 1984/50 (see Appendix 8, p. 413). Subsequently endorsed by GA Res. 39/118.

of South Africa.[10] The basic organ for the implementation of the *African Charter* is the African Commission on Human and Peoples' Rights.[11] States parties to the *Charter* are required to submit periodic reports, although compliance is irregular and those that do report rarely refer to capital punishment.[12]

At its twenty-sixth ordinary session, held in Kigali, Rwanda, in November 1999, the African Commission on Human and Peoples' Rights adopted a 'Resolution Urging States to Envisage a Moratorium on the Death Penalty'.[13] The preamble to the resolution notes that article 4 of the *African Charter* 'affirms the rights of everyone to life'. Reference is also made in the preamble to recent resolutions of the United Nations Commission on Human Rights and the Sub-Commission on the Promotion and Protection of Human Rights calling for a moratorium on the death penalty. The preamble notes that three African States have ratified the *Second Optional Protocol to the International Covenant on Civil and Political Rights*, and that nineteen African States have abolished the death penalty either *de facto* or *de jure*. Concern is expressed that some States parties to the *African Charter* impose the death penalty under conditions not in conformity with the rights to a fair trial guaranteed therein. Reference is also made to the exclusion of the death penalty in the statutes of the two *ad hoc* tribunals but, noticeably, there is no similar reference to the *Rome Statute of the International Criminal Court*.

The operative paragraphs of the resolution read as follows:

> 1. *Urges* all States parties to the African Charter on Human and Peoples' Rights that still maintain the death penalty to comply fully with their obligations under the treaty and to ensure that persons accused of crimes for which the death penalty is a competent sentence are afforded all the guarantees in the African Charter;
> 2. *Calls* upon all States parties that still maintain the death penalty to:

[10] Manfred Nowak, 'Is the Death Penalty an Inhuman Punishment?', in Theodore S. Orlin, Allan Rosas and Martin Scheinin, *The Jurisprudence of Human Rights Law: A Comparative Interpretive Approach*, Turku, Finland: Institute for Human Rights, Åbo Akademi University, 2000, pp. 27–45, at pp. 42–43.

[11] *African Charter on Human and Peoples' Rights*, arts. 30 *et seq.*

[12] Nigeria, in its periodic report dated 1993, referred to abolition of the death penalty for drug trafficking, unlawful dealing in petroleum products and coounterfeiting of currency, and its replacement with life imprisonment. 'Periodic Report of Nigeria', OAU Doc. ACHPR/MOC/XIII/006. But other States make no reference whatsoever to the death penalty in their reports: e.g. 'Periodic Report of Ghana', OAU Doc. ACHPR/MOC/XIII/009; 'Periodic Report of Ghana', OAU Doc. ACHPR/MOC/XIII/008; 'Periodic Report of Togo', OAU Doc. ACHPR/MOC/XIII/010. On the reporting procedure, see: Astrid Danielsen, *The State Reporting Procedure under the African Charter*, Copenhagen: Danish Centre for Human Rights, 1994; Felice D. Gaer, 'First Fruits: Reporting by States under the African Charter on Human and Peoples' Rights', (1992) 10 *Netherlands Quarterly of Human Rights* 29; Philip Vuciri Ramaga, 'The Tenth Session of the African Commission on Human and People's Rights, Banjul, The Gambia, 8–15 October 1991', (1992) 10 *Netherlands Quarterly of Human Rights* 356; Claude E. Welch Jr., 'The African Commission on Human and Peoples' Rights: A Five-Year Report and Assessment', (1992) 14 *Human Rights Quarterly* 43.

[13] 'Resolution Urging States to Envisage a Moratorium on the Death Penalty, 13th Activity Report of the African Commission on Human and People's Rights', OAU Doc. AHG/Dec.153(XXXVI), Annex IV.

(a) limit the imposition of the death penalty only to the most serious crimes;
(b) consider establishing a moratorium on executions of death penalty;
(c) reflect on the possibility of abolishing the death penalty.

The resolution was a response to concerns expressed by non-governmental organizations about death sentences recently carried out in African countries. The Commission's Special *Rapporteur* on Summary, Arbitrary and Extrajudicial Executions, Mohamed Hatem Ben Salem,[14] noting international activity aimed at abolition of the death penalty, proposed that the Commission make a statement on the subject and call for a moratorium. Ben Salem agreed with a request from the Chair to prepare a draft text. During debate, representatives of Rwanda and Sudan opposed the resolution, adopting positions similar to those taken by these countries in the United Nations Commission on Human Rights.

A year earlier, Rwanda itself had been targeted by a resolution of the African Commission on Human and Peoples' Rights with respect to its proposed execution of twenty-three persons convicted of genocide. The scheduled executions coincided with the twenty-third ordinary session of the Commission, being held in the Gambia, in April 1998. The Commission issued an urgent appeal to the government of Rwanda for postponement of the executions, stating this would violate article 4 of the *African Charter of Human and Peoples' Rights*, which guarantees the right to life. The Commission called for a proper investigation of the allegations against the accused and a new trial with adequate legal assistance.[15]

The individual petition mechanism of the *African Charter on Human and Peoples' Rights* is vaguely worded, compared with comparable provisions in other regional and universal human rights instruments.[16] Only recently, the process has become relatively public and transparent with the publication of the Commission's views on individual communications. In several cases, the African Commission has touched upon issues related to the death penalty. The most important of these concerned the execution of human rights defender Ken Saro-Wiwa by Nigeria in November 1995. The Commission had issued a provisional measures request to Nigeria not to execute Saro-Wiwa while his petition was being considered, but this was ignored by the Nigerian authorities. In its reasons issued in October 1998, the Commission held that in violating the provisional

---

[14] Ben Salem was appointed Special *Rapporteur* on Summary, Arbitrary and Extrajudicial Executions in 1994. He resigned from the position in 2001. There is no evidence in his work of any activity concerning capital punishment that might be comparable to that undertaken by the parallel *rapporteur* of the United Nations Commission on Human Rights.

[15] Amnesty International, *Africa Update*, October 1998, AI Index: AFR 01/05/98, p. 2.

[16] *African Charter on Human and Peoples' Rights*, art. 55. See: Chidi Anselm Odinkalu, 'The Individual Complaints Procedures of the African Commission on Human and Peoples' Rights: A Preliminary Assessment', (1998) 8 *Transnational Law and Contemporary Problems* 359; Rachel Murray, 'Decisions by the African Commission on Individual Communications Under the African Charter on Human and Peoples' Rights', (1998) 46 *International and Comparative Law Quarterly* 412.

measures request, Nigeria had breached article 1 of the *African Charter*.[17] The execution and related events prompted the Commission to hold an extraordinary session in Kampala and eventually to send a mission of inquiry to Nigeria.

With respect to article 4 of the *Charter*, which protects the right to life, the Commission observed:

> Given that the trial which ordered the executions itself violates Article 7, any subsequent implementation of sentences renders the resulting deprivation of life arbitrary and in violation of Article 4. The violation is compounded by the fact that there were pending communications before the African Commission at the time of the executions, and the Commission had requested the government to avoid causing any 'irreparable prejudice' to the subjects of the communications before the Commission had concluded its consideration. Executions had been stayed in Nigeria in the past on the invocation by the Commission of its rule on provisional measures (Rule 109 now 111) and the Commission had hoped that a similar situation will obtain in the case of Ken Saro-Wiwa and others. It is a matter of deep regret that this did not happen. The protection of the right to life in Article 4 also includes a duty for the state not to purposefully let a person die while in its custody. Here at least one of the victims' lives was seriously endangered by the denial of medication during detention. Thus, there are multiple violations of Article 4.[18]

The Commission found that a number of other provisions of the Charter, concerning such matters as freedom of expression, opinion and peaceful assembly, were also violated by Nigeria.

> Communication 154 alleges that the actual reason for the trial and the ultimate death sentences was the peaceful expression of views by the accused persons. The victims were disseminating information and opinions on the rights of the people who live in the oil producing area of Ogoniland, through MOSOP and specifically a rally. These allegations have not been contradicted by the government, which has already been shown to be highly prejudiced against MOSOP, without giving concrete justifications. MOSOP was founded specifically for the expression of views of the people who live in the oil producing areas, and the rally was organised with this in view. The Government's actions is [*sic*] inconsistent with Article 9.2 implicit when it violated Articles 10.1 and 11.[19]

The Commission described the execution of Ken Saro-Wiwa as 'a blot on the legal system of Nigeria which will not be easy to erase'. It added: 'To have carried out the execution in the face of pleas to the contrary by the Commission

---

[17] *International Pen, Constitutional Rights Project, Interights on behalf of Ken Saro-Wiwa Jr. and Civil Liberties Organisation* v. *Nigeria* (Comm. No. 137/94, 139/94, 154/96 and 161/97), Twelfth Activity Report of the African Commission on Human and Peoples' Rights, 1998–1999, OAU Doc. ACHPR/RPT/12th, Annex V, (2000) 7 IHRR 274. The *African Charter* has also been invoked before Nigeria's domestic courts in death penalty litigation: *Nemi* v. *The State*, [1994] 1 LRC 376 (Supreme Court, Nigeria), at p. 386 (Bello CJN); also at p. 400 (Uwais JSC). On the death penalty in Nigeria, see: Mike Ikhariale, 'Death Penalty in Nigeria: A Constitutional Aberration', (1991) 1 *Journal of Human Rights Law and Practice* 40.

[18] *Ibid.*, paras. 103–104. [19] *Ibid.*, para. 110.

and world opinion is something which we pray will never happen again. That it is a violation of the Charter is an understatement.'[20] The Commission concluded, *inter alia*, that there had been a violation of articles 4 and 7 'in relation to the conduct of the trial and the execution of the victims'.

Another series of petitions directed against Nigeria concerned an expedited procedure in capital trials developed for crimes involving firearms and robbery. The Commission held that the Robbery and Firearms (Special Provision) Decree No. 5 of 1984 which imposes capital punishment without the possibility of an appeal breaches the right to an appeal, which is ensured by article 7§1(a) of the *African Charter.*[21]

In a series of four cases filed against Sudan by non-governmental organisations, petitioners raised the issue of the death penalty being available for a broad range of offences pursuant to the 1983 Penal Code, including political offences such as subversion, failure to report a planned mutiny, upsetting the national economy, organizing a strike, possession of undeclared foreign currency and drug offences. They also alleged that there is no appeal of a death sentence, and that legal representation is denied at new trials.[22] One of the petitions charged that twenty-eight army officers who had been executed in April 1990 were allowed no legal representation.[23] The Commission observed that Sudan's insistence that these executions were carried out in accordance with the law in force were 'insufficient', and concluded there had been a violation of the right to fair trial, protected by article 7 of the *African Charter.*[24] The Commission also declared there had been a violation of article 4, but it is unclear whether this related to the capital punishment of the army officers or to various summary executions carried out within Sudan. No specific comment by the Commission addressed the issue of the number and nature of crimes for which the death penalty is available.

A petition filed against Botswana by Mariette Bosch invoked the *African Charter* to challenge her death sentence. Botswana went ahead with the hanging despite the pending proceedings.

The *African Charter of the Rights and Welfare of the Child,* which was adopted in 1990 but which only came into force on 29 November 1999, establishes that: 'Death sentence shall not be pronounced for crimes committed

---

[20] *Ibid.*, para. 115.
[21] *Constitutional Rights Project* v. *Nigeria* (Comm. No. 60/91), (1986–97) LRAC, Series A, Vol. 1, p. 54, 3 IHRR 132. See also: *Constitutional Rights Project (in respect of Zamani Lekwot and six others)* v. *Nigeria* (Comm. no. 87/93), (1986–97) LRAC, Series A, Vol. 1, p. 82, 3 IHRR 137.
[22] *Amnesty International, Comité Loosli Bachelard, Lawyers Committee for Human Rights and Association of Members of the Episcopal Conference of East Africa* v. *Sudan* (Comm. No. 48/90, 50/91, 52/91, 89/93), Thirteenth Activity Report of the African Commission on Human and Peoples' Rights, 1999–2000, OAU Doc. AHG/222/36th, Annex V.
[23] *Ibid.*, para. 13.   [24] *Ibid.*, para. 6.

by children.'[25] As in the United Nations *Convention on the Rights of the Child,* a child is defined as 'every human being below the age of 18 years'.[26] The *Charter* also states that children should not be subject to inhuman or degrading treatment, and that the essential purpose of the criminal justice system is to promote reintegration in the family and rehabilitation.[27] Like the *African Charter of Human and Peoples' Rights,* the *Charter of Rights of the Child* should be construed with reference to international human rights law, and specifically the *Convention on the Rights of the Child* and the *Universal Declaration of Human Rights.*[28] The African Committee of Experts on the Rights and Welfare of the Child is charged with implementation of the instrument.[29]

---

[25] *African Charter on the Rights and Welfare of the Child,* OAU Doc. CAB/LEG/24.9/49, art. 5§3.
[26] *Ibid.,* art. 2.   [27] *Ibid.,* art. 17.   [28] *Ibid.,* art. 46.   [29] *Ibid.,* arts. 32 *et seq.*

Conclusion

Victor Hugo described the death penalty as 'le signe spécial et éternel de la barbarie'.[1] The archetypal form of State-authorized premeditated homicide, it is eternal in the sense that it has been with mankind since antiquity. Yet its abolition has been envisaged for at least two centuries, and with the accelerating progress of the movement for abolition, the end of this dark tunnel is now in sight. There are many ways to measure society's progress away from barbarism and towards a more humane condition. One is by the progressive development of legal norms.

The abolitionist movement's origins can be traced to the eighteenth century, and several States had eliminated the death penalty by the nineteenth century. However, the spread of abolitionist legislation is generally a post-Second World War phenomenon or, to put it another way, a development dating from the adoption of the *Universal Declaration of Human Rights*, on 10 December 1948. Of seventy-four countries described as abolitionist for all crimes as of December 1999, sixty-six have abolished the death penalty since 1948. Of the forty-nine States that are abolitionist for ordinary crimes[2] or abolitionist *de facto*,[3] all have conducted executions since 1948; in other words, such partial or *de facto* abolition is a relatively recent development.

Slightly more than a decade ago, in 1989, Amnesty International published a seminal volume on the issue of capital punishment, entitled *When the State Kills*. Amnesty International surveyed the international situation, distinguishing between countries that were abolitionist for all crimes (i.e. countries whose laws do not provide for the death penalty for any crime), countries that were abolitionist for ordinary crimes only (i.e. countries whose laws provide for the death penalty only for exceptional crimes under military law or crimes committed in exceptional circumstances such as wartime), countries that were

[1] Victor Hugo, *Écrits sur la peine de mort*, Avignon: Actes Sud, 1979.
[2] That is, crimes contrary to military law or committed in wartime or other exceptional circumstances.
[3] States that have not conducted executions for ten years are deemed to be *de facto* abolitionist.

abolitionist in practice (i.e. countries and territories which retain the death penalty for ordinary crimes but have not executed anyone during the past ten years or more); and retentionist countries (i.e. countries and territories which retain and use the death penalty for ordinary crimes).[4] The statistical portrait was as follows:

Abolition for all crimes	35
Abolition for ordinary crimes only	18
Abolitionist in practice	27
Retentionist	100

Amnesty International also provided the relevant dates of abolition, where applicable. These indicated an unmistakable trend towards abolition, one that was constantly growing in momentum. For example, of the thirty-five countries that were abolitionist for all crimes, twenty-seven had abolished the death penalty since 1948. Moreover, with each decade subsequent to 1948, the number of States abolishing capital punishment increased. However, the figures also indicated that a majority of States continued to employ capital punishment.

Sometime in the middle of the 1990s, the majority shifted from one favouring capital punishment to one opposing it. According to the report of the Secretary-General of the United Nations, issued on 31 March 2000,[5] the numbers are as follows:

Abolitionist for all crimes	74
Abolitionist for ordinary crimes only	11
Abolitionist in practice	38
Retentionist	71

The change throughout the 1990s, since the Amnesty International study, is most dramatic. Thus, whereas in 1989, some 44 per cent of States were abolitionist in one form or another, by the year 2000 they made up 64 per cent of the total.

That this is a growing trend since the Second World War can be seen by comparing the dates of abolition (or, in the case of *de facto* abolition, the date of last execution). During the decade 1948–1957, seven countries put an end to the death penalty.[6] During the decade 1958–1967, the figure was eight.[7] From 1968

---

[4] Amnesty International, *When the State Kills. . . , The Death Penalty: A Human Rights Issue*, New York: Amnesty International, 1989, pp. 259–262.

[5] 'Capital Punishment and Implementation of the Safeguards Guaranteeing Protection of the Rights of Those Facing the Death Penalty, Report of the Secretary-General,' U.N. Doc. E/2000/3. The report was prepared by the distinguished English criminologist Professor Roger Hood. Amnesty International's latest figures, dated 1 January 2001, are somewhat different. They show slight increases in the *de jure* categories but are somewhat less optimistic about the number of *de facto* abolitionist States: abolitionist for all crimes, 75; abolitionist for ordinary crimes only, 13; abolitionist in practice, 20; retentionist, 87.

[6] Austria, Brunei Darussalam, Finland, Honduras, Israel, Maldives, Papua New Guinea.

[7] Bhutan, Dominican Republic, Madagascar, Monaco, New Zealand, Samoa, Senegal, Solomon Islands.

to 1977, the total was nine.[8] Then, the process began to accelerate dramatically. Between 1978 and 1987, twenty-nine countries abolished or ceased to employ capital punishment.[9] Forty-three countries joined this group between 1988 and 1996.[10] In the three-year period from 1998 to 2000, thirteen additional countries were declared abolitionist.[11]

In the first edition of this work, published in 1993, I wrote: '[I]f the trend continues uninterrupted, sometime prior to the year 2000 a majority of the world's states will have abolished the death penalty.' Some critics suggested that I was overly optimistic about the spread of abolitionism. In fact, I was too conservative.

On a regional level, Europe and Latin America stand far in front. Europe is now for all intents and purposes abolitionist, although this is a phenomenon of recent decades. With the abolition of the death penalty in the Russian Federation, we may now speak of a portion of the world that is approximately north of the fiftieth parallel where capital punishment no longer exists, with the exception of Belarus. Latin America, another bastion of abolitionism, has strong abolitionist traditions dating to the beginning of the twentieth century and even before. It too has its rare exceptions, but they only serve to prove the rule. Africa is the region where the progress has been most stunning in recent years. Prior to 1990, the vast majority of African States still provided for the death penalty. Since then, many have formally abolished it, and in several others it has fallen into disuse. If the Arab countries of North Africa are removed from the calculation, close to a majority of African States have now abolished the death penalty. Southern Africa is now essentially free of the scourge of capital punishment.

The United States remains one of the more steadfast advocates of capital punishment.[12] Nevertheless, popular enthusiasm for the death penalty has dropped dramatically since the mid-1990s, recalling an abolitionist maxim: 'Public support for capital punishment is a mile wide but an inch deep.' Several English-speaking Caribbean States and Cuba also continue to inflict the death penalty. On the Asian continent, China, Iran and Iraq all make extensive use of the death penalty. Islamic law is regularly cited as an insurmountable obstacle

---

[8] Canada, Central African Republic, Holy See, Malta, Naura, Niger, Sri Lanka, Tuvalu, United Kingdom.
[9] Argentina, Australia, Barbados, Brazil, Cape Verde, Congo, Cyprus, Dominica, El Salvador, France, Gambia, Germany, Grenada, Guinea, Haiti, Kiribati, Liechtenstein, Luxemburg, Mali, Marshall Islands, Micronesia, Nicaragua, Peru, Spain, Suriname, Togo, Tonga, Turkey, Vanuatu.
[10] Andorra, Angola, Antigua and Barbuda, Armenia, Belgium, Belize, Benin, Bolivia, Bosnia and Herzegovina, Burkina Faso, Cambodia, Croatia, Czech Republic, Djibouti, Eritrea, Gabon, Georgia, Greece, Guinea-Bissau, Hungary, Ireland, Jamaica, Laos, Mauritania, Mauritius, Mozambique, Myanmar, Namibia, Nepal, Palau, Paraguay, Poland, Qatar, Macedonia, Moldova, Romania, Sao Tome and Principe, Seychelles, Slovakia, Slovenia, South Africa, Swaziland, Yugoslavia.
[11] Albania, Armenia, Azerbaijan, Benin, Bulgaria, Côte d'Ivoire, East Timor, Estonia, Fiji, Latvia, Lithuania, Turkmenistan, Ukraine.
[12] See: Hugo Adam Bedau, ed., *The Death Penalty in America*, Oxford: Oxford University Press, 1987.

to abolition of the death penalty, although it would seem that ancient religious texts are more of a pretext than anything else for the enthusiastic resort to capital punishment by what are profoundly undemocratic and repressive States.

Analysis of trends in national legislation was not the purpose of this study. That task has been and continues to be well fulfilled by the quinquennial reports of the Secretary-General of the United Nations and their annual updates, by other international organizations such as the Council of Europe, the European Union and the Organization for Security and Cooperation in Europe, and by the thorough monitoring work of Amnesty International, a non-governmental organization whose pre-eminent role in the abolitionist movement is undisputed. That these developments can be measured in conjunction with an equally pronounced trend in the evolution of international human rights norms is what this study has endeavoured to demonstrate.

The first limitation on the death penalty in positive international law appeared in the 1929 *Geneva Convention*, dealing with prisoners of war taken in international armed conflicts.[13] It did not prevent execution but provided for certain controls, in the hope that international pressure and prisoner exchanges might reduce the incidence of the death penalty. Outrage at the abuses of the death penalty during the Second World War, particularly with respect to civilian populations, led to the recognition of the 'right to life' as a normative objective, a 'common standard of achievement for all peoples and nations', in the words of the preamble to the *Universal Declaration of Human Rights*. Hitherto, the right to life had appeared in some national constitutions, and in the post-war minorities treaties, but usually with its awkward and inconsistent appendage, the exception of capital punishment. When the United States *Constitution* stated that no person 'shall be deprived of life . . . without due process of law', it legitimized the death penalty, subject to certain limitations. But the *Universal Declaration of Human Rights*, adopted in 1948, and its contemporary in the Inter-American regional system, the *American Declaration of the Rights and Duties of Man*, let the right to life stand alone, unblemished by any limitation. The mission of these instruments was not to outline precise legal norms aimed at immediate implementation but rather to set a common goal that would be attained and perfected in the future. Their drafters contemplated abolition of the death penalty but were reluctant to proclaim it openly, given contemporary State practice. Yet the general recognition of the right to life in 1948, without exception, has proven far-sighted, for it has allowed the two declarations to retain their relevance and to grow as part of an abolitionist future that their authors only faintly discerned.

In 1949, the *Geneva Conventions* were revised and expanded. Only on closer examination is it evident that their goal is not regulation but elimination of

---

[13] *International Convention Relative to the Treatment of Prisoners of War*, (1932–33) 118 LNTS 343, art. 66.

the death penalty.[14] By providing, in article 68§2 of the civilian *Convention*, that the death penalty cannot be imposed on civilians in an occupied territory whose law, prior to invasion, did not provide for capital punishment, States were subtly invited to abolish the death penalty. Their citizens could only be protected from abuse by another State, in the event of wartime occupation, to the extent that they would protect them from abuse by their own judicial system in peacetime. The third and fourth *Conventions* added further procedural standards in the implementation of the death penalty, excluded civilian juveniles from execution altogether, and provided, in common article 3, a core due process guarantee in capital cases during international armed conflicts.

During the 1950s and 1960s, three international human rights treaties were drafted that provided expressly for the death penalty as a limit to the right to life. The first of the three, the *European Convention on Human Rights*,[15] adopted in 1950, imposed few explicit restraints on the death penalty, although the scope of any implicit limits was never tested because the death penalty soon fell into virtual disuse in Europe. Before the end of the 1950s, the United Nations General Assembly had prepared a far more progressive provision concerning the right to life, one that limited the death penalty and even excluded it for certain categories of individuals.[16] Even more advanced was its call for abolition of the death penalty, something which belonged more in a declaration than in a treaty but which was included as a compromise to satisfy the many States who felt that a right to life provision should not appear to sanction the death penalty: 'Nothing in this article shall be invoked to delay or to prevent the abolition of capital punishment by any State Party to the present Covenant.'[17] The third of the three treaties, the *American Convention on Human Rights*,[18] was drafted during the 1960s, and went even further towards abolition than the *International Covenant on Civil and Political Rights*. It was in reality an abolitionist treaty, at least for those States that had already abolished the death penalty, because it provided that capital punishment may not be reintroduced once it has disappeared from a State's statute books.

All three instruments approach the death penalty as an express limitation on the right to life. It may not, however, be entirely appropriate to use the term

---

[14] *Geneva Convention of August 12, 1949 Relative to the Treatment of Prisoners of War*, (1950) 75 UNTS 135, art. 100, 101 (see Appendix 9, p. 414); *Geneva Convention of August 12, 1949 Relative to the Protection of Civilians*, (1950) 75 UNTS 287, arts. 68, 75 (see Appendix 10, p. 416).

[15] *Convention for the Protection of Human Rights and Fundamental Freedoms*, (1955) 213 UNTS 221, ETS 5, art. 2 (see Appendix 14, p. 423).

[16] *International Covenant on Civil and Political Rights*, (1976) 999 UNTS 171, art. 6 (see Appendix 2, p. 380). The drafting of article 6 of the *Covenant* was completed by the Third Committee of the General Assembly in 1957, although the entire instrument was not adopted until 1966, and did not come into force until 1976.

[17] *Ibid.*, art. 6§6.

[18] (1979) 1144 UNTS 123, OASTS 36 (see Appendix 20, p. 436). Adopted in 1969, it came into force in 1978.

'limitation' to describe the death penalty in the right to life provisions. Limitations are a phenomenon common to human rights instruments in both domestic and international law. They are not always formulated similarly in the various systems, indeed, they are often expressed differently within the same instrument, depending on the right which is being limited. From a theoretical standpoint, however, they are invariably justified only to the extent that they protect a valid and competing interest.[19] For example, freedom of expression may be limited in the case of hate propaganda, recognizing the valid competing interest of individuals and groups to be protected from discrimination. The death penalty, although it appears in the international instruments as such a limitation, does not meet this standard of a valid and competing interest. Admittedly, it may be argued that the death penalty is necessary in order to deter anti-social behaviour. But this argument, a favourite of retentionists, was virtually absent as a consideration of the drafters of the *International Covenant on Civil and Political Rights*, the *European Convention* and the *American Convention*. The death penalty is a limit unlike any other in the international human rights instruments, a limit whose sole justification is the prudence of its drafters, aware of its anomaly but fearful of alienating retentionist States and discouraging them from ratification.

The *International Covenant on Civil and Political Rights* and the *American Convention* had barely come into force when international organizations charged with the protection of human rights began preparing for a further development, the adoption of protocols to the international human rights treaties that would abolish the death penalty. The European regional system was the first to take this step, and *Protocol No. 6* to the *European Convention* abolishing the death penalty came into force in 1985,[20] followed at the end of the decade by its United Nations[21] and Inter-American[22] counterparts. The common standard of achievement, only dimly envisaged by the drafters of the *Universal Declaration* in 1948, has become, with the protocols, a legal reality.

The three protocols still tolerate the death penalty in time of war. This final exception was included in order to encourage ratification by the many States that are not prepared to renounce use of capital punishment during armed conflict.

---

[19] Albert Beckman and Michael Bothe, 'General Report on the Theory of Limitations on Human Rights', in Armand de Mestral et al., *The Limitations of Human Rights in Comparative Constitutional Law*, Cowansville, Québec: Editions Yvon Blais, 1986, pp. 105–112, at p. 107.

[20] *Protocol No. 6 to the Convention for the Protection of Human Rights and Fundamental Freedoms Concerning the Abolition of the Death Penalty*, ETS no. 114 (see Appendix 15, p. 424).

[21] *Second Optional Protocol to the International Covenant on Civil and Political Rights Aimed at Abolition of the Death Penalty*, GA Res. 44/128 (see Appendix 4, p. 397). The *Second Optional Protocol* was adopted in 1989 and came into force in 1991.

[22] *Additional Protocol to the American Convention on Human Rights to Abolish the Death Penalty*, OASTS 73, 29 ILM 1447 (see Appendix 21, p. 438). The *Additional Protocol* was adopted in 1990, and came into force in 1991.

Indeed, it is in time of war when the greatest abuse of the death penalty occurs. Criteria of expediency and State terror stampede panicked governments towards inhumane excesses that would be unthinkable in time of peace. Strangely, the principal argument in favour of the death penalty in time of war, deterrence, has been discredited by criminologists. If States reject deterrence as a rationale for capital punishment in peacetime, why should it be valid in time of war? Until international law thoroughly abolishes the death penalty, in war as well as in peace, the norms of international humanitarian law will retain their relevance. The limitations on use of the death penalty in the 1949 *Geneva Conventions* were strengthened somewhat in 1977 by the two additional protocols.[23] These have expanded the categories of individuals covered by limitations and restrictions on capital punishment. Nevertheless, some common declaration of humanitarian principles, bridging human rights law and the law of armed conflict, and prohibiting capital punishment at all times, is desirable.

Most of the legal norms that have been developed since 1948 concern limitation of the death penalty, that is, its partial abolition. They deal with procedural safeguards, with restrictions *ratione personae* and *ratione materiae*, and with the right to seek pardon, reprieve, commutation and amnesty. Some of them have undoubtedly acquired the status of customary norms of international law, in that they represent the general practice of states and are accepted as law (*opinio juris*).[24]

That procedural safeguards must be respected in all capital trials is without doubt a norm of customary law.[25] Its universal recognition is confirmed in common article 3 to the *Geneva Conventions* of 1949, which proscribes the carrying out of executions 'without previous judgment pronounced by a regularly constituted court, affording all the judicial guarantees which are recognized as indispensable by civilized peoples'.[26] These minimum standards apply, according to the *Conventions*, in armed conflicts not of an international character.

---

[23] *Protocol Additional I to the 1949 Geneva Conventions and Relating to the Protection of Victims of International Armed Conflicts*, (1979) 1125 UNTS 3, arts. 76§3, 77§5 (see Appendix 11, p. 420); *Protocol Additional II to the 1949 Geneva Conventions and Relating to the Protection of Victims of Non-International Armed Conflicts*, (1979) 1125 UNTS 609, art. 6§4 (see Appendix 12, p. 421).

[24] Theodor Meron, *Human Rights and Humanitarian Norms as Customary Law*, Oxford: Clarendon Press, 1989; M. Akehurst, 'Custom as a Source of International Law', (1974–75) 47 *BYIL* 1.

[25] Phrased another way, a comment to the *Restatement (Third) of the Foreign Relations Law of the United States* declares: 'Capital punishment, imposed pursuant to conviction in accordance with due process of law, has not been recognized as a violation of the customary law of human rights.' Theodor Meron considers the 'core' of article 14 of the *International Covenant on Civil and Political Rights*, which enumerates the procedural safeguards in all criminal proceedings, to be customary law: Meron, *Human Rights*, p. 96.

[26] *Geneva Convention of August 12, 1949 for the Amelioration of the Condition of the Wounded and Sick in Armed Forces in the Field*, (1950) 75 UNTS 31, art. 3; *Geneva Convention of August 12, 1949 for the Amelioration of the Condition of Wounded, Sick and Shipwrecked Members of Armed Forces at Sea*, (1950) 75 UNTS 85, art. 3; *Geneva Convention of August 12, 1949 Relative to the Treatment of Prisoners of War*, art. 3; *Geneva Convention of August 12, 1949 Relative to the Protection of Civilians*, art. 3.

The *Geneva Conventions* of 1949 have been ratified by virtually every State in the world, and common article 3 has been recognized as expressing norms of customary international law.[27] If the norms of common article 3 are accepted in the extreme conditions of non-international armed conflict as the lowest common denominator of humane conduct, then *a fortiori* they most surely obtain during international armed conflict and in time of peace. But what are these judicial guarantees that are 'recognized as indispensable by civilized peoples'? The answer will be found in the more detailed provisions of the international treaties, the 'soft law' resolutions of bodies such as the Economic and Social Council and the General Assembly of the United Nations, and the declarations by States in their reports to the Secretary-General and in their periodic reports to the Human Rights Committee.

No person can be sentenced to death without a 'trial'.[28] As elementary as this proposition seems, its importance is understood with reference to the innumerable executions, notably in wartime, that have taken place merely as a result of the superior orders of a head of state, a justice minister or a ranking military officer. In order to merit the name 'trial', such proceedings must ensure that the accused is presumed innocent,[29] that he or she is entitled to legal counsel[30] and adequate time to prepare a defence,[31] that the trial be held without undue delay,[32] that the tribunal be impartial.[33] Many of these specific rights cannot be fully appreciated in the absence of a precise fact situation. For example, the right to counsel may in some cases necessitate State-funded assistance. Yet perfunctory recognition of this right, in the form of poorly remunerated junior

---

[27] *Military and Paramilitary Activities in and Against Nicaragua (Nicaragua* v. *United States)*, [1986] ICJ Reports 14, paras. 218, 255, 292(9).

[28] *International Covenant on Civil and Political Rights*, arts. 6§2, 14§1; *European Convention*, arts. 2§1, 6; *American Convention*, arts. 4§2, 8; *African Charter on Human and Peoples' Rights*, OAU Doc. CAB/LEG/67/3 rev.5, 4 EHRR 417, 21 *ILM* 58, art. 7 (see Appendix 22, p. 440); 'Safeguards Guaranteeing Protection of the Rights of Those Facing the Death Penalty', ESC Res. 1984/50, art. 5 (see Appendix 8, p. 413); 'Implementation of the Safeguards Guaranteeing Protection of the Rights of Those Facing the Death Penalty', ESC Res. 1989/64; ESC Res. 1996/15.

[29] *International Covenant on Civil and Political Rights*, art. 14§2; *European Convention*, art. 6§2; *American Convention*, art. 8§2; *African Charter*, art. 7§1(b); 'Safeguards', art. 4. The 'Safeguards' add that guilt must be based 'upon clear and convincing evidence leaving no room for an alternative explanation of the facts'.

[30] *International Covenant on Civil and Political Rights*, art. 14§3(d); *European Convention*, art. 6§2(c); *American Convention*, art. 8§2(d); 'Safeguards', art. 5; 'Implementation of the Safeguards'; 'Extrajudicial, Summary or Arbitrary Executions: Report by the Special Rapporteur', UN Doc. E/CN.4/1997/60, para. 81.

[31] *International Covenant on Civil and Political Rights*, art. 14§3(b); *European Convention*, art. 6§2(b); *American Convention*, art. 8§2(c); *African Charter*, art. 7§1(c); 'Safeguards', art. 5; 'Implementation of the Safeguards'.

[32] *International Covenant on Civil and Political Rights*, art. 14§3(c); *European Convention*, art. 6§1; *American Convention*, art. 8§1; *African Charter*, art. 7§1(d); 'Safeguards', art. 5.

[33] *International Covenant on Civil and Political Rights*, art. 14§1; *European Convention*, art. 6§1; *American Convention*, art. 8§1; *African Charter*, art. 7§1(b); 'Safeguards', art. 5.

attorneys, may in reality be a means to violate the right and to ensure summary conviction of the accused.[34]

The right to seek pardon, clemency, reprieve or commutation is widely admitted and rarely poses much of a real problem for States, because it is an inexpensive concession.[35] This right is very important, because, in many States, executive clemency has often preceded legislative change and tempered the extremes of public and judicial opinion.[36] There should be adequate time between sentence and execution in order to permit a realistic right of appeal or application for clemency. An Economic and Social Council resolution recognizes an obligation upon States 'to allow adequate time for the preparation of appeals to a court of higher jurisdiction and for the completion of appeal proceedings, as well as petitions for clemency'.[37] Obviously execution should not be carried out while appeal or petition for clemency is pending.[38] These principles should also apply in the case of communications or applications to international human rights bodies, where the right of petition has been recognized. Officials involved in executions must be informed of the status of appeals and petitions for clemency.[39]

One of the most difficult issues concerns the so-called 'death row phenomenon'. Obviously, all prisoners are entitled to be treated with humanity, whatever their sentence. The Economic and Social Council has urged death penalty states 'to effectively apply the Standard Minimum Rules for the Treatment of Prisoners, in order to keep to a minimum the suffering of prisoners under sentence of death and to avoid any exacerbation of such suffering'.[40] But it is also argued that prolonged detention of a person awaiting execution is, *per se*, cruel, inhuman and degrading treatment or punishment. The European Court

---

[34] Several decisions of the Human Rights Committee have insisted upon this point. See, for example: *Little* v. *Jamaica* (No. 283/1988), UN Doc. A/47/40, p. 276.

[35] *International Covenant on Civil and Political Rights*, art. 6§4; Safeguard 7; 'Implementation of the Safeguards Guaranteeing Protection of the Rights of Those Facing the Death Penalty', ESC Res. 1989/64; 'Extrajudicial, Summary or Arbitrary Executions: Report by the Special Rapporteur', UN Doc E/CN.4/1998/68, para. 118.

[36] In Canada, for example, executive clemency *de facto* abolished the death penalty fourteen years before Parliament. It was even invoked by Canadian officials during presentation of Canada's initial report to the Human Rights Committee as the major protection against abusive use of the military death penalty: UN Doc. CCPR/C/1/Add.43.

[37] 'Implementation of the Safeguards Guaranteeing Protection of the Rights of Those Facing the Death Penalty', ESC Res. 1989/64. Also 'Extrajudicial, Summary or Arbitrary Executions: Report by the Special Rapporteur', UN Doc E/CN.4/1996/4, para. 556; 'Extrajudicial, Summary or Arbitrary Executions: Report by the Special Rapporteur', UN Doc E/CN.4/1998/68, para. 118; 'Extrajudicial, Summary or Arbitrary Executions: Report by the Special Rapporteur', UN Doc E/CN.4/1998/68/Add.1, para. 178; *Geneva Convention of August 12, 1949 Relative to the Treatment of Prisoners of War*, art. 101; *Geneva Convention of August 12, 1949 Relative to the Protection of Civilians*, art. 75.

[38] 'Safeguards', art. 8.

[39] ESC Res. 1996/15; 'Extrajudicial, Summary or Arbitrary Executions: Report by the Special Rapporteur', UN Doc E/CN.4/1996/4, para. 556.

[40] ESC Res. 1996/15.

of Human Rights established the precedent in *Soering*, which involved probable detention of six to eight years between conviction and execution. It held the 'death row phenomenon' contrary to the *European Convention on Human Rights*.[41] The European Court's views were echoed a few years later by the Judicial Committee of the Privy Council.[42] However, the Human Rights Committee and the Special *Rapporteur* on Extrajudicial, Summary and Arbitrary Executions have refused to follow the same approach, apparently out of concerns that any condemnation of delayed execution can only incite States to accelerate the pace.[43]

The Human Rights Committee has recognized that the procedural protections of article 14 of the *International Covenant* are incorporated into article 6. This makes them non-derogable in death penalty cases, because article 6 cannot be suspended in time of emergency.[44] The *American Convention on Human Rights* is the clearest of the three treaties in this respect, being 'the first international human rights instrument to include among the rights that may not be suspended essential judicial guarantees for the protection of the nonderogable rights'.[45] The Inter-American Court of Human Rights has held that 'due process' cannot be suspended in the case of a non-derogable right, such as the right to life, even in emergency situations.[46] Under customary international law, the classic procedural guarantees must apply in death penalty cases, because they are the 'judicial guarantees which are recognized as indispensable by civilized peoples', in accordance with common article 3 to the *Geneva Conventions*.

The prohibition against retroactive imposition of the death penalty is without any doubt among those customary norms subsumed in common article 3 of the *Geneva Conventions*. It is recognized in all the major international treaties[47]

---

[41] *Soering* v. *United Kingdom and Germany*, 7 July 1989, Series A, Vol. 161, 11 EHRR 439.

[42] *Pratt* et al. v. *Attorney General for Jamaica* et al., [1993] 4 All.ER 769, [1993] 2 LRC 349, [1994] 2 AC 1, 14 *HRLJ* 338, 33 ILM 364 (JCPC).

[43] *Errol Johnson* v. *Jamaica* (No. 588/1994), UN Doc. CCPR/C/56/D/588/1994; 'Report by the Special Rapporteur, Mr. Bacre Waly Ndiaye, Submitted Pursuant to Commission on Human Rights Resolution 1993/71', UN Doc. E/CN.4/1994/7, para. 682. But see: 'Situation of Human Rights in Bosnia and Herzegovina: Report of the Special Rapporteur', UN Doc. E/CN.4/1998/13, para. 75.

[44] *General Comment 6(16)*, U.N. Doc CCPR/C/21/Add.1, U.N. Doc A/37/40, Annex V, U.N. Doc CCPR/3/Add.1, pp. 382–3 (see Appendix 5, p. 402); *Pinto* v. *Trinidad and Tobago* (No. 232/1987), UN Doc. A/45/40, Vol. II, p. 69; *Reid* v. *Jamaica* (No. 250/1987), UN Doc. A/45/40, Vol. II, p. 85, 11 *HRLJ* 319. A new additional protocol to the *International Covenant* making article 14 a non-derogable provision has been proposed: UN Doc. E/CN.4/Sub.2/1990/34, para. 150, UN Doc. E/CN.4/Sub.2/1991/29.

[45] *Habeas Corpus in Emergency Situations (Arts. 27(2), 25(1) and 7(6) American Convention on Human Rights)*, Advisory Opinion OC-8/87 of 30 January 1987, Series A, No. 8, para. 36.

[46] *Judicial Guarantees in States of Emergency (Arts. 27(2), 25(1) and 8 American Convention on Human Rights)*, Advisory Opinion OC-9/87 of 6 October 1987, Series A, No. 9, paras. 29–30.

[47] *International Covenant on Civil and Political Rights*, arts. 6§2, 15; *European Convention*, art. 7; *American Convention*, art. 9; *African Charter*, art. 7§2; 'Safeguards', art. 5.

and makes up the core of human rights from which there can be no derogation, even in time of war.[48]

Conventional international law has also sought to limit the scope *ratione materiae* of the death penalty, with such expressions as 'the most serious crimes'.[49] The problem is not with the existence of a norm but rather with the varying definitions that States provide for it, it being universally accepted that the death penalty should not be used for petty offences. The periodic reports to the Human Rights Committee show that many States consider this term to encompass political offences and economic crimes, although this view is not shared by members of the Committee. Islamic law even recognizes the death penalty for such crimes as adultery and apostasy. The 'Safeguards' adopted by the Economic and Social Council state that the scope of such crimes 'should not go beyond intentional crimes, with lethal or other extremely grave consequences'.[50] The Special *Rapporteur* on Extrajudicial, Summary or Arbitrary Executions has said 'the death penalty should be eliminated for crimes such as economic crimes and drug-related offences'.[51] There is also support in international instruments for norms promoting the progressive reduction in capital offences,[52] the non-extension of the scope of the death penalty,[53] and a prohibition on the reintroduction of capital punishment if it has been abolished.[54]

Several categories of persons have been excluded from the scope of the death penalty by conventional norms. The prohibition on the execution of pregnant women or of mothers of young children is recognized in virtually all of the international instruments,[55] and, as the reports to the Secretary-General and the Human Rights Committee attest, this is also consistent with State practice. After birth, the length of any moratorium varies in different States and is sometimes no more than a forty-day confinement period.[56] Considerable attention was devoted to this problem at the 1977 Diplomatic Conference on the *Additional Protocols*. In practice, the execution of pregnant women or mothers of young children is

---

[48] *International Covenant on Civil and Political Rights*, art. 4§2; *European Convention*, art. 15§2; *American Convention*, art. 27§2.

[49] *International Covenant on Civil and Political Rights*, art. 6§2; 'Safeguards', art. 1; 'Resolution Urging States to Envisage a Moratorium on the Death Penalty, 13th Activity Report of the African Commission on Human and People's Rights', OAU Doc. AHG/Dec.153(XXXVI), Annex IV, art. 2(a).

[50] 'Safeguards', art. 1.

[51] 'Extrajudicial, summary or arbitrary executions: Report by the Special Rapporteur', UN Doc E/CN.4/1997/60, para. 91.

[52] GA Res. 32/61; CHR Res. 1998/8.   [53] *American Convention*, art. 4§2.   [54] *Ibid.*

[55] *International Covenant on Civil and Political Rights*, art. 6§5; *American Convention*, art. 4§5; *Protocol Additional I to the 1949 Geneva Conventions and Relating to the Protection of Victims of International Armed Conflicts*, art. 76§3; *Protocol Additional II to the 1949 Geneva Conventions and Relating to the Protection of Victims of Non-International Armed Conflicts*, art. 6§4.

[56] 'Initial Report of Morocco', UN Doc. CCPR/C/10/Add.10; UN Doc. CCPR/C/SR.327, para. 8 (Mali).

extremely rare in peacetime,[57] although it may be increasingly common during war, especially as women play a more active role as combatants.

The *American Convention on Human Rights* is the only international instrument to prohibit execution of the elderly.[58] The concept provoked virtually no discussion or debate during the drafting of the *Convention*. The question did not even arise in the preparation of other international instruments, such as the *International Covenant on Civil and Political Rights* or the *Additional Protocols* to the *Geneva Conventions*. Although proposed for inclusion in the 'Safeguards', it was cut from the final draft, only to be added four years later in an Economic and Social Council resolution.[59] It is hard to find the requisite elements of custom with respect to execution of the elderly.

The same is not the case, however, for the prohibition of execution of persons for crimes committed while under eighteen years of age. State practice, with a few lingering exceptions, is consistent with such a ban. The treaty norm prohibiting such executions, in the *Convention on the Rights of the Child*, has been ratified without any reservation by all States with the exception of the United States, and it has signed the instrument.[60] The norm was recognized without protest during the adoption of several other international human rights or humanitarian instruments.[61] The Human Rights Committee has stated that the prohibition of execution of children constitutes a customary norm, although it did not precisely specify the cut-off age.[62] In declaring that the United States' reservation to article 6§5 of the *Covenant* was incompatible with the object and purpose of the instrument, it may have implicitly recognized that execution for crimes committed under the age of eighteen was contrary to a customary norm.[63]

The issue of whether the prohibition of juvenile executions is a customary norm has been litigated before the Inter-American Commission on Human Rights, which concluded that there was such a norm prohibiting execution of children but that a specific age such as eighteen could not be determined as a cut-off for exposure to the death penalty.[64] The Commission's reasoning on this point is unclear and it seemed more impressed by a different finding, namely that

---

[57] *United States* v. *Rosenberg*, 195 F.2d 583 (2nd Cir.), *cert. denied*, 344 US 838 (1952). Two boys under five were orphaned by the simultaneous execution of their parents.

[58] *American Convention*, art. 4§5.   [59] 'Implementation of the Safeguards', ESC Res. 1989/64.

[60] *Convention on the Rights of the Child*, GA Res. 44/25, art. 37§a.

[61] *Geneva Convention of August 12, 1949 Relative to the Protection of Civilians*, art. 68§4; *International Covenant on Civil and Political Rights*, art. 6§5; 'Safeguards', art. 3; *Convention on the Rights of the Child*, art. 37§a.

[62] *General Comment 24 (52)*, UN Doc. CCPR/C/21/Rev.1/Add.6, (1994) 15 *HRLJ* 464, para. 8.

[63] 'Initial Report of the United States', UN Doc. CCPR/C/79/Add.50 (1995), para. 14.

[64] *Roach and Pinkerton* v. *United States* (Case No. 9647), Resolution No. 3/87, reported in OAS Doc. OEA/Ser.L/V/II.71 doc. 9 rev.1, p. 147, *Inter-American Yearbook on Human Rights*, 1987, Dordrecht/Boston/London: Martinus Nijhoff, 1990, p. 328, 8 *HRLJ* 345.

the United States had protested the emergence of such a norm. But the United States did not protest article 68§4 of the fourth *Geneva Convention* or article 6 of the *International Covenant* during the drafting of those instruments, at which it was present. The International Court of Justice has held that objection to formation of a customary norm must be made 'consistently and uninterruptedly'.[65] An equivocal challenge to the provision during the drafting of the *American Convention* was later withdrawn by the representative of the United States. If a State does not protest the formation of a norm in a timely fashion, a subsequent objection is insufficient. A genuinely persistent objector may legitimately argue that the customary norm, even if it exists, is not opposable to it,[66] although this rule does not apply if the norm is one of *jus cogens*.[67]

The Economic and Social Council 'Safeguards' added the insane to the list of those who cannot be executed. Insane persons do not normally stand trial, but it is well documented that individuals who are fit to stand trial and are properly convicted sometimes become insane before sentence is carried out. The addition of this category to the 'Safeguards' was not challenged, and it is consistent with State practice, no State having indicated in any of the reports filed with the United Nations that it will execute the insane. It is therefore a norm of customary law that the insane may not be executed.[68] There is some evidence of a prohibitive norm in the distinct though related category of the mentally disabled.[69]

Progressive development of attitudes to capital punishment within national legal systems is perhaps best demonstrated by attempts to render the execution itself more humane, and to suppress such horrors as public execution. Little attention has been given to these matters by international human rights law. The Human Rights Committee has applied the prohibition on cruel, inhuman and degrading treatment or punishment in ruling the gas chamber, as used in California, to be contrary to the *International Covenant on Civil and Political Rights*.[70] In another case, it found execution by lethal injection, as practised in Pennsylvania, to be acceptable.[71] A pending case before the European Court of

---

[65] *Anglo Norwegian Fisheries Case (United Kingdom v. Norway)*, [1951] ICJ Reports 116, at p. 138.
[66] Ian Brownlie, *Principles of Public International Law*, Oxford: Clarendon Press, 1979, pp. 10–11; *Anglo Norwegian Fisheries Case (United Kingdom v. Norway)*, [1951] ICJ Reports 116, at p. 131; *North Sea Continental Shelf Cases (Federal Republic of Germany v. Denmark* and v. *Netherlands)*, [1969] ICJ Reports 3, at p. 46; *Nuclear Tests Case (Australia v. France)*, [1974] ICJ Reports 253, pp. 286–289.
[67] Nguyen Quoc Dinh, Patrick Daillier and Alain Pellet, *Droit international public*, 3rd edn, Paris: Librairie générale de droit et de jurisprudence, 1987, p. 302.
[68] William A. Schabas, 'International Norms on Execution of the Insane and the Mentally Retarded', (1993) 4 *Criminal Law Forum* 95.
[69] 'Implementation of the Safeguards'. Also: 'Extradjudicial, Summary or Arbitrary Executions: Report by the Special Rapporteur', UN Doc. E/CN.4/1994/7, para. 686; 'Extradjudicial, Summary or Arbitrary Executions: Report by the Special Rapporteur', UN Doc. E/CN.4/1998/68, para. 117.
[70] *Ng v. Canada* (No. 469/1991), UN Doc. A/49/40, Vol. II, p. 189, 15 *HRLJ* 149.
[71] *Cox v. Canada* (No. 539/1993), UN Doc. CCPR/C/52/D/539/1993, (1995) 15 *HRLJ* 410.

Human Rights challenges whether execution by hanging is compatible with the *European Convention on Human Rights*.[72] Nothing in any of the instruments speaks to the issue of public executions. The Human Rights Committee has stated that '[p]ublic executions are . . . incompatible with human dignity'.[73]

It has been suggested that at least some of the international law norms respecting the death penalty have acquired the status of *jus cogens*, that is, a peremptory rule of international law that trumps an inconsistent treaty.[74] Several publicists have claimed that the prohibition of execution of prisoners of war is a norm of *jus cogens*.[75] It has also been argued that the right to life is a norm of *jus cogens*.[76] Even a persistent objector to the formation of a customary norm of international law cannot avoid a rule of *jus cogens*.[77]

One of the most common arguments opposing the abolitionist movement is continuing public support for the death penalty. Public opinion polls have not inhibited many legislators in voting to abolish the death penalty. Nevertheless, a change in public attitudes in such countries as the United States could have a decisive effect on the future of capital punishment throughout the world. International law may assist considerably in the battle for public opinion, by demonstrating a growing world-wide consensus as to the fundamental principles of world order. The ratification of several human rights treaties, including the *International Covenant on Civil and Political Rights*, by the United States demonstrates that it feels it can no longer remain outside the international human rights systems. Since the 'Dulles doctrine' of 1953, the United States had hoped that international human rights would simply go away. When it did not, it found itself compelled to revise its position and ratify several major instruments. Because these instruments, and specifically article 6 of the *International Covenant on Civil and Political Rights*, conflict with its own domestic law, the United States has attempted to ratify with reservations. But these reservations have been met with objections and outright rejection by the principal human rights treaty body, the Human Rights Committee. In this way, international law is exercising considerable pressure on United States policy. Politicians and bureaucrats in Washington are intensely and increasingly aware of their isolation internationally on this question.

---

[72] *Öcalan* v. *Turkey* (No. 46221/99), Admissibility, 14 December 2000.

[73] 'Concluding Observations, Nigeria', UN Doc CCPR/C/79/Add.16, para. 16.

[74] *Roach and Pinkerton* v. *United States*, para. 56: 'The Commission finds that in the member States of the OAS there is recognized a norm of *jus cogens* which prohibits the State execution of children.' See also the speech of Commissioner Monroy Cabra to the Inter-American Court of Human Rights in *Restrictions to the Death Penalty (Arts. 4(2) and 4(4) American Convention on Human Rights)*, Advisory Opinion OC-3/83 of 8 September 1983, Series B, No. 3, p. 218.

[75] A. Verdross, 'Jus Dispositivum and Jus Cogens in International Law', (1966) 60 *AJIL* 55.

[76] W. Paul Gormley, 'The Right to Life and the Rule of Non-Derogability: Peremptory Norms of Jus Cogens', in Bertrand G. Ramcharan, ed., *The Right to Life in International Law*, Boston: Martinus Nijhoff, 1985, pp. 120–159, at p. 125; 'Human Rights in Chile', UN Doc. E/CN.4/1983/9.

[77] Nguyen, Daillier & Pellet, *Droit international public*, p. 302.

International law arguments may be less convincing in the Islamic world, where an entrenched and immutable religious doctrine insists upon the death penalty in certain cases. Perhaps there is a role for Islamic legal scholars who can demonstrate an alternative and more progressive view of religious law. The intransigence of Islamic States on the subject raises the whole issue of cultural relativism. If there is no universal agreement on the most fundamental of human rights, the right to life, how can anything more be expected in the rest of the catalogue of human rights? Yet other truly universal norms – the prohibition of slavery, of torture, and of the murder of prisoners of war – could not be defeated simply because an ancient sacred text might suggest otherwise. The death penalty is only one of many human rights issues in these intensely conservative States. Progressive change in other areas should also impact upon the status of capital punishment in these countries.

Relying on the second edition of this book, dissenting members of the Supreme Court of the Philippines argued that international legal developments showed the indisputable emergence of an international norm abolishing the death penalty. They insisted that the Philippines' Constitution should be interpreted in the spirit of this international norm, and that the death penalty be declared unconstitutional.[78] But more often, judges and government officials in death penalty States declare that international law does not prohibit the death penalty. The argument is flawed, in that nearly seventy States are now bound, as a question of international law, not to impose capital punishment and not to reintroduce it. This is the result of their adhesion to one of the three abolitionist protocols, or to the *American Convention on Human Rights*. Perhaps what they mean to say is that *customary* international law does not prohibit capital punishment. This is still true, but trends in State practice, in the development of international norms, and in fundamental human values suggest that it will not be true for very long.

This study was dedicated to several famous victims of the death penalty: Socrates, Spartacus and Jesus Christ, Joan of Arc, Danton and Robespierre, John Brown, Louis Riel, Roger Casemen, Sacco and Vanzetti, the Rosenbergs and Ken Saro-Wiwa. What is remarkable about such a list is how it permits history to be measured by executions: the apex of Greek philosophy, the decline of Rome and the birth of Christianity, the beginnings of the Renaissance, the French Revolution, the Cold War. It is a gruesome yardstick indeed of human 'progress', but, like every yardstick, it must have an end. The constant attention of international human rights law to the abolition of capital punishment has brought that end into sight.

[78] *Echegaray v. Secretary of Justice*, (1998) 297 SCR 754 (Supreme Court, Philipppines), p. 811.

Appendices

1 Universal Declaration of Human Rights

Article 3
Everyone has the right to life, liberty and security of the person.

2 International Covenant on Civil and Political Rights

Article 6

1. Every human being has the inherent right to life. This right shall be protected by law. No one shall be arbitrarily deprived of his life.

2. In countries which have not abolished the death penalty, sentence of death may be imposed only for the most serious crimes in accordance with the law in force at the time of the commission of the crime and not contrary to the provisions of the present Covenant and to the Convention on the Prevention and Punishment of the Crime of Genocide. This penalty can only be carried out pursuant to a final judgment rendered by a competent court.

3. When deprivation of life constitutes the crime of genocide, it is understood that nothing in this article shall authorize any State Party to the present Covenant to derogate in any way from any obligation assumed under the provisions of the Convention on the Prevention and Punishment of the Crime of Genocide.

4. Anyone sentenced to death shall have the right to seek pardon or commutation of the sentence. Amnesty, pardon or commutation of the sentence of death may be granted in all cases.

5. Sentence of death shall not be imposed for crimes committed by persons below eighteen years of age and shall not be carried out on pregnant women.

6. Nothing in this article shall be invoked to delay or to prevent the abolition of capital punishment by any State Party to the present Covenant.

Article 7

No one shall be subjected to torture or to cruel, inhuman or degrading treatment or punishment. In particular, no one shall be subjected without his free consent to medical or scientific experimentation.

Article 14

1. All persons shall be equal before the courts and tribunals. In the determination of any criminal charge against him, or of his rights and obligations in a suit at law, everyone shall be entitled to a fair and public hearing by a competent, independent and impartial tribunal established by law. The press and the public may be excluded from all or part of a trial for reasons of morals, public order (*ordre public*) or national security in a democratic society, or when the interest of the private lives of the parties so requires, or to the extent strictly necessary in the opinion of the court in special circumstances where publicity would prejudice the interests of justice; but any judgment rendered in a criminal case or in a suit at law shall be made public except where the interest of juvenile

persons otherwise requires or the proceedings concern matrimonial disputes or the guardianship of children.

2. Everyone charged with a criminal offence shall have the right to be presumed innocent until proved guilty according to law.

3. In the determination of any criminal charge against him, everyone shall be entitled to the following minimum guarantees, in full equality:

(a) To be informed promptly and in detail in a language which he understands of the nature and cause of the charge against him;

(b) To have adequate time and facilities for the preparation of his defence and to communicate with counsel of his own choosing;

(c) To be tried without undue delay;

(d) To be tried in his presence, and to defend himself in person or through legal assistance of his own choosing; to be informed, if he does not have legal assistance, of this right; and to have legal assistance assigned to him, in any case where the interests of justice so require, and without payment by him in any such case if he does not have sufficient means to pay for it;

(e) To examine, or have examined, the witnesses against him and to obtain the attendance and examination of witnesses on his behalf under the same conditions as witnesses against him;

(f) To have the free assistance of an interpreter if he cannot understand or speak the language used in court;

(g) Not to be compelled to testify against himself or to confess guilt.

4. In the case of juvenile persons, the procedure shall be such as will take account of their age and the desirability of promoting their rehabilitation.

5. Everyone convicted of a crime shall have the right to his conviction and sentence being reviewed by a higher tribunal according to law.

6. When a person has by a final decision been convicted of a criminal offence and when subsequently his conviction has been reversed or he has been pardoned on the ground that a new or newly discovered fact shows conclusively that there has been a miscarriage of justice, the person who has suffered punishment as a result of such conviction shall be compensated according to law, unless it is proved that the non-disclosure of the unknown fact in time is wholly or partly attributable to him.

7. No one shall be liable to be tried or punished again for an offence for which he has already been finally convicted or acquitted in accordance with the law and penal procedure of each country.

Article 15

1. No one shall be guilty of any criminal offence on account of any act or omission which did not constitute a criminal offence, under national or international law, at the time when it was committed. Nor shall a heavier penalty

be imposed than the one that was applicable at the time when the criminal offence was committed. If, subsequent to the commission of the offence, provision is made by law for the imposition of a lighter penalty, the offender shall benefit thereby.

2. Nothing in this article shall prejudice the trial and punishment of any person for any act or omission which, at the time when it was committed, was criminal according to the general principles of law recognized by the community of nations.

In force: 23 March 1976.

Ratifications as of 1 May 2001: 147.

Reservations concerning articles 6 and 7

Norway: 'Norway enters reservations with respect to: article 6, paragraph 4, . . .' Norway's reservation to article 6§4 was withdrawn on 12 December 1979.

Ireland: 'Article 6, paragraph 5. Pending the introduction of further legislation to give full effect to the provisions of paragraph 5 of article 6, should a case arise which is not covered by the provisions of existing law, the Government of Ireland will have regard to its obligations under the Covenant in the exercise of its power to advise commutation of the sentence of death.' Ireland's reservation to article 6§4 was withdrawn on 12 April 1994.

United States: 'The United States reserves the right, subject to its Constitutional constraints, to impose capital punishment on any person (other than a pregnant woman) duly convicted under existing or future laws permitting the imposition of capital punishment, including such punishment for crimes committed by persons below eighteen years of age.

The United States considers itself bound by Article 7 to the extent that "cruel, inhuman or degrading treatment or punishment" means the cruel and unusual treatment or punishment prohibited by the Fifth, Eighth or Fourteenth Amendments to the Constitution of the United States.'

Botswana: 'Reservations made upon signature and confirmed upon ratification: The Government of the Republic of Botswana considers itself bound by: a) Article 7 of the Covenant to the extent that "torture, cruel, inhuman or degrading treatment" means torture inhuman or degrading punishment or other treatment prohibited by Section 7 of the Constitution of the Republic of Botswana.'

Thailand: 'Interpretative declarations: The Government of Thailand declares that: With respect to article 6, paragraph 5 of the Covenant, the Thai Penal Code enjoins, or in some cases allows much latitude for, the Court to take into account the offender's youth as a mitigating factor in handing down sentences. Whereas Section 74 of the code does not allow any kind of punishment levied upon any person below fourteen years of age, Section 75 of the same Code provides that whenever any person over fourteen years but not yet over seventeen years of age commits any act provided by the law to be an offence, the Court shall take into account the sense of responsibility and all other things concerning him in order to come to decision as to whether it is appropriate to pass judgment inflicting punishment on him or not. If the court does not deem it appropriate to pass judgment inflicting punishment, it shall proceed according to Section 74 (*viz.* to adopt other correction measures short of punishment) or if the court deems it appropriate to pass judgment inflicting punishment, it shall reduce the scale of punishment provided for such offence by one half. Section 76 of the same Code also states that whenever any person over seventeen years but not yet over twenty years of age, commits any act provided by the law to be an offence, the Court *may*, if it thinks fit, reduce the scale of the punishment provided for such offence by one third or one half. The reduction of the said scale will prevent the Court from passing any sentence of death. As a result, though in theory, sentence of death may be imposed for crimes committed by persons below eighteen years, but not below seventeen years of age, the Court always exercises its discretion under Section 75 to reduce the said scale of punishment, and in practice the death penalty has not been imposed upon any persons below eighteen years of age. Consequently, Thailand considers that in real terms it has already complied with the principles enshrined herein.'

Objections to reservations concerning articles 6 and 7

Sweden (18 June 1993): 'With regard to interpretative declarations made by the United States of America: . . . In this context the Government recalls that under international treaty law, the name assigned to a statement whereby the legal effect of certain provisions of a treaty is excluded or modified, does not determine its status as a reservation to the treaty. Thus, the Government considers that some of the understandings made by the United States in substance constitute reservations to the Covenant.

A reservation by which a State modifies or excludes the application of the most fundamental provisions of the Covenant or limits its responsibilities under that treaty by invoking general principles of national law, may cast doubts upon the commitment of the reserving State to the object and purpose of the Covenant. The reservations made by the United States of America include both reservations to essential and non-derogable provisions, and general references to national legislation. Reservations of this nature contribute to undermining the basis of international treaty law. All States Parties share a common interest in the respect for the object and purpose of the treaty to which they have chosen to become parties.

Sweden therefore objects to the reservations made by the United States to:
- article 2; cf. Understanding (1)
- article 4; cf. Understanding (1)
- article 6; cf. Reservation (2)
- article 7; cf. Reservation (3)
- article 15; cf. Reservation (4)
- article 26; cf. Understanding (1).

This objection does not constitute an obstacle to the entry into force of the Covenant between Sweden and the United States of America.

Finland (28 September 1993): 'The Government of Finland has taken note of the reservations, understandings and declarations made by the United States of America upon ratification of the Covenant. It is recalled that under international treaty law, the name assigned to a statement whereby the legal effect of certain provisions of a treaty is excluded or modified, does not determine its status as a reservation to the treaty. Understanding (1) pertaining to articles 2, 4 and 26 of the Covenant is therefore considered to constitute in substance a reservation to the Covenant, directed at some of its most essential provisions, namely those concerning the prohibition of discrimination. In the view of the Government of Finland, reservation of this kind is contrary to the object and purpose of the Covenant, as specified in article 19(c) of the Vienna Convention on the Law of Treaties.

As regards reservation (2) concerning article 6 of the Covenant, it is recalled that according to article 4(2), no restrictions of articles 6 and 7 of the Covenant are allowed for. In the view of the Government of Finland, the right to life is of fundamental importance in the Covenant and the said reservation therefore is incompatible with the object and purpose of the Covenant.

As regards reservation (3), it is in the view of the Government of Finland subject to the general principle of treaty interpretation according to which a party may not invoke the provisions of its internal law a justification for failure to perform a treaty.

For the above reasons the Government of Finland objects to reservations made by the United States to article 2, 4 and 26 (cf. Understanding (1)), to article 6 (cf. Reservation (2)) and to article 7 (cf. Reservation (3)). However, the Government of Finland does not consider that this objection constitutes an obstacle to the entry into force of the Covenant between Finland and the United States of America.

Netherlands (28 September 1993): 'With regard to the reservations to articles 6 and 7 made by the United States of America: The Government of the Kingdom of the Netherlands objects to the reservations with respect to capital punishment for crimes committed by persons below eighteen years of age, since it follows from the text and history of the Covenant that the said reservation is incompatible with the text, the object and purpose of article 6 of the Covenant, which according to article 4 lays down the minimum standard for the protection of the right to life. The Government of the Kingdom of the Netherlands objects to the reservation with respect to article 7 of the Covenant, since it follows from the text and the interpretation of this article that the said reservation is incompatible with the object and purpose of the Covenant. In the opinion of the Government of the Kingdom of the Netherlands this reservation has the same effect as a general derogation from this article, while according to article 4 of the Covenant, no derogations, not even in times of public emergency, are permitted. It is the understanding of the Government of the Kingdom of the Netherlands that the understandings and declarations of the United States do not exclude or modify the legal effect of provisions of the Covenant in their application to the United States, and do not in any way limit the competence of the Human Rights Committee to interpret these provisions in their application to the United States. Subject to the proviso of article 21, paragraph 3 of the Vienna Convention of the Law of Treaties, these objections do not constitute an obstacle to the entry into force of the Covenant between the Kingdom of the Netherlands and the United States.'

Germany (29 September 1993): 'The Government of the Federal Republic of Germany objects to the United States' reservation referring to article 6, paragraph 5 of the Covenant, which prohibits capital punishment for crimes committed by persons below eighteen years of age. The reservation referring to this provision is incompatible with the text as well as the object and purpose of article 6, which, as made clear by paragraph 2 of article 4, lays down the minimum standard for the protection of the right to life. The Government of the Federal Republic of Germany interprets the United States 'reservation' with regard to article 7 of the Covenant as a reference to article 2 of the Covenant, thus not in any way affecting the obligations of the United States of America as a state party to the Covenant.'

Denmark (1 October 1993): 'With regard to the reservations made by the United States of America: Having examined the contents of the reservation made by the United States of America, Denmark would like to recall article 4, para. 2 of the Covenant according to which no derogation from a number of fundamental articles, *inter alia* 6 and 7, may be made by a State Party even in time of public emergency which threatens the life of the nation. In the opinion of Denmark, reservation (2) of the United States with respect to capital punishment for crimes committed by persons below eighteen years of age as well as reservation (3) with respect to article 7 constitute general derogations from articles 6 and 7, while according to article 4, para. 2 of the Covenant such derogations are not permitted. Therefore, and taking into account that articles 6 and 7 are protecting two of the most basic rights contained in the Covenant, the Government of Denmark regards the said reservations as incompatible with the object and purpose of the Covenant, and consequent [*sic*] Denmark objects to the reservations. These objections do not constitute an obstacle to the entry into force of the Covenant between Denmark and the United States.'

France (4 October 1993): At the time of the ratification of [the said Covenant], the United States of America expressed a reservation relating to article 6, paragraph 5, of the Covenant, which prohibits the imposition of the death penalty for crimes committed by persons below 18 years of age. France considers that this United States reservation is not valid, inasmuch as it is incompatible with the object and purpose of the Convention [*sic*]. Such objection does not constitute an obstacle to the entry into force of the Covenant between France and the United States.'

Norway (4 October 1993): 'With regard to reservations to articles 6 and 7 made by the United States of America: 1. In the view of the Government of Norway, the reservation (2) concerning capital punishment for crimes committed by persons below eighteen years of age is according to the text and history of the Covenant, incompatible with the object and purpose of article 6 of the Covenant. According to article 4(2), no derogations from article 6 may be made, not even in times of public emergency. For these reasons the Government of Norway objects to this reservation. 2. In the view of the Government of Norway, the reservation (3) concerning article 7 of the Covenant is according to the text and interpretation of this article incompatible with the object and purpose of the Covenant. According to article 4(2), article 7 is a non-derogable provision, even in times of public emergency. For these reasons, the Government of Norway objects to this reservation. The Government of Norway does not consider this objection to constitute an obstacle to the entry into force of the Covenant between Norway and the United States of America.'

Belgium (5 October 1993): 'The Government of Belgium wishes to raise an objection to the reservation made by the United States of America regarding article 6, paragraph 5, of the Covenant, which prohibits the imposition of the sentence of death for crimes committed by persons below 18 years of age. The Government of Belgium considers the reservation to be incompatible with the provisions and intent of article 6 of the Covenant which, as is made clear by article 4, paragraph 2, of the Covenant, establishes minimum measures to protect the right to life. The expression of this objection does not constitute an obstacle to the entry into force of the Covenant between Belgium and the United States of America.'

Italy (5 October 1993): 'The Government of Italy . . . objects to the reservation to art. 6 paragraph 5 which the United States of America included in its instrument of ratification. In the opinion of Italy reservations to the provisions contained in art. 6 are not permitted, as specified in art. 4, para. 2, of the Covenant. Therefore this reservation is null and void since it is incompatible with the object and purpose of art. 6 of the Covenant. Furthermore in the interpretation of the Government of Italy, the reservation to art. 7 of the Covenant does not affect obligations assumed by States that are parties to the Covenant on the basis of article 2 of the same Covenant. These objections do not constitute an obstacle to the entry into force of the Covenant between Italy and the United States.'

Portugal (5 October 1993): 'With regard to the reservations made by the United States of America: The Government of Portugal considers that the reservation made by the United States of America referring to article 6, paragraph 5 of the Covenant which prohibits capital punishment for crimes committed by persons below eighteen years of age is incompatible with article 6 which, as made clear by paragraph 2 of article 4, lays down the minimum standard for the protection of the right to life. The Government of Portugal also considers that the reservation with regard to article 7 in which a State limits its responsibilities under the Covenant by invoking general principles of National Law may create doubt on the commitments of the Reserving State to the object and purpose of the Covenant and, moreover, contribute to undermining the basis of International Law. The Government of Portugal therefore objects to the reservations made by the United States of America. These objections shall not constitute an obstacle to the entry into force of the Covenant between Portugal and the United States of America.'

Spain (5 October 1993): 'With regard to the reservations made by the United States of America: . . . After careful consideration of the reservations made by the United States of America, Spain wishes to point out that pursuant to article 4, paragraph 2, of the Covenant, a State Party may not derogate from several basic articles, among them articles 6 and 7, including in time of public emergency which threatens the life of the nation. The Government of Spain takes the view that reservation (2) of the United States having regard to capital punishment for crimes committed by individuals under 18 years of age, in addition to reservation

(3) having regard to article 7, constitute general derogations from articles 6 and 7, whereas, according to article 4, paragraph 2, of the Covenant, such derogations are not to be permitted. Therefore, and bearing in mind that articles 6 and 7 protect two of the most fundamental rights embodied in the Covenant, the Government of Spain considers that these reservations are incompatible with the object and purpose of the Covenant and, consequently, objects to them. This position does not constitute an obstacle to the entry into force of the Covenant between the Kingdom of Spain and the United States of America.'

Netherlands (26 December 1997): 'With regard to the interpretative declaration concerning article 6 paragraph 5 made by Thailand: The Government of the Kingdom of the Netherlands considers this declaration as a reservation. The Government of the Kingdom of the Netherlands objects to the aforesaid declaration, since it follows from the text and history of the Covenant that the declaration is incompatible with the text, the object and purpose of article 6 of the Covenant, which according to article 4 lays down the minimum standard for the protection of the right to life. This objection shall not preclude the entry into force of the Covenant between the Kingdom of the Netherlands and the Kingdom of Thailand.'

3 Optional Protocol to the International Covenant on Civil and Political Rights

The *Optional Protocol* authorises individual communications or petitions to the Human Rights Committee for breaches of the *International Covenant on Civil and Political Rights*. More than 100 such communications have been presented by persons threatened with the death penalty. The text of the instrument can be found at (1976) 999 U.N.T.S. 302.

In force: 23 March 1976

Ratifications as of 1 May 2001: 98

Reservations concerning capital punishment

Guyana: 'Reservation.... Guyana re-accedes to the Optional Protocol to the International Covenant on Civil and Political Rights with a Reservation to article 6 thereof with the result that the Human Rights Committee shall not be competent to receive and consider communications from any persons who is under sentence of death for the offences of murder and treason in respect of any matter relating to his prosecution, detention, trial, conviction, sentence or execution of the death sentence and any matter connected therewith. Accepting the principle that States cannot generally use the Optional Protocol as a vehicle to enter reservations to the International Covenant on Civil and Political Rights itself, the Government of Guyana stresses that its Reservation to the Optional Protocol in no way detracts from its obligations and engagements under the Covenant, including its undertaking to respect and ensure to all individuals within the territory of Guyana and subject to its jurisdiction the rights recognised in the Covenant (in so far as not already reserved against) as set out in article 2 thereof, as well as its undertaking to report to the Human Rights Committee under the monitoring mechanism established by article 40 thereof.'

Trinidad and Tobago: 'Reservation: ... Trinidad and Tobago re-accedes to the Optional Protocol to the International Covenant on Civil and Political Rights with a Reservation to article 1 thereof to the effect that the Human Rights Committee shall not be competent to receive and consider communications relating to any prisoner who is under sentence of death in respect of any matter relating to his prosecution, his detention, his trial, his conviction, his sentence or the carrying out of the death sentence on him and any matter connected therewith. Accepting the principle that States cannot use the Optional Protocol as a vehicle to enter reservations to the International Covenant on Civil and

Political Rights itself, the Government of Trinidad and Tobago stresses that its Reservation to the Optional Protocol in no way detracts from its obligations and engagements under the Covenant, including its undertaking to respect and ensure to all individuals within the territory of Trinidad and Tobago and subject to its jurisdiction the rights recognised in the Covenant (in so far as not already reserved against) as set out in article 2 thereof, as well as its undertaking to report to the Human Rights Committee under the monitoring mechanism established by article 40 thereof.'

Objections to reservations concerning capital punishment

Denmark (6 August 1999): 'With regard to the reservation made by Trinidad and Tobago upon accession: The Government of the Kingdom of Denmark finds that the reservation made by the Government of Trinidad and Tobago at the time of its re-accession to the Optional Protocol to the International Covenant on Civil and Political Rights raises doubts as to the commitment of Trinidad and Tobago to the object and purpose of the Optional Protocol. The reservation seeks to limit the obligations of the reserving State towards individuals under sentence of death. The purpose of the Optional Protocol to the International Covenant on Civil and Political Rights is to strengthen the position of the individual under the Covenant. Denying the benefits of the Optional Protocol to a group of individuals under the most severe sentence is not in conformity with the object and purpose of the Optional Protocol. The procedure followed by Trinidad and Tobago, of denouncing the Optional Protocol followed by a re-accession with a reservation circumvents the rules of the law of treaties that prohibit the formulation of reservations after ratification. The Government of the Kingdom of Denmark therefore objects to the aforementioned reservation made by the Government of Trinidad and Tobago to the Optional Protocol to the International Covenant on Civil and Political Rights. The objection shall not preclude the entry into force of the Optional Protocol between the Government of the Kingdom of Denmark and the Government of Trinidad and Tobago.'

Norway (6 August 1999): 'With regard to the reservation made by Trinidad and Tobago upon accession: The Government of Norway considers that the object and purpose of the Optional Protocol is to contribute to securing the compliance with the provisions of the International Covenant on Civil and Political Rights by strengthening the position of the individual under the Covenant. Due to the universality of all Human Rights, the right to petition, which is enshrined in article 1 of the Optional Protocol, must apply to all individuals that are subject to the State Party's jurisdiction. Further, denying the benefits of the Optional Protocol in relation to the Covenant to a vulnerable group of individuals will contribute to further weakening of that group's position which the Government of Norway considers to be contrary to the object and purpose of the Optional Protocol. Further, the Government of Norway is concerned with regard to the procedure followed by Trinidad and Tobago. The Government of Norway considers the denunciation of the Optional Protocol followed by a re-accession upon which a reservation is entered, as a circumvention of established rules of the law of treaties that prohibit the submission of reservations after ratification. For these reasons, the Government of Norway objects to the reservation made by Trinidad and Tobago. This objection shall not preclude the entry into force of the Optional Protocol between the Kingdom of Norway and Trinidad and Tobago.'

Netherlands (6 August 1999): '2. The Government of the Kingdom of the Netherlands is of the view that this reservation, which seeks to limit the obligations of the reserving State towards individuals under sentence of death, raises doubts as to the commitment of Trinidad and Tobago to the object and purpose of the Optional Protocol. 3. The Government of the Kingdom of the Netherlands considers that the purpose of the Optional Protocol to the International Covenant on Civil and Political Rights is to strengthen the position of the individual under the Covenant. Denying the benefits of the Optional Protocol in relation to the Covenant to a group of individuals under the most severe sentence is fundamentally in conflict with the object and purpose of the Optional Protocol. 4. Also the Government of the Kingdom of the Netherlands considers the procedure followed by Trinidad and Tobago, of denouncing the Optional Protocol followed by a re-accession with reservations, as contrary to the rules of the law of treaties that prohibit the formulation of reservations after ratification. The procedure followed by Trinidad and Tobago circumvents such well-established rules. 5. The Government of the Kingdom of the Netherlands therefore objects to the aforementioned reservation made by the Government of Trinidad and Tobago to the Protocol of the International Covenant on Civil and Political Rights. 6. This objection shall not preclude the entry into force of the Optional Protocol between the Kingdom of the Netherlands and Trinidad and Tobago.'

Germany (13 August 1999): 'The purpose of the Protocol is to strengthen the position of the individual under the Covenant. While the Government of the Federal Republic of Germany welcomes the decision of the Government of Trinidad and Tobago to reaccede to the Optional Protocol it holds the view that the benefits of the Optional Protocol should not be denied to individuals who are under the most severe sentence, the sentence of death. Furthermore, the Government of the Federal Republic of Germany is of the view that denunciation of an international human rights instrument followed by immediate reaccession under a far reaching reservation may set a bad precedent. The Government of the Federal Republic of Germany objects to the reservation. This objection shall not preclude the entry into force of the Optional Protocol between the Federal Republic of Germany and Trinidad and Tobago.'

Sweden (17 August 1999): 'The Government of Sweden notes that the Government of Trinidad and Tobago accepts the principle that States cannot use the Optional Protocol as a vehicle to enter reservations to the International Covenant on Civil and Political Rights itself, and it stresses that its reservation in no way detracts from its obligations and engagements under the Covenant. Nevertheless the Government of Sweden has serious doubts as to the propriety of the procedure followed by the Government of Trinidad and Tobago in that denunciation of the Optional Protocol succeeded by re-accession with a reservation undermines the basis of international treaty law as well as the international protection of human rights. The Government of Sweden therefore wishes to declare its grave concern over this method of proceeding. Furthermore the reservation seeks to limit the international obligations of Trinidad and Tobago towards individuals under sentence to death. The Government of Sweden is of the view that the right to life is fundamental and that the death penalty cannot be accepted. It is therefore of utmost importance that states that persist in this practice refrain from further weakening the position of that group of individuals.'

Ireland (23 August 1999): '2. The Government of Ireland is of the view that this reservation raises doubts as to the commitment of Trinidad and Tobago to the object and purpose of the Optional Protocol, which is to strengthen the position of the individual in respect of the rights protected by the International Covenant on Civil and Political Rights. The reservation on the contrary seeks to limit the international obligations of Trinidad and Tobago towards individuals under sentence of death. 3. The Government of Ireland also has doubts as to the propriety of the procedure followed by the Government of Trinidad and Tobago in that denunciation of the Optional Protocol, succeeded by re-accession with a reservation, compromises the ratification process and undermines the international protection of human rights. 4. The Government of Ireland therefore objects to the aforementioned reservation made by the Government of Trinidad and Tobago to the Optional Protocol to the International Covenant on Civil and Political Rights. 5. The objection shall not preclude the entry into force of the Optional Protocol between Ireland and Trinidad and Tobago.'

Spain (25 August 1999): 'The Government of the Kingdom of Spain believes that this reservation casts doubt on the commitment of Trinidad and Tobago to the object and purpose of the Optional Protocol, which is clearly to strengthen the individual's position with respect to the rights enshrined in the International

Covenant on Civil and Political Rights. On the contrary, the aim of the reservation is to limit the international obligations of Trinidad and Tobago towards individuals under sentence of death. The Government of the Kingdom of Spain also has reservations about whether the Government of Trinidad and Tobago has followed the proper procedure; the denunciation of the Optional Protocol, followed by re-accession to it with a reservation, prejudices the ratification process and undermines the international protection of human rights. Accordingly, the Government of Spain objects to this reservation made by the Government of Trinidad and Tobago to the Optional Protocol to the International Covenant on Civil and Political Rights. This objection does not preclude the entry into force of the Optional Protocol as between the Kingdom of Spain and Trinidad and Tobago.'

Germany (26 August 1999): 'With regard to the reservation made by Guyana upon accession: The purpose of the Protocol is to strengthen the position of the individual under the Covenant. While the Government of the Federal Republic of Germany welcomes the decision of the Government of Guyana to reaccede to the Optional Protocol it holds the view that the benefits of the Optional Protocol should not be denied to individuals who are under the most severe sentence, the sentence of death. Furthermore, the Government of the Federal Republic of Germany is of the view that denunciation of an international human rights instrument followed by immediate reaccession under a far reaching reservation may set a bad precedent. The Government of the Federal Republic of Germany objects to the reservation. This objection shall not preclude the entry into force of the Optional Protocol between the Federal Republic of Germany and Guyana.'

France (9 September 1999): 'While article 12, paragraph 1, of the Protocol provides that any State Party may denounce the Protocol "at any time" and that the denunciation shall take effect "three months after the date of receipt of the notification by the Secretary-General", the denunciation of the Protocol may in no case be used by a State Party for the sole purpose of formulating reservations to that instrument after having signed, ratified or acceded to it. Such a practice would undermine international commitments by constituting a form of misuse of procedure, would be manifestly contrary to the principle of good faith prevailing in international law and would contravene the rule of pacta sunt servanda. The means used (denunciation and accession on the same day to the same instrument, but with a reservation) cannot but prompt a negative reaction, irrespective of the doubts which may arise as to the compatibility of this reservation with the goal and purpose of the treaty. Consequently, the Government of the French Republic expresses its disapproval of the reservation formulated by Trinidad and Tobago.'

Italy (17 September 1999): 'The Government of the Italian Republic finds that the reservation made by the Government of Trinidad and Tobago at the time of its re-accession to the Optional Protocol to the International Covenant on Civil and Political Rights raises doubts as to the commitment of Trinidad and Tobago to the object and purpose of the Optional Protocol which is to strengthen the position of the individual in respect of the rights under the Covenant. The reservation on the contrary seeks to limit the international obligations of Trinidad and Tobago towards individuals under sentence of death. The Government of the Italian Republic also has doubts as to the propriety of the procedure followed by the Government of Trinidad and Tobago in that denunciation of the Optional Protocol, succeeded by a re-accession with a reservation compromises the ratification process and undermines the international protection of human rights. The Government of the Italian Republic therefore objects to the aforementioned reservation made by the Government of Trinidad and Tobago to the Optional Protocol to the International Covenant on Civil and Political Rights. This objection shall not preclude the entry into force of the Optional Protocol between Italy and Trinidad and Tobago.'

Netherlands (22 October 1999): 'With regard to the reservation made by Guyana upon accession: ... 2. The Government of the Kingdom of the Netherlands is of the view that this reservation, which seeks to limit the obligations of the reserving State towards individuals under sentence of death, raises doubts as to the object and purpose of the Optional Protocol. 3. The Government of the Netherlands considers that the purpose of the Optional Protocol is to strengthen the position of the individual under the Covenant. Denying the benefits of the Optional Protocol in relation to the Covenant to a group of individuals under the most severe sentence is fundamentally in conflict with the object and purpose of the Optional Protocol. 4. Also the Government of the Kingdom of the Netherlands considers the procedure followed by Guyana, of denouncing the Optional Protocol followed by a re-accession with reservations, as contrary to the rules of the law of treaties that prohibit the formulation of reservations after ratification. The procedure followed by Guyana circumvents such well-established rules. 5. The Government of the Kingdom of the Netherlands therefore objects to the aforementioned reservation made by the Government of Guyana to the Optional Protocol to the International Covenant on Civil and Political Rights. 6. This objection shall not preclude the entry into force of the Optional Protocol between the Kingdom of the Netherlands and Guyana.'

Spain (1 December 1999): 'With regard to the reservation made by Guyana upon accession: The Government of the Kingdom of Spain considers that this reservation raises doubts about the commitment of the Republic of Guyana to the purpose and goal of the Optional Protocol, which is to strengthen the position of the individual with regard to the rights protected by the International Covenant on Civil and Political Rights. The reservation, on the other hand, seeks to limit the international obligations of Guyana towards individuals who are under sentence of death. The Government of Spain also has doubts about the correctness of the procedure followed by the Government of Guyana, inasmuch as denunciation of the Optional Protocol followed by re-accession to it with a reservation prejudices the ratification process and undermines the international protection of human rights. Consequently, the Government of Spain objects to the aforesaid reservation made by the Government of the Republic of Guyana to the Optional Protocol to the International Covenant on Civil and Political Rights. This objection does not prevent the entry into force of the Optional Protocol between the Kingdom of Spain and the Republic of Guyana.'

France (28 January 2000): 'With regard to the reservation made by Guyana upon accession: . . . While article 12, paragraph 1, of the Protocol provides that any State Party may denounce the Protocol "at any time", with the denunciation taking effect "three months after the date of receipt of the notification by the Secretary-General", denunciation of the Protocol may not in any case be used by a State Party for the purpose of formulating reservations to the Covenant well after the party has signed, ratified or acceded thereto. Such a practice would call into question international commitments by a sort of abuse of process; it would be a clear violation of the principle of good faith that prevails in international law and would be incompatible with the rule of pacta sunt servanda. The means used (denunciation and accession on the same day to the same instrument but with a reservation) cannot but elicit a negative reaction. Consequently, the Government of the French Republic expresses its objection to the reservation made by Guyana.'

Finland (17 March 2000): 'The Government of Finland is of the view that denying the rights recognised in the Optional Protocol from individuals under the most severe sentence is in contradiction with the object and purpose of the said Protocol. Furthermore, the Government of Finland wishes to express its serious concern as to the procedure followed by Guyana, of denouncing the Optional Protocol (to which it did not have any reservations) followed by an immediate re-accession with a reservation. The Government of Finland is of the view that such a procedure is highly undesirable as circumventing the rule of the law of treaties that prohibits the formulation of reservations after accession. The Government of Finland therefore objects to the reservation made by the Government of Guyana to the said Protocol. This objection does not preclude the entry into force of the Optional Protocol between Guyana and Finland. The

Optional Protocol will thus become operative between the two states without Guyana benefitting from the reservation.'

Sweden (27 April 2000): 'The Government of Sweden has examined the reservation to article 1 made by the Government of Guyana at the time of its re-accession to the Optional Protocol. The Government of Sweden notes that the Government of Guyana accepts the principle that States cannot use the Optional Protocol as a vehicle to enter reservations to the International Covenant on Civil and Political Rights itself, and that it stresses that its reservation in no way detracts from its obligations and engagements under the Covenant. Nevertheless, the Government of Sweden has serious doubts as to the propriety of the procedure followed by the Government of Guyana. While article 12, paragraph 1 of the Protocol provides that any State Party may denounce the Protocol 'at any time', the denunciation may in no case be used by a State Party for the sole purpose of formulating reservations to that instrument after having re-acceeded to it. Such a practice would constitute a misuse of the procedure and would be manifestly contrary to the principle of good faith. It further contravenes the rule of pacta sunt servanda. As such, it undermines the basis of international treaty law and the protection of human rights. The Government of Sweden therefore wishes to declare its grave concern over this method of proceeding. Furthermore, the reservation seeks to limit the international obligations of Guyana towards individuals under sentence of death. The Government of Sweden is of the view that the right to life is fundamental and that the death penalty cannot be accepted. It is therefore of utmost importance that states that persist in this practice refrain from further weakening the position of that group of individuals.'

Poland (8 August 2000): 'The Government of the Republic of Poland believes that this reservation seeks to deny the benefits of the Optional Protocol towards a group of individuals under the sentence of death. This reservation is contrary to the object and purpose of the Protocol which is to strengthen the position of individuals in respect of the human rights protected by the Covenant. Furthermore the Government of the Republic of Poland considers the procedure followed by the Government of the Republic of Guyana in the denunciation of the Optional Protocol, and its subsequent re-accession with reservation as not consistent with the law of treaties and clearly undermining the Protocol. The Government of the Republic of Poland therefore objects to the above mentioned reservation made by the Government of the Republic of Guyana. This objection does not preclude the entry into force of the Optional Protocol between the Republic of Poland and the Republic of Guyana.'

4 Second Optional Protocol to the International Covenant on Civil and Political Rights Aiming at the Abolition of the Death Penalty

The States Parties to the present Protocol,

Believing that abolition of the death penalty contributes to enhancement of human dignity and progressive development of human rights,

Recalling article 3 of the Universal Declaration of Human Rights adopted on 10 December 1948 and article 6 of the International Convenant on Civil and Political Rights adopted on 16 December 1966,

Noting that article 6 of the International Covenant on Civil and Political Rights refers to abolition of the death penalty in terms that strongly suggest that abolition is desirable,

Convinced that all measures of abolition of the death penalty should be considered as progress in the enjoyment of the right to life,

Desirous to undertake hereby an international commitment to abolish the death penalty,

Have agreed as follows:

Article 1

1. No one within the jurisdiction of a State Party to the present Optional Protocol shall be executed.

2. Each State Party shall take all necessary measures to abolish the death penalty within its jurisdiction.

Article 2

1. No reservation is admissible to the present Protocol, except for a reservation made at the time of ratification or accession that provides for the application of the death penalty in time of war pursuant to a conviction for a most serious crime of a military nature committed during wartime.

2. The State Party making such a reservation shall at the time of ratification or accession communicate to the Secretary-General of the United Nations the relevant provisions of its national legislation applicable during wartime.

3. The State Party having made such a reservation shall notify the Secretary-General of the United Nations of any beginning or ending of a state of war applicable to its territory.

Article 3

The States Parties to the present Protocol shall include in the reports they submit to the Human Rights Committee, in accordance with article 40 of the Covenant, information on the measures that they have adopted to give effect to the present Protocol.

Article 4

With respect to the States Parties to the Covenant that have made a declaration under article 41, the competence of the Human Rights Committee to receive and consider communications when a State Party claims that another State Party is not fulfilling its obligations shall extend to the provisions of the present Protocol, unless the State Party concerned has made a statement to the contrary at the moment of ratification or accession.

Article 5

With respect to the States Parties to the (First) Optional Protocol to the International Covenant on Civil and Political Rights, adopted on 16 December 1966, the competence of the Human Rights Committee to receive and consider communications from individuals subject to its jurisdiction shall extend to the provision of the present Protocol, unless the State Party concerned has made a statement to the contrary at the moment of ratification or accession.

Article 6

1. The provisions of the present Protocol shall apply as additional provisions to the Covenant.

2. Without prejudice to the possibility of a reservation under article 2 of the present Protocol, the right guaranteed in article 1, paragraph 1, of the present Protocol shall not be subject to any derogation under article 4 of the Covenant.

Article 7

1. The present Protocol is open for signature by any State that has signed the Covenant.

2. The present Protocol is subject to ratification by any State that has ratified the Covenant or acceded to it. Instruments of ratification shall be deposited with the Secretary-General of the United Nations.

3. The present Protocol shall be open to accession by any State that has ratified the Covenant or acceded to it.

4. Accession shall be effected by the deposit of an instrument of accession with the Secretary-General of the United Nations.

5. The Secretary-General of the United Nations shall inform all States that have signed the present Protocol or acceded to it of the deposit of each instrument of ratification or accession.

Article 8

1. The present Protocol shall enter into force three months after the date of the deposit with the Secretary-General of the United Nations of the tenth instrument of ratification or accession.

2. For each State ratifying the present Protocol or acceding to it after the deposit of the tenth instrument of ratification or accession, the present Protocol shall enter into force three months after the date of the deposit of its own instrument of ratification or accession.

Article 9

The provisions of the present Protocol shall extend to all parts of federal States without any limitations or exceptions.

Article 10

The Secretary-General of the United Nations shall inform all States referred to in article 48, paragraph 1, of the Covenant of the following particulars:

(a) Reservations, communications and notifications under article 2 of the present Protocol;

(b) Statements made under its article 4 or 5;

(c) Signatures, ratifications and accessions under its article 7;

(d) The date of entry into force of the present Protocol under its article 8.

Article 11

1. The present Protocol, of which the Arabic, Chinese, English, French, Russian and Spanish texts are equally authentic, shall be deposited in the archives of the United Nations.

2. The Secretary-General of the United Nations shall transmit certified copies of the present Protocol to all States referred to in article 48 of the Covenant.

In force: 11 July 1991

Ratifications as of 1 May 2001: 44

Reservations and objections

Spain: 'Pursuant to article 2, Spain reserves the right to apply the death penalty in the exceptional and extremely serious cases provided for in Fundamental Act No. 13/1985 of 9 December 1985 regulating the Military Criminal Code, in wartime as defined in article 25 of that Act.' The reservation was withdrawn on 13 January 1998.

Malta: 'Pursuant to article 2, Malta reserves the right to apply the death penalty to persons subject to the Malta Armed Force Act (Chapter 220 of the revised edition of the Laws of Malta), which Act provides that the death penalty may be awarded in exceptional and serious cases defined therein, but only in times of war.' The reservation was withdrawn on 15 June 2000.

Azerbaijan: 'The Republic of Azerbaijan, adopting the [said Protocol], in exceptional cases, adopting the special law, allows the application of death penalty for the grave crimes, committed during the war or in condition of the threat of war. It is provided for the application of the death penalty in time of war pursuant to a conviction of a person for a most serious crime of a military nature committed during wartime.' On 28 September 2000, the Government of Azerbaijan communicated to the Secretary-General a modification to its reservation made upon accession: 'It is provided for the application of the death penalty in time of war pursuant to a conviction of a person for a most serious crime of a military nature committed during wartime.' According to the Secretary-General, '[I]n keeping with the depositary practice followed in similar cases, the Secretary-General proposes to receive the modification in question for deposit in the absence of any objection on the part of any of the Contracting States, either to the deposit itself or to the procedure envisaged, within a period of twelve months from the date of the present depositary notification. In the absence of any such objection, the above modification will be accepted for deposit upon the expiration of the above-stipulated twelve-month period, that is on 5 October 2001.'

Cyprus: 'The Republic of Cyprus in accordance with article 2.1 of the... Protocol reserves the right to apply the Death Penalty in time of war pursuant to a conviction of a most serious crime of a military nature committed during wartime.'

Greece: 'Subject to article 2 for the application of the death penalty in time of war pursuant to a conviction for a most serious crime of a military nature committed during wartime.'

Objections to reservations concerning capital punishment

Finland (17 March 2000): 'The Government of Finland notes that, according to Article 2 of the Second Optional Protocol, a reservation other than the kind referred to in the same Article is not acceptable. The reservation made by the Government of Azerbaijan is partly in contradiction with Article 2 as it does not limit the application of death penalty to the most serious crimes of a military nature committed during the time of war. The Government of Finland therefore objects to the reservation made by the Government of Azerbaijan to the said Protocol. This objection does not preclude the entry into force of the Second Optional Protocol between Azerbaijan and Finland. The Optional Protocol will thus become operative between the two states without Azerbaijan benefiting from the reservation.'

Germany (3 March 2000): 'The reservation allows the application of the death penalty for grave crimes committed during war "or in condition of the threat of war". Thus the reservation is partly in contradiction of article 2 of the Protocol since it does not limit the application of the death penalty to the most serious crimes of a military nature committed during the time of war. The Government of the Federal Republic of Germany therefore objects to the reservation by the Government of Azerbaijan. This objection does not preclude the entry into force of the Protocol between Azerbaijan and Germany.'

Sweden (27 April 2000): 'The Government of Sweden recalls that reservations other than the kind referred to in Article 2 of the Protocol are not permitted. The reservation made by the Government of Azerbaijan goes beyond the limit of Article 2 of the Protocol, as it does not limit the application of the death penalty to the most serious crimes of a military nature committed during the time of war. The Government of Sweden therefore objects to the aforesaid reservation made by the Government of Azerbaijan to the Second Optional Protocol to the International Covenant on Civil and Political Rights. This shall not preclude the entry into force of the Second Optional Protocol to the International Covenant on Civil and Political Rights between the Republic of Azerbaijan and the Kingdom of Sweden, without Azerbaijan benefiting from the reservation.'

Netherlands (17 July 2000): 'The Government of the Kingdom of the Netherlands notes that, according to Article 2 of the Second Optional Protocol, a reservation other than the kind referred to in the same Article is not acceptable. The reservation made by the Government of Azerbaijan is in contradiction with Article 2 as it does not limit the application of death penalty to the most serious crimes of a military nature committed during the time of war. The Government of the Kingdom of the Netherlands therefore objects to the aforesaid reservation made by the Government of Azerbaijan. This objection shall not preclude the entry into force of the Convention between the Kingdom of the Netherlands and Azerbaijan.'

5 General Comment on Article 6 of the International Covenant on Civil and Political Rights (General Comment 6(16))

1. The right to life enunciated in Article 6 of the Covenant has been dealt with in all State reports. It is the supreme right from which no derogation is permitted even in time of public emergency which threatens the life of the nation (Article 4) . . . It is a right which should not be interpreted narrowly.

. . .

6. While it follows from Article 6(2) to (6) that States parties are not obliged to abolish the death penalty totally, they are obliged to limit its use and, in particular, to abolish it for other than the 'most serious crimes'. Accordingly, they ought to consider reviewing their criminal laws in this light and, in any event, are obliged to restrict the application of the death penalty to the 'most serious crimes'. The article also refers generally to abolition in terms which strongly suggest (paras. 2(2) and (6)) that abolition is desirable. The Committee concludes that all measures of abolition should be considered as progress in the enjoyment of the right to life within the meaning of Article 40, and should as such be reported to the Committee. The Committee notes that a number of States have already abolished the death penalty or suspended its application. Nevertheless, States' reports show that progress made towards abolishing or limiting the application of the death penalty is quite inadequate.

7. The Committee is of the opinion that the expression 'most serious crimes' must be read restrictively to mean that the death penalty should be a quite exceptional measure. It also follows from the express terms of Article 6 that it can only be imposed in accordance with the law in force at the time of the commission of the crime and not contrary to the Covenant. The procedural guarantees therein prescribed must be observed, including the right to a fair hearing by an independent tribunal, the presumption of innocence, the minimum guarantees for the defence, and the right to review by a higher tribunal. These rights are applicable in addition to the particular right to seek pardon or commutation of the sentence.

6 Convention Against Torture and Other Forms of Cruel, Inhuman or Degrading Treatment or Punishment

Article 1

1. For the purposes of this Convention, the term 'torture' means any act by which severe pain or suffering, whether physical or mental, is intentionally inflicted on a person for such purposes as obtaining from him or a third person information or a confession, punishing him for an act he or a third person has committed or is suspected of having committed, or intimidating or coercing him or a third person, or for any reason based on discrimination of any kind, when such pain or suffering is inflicted by or at the instigation of or with the consent or acquiescence of a public official or other person acting in an official capacity. It does not include pain or suffering arising only from, inherent in or incidental to lawful sanctions.

Article 16

2. Each State Party shall undertake to prevent in any territory under its jurisdiction other acts of cruel, inhuman or degrading treatment or punishment which do not amount to torture as defined in article 1, when such acts are committed by or at the instigation of or with the consent or acquiescence of a public official or other person acting in an official capacity. In particular, the obligations contained in articles 10, 11, 12 and 13 shall apply with the substitution for references to torture of references to other forms of cruel, inhuman or degrading treatment or punishment.

In force: 26 June 1987

Ratifications as of 1 May 2001: 124

Reservations concerning the death penalty

United States of America: 'I. The Senate's advice and consent is subject to the following reservations:

(1) That the United States considers itself bound by the obligation under article 16 to prevent 'cruel, inhuman or degrading treatment or punishment', only insofar as the term 'cruel, inhuman or degrading treatment or punishment' means the cruel, unusual and inhumane treatment or punishment prohibited by the Fifth, Eighth and/or Fourteenth Amendments to the Constitution of the United States . . .

II. The Senate's advice and consent is subject to the following understandings, which shall apply to the obligations of the United States under the Convention:

' ...

(4) That the United States understands that international law does not prohibit the death penalty, and does not consider this convention to restrict or prohibit the United States from applying the death penalty consistent with the Fifth, Eighth and/or Fourteenth Amendments to the Constitution of the United States, including any constitutional period of confinement prior to the imposition of the death penalty.'

Objections to reservations concerning the death penalty

Finland (27 February 1996): 'A reservation which consists of a general reference to national law without specifying its contents does not clearly define to the other Parties of the Convention the extent to which the reserving State commits itself to the Convention and therefore may cast doubts about the commitment of the reserving State to fulfil its obligations under the Convention. Such a reservation is also, in the view of the Government of Finland, subject to the general principle of treaty interpretation according to which a party may not invoke the provisions of its internal law as justification for failure to perform a treaty. The Government of Finland therefore objects to the reservation made by the United States to article 16 of the Convention [(cf. Reservation I.(1)]. In this connection the Government of Finland would also like to refer to its objection to the reservation entered by the United States with regard to article 7 of the International Covenant on Civil and Political Rights.'

Netherlands (26 February 1996): 'The Government of the Netherlands considers the reservation made by the United States of America regarding the article 16 of [the Convention] to be incompatible with the object and purpose of the Convention, to which the obligation laid down in article 16 is essential. Moreover, it is not clear how the provisions of the Constitution of the United States of America relate to the obligations under the Convention. The Government of the Kingdom of the Netherlands therefore objects to the said reservation. This objection shall not preclude the entry into force of the Convention between the Kingdom of the Netherlands and the United States of America. The Government of the Kingdom of the Netherlands considers the following understandings to have no impact on the obligations of the United States of America under the Convention: II. 1a This understanding appears to restrict the scope of the definition of torture under article 1 of the Convention. 1d This understanding diminishes the continuous responsibility of public officials for behaviour of their subordinates. The Government of the Kingdom of the Netherlands reserves its position with regard to the understandings II. 1b, 1c and 2 as the contents thereof are insufficiently clear.'

Sweden (27 February 1996): The Government of Sweden would like to refer to its objections to the reservations entered by the United States of America with regard to article 7 of the International Covenant on Civil and Political Rights. The same reasons for objection apply to the now entered reservation with regard to article 16 reservation I (1) of [the Convention]. The Government of Sweden therefore objects to that reservation. It is the view of the Government of Sweden that the understandings expressed by the United States of America do not relieve the United States of America as a party to the Convention from the responsibility to fulfil the obligations undertaken therein.'

7 Convention on the Rights of the Child

Article 37

a. No child shall be subjected to torture or other cruel, inhuman or degrading treatment or punishment. Neither capital punishment nor life imprisonment shall be imposed for offences committed by persons below 18 years of age.

In force: 2 September 1990

Ratifications as of 1 May 2001: 191

Reservations concerning article 37§1

Myanmar: 'The Union of Myanmar accepts in principle the provisions of article 37 as they are in consonance with its laws, rules, regulations, procedures and practice as well as with its traditional, cultural and religious values. However, having regard to the exigencies of the situation obtaining in the country at present, the Union of Myanmar states as follows: 1. Nothing contained in Article 37 shall prevent, or be construed as preventing, the Government of the Union of Myanmar from assuming or exercising, in conformity with the laws for the time being in force in the country and the procedures established thereunder, such powers as are required by the exigencies of the situation for the preservation and strengthening of the rule of law, the maintenance of public order (*ordre public*) and, in particular, the protection of the supreme national interest, namely, the non-disintegration of the Union, the non-disintegration of national solidarity and the perpetuation of national sovereignty, which constitute the paramount national causes of the Union of Myanmar. 2. Such powers shall include the powers of arrest, detention, imprisonment, exclusion, interrogation, enquiry and investigation.' The reservation was withdrawn on 19 October 1993.

Singapore: 'Declarations: . . . (2) The Republic of Singapore considers that articles 19 and 37 of the Convention do not prohibit – (a) the application of any prevailing measures prescribed by law for maintaining law and order in the Republic of Singapore; (b) measures and restrictions which are prescribed by law and which are necessary in the interests of national security, public safety, public order, the protection of public health or the protection of the rights and freedoms of others . . .'

Malaysia: 'Reservation: The Government of Malaysia accepts the provisions of the Convention on the Rights of the Child but expresses reservations with respect to [. . . paragraph 1(a) of article] 37, . . . of the Convention and declares that the said provisions shall be applicable only if they are in conformity with the Constitution, national laws and national policies of the Government of Malaysia.'

Objections to reservations concerning article 37(a)

Germany (25 June 1992): 'The Federal Republic of Germany considers that the reservations made by the Union of Myanmar concerning articles 15 and 37 of the Convention on the Rights of the Child are incompatible with the object and purpose of the Convention (article 51, paragraph 2); accordingly it objects to them. This objection shall not preclude the entry into force of the Convention as between the Union of Myanmar and the Federal Republic of Germany.'

Portugal (15 July 1992): 'The Government of Portugal considers that reservations by which a State limits its responsibilities under the Convention by invoking general principles of National law may create doubts on the commitments of the reserving State to the object and purpose of the Convention and, moreover, contribute to undermining the basis of International law. It is in the common interest of States that Treaties to which they have chosen to become parties also are respected, as to object and purpose, by all parties. The Government therefore objects to the reservations. This objection shall not constitute an obstacle to the entry into force of the Convention between Portugal and Myanmar.'

Ireland (5 September 1995): With regard to the reservation made by Myanmar upon ratification: 'The Government of Ireland consider that such reservations, which seek to limit the responsibilities of the reserving State under the Convention, by invoking general principles of national law, may create doubts as to the commitment of those States to the object and purpose of the Convention. This objection shall not constitute an obstacle to the entry into force of the Convention between Ireland and [Myanmar].'

Portugal (4 December 1995): Same objection with respect to Malaysia as for Myanmar *mutatis mutandis*.

Germany (20 March 1996): 'The Government of the Federal Republic of Germany considers that such a reservation, which seeks to limit the responsibilities of [Malaysia] under the Convention by invoking general principles of national law, may raise doubts as to the commitment of [Malaysia] to the object and purpose of the Convention and, moreover, contributes to undermining the basis of international treaty law. It is the common interest of states that treaties to which they have chosen to become parties should be respected, as to object and purpose, by all parties. The Government of the Federal Republic of Germany therefore objects to the said reservation. This objection does not constitute an obstacle to the entry into force of the Convention between the Federal Republic of Germany and [Malaysia].'

Finland (14 June 1996): 'The reservation made by Malaysia covers several central provisions of the [said Convention]. The broad nature of the said reservation leaves open to what extent Malaysia commits itself to the Convention and to the fulfilment of its obligations under the Convention. In the view of the Government of Finland reservations of such comprehensive nature may contribute to undermining the basis of international human rights treaties. The Government of Finland also recalls that the said reservation is subject to the general principle of the observance of the treaties according to which a party may not invoke its internal law, much less its national policies, as justification for its failure to perform its treaty obligations. It is in the common interest of the States that contracting parties to international treaties are prepared to undertake the necessary legislative changes in order to fulfil the object and purpose of the treaty. Moreover, the internal legislation as well as the national policies are also subject to changes which might further expand the unknown effects of the reservation. In its present formulation the reservation is clearly incompatible with the object and purpose of the Convention and therefore inadmissible under article 51, paragraph 2, of the [said Convention]. Therefore the Government of Finland objects to such reservation. The Government of Finland further notes that the reservation made by the Government of Malaysia is devoid of legal effect. The Government of Finland recommends the Government of Malaysia to reconsider its reservation to the [said Convention].'

Austria (18 June 1996): 'Under article 19 of the Vienna Convention on the Law of Treaties which is reflected in article 51 of the [Convention] a reservation, in order to be admissible under international law, has to be compatible with the object and purpose of the treaty concerned. A reservation is incompatible with the object and purpose of a treaty if it intends to derogate from provisions the implementation of which is essential to fulfilling its object and purpose. The Government of Austria has examined the reservation made by Malaysia to the [Convention]. Given the general character of these reservations a final assessment as to its admissibility under international law cannot be made without further clarification. Until the scope of the legal effects of this reservation is sufficiently specified by Malaysia, the Republic of Austria considers these reservations as not affecting any provision the implementation of which is essential to fulfilling the object and purpose of the [Convention]. Austria, however, objects to the admissibility of the reservations in question if the application of this reservation negatively affects the compliance of Malaysia . . . with its obligations under the [Convention] essential for the fulfilment of its object and purpose. Austria could not consider the reservation made by Malaysia . . . as admissible under the regime of article 51 of the [Convention] and article 19 of the Vienna Convention on the Law of Treaties unless Malaysia . . . by providing additional information or through subsequent practice ensure[s] that the reservations are compatible with the provisions essential for the implementation of the object and purpose of the [Convention].'

Netherlands (25 June 1996): 'With regard to the reservation made by Malaysia upon accession: The Government of the Kingdom of the Netherlands considers that such reservations, which seek to limit the responsibilities of the reserving State under the Convention by invoking general principles of national law, may raise doubts as to the commitment of these States to the object and purpose of the Convention and moreover, contribute to undermining the basis of international treaty law. It is in the common interest of States that treaties to which they have chosen to become parties should be respected, as to object and purpose, by all parties. the Government of the Kingdom of the Netherlands therefore objects to these reservations. This objection does not constitute an obstacle to the entry into force of the Convention between the Kingdom of the Netherlands and Malaysia.'

Sweden (26 June 1996): 'A reservation by which a State party limits its responsibilities under the Convention by invoking general principles of national law may cast doubts on the commitments of the reserving state to the object and purpose of the Convention and, moreover, contribute to undermining the basis of international treaty law. It is in the common interest of states that treaties to which they have chosen to become parties also are respected, as to object and purpose, by all parties. The Government of Sweden therefore objects to the reservations. This objection does not constitute an obstacle to the entry into force of the Convention between Sweden and Malaysia.'

Norway (27 June 1996): 'The Government of Norway considers that the reservation made by the Government of Malaysia, due to its very broad scope and undefined character, is incompatible with the object and purpose of the Convention, and thus not permitted under article 51, paragraph 2, of the Convention. Moreover, the Government of Norway considers that the monitoring system established under the Convention is not optional and that, accordingly, reservations with respect to articles 44 and 45 of the Convention are not permissible. For these reasons, the Government of Norway objects to the reservation made by the Government of Malaysia. The Government of Norway does not consider this objection to preclude the entry into force of the Convention between the Kingdom of Norway and Malaysia.'

Belgium (1 July 1996): 'The Belgian Government believes that this reservation is incompatible with the object and purpose of the Convention and that, consequently, in accordance with article 51, paragraph 2, of the Convention, it is not permitted . . . Accordingly, Belgium wishes to be bound by the Convention in its entirety as regards [the State of Malaysia] which [has] expressed reservations prohibited by the [said] Convention. Moreover, as the twelve month period specified in article 20.5 of the Vienna Convention on the Law of Treaties is not applicable to reservations which are null and void, Belgium's objection to such reservations is not subject to any particular time-limit.'

Denmark (2 July 1996): 'The reservation is covering multiple provisions, including central provisions of the Convention. Furthermore, it is a general principle of international law that internal law may not be invoked as justification for failure to perform treaty obligations. Consequently, the Government of Denmark considers the said reservation as being incompatible with the object and purpose of the Convention and accordingly inadmissible and without effect under international law. The Convention remains in force in its entirety between Malaysia and Denmark. It is the opinion of the Government of Denmark that no time limit applies to objections against reservations, which are inadmissible under international law. The Government of Denmark recommends the Government of Malaysia to reconsider its reservation to the said Convention.'

Germany (4 September 1996): Same objection with respect to Singapore as for Malaysia *mutatis mutandis*.

Belgium (26 September 1996): 'With regard to the reservations made by Singapore upon ratification: The Government considers that paragraph 2 of the declarations, concerning articles 19 and 37 of the Convention and paragraph 3 of the reservations, concerning the constitutional limits upon the acceptance of the obligations contained in the Convention, are contrary to the purposes of the Convention and are consequently without effect under international law.'

Italy (4 October 1996): 'The Government of the Italian Republic considers that such a reservation, which seeks to limit the responsibilities of Singapore under the Convention by invoking general principles of national law, may raise doubts as to the commitment of Qatar to the object and purpose of the Convention and, moreover, contributes to undermining the basis of international treaty law.'

It is [in the] common interest of States that treaties to which they have chosen to become Parties should be respected, as to the objects and the purpose, by all Parties. The Government of the Italian Republic therefore objects to this reservation. This objection does not constitute an obstacle to the entry into force of the Convention between the Government of the Italian Republic and the State of Singapore.'

Netherlands (6 November 1996): Same objection with respect to Singapore as for Malaysia *mutatis mutandis.*

Finland (26 November 1996): 'The reservations made in paragraphs 2 and 3 by the Republic of Singapore, consisting of a general reference to national law without stating unequivocally the provisions the legal effect of which may be excluded or modified, do not clearly define to the other Parties of the Convention the extent to which the reserving State commits itself to the Convention and therefore create doubts about the commitment of the reserving State to fulfil its obligations under the said Convention. Reservations of such unspecified nature may contribute to undermining the basis of international human rights treaties. The Government of Finland also recalls that these reservations of the Republic of Singapore are subject to the general principle of observance of treaties according to which a party may not invoke the provisions of its internal law as justification for failure to perform its treaty obligations. It is in the common interest of States that Parties to international treaties are prepared to take the necessary legislative changes in order to fulfil the object and purpose of the treaty. The Government of Finland considers that in their present formulation these reservations made by the Republic of Singapore are incompatible with the object and purpose of the said Convention and therefore, inadmissible under article 51, paragraph 2, of the said Convention. In view of the above, the Government of Finland objects to these reservations and notes that they are devoid of legal effect.'

Norway (29 November 1996): 'The Government of Norway considers that reservation (3) made by the Republic of Singapore, due to its unlimited scope and undefined character, is contrary to the object and purpose of the Convention, and thus impermissible under article 51, paragraph 2, of the Convention. Furthermore, the Government of Norway considers that declaration (2) made by the Republic of Singapore, in so far as it purports to exclude or to modify the legal effect of articles 19 and 37 of the Convention, also constitutes a reservation impermissible under the Convention, due to the fundamental nature of the rights concerned and the unspecified reference to domestic law. For these reasons, the Government of Norway objects to the said reservations made by the Government of Singapore. The Government of Norway does not consider this objection to preclude the entry into force of the Convention between the Kingdom of Norway and the Republic of Singapore.'

Portugal (3 December 1996): Same objection with respect to Singapore as for Myanmar *mutatis mutandis.*

Sweden (13 August 1997): Same objection for Singapore as for Malaysia *mutatis mutandis.*

Ireland (13 March 1997): With regard to the reservation made by Malaysia upon accession: 'Ireland considers that this reservation is incompatible with the object and purpose of the Convention and is therefore prohibited by article 51(2) of the Convention. The Government of Ireland also considers that it contributes to undermining the basis of international treaty law. The Government of Ireland therefore objects to the said reservation.'

8 Safeguards Guaranteeing Protection of the Rights of Those Facing the Death Penalty

1. In countries which have not abolished the death penalty, capital punishment may be imposed only for the most serious crimes, it being understood that their scope should not go beyond intentional crimes, with lethal or other extremely grave consequences.

2. Capital punishment may be imposed only for a crime for which the death penalty is prescribed by law at the time of its commission, it being understood that if, subsequent to the commission of the crime, provision is made by law for the imposition of a lighter penalty, the offender shall benefit thereby.

3. Persons below 18 years of age at the time of the commission of the crime shall not be sentenced to death, nor shall the death penalty be carried out on pregnant women, or on new mothers or on persons who have become insane.

4. Capital punishment may be imposed only when the guilt of the person charged is based upon clear and convincing evidence leaving no room for an alternative explanation of the facts.

5. Capital punishment may only be carried out pursuant to a final judgment rendered by a competent court after legal process which gives all possible safeguards to ensure a fair trial, at least equal to those contained in Article 14 of the International Covenant on Civil and Political Rights, including the right of anyone suspected of or charged with a crime for which capital punishment may be imposed to adequate legal assistance at all stages of the proceedings.

6. Anyone sentenced to death shall have the right to appeal to a court of higher jurisdiction, and steps should be taken to ensure that such appeals shall become mandatory.

7. Anyone sentenced to death shall have the right to seek pardon, or commutation of sentence; pardon or commutation of sentence may be granted in all cases of capital punishment.

8. Capital punishment shall not be carried out pending any appeal or other recourse procedure or other proceeding relating to pardon or commutation of the sentence.

9. Where capital punishment occurs, it shall be carried out so as to inflict the minimum possible suffering.

9 Geneva Convention Relative to the Treatment of Prisoners of War

Article 3

In the case of armed conflict not of an international character occurring in the territory of one of the High Contracting Parties, each Party to the conflict shall be bound to apply, as a minimum, the following provisions:

(I) Persons taking no active part in the hostilities, including members of armed forces who have laid down their arms and those placed hors de combat by sickness, wounds, detention, or any other cause, shall in all circumstances be treated humanely, without any adverse distinction founded on race, colour, religion or faith, sex, birth or wealth, or any other similar criteria.

To this end the following acts are and shall remain prohibited at any time and in any place whatsoever with respect to the above-mentioned persons:

. . .

(d) the passing of sentences and the carrying out of executions without previous judgment pronounced by a regularly constituted court affording all the judicial guarantees which are recognized as indispensable by civilized peoples.

Article 87§2

When fixing the penalty, the courts or authorities of the Detaining Power shall take into consideration, to the widest extent possible, the fact that the accused, not being a national of the Detaining Power, is not bound to it by any duty of allegiance, and that he is in its power as the result of circumstances independent of his own will. The said courts or authorities shall be at liberty to reduce the penalty provided for the violation of which the prisoner of war is accused, and shall therefore not be bound to apply the minimum penalty prescribed.

Article 100

Prisoners of war and the Protecting Powers shall be informed, as soon as possible, of the offences which are punishable by the death sentence under the laws of the Detaining Power.

Other offences shall not therefore be made punishable by the death penalty without the concurrence of the Power upon which the prisoners of war depend.

The death sentence cannot be pronounced on a prisoner of war unless the attention of the court has, in accordance with Article 87, second paragraph, been particularly called to the fact that since the accused is not a national of the Detaining Power, he is not bound to it by any duty of allegiance, and that he is in its power as the result of circumstances independent of his will.

Article 101

If the death penalty is pronounced on a prisoner of war, the sentence shall not be executed before the expiration of a period of at least six months from the date when the Protecting Power receives, at an indicated address, the detailed communication provided for in Article 107.

Article 107

Any judgment and sentence pronounced upon a prisoner of war shall be immediately reported to the Protecting Power in the form of a summary communication, which shall also indicate whether he has the right of appeal with a view to the quashing of the sentence or the reopening of the trial. This communication shall likewise be sent to the prisoners' representative concerned. It shall also be sent to the accused prisoner of war in a language he understands, if the sentence was not pronounced in his presence. The Detaining Power shall also immediately communicate to the Protecting Power the decision of the prisoner of war to use or to waive his right of appeal.

Furthermore, if a prisoner of war is finally convicted or if a sentence pronounced on a prisoner of war in the first instance is a death sentence, the Detaining Power shall as soon as possible address to the Protecting Power a detailed communication containing:

(1) the precise wording of the finding and sentence;
(2) a summarized report of any preliminary investigation and of the trial, emphasizing in particular the elements of the prosecution and the defence;
(3) notification, where applicable, of the establishment where the sentence will be served.

The communications provided for in the foregoing sub-paragraphs shall be sent to the Protecting Power at the address previously made known to the Detaining Power.

In force: 21 October 1950

Ratifications as of 1 May 2001: 189

Reservations to articles concerning the death penalty: none

10 Geneva Convention Relative to the Protection of Civilians

Article 3

In the case of armed conflict not of an international character occurring in the territory of one of the High Contracting Parties, each Party to the conflict shall be bound to apply, as a minimum, the following provisions:

(I) Persons taking no active part in the hostilities, including members of armed forces who have laid down their arms and those placed hors de combat by sickness, wounds, detention, or any other cause, shall in all circumstances be treated humanely, without any adverse distinction founded on race, colour, religion or faith, sex, birth or wealth, or any other similar criteria.

To this end the following acts are and shall remain prohibited at any time and in any place whatsoever with respect to the above-mentioned persons:

. . .

(d) the passing of sentences and the carrying out of executions without previous judgment pronounced by a regularly constituted court affording all the judicial guarantees which are recognized as indispensable by civilized peoples.

Article 68

Protected persons who commit an offence which is solely intended to harm the Occupying Power, but which does not constitute an attempt on the life or limb of members of the occupying forces or administration, nor a grave collective danger, nor seriously damage the property of the occupying forces or administration or other installations used by them, shall be liable to internment or simple imprisonment, provided the duration of such internment or imprisonment is proportionate to the offence committed. Furthermore, internment or imprisonment shall, for such offences, be the only measure adopted for depriving protected persons of liberty. The courts provided for under Article 66 of the present Convention may at their discretion convert a sentence of imprisonment to one of internment for the same period.

The penal provisions promulgated by the Occupying Power in accordance with Articles 64 and 65 may impose the death penalty on a protected person only in cases where the person is guilty of espionage, of serious acts of sabotage against the military installations of the Occupying Power or of intentional offences which have caused the death of one or more persons, provided that such offences were punishable by death under the law of the occupied territory in force before the occupation began.

The death penalty may not be pronounced on a protected person unless the attention of the court has been particularly called to the fact that since the accused is not a national of the Occupying Power, he is not bound to it by any duty of allegiance.

In any case, the death penalty may not be pronounced on a protected person who was under eighteen years of age at the time of the offence.

Article 74§2
Any judgment involving a sentence of death, or imprisonment for two years or more, shall be communicated, with the relevant grounds, as rapidly as possible to the Protecting Power. The notification shall contain a reference to the notification made under Article 71 . . . Any period allowed for appeal in the case of sentences involving the death penalty, or imprisonment of two years or more, shall not run until notification of judgment has been received by the Protecting Power.

Article 75
In no case shall persons condemned to death be deprived of the right of petition for pardon or reprieve.

No death sentence shall be carried out before the expiration of a period of at least six months from the date of receipt by the Protecting Power of the notification of the final judgment confirming such death sentence, or of an order denying pardon or reprieve.

The six months period of suspension of the death sentence herein prescribed may be reduced in individual cases in circumstances of grave emergency involving an organized threat to the security of the Occupying power or its forces, provided always that the Protecting Power is notified of such reduction and is given reasonable time and opportunity to make representations to the competent occupying authorities in respect of such death sentences.

In force: 21 October 1950

Ratifications as of 1 May 2001: 189

Reservations concerning article 68

Argentina: 'Argentina, Gentlemen, has always taken a leading place among many other nations on the questions which have formed the subject of our discussions. I shall, therefore, sign the four Conventions in the name of my Government and subject to ratification, with the reservation that Article 3, common to all four Conventions, shall be the only Article, to the exclusion of all others, which shall be applicable in the case of armed conflicts not of an international character. I shall likewise sign the Convention relative to the Protection of Civilian Persons with a reservation in respect of Article 68.' Argentina neither maintained nor withdrew its reservation at the time of ratification.

Australia: 'In ratifying the Geneva Convention relative to the Protection of Civilian Persons in Time of War, the Government of the Commonwealth of Australia RESERVES the right to impose the death penalty in accordance with the provisions of paragraph 2 of Article 68 of the said Convention without regard to whether the offences referred to therein are punishable by death under the law of the occupied territory at the time the occupation begins and DECLARES that it interprets the term 'military installations' in paragraph 2 of Article 68 of the said Convention as meaning installations having an essential military interest for an Occupying Power.' Australia's reservation was withdrawn on 21 February 1974.

Canada: 'Canada reserves the right to impose the death penalty in accordance with the provisions of Article 68, paragraph 2, without regard to whether the offences referred to therein are punishable by death under the law of the occupied territory at the time the occupation begins.' Canada's reservation was withdrawn when it ratified the *Convention*.

Netherlands: 'The Kingdom of the Netherlands reserves the right to impose the death penalty in accordance with the provisions of Article 68, paragraph 2, without regard to whether the offences referred to therein are punishable by death under the law of the occupied territory at the time the occupation begins.' The Netherlands confirmed its reservation when it ratified the *Convention*. The reservation was withdrawn on 7 February 1983.

New Zealand: 'New Zealand reserves the right to impose the death penalty in accordance with the provisions of Article 68, paragraph 2, without regard to whether the offences referred to therein are punishable by death under the law of the occupied territory at the time the occupation begins.' New Zealand's reservation was maintained at the time of ratification, and withdrawn on 2 March 1976.

Pakistan: Pakistan ratified the *Convention* on 12 December 1951, making the same reservation as the Netherlands.

Republic of Korea: 'The Republic of Korea reserves the right to impose the death penalty in accordance with the provisions of Article 68, paragraph 2, without regard to whether the offences referred to therein are punishable by death under the law of the occupied territory at the time the occupation begins.'

Romania: 'The Government of the Socialist Republic of Romania cannot accept the reservations made by the South Korean authorities with regard to Article 118 of the Convention relative to the treatment of prisoners of war and to Article 68 of the Convention relative to the protection of civilian persons in time of war. It regards those reservations as incompatible with the purposes of the aforementioned Conventions.'

Suriname: 'The Republic of Suriname declares that it considers itself to be bound by the following reservation made by the Kingdom of the Netherlands on behalf of Suriname: "The Kingdom of the Netherlands reserves the right to impose the death penalty in accordance with the provisions of Article 68, paragraph 2, without regard to whether the offences referred to therein are punishable by death under the law of the occupied territory at the time the occupation begins."'

United Kingdom: 'The United Kingdom of Great Britain and Northern Ireland reserves the right to impose the death penalty in accordance with the provisions of Article 68, paragraph 2, without regard to whether the offences referred to therein are punishable by death under the law of the occupied territory at the time the occupation begins.' The United Kingdom's reservation was maintained at the time of ratification, and withdrawn on 2 February 1972.

United States of America: 'The United States reserves the right to impose the death penalty in accordance with the provisions of Article 68, paragraph 2, without regard to whether the offences referred to therein are punishable by death under the law of the occupied territory at the time the occupation begins.' The United States of America maintained its reservation when it ratified the *Convention.*

11 Protocol Additional I to the 1949 Geneva Conventions and Relating to the Protection of Victims of International Armed Conflicts

Article 76§3

To the maximum extent feasible, the Parties to the conflict shall endeavour to avoid the pronouncement of the death penalty on pregnant women or mothers having dependent infants, for an offence related to the armed conflict. The death penalty for such offences shall not be executed on such women.

Article 77§5

The death penalty for an offence related to the armed conflict shall not be executed on persons who had not attained the age of eighteen years at the time the offence was committed.

In force: 12 December 1978

Ratifications as of 1 May 2001: 158

Reservations concerning articles 76§3 or 77§5: none

12 Protocol Additional II to the 1949 Geneva Conventions and Relating to the Protection of Victims of Non-International Armed Conflicts

Article 6

4. The death penalty shall not be pronounced on persons who were under the age of eighteen years at the time of the offence and shall not be carried out on pregnant women or mothers of young children.

In force: 7 December 1978

Ratifications as of 1 May 2001: 158

Reservations concerning article 6§4: none

13 Rome Statute of the International Criminal Court

Article 77 Applicable penalties

1. Subject to article 110, the Court may impose one of the following penalties on a person convicted of a crime under article 5 of this Statute:

(a) Imprisonment for a specified number of years, which may not exceed a maximum of 30 years; or

(b) A term of life imprisonment when justified by the extreme gravity of the crime and the individual circumstances of the convicted person.

2. In addition to imprisonment, the Court may order:

(a) A fine under the criteria provided for in the Rules of Procedure and Evidence;

(b) A forfeiture of proceeds, property and assets derived directly or indirectly from that crime, without prejudice to the rights of bona fide third parties.

Article 80 Non-prejudice to national application of penalties and national laws

Nothing in this Part of the Statute affects the application by States of penalties prescribed by their national law, nor the law of States which do not provide for penalties prescribed in this Part.

In force: 1 July 2002

Ratifications as of 1 May 2001: 32

14 Convention for the Protection of Human Rights and Fundamental Freedoms (European Convention on Human Rights)

Article 2

1. Everyone's right to life shall be protected by law. No one shall be deprived of his life intentionally save in the execution of a sentence of a court following his conviction of a crime for which this penalty is provided by law.

2. Deprivation of life shall not be regarded as inflicted in contravention of this Article when it results from the use of force which is no more than absolutely necessary:

(a) in defence of any person from unlawful violence;
(b) in order to effect a lawful arrest or to prevent the escape of a person lawfully detained;
(c) in action lawfully taken for the purpose of quelling a riot or insurrection.

Article 3

No one shall be subjected to torture or to inhuman or degrading treatment or punishment.

In force: 3 September 1953

Ratifications as of 1 May 2001: 41

Reservations concerning the death penalty: none

15 Protocol No. 6 to the Convention for the Protection of Human Rights and Fundamental Freedoms Concerning the Abolition of the Death Penalty

The member States of the Council of Europe, signatory to this Protocol to the Convention for the Protection of Human Rights and Fundamental Freedoms, signed at Rome on 4 November 1950 (hereinafter referred to as 'the Convention');

Considering that the evolution that has occurred in several member States of the Council of Europe expresses a general tendency in favour of abolition of the death penalty;

Have agreed as follows:

Article 1

The death penalty shall be abolished. No one shall be condemned to such penalty or executed.

Article 2

A State may make provision in its law for the death penalty in respect of acts committed in time of war or of imminent threat of war; such penalty shall be applied only in the instances laid down in the law and in accordance with its provisions. The State shall communicate to the Secretary General of the Council of Europe the relevant provisions of that law.

Article 3

No derogation from the provisions of this Protocol shall be made under Article 15 of the Convention.

Article 4

No reservation may be made under Article 64 of the Convention in respect of the provisions of this Protocol.

Article 5

1. Any State may at the time of signature or when depositing its instrument of ratification, acceptance or approval, specify the territory or territories to which this Protocol shall apply.

2. Any State may at any later date, by a declaration addressed to the Secretary General of the Council of Europe, extend the application of this Protocol to any other territory specified in the declaration. In respect of such territory the

Protocol shall enter into force on the first day of the month following the date of receipt of such declaration by the Secretary General.

3. Any declaration made under the two preceding paragraphs may, in respect of any territory specified in such declaration, be withdrawn by a notification addressed to the Secretary General. The withdrawal shall become effective on the first day of the month following the date of receipt of such notification by the Secretary General.

Article 6

As between the States Parties the provisions of Articles 1 to 5 of this Protocol shall be regarded as additional articles to the Convention and all the provisions of the Convention shall apply accordingly.

Article 7

This Protocol shall be open for signature by the member States of the Council of Europe, signatories to the Convention. It shall be subject to ratification, acceptance or approval. A member State of the Council of Europe may not ratify, accept or approve this Protocol unless it has, simultaneously or previously, ratified the Convention. Instruments of ratification, acceptance or approval shall be deposited with the Secretary General of the Council of Europe.

Article 8

1. This Protocol shall enter into force on the first day of the month following the date on which five member States of the Council of Europe have expressed their consent to be bound by the Protocol in accordance with the provisions of Article 7.

2. In respect of any member State which subsequently expresses its consent to be bound by it, the Protocol shall enter into force on the first day of the month following the date of the deposit of the instrument of ratification, acceptance or approval.

Article 9

The Secretary General of the Council of Europe shall notify the member States of the Council of:

(a) any signature;
(b) the deposit of any instrument of ratification, acceptance or approval;
(c) the date of entry into force of this Protocol in accordance with Articles 5 and 8;
(d) any other act, notification or communication relating to this Protocol.

In force: 1 March 1985

Ratifications as of 1 May 2001: 39

Declarations

Netherlands: 'On the occasion of the deposit today of the instrument of acceptance by the Kingdom of the Netherlands of Protocol No. 6 to the Convention for the Protection of Human Rights and Fundamental Freedoms concerning the Abolition of the Death Penalty, done at Strasbourg on 28 April 1983, I have the honour to state, on behalf of the Government of the Kingdom of the Netherlands, that the bills for the abolition of capital punishment, insofar as it is still provided for under Dutch military law and Dutch regulations governing wartime offences, have been before parliament since 1981. It should be noted, however, that under the provisions of the Constitution of the Netherlands, which came into force on 17 February 1983, capital punishment may not be imposed.

Furthermore, I have the honour to communicate herewith in accordance with article 2 of the said protocol, sections 103 and 108 of the Criminal Code of the Netherlands Antilles and Aruba:

Sections 103 and 108 of the Criminal Code of the Netherlands Antilles and Aruba:

103. Any person who enters into an understanding with a foreign power with a view to inducing that power to engage in hostilities or war against the State, to strengthening its resolve to do so, or to promising or providing assistance in the preparation of such acts, shall be liable to a prison sentence of a maximum of fifteen years.

If the hostilities are carried out or a state of war occurs, the death sentence, life imprisonment, or a determinate prison sentence of a maximum of twenty years shall be imposed.

108. Any person who, in time of war, intentionally aids an enemy of the State, or disadvantages the State in relation to any enemy, shall be liable to a determinate prison sentence of a maximum of fifteen years. Life imprisonment or a determinate prison sentence of a maximum of twenty years shall be imposed if the offender:

1. informs or gives the enemy possession of any maps, plans, drawings or descriptions of military facilities or supplies any information relating to military operations or plans; or
2. acts as a spy for the enemy or assists, shelters or conceals an enemy spy.

The death penalty, life imprisonment or a determinate prison sentence of a maximum of twenty years shall be imposed if the offender:

1. destroys, renders unusable or betrays to the enemy or puts the enemy in possession of any fortified or manned location or post, any means of communication, any depot, any military supplies, any war funds, any restricted area (PB 1965, 69), or the navy or army or any part thereof, or if he hinders, impedes or sabotages any defensive or offensive flooding operations, whether planned or executed, or any other military operation;
2. causes or incites insurrection, mutiny or desertion among service personnel.'

Switzerland: 'In connection with the deposit of the instrument of ratification of Protocol No. 6 to the Convention for the Protection of Human Rights and Fundamental Freedoms, concerning the abolition of the death penalty, we wish to notify you of the following on behalf of the Swiss Federal Council in respect of Article 2 of the Protocol:

The Swiss legal system allows the death penalty to be reintroduced in time of war or in the event of an imminent threat of war, in pursuance of Articles 5 and 27 of the Military Criminal Code of 13 June 1927.

The Swiss legal system also allows the death penalty to be reintroduced on grounds of necessity ("droit de nécessité"). The Federal Council did this on 28 May 1940 by legislating on the basis of an ordinance issued in pursuance of the full powers conferred on it by the Federal Assembly on 30 August 1939, at the outbreak of the second world war. Consequently, in time of war or of imminent threat of war, within the meaning of article 2 of Protocol No. 6, the death penalty could be applied in Switzerland in the cases provided for in ordinary legislation (articles 5 and 27 of the Military Criminal Code) or in legislation adopted by the Federal Council on grounds of necessity ("droit de nécessité").

Copies of the following provisions of the relevant Swiss legislation are attached:
- article 5 of the Military Criminal Code of 13 June 1927,
- article 27 of the Military Criminal Code of 13 June 1927,
- Section 6 of the Federal Council Ordinance of 28 May 1940, amending and supplementing the Military Criminal Code (this legislative ordinance was abrogated with effect from 21 August 1945).

To indicate the background to this last-named provision, copies are also attached of the Federal Council's message of 29 August 1939 to the Federal Assembly on measures for ensuring the security of the country and maintaining its neutrality (Ff 1939 II 217); the Federal Assembly's order of 30 August 1939 on measures for ensuring the security of the country and maintaining its neutrality ("Full Powers" Federal order, RO 55 (1939), p. 781); the 3rd report of 19 November 1940 from the Federal Council to the Federal Assembly on Measures taken by it in pursuance of its extraordinary powers (FF 1940 I 1226, spec. 1233); and the Federal Council's order of 3 August 1945 terminating active service and abrogating the legislative ordinance of 28 May 1940 (RO 61 (1945), p. 561).

When appropriate, the Federal Council would notify you immediately of the entry into force of the above-mentioned statutory provisions.'

Germany 'In connection with the deposit of the instrument of ratification to Protocol No. 6 of 28 April 1983 to the Convention for the Protection of Human Rights and Fundamental Freedoms concerning the Abolition of the Death Penalty I have the honour to declare on behalf of the Government of the Federal Republic of Germany that Protocol No. 6 shall also apply to Land Berlin with effect from the date on which it enters into force for the Federal Republic of Germany.'

In connection with the deposit of the instrument of ratification to Protocol No. 6 of 28 April 1983 to the Convention for the Protection of Human Rights and Fundamental Freedoms concerning the Abolition of the Death Penalty I have the honour to declare on behalf of the Government of the Federal Republic of Germany that, in its view, the obligations deriving from Protocol No. 6 are confined to the abolition of the death penalty within the Protocol's area of application in the respective State and that national noncriminal legislation is not affected. The Federal Republic of Germany has already met its obligations under the Protocol by means of Article 102 of the Basic Law.'

Cyprus: 'It is hereby communicated, in accordance with Article 2 of the Protocol, that the death penalty is retained for the following offences under the Military Criminal Code and Procedure Law no. 40 of 1964 as amended: – Treason (section 13), – Surrender of entrusted post by military commander (section 14), – Capitulation in open place by officer in command (section 15(a), – Instigating or leading a revolt within the armed forces (section 42(2)), – Transmission of military secrets to a foreign state, spy of agent (section 70(1)), – Instigating or leading a revolt among war prisoners (section 95(2)). An English translation of the provisions of the above offences is attached as Appendix I to this Communication. It is further communicated that by virtue of the provisions of the Military Criminal Code and Procedure (Amendment) Law no. 91(I) of 1995, the death penalty, wherever provided for in the principal law, is imposed only when the offence is committed in time of war. According to the same provisions, the death penalty is not a mandatory sanction, but may, on the discretion of the Court, be substituted by imprisonment for life or for a shorter period. An English translation of the provisions of the Military Criminal Code and Procedure (Amendment) Law no. 91(I) of 1995 is attached as Appendix II.'

Ukraine: 'On 29 December 1999, the Constitutional Court of Ukraine ruled that the provisions of the Criminal Code of Ukraine which provided for death penalty were unconstitutional. According to the Law of Ukraine of 22 February 2000 "On the Introduction of Amendments to the Criminal, Criminal Procedure and Correctional Labour Codes of Ukraine", the Criminal Code of Ukraine has been brought into conformity with the above-mentioned ruling of the Constitutional Court of Ukraine. The death penalty was replaced by life imprisonment (Article 25 of the Criminal Code of Ukraine). The Law of Ukraine "On the Ratification of Protocol No. 6 to the Convention for the Protection of Human Rights and Fundamental Freedoms Concerning the Abolition of the Death Penalty, of 1983" envisages retaining of application of the death penalty for offences committed in time of war by means of introduction of appropriate amendments to the legislation in force. Pursuant to Article 2 of the Protocol No. 6 to the Convention for the Protection of Human Rights and Fundamental Freedoms, Ukraine will notify the Secretary General of the Council of Europe in case of introduction of these amendments.'

16 Charter of Fundamental Rights of the European Union

Article 2 Right to life
1. Everyone has the right to life.
2. No one shall be condemned to the death penalty, or executed.

Article 19 Protection in the event of removal, expulsion or extradition
1. Collective expulsions are prohibited.
2. No one may be removed, expelled or extradited to a State where there is a serious risk that he or she would be subjected to the death penalty, torture or other inhuman or degrading treatment or punishment.

17 European Union Minimum Standards Paper

Where states insist on maintaining the death penalty, the EU considers it important that the following minimum standards should be met:

(i) Capital punishment may be imposed only for the most serious crimes, it being understood that their scope should not go beyond intentional crimes with lethal or other extremely grave consequences. The death penalty should not be imposed for non-violent financial crimes or for non-violent religious practice or expression of conscience.

(ii) Capital punishment may be imposed only for a crime for which the death penalty was prescribed at the time of its commission, it being understood that if, subsequent to the commission of the crime, provision is made by law for the imposition of a lighter penalty, the offender shall benefit thereby.

(iii) Capital punishment may not be imposed on:
– persons below 18 years of age at the time of the commission of their crime;
– pregnant women or new mothers;
– persons who have become insane.

(iv) Capital punishment may be imposed only when the guilt of the person charged is based upon clear and convincing evidence leaving no room for alternative explanation of the facts.

(v) Capital punishment must only be carried out pursuant to a final judgment rendered by a competent court after legal process which gives all possible safeguards to ensure a fair trial, at least equal to those contained in Article 14 of the International Covenant on Civil and Political Rights, including the right of anyone suspected of or charged with a crime for which capital punishment may be imposed to adequate legal assistance at all stages of the proceedings, and where appropriate, the right to contact a consular representative.

(vi) Anyone sentenced to death shall have an effective right to appeal to a court of higher jurisdiction, and steps should be taken to ensure that such appeals become mandatory.

(vii) Where applicable, anyone sentenced to death shall have the right to submit an individual complaint under international procedures; the death sentence will not be carried out while the complaint remains under consideration under those procedures.

(viii) Anyone sentenced to death shall have the right to seek pardon or commutation of the sentence. Amnesty, pardon or commutation of the sentence of death may be granted in all cases of capital punishment.

(ix) Capital punishment may not be carried out in contravention of a state's international commitments.

(x) The length of time spent after having been sentenced to death may also be a factor.

(xi) Where capital punishment occurs, it shall be carried out so as to inflict the minimum possible suffering. It may not be carried out in public or in any other degrading manner.

(xii) The death penalty should not be imposed as an act of political revenge in contravention of the minimum standards, e.g. against coup plotters.

18 Organisation for Security and Cooperation in Europe Commitments

Concluding Document of the 1989 Vienna Follow-up Meeting

(24) With regard to the question of capital punishment, the participating States note that capital punishment has been abolished in a number of them. In participating States where capital punishment has not been abolished, sentence of death may be imposed only for the most serious crimes in accordance with the law in force at the time of the commission of the crime and not contrary to their international commitments. This question will be kept under consideration. In this context, the participating States will co-operate within relevant international organizations.

Document of the 1990 Copenhagen Meeting of the Conference on the Human Dimension of the Conference on Security and Cooperation in Europe

17.   The participating States

17.1 recall the commitments undertaken in the Vienna Concluding Document to keep the question of capital punishment under consideration and to co-operate within relevant international organizations;

17.2 recall, in this context, the adoption by the General Assembly of the United Nations, on 15 December 1989, of the Second Optional Protocol to the International Covenant on Civil and Political Rights, aiming at the abolition of the death penalty;

17.3 note the restrictions and safeguards regarding the use of the death penalty which have been adopted by the international community, in particular Article 6 of the International Covenant on Civil and Political Rights;

17.4 note the provisions of the Sixth Protocol to the European Convention for the Protection of Human Rights and Fundamental Freedoms, concerning the abolition of the death penalty;

17.5 note recent measures taken by a number of participating States towards the abolition of capital punishment;

17.6 note the activities of several non-governmental organizations on the question of the death penalty;

17.7 will exchange information within the framework of the Conference on the Human Dimension on the question of the abolition of the death penalty and keep that question under consideration;

17.8 will make available to the public information regarding the use of the death penalty.

Document of the 1991 Moscow Meeting of the Conference on the Human Dimension of the Conference on Security and Cooperation in Europe

(36) The participating States recall their commitment in the Vienna Concluding Document to keep the question of capital punishment under consideration and reaffirm their undertakings in the Document of the Copenhagen Meeting to exchange information on the question of the abolition of the death penalty and to make available to the public information regarding the use of the death penalty.

(36.1) They note
(i) that the Second Optional Protocol to the International Covenant on Civil and Political Rights aiming at the abolition of the death penalty entered into force on 11 July 1991;
(ii) that a number of participating States have recently taken steps towards the abolition of capital punishment;
(iii) the activities of several non-governmental organizations concerning the question of the death penalty.

Concluding Document of the 1992 Helsinki Summit

The participating States
. . .
(58) Confirm their commitments in the Copenhagen and Moscow Documents concerning the question of capital punishment.

Concluding Document of the 1994 Budapest Summit

19. The participating States reconfirm their commitments in the Copenhagen and Moscow Documents concerning the question of capital punishment.

19 American Declaration on the Rights and Duties of Man

Article 1
Every human being has the right to life, liberty and the security of his person.

20 American Convention on Human Rights

Article 4

1. Every person has the right to have his life respected. This right shall be protected by law and, in general, from the moment of conception. No one shall be arbitrarily deprived of his life.

2. In countries that have not abolished the death penalty, it may be imposed only for the most serious crimes and pursuant to a final judgment rendered by a competent court and in accordance with a law establishing such punishment, enacted prior to the commission of the crime. The application of such punishment shall not be extended to crimes to which it does not presently apply.

3. The death penalty shall not be reestablished in states that have abolished it.

4. In no case shall capital punishment be inflicted for political offenses or related common crimes.

5. Capital punishment shall not be imposed upon persons who, at the time the crime was committed, were under 18 years of age or over 70 years of age; nor shall it be applied to pregnant women.

6. Every person condemned to death shall have the right to apply for amnesty, pardon, or commutation of sentence, which may be granted in all cases. Capital punishment shall not be imposed while such a petition is pending decision by the competent authority.

Article 5

1. Every person has the right to have his physical, mental, and moral integrity respected.

2. No one shall be subjected to torture or to cruel, inhuman, or degrading punishment or treatment. All persons deprived of their liberty shall be treated with respect for the inherent dignity of the human person.

In force: 18 July 1978

Ratifications as of 1 May 2001: 25

Reservations concerning capital punishment

Dominican Republic: 'The Dominican Republic, upon signing the American Convention on Human Rights, aspires that the principle pertaining to the abolition of the death penalty shall become purely and simply that, with general application throughout the states of the American region, and likewise maintains the observations and comments made on the aforementioned Draft Convention which it distributed to the delegations to the council of the Organization of American States on 20 June 1969.'

Barbados: 'In respect of 4(4) the Criminal Code of Barbados provides for death by hanging as a penalty for murder and treason. The Government is at present reviewing the whole matter of the death penalty which is only rarely inflicted but wishes to enter a reservation on this point in as much as treason in certain circumstances might be regarded as a political offence and falling within the terms of section 4(4). In respect of 4(5) while the youth or old age of an offender may be matters which the Privy Council, the highest Court of Appeal, might take into account in considering whether the sentence of death should be carried out, persons of 16 years and over, or over 70 years of age, may be executed under Barbadian law.'

Guatemala: 'The Government of the Republic of Guatemala, ratifies the American Convention on Human Rights, signed in San José, Costa Rica, on the 22nd of November of 1969, making a reservation with regard to Article 4, paragraph 4 of the same, inasmuch as the Constitution of the Republic of Guatemala, in its Article 54, only excludes from the application of the death penalty, political crimes, but not common crimes related to political crimes.'

This reservation was withdrawn on 12 August 1986: 'The Government of Guatemala, by Government Agreement No. 281–86, dated 20 May 1986, has withdrawn the above-mentioned reservation, which was included in its instrument of ratification dated 27 April 1978, considering that it is no longer supported by the Constitution in the light of the new legal system in force. The withdrawal of the reservation will become effective as of 12 August 1986, in conformity with Article 22 of the Vienna Convention on the Law of Treaties of 1969, in application of Article 75 of the American Convention on Human Rights.'

Trinidad and Tobago: 'As regards Article 4(5) of the Convention the Government of The Republic of Trinidad and Tobago makes reservation in that under the laws of Trinidad and Tobago there is no prohibition against the carrying out of a sentence of death on a person over seventy (70) years of age.'

Dominica: 'Article 4.4. Reservation is made in respect of the words 'or related crimes'.'

21 Additional Protocol to the American Convention on Human Rights to Abolish the Death Penalty

The States Parties to this Protocol

Considering:

That Article 4 of the American Convention on Human Rights recognizes the right to life and restricts the application of the death penalty;

That everyone has the inalienable right to respect for his life, a right that cannot be suspended for any reason;

That the tendency among the American States is to be in favour of abolition of the death penalty;

That application of the death penalty has irrevocable consequences, forecloses the correction of judicial error, and precludes the possibility of changing or rehabilitating those convicted;

That the abolition of the death penalty helps to ensure more effective protection of the right to life;

That an international agreement must be arrived at that will entail a progressive development of the American Convention on Human Rights; and

That States Parties to the American Convention on Human Rights have expressed their intention to adopt an international agreement with a view to consolidating the practice of not applying the death penalty in the Americas.

Have agreed to sign the following Protocol to the American Convention on Human Rights to Abolish the Death Penalty

Article 1

The States Parties to this Protocol shall not apply the death penalty in their territory to any person subject to their jurisdiction.

Article 2

1. No reservations may be made to this Protocol. However, at the time of ratification or accession, the States Parties to this instrument may declare that they reserve the right to apply the death penalty in wartime in accordance with international law, for extremely serious crimes of a military nature.

2. The State Party making this reservation shall, upon ratification or accession, inform the Secretary General of the Organization of American States of the pertinent provisions of its national legislation applicable in wartime, as referred to in the preceding paragraph.

3. Said State Party shall notify the Secretary General of the Organization of American States of the beginning or end of any state of war in effect in its territory.

Article 3

This Protocol shall be open for signature and ratification or accession by any State Party to the American Convention on Human Rights.

Ratification of this Protocol or accession thereto shall be made through the deposit of an instrument of ratification or accession with the General Secretariat of the Organization of American States.

Article 4

This Protocol shall enter into force among the States that ratify or accede to it when they deposit their respective instruments of ratification or accession with the General Secretariat of the Organization of American States.

In force: 28 August 1991

Ratifications as of 1 May 2001: 8

Reservation

Brazil: 'In ratifying the Protocol to Abolish the Death Penalty, adopted in Asunción on June 8, 1990, I make hereby, in compliance with constitutional requirements, a reservation under the terms of Article 2 of the said Protocol, which guarantees states parties the right to apply the death penalty in wartime in accordance with international law, for extremely serious crimes of a military nature.'

22 African Charter of Human and Peoples' Rights

Article 4

Human beings are inviolable. Every human being shall be entitled to respect for his life and the integrity of his person. No one may be arbitrarily deprived of this right.

Article 5

Every individual shall have the right to the respect of the dignity inherent in a human being and to the recognition of his legal status. All forms of exploitation and degradation of man particularly slavery, slave trade, torture, cruel, inhuman or degrading punishment and treatment shall be prohibited.

In force: 21 October 1986

Ratifications as of 1 May 2001: 52

23 African Charter on the Rights and Welfare of the Child

Article 5 Survival and development

1. Every child has an inherent right to life. This right shall be protected by law.

2. States Parties to the present Charter shall ensure, to the maximum extent possible, the survival, protection and development of the child.

3. Death sentence shall not be pronounced for crimes committed by children.

In force: 29 November 1999

Ratifications as of 1 May 2001: 22

24 Arab Charter on Human Rights

Article 5
Every individual has the right to life, liberty and security of person. These rights shall be protected by law.

Article 10
The death penalty may be imposed only for the most serious crimes and anyone sentenced to death shall have the right to seek pardon or commutation of the sentence.

Article 11
The death penalty shall under no circumstances be imposed for a political offence.

Article 12
The death penalty shall not be inflicted on a person under 18 years of age, on a pregnant woman prior to her delivery or on a nursing mother within two years from the date on which she gave birth.

Article 13
(a) The States parties shall protect every person in their territory from being subjected to physical or mental torture or cruel, inhuman or degrading treatment. They shall take effective measures to prevent such acts and shall regard the practice thereof, or participation therein, as a punishable offence.

(b) No medical or scientific experimentation shall be carried out on any person without his free consent.

In force: The Charter will come into force following the seventh ratification.

Ratifications as of 1 May 2001: 1

Bibliography

Monographs

Amnesty International, *The Death Penalty*, London: Amnesty International, 1979

    United States of America: The Death Penalty and Juvenile Offenders, London: Amnesty International, 1991

    When the State Kills . . . The Death Penalty: A Human Rights Issue, New York: Amnesty International, 1989

Ancel, Marc, *Capital Punishment*, UN Doc. ST/SOA/SD/9, U.N. Publication, Sales No. 62.IV.2

    The Death Penalty in European Countries, Strasbourg: Council of Europe, 1962

Baird, Robert M., and Rosenbaum, Stuart E., *Punishment and the Death Penalty: The Current Debate*, New York: Prometheus Books, 1995

Baldus, David C., Woodworth, George, and Pulaski Jr., Charles A., *Equal Justice and the Death Penalty: A Legal and Empirical Analysis*, Boston: Northeastern University Press, 1990

Beccaria, Cesare, *On Crimes and Punishments*, trans. Henry Paolucci, Indianapolis: Bobbs-Merrill, 1963

Bedau, Hugo Adam, ed., *The Death Penalty in America*, Oxford: Oxford University Press, 1997

Cario, Robert, ed., *La peine de mort au seuil du troisième millenaire*, Toulouse: Editions Erès, 1993

Clark, Roger S., *The United Nations Crime Prevention and Criminal Justice Program, Formulation of Standards and Efforts at Their Implementation*, Philadelphia: University of Pennsylvania Press, 1994

Danielsen, Astrid, *The State Reporting Procedure under the African Charter*, Copenhagen: Danish Centre for Human Rights, 1994

Dormenval, Agnès, *Procédures onusiennes de mise en oeuvre des droits de l'homme: limites ou défauts*, Geneva: Presses universitaires de France, 1991

Epstein, Lee, and Kobylka, Joseph F., *The Supreme Court and Legal Change: Abortion and the Death Penalty*, Chapel Hill: University of North Carolina Press, 1992

Evans, Richard J., *Rituals of Retribution, Capital Punishment in Germany 1600–1987*, Oxford: Clarendon Press, 1996

Gross, Samuel R., & Mauro, Robert, *Death and Discrimination, Racial Disparities in Capital Sentencing*, Boston: Northeastern, 1989

Harlow, Enid, Matas, David, and Rocamora, Jane, eds., *The Machinery of Death*, New York: Amnesty International, 1995

Henkin, Louis, ed., *The International Bill of Rights: The Covenant on Civil and Political Rights*, New York: Columbia University Press, 1981

Hodgkinson, Peter, & Rutherford, Andrew, *Capital Punishment: Global Issues and Prospects*, London: Waterside Press, 1996

Hood, Roger, *The Death Penalty, A World-wide Perspective*, Oxford: Clarendon Press, 1997

Imbert, Jean, *La peine de mort*, 3rd ed., Paris: Presses universitaires de France, 1998

Jackson, Robert H., *Report of Robert H. Jackson, United States Representative to the International Conference on Military Trials*, Washington: U.S. Government Printing Office, 1949

Joseph, Sarah, Schultz, Jenny, & Castan, Melissa, *The International Covenant on Civil and Political Rights, Cases, Materials and Commentary*, Oxford: Oxford University Press, 2000

Joyce, James Avery, *Capital Punishment, A World View*, New York: Thomas Nelson, 1961

Lee, Roy, ed., *The International Criminal Court, The Making of the Rome Statute*, Dordrecht/London/Boston: Kluwer Law, 1999

Mbaye, Keba, *Les droits de l'homme en Afrique*, Paris: Pedone, 1992

McGoldrick, Dominic, *The Human Rights Committee*, Oxford: Clarendon Press, 1991

Meron, Theodor, *Human Rights and Humanitarian Norms as Customary International Law*, Oxford: Clarendon Press, 1989

Miller, Kent S., and Radelet, Michael L., *Executing the Mentally Ill*, Newbury Park, CA: Sage Publications, 1993

Morsink, Johannes, *The Universal Declaration of Human Rights, Origins, Drafting & Intent*, Philadelphia: University of Pennsylvania Press, 1998

Nowak, Manfred, *CCPR Commentary*, Kehl: Engel, 1993

Nowak, Manfred, & Xin, Chunying, *EU–China Human Rights Dialogue*, Vienna: Verlag Osterreich, 2000

Orlin, Theodore S., Rosas, Allan, and Scheinin, Martin, *The Jurisprudence of Human Rights Law: A Comparative Interpretive Approach*, Turku, Finland: Institute for Human Rights, Åbo Akademi University, 2000

Ouguergouz, Fatsah, *La Charte africaine des droits de l'homme et des peuples*, Geneva: Presses universitaires de France, 1993

Pannick, David, *Judicial Review of the Death Penalty*, London: Duckworth, 1982

Pettiti, L. E., Decaux, E., & Imbert, P.-H., *La Convention européenne des droits de l'homme, commentaire article par article*, Paris: Economica, 1995

Potter, Harry, *Hanging in Judgment, Religion and the Death Penalty in England from the Bloody Code to Abolition*, London: SCM Press, 1993

Prejean, Helen, *Dead Man Walking*, New York: Random House, 1993

Prémont, Daniel, ed., *Essais sur le concept de 'droit de vivre' en mémoire de Yougindra Khushalani*, Brussels: Bruylant, 1988

Radelet, Michael L., Bedau, Hugo Adam, and Putnam, Constance E., *In Spite of Innocence*, Boston: Northeastern University Press, 1992

Ramcharan, Bertrand G., ed., *The Right to Life in International Law*, Dordrecht/Boston/Lancaster: Martinus Nijhoff Publishers, 1985

Rodley, Nigel, *The Treatment of Prisoners Under International Law*, 2nd ed., Oxford: Clarendon Press, 1999

Savage, David G., *Turning Right, The Making of the Rehnquist Supreme Court*, New York: Wiley, 1992

Schabas, William A., *Genocide in International Law*, Cambridge: Cambridge University Press, 2000

    Introduction to the International Criminal Court, Cambridge: Cambridge University Press, 2001

    ed., *Sourcebook on the Abolition of the Death Penalty*, Boston: Northeastern University Press, 1997

    The Death Penalty as Cruel Treatment and Torture, Boston: Northeastern University Press, 1996

Streib, Victor L., *Death Penalty for Juveniles*, Bloomington and Indianapolis: Indiana University Press, 1987

Triffterer, Otto, ed., *Commentary on the Rome Statute of the International Criminal Court, Observers' Notes, Article by Article*, Baden-Baden: Nomos, 1999

Trombley, Stephen, *The Execution Protocol*, London: Century, 1993

United Kingdom, *Royal Commission on Capital Punishment, 1949–1953, Report*, London: Her Majesty's Stationery Office, 1953

van Aggelen, Johannes G. C., *Le rôle des organisations internationales dans la protection du droit à la vie*, Brussels: Story-Scientia, 1986

van den Wijngaert, Christine, *The Political Offence Exception to Extradition*, Deventer: Kluwer, 1980

Vasak, Karl, *La Commission Interaméricaine des droits de l'homme*, Paris: Bibliothèque constitutionnelle et de science politique, 1968

Velu, Jacques, and Ergec, Rusen, *La Convention européenne des droits de l'homme*, Brussels: Bruylant, 1990

Verdoodt, Albert, *Naissance et signification de la déclaration universelle des droits de l'homme*, Louvain, Paris: Nauwelaerts, 1963

von Drehle, David, *Among the Lowest of the Dead, The Culture of Death Row*, New York: Random House, 1995

White, Welsh S., *The Death Penalty in the Nineties*, Ann Arbor: University of Michigan Press, 1991

Articles

Aceves, W. J., 'Individual Rights Under Vienna Convention on Consular Relations – Duty to Inform Detained Foreign Nationals of Right to Seek Consular Assistance – Protections Against Arbitrary Deprivation of Life – Advisory Jurisdiction of the Inter-American Court of Human Rights', (2000) 94 *American Journal of International Law* 555

Adeyemi, A. A., 'Death Penalty: Criminological Perspectives. The Nigerian Situation', (1987) 58 *Revue internationale de droit pénal* 485

Adinolfi, A., 'Premier instrument international sur l'abolition de la peine de mort', (1987) 58 *Revue internationale de droit pénal* 321

Aguilar-Urbina, Francisco José, 'An Overview of the Main Differences Between the Systems Established by the Optional Protocol to the ICCPR and the ACHR as Regards Individual Communications', [1991–92] *CHRY* 127

Alexis, J., M., and De Merieux, M. 'Inordinately Delayed Hanging: Whether an Inhuman Punishment', (1987) 29 *Journal of the Indian Law Institute* 356

Angus, Laurel, 'Delay Before Execution: Is it Inhuman and Degrading Treatment', (1993) 9 *South African Journal of Human Rights* 432

Antoine, R. M. B., 'International Law and the Right to Legal Representation in Capital Offence Cases – A Comparative Approach', (1992) 12 *Oxford Journal of Legal Studies* 284

'The Judicial Committee of the Privy Council – An Inadequate Remedy for Death Row Prisoners', (1992) 41 *ICLQ* 179

Badinter, Robert, 'France: The Abolition of Capital Punishment: The French Experience', (1984) 11 *Crime Prevention and Criminal Justice Newsletter* 17

Baldus, D. C., Pulaski, C., & Woodworth, G., 'Arbitrariness and Discrimination in the Administration of the Death Penalty', (1986) 15 *Stetson Law Review* 133

Bantekas, Ilias, and Hodgkinson, Peter, 'Capital Punishment at the United Nations: Recent Developments', (2000) 11 *Criminal Law Forum* 23

Barry, Donald D., and Williams, Eric J., 'Russia's Death Penalty Dilemmas', (1997) 8 *Criminal Law Forum* 231

Bassiouni, M. Cherif, 'Reflections on the Ratification by the United States of the International Covenant on Civil and Political Rights by the United States Senate', (1993) 42 *Depaul Law Review* 1169

Bello, E. G., 'The African Charter on Human and People's Rights. A Legal Analysis', (1985) 194 *RCADI* 91

Bentele, U., 'Back to an International Perspective on the Death Penalty as a Cruel Punishment: The Example of South Africa', (1998) 73 *Tulane Law Review* 251

Bishop, Norman, 'L'activité du Comité européen pour les problèmes criminels du Conseil de l'Europe', (1966) 21 (n.s.) *Revue de science criminelle et du droit pénal comparé* 427

Bossuyt, Marc J., 'The Death Penalty in the "Travaux Préparatoires" of the International Covenant on Civil and Political Rights', in Daniel Prémont, ed., *Essais sur le concept de 'droit de vivre' en mémoire de Yougindra Khushalani*, Brussels: Bruylant, 1988, pp. 252–265

Boyle, C. K., 'The Concept of Arbitrary Deprivation of Life', in Bertrand G. Ramcharan, ed., *The Right to Life in International Law*, Boston: Martinus Nijhoff, 1985, pp. 221–244

Breillat, Dominique, 'L'abolition mondiale de la peine de mort. À propos du 2e Protocole facultatif se rapportant au Pacte international relatif aux droits civils et politiques, visant à abolir la peine de mort', [1991] *Revue de science criminelle et de droit pénal comparé* 261

Buergenthal, Thomas, 'The American and European Conventions on Human Rights: Similarities and Differences', (1980) 30 *American University Law Review* 155

'The Revised OAS Charter and the Protection of Human Rights', (1975) 69 *AJIL* 828

Campos, Francisco, del Rio, F. Nieto, Fenwick, Charles G., and Robledo, A. Gómez, 'Report to Accompany the Draft Declaration of the International Rights and Duties of Man', (1946) 40 *AJIL Supp.* 100

Cançado Trindade, A. A., 'Co-existence and Co-ordination of Mechanisms of International Protection of Human Rights (At Global and Regional Levels)', (1987) 202 *RCADI* 9

'El Brasil contre il pena de meurte', (1994) 19 *Revista IIDH* 547

Centre des études de sécurité (Arabie Saoudite), 'L'égalité et commodité de la peine de mort en droit musulman', (1987) 58 *Revue internationale de droit pénal* 431

Cerna, Christina M., 'Universality of Human Rights: The Case of the Death Penalty', (1997) 3 *ILSA Journal of International and Comparative Law* 465

'US Death Penalty Tested Before the Inter-American Commission on Human Rights', (1992) 10 *Netherlands Quarterly of Human Rights* 155

Clark, Roger S., 'Human Rights and the U.N. Committee on Crime Prevention and Control', (1989) 506 *Annals of the American Association of Political and Social Science* 68

'The Eighth United Nations Congress on the Prevention of Crime and the Treatment of Offenders, Havana, Cuba, August 27–September 7, 1990', (1990) 1 *Criminal Law Forum* 513

Clifford, William, 'The Committee on Crime Prevention and Control', (1978) 34 *International Review of Criminal Policy* 11

Cohen-Jonathan, Gérard, 'La décision du Comité des droits de l'homme des Nations unies du 2 novembre 1999 dans l'affaire *Kennedy contre Trinité-et-Tobago*, Des réserves au premier protocole facultatif', (2000) 12 *Revue universelle des droits de l'homme* 209

Cottrell, Jim, 'Wrestling with the Death Penalty in India', (1991) 7 *South African Journal of Human Rights* 185

Dawtry, F., 'The Abolition of the Death Penalty in Britain', (1966) 6 *British Journal of Criminology* 183

De la Vega, Connie, and Brown, Jennifer, 'Can a United States Treaty Reservation Provide a Sanctuary for the Juvenine Death Penalty', (1998) 32 *USF Law Review* 735

Degni-Segui, René, 'L'apport de la Charte africaine des droits de l'homme et des peuples au droit international de l'homme' (1991) 3 *African Journal of International and Comparative Law* 699

Denno, Deborah, W., 'Is Electrocution an Unconstitutional Method of Execution? The Engineering of Death Over the Century', (1994) 35 *William and Mary Law Review* 551

Desch, T., 'The Concept and Dimensions of the Right to Life – As Defined in International Standards and in International and Comparative Jurisprudence', (1985–86) 36 *Osterreichische Zeitschrift für Öffentliches Recht und Volkerrecht* 77

DeWitt, M. E., 'Extradition Enigma: Italy and Human Rights vs. America and the Death Penalty', (1998) 47 *Catholic University Law Review* 535

Duxbury, Alison, 'Saving Lives in the International Court of Justice: The Use of Provisional Measures to Protect Human Rights', (2000) 31 *California Western International Law Journal* 141

Edwards, William, 'Execution of People with Mental Retardation: A Violation of National and International Customary International Law', (2000) 38 *Mental Retardation* 173

Eldred, Charles Kenneth, 'The New Federal Death Penalties', (1994) 22 *American Journal of Criminal Law* 10

Espiell, Hector Gros, 'The Right to Life and the Right to Live', in Daniel Prémont, ed., *Essais sur le concept de 'droit de vivre' en mémoire de Yougindra Khushalani*, Brussels: Bruylant, 1988, pp. 45–53

Fattah, Ezzat A., 'Canada's Successful Experience with the Abolition of the Death Penalty', (1987) 25 *Canadian Journal of Criminology* 421

'The Use of the Death Penalty for Drug Offences and for Economic Crimes – A Discussion and a Critique', (1987) 58 *Revue internationale de droit pénal* 723

Favoreu, Louis, 'La décision du conseil constitutionnel du 22 mai 1985 relative au protocole no 6 additionnel à la Convention européenne des droits de l'homme', [1985] *Annuaire français du droit international* 868

Feria Tinta, Monica, 'Due Process and the Right to Life in the Context of the Vienna Convention on Consular Relations: Arguing the LaGrand Case', (2001) 12 *European Journal of International Law* 363

Fitzpatrick, Joan, and Miller, Alice, 'International Standards on the Death Penalty: Shifting Discourse', (1993) 19 *Brooklyn Journal of International Law* 273

Fox, T. D., 'Inter-American Commission of Human Rights Finds United States in Violation', (1988) 82 *AJIL* 601

Frowein, Jochen Abr., 'The European and the American Conventions on Human Rights – A Comparison', (1980) 1 *Human Rights Law Journal* 44

Gaer, Felice D., 'First Fruits: Reporting by States under the African Charter on Human and Peoples' Rights', (1992) 10 *Netherlands Quarterly of Human Rights* 29

Gappa, David L., 'European Court of Human Rights – Extradition – Inhuman or Degrading Treatment or Punishment, Soering Case', (1990) 20 *Georgia Journal of International and Comparative Law* 463

Giegerich, Thomas, 'Richtermacht und Todesstrafe in den USA: Gewaltenteilung, ver-fassungsstaatliche und völkerrechtliche Humanitätsstandards in Kollision', (1995) 22 *Europäische Grundrechte Zeitschrift* 1

Harremoes, Erik, 'L'activité du Comité européen pour les problèmes criminels du Conseil de l'Europe 1966–1974', [1975] *Revue de science criminelle et de droit pénal comparé* 327
'The Council of Europe and Its Efforts to Promote the Abolition of the Death Penalty', (1986) 12–13 *Crime Prevention and Criminal Justice Newsletter* 62

Harring, S. L., 'Death, Drugs and Development: Malaysia's Mandatory Death Penalty for Traffickers and the International War on Drugs', (1991) 29 *Columbia Journal of Transnational Law* 364

Hatchard, John, 'Capital Punishment in Southern Africa: Some Recent Developments', (1994) 43 *International and Comparative Law Quarterly* 923

Hatchard, John, & Coldham, Simon, 'Commonwealth Africa', in Peter Hodgkinson & Andrew Rutherford, eds., *Capital Punishment: Global Issues and Prospects*, London: Waterside Press, 1996, pp. 155–191

Henkin, Louis, 'U.S. Ratification of Human Rights Conventions: The Ghost of Senator Bricker', (1995) 89 *AJIL* 341

Henry, J. E., 'Overcoming Federalism in Internationalized Death Penalty Cases', (2000) 35 *Texas International Law Journal* 459

Hood, Roger, 'The Death Penalty: The USA in World Perspective', (1997) 6 *Florida State University Journal of Transnational Law and Policy* 517

Horvath, Tibor, 'L'abolition de la peine de mort en Hongrie', [1992] 2 *Revue internationale de criminologie et de police technique* 167

Hosni, N., 'La peine de mort en droit égyptien et en droit islamique', (1987) 58 *Revue internationale de droit pénal* 407

Hudson, Patrick, 'Does the Death Row Phenomenon Violate a Prisoner's Human Rights Under International Law?' (2000) 11 *European Journal of International law* 833

Ikhariale, Mike, 'Death Penalty in Nigeria: A Constitutional Aberration', (1991) 1 *Journal of Human Rights Law and Practice* 40

International Commission of Jurists, 'Report of a Mission Concerniing the Administration of the Death Penalty in the United States', (1997) 19 *HRQ* 165

Kennedy, R. L., 'McCleskey v. Kemp: Race, Capital Punishment and the Supreme Court', (1988) 101 *Harvard Law Review* 1388

King, Faiza P., and La Rosa, Anne-Marie, 'Penalties Under the ICC Statute', in Flavia Lattanzi and William A. Schabas, eds., *Essays on the Rome Statute of the ICC*, Rome: Editrice il Sirente, 2000, pp. 311–338

Kiss, A.-C., and Marie, J.-B., 'Le droit à la vie', (1974) 7 HRJ 338

Labayle, Henri, 'Droits de l'homme, traitement inhumain et peine capitale: Réflexions sur l'édification d'un ordre public européen en matière d'extradition par la Cour européenne des droits de l'homme', (1990) 64 *Semaine juridique* 3452

Landerer, Lilly E., 'Capital Punishment as a Human Rights Issue Before the United Nations', (1971) 4 *HRJ* 511

Lenihan, James M., 'Soering's Case: Waiting for Godot – Cruel and Unusual Punishment?', (1992) 4 *Pace Yearbook of International Law* 157

Leone, U., 'International Bibliography on Capital Punishment', (1987) 58 *Revue internationale de droit pénal* 823

'UNSDRI's Activities Related to the Death Penalty Issue', (1987) 58 *Revue internationale de droit pénal* 325

Lepper, S. J., 'Short v. The Kingdom of the Netherlands: Is it Time to Renegotiate the NATO Status of Forces Agreement?', (1991) 24 *Vanderbilt Journal of Transnational Law* 867

Leuprecht, Peter, 'The First International Instrument for the Abolition of the Death Penalty', (1983) 2 *Forum* 2

Lillich, Richard B., 'Harmonizing Human Rights Law Nationally and Internationally: The Death Row Phenomenon as a Case Study', (1996) 40 *St. Louis Law Journal* 699

'The Soering Case', (1991) 85 *AJIL* 128

Madhuku, Lovemore, 'Delay Before Execution: More on it Being Inhuman and Degrading', (1994) 10 *South African Journal of Human Rights* 276

Malhuku, Lovemore, 'Incompatability of the Death Penalty and Human Rights', (1997) 13 *South African Journal of Human Rights* 151

Marks, Susan, 'Yes, Virginia, Extradition May Breach the European Convention on Human Rights', (1990) 49 *Cambridge Law Journal* 194

Mbaya, Etienne-Richard, 'À la recherche du noyau intangible dans la Charte africaine', in *Le noyau intangible des droits de l'homme*, Fribourg: Éditions universitaires Fribourg Suisse, 1991, pp. 207–211

Murray, Rachel, 'Decisions by the African Commission on Individual Communications Under the African Charter on Human and Peoples' Rights', (1998) 46 *International and Comparative Law Quarterly* 412

Naldi, Gino J., 'United Nations Seeks to Abolish the Death Penalty', (1991) 40 *International and Comparative Law Quarterly* 948

Nanda, Ved. P., 'Bases for Refusing International Extradition Requests – Capital Punishment and Torture', (2000) 23 *Fordham International Law Journal* 1369

'Recent Developments in the United States and Internationally Regarding Capital Punishment – An Appraisal', (1993) 67 *St. John's Law Review* 523

'The U.S. Reservation to the Ban on the Death Penalty for Juvenile Offenders: An Appraisal Under the International Covenant on Civil and Political Rights', (1993) 42 *DePaul Law Review* 1311

Neier, Aryeh, 'Political Consequences of the United States Ratification of the International Covenant on Civil and Political Rights', (1993) 42 *DePaul Law Review* 1233

O'Driscoll, C. S., 'The Execution of Foreign Nationals in Arizona: Violations of the Vienna Convention on Consular Relations', (2000) 32 *Arizona State Law Journal* 323

O'Boyle, Michael, 'Extradition and Expulsion under the European Convention on Human Rights, Reflections on the Soering Case', in James O'Reilly, ed., *Human Rights and Constitutional Law, Essays in Honour of Brian Walsh*, Dublin: Round Hall Press, 1992, pp. 93–107

Odinkalu, Chidi Anselm, 'The Individual Complaints Procedures of the African Commission on Human and Peoples' Rights: A Preliminary Assessment', (1998) 8 *Transnational Law and Contemporary Problems* 359

Orlin, Theodore S., 'The Prohibition of the Death Penalty: An Emerging International Norm', in Allan Rosas, Jan Helgesen and Donna Gomien, *Human Rights in a Changing East–West Perspective*, London, New York: Pinter Publishers, 1990, pp. 136–173

Pak, John, 'Canadian Extradition and the Death Penalty: Seeking a Constitutional Assurance of Life', (1993) 26 *Cornell International Law Journal* 239

Parkerson, J. E. Jr., and Stoehr, C. S., 'The U.S. Military Death Penalty in Europe: Threats from Recent European Human Rights Developments', (1990) 129 *Military Law Review* 41

Parkerson, John E. Jr, and Lepper, Steven J., 'Commentary on Short vs Netherlands', (1991) 85 *AJIL* 698

Pettiti, L. E., 'Arrêt Soering c./Grande-Bretagne du 8 juillet 1989', [1989] *Revue de science criminelle et de droit pénal comparé* 786

Pickard, Daniel B., 'Proposed Sentencing Guidelines for the International Criminal Court', (1997) 20 *Loyola of Los Angeles International and Comparative Law Journal* 123

Pilloud, Claude, 'La protection pénale des conventions humanitaires internationales', [1953] *Revue internationale de la Croix-rouge* 842

'Reservations to the 1949 Geneva Conventions', [1958] *International Review of the Red Cross* 193

'Reservations to the Geneva Conventions of 1949', [1976] *International Review of the Red Cross* 163

Piragoff, Donald K., and Kran, Marcia V. J., 'The Impact of Human Rights Principles on Extradition from Canada and the United States: The Role of National Courts', (1992) 3 *Criminal Law Forum* 191

Przetacnik, F., 'The Right to Life as a Basic Human Right', (1976) 9 *HRJ* 585

'The Right to Life as a Basic Human Right', (1978) *Revue de droit international de science diplomatique* 23

Quigley, John, 'Criminal Law and Human Rights: Implications of the United States Ratification of the International Covenant on Civil and Political Rights', (1993) 6 *Harvard Human Rights Journal* 59

Quigley, John, and Shank, J., 'Death Row as a Violation of Human Rights: Is it Illegal to Extradite to Virginia?', (1989) 30 *Virginia International Law Journal* 251

Radelet, Michael L., and Borg, Marian J., 'The Changing Nature of Death Penalty Debates', (2000) 26 *Annual Review of Sociology* 43

Ramcharan, Bertrand G., 'The Right to Life', (1983) 30 *Netherlands International Law Review* 297

Rieter, Eva, 'Interim Measures by the World Court to Suspend the Execution of an Individual: The Breard Case', (1998) 16 *Netherlands Quarterly of Human Rights* 475

Roecks, Craig R., 'Extradition, Human Rights and the Death Penalty: When Nations Must Refuse to Extradite a Person Charged with a Capital Crime', (1995) 25 *California Western International Law Journal* 189

Rosen, Sonia, and Journey, Stephen, 'Abolition of the Death Penalty: An Emerging Norm of International Law', (1993) 14 *Hamline Journal of Public Law and Policy* 163

Röstad, H., 'The International Penal and Penitentiary Foundation and the Death Penalty', (1987) 58 *Revue internationale de droit pénal* 345

Schabas, William A., 'Canadian Ratification of the American Convention on Human Rights' (1998) 16 *Netherlands Quarterly of Human Rights* 315

'Case Comment: Pratt and Morgan v. Jamaica', (1994) 5 *Criminal Law Forum* 180

'Extradition et la peine de mort: le Canada renvoie deux fugitifs au couloir de la mort', (1992) 4 *Revue universelle des droits de l'homme* 65–70

'Illegal Reservations to Human Rights Treaties: Spare the RUD and Spoil the Treaty', in David P. Forsythe, ed., *The United States and Human Rights: Looking Inward and Outward*, Lincoln: University of Nebraska Press, 2000, pp. 110–125

'International Law and the Abolition of the Death Penalty', (1998) 55 *Washington and Lee Law Review* 797

'International Law and the Death Penalty: Recent Developments', (1998) 4 *ILSA Journal of International and Comparative Law* 535

'International Law and the Death Penalty', (1994) 22 *American Journal of Criminal Law* 250

'International Norms on Execution of the Insane and the Mentally Retarded', (1993) 4 *Criminal Law Forum* 95

'Is the United States Still a Party to the *International Covenant on Civil and Political Rights?*', (1995) 21 *Brooklyn Journal of International Law* 277

'Islam and the Death Penalty', (2000) 9 *William & Mary Bill of Rights Journal* 223

'Kindler v. Canada', (1993) 87 *AJIL* 128

'L'abolition de la peine de mort en droit international des droits de l'homme: développements récents', (2000) 26 *Publications de la Revue marocaine d'administration locale et de développement* 57

'Les réserves des États-Unis d'Amérique aux articles 6 et 7 du Pacte international relatif aux droits civils et politiques', (1994) 6 *Revue universelle des droits de l'homme* 137

'Life, Death and the Crime of Crimes: Supreme Penalties and the ICC Statute', (2000) 2 *Punishment & Society* 263

'Penalties', in Antonio Cassese, ed., *International Criminal Court: A Commentary on the Rome Statute for an International Criminal Court*, Oxford: Oxford University Press (forthcoming)

'Penalties', in Flavia Lattanzi, ed., *The International Criminal Court, Comments on the Draft Statute*, Naples: Editoriale Scientifica, 1998, pp. 273–299

'Perverse Effects of the Nulla Poena Principle: National Practice and the Ad Hoc Tribunals', (2000) 11 *European Journal of International Law* 521

'Reservations to International Human Rights Treaties', (1995) 32 *Canadian Yearbook of International Law* 39

'Soering's Legacy: The Human Rights Committee and the Judicial Committee of the Privy Council Take a Walk Down Death Row', (1994) 43 *International and Comparative Law Quarterly* 913

'South Africa's Constitutional Court Outlaws the Death Penalty', (1995) 16 *Human Rights Law Journal* 133–148

'The Death Penalty for Crimes Committed by Persons Under Eighteen Years of Age', in Eugen Verhellen, ed., *Monitoring Children's Rights*, Dordrecht: Martinus Nijhoff, 1996, pp. 603–619

'The Penalties Provisions in the ICC Statute', in Dinah Shelton, ed., *International Crimes, Peace, and Human Rights: The Role of the International Criminal Court*, Ardsley, NY: Transnational Publishers, 2000, pp. 105–136

'Universal Norms and International Tribunals: The Case of Cruel Treatment and the Death Row Phenomenon', in Thomas J. Schoenbaum, Junji Nakagawa and Linda Reif, eds., *Trilateral Perspectives on International Legal Issues: From Theory into Practice*, Irvington, NY: Transnational Publishers, 1998, pp. 173–208

'War Crimes, Crimes Against Humanity and the Death Penalty', (1997) 60 *Albany Law Journal* 736

Schmidt, Markus G., 'The Complementarity of the Covenant and the European Convention on Human Rights – Recent Developments', in D. H. Harris, ed., *The ICCPR – Its Impact on United Kingdom Law*, Oxford: Oxford University Press, 1995, pp. 635–665

'Universality of Human Rights and the Death Penalty – The Approach of the Human Rights Committee', (1997) 3 *ILSA Journal of International and Comparative Law* 477

Schulte, Constanze, 'Jurisprudence of the International Court of Justice: Order Issued in the Case Concerning the Vienna Convention on Consular Relations (Paraguay v. United States of America)', (1998) 9 *European Journal of International Law* 761

Scobell, Andrew, 'Strung Up or Shot Down? The Death Penalty in Hong Kong and China and Implications for Post-1997', (1988) 20 *Case Western Reserve Journal of International Law* 147

'The Death Penalty Under Socialism, 1917–90: China, the Soviet Union, Cuba, and the German Democratic Republic', (1991) 12 *Criminal Justice History* 189

Separavic, Z. P., 'Political Crimes and the Death Penalty', (1987) 58 *Revue internationale de droit pénal* 755

Shelton, Dinah, 'Application of Death Penalty on Juveniles in the U.S.', (1987) 8 *HRLJ* 355

'The Prohibition of Juvenile Executions in International Law', (1987) 58 *Revue internationale de droit pénal* 773

Sherlock, Ann, 'Extradition, Death Row and the Convention', (1990) 15 *European Law Review* 87

Sherman Jr., E. F., 'The U.S. Death Penalty Reservation to the International Covenant on Civil and Political Rights – Exposing the Limitations of the Flexible System Governing Treaty Formation', (1994) 29 *Texas International Law Journal* 69

Simmons, D. A. C., 'Conflicts of Law and Policy in the Caribbean – Human Rights and the Enforcement of the Death Penalty – Between a Rock and a Hard Place', (2000) 9 *Journal of Transnational Law and Policy* 263

Sottile, Antoine, 'Le terrorisme international', [1938] III *Recueil de cours de l'Académie de droit international* 89

Spielman, Alphonse, 'La Convention européenne des droits de l'homme et la peine de mort', in *Présence du droit public et les droits de l'homme, Mélanges offerts à Jacques Vélu*, Brussels: Bruylant, 1992, pp. 1503–1527

Stavros, Stephanos, 'The Right to a Fair Trial in Emergency Situations', (1992) 41 *International and Comparative Law Quarterly* 343

Stewart, David P., 'U.S. Ratification of the Covenant on Civil and Political Rights: The Significance of the Reservations, Understandings and Declarations' (1993) 14 *HRLJ* 77

Sudre, Frédéric, 'Extradition et peine de mort – arrêt Soering de la Cour européenne des droits de l'homme du 7 juillet 1989', (1990) *Revue générale de droit international public* 103

Tardu, M., 'The Protocol to the United Nations Covenant on Civil and Political Rights and the Inter-American System: A Study of Coexisting Petition Procedures', (1976) 70 *AJIL* 778

Templeton, Erica, 'Killing Kids: The Impact of Domingues v. Nevada on the Juvenile Death Penalty as a Violation of International Law', (2000) 41 *BC Law Review* 1175

van den Wyngaert, Christine, 'Applying the European Convention on Human Rights to Extradition: Opening Pandora's Box?', (1990) 39 *International and Comparative Law Quarterly* 757

'Military Offences, International Crimes and the Death Penalty', (1987) 58 *Revue internationale de droit pénal* 737

van der Meersch, W. Ganshof, 'L'extradition et la Convention européenne des droits de l'homme. L'affaire Soering', (1990) *Revue trimestrielle des droits de l'homme* 5

Wako, Amos, 'Comparison of the African Charter of Human and Peoples' Rights and the Optional Protocol to the International Covenant on Civil and Political Rights', [1991–92] *Canadian Human Rights Yearbook* 145

Warbrick, C., 'Coherence and the European Court of Human Rights: The Adjudicative Background to the Soering Case', (1989–90) 11 *Michigan Journal of International Law* 1073

Wattendorff, H., and du Perron, E., 'Human Rights v. Extradition: The Soering Case', (1990) 11 *Michigan Journal of International Law* 845

Weissbrodt, David, 'Execution of Juvenile Offenders by the United States Violates International Human Rights Law', (1988) 3 *American University Journal of International Law and Policy* 339

Welch, Claude E., Jr., 'The African Commission on Human and Peoples' Rights: A Five-Year Report and Assessment', (1992) 14 *HRQ* 43

Williams, Sharon A., 'Extradition and the Death Penalty Exception in Canada: Resolving the Ng and Kindler Cases', (1991) 13 *Loyola of Los Angeles International and Comparative Law Journal* 799

'Extradition to a State that Imposes the Death Penalty', [1990] *Canadian Yearbook of International Law* 117

'Human Rights Safeguards and International Cooperation in Extradition: Striking the Balance', (1992) 3 *Criminal Law Forum* 191

'Nationality, Double Jeopardy, Prescription and the Death Sentence as Bases for Refusing Extradition', (1991) 62 *International Review of Penal Law* 259

Wyman, James H., 'Vengeance is Whose? The Death Penalty and Cultural Relativism in International law', (1997) 6 *Journal of Transnational Law and Policy* 543

Index